658. 1511 A

L

MANAGEMENT ACCOUNTING
FOR DECISION MAKERS

NINTH EDITION

MANAGEMENT ACCOUNTING
FOR DECISION MAKERS

Peter Atrill and
Eddie McLaney

Harlow, England • London • New York • Boston • San Francisco • Toronto • Sydney
Dubai • Singapore • Hong Kong • Tokyo • Seoul • Taipei • New Delhi
Cape Town • São Paulo • Mexico City • Madrid • Amsterdam • Munich • Paris • Milan

PEARSON EDUCATION LIMITED
KAO TWO
KAO PARK
Harlow CM17 9NA
United Kingdom
Tel: +44 (0)1279 623623
Web: www.pearson.com/uk

First published 1995 by Prentice Hall Europe (print)
Second edition published 1999 by Prentice Hall Europe (print)
Third edition published 2002 by Pearson Education Limited (print)
Fourth edition published 2005 (print)
Fifth edition published 2007 (print)
Sixth edition published 2009 (print)
Seventh edition published 2012 (print and electronic)
Eighth edition published 2015 (print and electronic)
Ninth edition published 2018 (print and electronic)

© Prentice Hall Europe 1995, 1999 (print)
© Pearson Education Limited 2002, 2005, 2007, 2009 (print)
© Pearson Education Limited 2012, 2015, 2018 (print and electronic)

The Financial Times. With a worldwide network of highly respected journalists, *The Financial Times* provides global business news, insightful opinion and expert analysis of business, finance and politics. With over 500 journalists reporting from 50 countries worldwide, our in-depth coverage of international news is objectively reported and analysed from an independent, global perspective. To find out more, visit www.ft.com/pearsonoffer.

ISBN: 978-1-292-20457-4 (print)
       978-1-292-20460-4 (PDF)
       978-1-292-20462-8 (ePub)

British Library Cataloguing-in-Publication Data
A catalogue record for the print edition is available from the British Library

Library of Congress Cataloging-in-Publication Data
Names: Atrill, Peter, author. | McLaney, E. J., author.
Title: Management accounting for decision makers / Peter Atrill, Eddie
    McLaney.
Description: Ninth edition. | Harlow, United Kingdom : Pearson Education, [2018]
Identifiers: LCCN 2017048338 | ISBN 9781292204574 (print) | ISBN 9781292204604
    (PDF) | ISBN 9781292204628 (ePub)
Subjects: LCSH: Managerial accounting. | Decision making.
Classification: LCC HF5657.4.A873 2018 | DDC 658.15/11—dc23
LC record available at https://lccn.loc.gov/2017048338

10 9 8 7 6 5 4 3 2
22 21 20 19 18

Front cover image © Shutterstock Premier/Allies Interactive

Print edition typeset in 9.25/13 HelveticaNeueLTW1G by iEnergizer Aptara®, Ltd.
Printed and bound by Vivar, Malaysia.

NOTE THAT ANY PAGE CROSS REFERENCES REFER TO THE PRINT EDITION

Brief Contents

Contents

6 Budgeting 193

12 Managing working capital 453

Lecturer Resources

For password-protected online resources tailored to
support the use of this textbook in teaching, please visit
www.pearsoned.co.uk/atrillmclaney

Preface

This book is directed primarily at those following an introductory course in management accounting. Many readers will be studying at a university or college, perhaps majoring in accounting or in another area, such as business studies, IT, tourism or engineering. Other readers, however, may be studying independently, perhaps with no qualification in mind.

The book is written in an 'open learning' style, which has been adopted because we believe that readers will find it to be more 'user-friendly' than the traditional approach. Whether they are using the book as part of a taught course or for personal study, we feel that the open learning approach makes it easier for readers to learn.

Management accounting is concerned with ensuring that managers have the information needed to plan and control the direction of their organisation. In writing a book on this subject, we have taken into account the fact that most readers will not have studied the subject before. We have therefore tried to write in an accessible style, avoiding technical jargon. Where technical terminology is unavoidable, we have tried to give clear explanations. At the end of the book (in Appendix A) there is a glossary of technical terms, which readers can use to refresh their memory where they come across a term whose meaning is in doubt. We have tried to introduce topics gradually, explaining everything as we go. We have included a variety of questions and tasks designed to help readers to grasp the subject more thoroughly, just as a good lecturer might do in lectures and tutorials. In framing these questions and tasks, we have tried to encourage critical thinking by requiring analysis and evaluation of various concepts and techniques. To help broaden understanding, questions and tasks often require readers to go beyond the material in the text and/or to link the current topic with material covered earlier in the book. More detail on the nature and use of these questions and tasks is given in the 'How to use this book' section immediately following this preface.

The book covers all the areas required to gain a firm foundation in the subject. Chapter 1 provides a broad introduction to the nature and purpose of management accounting. Chapters 2, 3, 4 and 5 are concerned with identifying cost information and using it to make short-term and medium-term decisions. Chapters 6 and 7 deal with the ways in which management accounting can be used in making plans and in trying to ensure that those plans are actually achieved. Chapter 8 considers the use of management-accounting information in making investment decisions, typically long-term ones. Chapter 9 is concerned with the all-important area of risk in financial decision making and how to handle it. Chapter 10 deals with performance evaluation and pricing, including strategic management accounting. This is an increasingly important area of management accounting that focuses on factors outside the organisation but which have a significant effect on its success. Chapter 11 deals with the problems of measuring performance where the business operates through a divisional organisation structure, which is common among large businesses. It also considers the use of non-financial measures in measuring performance. Finally, Chapter 12 looks at the way in which management accounting can help in the control of short-term assets, such as inventories (stock) and cash.

In this ninth edition, we have taken the opportunity to improve the book. We have introduced a new chapter, Chapter 9, which focuses on risk in decision making. In earlier editions of the book, risk had been covered, but we decided that it should be given greater emphasis, thereby justifying a separate chapter. The new chapter expands on the coverage of risk in the earlier editions. We have continued to highlight the changing role of management accountants, enabling them to retain their place at the centre of the decision-making and planning process. We have also added more, as well as more up-to-date, examples of management accounting in practice.

We would like to thank those at Pearson Education who were involved with this book for their support and encouragement. Without their help it would not have materialised.

We hope that readers will find the book readable and helpful.

Peter Atrill
Eddie McLaney

How to use this book

Whether you are using the book as part of a lecture/tutorial-based course or as the basis for a more independent mode of study, the same approach should be broadly followed.

Order of dealing with the material

The contents of the book have been ordered in what is meant to be a logical sequence. For this reason, it is suggested that you work through the book in the order in which it is presented. Every effort has been made to ensure that earlier chapters do not refer to concepts or terms which are not explained until a later chapter. If you work through the chapters in the 'wrong' order, you may encounter points that have been explained in an earlier chapter which you have not read.

Working through the chapters

You are advised to work through the chapters from start to finish, but not necessarily in one sitting. Activities are interspersed within the text. These are meant to be like the sort of questions which a good lecturer will throw at students during a lecture or tutorial. Activities seek to serve two purposes:

- To give you the opportunity to check that you understand what has been covered so far.
- To try to encourage you to think beyond the topic that you have just covered, sometimes so that you can see a link between that topic and others with which you are already familiar. Sometimes, activities are used as a means of linking the topic just covered to the next one.

You are strongly advised to do all the activities. The answers are provided immediately after the activity. These answers should be covered up until you have arrived at a solution, which should then be compared with the suggested answer provided.

Towards the end of Chapters 2–12, there is a 'self-assessment question'. This is rather more demanding and comprehensive than any of the activities. It is intended to give you an opportunity to see whether you understand the main body of material covered in the chapter. The solutions to the self-assessment questions are provided in Appendix B at the end of the book. As with the activities, it is very important that you make a thorough attempt at the question before referring to the solution. If you have real difficulty with a self-assessment question you should go over the chapter again, since it should be the case that careful study of the chapter will enable completion of the self-assessment question.

End-of-chapter assessment material

At the end of each chapter, there are four 'review' questions. These are short questions requiring a narrative answer and intended to enable you to assess how well you can recall main points covered in the chapter. Suggested answers to these questions are provided in

Appendix C at the end of the book. Again, a serious attempt should be made to answer these questions before referring to the solutions.

At the end of each chapter, there are normally eight exercises. These are more demanding and extensive questions, mostly computational, and should further reinforce your knowledge and understanding. We have attempted to provide questions of varying complexity.

Answers to five out of the eight exercises in each chapter are provided in Appendix D at the end of the book. These exercises are marked with a coloured number, but a thorough attempt should be made to answer these questions before referring to the answers. Answers to the three exercises that are not marked with a coloured number are given in a separate teacher's manual.

Acknowledgements

The publisher thanks the following reviewers for their very valuable comments on the book:

John Currie
Bianca A.C. Groen
Khamid Irgashev
Celani John Nyide

Figures

Figure 1.3 from Rigby, D. and Bilodeau, B. (2015) *Management Tools and Trends 2015*, Bain and Company; Figure 3.13 from www.statista.com. with Oil price information taken from www.nasdaq.com and www. statista.com accessed 12 November 2016; Figure 4.2 from Al-Omiri, M. and Drury, C. (2007) A survey of factors influencing the choice of product costing systems in UK organizations, *Management Accounting Research*, Vol. 18 (4), pp. 399-424. Copyright © 2007 Elsevier Ltd. With permission from Elsevier; Figures 4.13, 5.5, 5.7, 7.11, 7.13 adapted from CIMA (2009) *Management Accounting Tools for Today and Tomorrow*, p. 12; Figure 5.2 adapted from Innes, J. and Mitchell, F. (1990) *Activity Based Costing: A Review With Case Studies*, CIMA Publishing. With kind permission of Elsevier; Figure 5.10 adapted from Porter, M.E. (1985) *Competitive Advantage: Creating and Sustaining Superior Performance*, The Free Press. Copyright © 1985, 1998 by Michael E. Porter. All rights reserved. With the permission of The Free Press, a Division of Simon & Schuster, Inc.; Figure 5.11 adapted from CIMA (2009) *Management Accounting Tools for Today and Tomorrow*, p. 19; Figure 5.13 from Rigby, D. (2015) *Insights Management Tools, Benchmarking*, Bain & Company, http://www.bain.com, 10 June; Figure 5.15 from Rigby, D. (2015) *Insights Management Tools, Total Quality Management*, Bain & Company, http://www.bain.com, 10 June; Figure 6.6 from BPM Forum (2008) *Perfect How You Project*; Figures 6.7, 6.8, 6.10, 6.13 adapted from CIMA (2009) *Management Accounting Tools for Today and Tomorrow*, p. 15; Figure 6.12 from *Beyond Budgeting*, aawww.bbrt.org; Figure 8.7 adapted from CIMA (2009) *Management Accounting Tools for Today and Tomorrow*, p. 18; Figures 10.5, 10.6 from Deloitte (2016) *Thriving in Uncertainty: Cost improvement practices and trends in the Fortune 1000*, www2. Deloitte.com, April; Figure 10.7 adapted from Kaplan, R. and Norton, D. (1996) *The Balanced Scorecard*, Harvard Business School Press. Copyright © 1996 by the Harvard Business School Publishing Corporation. All rights reserved. Reprinted by permission of Harvard Business School Press; Figure 10.9 from Rigby, D. (2015) *Insights Management Tools, Balanced Scorecard*, Bain & Company, http://www.bain.com/publications/articles/management-tools-balanced-scorecard.aspx, 10 June, used with permission from Bain & Company; Figures 10.17, 10.18 adapted from CIMA (2009) *Management Accounting Tools for Today and Tomorrow*, p. 13; Figure 11.1 from Savills plc, www.savills.co.uk, accessed 26 October 2016; Figure 11.4 after Drury, C. and El-Shishini, E. (2005) *Divisional Performance Measurement: An Examination of Potential Explanatory Factors*, CIMA Research Report, August, p. 32. With the kind permission of Professor C Drury; Figure 11.9 from Abdel-Maksoud, A., Dugdale, D. and Luther, R. (2005) Non-financial performance measurement in manufacturing companies, *The British Accounting Review*, Vol. 37, Issue 3, pp. 261-297. Copyright © 2005 Elsevier Ltd.

Text

Article 1.1 from http://www.icmi.com/Resources/Customer-Experience/2015/10/Yes-the-Customer-is-Still-King; Extract 1.2 from Ruddick, G. (2016), *Rolls-Royce to scrap two divisions amid restructuring* www.theguardian.com, 16 December; Extract 1.5 from Gallivan, R. (2016), *News Corp Buys Wireless Group for $296 Million*, The Wall Street Journal, 25 June; Extract 1.6 from Allarey, R (2015) *This Is How Nike Managed to Clean Up Its Sweatshop Reputation*, www.complex.com, 8 June.; Article 1.7 adapted from Goyder, M., (2009) How we've poisoned the well of wealth, *Financial Times* ,15 February. © The Financial Times Limited 2009. All rights reserved. We would like to thank Mark Goyder, Founder Director of Tomorrow's Company for permission to quote his article 'How we've poisoned the well of wealth' as published in the *Financial Times*; Extract 1.9 from Paltrow, S. (2016) *U.S. Army fudged its accounts by trillions of dollars, auditor finds*, www.reuters.com, 19 August; Article 2.1 adapted from Anderson, L., (2012) *Something for the weekend*, ft.com, 16 November. © The Financial Times Limited 2012. All rights reserved; Extract 2.2 from Burite, J., (2016) *Tullow Sees Opportunity Cost If Kenya-Uganda Pipeline Plan Fails*, www.bloomberg.com, 30 March; Extract 2.3 from the FT editorial (2013), *UK taxpayer will lose in rush to exit*, ft.com, 5 May, © The Financial Times Limited. All Rights Reserved; Extract 3.2 from McGee, P. and Parker, A. (2015), *Disaster-plagued Malaysian Airways seeks break-even by 2018*, ft.com, 1 June. © The Financial Times Limited. All Rights Reserved; Extract 3.4 from Jimmy Choo plc, Preliminary results statement for the six months ended 30 June 2016, www.jimmychooplc.com, 25 August 2016; Extract 3.6 from Murray, D. (2016) *Wheat price is below break-even point. Record-setting wheat crop adds to international glut*, www.greatfalltribune.com, 7 August; Extract 3.8 from Proactive Investors United Kingdom (2016) *Image scan to break even thanks to large June x-ray order*. www.proactiveinvestors.co.uk, 22 August; Extract 3.11 from Stern, S. (2013) *Logic of outsourcing can be hard to resist,* ft.com, 20 September. © The Financial Times Limited 2013. All rights reserved.; Extract 4.1 from Morgan, J. (2016) Cambridge's 'cost of education' rises to £18K per student *Times Higher Education Supplement*, 8 September; Extract 5.10 from Rigby, D. (2015) *Insights Management Tools, Total Quality Management*, Bain & Company, http://www.bain.com, 10 June; Extract 5.11 from Song, J. and Bradshaw, T. (2016) Samsung recall debacle fuels brand concerns, ft.com, 11 October. © The Financial Times Limited. All Rights Reserved; Extract 6.1 from Greene King plc Annual Report 2016, p.48; Extract 6.2 from Rolls-Royce Holdings plc, Annual Report 2016, p. 64; Extract 6.6 from CIMA (2009) *Management Accounting Tools for Today and Tomorrow*, p. 15 and McLaughlin, T. (2017), *Back to zero: Companies use 1970s budget tool to cut costs as they hunt for growth*, Reuter Business News, uk.reuter.com, 30 January; Article 6.8 from John Timpson (2011), The management column, *Daily Telegraph Business*, 5 June. Copyright © Telegraph Media Group Limited 2011; Extract 7.10 from Marginson, D. and Ogden, S. (2005) Budgeting and innovation, *Financial Management,* April, pp. 29-31; Extract 8.4 from Bland, B. (2016), *China's robot revolution*, ft.com, 6 June. © The Financial Times Limited. All Rights Reserved; Extract 8.5 from Guthrie, J. (2016), *Kiwi combo, Lombard*, ft.com, 9 June. © The Financial Times Limited. All Rights Reserved; Extract 8.6 from Stothard. M. (2016), *Hinkley Point is risk for overstretched EDF, warn critics*, ft.com, 15 September. © The Financial Times Limited. All Rights Reserved; Article 8.10 from Rolls Royce Holdings plc Annual Report 2016, p. 185; Extract 8.11 from Grant, J. (2015) *CRH adds CR Laurence to acquisitions tally for $1.3bn*, ft.com, 27 August. © The Financial Times Limited. All Rights Reserved; Article 8.14 adapted from Kingfisher plc *Annual Report 2015/16*, p. 28, (www.kingfisher.co.uk); Extract 9.2 from Minco Plc (2014), Woodstock Mn - New Brunswick, www.mincoplc.com, 10 July; Extract 9.3 from Alkaraan, F. and Northcott, D. (2006). Strategic capital investment decision-making: a role for emergent analysis tools? A study of practice in large UK manufacturing companies, *British Accounting Review*, Vol. 38 pp. 149-173; Cohen, G. and Yagil, J. (2010). Sectoral differences in corporate financial behaviour: an international survey, *The European Journal of Finance*, Vol. 16, pp. 245-262; Article 10.1 adapted from 'How companies respond to competitors: a McKinsey global survey', *The McKinsey Quarterly*, mckinseyquarterly.com,   May 2008. Reprinted with permission; Article 10.6 from Kaplan, R. and Norton, D. (1996) *The Balanced Scorecard*, Harvard Business School Press. Copyright © 1996 by the Harvard Business School Publishing Corporation. All rights reserved. Reprinted by permission of Harvard Business School Press; Extract 10.7 from When misuse leads to failure, *Financial Times*, 24 May 2006. © The Financial Times Limited 2006. All rights reserved; Extract 10.8 from Stock Analysis on Net, www.stock-analysis-on.net, accessed 16 March 2017; Article 10.11 from Robinson, D. (2012) Pricing strategies amid uncertainty, ft.com, 30 July. © The Financial Times Limited 2012. All rights reserved. Used with permission of the author; Article 10.12 from Guilding, C., Drury, C. and Tayles, M. (2005) An empirical investigation of the importance of cost-plus pricing, *Management Auditing Journal*, Vol. 20, No. 2, pp.125 – 137; CIMA (2009) *Management Accounting Tools for Today and Tomorrow*, p. 13; Extract 11.1 from Timpson, About Timpson, www.timpson.co.uk/about-timpson accessed on

16 March 2017; Article 11.3 from Associated British Foods plc, Annual Report 2015, p. 9; Article 11.5 from Drury, C. and El-Shishini, E. (2005) *Divisional Performance Measurement: An Examination of Potential Explanatory Factors*, CIMA Research Report, August, p. 30. With the kind permission of Professor C Drury; Extract 11.7 from Miller, H. and Pope, T. (2016) What does the row over Google's tax bill tell us about the corporate tax systems, Institute for Fiscal Studies, 26 January; Article 11.8 from *In the spotlight: a new era of transparency and risk for transfer pricing 2016*, EY Transfer Pricing Survey Series, www.ey.com pp. 3 and 4; Extract 11.11 from Swallow, B. (2014) ESQi: *Why is a 20-year-old service measure still so influential?* http://www.mycustomer.com/service/management/esqi-why-is-a-20-year-old-service-measure-still-so-influential, May; Extract 12.3 from McFarlane, S. and Zhdannikov, D. (2015), *Glencore shrinking its $18 bn commodity inventory mountain*, www.reuters.com, 29 October; Extract 12.6 from Hurley, J. (2016) Suppliers 'routinely kept waiting by supermarkets', www.thetimes.co.uk, 25 January; Extract 12.11 from Davies, R. and Merin, D. (2014), *Uncovering cash and insights from working capital*, McKinsey and Company, www.mckinsey.com, July. Copyright (c) 2017, McKinsey & Company; Extract 12.12 from REL Consulting, *The Working Capitalist – Spring 2016*, p. 8 www.relconsultancy.com.

Chapter 1

INTRODUCTION TO MANAGEMENT ACCOUNTING

INTRODUCTION

Welcome to the world of management accounting! Management accounting is concerned with collecting and analysing financial and other information and then communicating this information to managers. This information is intended help mangers within businesses and other organisations make better decisions. In this introductory chapter, we examine the role of management accounting within a business. To understand the context for management accounting, we begin by examining the nature and purpose of a business. Thus, we first consider what businesses seek to achieve, how they are organised and how they are managed. Having done this, we go on to explore how management-accounting information can be used within a business to improve the quality of managers' decisions. We also identify the characteristics that management-accounting information must possess to fulfil its role. Management accounting has undergone many changes in response to developments in the business environment and to the increasing size and complexity of businesses. In this chapter we shall discuss some of the more important changes that have occurred.

Learning outcomes

When you have completed this chapter, you should be able to:

- Identify the purpose of a business and discuss the ways in which a business may be organised and managed.

- Discuss the issues to be considered when setting the long-term direction of a business.

- Explain the role of management accounting within a business and describe the key qualities that management-accounting information should possess.

- Explain the changes that have occurred over time in both the role of the management accountant and the type of information provided by management-accounting systems.

WHAT IS THE PURPOSE OF A BUSINESS?

Peter Drucker, an eminent management thinker, has argued that '*The purpose of business is to create and keep a customer*' (see reference 1 at the end of the chapter). Drucker defined the purpose of a business in this way in 1967, at a time when most businesses did not adopt this strong customer focus. His view therefore represented a radical challenge to the accepted view of what businesses do. Fifty years later, however, his approach is part of the conventional wisdom. It is now widely accepted that, in order to succeed, businesses must focus on satisfying the needs of the customer.

Although the customer has always provided the main source of revenue for a business, this has often been taken for granted. In the past, too many businesses assumed that the customer would readily accept whatever services or products were on offer. When competition was weak and customers were passive, businesses could operate under this assumption and still make a profit. However, the era of weak competition has passed. Today, customers have much greater choice and are much more assertive concerning their needs. They now demand higher quality services and goods at cheaper prices. They also require that services and goods be delivered faster with an increasing emphasis on the product being tailored to their individual needs. If a business cannot meet these needs, a competitor often can. Thus the business mantra for the current era is '*the customer is king*'. Most businesses now recognise this fact and organise themselves accordingly.

Real World 1.1 describes how the internet and social media have given added weight to this mantra. It points out that dissatisfied customers now have a powerful medium for broadcasting their complaints.

Real World 1.1

The customer is king

The mantra that the "customer is king" has gained even greater significance among businesses in recent years because of the rise of the internet and social media. In the past, a dissatisfied customer might tell only a few friends about a bad buying experience. As a result, the damage to the reputation of the business concerned would normally be fairly limited. However, nowadays, through the magic of the internet, several hundred people, or more, can be very speedily informed of a bad buying experience.

Businesses are understandably concerned about the potential of the internet to damage reputations, but are their concerns justified? Do customer complaints, which wing their way through cyberspace, have any real effect on the businesses concerned? A Harris Poll survey of 2,000 adults in the UK and US suggests they do and so businesses should be concerned. It seems that social media can exert a big influence on customer buying decisions.

The Harris Poll survey, which was conducted online, found that around 20 per cent of those surveyed use social media when making buying decisions. For those in the 18-34 age range, the figure rises to almost forty per cent. Furthermore, 60 percent of those surveyed indicated that they would avoid buying from a business that receives poor customer reviews for its products or services.

The moral of this tale appears to be that, in this internet age, businesses must work even harder to keep their customers happy if they are to survive and prosper.

Source: Based on information in Miesbach, A.(2015) *Yes, the Customer is Still King*, 30 October www.icmi.com

HOW ARE BUSINESSES ORGANISED?

Nearly all businesses that involve more than a few owners and/or employees are set up as limited companies. Finance will come from the owners (shareholders) both in the form of a direct cash investment to buy shares (in the ownership of the business) and through the shareholders allowing past profits, which belong to them, to be reinvested in the business. Finance will also come from lenders (banks, for example) as well as through suppliers providing goods and services on credit.

In larger limited companies, the owners (shareholders) tend not to be involved in the daily running of the business; instead they appoint a board of directors to manage the business on their behalf. The board is charged with three major tasks:

- setting the overall direction for the business;
- monitoring and controlling the activities of the business; and
- communicating with shareholders and others connected with the business.

Each board has a chairman who is elected by the directors. The chairman is responsible for the smooth running of the board. In addition, each board has a chief executive officer (CEO) who leads the team that is responsible for running the business on a day-to-day basis. Occasionally, the roles of chairman and CEO are combined, although it is usually considered to be good practice to separate them. It prevents a single individual having excessive power.

The board of directors represents the most senior level of management. Below this level, managers are employed, with each manager being given responsibility for a particular part of the business's operations.

Activity 1.1

Why are larger businesses *not* managed as a single unit by just one manager? Try to think of at least one reason.

Three common reasons are:

- The sheer volume of activity or number of employees makes it impossible for one person to manage them.
- Certain business operations may require specialised knowledge or expertise.
- Geographical remoteness of part of the business operations may make it more practical to manage each location as a separate part, or set of separate parts.

The operations of a business may be divided for management purposes in different ways. For smaller businesses offering a single product or service, separate departments are often created. Tasks are grouped according to functions (such as marketing, human resources and finance) with each department responsible for a particular function. The managers of each department will then be accountable to the board of directors. In some cases, a departmental manager may also be a board member. A typical departmental structure, organised along functional lines, is shown in Figure 1.1.

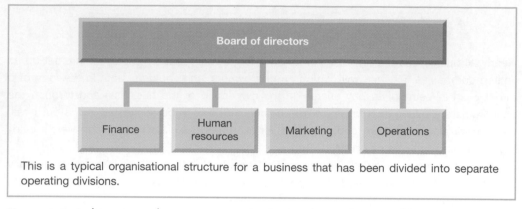

This is a typical organisational structure for a business that has been divided into separate operating divisions.

Figure 1.1 A departmental structure organised according to business functions

Departments based around functions permit greater specialisation, which, in turn, can promote greater efficiency. The departmental structure, however, can become too rigid. This can lead to poor communication between departments and, perhaps, a lack of responsiveness to changing market conditions.

The structure set out in Figure 1.1 may be adapted according to the particular needs of the business. Where, for example, a business has few employees, the human resources function may not form a separate department but rather form part of another department. Where business operations are specialised, separate departments may be created to deal with each specialist area. Example 1.1 illustrates how Figure 1.1 may be modified to meet the needs of a particular business.

Example 1.1

Supercoach Ltd owns a small fleet of coaches that it hires out with drivers for private group travel. The business employs about 60 people. It could be departmentalised as follows:

- *Marketing department*, dealing with advertising, dealing with enquiries from potential customers, maintaining good relationships with existing customers and entering into contracts with customers.
- *Routing and human resources department*, responsible for the coach drivers' routes, schedules, staff duties and rotas and problems that arise during a particular job or contract.
- *Coach maintenance department*, looking after repair and maintenance of the coaches, buying spares, and giving advice on the need to replace old or inefficient coaches.
- *Finance department*, responsible for managing cash flows, costing business activities, pricing new proposals, measuring financial performance, preparing budgets, borrowing, paying wages and salaries, billing and collecting amounts due from customers, and processing and paying invoices from suppliers.

For large businesses with a diverse geographical spread and/or a wide product range, the simple departmental structure set out in Figure 1.1 will usually have to be adapted. Separate divisions are often created for each geographical area and/or major product group. Each division will be managed separately and will usually enjoy a degree of autonomy. This can produce more agile responses to changing market conditions. Within each division, however, departments are often created and organised along functional lines. Those functions that provide support across the various divisions, such as human resources, may be carried out at head office to avoid duplication. The managers of each division will be accountable to the board of directors. In some cases, individual board members may also be divisional managers.

A typical divisional organisational structure is set out in Figure 1.2. Here the main basis of the structure is geographical. Thus, North Division deals with production and sales in the north and so on.

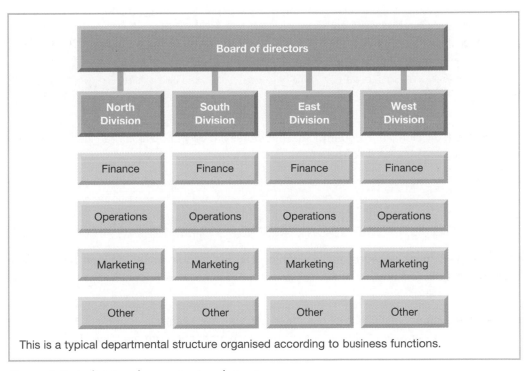

This is a typical departmental structure organised according to business functions.

Figure 1.2 A divisional organisational structure

Once a particular divisional structure has been established, it need not be permanent. Successful businesses constantly strive to improve their operational efficiency. This could well result in revising their divisional structure. **Real World 1.2** is an extract from an article that describes how one well-known business has reorganised in order to simplify operations and to reduce costs.

Real World 1.2

Engineering change

The chief executive of Rolls-Royce has shaken up its senior management team and scrapped two divisions as part of his attempt to turnaround the struggling engineer. Warren East will scrap the aerospace and land & sea divisions that split Rolls into two parts.

The move means that Rolls will operate with five smaller businesses all reporting directly to East. The Rolls chief executive plans to bring in a chief operating officer to assist him in running the company. Rolls said the revamp will "simplify the organisation, drive operational excellence and reduce cost".

The Rolls boss is overhauling the company after it issued five profit warnings in less than two years. East wants to cut costs by between £150m and £200m a year. The level of concern about the future of Rolls was underlined earlier this week when it emerged the government has drawn up contingency plans to nationalise its nuclear submarine business or force it to merge with defence manufacturer BAE Systems in the event the company's performance worsens.

East said: "The changes we are announcing today are the first important steps in driving operational excellence and returning Rolls-Royce to its long-term trend of profitable growth. This is a company with world-class engineering capability, strong market positions and exceptional long-term prospects."

Under the new structure Rolls will operate with five divisions from January 1 2016 – civil aerospace, defence aerospace, marine, nuclear, and power systems.

Source: Extracts from Ruddick, G. (2016), Rolls-Royce to scrap two divisions amid restructuring, www.theguardian.com, 16 December.

While both divisional and departmental structures are very popular in practice, it should be noted that other organisational structures may be found.

HOW ARE BUSINESSES MANAGED?

Over the past three decades, the environment in which businesses operate has become increasingly turbulent and competitive. Various reasons have been identified to explain these changes, including:

- the increasing sophistication of customers (as we have seen);
- the development of a global economy where national frontiers have become less important;
- rapid changes in technology;
- the deregulation of domestic markets (for example, electricity, water and gas);
- increasing pressure from owners (shareholders) for competitive economic returns; and
- the increasing volatility of financial markets.

The effect of these environmental changes has been to make the role of managers more complex and demanding. This, along with the increasing size of many businesses, has led managers to search for new ways to manage their businesses. One important tool that has been developed in response to managers' needs is **strategic management**. This is concerned with establishing the long-term direction for the business. It involves setting long-term goals and then ensuring that they are implemented effectively. To help the business develop a competitive edge, strategic management focuses on doing things differently rather than simply doing things better.

Strategic management provides a business with a clear sense of purpose along with a series of steps to achieve that purpose. The steps taken should link the internal resources of the business to the external environment of competitors, suppliers, customers and so on. This should be done in such a way that any business strengths, such as having a skilled workforce, are exploited and any weaknesses, such as being short of investment finance, are not exposed. To achieve this requires the development of strategies and plans that take account of the business's strengths and weaknesses, as well as the opportunities offered and threats posed by the external environment. Access to a new, expanding market is an example of an opportunity; the decision of a major competitor to reduce prices is an example of a threat.

Real World 1.3 provides an indication of the extent to which strategic planning is carried out in practice.

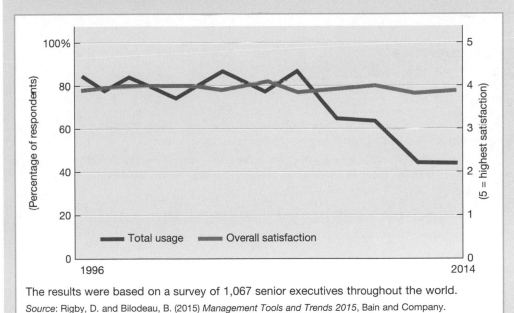
The strategic management process may be approached in different ways. One popular approach, involving five steps, is described below.

1 Establish mission, vision and objectives

The first step is to establish the mission of a business, which may be set out in the form of a **mission statement**. This is a concise declaration of the overriding purpose of the business. It addresses the question '*What business are we in?*' To answer this question, managers should focus on those customer needs that the business seeks to satisfy rather than on the products currently produced. Thus, a publisher of novels might, for example, conclude that it is really in the entertainment business. The **vision statement** is closely connected to the mission statement and declares the business's aspirations. It addresses the question '*What do we want to achieve?*' Once again, it should be in as concise a form as possible. By answering both questions, managers are provided with a clear focus for decision making.

Activity 1.2

Can you think why mission statements and vision statements should be concise?

Having to produce concise statements will force managers to think very carefully about the essential nature of their business and the aspirations that they have for it. In practice, this can prove more difficult than it may sound. Concise statements have the added advantages that they are easier to remember and to communicate to employees, owners and others.

The mission and vision of a business will often adorn its website. **Real World 1.4** provides an example of these strategic statements for one large business.

Real World 1.4

Power trip

Aggreko plc provides power generation and temperature control solutions to customers who need them quickly or for a short period of time. Its mission is:

> To offer specialist energy solutions that are delivered by our high-quality people in such a way that we continually grow our global list of satisfied and long-term customers.

Its stated vision is:

> To be the leading global player in the specialist energy marketplace.

Source: www.aggreko.com, accessed 7 November 2016.

Having established the purpose and aspirations of the business, objectives must be developed in order to translate these into specific commitments. Objectives help to bring real discipline into the strategy process. They should provide clear targets, or outcomes, which are both challenging and achievable. They should also provide the basis for assessing actual performance. Although quantifiable objectives provide the clearest targets, some areas of performance, such as employee satisfaction, may be capable of only partial quantification. Other areas, such as business ethics, may be impossible to quantify.

In practice, the objectives set by a business are likely to range across all key areas and might include a commitment to achieve:

- a specified percentage share of the market in which the business competes;
- a high level of customer satisfaction;
- a high degree of employee involvement;
- a specified percentage of sales revenue being generated from newly-developed products;
- high standards of ethical behaviour in business dealings;

- a specified percentage operating profit margin (operating profit as a percentage of sales revenue); and
- a specified percentage return on capital employed.

Businesses do not normally make their statement of objectives public.

Activity 1.3

Can you think why they may not wish to do so?

It is often because they do not wish to make their intentions clear to their competitors.

2 Undertake a position analysis

The **position analysis** seeks to discover how, given its attributes, the business is placed in relation to its environment (customers, competitors, suppliers, technology, the economy, political climate and so on). This will be carried out in the context of its mission, vision and objectives. The position analysis is often approached within the framework of the business's strengths, weaknesses, opportunities and threats (a **SWOT analysis**). It involves identifying the business's strengths and weaknesses as well as the opportunities provided and threats posed by the external environment. Strengths and weaknesses are internal attributes of the business, whereas opportunities and threats are present in the environment within which the business operates.

Activity 1.4

Ryanair Holdings plc is a highly successful 'no-frills' airline. Can you suggest some factors that could be strengths, weaknesses, opportunities and threats for this business? Try to think of two for each of these (eight in all).

Strengths could include such things as:

- a strong, well-recognised brand name;
- a modern fleet of aircraft requiring less maintenance;
- reliable customer service concerning punctuality and baggage loss; and
- an Internet booking facility used by virtually all passengers, which reduces administration costs.

Weaknesses might include:

- limited range of destinations;
- use of secondary airports situated some distance from city centres;
- poor facilities at secondary airports; and
- poor customer service concerning complaints.

Opportunities might include:

- new destinations becoming available, particularly in eastern Europe;
- increasing acceptance of 'no-frills' air travel among business travellers; and
- the development of new fuel-efficient aircraft.

Threats to the business might come from:

■ increased competition – either new low-fare competitors entering the market or traditional airlines reducing fares to compete;
■ increases in fuel prices and airport charges;
■ increasing congestion at airports, making it more difficult to turn aircraft around quickly;
■ changes in the regulatory environment (for example, changes in regulations concerning the maximum monthly flying hours for a pilot) making it harder to operate; and
■ vulnerability to a downturn in economic conditions.

You may have thought of others.

The SWOT framework is not the only way to carry out a position analysis; nevertheless, it seems to be very popular. A 2009 survey of businesses covering different industry sectors, geographical locations and size found that about 65 per cent of the total used SWOT analysis (see reference 2 at the end of the chapter).

3 Identify and assess the strategic options

This involves trying to identify possible courses of action. Each of the options identified should assist the business in reaching its objectives by using its strengths to exploit opportunities while not exposing its weaknesses to threats. The strengths, weaknesses, opportunities and threats are, of course, those identified using SWOT analysis. Having identified the available strategic options, each will then be assessed according to agreed criteria.

4 Select strategic options and formulate plans

The business will select what appears to be the best of the courses of action or strategies (identified in Step 3) available. When doing this, the potential for the selected strategies to achieve the mission, vision and objectives must be the key criterion. While the strategies selected provide a the broad outline, a more detailed plan is required to specify the particular actions to be taken. This overall plan will normally be broken down into a series of plans, one for each aspect of the business.

In an effort to match the chosen strategies with the opportunities available, a business may decide to acquire other businesses. **Real World 1.5** is an extract from a *Wall Street Journal* article that discusses an example of an acquisition made because of its 'strategic fit'.

Real World 1.5

Fit for purpose

News Corp is buying the owner of the radio station talkSPORT for £220.3 million ($296 million), the latest move by the media company to increase its exposure to U.K. sports content including the lucrative English Premier League soccer competition.

News Corp said the purchase of Wireless Group plc "represents an excellent strategic fit with its existing operations, broadening News Corp's range of services in the U.K., Ireland and internationally."

Source: Extract from Gallivan, R. (2016), News Corp Buys Wireless Group for $296 Million *The Wall Street Journal*, 25 June.

The fact that News Corp describes the acquisition as an 'excellent strategic fit', suggests that it represented better value to News Corp than it would for a different acquirer, paying the same price, but for which the strategic fit was not as good.

5 Perform, review and control

Finally, the business must implement the plans derived in Step 4. The actual outcome will be monitored and compared with the plans to see whether things are progressing satisfactorily. Steps must be taken to exercise control where actual performance fails to match earlier planned performance.

Figure 1.4 shows the strategic management framework in diagrammatic form. This framework will be considered further in later chapters. We shall see, for example, how the business's mission and vision links, through objectives and long-term plans, to detailed budgets in Chapters 6 and 7.

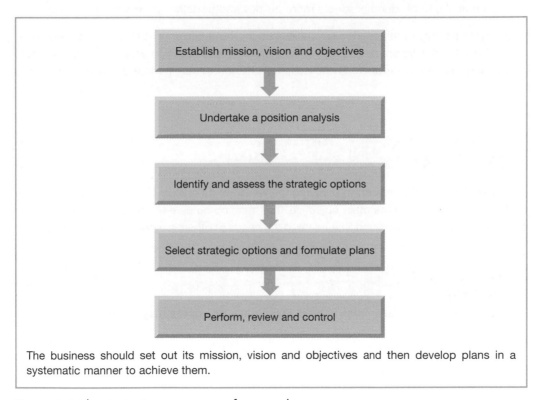

The business should set out its mission, vision and objectives and then develop plans in a systematic manner to achieve them.

Figure 1.4 The strategic management framework

THE CHANGING BUSINESS LANDSCAPE

Factors such as increased global competition and advances in technology, mentioned earlier, have had a tremendous impact on the kind of businesses that survive and prosper. They have also had an impact on the kind of business structures and processes adopted. Examples of the changes that have occurred in many countries in recent years, including the UK, are:

- *The growth of the service sector.* This includes businesses such as financial services, communications, tourism, transportation, consultancy, leisure and so on. This growth of the service sector has been matched by the decline of the manufacturing and extractive (for example, coal mining) sectors.

- *The emergence of new industries.* This includes science-based industries such as genetic engineering and biotechnology.
- *The growth of e-commerce.* Consumers are increasingly drawn to buying a wide range of goods including groceries, books, music and computers online. Businesses also use e-commerce to order supplies, monitor deliveries and distribute products.
- *Automated manufacturing.* Many manufacturing processes are now fully automated and computers are used to control the production process.
- *Lean manufacturing.* This involves a systematic attempt to identify and eliminate waste, surplus production, delays, defects and so on in the production process.
- *Greater product innovation.* There is much greater pressure to produce new, innovative products. The effect has been to increase the range of products available and to shorten the life cycles of many products.
- *Faster response times.* There is increasing pressure on businesses to develop products more quickly, to produce products more quickly and to deliver products more quickly.

These changes have presented huge challenges for the management accountant. New techniques have been developed and existing techniques adapted to try to ensure that management accounting retains its relevance. These issues will be considered in more detail as we progress through the book.

WHAT IS THE FINANCIAL OBJECTIVE OF A BUSINESS?

A business is normally created to enhance the wealth of its owners. Throughout this book we shall assume that this is its main objective. This may come as a surprise, as there are other objectives that may be pursued that relate to the needs of others associated with the business.

Activity 1.5

Can you think of two examples of what these other objectives may be?

A business may seek to:

- provide good working conditions for its employees;
- conserve the environment for the local community;
- develop safer products for its customers; and
- offer fair trading terms to suppliers in underdeveloped countries.

You may have thought of others.

While a business may pursue these objectives, it is normally set up primarily with a view to increasing the wealth of its owners. In practice, the behaviour of businesses over time appears to be consistent with this objective.

Within a market economy there are strong competitive forces at work that ensure that failure to enhance owners' wealth will not be tolerated for long. Competition for the funds provided by the owners and competition for managers' jobs will normally mean that the owners' interests will prevail. If the managers do not provide the expected increase in ownership wealth, the owners have the power to replace the existing management team with a new team that is more responsive to owners' needs. Does this mean that the needs of other groups associated with the business (employees, customers, suppliers, the community and so on) are not really important? The answer to this question is almost certainly no, if the business wishes to survive and prosper over the longer term.

Satisfying the needs of other groups is usually consistent with increasing the wealth of the owners over the longer term. Disaffected customers, for example, may turn to another supplier, resulting in a loss of shareholder wealth for the original supplier. A dissatisfied workforce may result in low productivity, strikes, high labour turnover rates and so forth, which will in turn have an adverse effect on owners' wealth. Similarly, a business that upsets the local community by unacceptable behaviour, such as polluting the environment, may attract bad publicity, resulting in a loss of customers and heavy fines.

Real World 1.6 is an article that discusses how one well-known business responded to damaging allegations.

We should be clear that generating wealth for the owners is not the same as seeking to maximise the current year's profit. Wealth creation is concerned with the longer term and so it relates not only to this year's profit but to that of future years as well. In the short term, corners can be cut and risks taken that improve current profit at the expense of future profit. **Real World 1.7** is a *Financial Times* article that provides some examples of how emphasis on short-term profit can be damaging.

Short-term gains, long-term problems

For many years, under the guise of defending capitalism, we have been allowing ourselves to degrade it. We have been poisoning the well from which we have drawn wealth. We have misunderstood the importance of values to capitalism. We have surrendered to the idea that success is pursued by making as much money as the law allowed without regard to how it was made.

Thirty years ago, retailers would be quite content to source the shoes they wanted to sell as cheaply as possible. The working conditions of those who produced them was not their concern. Then headlines and protests developed. Society started to hold them responsible for previously invisible working conditions. Companies like Nike went through a transformation. They realised they were polluting their brand. Global sourcing became visible. It was no longer viable to define success simply in terms of buying at the lowest price and selling at the highest.

Financial services and investment are today where footwear was thirty years ago. Public anger at the crisis will make visible what was previously hidden. Take the building up of huge portfolios of loans to poor people on US trailer parks. These loans were authorised without proper scrutiny of the circumstances of the borrowers. Somebody else then deemed them fit to be securitised and so on through credit default swaps and the rest without anyone seeing the transaction in terms of its ultimate human origin.

Each of the decision makers thought it okay to act like the thoughtless footwear buyer of the 1970s. The price was attractive. There was money to make on the deal. Was it responsible? Irrelevant. It was legal, and others were making money that way. And the consequences for the banking system if everybody did it? Not our problem.

The consumer has had a profound shock. Surely we could have expected the clever and wise people who invested our money to be better at risk management than they have shown themselves to be in the present crisis? How could they have been so gullible in not challenging the bankers whose lending proved so flaky? How could they have believed that the levels of bonuses that were, at least in part, coming out of their savings could have been justified in 'incentivising' a better performance? How could they have believed that a 'better' performance would be one that is achieved for one bank without regard to its effect on the whole banking system? Where was the stewardship from those exercising investment on their behalf?

The answer has been that very few of them do exercise that stewardship. Most have stood back and said it doesn't really pay them to do so. The failure of stewardship comes from the same mindset that created the irresponsible lending in the first place. We are back to the mindset that has allowed us to poison the well: never mind the health of the system as a whole, I'm making money out of it at the moment. Responsibility means awareness for the system consequences of our actions. It is not a luxury. It is the cornerstone of prudence.

 Source: Adapted from Goyder, M. (2009) How we've poisoned the well of wealth, *Financial Times*, 15 February.
© The Financial Times Limited 2009. All Rights Reserved. We would like to thank Mark Goyder, Founder Director of Tomorrow's Company for permission to quote his article 'How we've poisoned the well of wealth' as published in the *Financial Times*.

BALANCING RISK AND RETURN

All decisions attempt to influence future outcomes, and financial decisions are no exception. The only thing certain about the future, however, is that we cannot be sure what will happen. There is a risk that things may not turn out as planned and this should be taken into account when making financial decisions.

As in other aspects of life, risk and return tend to be related. Evidence shows that returns relate to risk in something like the way shown in Figure 1.5.

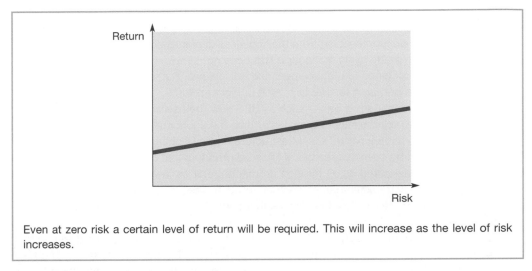

Even at zero risk a certain level of return will be required. This will increase as the level of risk increases.

Figure 1.5 Relationship between risk and return

Activity 1.6

Look at Figure 1.5 and state, in broad terms, where an investment in

(a) a government savings account and
(b) a lottery ticket

should be placed on the risk–return line.

A government savings account is normally a very safe investment. Even if the government is in financial difficulties, it can always print more money to repay investors. Returns from this form of investment, however, are normally very low.

Investing in a lottery ticket runs a very high risk of losing the whole amount invested. This is because the probability of winning is normally very low. However, a winning ticket can produce enormous returns.

Thus, the government savings account should be placed towards the far left of the risk–return line and the lottery ticket towards the far right.

This relationship between risk and return has important implications for setting financial objectives for a business. The owners will require a minimum return to induce them to invest at all, but will require an additional return to compensate for taking risks; the higher the risk, the higher the required return. Managers must be aware of this and must strike the appropriate balance between risk and return when setting objectives and pursuing particular courses of action.

The turmoil in the banking sector has shown, however, that the right balance is not always struck. Some banks have taken excessive risks in pursuit of higher returns and, as a consequence, have incurred massive losses. They are now being kept afloat with taxpayers' money. **Real World 1.8** discusses the collapse of one leading bank, in which the UK government took a majority stake, and argues that the risk appetite of banks must now change.

Banking on change

The taxpayer has become the majority shareholder in the Royal Bank of Scotland (RBS). This change in ownership, resulting from the huge losses sustained by the bank, will shape the future decisions made by its managers. This does not simply mean that it will affect the amount that the bank lends to homeowners and businesses. Rather it is about the amount of risk that it will be prepared to take in pursuit of higher returns.

In the past, those managing banks such as RBS saw themselves as producers of financial products that enabled banks to grow faster than the economy as a whole. They did not want to be seen as simply part of the infrastructure of the economy. It was too dull. It was far more exciting to be seen as creators of financial products that created huge profits and, at the same time, benefited us all through unlimited credit as low rates of interest. These financial products, with exotic names such as 'collateralised debt obligations' and 'credit default swaps', ultimately led to huge losses that taxpayers had to absorb in order to prevent the banks from collapse.

Now that many banks throughout the world are in taxpayers' hands, they are destined to lead a much quieter life. They will have to focus more on the basics such as taking deposits, transferring funds and making simple loans to customers. Is that such a bad thing?

The history of banks has reflected a tension between carrying out their core functions and the quest for high returns through high risk strategies. It seems, however, that for some time to come they will have to concentrate on the former and will be unable to speculate with depositors' cash.

Source: Based on information in Peston, Robert (2008) We own Royal Bank, *BBC News*, www.bbc.co.uk, 28 November.

WHAT IS MANAGEMENT ACCOUNTING?

Having considered what businesses are and how they are organised and managed, we can now turn our attention to the role of **management accounting**. A useful starting point for our discussion is to understand the general role of accounting, which is to help people make informed business decisions. All forms of accounting, including management accounting, are concerned with collecting and analysing financial, and other, information and then communicating this information to those making decisions. This decision-making perspective of accounting provides the theme for the book and shapes the way that we deal with each topic.

For accounting information to be useful for decision making, the accountant must be clear about *for whom* the information is being prepared and *for what purpose* it will be used. In practice there are various groups of people (known as 'user groups') with an interest in a particular organisation, in the sense of needing to make decisions about that organisation. For the typical private-sector business, the most important of these groups of users of accounting information are shown in Figure 1.6. Each of these groups will have different needs.

This book is concerned with providing accounting information for only one of the groups identified – the managers. It is, however, a particularly important user group. Managers are responsible for running the business, and their decisions and actions play a vital role in

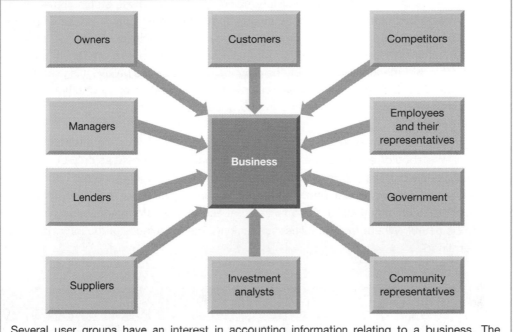

Several user groups have an interest in accounting information relating to a business. The majority of these are outside the business but, nevertheless, have a stake in it. This is not meant to be an exhaustive list of potential users; however, the groups identified are normally the most important.

Figure 1.6 Main users of accounting information relating to a business

determining its success. Planning for the future and exercising day-to-day control over a business involves a wide range of decisions being made. For example, managers may need to decide whether to:

■ develop new products or services (as with a computer manufacturer developing a new range of computers);
■ increase or decrease the price or quantity of existing products or services (as with a tele-communications business changing its mobile phone call and text charges);
■ increase or decrease the operating capacity of the business (as with a beef farming business reviewing the size of its herd); and/or
■ change the methods of purchasing, production or distribution (as with a clothes retailer switching from local to overseas suppliers).

The accounting information provided should help in identifying and assessing the financial consequences of the kind of decisions listed above. In later chapters, we shall consider each of the types of decisions in the list and see how their financial consequences can be assessed.

HOW USEFUL IS MANAGEMENT-ACCOUNTING INFORMATION?

There are arguments and convincing evidence that managers regard management-accounting information as useful. There have been numerous research surveys that have asked managers to rank the importance of management-accounting information, in relation to other sources of information, for decision-making purposes. These studies have almost invariably found that managers rank accounting information very highly. It is also worth noting that businesses of any size will normally produce management-accounting information even though there is no legal compulsion for businesses to do so. Presumably, the cost of producing this information is justified on the grounds that managers believe it is useful. Such arguments and evidence, however, leave unanswered the question as to whether the information is *actually* useful for decision-making purposes: that is, does it really affect managers' behaviour?

It is impossible to measure just how useful management-accounting information is to managers. We should remember that this information usually represents only one input to a particular decision. The precise weight attached to it by managers, and the benefits that flow as a result, cannot be accurately assessed. We shall shortly see, however, that it is at least possible to identify the kinds of qualities that accounting information must possess in order to be useful. Where these qualities are lacking, the usefulness of the information will be undermined.

PROVIDING A SERVICE

One way of viewing management accounting is as a form of service. Management accountants provide economic information to their 'clients', the managers. The value of this service can be judged according to whether the managers' information needs have been met.

To be useful, management-accounting information should possess certain qualities, or characteristics. In particular, it must be relevant and it must faithfully represent what it is supposed to represent. These two qualities, **relevance** and **faithful representation**, are regarded as fundamental qualities and are now explained in more detail.

■ *Relevance*. Management-accounting information should make a difference. That is, it should be capable of influencing managers' decisions. To do this, it must help to *predict future events* (such as predicting the next year's profit), or help to *confirm past events* (such as establishing the previous year's profit), or do both. By confirming past events, managers can check on the accuracy of their earlier predictions. This may, in turn, help them to improve the ways in which they make predictions in the future.

Management-accounting information often relies on the use of estimates. These can cover a wide range and may, for example, include estimates of future sales, costs and cash flows. By their very nature, however, estimates contain a degree of uncertainty.

Activity 1.7

Do you think that the use of estimates will weaken the relevance of accounting information provided to managers?

Estimates will vary in the degree of uncertainty that they contain. The higher the degree of uncertainty, the less relevant estimates are likely to be.

This does not imply, however, that estimates with a high degree of uncertainty should not be reported. There may be situations where they still provide managers with the most relevant information available.

To be relevant, management-accounting information must cross a threshold of **materiality**. An item of information should be considered material, or significant, if its omission or mis-statement could alter the decisions that managers make.

Activity 1.8

Do you think that information that is material for one business will also be material for all other businesses?

No. It will often vary from one business to the next. What is material will normally depend on factors such as the size of the business, the nature of the information and the amounts involved.

Ultimately, what is considered material is a matter of judgement. In making this judgement, consideration should be given as to how this information is likely to be used by managers. Where a piece of information is not material, it should not be included within the management-accounting reports. It will merely clutter them up and, perhaps, interfere with the managers' ability to interpret them.

■ *Faithful representation*. Management-accounting information should represent what it is supposed to represent. To do so, the information provided must reflect the substance of what has occurred rather than its legal form. Take, for example, a manufacturer that provides goods to a retailer on a sale-or-return basis. The manufacturer may wish to treat this arrangement as two separate transactions. Thus, a contract may be agreed for the sale of the goods and a separate contract agreed for the return of the goods if unsold by the retailer. This may result in a sale being reported as soon as the goods are delivered to the retailer even though they are returned at a later date. The economic substance, however, is that the manufacturer has made no sale as the goods were subsequently returned. They have simply been moved from the manufacturer's business to the retailer's business and then back again. Management-accounting reports should reflect this economic substance. To do otherwise would be misleading.

To provide a perfectly faithful representation, the information provided should be *complete.* In other words, it should incorporate everything needed for managers to understand what is being portrayed. It should also be *neutral*, which means that the information should be presented and selected without bias. Finally, it should be *free from error*. This is not the same as saying that information must be perfectly accurate; this may not be possible. We saw earlier that management-accounting information often contains estimates and these may turn out to be inaccurate. Nevertheless, estimates can still be faithfully represented provided they are properly described and prepared. In practice, management-accounting information is unlikely to reflect perfectly these three aspects of faithful representation. It should aim to do so, however, insofar as possible.

Management-accounting information must contain *both* of these fundamental qualities if it is to be useful. There is little point in producing information that is relevant, but which lacks faithful representation, or producing information that is irrelevant, even if it is faithfully represented.

Further qualities

Where management-accounting information is both relevant and faithfully represented, there are other qualities that, if present, can *enhance* its usefulness. These are **comparability**, **verifiability**, **timeliness** and **understandability**. Each of these qualities is now considered.

- *Comparability.* When using management-accounting information, managers often want to make comparisons. They may want to compare performance of the business over time (for example, profit this year compared to last year). They may also want to compare certain *aspects* of business performance to those of similar businesses (such as the level of sales achieved during the year). Better comparisons can be made where the management-accounting system treats items that are basically the same in the same way and where policies for measuring and presenting management-accounting information are made clear.

- *Verifiability.* This quality provides assurance to users that the management-accounting information provided faithfully represents what it is supposed to represent. Management accounting information is verifiable where different, independent experts could reach a consensus that it provides a faithful portrayal. Verifiable information tends to be supported by evidence, such as an invoice stating the cost of some item of inventories.

- *Timeliness.* Management-accounting information should be produced in time for managers to make their decisions. A lack of timeliness will undermine the usefulness of the information. Normally, the later management-accounting information is produced, the less useful it becomes.

- *Understandability.* Management-accounting information should be set out as clearly and concisely as possible so as to help those managers at whom the information is aimed.

Activity 1.9

Do you think that management-accounting reports should be understandable to those who have not studied management accounting?

It would be very helpful if everyone could understand management-accounting reports. This, however, is unrealistic, as it is not normally possible to express complex financial events and transactions in simple, non-technical terms. Any attempts to do so are likely to provide a distorted picture of reality.

It is probably best that we regard management-accounting reports in the same way that we regard a report written in a foreign language. To understand either of these, we need to have had some preparation. When management-accounting reports are produced, it is normally assumed that the relevant manager not only has a reasonable knowledge of business and accounting but is also prepared to invest some time in studying the reports. Nevertheless, the onus is clearly on management accountants to provide information in a way that makes it as understandable as possible to non-accountants.

It is worth emphasising that the four qualities just discussed cannot make management-accounting information useful. They can only enhance the usefulness of information that is already relevant and faithfully represented.

WEIGHING UP THE COSTS AND BENEFITS

Even though a piece of management-accounting information may have all the qualities described, it does not automatically mean that it should be collected and reported to users. There is still one more hurdle to jump. Consider Activity 1.10.

Activity 1.10

Suppose that an item of information is capable of being provided. It is relevant to a particular decision and can be faithfully represented. It is also comparable, verifiable and timely, and could be understood by the manager.

Can you think of a good reason why, in practice, you might decide not to produce the information?

The reason is that you judge the cost of doing so to be greater than the potential benefit of having the information. This cost–benefit issue will limit the amount of management accounting information provided.

In theory, a particular item of management-accounting information should only be produced if the costs of providing it are less than the benefits, or value, to be derived from its use. Figure 1.7 shows the relationship between the costs and value of providing additional management-accounting information.

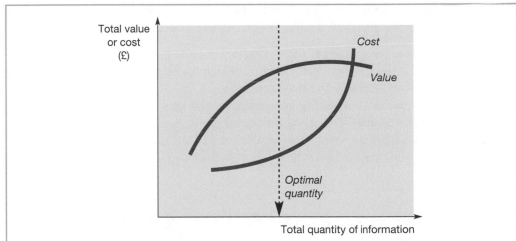

The benefits of management-accounting information eventually decline. The cost of providing the information, however, will rise with each additional piece of information. The optimal level of information provision is where the gap between the value of the information and the cost of providing it is at its greatest.

Figure 1.7 Relationship between the cost and value of providing additional management-accounting information

Figure 1.7 shows how the total value of information received by the manager eventually begins to decline. This is, perhaps, because additional information becomes less relevant, or because of the problems that a manager may have in processing the sheer quantity of information provided. The total cost of providing the information, however, will increase with each additional piece of information. The broken line indicates the point at which the gap between the value of information and the cost of providing that information is at its greatest. This represents the optimal amount of information that should be provided. Beyond this optimal level, each additional piece of information will cost more than the value of having it. This theoretical model, however, poses a number of problems in practice, which we shall now discuss.

To illustrate the practical problems of establishing the value of information, let us assume that when parking our car, we accidentally reversed our car into a wall in a car park. This resulted in a dented boot and scraped paintwork. We want to have the dent taken out and the paintwork resprayed at a local garage. We have discovered that the nearest garage would charge £400, but we believe that other local garages may offer to do the job for a lower price. The only way of finding out the prices at other garages is to visit them, so that they can see the extent of the damage. Visiting the garages will involve using some fuel and will take up some of our time. Is it worth the cost of finding out the price for the job at the various local garages? The answer, as we have seen, is that if the cost of discovering the price is less than the potential benefit, it is worth having that information.

To identify the various prices for the job, there are several points to be considered, including:

- How many garages shall we visit?
- What is the cost of fuel to visit each garage?
- How long will it take to make all the garage visits?
- At what price do we value our time?

The economic benefit of having the information on the price of the job is probably even harder to assess, in advance. The following points need to be considered:

- What is the cheapest price that we might be quoted for the job?
- How likely is it that we shall be quoted a price cheaper than £400?

As we can imagine, the answers to these questions may be far from clear – remember that we have only contacted the local garage so far. When assessing the value of accounting information, we are confronted with similar problems.

Producing management-accounting information can be very costly. The costs, however, are often difficult to quantify. Direct, out-of-pocket costs, such as salaries of accounting staff, are not usually a problem, but these are only part of the total costs involved. There are other costs such as the cost of users' time spent on analysing and interpreting the information provided.

Activity 1.11

What about the economic benefits of producing management-accounting information? Do you think it is easier, or harder, to assess the economic benefits of management-accounting information than to assess the costs of producing it?

It is normally much harder to assess the benefits. We saw earlier that, even if we could accurately measure the economic benefits arising from a particular decision, we must bear in mind that management-accounting information will be only one factor influencing that decision. Other factors will also be taken into account. Furthermore, the precise weight attached to the management-accounting information by the decision maker cannot normally be established.

There are no easy answers to the problem of weighing costs and benefits. Although it is possible to apply some 'science' to the problem, a lot of subjective judgement is normally involved.

The qualities, or characteristics, influencing the usefulness of management-accounting information that have been discussed above are summarised in Figure 1.8.

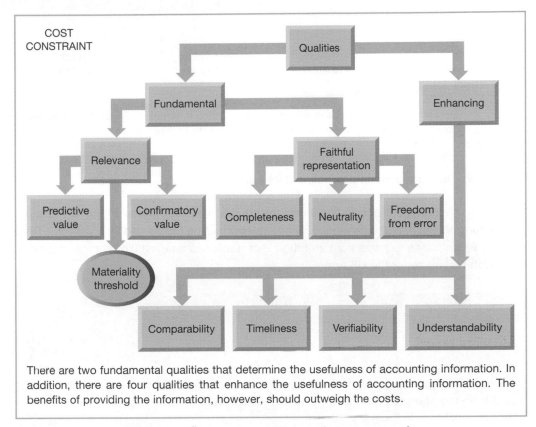

There are two fundamental qualities that determine the usefulness of accounting information. In addition, there are four qualities that enhance the usefulness of accounting information. The benefits of providing the information, however, should outweigh the costs.

Figure 1.8 The qualities that influence the usefulness of accounting information

MANAGEMENT ACCOUNTING AS AN INFORMATION SYSTEM

We have already seen that management accounting can be seen as the provision of a service to its 'clients', the managers. Another way of viewing management accounting is as a part of the business's total information system. Managers have to make decisions concerning the allocation of scarce economic resources. To ensure that these resources are efficiently allocated, managers often require economic information on which to base their decisions. It is the role of the management-accounting system to provide that information.

The **management-accounting information system** has certain features that are common to all information systems within a business. These are:

■ identifying and capturing relevant information (in this case, economic information);
■ recording the information collected in a systematic manner;
■ analysing and interpreting the information collected; and
■ reporting the information in a manner that suits the needs of individual managers.

The relationship between these features is set out in Figure 1.9.

Given the decision-making emphasis of this book, we shall be concerned primarily with the last two elements of the process – the analysis and reporting of management-accounting information. We shall consider the way in which information is used by, and is useful to, managers rather than the way in which it is identified and recorded.

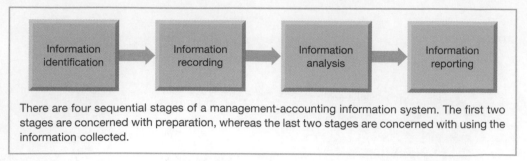

There are four sequential stages of a management-accounting information system. The first two stages are concerned with preparation, whereas the last two stages are concerned with using the information collected.

Figure 1.9 The management-accounting information system

Efficient management-accounting systems are an essential ingredient of an efficient organisation. When management-accounting systems fail, the results can be disastrous. **Real World 1.9** comprises extracts from an article that discusses an example of an almost complete systems failure for the US Army.

IT'S JUST A PHASE

Although management accounting has always been concerned with helping managers to manage, the information provided has undergone profound changes over the years. This has been in response to changes in both the business environment and in business methods. The development of management accounting can be seen as having four distinct phases.

Phase 1

Until 1950, or thereabouts, businesses enjoyed a fairly benign economic environment. Competition was weak and, as products could easily be sold, there was no pressing need for product innovation. The main focus of management attention was on the internal processes of the business. In particular, there was a concern for determining the cost of goods and services produced and for exercising financial control over the relatively simple production processes that existed during that period. In this early phase, management-accounting information was not a major influence on decision making. Although cost and budget information was produced, it was not widely supplied to managers at all levels of seniority.

Phase 2

During the 1950s and 1960s management-accounting information remained inwardly focused; however, the emphasis shifted towards producing information for short-term planning and control purposes. Management accounting came to be seen as an important part of the system of management control and of particular value in controlling the production and other internal processes of the business. The controls developed, however, were largely reactive in nature. Problems were often identified as a result of actual performance deviating from planned performance. Only then would corrective action be taken.

Phase 3

During the 1970s and early 1980s the world experienced considerable upheaval as a result of oil price rises and economic recession. This was also a period of rapid technological change and increased competition. These factors conspired to produce new techniques of production, such as robotics and computer-aided design. These new techniques led to a greater concern for controlling costs, particularly through waste reduction. Waste arising from delays, defects, excess production and so on was identified as a non-value-added activity – that is, an activity that increases costs, but does not generate additional revenue. Various techniques were developed to reduce or eliminate waste. To compete effectively, managers and employees were given greater freedom to make decisions and this in turn has led to the need for management-accounting information to be made more widely available. Advances in computing, such as the personal computer, changed the nature, amount and availability of management-accounting information. Increasing the volume and availability of information to managers meant that greater attention had to be paid to the design of management-accounting information systems.

Phase 4

During the 1990s and 2000s advances in manufacturing technology and in information technology, such as the World Wide Web, continued unabated. This further increased the level of competition which, in turn, led to a further shift in emphasis. Increased competition provoked a concern for the more effective use of resources, with particular emphasis on creating value for shareholders by understanding customer needs (see reference 3 at the end of the chapter). This change resulted in management-accounting information becoming more outwardly focused. The attitudes and behaviour of customers have become the object of much information gathering. Increasingly, successful businesses are those that are able to secure and maintain competitive advantage over their rivals through a greater understanding of customer needs. Thus, information that provides details of customers and the market has become vitally important. Such information might include customers' evaluation of services provided (perhaps through the use of opinion surveys) and data on the share of the market enjoyed by the particular business.

It should be emphasised that the effect of these four phases is cumulative. That is to say that each successive phase built on what already existed as common practice, rather than replacing it. For example, the activities of Phase 1 (principally, cost determination) remain an important part of the work of the management accountant during Phase 4.

Figure 1.10 summarises the four phases in the development of modern management accounting.

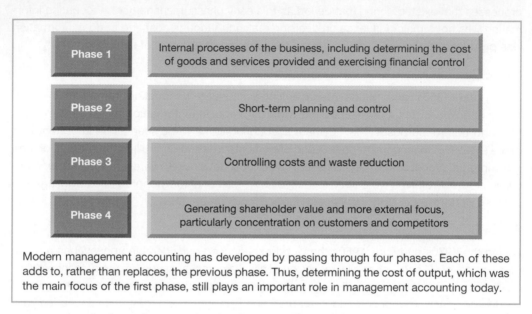

Modern management accounting has developed by passing through four phases. Each of these adds to, rather than replaces, the previous phase. Thus, determining the cost of output, which was the main focus of the first phase, still plays an important role in management accounting today.

Figure 1.10 The four phases in the development of management accounting

WHAT INFORMATION DO MANAGERS NEED?

We have seen that management accounting can be regarded as a form of service where managers are the 'clients'. This raises the question, however, as to what kind of information these 'clients' require. It is possible to identify four broad areas of decision making where management-accounting information is required:

- *Developing objectives and plans.* We have seen that managers are responsible for establishing the objectives of the business and then developing appropriate strategies to achieve them. Management-accounting information can help in developing objectives and in identifying the various strategies available. It can also generate financial plans to reveal likely outcomes from implementing the various strategies identified. These plans should help managers to evaluate each strategy and to select the most appropriate.
- *Performance evaluation and control.* Management-accounting information can help in reviewing the performance of the business against agreed criteria. Controls need to be in place to try to ensure that actual performance conforms to planned performance. Actual outcomes will, therefore, be compared with plans to see whether the performance is better or worse than expected. Where there is a significant difference, some investigation should be carried out and corrective action taken where necessary.
- *Allocating resources.* Resources available to a business are limited and it is the duty of managers to ensure that they are used as efficiently and effectively as possible. Management-accounting information can play a key role in carrying out this duty.

Decisions such as the optimum level of output, the appropriate location for production facilities, the optimum mix of products and the appropriate type of investment in new equipment rely heavily on management-accounting information.

■ *Determining costs and benefits.* Many management decisions require knowledge of the costs and benefits of pursuing a particular course of action such as providing a service, producing a new product or closing down a department. The decision will involve weighing the costs against the benefits. The management accountant can help managers by providing details of particular costs and benefits. In some cases, these may be extremely difficult to quantify; however, some approximation is usually better than nothing at all.

These areas of management decision making are set out in Figure 1.11.

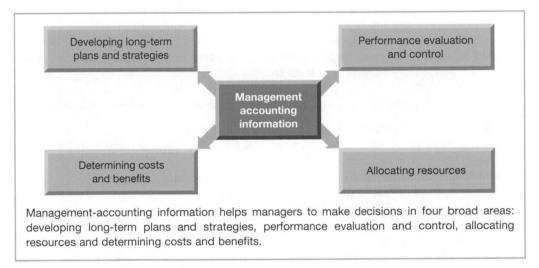

Management-accounting information helps managers to make decisions in four broad areas: developing long-term plans and strategies, performance evaluation and control, allocating resources and determining costs and benefits.

Figure 1.11 Decisions requiring management-accounting information

REPORTING NON-FINANCIAL INFORMATION

Adopting a more strategic and customer-focused approach to running a business has highlighted the fact that many factors, which are often critical to success, cannot be measured in purely financial terms. Many businesses have developed **key performance indicators (KPIs)**. These include the traditional financial measures, such as return on capital employed. However, KPIs often include a large proportion of non-financial indicators to help assess the prospects of long-term success. As the major provider of decision-making information, the management accountant has increasingly shouldered responsibility for reporting non-financial measures regarding quality, product innovation, product cycle times, delivery times and so on.

Activity 1.12

It can be argued that non-financial measures, such as those mentioned above, do not, strictly speaking, fall within the scope of accounting information and, therefore, could (or should) be provided by others. What do you think?

It is true that others could collect this kind of information. As stated, however, management accountants are major information providers to managers and may see it as their role to provide a broad range of information for decision making.

The boundaries of management accounting are not fixed. Non-financial information is often inextricably linked to financial outcomes. A lack of new product innovation, for example, may lead to a decline in sales revenue. Management accountants may, therefore, feel obliged to report the relationship between the two. To do this will involve collecting both financial and non-financial information.

Activity 1.13 considers the kind of information that may be expressed in non-financial terms and which the management accountant may provide for an airline business.

Activity 1.13

Imagine that you are the chief executive of the 'no-frills' airline Ryanair Holdings plc. What kinds of non-financial information (that is, information not containing monetary values) may be relevant to help you evaluate the performance of the business for a particular period? Try to think of at least six.

Here are some possibilities, although there are many more that might have been chosen:

- volume of passengers transported to various destinations;
- average load factor (that is, percentage of total passenger seats occupied) per trip;
- market share of air passenger travel;
- number of new routes established by Ryanair during a period;
- percentage of total passenger volume generated by these new routes;
- aircraft turnaround times at airports;
- punctuality of flights;
- levels of aircraft utilisation;
- number of flight cancellations;
- percentage of baggage losses;
- levels of customer satisfaction;
- levels of employee satisfaction;
- percentage of bookings made over the Internet; and
- maintenance hours per aircraft.

In Chapter 10 we shall look at some of the financial and non-financial KPIs that are used in practice.

INFLUENCING MANAGERS' BEHAVIOUR

We have seen that management accounting attempts to measure various aspects of business performance. Its ultimate purpose is to improve the quality of managers' decisions. In other words, the various measures are intended to have a positive effect on managers' behaviour. Occasionally, however, things may not turn out this way.

A potential problem is that managers will focus their attention and efforts on those aspects of the business that are being measured and will ignore other aspects. This is because the aspects being measured are often those used to evaluate managers' performance. They may therefore conclude that 'the things that count are the things that get counted'. Such a narrow focus, however, can have undesirable consequences for the business.

A departmental manager has been given responsibility for controlling departmental costs and this forms an important part of her annual performance appraisal. The manager is allocated an amount of money to spend on staff training each year. How might the manager's focus on 'the things that get counted' result in undesirable consequences?

To demonstrate cost consciousness, the manager may underspend during the year by cutting back on staff training. Although this may help to exert control over costs, staff morale and longer-term profitability may be adversely affected. These adverse effects may go unrecognised, at least in the short term, as cost control will be the focus of attention.

There is also the potential problem that a particular measure will be manipulated. Where, for example, profit is seen as important, a manager may attempt to boost this measure by continuing to use old, fully depreciated, pieces of equipment in order to keep depreciation charges low. This may be done despite the fact that the purchase of new equipment would produce higher quality products and would help the business to flourish over the longer term. The incentive for such behaviour is often linked to managers' rewards. In the case just described, for example, annual, profit-related bonuses may be the key motivation behind the manager's actions.

A further potential problem is that the targets against which performance is measured may be 'gamed'. A sales manager, for example, may provide a deliberately low sales forecast for a period where it will be used as the basis for a sales target. The incentive to do so may again be related to management rewards, such as when bonuses are given for exceeding sales targets. It may also be done, however, to ensure that future sales targets can be achieved with relatively little effort.

Management accountants must be aware of the unintended consequences of accounting measures on the behaviour of managers. When developing measures, every effort should be made to take account of all key aspects of performance, even though some may be difficult to quantify. Furthermore, they must be alert to any signs that managers are manipulating measures or 'gaming' targets rather than striving to achieve the objectives of the business.

REAPING THE BENEFITS OF INFORMATION TECHNOLOGY

The impact of information technology (IT) on the volume, quality and timeliness of management-accounting information, as well as other information, reported to managers is difficult to overstate. The ability of computers to process large amounts of information means that routine reports can be produced quickly and accurately. Some reports may be produced on a daily, or even a real-time, basis. This can be vital for businesses operating in a highly competitive environment, which risk losing competitive advantage through making decisions based on inaccurate, or out-of-date, reports. IT has also enabled information to be more widely available throughout the business. Increasingly, employees at all levels can gain access to relevant information and reports to guide their decisions and actions through their personal computers.

IT has allowed management reports to be produced in greater detail and in greater variety than could be contemplated under a manual system. It has also allowed sophisticated measurement systems to be provided at relatively low cost. IT makes it much easier to assess proposals by allowing variables (such as estimates of product price, output, product cost and so on) to be changed easily. By just a few keystrokes, the estimated size of key variables may be increased or decreased so as to create a range of possible scenarios.

In recent years, enterprise resource planning (ERP) systems have been developed. These systems provide an integrated suite of applications, or modules, to track resources across the whole of the business. They operate in real time and offer modules covering a range of business functions including accounting, manufacturing, marketing and sales, human resources and project management. ERP systems offer timeliness and accuracy in reporting and generate a wealth of data relating to the various business operations. Managers are, therefore, better able to plan and control a range of business operations.

The IT revolution continues and its impact on businesses shows no sign of easing. One development that has a potentially profound effect on the role of management accountants is that of **big data**. This term is used to describe the huge volume of data that businesses now collect relating to customers, to competitors and to the broader business environment. These data, which are varied and often generated at great velocity, are collected from multiple sources such as credit cards, the Internet, social media and so on. Big data poses a major challenge to businesses because its volume and complexity is too much for traditional data processing systems to handle. Those businesses, however, which are able to capture, shape and analyse big data gain a huge competitive advantage. They can scan the environment in order to detect trends and patterns to be fed into the planning and decision-making process.

FROM BEAN COUNTER TO TEAM MEMBER

Given the changes described above, it is not surprising that the role of the management accountant within a business has been transformed. IT has released the management accountant from much of the routine work associated with preparation of management-accounting reports. This has allowed more time to focus on the design of information systems and the analysis and interpretation of the information produced.

The release from routine work has also enabled management accountants to take a more proactive role within the business. Their reach now extends beyond providing information, and perhaps advice, to managers. Increasingly, they are regarded as part of the management team. By taking a lead in the design of information systems and by shaping and interpreting their output, they become more directly involved in planning and decision making.

Management accountants are gradually assuming a broader role as information managers within a business. They are well placed to do so as their core skills in structuring, analysing and reporting information can be applied to both financial and non-financial information. Furthermore, these skills are underpinned by commercial awareness as well as an understanding of managers' needs. To carry out this broader role, management accountants must work closely with IT professionals. Often, they can provide a bridge between IT professionals and the management team.

The enhanced role for management accountants should add value to the business and improve its competitive position. However, it requires a wider set of skills than required from their more traditional role.

Changes to the role of the management accountant should benefit the development of management accounting as a discipline. While working as part of a cross-functional team, there is an opportunity to gain a greater awareness of strategic and operational matters, an increased understanding of the information needs of managers and a deeper appreciation of the importance of value creation. This is likely to have a positive effect on the design and development of management-accounting systems. As a consequence, we should see increasing evidence that management accounting systems are being designed to fit the particular structure and processes of the business rather than the other way round.

REASONS TO BE ETHICAL

The extent to which a business displays honesty, fairness and transparency when dealing with its stakeholders (customers, employees, suppliers, the community, the shareholders and so on) has become a key issue. There have been many examples of businesses, some of them very well known, acting in ways that most people would regard as unethical and unacceptable. Such actions include:

- paying bribes to encourage employees of a competitor business to reveal information about the competitor that could be useful;
- oppressive treatment of suppliers, for example, making suppliers wait excessive periods before payment; and
- manipulating the financial statements, for example, overstating profit so that senior managers become eligible for performance bonuses.

Despite the many examples of unethical acts that have attracted publicity over recent years, it would be very unfair to conclude that most businesses are involved in unethical activities. Nevertheless, revelations of unethical practice can be damaging to the entire business community. Dishonest, bullying and underhand behaviour can lead to a loss of confidence in business generally, perhaps leading to the imposition of tighter regulatory burdens. Most businesses are aware of these consequences and try, therefore, to demonstrate their commitment to high standards of behaviour.

As an additional incentive to behave ethically, there is evidence to suggest a link between high ethical standards and superior financial performance. **Real World 1.10** describes the findings of one study claiming to find such a link.

Business karma?

The Ethisphere Institute is a well-known organisation that promotes ethical business practices. Each year it produces a list of the World's Most Ethical Companies. The criteria used for evaluating businesses cover various aspects including corporate governance, compliance programmes, culture of ethics, reputation and corporate citizenship.

To see whether investing in ethical businesses led to superior investor returns, one study created an investment portfolio of businesses that were included in the list of the World's Most Ethical Companies as well as being listed on a US stock market. For the period 2007–2011, returns from this portfolio were then compared to the market returns, as measured by a market index (S&P 500). After adjusting for differences in risk, the study found that the portfolio of ethical businesses consistently outperformed the market. Investing in the portfolio generated returns up to 8 per cent higher than expected returns during periods when the market was rising as well as when it was falling. The authors of the study argued that this latter finding suggested that ethical businesses benefit from special protection in times of crises.

Source: Areal, N. and Carvalho, A. (2012) The World's Most Ethical Companies: does the fame translate into gain? www.efmaefm.org. pp. 1–41.

While the above findings are interesting, we should be cautious in drawing conclusions. Perhaps ethical practices do not drive superior performance but rather well-managed, high-performing, businesses tend to adopt ethical practices.

Management accountants are likely to find themselves at the forefront with issues relating to business ethics. In the three examples of unethical business activity mentioned above, a management accountant would probably have to be involved either in helping to commit the unethical act or in covering it up. Management accountants are, therefore, particularly vulnerable to being put under pressure to engage in unethical acts. Many businesses recognise this risk and produce an ethical code for their finance and accounting staff. **Real World 1.11** provides an example of one such code.

The only way is ethics

BT plc, the telecommunications business, has a code of ethics for its senior finance and accounting staff which states that they must:

- Act with honesty and integrity, including ethically handling actual or apparent conflicts of interest between their personal relationships or financial or commercial interests and their responsibilities to BT;
- Promote full, fair, accurate, timely and understandable disclosure in all reports and documents that BT files with, or submits to, the US Securities and Exchange Commission or otherwise makes public;
- Comply with all laws, rules and regulations applicable to BT and to its relationship with its shareholders;
- Report known or suspected violations of this code of ethics promptly to the chairman of the Nominating & Governance Committee; and
- Ensure that their actions comply not only with the letter but the spirit of this code of ethics and foster a culture in which BT operates in compliance with the law and BT's policies.

Source: BT plc, Our Business Practice and Code of Ethics, www.BT.com, accessed 8 November 2016.

MANAGEMENT ACCOUNTING AND FINANCIAL ACCOUNTING

Management accounting is one of two main strands in accounting; the other strand is **financial accounting**. The difference between the two is based on the user groups to which each is addressed. Management accounting seeks to meet the needs of managers, whereas financial accounting seeks to meet the accounting needs of the other users that were identified earlier in Figure 1.6 (see p. 17).

The difference in their targeted user groups has led to each strand of accounting developing along different lines. The main areas of difference are as follows:

- *Nature of the reports produced.* Financial accounting reports tend to be general-purpose. Although they are aimed primarily at providers of finance such as owners and lenders, they contain financial information that will be useful for a broad range of users and decisions. Management accounting reports, on the other hand, are often specific-purpose reports. They are often designed with a particular decision in mind and/or for a particular manager.

- *Level of detail.* Financial accounting reports provide users with a broad overview of the performance and position of the business for a period. As a result, information is aggregated (that is, added together) and detail is often lost. Management accounting reports, however, often provide managers with considerable detail to help them with a particular operational decision.

- *Regulations.* The financial accounting reports of many businesses are subject to regulations imposed by the law and by accounting rule makers. These regulations often require a standard content and, perhaps, a standard format to be adopted. As management accounting reports are for internal use only, there are no regulations from external sources concerning their content and form. They can be designed to meet the needs of particular managers.

- *Reporting interval.* For most businesses, financial accounting reports are produced on an annual basis, although some large businesses produce half-yearly reports and a few produce quarterly ones. Management accounting reports will be produced as frequently as is needed. A sales manager, for example, may require routine sales reports on a daily, weekly or monthly basis so as to monitor performance closely. Special-purpose reports can also be prepared when the occasion demands: for example, where an evaluation is required of a proposed investment in new equipment.

- *Time orientation.* Financial accounting reports reveal the performance and position of a business for the past period. In essence, they are backward-looking. Management accounting reports, on the other hand, often provide information concerning future performance as well as past performance. It is an oversimplification, however, to suggest that financial accounting reports never incorporate expectations concerning the future. Occasionally, businesses will release forward-looking information to other users in an attempt to raise finance or to fight off unwanted takeover bids. Even preparation of financial accounting reports for the past period typically requires making some judgements about the future, for example the residual value of a depreciating asset.

- *Range and quality of information.* Two key points are worth mentioning here. Firstly, financial accounting reports concentrate on information that can be quantified in monetary terms. Management accounting also produces such reports, but is also more likely to produce reports that contain information of a non-financial nature, such as physical volume of inventories, number of sales orders received, number of new products launched, physical output per employee and so on. Secondly, financial accounting places greater emphasis on the use of objective, verifiable evidence when preparing reports. Management accounting reports may use information that is less objective and verifiable, but nevertheless provide managers with the information they need.

We can see from this that management accounting is less constrained than financial accounting. It may draw from a variety of sources and use information that has varying degrees of reliability. The only real test to be applied when assessing the value of the information produced for managers is whether or not it improves the quality of the decisions made.

The main differences between financial accounting and management accounting reports are summarised in Figure 1.12.

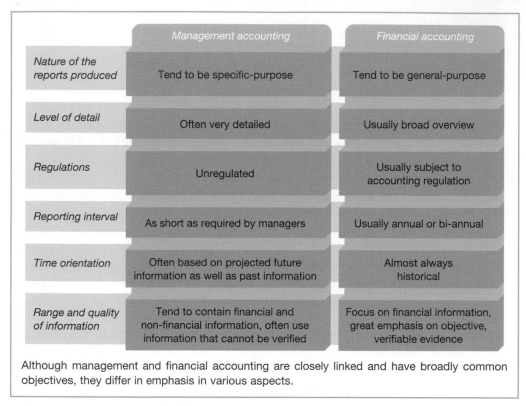

	Management accounting	Financial accounting
Nature of the reports produced	Tend to be specific-purpose	Tend to be general-purpose
Level of detail	Often very detailed	Usually broad overview
Regulations	Unregulated	Usually subject to accounting regulation
Reporting interval	As short as required by managers	Usually annual or bi-annual
Time orientation	Often based on projected future information as well as past information	Almost always historical
Range and quality of information	Tend to contain financial and non-financial information, often use information that cannot be verified	Focus on financial information, great emphasis on objective, verifiable evidence

Although management and financial accounting are closely linked and have broadly common objectives, they differ in emphasis in various aspects.

Figure 1.12 Management and financial accounting reports compared

The differences between management accounting and financial accounting reports suggest differences in the information needs of managers and those of other users. While differences undoubtedly exist, there is also a good deal of overlap between the information needs of both.

Activity 1.16

Can you think of any areas of overlap between the information needs of managers and those of other users? (*Hint*: Think about the time orientation and the level of detail of accounting information.)

Two points that spring to mind are:

■ Managers will, at times, be interested in receiving a historical overview of business operations of the sort provided to other users.
■ Other users would be interested in receiving detailed information relating to the future, such as the planned level of profits, and non-financial information, such as the state of the sales order book and the extent of product innovations.

To some extent, differences between the two strands of accounting reflect differences in access to financial information. Managers have total control over the form and content of the information that they receive. Other users have to rely on what managers are prepared to provide or what financial reporting regulations insist must be provided. Although the scope of financial accounting reports has increased over time, fears concerning loss of competitive advantage and user ignorance about the reliability of forward-looking data have meant that other users do not receive the same detailed and wide-ranging information as that available to managers.

In the past it has been argued that accounting systems are biased in favour of providing information for external users. Financial accounting requirements have been the main priority and management accounting has suffered as a result. More recent survey evidence suggests, however, that this argument has lost its force. Nowadays, management accounting systems will usually provide managers with information that is relevant to their needs rather than that determined by external reporting requirements. External reporting cycles, however, retain some influence over management accounting. Managers tend to be aware of external users' expectations (see reference 4 at the end of the chapter).

SUMMARY

The main points of this chapter may be summarised as follows:

What is the purpose of a business?

- To create and keep a customer.

How are businesses organised and managed?

- Most businesses of any size are set up as limited companies.
- A board of directors is appointed by shareholders to oversee the running of the business.
- Businesses are often divided into departments and organised along functional lines; however, larger businesses may be divisionalised along geographical and/or product lines.

Strategic management

- The development of strategic management is in response to changes in the competitive environment and to the increase in size of many businesses.
- Strategic management involves five steps:
  1 Establish mission, vision and objectives.
  2 Undertake a position analysis (for example, a SWOT analysis).
  3 Identify and assess strategic options.
  4 Select strategic options and formulate plans.
  5 Perform, review and control.

The changing business landscape

- Increased competition and advances in technology have changed the business landscape.
- There have been changes in the kind of businesses in existence as well as changes in business structures and processes.

Setting financial aims and objectives

■ A key financial objective for a business is to enhance the owners' (shareholders') wealth.

■ When setting financial objectives the right balance must be struck between risk and return.

Management accounting and user needs

■ For management accounting to be useful, it must be clear *for whom* and *for what purpose* the information will be used.

■ Managers are an important type of user of financial information concerning the business, but there are several others including owners, employees, lenders and government.

Providing a service

■ Management accounting can be viewed as a form of service as it involves providing information to 'clients' – the managers.

■ To provide a useful service, management accounting information must possess certain qualities, or characteristics.

■ The fundamental qualities are relevance and faithful representation. Other qualities that enhance the usefulness of accounting information are comparability, verifiability, timeliness and understandability.

■ Providing a service to managers can be costly and information should be produced only if the cost of providing the information is less than the benefits gained.

Management accounting as an information system

■ Management accounting is part of the total information system within a business. It shares the features that are common to all information systems within a business, which are the identification, recording, analysis and reporting of information.

What information do managers need?

■ To meet managers' needs, information relating to the following broad areas is required:
  ■ developing objectives and plans;
  ■ performance evaluation and control;
  ■ allocating resources; and
  ■ determining costs and benefits.

■ Providing non-financial information has become an increasingly important part of the management accountant's role.

Influencing managers' behaviour

■ The main purpose of management accounting is to affect people's behaviour.

■ Doing so, however, is not always beneficial and may have unintended consequences.

Reaping the benefits of IT

- IT has had a major effect on the ability to provide accurate, detailed and timely information.
- Developments in IT have enabled information and reports to be more widely disseminated throughout the business.
- IT has had a profound impact on the role of the management accountant.

Changing role of the management accountant

- Management accounting has changed over the years in response to changes in the business environment (including the IT revolution) and in business methods.
- Less time is spent preparing reports and more time is spent on analysis and on providing business advice.
- The management accountant is often a key member of the management team, which requires greater interpersonal, leadership and management skills.
- The management accountant often takes on a broader role of information manager within a business.
- This new dimension to the management accountant's role should benefit the design of more relevant management accounting information systems.

Ethical behaviour

- Management accountants may be put under pressure to commit unethical acts.
- Many businesses now publish a code of ethics governing the behaviour of accounting staff.

Management accounting and financial accounting

- Accounting has two main strands – management accounting and financial accounting.
- Management accounting seeks to meet the needs of the business's managers, and financial accounting seeks to meet the needs of providers of finance but will also be of use to other user groups.
- These two strands differ in terms of the types of reports produced, the level of reporting detail, the time orientation, the degree of regulation and the range and quality of information provided.

KEY TERMS

For definitions of these terms, see Appendix A.

REFERENCES

1 Drucker, P. (1967) *The Effective Executive*, Heinemann.

2 Chartered Institute of Management Accounting (2009) *Management Accounting Tools for Today and Tomorrow*, CIMA.

3 Abdel-Kader, M. and Luther, R. (2008) The impact of firm characteristics on management accounting practices: a UK-based empirical analysis, *British Accounting Review*, March.

4 Dugdale, D., Jones, C. and Green, S. (2006) *Contemporary Management Accounting Practices in UK Manufacturing*, Elsevier.

FURTHER READING

If you would like to explore the topics covered in this chapter in more depth, we recommend the following:

Bhimani, A., Horngren, C., Datar, S. and Rajan, M. (2015) *Management and Cost Accounting*, 6th edn, Pearson, Chapter 1.

Crane, A. and Matten, D. (2016) *Business Ethics: Managing Corporate Citizenship and Sustainability in the Age of Globalization,* 4th edn, Oxford University Press, Chapter 1.

Hilton, R. and Platt, D. (2014) *Managerial Accounting*, 10th edn, McGraw-Hill Higher Education, Chapter 1.

Johnson, G., Whittington D., Scholes, K., Angwin, D. and Regner, P. (2014) *Exploring Strategy: Text and Cases*, 10th edn, Pearson, Chapters 1–3.

REVIEW QUESTIONS

Solutions to these questions can be found at the back of the book on pp. 526–527.

1.1 Identify the main users of accounting information for a university. For what purposes would different user groups need information? Would these groups use the accounting information in a different way from the equivalent groups in private-sector businesses?

1.2 Management accounting has been described as 'the eyes and ears of management'. What do you think this expression means?

1.3 Assume that you are a manager considering the launch of a new service. What accounting information might be useful to help in making a decision?

1.4 'Management accounting information should be understandable. As some managers have a poor knowledge of accounting we should produce simplified financial reports to help them.' To what extent do you agree with this view?

EXERCISES

Solutions to these exercises can be found at the back of the book on pp. 535–536.

Basic-level exercise

1.1 You have been speaking to a friend who owns a small business, and she has said that she has read something about strategic management and that no modern business can afford not to get involved with it. Your friend has little idea what strategic management involves.

Required:

Briefly outline the steps in strategic management, summarising what each step involves.

Advanced-level exercise

1.2 Jones Dairy Ltd (Jones) operates a 'doorstep' fresh milk delivery service. Two brothers carry on the business that they inherited from their father in the early 1980s. They are the business's only directors. The business operates from a yard on the outskirts of Trepont, a substantial town in mid Wales.

Jones expanded steadily from when the brothers took over until the early 1980s, by which time it employed 25 full-time rounds staff. This was achieved because of four factors: (1) some expansion of the permanent population of Trepont; (2) expanding Jones's geographical range to the villages surrounding the town; (3) an expanding tourist trade in the area; and (4) a positive attitude to 'marketing'.

As an example of the marketing effort, when new residents move into the area, the member of the rounds staff concerned reports this back. One of the directors immediately visits the potential customer with an introductory gift, usually a bottle of milk, a bottle of wine and a bunch of flowers. He then attempts to obtain a regular milk order. Similar methods are used to persuade existing residents to place orders for delivered milk.

By the mid-1990s Jones had a monopoly of doorstep delivery in the Trepont area. A combination of losing market share to Jones and the town's relative remoteness had discouraged the national doorstep suppliers. The little locally-based competition there once was had gone out of business.

Supplies of milk come from a bottling plant, owned by one of the national dairy businesses, which is located 50 miles from Trepont. The bottlers deliver nightly, except Saturday nights, to Jones's depot. Jones delivers daily, except on Sundays.

Profits, after adjusting for inflation, have fallen since the early 1990s. Sales volumes have fallen by about a third, compared with a decline of about 50 per cent for doorstep deliveries nationally over the same period. New customers are increasingly difficult to find, despite a continuing policy of encouraging them. Many existing customers tend to have less milk delivered. A sufficient profit has been made to enable the directors to enjoy a reasonable income compared with their needs, but only by raising prices. Currently Jones charges 81p for a standard pint, delivered. This is fairly typical of prices for milk delivered to the doorstep around the UK. The Trepont supermarket, which is located in the centre of town, charges 50p a pint and other local stores charge between 55p and 60p.

Currently Jones employs 15 full-time rounds staff, a van maintenance mechanic, a secretary/bookkeeper and the two directors. Jones is regarded locally as a good employer. Regular employment opportunities in the area are generally few. Rounds staff are expected to, and generally do, give customers a friendly, cheerful and helpful service.

The two brothers continue to be the only shareholders and directors and comprise the only level of management. One of the directors devotes most of his time to dealing with the supplier and with issues connected with details of the rounds. The other director looks after administrative matters, such as the accounts and human resources issues. Both directors undertake rounds to cover for sickness and holidays.

Required:

As far as the information given in the question will allow, undertake an analysis of the strengths, weaknesses, opportunities and threats (a SWOT analysis) of the business.

Chapter 2

RELEVANT COSTS AND BENEFITS FOR DECISION MAKING

INTRODUCTION

This chapter considers how we should identify relevant costs and benefits when making management decisions. The principles outlined will provide the basis for much of the rest of the book.

Management decisions should aim to achieve the objectives of the business. When considering a proposed course of action, this involves weighing the relevant benefits and associated costs. We shall see that not all of benefits and costs that can be identified may be relevant to the particular course of action. It is important, therefore, to distinguish carefully between the costs and benefits that are relevant and those that are not. Failure to do so can easily lead to poor decisions being made.

Learning outcomes

When you have completed this chapter, you should be able to:

■ Define and distinguish between relevant costs, outlay costs and opportunity costs.

■ Identify and quantify the costs and benefits that are relevant to a particular decision.

■ Use relevant costs and benefits to make decisions.

■ Set out relevant costs and benefits analysis in a logical form so that the results can be clearly communicated to managers.

COST–BENEFIT ANALYSIS

Managers spend much of their time making plans and decisions. As part of this process, they try to assess the likely outcome from each course of action being considered. This involves a careful weighing of the prospective **benefits** against the **costs** involved. Benefits are those outcomes, resulting from a course of action, that help a business to achieve its objectives. Costs, on the other hand, represent the sacrifice of resources needed to achieve those benefits. For a proposed plan, or decision, to be worthwhile, the likely benefits should exceed the associated costs.

Real World 2.1 provides an interesting example of where **cost–benefit analysis** was used to evaluate a possible course of action designed to solve a serious problem faced by many businesses.

Real World 2.1

Stocktaking

Light-fingered employees are a problem for all employers; however, the issue is particularly severe in the retail trade. Tatiana Sandino, an associate professor in accounting and management at Harvard Business School, and co-author Clara Xiaoling Chen, an assistant professor of accountancy at the University of Illinois at Urbana–Champaign, cite figures from the National Retail Security survey in the USA which says that employee theft of inventories contributed to a loss of $15.9bn in 2008.

To try to discover what might dissuade employees from stealing, the two academics wondered if higher remuneration might help. They hypothesised that higher wages might encourage employees to feel more warmly towards their employers, that these employees – if they were paid more – would be less inclined to steal because they would not want to lose their jobs and paying a larger sum in the first place would attract more honest employees.

Using two data sets and including factors such as workers' different socio-economic environments and how many people the stores employed, the authors found that paying a larger salary caused a drop in employee theft and could, in certain circumstances, make fiscal sense.

A cost–benefit analysis found that what an employer saved in cash and inventories theft covered about 39 per cent of the cost of the wage increase. 'Our study suggests that an increase in wages will decrease theft, but won't fully pay off,' says Prof. Sandino. The pair suggest that raising salaries might be the right course of action if other benefits – such as reduced employee turnover or higher employee productivity – account for at least 61 per cent of the wage increase.

 Source: Adapted from Anderson, L. (2012) Something for the weekend, ft.com, 16 November.
© The Financial Times Limited 2012. All Rights Reserved.

To help weigh costs and benefits arising from a particular decision, it would be useful if both could be measured in monetary terms. This would then provide a common denominator for cost–benefit analysis. Some costs and benefits, however, may elude attempts to place a reliable monetary value on them. Take, for example, the likely problems of trying to measure the costs, in terms of loss of reputation, incurred by selling customers faulty products or the benefits accruing from steps taken to lift morale among the workforce. To add to the measurement problems, the timing and duration of these costs and benefits may be difficult to estimate. Nevertheless, the costs just described can have a significant effect on the achievement of business objectives. They should not, therefore, be ignored or given less weight when making decisions. There is always a risk that managers will take too narrow a view and act on the basis that 'the things that count are the things that get counted'. That is, attention will be paid to those aspects where it is easy to assign a monetary value, but aspects that are difficult to value are ignored. We shall return to this point a little later in the chapter.

WHAT IS MEANT BY 'COST'?

The term 'cost' is a slippery concept. Although a very broad description was given earlier when discussing cost–benefit analysis, it can be defined in different ways. Managers therefore need to be clear what it means in the context of decision making. This is an important issue to which we now turn.

Identifying and measuring cost may seem, at first sight, to be pretty straightforward: it is simply the amount paid for the goods supplied or the service provided. When measuring cost *for decision-making purposes*, however, things are not quite that simple. The following activity illustrates why this is the case.

Activity 2.1

You own a motor car, for which you paid a purchase price of £5,000 – much below the list price – at a recent car auction. You have just been offered £6,000 for this car.

What is the cost to you of keeping the car for your own use? *Note*: Ignore running costs and so on; just consider the 'capital' cost of the car.

By retaining the car, you are forgoing a cash receipt of £6,000. Thus, the real sacrifice, or cost, incurred by keeping the car for your own use is £6,000.

Any decision that you make with respect to the car's future should logically take account of the figure of £6,000. This is known as the **opportunity cost** since it is the value of the opportunity foregone in order to pursue the other course of action. (In this case, the other course of action is to retain the car.)

We can see that the cost of retaining the car is not the same as the purchase price. In one sense, of course, the cost of the car in Activity 2.1 is £5,000 because that is how much was paid for it. However, this cost, which for obvious reasons is known as the **historic cost**, is only of academic interest. It cannot logically ever be used to make a decision on the car's future. If we disagree with this point, we should ask ourselves how we should assess an offer of £5,500, from another person, for the car – assuming that the original offer still stood. The answer is that we should compare the offer price of £5,500 with the opportunity cost of £6,000. This should lead us to reject the offer as it is less than the £6,000 opportunity cost. In these circumstances, it would not be logical to accept the offer of £5,500 on the basis that it was more than the £5,000 that we originally paid. The only other figure that should concern us is the value to us, in terms of pleasure, usefulness and so on, of retaining the car. If we valued this more highly than the £6,000 opportunity cost, we should reject both offers.

We may still feel, however, that the £5,000 is relevant here because it will help us in assessing the profitability of the decision. If we sold the car, we should make a profit of either £500 (£5,500 − £5,000) or £1,000 (£6,000 − £5,000) depending on which offer we accept. Since we should seek to make the higher profit, the right decision is to sell the car for £6,000. However, we do not need to know the historic cost of the car to make the right decision. What decision should we make if the car cost us £4,000 to buy? Clearly we should still sell the car for £6,000 rather than for £5,500 as the important comparison is between the offer price and the opportunity cost. We should reach the same conclusion whatever the historic cost of the car.

To emphasise the above point, let us assume that the car cost £10,000. Even in this case the historic cost would still be irrelevant. Had we just bought a car for £10,000 and found shortly after that it is only worth £6,000, we might well be fuming with rage at our mistake, but this does not make the £10,000 a **relevant cost**. The only relevant factors, in a decision on whether to sell the car or to keep it, are the £6,000 opportunity cost and the value of the benefits of keeping it. Thus, the historic cost can never be relevant to a future decision.

To say that historic cost is an **irrelevant cost** is not to say that *the effects of having incurred that cost* are always irrelevant. The fact that we own the car, and are thus in a position to exercise choice as to how to use it, is not irrelevant. It is highly relevant.

Opportunity costs are rarely taken into account in the routine accounting processes, such as recording revenues, expenses, assets and claims. This is because they do not involve any out-of-pocket expenditure. It seems that they are only calculated where they are relevant to a particular management decision. Historic costs, on the other hand, do involve out-of-pocket expenditure and are recorded. They are used in preparing the annual financial statements, such as the statement of financial position and the income statement. This is logical, however, since these statements are intended to be accounts of what has actually happened and are drawn up after the event. The failure to use opportunity costs when preparing the traditional financial statements rather calls into question the usefulness of those statements for decision-making purposes. This point is beyond the scope of this book, however.

RELEVANT COSTS: OPPORTUNITY AND OUTLAY COSTS

We have just seen that, when we are making decisions concerning the future, **past costs** (that is, historic costs) are irrelevant. It is future opportunity costs and future **outlay costs** that are of concern. An opportunity cost can be defined as the value, in monetary terms, of being deprived of the next best opportunity in order to pursue the particular objective. An outlay cost is an amount of money that will have to be spent to achieve an objective. We shall shortly meet plenty of examples of both of these types of future cost.

To be relevant to a particular decision, a future outlay cost, or opportunity cost, must satisfy all three of the following criteria:

1 *It must relate to the objectives of the business.* Most businesses have enhancing owners' (shareholders') wealth as their key strategic objective. That is, they are trying to become richer (see Chapter 1). Thus, to be relevant to a particular decision, a cost must have an effect on the wealth of the business.

2 *It must be a future cost.* Past costs cannot be relevant to decisions being made about the future.

3 *It must vary with the decision.* Only costs that are different between outcomes can be used to distinguish between them. Take, for example, a road haulage business that has decided

that it will buy a new additional lorry and the decision lies between two different models. The purchase price, the load capacity, the fuel and maintenance costs are different for each lorry. The potential costs and benefits associated with these are relevant items. The lorry will require a driver, so the business will need to employ one, but a suitably qualified driver could drive either lorry equally well, for the same wage. The cost of employing the driver is thus irrelevant to the decision as to which lorry to buy. This is despite the fact that this cost is a future one.

Activity 2.2

If the decision did not concern a choice between two models of lorry but rather whether to operate an additional lorry or not, would the cost of employing the additional driver be relevant?

Yes – because it would then be a cost that would vary with the decision.

Figure 2.1 sets out in diagrammatic form how we determine which costs are relevant to a particular decision.

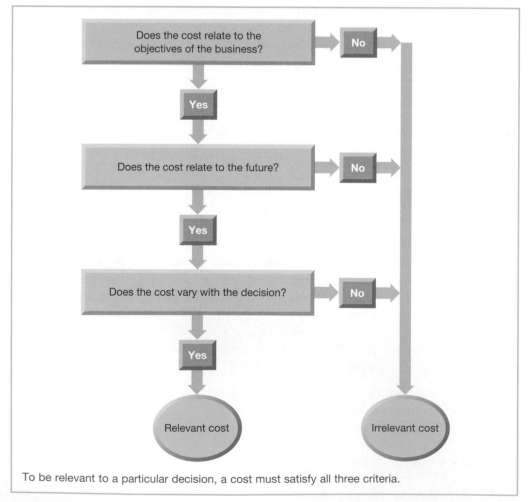

To be relevant to a particular decision, a cost must satisfy all three criteria.

Figure 2.1 A decision flow diagram for identifying relevant costs

To be relevant, the benefits arising from a particular course of action must also satisfy all three criteria mentioned. That is, they should relate to the objectives of the business, they should relate to the future and they should vary with the decision.

Activity 2.3

A garage has a car that it bought several months ago. The car needs new tyres before it is roadworthy. A tyre fitting business has offered to fit four new tyres on the car for £400.

The garage paid £9,000 to buy the car. Without the new tyres it could be sold for an estimated £10,500. What is the minimum price at which the garage should sell the car with new tyres?

The minimum price is the amount required to cover all the relevant costs. At this price, the benefits will exactly equal the costs and so neither a profit nor loss is made. Any price that is lower than this amount will mean the wealth of the business is reduced. In this case, the minimum price is:

	£
Opportunity cost of the car	10,500
Cost of the new tyres	400
Total	10,900

The original cost of the car is irrelevant for reasons already discussed. It is the opportunity cost of the car that concerns us. In this case, it is the sales value foregone. If the new tyres are purchased, the garage will have to pay £400; but will pay nothing if they are not. The £400 is, therefore, a relevant cost as it is a future cost that varies with the decision.

It should be emphasised that the garage will not try to sell the car with its new tyres for £10,900; it will try to get as much as possible for it. Any price above the £10,900, however, will make the garage better off than would be the case if it did not buy the new tyres.

Real World 2.2 is an extract from an article that discusses the opportunity cost of two countries building separate oil pipelines rather than cooperating in a joint venture.

Real World 2.2

Benefits foregone

Tullow Sees Opportunity Cost If Kenya-Uganda Pipeline Plan Fails

- Joint facilty has 'tangible economic value,' official says
- London-based oil company has discoveries in both countries

By Joseph Burite
(Bloomberg) — 03/30/2016

Tullow Oil plc, which has oil discoveries in Uganda and Kenya, sees an opportunity cost if the two countries don't collaborate on a pipeline to ship their crude to the Indian Ocean, a company official said.

Landlocked Uganda is deciding on whether the pipeline will traverse northern Kenya's desert to a proposed port at Lamu, or south past Lake Victoria to Tanga on Tanzania's coast. While Tullow, which discovered Uganda's oil, has a seat at the talks, the pipeline decision is "above our pay grade," Tim O'Hanlon, the London-based company's vice president for African business, said in an interview.

"For us we think of it as an East African integrated regional infrastructure and the opportunity cost of Uganda and Kenya not cooperating on the pipeline is enormous," he said Wednesday in Tanzania's commercial capital, Dar es Salaam. "A joint pipeline has real tangible economic value, measurable value for individual countries Uganda and Kenya, and East Africa in general."

Tanzanian President John Magufuli said earlier this month he'd agreed with his Ugandan counterpart, Yoweri Museveni, to route the conduit via his country at a cost of about $4 billion, with Total SA helping fund the project. Nagoya, Japan-based Toyota Tsusho Corp. estimates the Kenyan route may cost about $5 billion.

Separate Pipelines

A Ugandan decision to route the pipeline through Tanzania would probably mean Kenya would need its own facility to transport its oil, according to O'Hanlon. "We are talking about two separate pipelines or a joint pipeline through Kenya," he said.

Tullow along with Total SA and the China National Offshore Oil Corp. are developing Uganda's oil fields in the western region of Hoima. The Chinese company was awarded its production license in 2013, the only one so far issued by Uganda's government.

O'Hanlon said Tullow expects its first production in Uganda about three or four years after the company makes its final investment decision in 2017, and that it will be awarded production licenses in the next few weeks.

"It's taken time but it's going fine and it's of course one of the key issues that we have to have in place before we march into production," he said. To contact the reporter on this story:

Joseph Burite in Dar es Salaam at jburite@bloomberg.net

To contact the editors responsible for this story:

Paul Richardson at pmrichardson@bloomberg.net

Michael Gunn

Source: Direct extract from Burite, J. (2016) *Tullow Sees Opportunity Cost If Kenya-Uganda Pipeline Plan Fails*, www.bloomberg.com, 30 March.

IRRELEVANT COSTS: SUNK COSTS AND COMMITTED COSTS

A **sunk cost** is simply another way of referring to a past cost and so the terms 'sunk cost' and 'past cost' can be used interchangeably. A **committed cost** arises where an irrevocable decision has been made to incur the cost. This is often because a business has entered into a legally-binding contract. As a result, it is effectively the same as a past cost despite the fact that the cash may not be paid until some point in the future. Since the business must eventually pay, the cost will not vary with the decision. Thus, as with a past cost, a committed cost can never be a relevant cost for decision-making purposes.

Activity 2.4

Past costs are irrelevant costs. Does this mean that what happened in the past is irrelevant?

No, it does not mean this. The fact that the business has an asset that it can deploy in the future is highly relevant. What is not relevant is how much it cost to acquire that asset. This point was raised in the discussion that followed Activity 2.1.

Another reason why the past can be relevant is that it generally – though not always – provides us with our best guide to the future. Suppose that we need to estimate the cost of doing something in the future to help us to decide whether it is worth doing. In these circumstances our own experience, or that of others, on how much it has cost to do the thing in the past may provide us with a valuable guide to how much it is likely to cost in the future.

Real World 2.3 provides extracts from a *Financial Times* article that deals with the possible disposal by the UK government of its stake in a bank that came close to collapse during the recent recession and had to be rescued. It points out that what the government paid for its shares in the bank is a sunk cost and, therefore, an irrelevant one.

Real World 2.3

Bank transfer

Royal Bank of Scotland and George Osborne, the UK chancellor, are both eager to see the back of the other. RBS has declared that it should be healthy enough by next year for the government to start selling off its 81 per cent, and Mr Osborne has privately mooted a similar notion.

Last week, RBS displayed some encouraging signs of progress. For a long time, it seemed in such a dire state that it needed either to be fully nationalised, or split into good and bad banks and recapitalised by the taxpayer. Those risks, if not eliminated, have been reduced.

This does not mean the bank and its major shareholder can take a victory lap. RBS still has plenty of work to do, and concerns linger about whether it has fully acknowledged its bad loans. Its shares suffered when it announced its first-quarter results, revealing the rapid contraction of its investment arm.

The government must consider two factors before privatisation. The first is what price it can achieve, and whether it will match the book value paid by the Labour government in 2008. It need not get too hung up on the purchase price because that is a sunk cost. But neither should it be so enthusiastic to sell that it fails to get the best return for taxpayers.

 Source: Extracts from the FT editorial (2013), UK taxpayer will lose in rush to exit, ft.com, 5 May.

SUNK COST FALLACY

Although we should ignore past costs when considering future courses of action, this is often easier said than done. It seems that people often display an irrational commitment to past costs. We persist in continuing along a particular path because of our previous investment of time, effort or money. The end result is often to make poor decisions about the future direction. Managers can be as guilty of this kind of behaviour as anyone else.

In behavioural economics, the refusal to abandon an attachment to an irrecoverable investment is known as the **sunk cost fallacy**. Various reasons have been suggested as to why we act in this way. In **Real World 2.4** we consider some of these.

Real World 2.4

Clinging to the past

Perhaps you have said, or heard, the following sort of comments:

'I might as well finish this book. It's not very good but I paid for it and now I'm more than half was through.'

'I can't throw out these shoes. They are almost new and, although they hurt my feet, I paid a fortune for them'

'I really don't want to buy the car any more. However, I paid the dealer a non-refundable deposit and so I suppose I should go ahead.'

'I hate my job as an accountant but I've invested too many years of my life to achieve the qualifications just to throw it all away.'

These sort of comments show an attachment to past decisions rather than a concern for the future. They are irrational because costs previously incurred are not a good guide to maximising future utility. The investment of time, money or other resources should not be determined by what has already been spent.

Why do we do this? It may be because we suffer from loss aversion, which is a strong dislike of wasting resources. This is a strong negative emotion: the greater the amount wasted, the greater the suffering. The pain of incurring losses is usually much greater than the pleasure achieved by making equivalent gains. We may, therefore, stick with the book or the job in the hope that things improve in the future.

To abandon an investment may lead to feelings of regret and failure, which we may seek to avoid. It may also attract criticism. We may be blamed for giving up too easily or for making the original investment. This can make it difficult to own up to our poor decisions.. Finally we may not be able to see clearly the options available by not sticking with the investment. However, new opportunities may come into view once we have abandoned the sunk cost.

An example of the sunk cost fallacy in business occurred when the British and French governments agreed to develop the Concorde - a supersonic passenger jet. This turned out to be a very bad investment. Development costs were much higher than expected and it became clear, before the project was completed, that it would not be financially viable. Nevertheless, both governments decided to press ahead and complete the project rather than admit failure and write off the investment cost. Many believe that the decision to continue was largely determined by the costs already incurred. The Concorde was in operation from 1976 to 2003.

Source: Based on information in Leahy, R. (2014) *Letting go of sunk costs,* www.psychologytoday.com, 24 September and J. Blasingame (2011) *Beware of the Concorde fallacy* www.forbes.com 15 September.

DETERMINING THE RELEVANT COST OF LABOUR AND MATERIALS

Having set out the broad principles of what constitutes a relevant cost, let us now consider two key elements that go to make up the cost of a product or service – labour and materials. Determining the relevant costs of each can be quite tricky. This is because, in practice, they will vary according to the particular circumstances. By keeping in mind the principles just discussed, however, we should be able to separate the relevant costs arising from a course of action from any irrelevant costs.

Labour

The relevant cost of labour will vary according to whether the business is operating with spare capacity or whether it is operating at full capacity. In Activity 2.5 on the next page, we consider the situation where a business has temporary spare capacity but does not intend to lay off its workers.

Assume the same information set out in Activity 2.3 above. Further assume, however, that the car also needs a replacement engine before it can be driven. It is possible to buy a reconditioned engine for £1,200, which would take seven hours to fit by a mechanic who is paid £15 an hour. The garage is currently short of work, but the owners are reluctant to lay off any mechanics or even to cut down their basic working week. This is because skilled mechanics are difficult to find and an upturn in demand for their skills is expected soon.

What is the minimum price at which the garage should sell the car with a reconditioned engine and with new tyres fitted?

Again, the minimum price is the amount required to cover the relevant costs of the job. This minimum price will now be as follows:

	£
Opportunity cost of the car	10,500
Cost of new tyres	400
Cost of the reconditioned engine	1,200
Total	12,100

The cost of the new engine is a relevant cost for the same reason as the cost of new tyres: it is a future cost that varies with the decision. If the garage decides against fitting the engine, this cost will not be incurred. The cost of labour, on the other hand, is an irrelevant cost because it does not vary with the decision. As the mechanic will still be employed even though there is no work, the garage will incur the same cost whether or not the mechanic undertakes the engine-replacement job. If this job is not undertaken, the mechanic will be paid to do nothing. The additional labour cost for this job is, therefore, zero.

Where the business is working at full capacity the relevant cost of labour will depend on whether additional workers are employed to undertake the task or whether workers currently spending time on another task are redeployed. Let us first consider the situation where additional workers are employed to carry out a specified task.

Assume exactly the same circumstances as in Activity 2.5, except that the garage is currently working at full capacity. It is possible, however, to employ a recently-retired mechanic, on a casual basis, to fit the engine. The mechanic will be employed for seven hours and will be paid £15 an hour.

What is the minimum price at which the garage should sell the car, with a reconditioned engine fitted and new tyres, under these altered circumstances?

The minimum price is:

	£
Opportunity cost of the car	10,500
Cost of new tyres	400
Cost of mechanic (7 × £15)	105
Cost of the reconditioned engine	1,200
Total	12,205

$\rightarrow$

The opportunity cost of the car, the cost of the new tyres and the cost of the recondi-tioned engine are the same as in Activity 2.5. However, a charge for labour has now been added to obtain the minimum price. This is because it is now a future cost that varies with the decision. If the garage decides against fitting the engine, the mechanic will not be hired.

If overtime payments are made to existing workers to fit the engine, a similar situation to hiring a mechanic on a casual basis would arise. The overtime payments would be regarded as a relevant cost as they would vary with the decision.

Where a business is working at full capacity, it may be possible to redeploy the existing workforce in order to carry out a new task. This will mean that an opportunity cost is normally incurred as workers will be taken away from other revenue-generating tasks. Activity 2.7 considers this scenario.

Activity 2.7

Assume exactly the same circumstances as in Activity 2.6, except that the garage rede-ploys a mechanic to carry out the engine-replacement job. This means that other work, which the mechanic could have done during the seven hours, will not be undertaken. This other work could have been charged to a customer at the rate of £60 an hour. The mechanic, however, is only paid £15 an hour.

What is the minimum price at which the garage should sell the car, with new tyres and a reconditioned engine fitted, under these circumstances?

The minimum price is:

	£
Opportunity cost of the car	10,500
Cost of new tyres	400
Opportunity cost of mechanic (7 × £60)	420
Cost of the reconditioned engine	1,200
Total	12,520

The opportunity cost of the car, the cost of the new tyres and the cost of the recondi-tioned engine are the same as in Activity 2.6. However, the cost of labour is now different. It is the amount sacrificed in making time available to undertake the engine-replacement job. While the mechanic is working on this job, the opportunity to do other work, for which customers would pay £420, is lost.

Note that the £15 an hour mechanic's wage is still not relevant. The mechanic will be paid £15 an hour irrespective of whether it is the engine-replacement work or some other job that is undertaken.

The points made above concerning the relevant cost of labour are summarised in Figure 2.2 on the next page.

Materials

The relevant cost of materials will vary according to whether the materials are held in inven-tories and whether there is an intention to replace them. In Activity 2.8 on the next page, the materials required for a particular job are already held in inventories but not all need to be replaced. When attempting this activity, keep firmly in mind the principles discussed earlier.

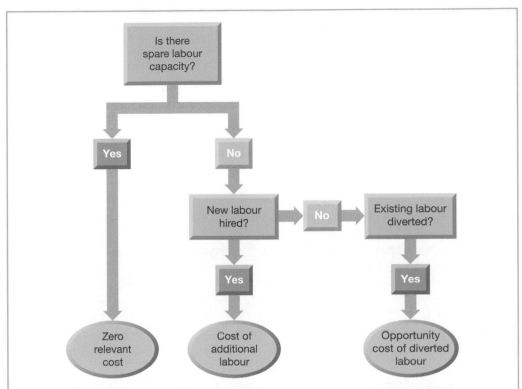

The starting point is to determine whether there is temporary spare capacity. In these circumstances, the relevant cost of labour is usually zero. Relevant labour costs often only arise where the business is operating a full capacity.

Figure 2.2 A decision flow diagram for identifying the relevant cost of labour

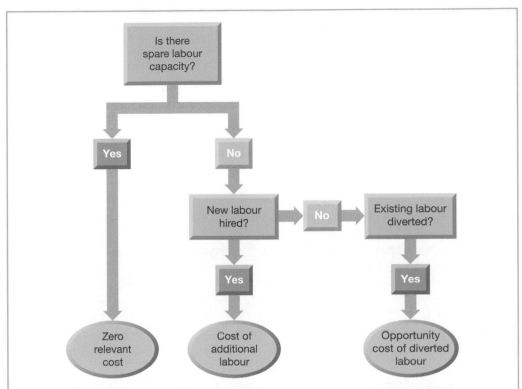

Activity 2.8

A business is considering making a bid to undertake a contract. The contract will require the use of two types of raw material – A1 and B2. Quantities of both of these materials are held by the business. If it chose to do so, the business could sell the raw materials in their present state. All of the inventories of these two raw materials will need to be used on the contract. Information on the raw materials concerned is as follows:

Inventories item	Quantity (units)	Historic cost (£/unit)	Sales value (£/unit)	Current purchase cost (£/unit)
A1	500	5	3	6
B2	800	7	8	10

Inventories item A1 is in frequent use in the business on a variety of work.

The inventories of item B2 were bought a year ago for a contract that was abandoned. It has recently become obvious that there is no likelihood of ever using this raw material unless the contract currently being considered proceeds.

Management wishes to deduce the minimum price at which the business could undertake the contract without reducing its wealth as a result (that is, the price at which the costs are exactly equal to the benefits). This can be used as the baseline in deducing the bid price.

How much should be included in the minimum price in respect of the two inventories items detailed above?

→

The minimum price must cover the relevant costs. The costs to be covered by the minimum price are:

A1	£6 × 500 = £3,000
B2	£8 × 800 = £6,400

We are told that the item A1 is in frequent use and so, if it is used on the contract, it will need to be replaced. The business will, therefore, have to buy 500 units additional to those which would have been required had the contract not been undertaken. The purchase cost of the materials is £6 per unit and so the relevant cost is 500 × £6.

Item B2 will never be used by the business unless the contract is undertaken. This means that if the contract is not undertaken, the only reasonable thing for the business to do is to sell the B2. If, however, the contract is undertaken and the B2 is used, it will have an opportunity cost equal to the potential proceeds from disposal, which is £8 a unit. In other words, the relevant cost will be the sales value of item B2 that has been foregone.

Note that the historic cost information about both materials is irrelevant. This will always be the case as it represents a sunk cost.

Where an item of materials is not held in inventories, it will have to be purchased specifically for the job. In this case, therefore, the purchase cost of the materials will be the relevant cost. It is a future cost that will vary with the decision.

Now have a go at Activity 2.9 below, which is a little more difficult than the previous activity.

The points made above concerning the relevant cost of materials are summarised in Figure 2.3 on the next page.

Activity 2.9

HLA Ltd is in the process of preparing a quotation for a special job for a customer. The job will have the following material requirements:

Material	Units required	Units currently held in inventories			Current purchase cost (£/unit)
		Quantity held (units)	Historic cost (£/unit)	Sales value (£/unit)	
P	400	0	–	–	40
Q	230	100	62	50	64
R	350	200	48	23	59
S	170	140	33	12	49
T	120	120	40	0	68

Material Q is used consistently by the business on various jobs.

The business holds materials R, S and T as the result of previous overbuying. No other use (apart from this special job) can be found for R, but the 140 units of S could be used in another job as a substitute for 225 units of material V that are about to be purchased at a price of £10 a unit. Material T has no other use, it is a dangerous material that is difficult to store and the business has been informed that it will cost £160 to dispose of the material currently held.

If it chose to, the business could sell the raw materials Q, R and S already held in their present state.

What is the relevant cost of the materials for the job specified above?

The relevant cost is as follows:

	£
Material P	
This will have to be purchased at £40 a unit (400 × £40)	16,000
Material Q	
Those units already held will have to be replaced and the remaining 130 units will have to be purchased, therefore the relevant cost is (230 × £64)	14,720
Material R	
200 units of this are held and these could be sold. The relevant cost of these is the sales value forgone (200 × £23)	4,600
The remaining 150 units of R would have to be purchased (150 × £59)	8,850
Material S	
This could be sold or used as a substitute for material V	
The existing inventories could be sold for £1,680 (that is, 140 × £12); however, the saving on material V is higher. This higher figure must be taken as the opportunity cost (225 × £10)	2,250
The remaining units of material S must be purchased (30 × £49)	1,470
Material T	
A saving on disposal will be made if material T is used	(160)
Total relevant cost	47,730

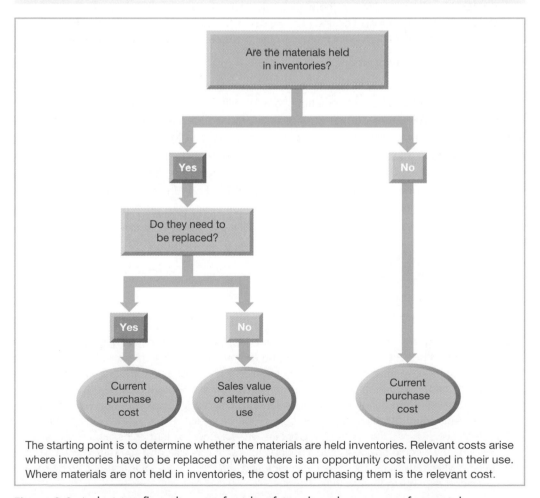

The starting point is to determine whether the materials are held inventories. Relevant costs arise where inventories have to be replaced or where there is an opportunity cost involved in their use. Where materials are not held in inventories, the cost of purchasing them is the relevant cost.

Figure 2.3 A decision flow diagram for identifying the relevant cost of materials

NON-MEASURABLE COSTS AND BENEFITS

It was mentioned at the beginning of the chapter that certain costs and benefits may defy measurement in monetary terms. These costs and benefits often have a broader, but less immediate, impact on the business. Ultimately, however, they are likely to affect the ability of a business to achieve its objectives.

Activity 2.10

Activities 2.5, 2.6 and 2.7 were concerned with the cost of putting a car into a marketable condition. Apart from the quantifiable items mentioned, are there other costs or benefits that are difficult to quantify, but which should, nevertheless, be taken into account in making a decision as to whether to do the work? Try to think of at least two.

We can think of four:

■ Turning away another job in order to do the engine replacement may result in customer dissatisfaction.
■ The quality of workmanship may be lower where casual labour is employed, which could damage the reputation of the business.
■ Demand for the car following the work carried out may be uncertain.
■ Benefits beyond the profit expected from the sale of the particular car may accrue. By offering a broader range of cars for sale, more car-buying customers may be attracted to the garage.

You may have thought of others.

These 'qualitative' costs and benefits should provide a further input to the final plans or decisions. To include these costs and benefits, managers must rely on judgement when attaching weightings to them. By taking them into account, however, the final picture may be quite different than that provided by only the quantifiable costs and benefits.

To end the chapter, **Real World 2.5** describes another case where the decision makers, quite correctly, ignored past costs and just concentrated on future options for the business concerned. It also highlights how two sets of managers can take quite different views of the worth of an investment, presumably based on similar sources of information.

Real World 2.5

Delivering for £1

In April 2013 Better Capital PCC Ltd, a private equity business, paid £1 to buy City Link, the delivery and courier business, from Rentokil Initial plc, the pest control and hygiene business.

Rentokil had bought City Link as part of the takeover of Target Express in 2006, but had never been able to make a success of its acquisition. An analyst at Espirito Santo, the investment bank, said 'City Link has been a persistent thorn in the side of [Rentokil's] management's efforts to deliver a turnround at Rentokil and has assumed both significant financial cost and management focus, detracting from the core of the business'. The management at Rentokil was clearly very pleased to rid itself of City Link without incurring further losses.

Better Capital could obviously see a brighter future for City Link and committed £40 million to fund additional working capital and restructuring, including the acquisition of new delivery vehicles and expanding the number of staff.

Despite Better Capital honouring its £40 million commitment, adverse trading results forced City Link to stop trading and into administration in December 2014, seemingly with Better Capital losing its investment and, probably more importantly, with the business's 2,700 employees losing their jobs.

Better Capital is no stranger to deals done for £1. In February 2014, it sold Readers Digest, a publishing business, for that sum. It had bought the business for £14 million in 2010 and subsequently invested £9 million in it.

Sources: Based on City Link (2014) City Link reaps benefits of Better Capital investment, www.city-link.co.uk/press/2014/news, January; Wembridge, M. (2013) Rentokil Initial sells City Link to John Moulton's buyout group, ft.com, 29 April; Armstrong, A. (2014) Reader's Digest sold for £1 by Better Capital, *Daily Telegraph*, 16 February; Szu, P. C. (2014) City Link collapses into administration leaving 2,700 jobs at risk, *Daily Telegraph*, 25 December.

Self-assessment question 2.1

JB Limited is a small specialist manufacturer of electronic components. Makers of aircraft, for both civil and military purposes, use much of its output. One of the aircraft makers has offered a contract to JB Limited for the supply, over the next 12 months, of 400 identical components. The data relating to the production of each component are as follows:

- *Material requirements:*
  3 kg of Material M1 (see Note 1 below)
  2 kg of Material P2 (see Note 2 below)
  1 bought-in component (part number 678) (see Note 3 below)

  Note 1: Material M1 is in continuous use by the business; 1,000 kg are currently held by the business. The original cost was £4.70/kg, but it is known that future purchases will cost £5.50/kg.

  Note 2: 1,200 kg of Material P2 are currently held. The original cost of this material was £4.30/kg. The material has not been required for the last two years. Its scrap value is £1.50/kg. The only foreseeable alternative use is as a substitute for Material P4 (in constant use), but this would involve further processing costs of £1.60/kg. The current cost of Material P4 is £3.60/kg.

  Note 3: It is estimated that the components (part number 678) could be bought in for £50 each.
- *Labour requirements:* Each component would require five hours of skilled labour and five hours of semi-skilled. A skilled employee is available and is currently paid £14/hour. A replacement would, however, have to be obtained at a rate of £12/hour for the work that would otherwise be done by the skilled employee. The current rate for semi-skilled work is £10/hour and an additional employee could be appointed for this work.
- *General manufacturing costs:* It is JB Limited's policy to charge a share of the general costs (rent, heating and so on) to each contract undertaken at the rate of £20 for each machine hour used on the contract. If the contract is undertaken, the general costs are expected to increase as a result of undertaking the contract by £3,200.

Spare machine capacity is available and each component would require four machine hours. A price of £200 a component has been offered by the potential customer.

Required:
(a) Should the contract be accepted? Support your conclusion with appropriate figures to present to management.
(b) What other factors ought management to consider that might influence the decision?

The solution to this question can be found at the back of the book on p. 514.

The main points of this chapter may be summarised as follows:

Cost–benefit analysis

- Involves a careful weighing of the costs and benefits of plans and decisions.
- To be worthwhile, benefits should exceed the associated costs.
- Not all costs and benefits can be measured in monetary terms.

Relevant and irrelevant costs

- Relevant costs must:
  - relate to the objective being pursued by the business;
  - be a future cost; and
  - vary with the decision.
- Relevant costs therefore include:
  - opportunity costs; and
  - differential future outlay costs.
- Irrelevant costs therefore include:
  - all past (or sunk) costs;
  - all committed costs; and
  - non-differential future outlay costs.

Relevant cost of labour and materials

- The relevant cost of labour will vary according to whether the business is operating with spare capacity or is operating at full capacity.
- The relevant cost of materials will vary according to whether the materials are held in inventories and whether they need to be replaced.

Non-measurable costs and benefits

- Should provide an input to the final plans or decisions.
- Managers must rely on judgement when attaching weights to these items.

KEY TERMS

For definitions of these terms, see Appendix A.

Benefit p. 41	**Irrelevant cost** p. 43
Cost p. 41	**Past cost** p. 43
Cost–benefit analysis p. 41	**Outlay cost** p. 43
Opportunity cost p. 42	**Sunk cost** p. 46
Historic cost p. 42	**Committed cost** p. 46
Relevant cost p. 43	**Sunk cost fallacy** p. 47

FURTHER READING

If you would like to explore the topics covered in this chapter in more depth, we recommend the following:

Drury, C. (2015) *Management and Cost Accounting*, 9th edn, Cengage Learning, Chapter 9.

Hilton, R. and Platt D. (2014) *Managerial Accounting*, Global edn, McGraw-Hill Education, Chapter 14.

Bhimani, A., Horngren, C., Datar, S. and Rajan, M. (2015) *Management and Cost Accounting*, 6th edn, Pearson, Chapter 10.

Kaplan, R., Atkinson, A., Matsumura, E. and Young, S.M. (2011) *Management Accounting*, 6th edn, Prentice Hall, Chapter 3.

REVIEW QUESTIONS

Solutions to these questions can be found at the back of the book on p. 527.

2.1 To be relevant to a particular decision, a cost must have three attributes. What are they?

2.2 Distinguish between a sunk cost and an opportunity cost.

2.3 Define the word 'cost' in the context of management accounting.

2.4 What is meant by the expression 'committed cost'? How do committed costs arise?

EXERCISES

Those with **coloured numbers** have solutions given at the back of the book on pp. 536–539.

Basic-level exercises

2.1 Lombard Ltd has been offered a contract for which there is available production capacity. The contract is for 20,000 identical items, manufactured by an intricate assembly operation, to be produced and delivered in the next few months at a price of £80 each. The specification for one item is as follows:

Assembly labour	4 hours
Component X	4 units
Component Y	3 units

There would also be the need to hire equipment, for the duration of the contract, at an outlay cost of £200,000.

The assembly is a highly skilled operation and the workforce is currently underutilised. It is the business's policy to retain this workforce on full pay in anticipation of high demand next year, for a new product currently being developed. There is sufficient available skilled labour to undertake the contract now under consideration. Skilled workers are paid £15 an hour.

Component X is used in a number of other sub-assemblies produced by the business. It is readily available. 50,000 units of Component X are currently held in inventories. Component Y was a special purchase in anticipation of an order that did not in the end materialise. It is, therefore, surplus to requirements and the 100,000 units that are currently held may have to be sold at a loss. An estimate of various values for Components X and Y provided by the materials planning department is as follows:

Component	X £/unit	Y £/unit
Historic cost	4	10
Replacement cost	5	11
Net realisable value	3	8

It is estimated that any additional relevant costs associated with the contract (beyond the above) will amount to £8 an item.

Required:
Analyse the information and advise Lombard Ltd on the desirability of the contract.

2.2 The local authority of a small town maintains a theatre and arts centre for the use of a local repertory company, other visiting groups and exhibitions. Management decisions are taken by a committee that meets regularly to review the financial statements and to plan the use of the facilities.

The theatre employs a full-time, non-performing staff and a number of artistes at total costs of £9,600 and £35,200 a month, respectively. The theatre mounts a new production every month for 20 performances. Other monthly costs of the theatre are as follows:

	£
Costumes	5,600
Scenery	3,300
Heat and light	10,300
A share of the administration costs of the local authority	16,000
Casual staff	3,520
Refreshments	2,360

On average the theatre is half full for the performances of the repertory company. The capacity and seat prices in the theatre are:

200 seats at £24 each
500 seats at £16 each
300 seats at £12 each

In addition, the theatre sells refreshments during the performances for £7,760 a month. Programme sales cover their costs, and advertising in the programme generates £6,720 a month.

The management committee has been approached by a popular touring group, which would like to take over the theatre for one month (25 performances). The group is prepared to pay the local authority half of its ticket income as a fee for the use of the theatre. The group expects to fill the theatre for 10 nights and achieve two-thirds capacity on the remaining 15 nights. The prices charged are £2 less than normally applies in the theatre.

The local authority will, as normal, pay for heat and light costs and will still honour the contracts of all artistes and pay the non-performing employees who will sell refreshments, programmes and so on. The committee does not expect any change in the level of refreshments or programme sales if they agree to this booking.

Note: The committee includes the share of the local authority administration costs when making profit calculations. It assumes occupancy applies equally across all seat prices.

Required:
(a) On financial grounds should the management committee agree to the approach from the touring group? Support your answer with appropriate workings.
(b) What other factors may have a bearing on the decision by the committee?

2.3 Andrews and Co. Ltd has been invited to tender for a contract. It is to produce 10,000 metres of an electrical cable in which the business specialises. The estimating department of the business has produced the following information relating to the contract:

- *Materials:* The cable will require a steel core, which the business buys in. The steel core is to be coated with a special plastic, also bought in, using a special process. Plastic for the covering will be required at the rate of 0.10 kg/metre of completed cable.

- *Direct labour:*

Skilled:	10 minutes/metre
Unskilled:	5 minutes/metre

The business already holds sufficient of each of the materials required to complete the contract. Information on the cost of the inventories is as follows:

	Steel core £/metre	Plastic £/kg
Historic cost	1.50	0.60
Current buying-in cost	2.10	0.70
Scrap value	1.40	0.10

The steel core is in constant use by the business for a variety of work that it regularly undertakes. The plastic is a surplus from a previous contract where a mistake was made and an excess quantity ordered. If the current contract does not go ahead, this plastic will be scrapped.

Unskilled labour, which is paid at the rate of £7.50 an hour, will need to be taken on specifically to undertake the contract. The business is fairly quiet at the moment which means that a pool of skilled labour exists that will still be employed at full pay of £12 an hour to do nothing if the contract does not proceed. The pool of skilled labour is sufficient to complete the contract.

Required:
Indicate the minimum price at which the contract could be undertaken, such that the business would be neither better nor worse off as a result of doing it.

Intermediate-level exercises

2.4 SJ Services Ltd has been asked to quote a price for a special contract to render a service that will take the business one week to complete. Information relating to labour for the contract is as follows:

Grade of labour	Hours required	Basic rate/hour
Skilled	27	£24
Semi-skilled	14	£18
Unskilled	20	£14

A shortage of skilled labour means that the necessary staff to undertake the contract would have to be moved from other work that is currently yielding an excess of sales revenue over labour and other costs of £8 an hour.

Semi-skilled labour is currently being paid at semi-skilled rates to undertake unskilled work. If the relevant members of staff are moved to work on the contract, unskilled labour will have to be employed for the week to replace them.

The unskilled labour actually needed to work on the contract will be specifically employed for the week of the contract.

All labour is charged to contracts at 50 per cent above the rate paid to the employees, so as to cover the contract's fair share of the business's general costs (rent, heating and so on). It is estimated that these general costs will increase by £50 as a result of undertaking the contract.

Undertaking the contract will require the use of a specialised machine for the week. This machine is currently being hired out to another business at a weekly rental of £175 on a week-by-week contract.

To derive the above estimates, the business has had to spend £300 on a specialised study. If the contract does not proceed, the results of the study can be sold for £250.

An estimate of the contract's fair share of the business's rent is £150 a week.

Required:

Deduce the minimum price at which SJ Services Ltd could undertake the contract such that it would be neither better nor worse off as a result of undertaking it.

2.5 A business in the food industry is currently holding 2,000 tonnes of material in bulk storage. This material deteriorates with time. In the near future, it will, therefore, be necessary for it to be repackaged for sale or sold in its present form.

The material was acquired in two batches: 800 tonnes at a price of £40 a tonne and 1,200 tonnes at a price of £44 a tonne. The current market price of any additional purchases is £48 a tonne. If the business were to dispose of the material, in its present state, it could sell any quantity but for only £36 a tonne; it does not have the contacts or reputation to command a higher price.

Processing this material may be undertaken to develop either Product A or Product X. No weight loss occurs with the processing, that is, 1 tonne of the material will make 1 tonne of A or X. For Product A, there is an additional cost of £60 a tonne, after which it will sell for £105 a tonne. The marketing department estimates that a maximum of 500 tonnes could be sold in this way.

With Product X, the business incurs additional costs of £80 a tonne for processing. A market price for X is not known and no minimum price has been agreed. The management is currently engaged in discussions over the minimum price that may be charged for Product X in the current circumstances. Management wants to know the relevant cost per tonne for Product X so as to provide a basis for negotiating a profitable selling price for the product.

Required:

Identify the relevant cost per tonne for Product X, given sales volumes of X of:

(a) up to 1,500 tonnes
(b) over 1,500 tonnes, up to 2,000 tonnes
(c) over 2,000 tonnes.

Explain your answer.

Advanced-level exercises

2.6 A local education authority is faced with a predicted decline in the demand for school places in its area. It is believed that some schools will have to close in order to remove up to 800 places from current capacity levels. The schools that may face closure are referenced as A, B, C and D. Their details are as follows:

■ *School A* (capacity 200) was built 15 years ago at a cost of £1.2 million. It is situated in a 'socially disadvantaged' community area. The authority has been offered £14 million for the site by a property developer.

- *School B* (capacity 500) was built 20 years ago and cost £1 million. It was renovated only two years ago at a cost of £3 million to improve its facilities. An offer of £8 million has been made for the site by a business planning a shopping complex in this affluent part of the area.
- *School C* (capacity 600) cost £5 million to build five years ago. The land for this school is rented from a local business for an annual cost of £300,000. The land rented for School C is based on a 100-year lease. If the school closes, the property reverts immediately to the owner. If School C is not closed, it will require a £3 million investment to improve safety at the school.
- *School D* (capacity 800) cost £7 million to build eight years ago; last year £1.5 million was spent on an extension. It has a considerable amount of grounds, which is currently used for sporting events. This factor makes it attractive to developers, who have recently offered £9 million for the site. If School D is closed, it will be necessary to pay £1.8 million to adapt facilities at other schools to accommodate the change.

In its accounting system, the local authority depreciates non-current assets based on 2 per cent a year on the original cost. It also differentiates between one-off, large items of capital expenditure or revenue, on the one hand, and annually recurring items, on the other.

The local authority has a central staff, which includes administrators for each school costing £200,000 a year for each school, and a chief education officer costing £80,000 a year in total.

Required:
(a) Prepare a summary of the relevant cash flows (costs and revenues, relative to not making any closures) under the following options:
  (1) closure of D only
  (2) closure of A and B
  (3) closure of A and C.
  Show separately the one-off effects and annually recurring items, rank the options open to the local authority and, briefly, interpret your answer. *Note*: Various approaches are acceptable provided that they are logical.
(b) Identify and comment on any two different types of irrelevant cost contained in the information given in the question.
(c) Discuss other factors that might have a bearing on the decision.

2.7 Rob Otics Ltd, a small business that specialises in manufacturing electronic-control equipment, has just received an enquiry from a potential customer for eight identical robotic units. These would be made using Rob Otics's own labour force and factory capacity. The product specification prepared by the estimating department shows the following:

- Material and labour requirements for each robotic unit:

Component X	2 per unit
Component Y	1 per unit
Component Z	4 per unit
Assembly labour	25 hours per unit (but see below)
Inspection labour	6 hours per unit

As part of the costing exercise, the business has collected the following information:

- *Component X.* This item is normally held by the business as it is in constant demand. There are 10 units currently held which were bought for £150 a unit. The sole supplier of Component X has announced a price rise of 20 per cent, effective immediately, for any further supplies. Rob Otics has not yet paid for the items currently held.

- *Component Y.* 25 units are currently held. This component is not normally used by Rob Otics, but the units currently held are because of a cancelled order following the bankruptcy of a customer. The units originally cost the business £4,000 in total, although Rob Otics has recouped £1,500 from the liquidator of the bankrupt business. As Rob Otics can see no use for these units (apart from the possible use of some of them in the order now being considered), the finance director proposes to scrap all 25 units (zero proceeds).
- *Component Z.* This is in regular use by Rob Otics. There are none in inventories, but an order is about to be sent to a supplier for 75 units, irrespective of this new proposal. The supplier charges £25 a unit on small orders but will reduce the price to £20 a unit for all units on any order over 100 units.
- *Other items.* These are expected to cost £250 in total.

Assembly labour is currently in short supply in the area and is paid at £10 an hour. If the order is accepted, all necessary labour will have to be transferred from existing work. As a result, other orders will be lost. It is estimated that for each hour transferred to this contract £38 will be lost (calculated as lost sales revenue £60, less materials £12 and labour £10). The production director suggests that, owing to a learning process, the time taken to make each unit will reduce, from 25 hours to make the first one, by one hour a unit made. (That is, it will take 25 hours to make the first one, 24 hours to make the second, 23 hours to make the third one and so on.)

Inspection labour can be provided by paying existing personnel overtime which is at a premium of 50 per cent over the standard rate of £12 an hour.

When the business is working out its contract prices, it normally adds an amount equal to £20 for each assembly labour hour to cover its general costs (such as rent and electricity). To the resulting total, 40 per cent is normally added as a profit mark-up.

Required:

(a) Prepare an estimate of the minimum price that you would recommend Rob Otics Ltd to charge for the proposed contract such that it would be neither better nor worse off as a result. Provide explanations for any items included.

(b) Identify any other factors that you would consider before fixing the final price.

2.8 A business places substantial emphasis on customer satisfaction and, to this end, delivers its product in special protective containers. These containers have been made in a department within the business. Management has recently become concerned that this internal supply of containers is very expensive. As a result, outside suppliers have been invited to submit tenders for the provision of these containers. A quote of £250,000 a year has been received for a volume that compares with current internal supply.

An investigation into the internal costs of container manufacture has been undertaken and the following emerges:

(a) The annual cost of material is £120,000, according to the stores records, maintained at actual historic cost. Three-quarters (by cost) of this represents material that is regularly stocked and replenished. The remaining 25 per cent of the material cost is a special foaming chemical. This chemical is not used by the business for any purpose other than making the containers. There are 40 tonnes of this chemical currently held. It was bought in bulk for £750 a tonne. Today's replacement price for this material is £1,050 a tonne, but it is unlikely that the business could realise more than £600 a tonne if it had to be disposed of owing to the high handling costs and special transport facilities required.

(b) The annual labour cost is £80,000 for this department. Most of this cost, however, relates to casual employees or recent starters. If an outside quote were accepted, therefore, little redundancy would be payable. There are, however, two long-serving employees who would each accept as a salary £15,000 a year until they reached retirement age in two years' time.

(c) The department manager has a salary of £30,000 a year. The closure of this department would release him to take over another department for which a vacancy is about to be advertised. The salary, status and prospects are similar.

(d) A rental charge of £9,750 a year, based on floor area, is allocated to the containers department. If the department were closed, the floor space released would be used for warehousing and, as a result, the business would give up the tenancy of an existing warehouse for which it is paying £15,750 a year.

(e) The plant cost £162,000 when it was bought five years ago. Its market value now is £28,000 and it could continue for another two years, at which time its market value would have fallen to zero. (The plant depreciates evenly over time.)

(f) Annual plant maintenance costs are £9,900 and allocated general administrative costs £33,750 for the coming year.

Required:

Calculate the annual cost of manufacturing containers for comparison with the quote using relevant figures for establishing the cost or benefit of accepting the quote. Indicate any assumptions or qualifications you wish to make.

Chapter 3

COST–VOLUME–PROFIT ANALYSIS

INTRODUCTION

This chapter considers the relationship between cost, the volume of activity and profit. We shall see how an understanding of this relationship, can be used to make decisions and to assess risk, particularly within the context of short-term decisions.

The theme of Chapter 2 concerning relevant costs is further developed in this chapter. We shall take a look at circumstances where a whole class of cost – fixed cost – can be treated as irrelevant for decision-making purposes.

Learning outcomes

When you have completed this chapter, you should be able to:

- Distinguish between fixed cost and variable cost and use this distinction to explain the relationship between cost, volume of activity and profit.

- Prepare a break-even chart and deduce the break-even point for some activity.

- Discuss the weaknesses of break-even analysis.

- Demonstrate the way in which marginal analysis can be used when making short-term decisions.

COST BEHAVIOUR

We saw in the previous chapter that cost represents the resources sacrificed to achieve benefits. Costs incurred by a business may be classified in various ways, and one useful way is according to how they behave in relation to changes in the volume of activity. Costs may be classified according to whether they:

■ remain constant (fixed) when changes occur to the volume of activity; or
■ vary according to the volume of activity.

These are known as **fixed costs** and **variable costs** respectively. Thus, in the case of a restaurant, the manager's salary would normally be a fixed cost while the cost of the unprepared food would be a variable cost.

As we shall see, knowing how much of each type of cost is associated with a particular activity can be of great value to the decision maker.

FIXED COST

The way in which a fixed cost behaves can be shown by preparing a graph that plots the fixed cost of a business against the level of activity, as in Figure 3.1. The distance 0F represents the amount of fixed cost, and this stays the same irrespective of the volume of activity.

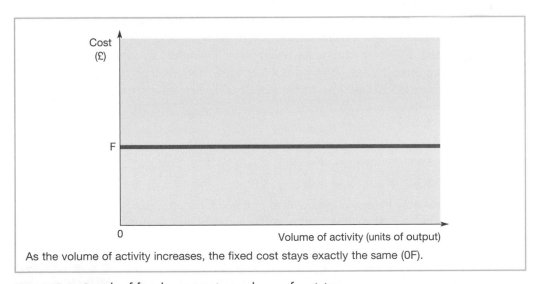

As the volume of activity increases, the fixed cost stays exactly the same (0F).

Figure 3.1 Graph of fixed cost against volume of activity

Can you give some examples of items of cost that are likely to be fixed for a hairdressing business?

We came up with the following:

- rent;
- insurance;
- cleaning cost; and
- staff salaries.

You may have thought of others.

These items of cost are likely to be the same irrespective of the number of customers having their hair cut or styled.

Staff salaries (or wages) are often assumed to be a variable cost but, in practice, they tend to be fixed. Members of staff are not normally paid according to the volume of output and it is unusual to dismiss staff when there is a short-term downturn in activity. Where there is a long-term downturn, or at least it seems that way to management, redundancies may occur with fixed cost savings. This, is, however, true of all types of fixed cost. For example, management may also decide to close some branches to make rental cost savings.

There are circumstances in which the labour cost is variable (for example, where staff are paid according to how much output they produce), but this is unusual. Whether labour cost is fixed or variable will depend on the particular circumstances.

It is important to be clear that 'fixed', in this context, means only that the cost is unaffected by changes in the volume of activity. Fixed cost is likely to be affected by inflation. If rent (a typical fixed cost) goes up because of inflation, a fixed cost will have increased, but not because of a change in the volume of activity.

Similarly, the level of fixed cost does not stay the same irrespective of the time period involved. Fixed cost elements are almost always *time-based*: that is, they vary with the length of time concerned. The rental charge for two months is normally twice that for one month. Thus, fixed cost normally varies with time, but (of course) not with the volume of output. This means that when we talk of fixed cost being, say, £1,000, we must add the period concerned, say, £1,000 a month.

Activity 3.2

Does fixed cost stay the same irrespective of the volume of output, even where there is a massive rise in that volume? Think in terms of the rent cost for the hairdressing business.

In fact, the rent is only fixed over a particular range (known as the 'relevant' range). If the number of people wanting to have their hair cut by the business increased, and the business wished to meet this increased demand, it would eventually have to expand its physical size. This might be achieved by opening an additional branch, or perhaps by moving the existing business to larger accommodation. It may be possible to cope with relatively minor increases in activity by using existing space more efficiently, or by having longer opening hours. If activity continued to increase, however, increased rent charges may be inevitable.

In practice, the situation described in Activity 3.2 would look something like Figure 3.2.

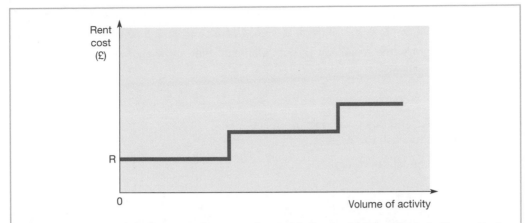

As the volume of activity increases from zero, the rent (a fixed cost) is unaffected. At a particular point, the volume of activity cannot increase further without additional space being rented. The cost of renting the additional space will cause a 'step' in the rent cost. The higher rent cost will continue unaffected if volume rises further until eventually another step point is reached.

Figure 3.2 Graph of rent cost against the volume of activity

At lower volumes of activity, the rent cost shown in Figure 3.2 would be 0R. As the volume of activity increases, a point will be reached where the existing accommodation becomes inadequate. To expand the business beyond this point, larger accommodation will be needed, which will mean a sharp increase in fixed cost. Where the volume of activity continues to increase, another point will be reached where the accommodation becomes inadequate. Hence, even larger accommodation will be needed, leading to a further sharp increase in fixed cost. Elements of fixed cost that behave in this way are often referred to as **stepped fixed costs**.

VARIABLE COST

We saw earlier that variable cost varies with the volume of activity. In a manufacturing business, for example, this would include the cost of raw materials used.

Variable cost can be represented graphically as in Figure 3.3. At zero volume of activity, the variable cost is zero. It then increases in a straight line as activity increases.

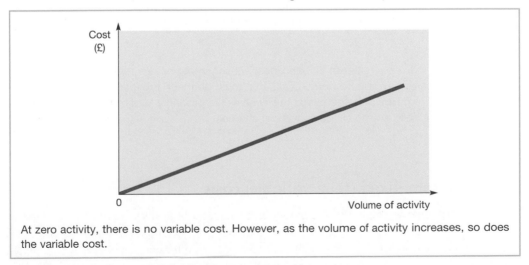

At zero activity, there is no variable cost. However, as the volume of activity increases, so does the variable cost.

Figure 3.3 Graph of variable cost against the volume of activity

As with many types of business activity, the variable cost incurred by hairdressers tends to be low in comparison with the fixed cost. Thus, fixed cost tends to make up the bulk of **total cost**.

The straight line for variable cost on this graph implies that this type of cost will be the same per unit of activity, irrespective of the volume of activity. We shall consider the practicality of this assumption a little later in this chapter.

SEMI-FIXED (SEMI-VARIABLE) COST

In some cases, a particular cost has an element of both fixed and variable cost. These can be described as **semi-fixed (semi-variable) costs**. An example might be the electricity cost for the hairdressing business. Some of this will be for heating and lighting, and this part is probably fixed, at least until the volume of activity increases to a point where longer opening hours or larger accommodation is necessary. The other part of the cost will vary with the volume of activity. Here we are talking about such things as power for hairdryers.

Analysing semi-fixed (semi-variable) costs

The fixed and variable elements of a particular cost may not always be clear. Past experience, however, can often provide some guidance. Let us again take the example of electricity. If we have data on what the electricity cost has been for various volumes of activity, say the relevant data over several three-month periods (electricity is usually billed by the quarter), we can estimate the fixed and variable elements. The easiest way to do this is to use the **high-low method**. This method involves taking the highest and lowest total electricity cost figures from the range of past quarterly data available. An assumption is then made that the difference between these two quarterly figures is caused entirely by the change in variable cost.

Example 3.1 demonstrates how the fixed and variable elements of electricity cost may be estimated using this method.

Example 3.1

Davos Ltd collected data relating to its electricity cost and volume of activity over several quarters and found the following:

	Lowest quarterly activity	*Highest quarterly activity*
Volume of activity	100,000 units	180,000 units
Total electricity cost	£80,000	£120,000

We can see that an increase in activity of 80,000 units (that is, from 100,000 to 180,000 units) led to an increase in total electricity cost of £40,000 (that is from £80,000 to £120,000). As it is assumed that this increase is caused by an increase in variable cost, the variable cost per unit of output must be £40,000/80,000 = £0.50 per unit.

The breakdown in total electricity cost for the highest and lowest quarters will therefore be as follows:

	Lowest quarterly activity	*Highest quarterly activity*
Volume of activity	100,000 units	180,000 units
	£	£
Variable cost		
100,000 × £0.50	50,000	
180,000 × £0.50		90,000
Fixed cost (balancing figure)	30,000	30,000
Total electricity cost	80,000	120,000

Activity 3.5

What do you think is the weakness of using the high–low approach?

The weakness of this method is that it relies on only two points in a range of information relating to quarterly electricity charges. It ignores all other information.

A more reliable estimate of the fixed and variable cost elements can be made if the full range of electricity cost for each quarter is used in the analysis. By plotting total electricity cost against the volume of activity for each quarter, a graph that looks like the one shown in Figure 3.4 may be produced.

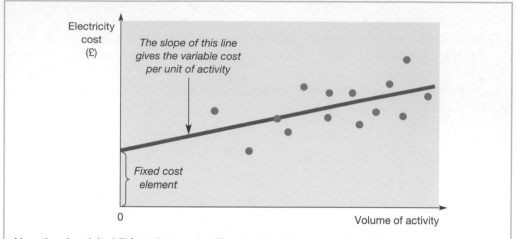

Here the electricity bill for a time period (for example, three months) is plotted against the volume of activity for that same period. This is done for a series of periods. A line is then drawn that best 'fits' the various points on the graph. From this line we can then deduce both the cost at zero activity (the fixed element) and the slope of the line (the variable element).

Figure 3.4 Graph of electricity cost against the volume of activity

Each of the dots in Figure 3.4 is the electricity charge for a particular quarter plotted against the volume of activity (probably measured in terms of sales revenue) for the same quarter. The diagonal line on the graph is the *line of best fit*. This means that this was the line that best seemed (to us, at least) to represent the data. A better estimate can usually be made using a statistical technique (*least squares regression*), which does not involve drawing graphs and making estimates. In terms of accuracy, however, there is probably little practical difference between the two approaches.

From the graph we can say that the fixed element of the electricity cost is the amount represented by the vertical distance from the origin at zero (bottom left-hand corner) to the point where the line of best fit crosses the vertical axis of the graph. The variable cost per unit is the amount that the graph line rises for each increase in the volume of activity.

Armed with knowledge of how much each element of cost represents for a particular product or service, it is possible to make predictions regarding total and per-unit cost at various projected levels of output. This information can be very useful to decision makers. Much of the rest of this chapter will be devoted to seeing how it can be useful, starting with **break-even (BE) analysis**.

FINDING THE BREAK-EVEN POINT

If, for a particular product or service, we know the fixed cost for a period and the variable cost per unit, we can produce a graph like the one shown in Figure 3.5. This graph shows the total cost over the possible range of volume of activity.

The bottom part of Figure 3.5 shows the fixed cost area. Added to this is the variable cost, the wedge-shaped portion at the top of the graph. The uppermost line represents the total cost over a range of volume of activity. For any particular volume, the total cost can be measured

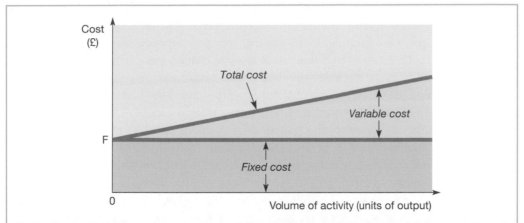

The bottom part of the graph represents the fixed cost element. To this is added the wedge-shaped top portion, which represents the variable cost. The two parts together represent total cost. At zero activity, the variable cost is zero, so total cost equals fixed cost. As activity increases so does total cost, but only because variable cost increases. We are assuming that there are no steps in the fixed cost.

Figure 3.5 Graph of total cost against volume of activity

by the vertical distance between the graph's horizontal axis and the relevant point on the uppermost line.

Logically, the total cost at zero activity is the amount of the fixed cost. This is because, even where there is nothing happening, the business will still be paying rent, salaries and so on, at least in the short term. As the volume of activity increases from zero, the fixed cost is augmented by the relevant variable cost to give the total cost.

If we take this total cost graph in Figure 3.5, and superimpose on it a line representing total revenue over the range of volume of activity, we obtain the **break-even (BE) chart**. This is shown in Figure 3.6.

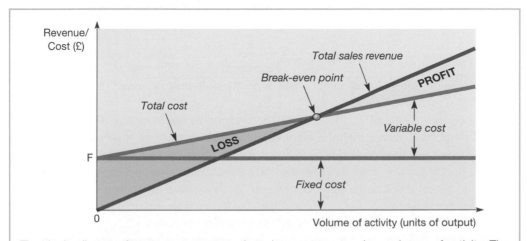

The sloping line starting at zero represents the sales revenue at various volumes of activity. The point at which this finally catches up with the sloping total cost line, which starts at F, is the break-even point (BEP). Below this point a loss is made, above it a profit.

Figure 3.6 Break-even chart

Note in Figure 3.6 that, at zero volume of activity (zero sales), there is zero sales revenue. The profit (loss), which is the difference between total sales revenue and total cost, for a particular volume of activity, is the vertical distance between the total sales revenue line and the total cost line at that volume of activity. Where there is no vertical distance between these two lines (total sales revenue equals total cost) the volume of activity is at **break-even point (BEP)**. At this point there is neither profit nor loss; that is, the activity *breaks even*. Where the volume of activity is below BEP, a loss will be incurred because total cost exceeds total sales revenue. Where the business operates at a volume of activity above BEP, there will be a profit because total sales revenue will exceed total cost. The further the volume of activity is below BEP, the higher the loss: the further above BEP it is, the higher the profit.

Deducing BEPs graphically is a laborious business. Since, however, the relationships in the graph are all linear (that is, the lines are all straight), it is easy to calculate the BEP.

We know that at BEP (but not at any other volume of activity)

Total sales revenue = Total cost

(At all other volumes of activity except the BEP, either total sales revenue will exceed total cost or the other way round. Only at BEP are they equal.) The above formula can be expanded so that

Total sales revenue = Fixed cost + Variable cost

If we call the number of units of output at BEP b, then

$$b \times \text{Sales revenue per unit} = \text{Fixed cost} + (b \times \text{Variable cost per unit})$$

so

$$(b \times \text{Sales revenue per unit}) - (b \times \text{Variable cost per unit}) = \text{Fixed cost}$$

and

$$b \times (\text{Sales revenue per unit} - \text{Variable cost per unit}) = \text{Fixed cost}$$

giving

$$b = \frac{\text{Fixed cost}}{\text{Sales revenue per unit} - \text{Variable cost per unit}}$$

If we look back at the BE chart in Figure 3.6, this formula seems logical. The total cost line starts off at point F, higher than the starting point for the total sales revenues line (zero) by amount F (the amount of the fixed cost). Because the sales revenue per unit is greater than the variable cost per unit, the sales revenue line will gradually catch up with the total cost line. The rate at which it will catch up is dependent on the relative steepness of the two lines. Bearing in mind that the slopes of the two lines are the variable cost per unit and the selling price per unit, the above equation for calculating b looks perfectly logical.

Although the BEP can be calculated quickly and simply without resorting to graphs, this does not mean that the BE chart is without value. The chart shows the relationship between cost, volume and profit over a range of activity and in a form that can easily be understood by non-financial managers. The BE chart can therefore be a useful device for explaining this relationship.

Example 3.2

Cottage Industries Ltd makes baskets. The fixed cost of operating the workshop for a month totals £500. Each basket requires materials that cost £2 and takes one hour to make. The business pays the basket makers £10 an hour. The basket makers are all on contracts such that if they do not work for any reason, they are not paid. The baskets are sold to a wholesaler for £14 each.

What is the BEP for basket making for the business?

Solution

The BEP (in number of baskets) is:

$$BEP = \frac{\text{Fixed cost}}{(\text{Sales revenue per unit} - \text{Variable cost per unit})}$$

$$= \frac{£500}{£14 - (£2 + £10)} = 250 \text{ baskets per month}$$

Note that the BEP must be expressed with respect to a period of time.

Real World 3.1 shows information on the BEPs of one well-known business.

Real World 3.1

BE at Ryanair

Commercial airlines seem to pay a lot of attention to their BEPs and their 'load factors', that is, their actual level of activity. Figure 3.7 shows the BEPs and load factors for Ryanair, the 'no-frills' carrier.

We can see that Ryanair made operating profits in each of the five years considered. This is because the airline's load factor was consistently greater than its BEP.

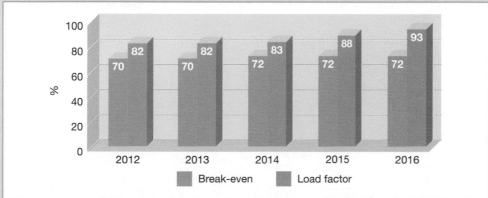

The chart shows that over the five-year period, Ryanair's load factor increased significantly, whereas its break-even point did not. For each year the load factor comfortably exceeded the break-even point.

Figure 3.7 Break-even and load factors at Ryanair

Source: Based on information contained in the Ryanair Holdings plc Annual Report 2016.

Activity 3.6

In Real World 3.1, we saw that Ryanair's BEP varied from 70 per cent to 72 per cent over the five-year period. Why was it not the same each year?

Break-even point depends on three broad factors. These are sales revenue, variable cost and fixed cost. Each of these can vary quite noticeably from one year to another. Ryanair's sales revenue could be affected by the level of disposable income among the travelling public and/or by levels of competition from other airlines. Costs can vary from one year to another, particularly the cost of aviation fuel.

[Interestingly, Ryanair's average fuel cost was €2.07 per gallon in 2012, €2.38 in 2013, €2.45 in 2014, €2.34 in 2015 and €2.21 in 2016. It seems that this major cost for the business can vary widely from one year to the next.]

Activity 3.7

Can you think of reasons why the managers of a business might find it useful to know the BEP of some activity that they are planning to undertake?

By knowing the BEP, it is possible to compare the expected, or planned, volume of activity with the BEP and so make a judgement about risk. If the volume of activity is expected to be only just above the BEP, this may suggest that it is a risky venture. Only a small fall from the expected volume of activity could lead to a loss.

Deriving BEP is not the only approach to risk assessment. In Chapter 9, we shall be considering the subject of risk, and its assessment and management, in some detail.

Activity 3.8

Cottage Industries Ltd (see Example 3.2) expects to sell 500 baskets a month. The business has the opportunity to rent a basket-making machine. Doing so would increase the total fixed cost of operating the workshop for a month to £3,000. Using the machine would reduce the labour time to half an hour per basket. The basket makers would still be paid £10 an hour.

(a) How much profit would the business make each month from selling baskets:
  - without the machine; and
  - with the machine?
(b) What is the BEP if the machine is rented?
(c) What do you notice about the figures that you calculate?

(a) Estimated monthly profit from basket making:

	Without the machine		With the machine	
	£	£	£	£
Sales revenue (500 × £14)		7,000		7,000
Materials (500 × £2)	(1,000)		(1,000)	
Labour (500 × 1 × £10)	(5,000)			
(500 × ½ × £10)			(2,500)	
Fixed cost	(500)		(3,000)	
		(6,500)		(6,500)
Profit		500		500

(b) The BEP (in number of baskets) with the machine:

$$BEP = \frac{\text{Fixed cost}}{\text{Sales revenue per unit} - \text{Variable cost per unit}}$$

$$= \frac{£3,000}{£14 - (£2 + £5)} = 429 \text{ baskets a month}$$

The BEP without the machine is 250 baskets per month (see Example 3.2).

(c) There is no difference between the two manufacturing strategies as regards to profit, at the expected sales volume. There is, however, a distinct difference between the two strategies regarding the BEP. Without the machine, the actual volume of sales could fall by 50 per cent of that expected (from 500 to 250) before the business fails to make a profit. With the machine, however, a reduction in the volume of sales of just 14 per cent (from 500 to 429) means that the business fails to make a profit. On the other hand, for each additional basket sold above the estimated 500, an additional profit of only £2 (that is, £14 − (£2 + £10)) would be made without the machine, whereas £7 (that is, £14 − (£2 + £5)) would be made with the machine. (Note how knowledge of the BEP and the planned volume of activity offers a basis for assessing the riskiness of the activity.)

Real World 3.2 reveals how ill-fated airline, Malaysian Airlines, which has failed to reach its BEP since 2010, aims to be profitable by 2018. The ways in which this is to be achieved brings into focus the relationship between cost, volume of activity and profit.

Real World 3.2

Approaching take off

Mayalsian Airways has been unprofitable since 2010. To make matters worse, it suffered two air disasters during 2014, which adversely affected passenger volumes and profitability.

In order to turn the business around, a new chief executive officer (CEO), Christopher Mueller, was appointed. The new CEO plans to lower costs and improve profits by:

- reducing the workforce from 20,000 employees to 14,000;
- reducing the number of flights and the size of the fleet;
- focusing on domestic and regional routes;
- stopping some long-haul, loss-making routes, for example, its only US route from Kuala Lumpur to Los Angeles;
- renegotiating some key contracts, including some of those with airports.

These are drastic steps. However, the new CEO believes they are necessary to achieve break even and to save the business.

FT *Source*: Information taken from McGee, P. and Parker, A. (2015) Disaster-plagued Malaysian Airways seeks break-even by 2018, ft.com, 1 June.

We shall take a closer look at the relationship between fixed cost, variable cost and profit together with any advice that we might give the management of Cottage Industries Ltd after we have briefly considered the notion of contribution.

CONTRIBUTION

The bottom part of the break-even formula (sales revenue per unit less variable cost per unit) is known as the **contribution per unit**. Thus, for the basket-making activity, without the machine the contribution per unit is £2 and with the machine it is £7. This can be quite a useful figure to know in a decision-making context. It is called 'contribution' because it contributes to meeting the fixed cost and, if there is any excess, it then contributes to profit.

We shall see, a little later in this chapter, how knowing the amount of the contribution generated by a particular activity can be valuable in making short-term decisions of various types, as well as being useful in the BEP calculation.

Contribution margin ratio

The **contribution margin ratio** is the contribution from an activity expressed as a percentage of the sales revenue, thus:

$$\text{Contribution margin ratio} = \frac{\text{Contribution}}{\text{Sales revenue}} \times 100\%$$

Contribution and sales revenue can both be expressed in per-unit or total terms. For Cottage Industries Ltd (Example 3.2 and Activity 3.8), the contribution margin ratios are:

$$\text{Without the machine, } \frac{14-12}{14} \times 100\% = 14\%$$

$$\text{With the machine, } \frac{14-7}{14} \times 100\% = 50\%$$

The ratio can provide an impression of the degree to which sales revenue is eaten away by variable cost.

MARGIN OF SAFETY

The **margin of safety** is the extent to which the planned volume of output or sales lies above the BEP. To illustrate how the margin of safety is calculated, we can use the information in Activity 3.8 relating to each option.

	Without the machine *(number of baskets)*	*With the machine* *(number of baskets)*
(a) Expected volume of sales	500	500
(b) BEP	250	429
Margin of safety (the difference between (a) and (b))	250	71
Expressed as a percentage of expected volume of sales	50%	14%

The margin of safety can be used as a partial measure of risk.

Activity 3.9

What advice would you give Cottage Industries Ltd about renting the machine, on the basis of the values for margin of safety?

It is a matter of personal judgement, which in turn is related to individual attitudes to risk, as to which strategy to adopt. Most people, however, would prefer the strategy of not renting the machine, since the margin of safety between the expected volume of activity and the BEP is much greater. Thus, for the same level of return, the risk will be lower without renting the machine.

The relative margins of safety are directly linked to the relationship between the selling price per basket, the variable cost per basket and the fixed cost per month. Without the machine the contribution (selling price less variable cost) per basket is £2; with the machine it is £7. On the other hand, without the machine the fixed cost is £500 a month; with the machine it is £3,000. This means that, with the machine, the contributions have more fixed cost to 'overcome' before the activity becomes profitable. However, the rate at which the contributions can overcome fixed cost is higher with the machine, because variable cost is lower. Thus, one additional, or one fewer, basket sold has a greater impact on profit than it does if the machine is not rented. The contrast between the two scenarios is shown graphically in Figure 3.8.

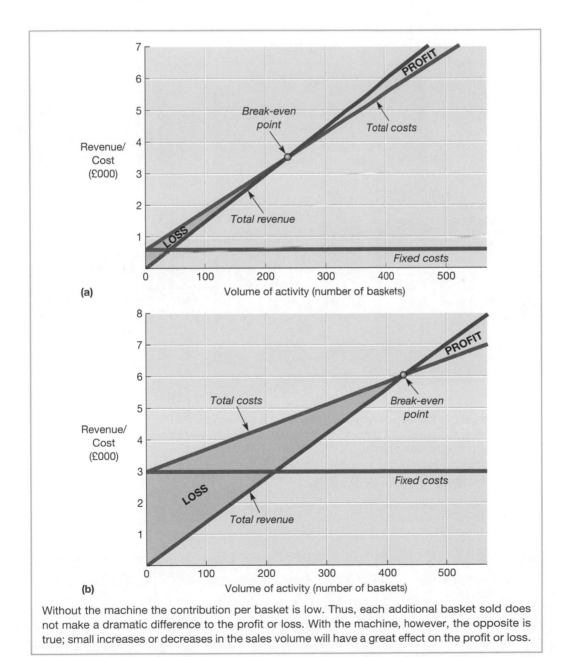

Without the machine the contribution per basket is low. Thus, each additional basket sold does not make a dramatic difference to the profit or loss. With the machine, however, the opposite is true; small increases or decreases in the sales volume will have a great effect on the profit or loss.

Figure 3.8 Break-even charts for Cottage Industries Ltd's basket-making activities (a) without the machine and (b) with the machine

Real World 3.3 goes into more detail on Ryanair's margin of safety and operating profit over recent years.

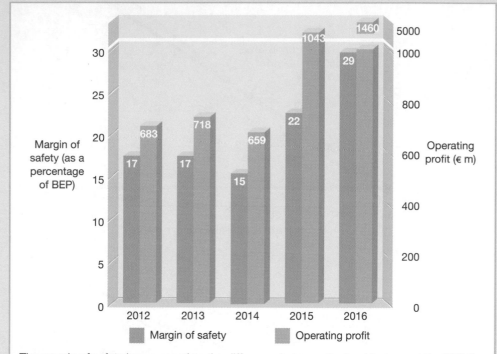
ACHIEVING A TARGET PROFIT

In the same way as we can derive the number of units of output necessary to break even, we can calculate the volume of activity required to achieve a particular level of profit. We can expand the equation given in the section 'Finding the break-even point' (on page 70) so that:

Total sales revenue = Fixed cost + Total variable cost + Target profit

If we let t be the required number of units of output to achieve the target profit, then

$t \times$ Sales revenue per unit $=$ Fixed cost $+ (t \times$ Variable cost per unit$) +$ Target profit

so

$(t \times$ Sales revenue per unit$) - (t \times$ Variable cost per unit$) =$ Fixed cost $+$ Target profit

and

$t \times$ (Sales revenue per unit $-$ Variable cost per unit$) =$ Fixed cost $+$ Target profit

giving

$$t = \frac{\text{Fixed cost} + \text{Target profit}}{\text{Sales revenue per unit} - \text{Variable cost per unit}}$$

Activity 3.10

Cottage Industries Ltd (see Example 3.2 and Activity 3.8) has a target profit of £4,000 a month. What volume of activity is required to achieve this

(a) without the machine; and
(b) with the machine?

(a) Using the formula above, the required volume of activity without the machine:

$$\frac{\text{Fixed cost} + \text{Target profit}}{\text{Sales revenue per unit} - \text{Variable cost per unit}}$$

$$= \frac{£500 + £4,000}{£14 - (£2 + £10)}$$

$= 2,250$ baskets a month

(b) The required volume of activity with the machine:

$$\frac{£3,000 + £4,000}{£14 - (£2 + £5)}$$

$= 1,000$ baskets a month

OPERATING GEARING AND ITS EFFECT ON PROFIT

The relationship between fixed cost and variable cost is known as **operating gearing** (or operational gearing). An activity with a relatively high fixed cost compared with its total variable cost, at its normal level of activity, is said to have high operating gearing. Thus, Cottage Industries Ltd has higher operating gearing using the machine than it has if not using it. Renting the machine increases the level of operating gearing quite dramatically because it causes an increase in fixed cost, but at the same time it leads to a reduction in variable cost per basket.

The reason why the word 'gearing' is used in this context is because, as with intermeshing gear wheels of different circumferences, a movement in one of the factors (volume of output) causes a more-than-proportionate movement in the other (profit) as illustrated by Figure 3.10.

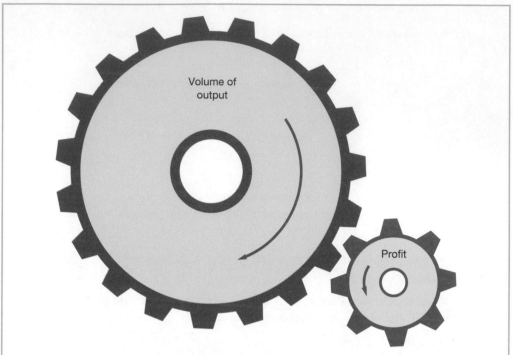

Where operating gearing is relatively high, as in the diagram, a small amount of motion in the volume wheel causes a relatively large amount of motion in the profit wheel. An increase in volume would cause a disproportionately greater increase in profit. The equivalent would also be true of a decrease in activity, however.

Figure 3.10 The effect of operating gearing

Increasing the level of operating gearing makes profit more sensitive to changes in the volume of activity. We can demonstrate operating gearing with Cottage Industries Ltd's basket-making activities as follows:

	Without the machine			*With the machine*		
Volume (number of bas kets)	500	1,000	1,500	500	1,000	1,500
	£	£	£	£	£	£
Contributions*	1,000	2,000	3,000	3,500	7,000	10,500
Fixed cost	(500)	(500)	(500)	(3,000)	(3,000)	(3,000)
Profit	500	1,500	2,500	500	4,000	7,500

* £2 per basket without the machine and £7 per basket with it.

Note that, without the machine (low operating gearing), a doubling of the output from 500 to 1,000 units brings a trebling of the profit. With the machine (high operating gearing), a doubling of output from 500 units causes profit to rise by eight times. At the same time, reductions in the volume of output tend to have a more damaging effect on profit where the operating gearing is higher.

Activity 3.11

What types of business activity are likely to have high operating gearing? (*Hint*: Cottage Industries Ltd might give you some idea.)

Activities that are capital intensive tend to have high operating gearing. This is because renting or owning capital equipment gives rise to additional fixed cost, but it can also give rise to lower variable cost.

Real World 3.4 shows how a well-known business has benefited from operating gearing.

PROFIT–VOLUME CHARTS

A slight variant of the break-even chart is the **profit–volume (PV) chart**. A typical PV chart is shown in Figure 3.11.

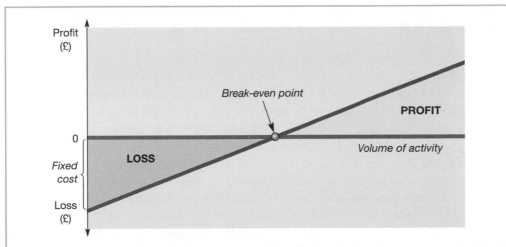

The sloping line is profit (loss) plotted against activity. As activity increases, so does total contribution (sales revenue less variable cost). At zero activity there is no contribution, so there will be a loss equal in amount to the total fixed cost.

Figure 3.11 Profit–volume chart

The PV chart is obtained by plotting loss or profit against volume of activity. The slope of the graph is equal to the contribution per unit, since each additional unit sold decreases the loss, or increases the profit, by the sales revenue per unit less the variable cost per unit. At zero volume of activity there is no contribution, so there is a loss equal to the amount of the fixed cost. As the volume of activity increases, the amount of the loss gradually decreases until BEP is reached. Beyond BEP a profit is made, which increases as the volume of activity increases.

As we can see, the PV chart does not tell us anything not shown by the break-even chart. It does, however, highlight key information concerning the profit (loss) arising at any volume of activity. The break-even chart shows this as the vertical distance between the total cost and total sales revenue lines. The PV chart, in effect, combines the total sales revenue and total variable cost lines, which means that profit (or loss) is directly readable.

THE ECONOMIST'S VIEW OF THE BREAK-EVEN CHART

So far in this chapter we have treated all the relationships as linear – that is, all of the lines in the graphs have been straight. However, this is usually not strictly valid in practice.

Consider, for example, the variable cost line in the break-even chart; accountants would normally treat this as being a straight line. In reality, however, the line may not be straight because, at high levels of output, **economies of scale** may occur. These are cost savings arising from an increase in the volume of activity.

Activity 3.12

How might a manufacturer benefit from economies of scale relating to its raw material requirements?

Raw material (a typical variable cost) may be capable of being used more efficiently with higher volumes of activity. Furthermore, buying larger quantities of raw material make the business eligible for bulk discounts, thereby lowering the cost.

It is possible, however, that a high volume of activity will lead to *diseconomies of scale*. In other words, it may lead to a higher variable cost per unit of output. For instance, high usage of a particular raw material may lead to shortages, which might cause higher prices to have to be paid for supplies. Where there are either economies or diseconomies of scale, the cost per unit will not be constant over all volumes of activity.

There is also a tendency for sales revenue per unit to reduce as volume is increased. To sell more of a particular product or service, it will usually be necessary to lower the price per unit.

Economists recognise that, in real life, the relationships portrayed in the break-even chart are usually non-linear. The typical economist's view of the chart is shown in Figure 3.12.

Note, in Figure 3.12, that the total variable cost line starts to rise quite steeply with volume but, around point A, economies of scale start to take effect. With further increases in volume, total variable cost does not rise as steeply because the variable cost *for each additional unit of output* is lowered. These economies of scale continue to have a benign effect on cost until a point is reached where the business is operating towards the end of its efficient range. Beyond this range, problems will emerge that adversely affect variable cost. For example, the business may be unable to find cheap supplies of the variable cost elements, as mentioned above, or may suffer production difficulties, such as machine breakdowns. As a result, the total variable cost line starts to rise more steeply.

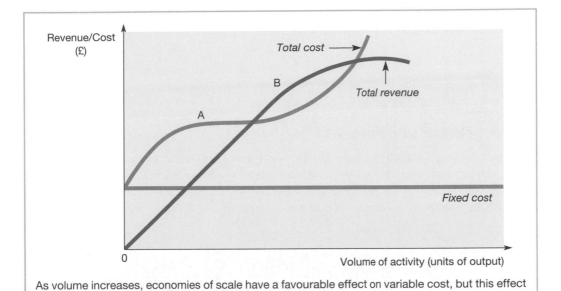

As volume increases, economies of scale have a favourable effect on variable cost, but this effect is reversed at still higher levels of output. At the same time, sales revenue per unit will tend to decrease at higher levels to encourage additional buyers.

Figure 3.12 The economist's view of the break-even chart

At low levels of output, sales may be made at a relatively high price per unit. To increase sales output beyond point B, however, it may be necessary to lower the average sales price per unit. This will mean that the total revenue line will not rise as steeply, and may even curve downwards. Note how this 'curvilinear' representation of the break-even chart can easily lead to the existence of more than one BEP.

Accountants justify their approach by arguing that, although the lines may not, in practice, be perfectly straight, this defect is not usually worth taking into account. This is partly because information used in the analysis is based on estimates of the future. These estimates will, inevitably, be flawed because of our inability to predict with great accuracy. It is pointless, it can be argued, to be concerned with the minor approximation of treating total cost and total revenue lines as straight. Only where significant economies or diseconomies of scale are involved should the non-linearity of variable cost be taken into account. Furthermore, for most businesses, the range of possible volumes of activity over which they operate (the **relevant range**) is quite narrow. When dealing with short distances, it may be perfectly reasonable to treat a curved line as being straight.

THE PROBLEM OF BREAKING EVEN

Most businesses struggle to break even at some point in their life; however, for some businesses, it can be a regular occurrence. Businesses whose fortunes are linked to the **business cycle** are particularly vulnerable to this risk. The business cycle refers to the contraction and expansion in activity arising within an economy over time. Businesses operating in industries such as construction, commodities and airlines are particularly sensitive to movements in this cycle. Hence, demand for their output can vary greatly. During a downturn in economic activity, breaking even may be beyond their reach.

Real World 3.5 reveals how the price of oil in 2016 fell significantly below the BEP for businesses extracting oil in the Middle East and Africa.

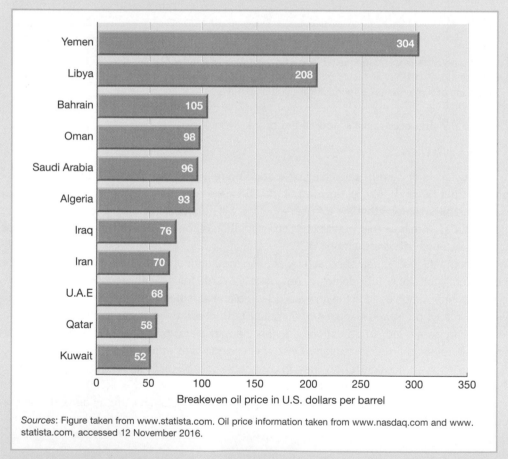
The agriculture industry can have its own cyclical pattern. Good years tend to be followed by bad years. **Real World 3.6** is an extract from an article which describe how US wheat farmers are currently finding it hard to break even.

Not reaping rewards

The U.S. Department of Agriculture reports that global stocks of wheat will exceed international demand by more than a quarter of a billion tons this year.

"From a financial perspective, the cost of production has not gone down nearly as much as the price of grain," said Adrian Doucette, president of Stockman Bank for northcentral Montana. Stockman Bank is Montana's single largest private agricultural lending institution. "An example we had the other day was someone who cut a phenomenal yield, but their inputs were $240 an acre," Doucette said. "So when you work that backward to $4 for a bushel of wheat, you've got to have a pretty good yield to make a profit."

That means that if the farmer was lucky enough to get $4 a bushel, his crop needs to average 60 bushels an acre just to break even. The 30-year average is 36 bushels an acre as reported by Montana State University extension offices.

Figures from the Chicago Board of Trade show that between January 2011 and March 2014, U.S. wheat prices fluctuated between $5.77 and $8.67 a bushel. But for the past two years, the price has consistently remained below $5 a bushel and has now slipped below $4. On July 14, NASS predicted the open market price for wheat will continue to fall, projecting a season-ending average price of around $3.70 a bushel. At those prices, only exceptional harvests have any hope of showing a profit.

"That is a concern," Doucette said. "We're seeing a lot of deals where, given normal yields, the breakeven price is higher than the current market price. That tells me people are going to have to use up some of their equity; either in real estate or other assets if they continue raising a crop that's not profitable. We never like to see anyone go backward, but it is going to happen if break evens are above the market price. For the ones who don't have the equity to fall back on, it's going to be a difficult fall."

Source: Extract from Murray, D. (2016) Wheat price is below break-even point. Record-setting wheat crop adds to international glut, www.greatfalltribune.com, 7 August.

WEAKNESSES OF BREAK-EVEN ANALYSIS

Although break-even analysis can provide useful insights concerning the relationship between cost, volume and profit, it does have its weaknesses. There are three general problems:

1 *Non-linear relationships.* Break-even analysis, as it is generally used, assumes that total variable cost and total revenue lines are perfectly straight when plotted against volume of output. In real life, this is unlikely to be the case. We saw earlier, however, that, in practice, minor variations from strict linearity are unlikely to be significant and that, over the relevant range of business operations, curved lines tend to be fairly straight.

2 *Stepped fixed cost.* Most types of fixed cost are not fixed over the whole range of activity. They tend to be 'stepped' in the way depicted in Figure 3.2. This means that, in practice, great care must be taken in making assumptions about fixed cost. The problem is amplified because many activities involve different types of fixed cost (for example, rent, supervisory salaries and administration cost), which are likely to have steps at different points.

3 *Multi-product businesses.* Most businesses provide more than one product (or service). This can be a problem for break-even analysis since additional sales of one product may affect sales of another of the business's products. There is also the problem of identifying the fixed cost associated with a particular product. Fixed cost may be incurred for the

benefit of more than one product – for example, several products may be made in the same factory. There are ways of apportioning the fixed cost of the factory between products, but they tend to be arbitrary, which undermines the value of break-even analysis.

Activity 3.13

We saw above that, in practice, relationships between costs, revenues and volumes of activity are not necessarily straight-line ones.

Can you think of at least three reasons, with examples, why this may be the case?

We thought of the following:

- *Economies of scale with labour.* A business may operate more economically at a higher volume of activity. For example, employees may be able to increase productivity by specialising in particular tasks.
- *Economies of scale with buying goods or services.* A business may find it cheaper to buy in goods and services where it is buying in bulk as discounts are often given.
- *Diseconomies of scale.* This may mean that the per-unit cost of output is higher at higher levels of activity. For example, it may be necessary to pay higher rates of pay to workers to recruit the additional staff needed at higher volumes of activity.
- *Lower sales prices at high levels of activity.* Some consumers may only be prepared to buy the particular product or service at a lower price. Thus, it may not be possible to achieve high levels of sales volume without lowering the price.

You may have thought of others.

Despite some practical problems, break-even analysis seems to be widely used. The media frequently refer to the BEP for businesses and other activities. Football is one example. There is often mention of the number of spectators required for a particular club to break even. Furthermore, UEFA has implemented a financial fair play rule for football clubs based on the concept of break even. Clubs participating, or wishing to participate, in its competitions must, as a minimum, balance their spending against the revenues generated over a three-year period. This is designed to prevent clubs recklessly spending money in pursuit of success and thereby placing their long-term future in jeopardy. Failure to adhere to this break-even rule can result in exclusion from UEFA competitions. **Real World 3.7** discusses an example of one such exclusion.

Real World 3.7

Penalty!

Galatasaray, the Turkish football champions, were not able to compete in either of the two competitions organised by UEFA, basically the Champions League and the Europa cup, for both the 2016/17 and 2017/18 seasons. The ban arose from the club breaching UEFA's fair play rules by overspending on staff remuneration during the previous years.

Source: Based on information in: *Champions Galatasaray get year-long ban from UEFA competitions*, www.espnfc. com, 2 March 2016.

The media also reports on particular businesses that are struggling to break even. **Real World 3.8** describes how one business is moving towards this point.

Real World 3.8

Seeing through the problem

X-ray screening supplier Image Scan Holdings plc is on track to break even when it announces final results later this year, after the impact from a large customer order. Last June, the group reported an £800,000 order for its ThreatScan-LS1 portable X-ray systems. Image Scan expects to have realised half this by the end of the financial year and therefore now expects to materially exceed current market expectations.

"For a company the size of Image Scan, large orders can present their own challenges. However excellent progress has been made with the planning for the recent orders and we have the commitments from our supply chain," said chairman and chief executive Bill Mawer. "I am delighted that as a consequence Image Scan will now approach break even in the current financial year".

Source: Proactive investors United Kingdom (2016) Image Scan to break even thanks to large June X-ray order, www.proactiveinvestors.co.uk, 22 August.

Real World 3.9 provides evidence concerning the extent to which managers use break-even analysis.

Real World 3.9

Break-even analysis in practice

A survey of management accounting practice in the USA was conducted in 2003. Nearly 2,000 businesses replied to the survey. These tended to be larger businesses, of which about 40 per cent were manufacturers and about 16 per cent financial services; the remainder were across a range of other industries.

The survey revealed that 62 per cent use break-even analysis extensively, with a further 22 per cent considering using the technique in the future.

The survey is now pretty old and covers only larger businesses. It should, therefore, be treated with caution. Nevertheless, it may provide some indication of what is current practice in the USA and elsewhere in the developed world.

A much more recent, and UK-based, survey of the practices of 11 small and medium sized businesses found a marked tendency to use break-even analysis.

Sources: Taken from the *2003 Survey of Management Accounting* by Ernst and Young, 2003; Lucas, M., Prowle, M. and Lowth, G. (2013) *Management Accounting Practices of UK Small-medium-sized Enterprises*, CIMA, July 2013.

USING CONTRIBUTION TO MAKE DECISIONS: MARGINAL ANALYSIS

In Chapter 2, where we discussed relevant costs for decision making, we saw that, when deciding between two or more possible courses of action, *only costs that vary with the decision should be included in the analysis*. This principle can be applied to the consideration of fixed cost.

For many decisions that involve:

- relatively small variations from existing practice, and/or
- relatively limited periods of time,

fixed cost is not relevant. It will be the same irrespective of the decision made. This is because fixed cost elements cannot, or will not, be altered in the short term.

Activity 3.14

Ali plc owns a workshop from which it provides an IT repair and maintenance service. There has recently been a downturn in demand for the service. It would be possible for Ali plc to carry on the business from smaller, cheaper accommodation.

Can you think of any reasons why the business might not immediately move to smaller, cheaper accommodation?

We thought of broadly three reasons:

1 It is not usually possible to find a buyer for the existing accommodation at very short notice and it may be difficult to find an available alternative property quickly.
2 It may be difficult to move accommodation quickly where there is, say, delicate equipment to be moved.
3 Management may feel that the downturn might not be permanent and would, therefore, be reluctant to take such a dramatic step and deny itself the opportunity to benefit from a possible revival of trade.

You may have throught of others.

We shall now consider some types of decisions where fixed cost can be regarded as irrelevant. In making these decisions, we should have as our key objective the enhancement of owners' (shareholders') wealth. Since these decisions are short-term in nature, generating as much net cash inflow as possible will normally increase wealth.

In **marginal analysis** only costs and revenues that vary with the decision are considered. This means that fixed cost can usually be ignored. This is because marginal analysis is usually applied to minor alterations in the level of activity. It tends to be true, therefore, that the variable cost per unit will be equal to the **marginal cost**, which is the additional cost of producing one more unit of output. While marginal cost normally equals variable cost, there may be times when producing one more unit will involve a step in the fixed cost. If this occurs, the marginal cost is not just the variable cost; it will include the increment, or step, in the fixed cost as well.

Marginal analysis may be used in four key areas of decision making:

- pricing/assessing opportunities to enter contracts;
- determining the most efficient use of scarce resources;
- make-or-buy decisions; and
- closing or continuation decisions.

Let us consider each of these areas in turn.

Pricing/assessing opportunities to enter contracts

To understand how marginal analysis may be used in assessing an opportunity, consider the following Activity.

Cottage Industries Ltd (see Example 3.2, page 73) has spare capacity as its basket makers have some spare time. An overseas retail chain has offered the business an order for 300 baskets at a price of £13 each.

Without considering any wider issues, should the business accept the order? (Assume that the business does not rent the machine.)

Since the fixed cost will be incurred in any case, it is not relevant to this decision. All we need to do is to see whether the price offered will yield a contribution. If it will, the business will be better off by accepting the contract than by refusing it.

	£
Additional revenue per unit	13
Additional cost per unit	(12)
Additional contribution per unit	1

For 300 units, the additional contribution will be £300 (that is, 300 × £1). Since no fixed cost increase is involved, irrespective of what else is happening to the business, it will be £300 better off by taking this contract than by refusing it.

As ever with decision making, there are other factors that are either difficult or impossible to quantify. These should be taken into account before reaching a final decision. In the case of Cottage Industries Ltd's decision concerning the overseas customer, these could include the following:

■ The possibility that spare capacity will have been 'sold off' cheaply when there might be another potential customer who will offer a higher price, but, by that time, the capacity will be fully committed. It is a matter of commercial judgement as to how likely this will be.
■ Selling the same product, but at different prices, could lead to a loss of customer goodwill. The fact that a different price will be set for customers in different countries (that is, in different markets) may be sufficient to avoid this potential problem.
■ If the business is going to suffer continually from being unable to sell its full production potential at the 'usual' price, it might be better, in the long run, to reduce capacity and make fixed cost savings. Using the spare capacity to produce marginal benefits may lead to the business failing to address this issue.
■ On a more positive note, the business may see this as a way of breaking into a different market. This is something that might be impossible to achieve if the business charges its usual price.

The marginal cost is the minimum price at which the business can offer a product or service for sale. It will result in the business being no better off as a result of making the sale than if it had not done so. Achieving more than this minimum price will generate a profit (an increase in owners' wealth).

A marginal cost approach to pricing would only be used where there is not the opportunity to sell at a price that will cover the full cost. In the long run, the business must more than cover all of its costs, both variable and fixed, if it is to be profitable.

A commercial aircraft is due to take off in one hour's time with 20 seats unsold. What is the minimum price at which these seats could be sold such that the airline would be no worse off as a result?

The answer is that any price above the additional cost of carrying one more passenger would represent an acceptable minimum. If there are no such costs, the minimum price is zero.

This is not to say that the airline will seek to charge the minimum price; it will presumably seek to charge the highest price that the market will bear. The fact that the market will not bear the full cost, plus a profit margin, should not, in principle, be sufficient for the airline to refuse to sell seats, where there is spare passenger capacity.

In practice, airlines are major users of a marginal costing approach. They often offer low priced tickets for off-peak travel, where there are not sufficient customers willing to pay 'normal' prices. By insisting on a Saturday stopover for return tickets, they tend to exclude 'business' travellers, who are probably forced to travel, but for whom a Saturday stopover may be unattractive. UK train operators often offer substantial discounts for off-peak travel. Similarly, hotels often charge very low rates for rooms at off-peak times. A hotel mainly used by business travellers may well offer very low room rates for Friday and Saturday occupancy.

Real World 3.10 explains how basing pharmaceutical prices that are set a little above marginal costs can be of real benefit to poorer countries and yet still be profitable for the businesses concerned

Real World 3.10

A shot in the arm for poorer countries

The large pharmaceutical businesses ('big pharma') seem to be viewed as villains by the general public as a result of recent large increases in the prices of their drugs output. It seems, however, that big pharma businesses can be commercially successful without taking advantage of the fact that they may represent the only source of a particular drug.

In the view of the former chief executive of one big pharma business, GlaxoSmithKline (GSK) it is possible to be beneficial to people and to be profitable at the same time. Businesses cannot survive unless they make a profit. This means that everything that they do meets the marginal costs, as a minimum. For GSK, this amounts to making a 'contribution' wherever they are selling their drugs, no matter how small that contribution may be.

GSK ranks each country by a wealth measure (gross national product per head of population) and then with particular types of drug, vaccines for example, it applies a sliding scale of pricing according to the wealth measure – poorer people pay less. This tends to lead to high sales volumes for GSK, so the small contribution per sale still leads to a sustainable business model for the business.

Source: Information taken from Mukherjee, S. (2016) *GSK's CEO Explains How Big Pharma Can Help the Poor and Still Make Money*, www.fortune.com, 2 November.

The most efficient use of scarce resources

Normally, the output of a business is determined by customer demand for the particular goods or services. In some cases, however, output will be restricted by the productive capacity of the business. Limited productive capacity might stem from a shortage of any factor of production – labour, raw materials, space, machine capacity and so on. Such scarce factors are often known as *key* or *limiting* factors.

Where productive capacity acts as a brake on output, management must decide on how best to deploy the scarce resource. That is, it must decide which products, from the range available, should be produced and how many of each should be produced. Marginal analysis can be useful to management in such circumstances. The guiding principle is that the most profitable combination of products will occur where the *contribution per unit of the scarce factor* is maximised. Example 3.3 illustrates this point.

Example 3.3

A business provides three different services, the details of which are as follows:

Service (code name)	AX107	AX109	AX220
	£	£	£
Selling price per unit	50	40	65
Variable cost per unit	(25)	(20)	(35)
Contribution per unit	25	20	30
Labour time per unit	2.5 hours	1.5 hours	3 hours

Within reason, the market will take as many units of each service as can be provided, but the ability to provide the service is limited by the availability of labour, all of which needs to be skilled. Fixed cost is not affected by the choice of service provided because all three services use the same facilities.

The most profitable service is AX109 because it generates a contribution of £13.33 (£20/1.5) an hour. The other two generate only £10 each an hour (£25/2.5 and £30/3). So, to maximise profit, priority should be given to the production that maximises the contribution per unit of limiting factor.

Our first reaction might be that the business should provide only service AX220, as this is the one that yields the highest contribution per unit sold. If so, we would have been making the mistake of thinking that it is the ability to sell that is the limiting factor. If the above analysis is not convincing, we can take a random number of available labour hours and ask ourselves what is the maximum contribution (and, therefore, profit) that could be made by providing each service exclusively. Bear in mind that there is no shortage of anything else, including market demand, just a shortage of labour.

Activity 3.17

A business makes three different products, the details of which are as follows:

Product (code name)	B14	B17	B22
Selling price per unit (£)	25	20	23
Variable cost per unit (£)	10	8	12
Weekly demand (units)	25	20	30
Machine time per unit (hours)	4	3	4

Fixed cost is not affected by the choice of product because all three products use the same machine. Machine time is limited to 148 hours a week.

Which combination of products should be manufactured if the business is to produce the highest profit?

Product (code name)	B14	B17	B22
	£	£	£
Selling price per unit	25	20	23
Variable cost per unit	(10)	(8)	(12)
Contribution per unit	15	12	11
Machine time per unit	4 hours	3 hours	4 hours
Contribution per machine hour	£3.75	£4.00	£2.75
Order of priority	2nd	1st	3rd

Therefore produce:

20 units of product B17 using	60 hours
22 units of product B14 using	88 hours
	148 hours

This leaves unsatisfied the market demand for a further three units of product B14 and 30 units of product B22.

Activity 3.18

What practical steps could be taken that might lead to a higher level of contribution for the business in Activity 3.17?

The possibilities for improving matters that occurred to us are as follows:

- Consider obtaining additional machine time. This could mean obtaining a new machine, subcontracting the machining to another business or, perhaps, squeezing a few more hours a week out of the business's own machine. Perhaps a combination of two or more of these is a possibility.
- Redesign the products in a way that requires less time per unit on the machine.
- Increase the price per unit of the three products. This might well have the effect of dampening demand, but the existing demand cannot be met at present. It may, therefore, be more profitable, in the long run, to make a greater contribution on each unit sold than to take one of the other courses of action to overcome the problem.

Activity 3.19

Going back to Activity 3.17, what is the maximum price that the business concerned would logically be prepared to pay to have the remaining B14s machined by a subcontractor, assuming that no fixed or variable cost would be saved as a result of not doing the machining in-house?

Would there be a different maximum if we were considering the B22s?

If the remaining three B14s were subcontracted at no cost, the business would be able to earn a contribution of £15 a unit, which it would not otherwise be able to gain. Therefore, any price up to £15 a unit would be worth paying to a subcontractor to undertake the machining. Naturally, the business would prefer to pay as little as possible, but anything up to £15 would still make it worthwhile subcontracting the machining.

This would not be true of the B22s because they have a different contribution per unit; £11 would be the relevant figure in their case.

Make-or-buy decisions

Businesses are frequently confronted by the need to decide whether to produce the product or service that they sell themselves, or to buy it in from some other business. Thus, a producer of electrical appliances might decide to subcontract the manufacture of one of its products to another business, perhaps because there is a shortage of production capacity in the producer's own factory, or because it believes it to be cheaper to subcontract than to make the appliance itself.

It might just be part of a product or service that is subcontracted. For example, the producer may have a component for the appliance made by another manufacturer. In principle, there is hardly any limit to the scope of make-or-buy decisions. Virtually any part, component or service that is required in production of the main product or service, or the main product or service itself, could be the subject of a make-or-buy decision. So, for example, the human resources function of a business, which is normally performed in-house, could be subcontracted. At the same time, electrical power, which is typically provided by an outside electrical utility business, could be generated in-house. Obtaining services or products from a subcontractor is referred to as **outsourcing**.

Activity 3.20

Shah Ltd needs a component for one of its products. It can outsource production of the component to a subcontractor who will provide the components for £20 each. Shah Ltd can produce the components internally for a total variable cost of £15 per component. Shah Ltd has spare capacity.

Should the component be subcontracted or produced internally?

The answer is that Shah Ltd should produce the component internally, since the variable cost of subcontracting is greater by £5 (that is, £20 − £15) than the variable cost of internal manufacture.

Activity 3.21

Now assume that Shah Ltd (Activity 3.20) has no spare capacity, so it can produce the component internally only by reducing its output of another of its products. While it is making each component, it will lose contributions of £12 from the other product.

Should the component be subcontracted or produced internally?

The answer is to subcontract. In this case, both the variable cost of production and the opportunity cost of lost contributions must be taken into account. Thus, the relevant cost of internal production of each component is:

	£
Variable cost of production of the component	15
Opportunity cost of lost production of the other product	12
	27

This is obviously more costly than the £20 per component that will have to be paid to the subcontractor.

Activity 3.22

What factors, other than the immediately financially quantifiable, would you consider when making a make-or-buy decision?

We feel that there are two major factors:

1 The general problems of subcontracting, particularly:
   (a) loss of control of quality; and
   (b) potential unreliability of supply.
2 Expertise and specialisation. Generally, businesses should focus on their core competences.

Picking up on the second point in Activity 3.22, it is possible for most businesses, with sufficient determination, to do virtually everything in-house. This may, however, require a level of skill and facilities that most businesses neither have nor wish to acquire. For example, while most businesses could generate their own electricity, their managements usually take the view that this is better done by a generator business. Specialists can often do things more cheaply, with less risk of things going wrong.

Real World 3.11 comprises extracts from an article that expands on the answer to Activity 3.22 in pointing out the limits to beneficial outsourcing.

Real World 3.11

Outsourcing can be neat, plausible and wrong

For every complicated problem, the journalist H.L. Mencken said, there is a solution that is neat, plausible and wrong. When outsourcing first became a popular business practice two decades ago, some executives mistakenly believed they had found a neat solution that was plausible, and right.

While there were obvious 'cost arbitrage' savings to be made by taking a business unit out of a high-wage area and transporting the activity to an emerging market – the so-called 'lift and shift' approach – it turned out that life was more complicated than that. Outsourcing was not and is not an easy option. Contracts take a lot of managing. Cheaper will not necessarily mean more efficient, and more efficient will not necessarily mean more effective. The 'people factor' is significant. Service level agreements have to be monitored and maintained. And initial cost savings can be eroded as wages rise in rapidly developing economies.

In any case, intelligent outsourcing is no longer simply about cost savings. 'That's just "table stakes",' says Anoop Sagoo, senior managing director at Accenture, the consulting firm. 'We've moved on a long way from what people used to think about when they discussed outsourcing,' he says.

Another interesting aspect of current thinking on outsourcing is the way it forces (or should force) businesses to ask hard and fundamental questions about how they operate, and what sort of business they really are. If growth is the ultimate goal this matters. Jonathan Cooper-Bagnall, head of shared services and outsourcing at PA Consulting, says that intelligent outsourcing can provide businesses with the sort of flexibility they need to be able to compete successfully, and grow. 'In the wake of the financial crisis, some companies have cut their cost base very deep, and are not in a position to rebuild that cost base,' he says. 'So they have to use third parties in a smart way. Say you were a bank or a retailer setting up in a new market. Do you really need to build your own systems, hire all your own people,' he asks. Mr Cooper-Bagnall goes further. 'What is really core to your business? Do you need your own R&D team? Or are you really a branding company? Other people can handle logistics, procurement, do the product development – your job is to market it.' This is where the logic of outsourcing ultimately takes you. How and where do you create value?

But before selling a too optimistic version of outsourcing, Mr Cooper-Bagnall adds: 'The talent needed to run these [outsourced] operations is in short supply, and expensive. Business acumen, managing suppliers, and those other sorts of relationship skills, are rarely found in one individual. How do you find and develop people for these roles? It's not easy.' In order to avoid classic outsourcing pitfalls, it is worth asking what the common characteristics of successful attempts to outsource are.

Outsourcing is not the answer to everything. It can be taken too far. Companies can lose control – or 'sight' – of far-flung operations. And some activities will, or should, always remain core. But the logic of outsourcing can be hard to resist. And for those looking to grow quickly, flexibly and sustainably, it is an unavoidable option.

FT   *Source*: Extracts from Stern, S. (2013) Logic of outsourcing can be hard to resist, ft.com, 20 September.
© The Financial Times Limited 2013. All Rights Reserved.

Closing or continuation decisions

It is quite common for businesses to produce separate financial statements for each department or section, to try to assess their relative performance. Example 3.4 considers how marginal analysis can help decide how to respond where it is found that a particular department underperforms.

Example 3.4

Goodsports Ltd is a retail shop that operates through three departments, all in the same accommodation. The three departments occupy roughly equal-sized areas of the accommodation. The projected trading results for next year are:

	Total £000	Sports equipment £000	Sports clothes £000	General clothes £000
Sales revenue	534	254	183	97
Cost	(482)	(213)	(163)	(106)
Profit/(loss)	52	41	20	(9)

It would appear that if the general clothes department were to close, the business would be more profitable, by £9,000 a year.

When the cost is analysed between that part that is variable and that part that is fixed, however, the contribution of each department can be deduced and the following results obtained:

	Total £000	Sports equipment £000	Sports clothes £000	General clothes £000
Sales revenue	534	254	183	97
Variable cost	(344)	(167)	(117)	(60)
Contribution	190	87	66	37
Fixed cost (rent and so on)	(138)	(46)	(46)	(46)
Profit/(loss)	52	41	20	(9)

Now it is obvious that closing the general clothes department, without any other developments, would make the business worse off by £37,000 (the department's contribution). The department should not be closed, because it makes a positive contribution. The fixed cost would continue whether the department was closed or not. As can be seen from the above analysis, distinguishing between variable and fixed cost, and deducing the contribution, can make the picture much clearer.

Activity 3.23

In considering Goodsports Ltd (in Example 3.4), we saw that the general clothes department should not be closed 'without any other developments'.

What 'other developments' could affect this decision, making continuation either more attractive or less attractive?

The things that we could think of are as follows:

- Expansion of the other departments or replacing the general clothes department with a completely new activity. This would make sense only if the space currently occupied by the general clothes department could generate contributions totalling at least £37,000 a year.
- Subletting the space occupied by the general clothes department. Once again, this would need to generate a net rent greater than £37,000 a year to make it more financially beneficial than keeping the department open.
- Keeping the department open, even if it generated no contribution whatsoever (assuming that there is no other use for the space), may still be beneficial. If customers are attracted into the shop because it has general clothing, they may then buy something from one of the other departments. In the same way, the activity of a subtenant might attract customers into the shop. (On the other hand, it might drive them away!)

You may have thought of others.

Figure 3.14 summarises the four key decision-making areas where marginal analysis tends to be used.

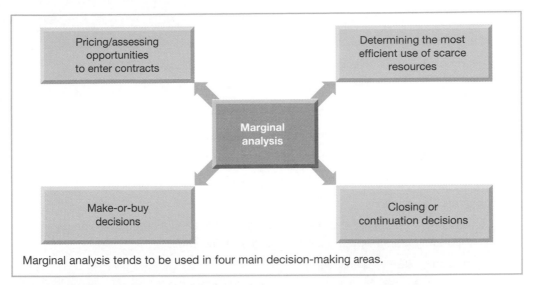

Marginal analysis tends to be used in four main decision-making areas.

Figure 3.14 The four key areas of decision making using marginal analysis

Self-assessment question 3.1

Khan Ltd can render three different types of service (Alpha, Beta and Gamma) using the same staff. Various estimates for next year have been made as follows:

Service	Alpha	Beta	Gamma
Selling price (£/unit)	30	39	20
Variable material cost (£/unit)	15	18	10
Other variable costs (£/unit)	6	10	5
Share of fixed cost (£/unit)	8	12	4
Staff time required (hours)	2	3	1

Fixed cost for next year is expected to total £40,000.

Required:

(a) If the business were to render only service Alpha next year, how many units of the service would it need to provide in order to break even? (Assume for this part of the question that there is no effective limit to market size and staffing level.)

(b) If the business has limited staff hours available next year, in which order of preference would the three services come?

(c) The maximum market for next year for the three services is as follows:

Alpha	3,000 units
Beta	2,000 units
Gamma	5,000 units

Khan Ltd has a maximum of 10,000 staff hours available next year.
What quantities of each service should the business provide next year and how much profit would this be expected to yield?

The solution to this question can be found at the back of the book on pp. 514–515.

SUMMARY

The main points of this chapter may be summarised as follows:

Cost behaviour

- Fixed cost is independent of the level of activity (for example, rent).
- Variable cost varies with the level of activity (for example, raw materials).
- Semi-fixed (semi-variable) cost is a mixture of fixed and variable costs (for example, electricity).

Break-even (BE) analysis

- The break-even point (BEP) is the level of activity (in units of output or sales revenue) at which total cost (fixed + variable) = total sales revenue.
- Calculation of BEP is as follows:

$$\text{BEP(in units of output)} = \frac{\text{Fixed cost for the period}}{\text{Contribution per unit}}$$

- Knowledge of the BEP for a particular activity can be used to help assess risk.
- Contribution per unit = sales revenue per unit less variable cost per unit.
- Contribution margin ratio = contribution/sales revenue ($\times$ 100%).
- Margin of safety = excess of planned volume (or sales revenue) of activity over volume (or sales revenue) at BEP.
- Calculation of the volume of activity (t) required to achieve a target profit is as follows:

$$t = \frac{\text{Fixed cost} + \text{Target profit}}{\text{Sales revenue per unit} - \text{Variable cost per unit}}$$

- Operating gearing is the extent to which the total cost of some activity is fixed rather than variable.
- The profit–volume (PV) chart is an alternative approach to the BE chart, which is probably easier to understand.
- Economists tend to take a different approach to BE, taking account of economies (and diseconomies) of scale and of the fact that, generally, to be able to sell large volumes, price per unit tends to fall.

Weaknesses of BE analysis

- There are non-linear relationships between cost, revenue and volume.
- There may be stepped fixed cost. Most elements of fixed cost are not fixed over all volumes of activity.
- Multi-product businesses have problems in allocating fixed cost to particular activities.

Marginal analysis (ignores fixed cost where this is not affected by the decision)

- Assessing contracts – we consider only the effect on contributions.
- Using scarce resources – the limiting factor is most effectively used by maximising its contribution per unit.
- Make-or-buy decisions – we take the action that leads to the highest total contributions.
- Closing/continuing an activity – should be assessed by net effect on total contributions.

FURTHER READING

If you would like to explore the topics covered in this chapter in more depth, we recommend the following:

Bhimani, A., Horngren, C., Datar, S. and Rajan, M. (2015) *Management and Cost Accounting*, 6th edn, Pearson, Chapters 8 and 9.

Burns, J., Quinn, M., Warren, L. and Oliveira, J. (2013) *Management Accounting*, McGraw-Hill Education, Chapters 11–13.

Drury, C. (2015) *Management and Cost Accounting*, 9th edn, Cengage Learning EMEA, Chapter 8.

Hilton, R. and Platt, D. (2014) *Managerial Accounting*, 10th edn, McGraw-Hill Higher Education, Chapters 6 and 7.

REVIEW QUESTIONS

Solutions to these questions can be found at the back of the book on pp. 527–528.

3.1 Define the terms *fixed cost* and *variable cost.* Explain how an understanding of the distinction between fixed cost and variable cost can be useful to managers.

3.2 What is meant by the BEP for an activity? How is the BEP calculated? Why is it useful to know the BEP?

3.3 When we say that some business activity has *high operating gearing*, what do we mean? What are the implications for the business of high operating gearing?

3.4 If there is a scarce resource that is restricting sales, how will the business maximise its profit? Explain the logic of the approach that you have identified for maximising profit.

Those with coloured numbers have solutions given at the back of the book on pp. 539–541.

Basic-level exercises

3.1 Motormusic Ltd makes a standard model of car radio, which it sells to car manufacturers for £60 each. Next year the business plans to make and sell 20,000 radios. The business's costs are as follows:

Manufacturing	
Variable materials	£20 per radio
Variable labour	£14 per radio
Other variable costs	£12 per radio
Fixed cost	£80,000 per year
Administration and selling	
Variable	£3 per radio
Fixed	£60,000 per year

Required:

(a) Calculate the BEP for next year, expressed both in quantity of radios and sales value.

(b) Calculate the margin of safety for next year, expressed both in quantity of radios and sales value.

3.2 Lannion and Co. is engaged in providing and marketing a standard advice service. Summarised results for the past two months reveal the following:

	October	November
Sales (units of the service)	200	300
Sales revenue (£)	5,000	7,500
Operating profit (£)	1,000	2,200

There were no price changes of any description during these two months.

Required:

(a) Deduce the BEP (in units of the service) for Lannion and Co.

(b) State why the business might find it useful to know its BEP.

Intermediate-level exercises

3.3 Gandhi Ltd renders a promotional service to small retailing businesses. There are three levels of service: the 'Basic', the 'Standard' and the 'Comprehensive'. The business plans next year to work at absolute full production capacity. Managers believe that the market will not accept more of any of the three services at the planned prices. The plans are:

Service	Number of units of the service	Selling price £	Variable cost per unit £
Basic	11,000	50	25
Standard	6,000	80	65
Comprehensive	16,000	120	90

The business's fixed cost totals £660,000 a year. Each service takes about the same length of time, irrespective of the level.

One of the accounts staff has just produced a report that seems to show that the Standard service is unprofitable. The relevant extract from the report is as follows:

Standard service cost analysis

	£	
Selling price per unit	80	
Variable cost per unit	(65)	
Fixed cost per unit	(20)	(£660,000/(11,000 + 6,000 + 16,000))
Loss	(5)	

The writer of the report suggests that the business should not offer the Standard service next year. The report goes on to suggest that, if the price of the Basic service were to be lowered, the market could be expanded.

Required:

(a) Should the Standard service be offered next year, assuming that the quantity of the other services could not be expanded to use the spare capacity?

(b) Should the Standard service be offered next year, assuming that the released capacity could be used to render a new service, the 'Nova', for which customers would be charged £75 per unit, and which would have a variable cost of £50 per unit and take twice as long per unit as each the other three services?

(c) What is the minimum price that could be accepted for the Basic service, assuming that the necessary capacity to expand it will come only from not offering the Standard service?

3.4 The management of a business is concerned about its inability to obtain enough fully trained labour to enable it to meet its present budget projection, which is as follows:

Service:	Alpha	Beta	Gamma	Total
	£000	£000	£000	£000
Variable cost:				
Materials	6	4	5	15
Labour	9	6	12	27
Expenses	3	2	2	7
Allocated fixed cost	6	15	12	33
Total cost	24	27	31	82
Profit	15	2	2	19
Sales revenue	39	29	33	101

The amount of labour likely to be available amounts to £20,000. All of the variable labour is paid at the same hourly rate. You have been asked to prepare a statement of plans, ensuring that at least 50 per cent of the budgeted sales revenues are achieved for each service and the balance of labour is used to produce the greatest profit.

Required:

(a) Prepare the statement, with explanations, showing the greatest profit available from the limited amount of skilled labour available, within the constraint stated. (*Hint*: Remember that all labour is paid at the same rate.)

(b) What steps could the business take in an attempt to improve profitability, in the light of the labour shortage?

3.5 A hotel group prepares financial statements on a quarterly basis. The senior management is reviewing the performance of one hotel and making plans for next year.

The managers have in front of them the results for this year (based on some actual results and some forecasts to the end of this year):

Quarter	Sales revenue	Profit/(loss)
	£000	£000
1	400	(280)
2	1,200	360
3	1,600	680
4	800	40
Total	4,000	800

The total estimated number of guests (guest nights) for this year is 50,000, with each guest night being charged at the same rate. The results follow a regular pattern; there are no unexpected cost fluctuations beyond the seasonal trading pattern shown above.

For next year, management anticipates an increase in unit variable cost of 10 per cent and a profit target for the hotel of £1 million. These will be incorporated into its plans.

Required:

(a) Calculate the total variable and total fixed cost of the hotel for this year. Show the provisional annual results for this year in total, showing variable and fixed cost separately. Show also the revenue and cost per guest.

(b) (1) If there is no increase in guests for next year, what will be the required revenue rate per hotel guest to meet the profit target?

(2) If the required revenue rate per guest is not raised above this year's level, how many guests will be required to meet the profit target?

(c) Outline and briefly discuss the assumptions, that are made in typical PV or break-even analysis, and assess whether they limit its usefulness.

Advanced-level exercises

3.6 A business makes three products, A, B and C. All three products require the use of two types of machine: cutting machines and assembling machines. Estimates for next year include the following:

Product	A	B	C
Selling price (£ per unit)	25	30	18
Sales demand (units)	2,500	3,400	5,100
Material cost (£ per unit)	12	13	10
Variable production cost (£ per unit)	7	4	3
Time required per unit on cutting machines (hours)	1.0	1.0	0.5
Time required per unit on assembling machines (hours)	0.5	1.0	0.5

Fixed cost for next year is expected to total £42,000.

The business has cutting machine capacity of 5,000 hours a year and assembling machine capacity of 8,000 hours a year.

Required:

(a) State, with supporting workings, which products in which quantities the business should plan to make next year on the basis of the above information. (*Hint*: First determine which machines will be a limiting factor (scarce resource).)

(b) State the maximum price per product that it would be worth the business paying to a subcontractor to carry out that part of the work that could not be done internally.

3.7 Darmor Ltd has three products, which require the same production facilities. Information about the production cost for one unit of its products is as follows:

Product	X	Y	Z
	£	£	£
Labour: Skilled	6	9	3
Unskilled	2	4	10
Materials	12	25	14
Other variable costs	3	7	7
Fixed cost	5	10	10

All labour and materials are variable costs. Skilled labour is paid £12 an hour and unskilled labour is paid £8 an hour. All references to labour cost above are based on basic rates of pay. Skilled labour is scarce, which means that the business could sell more than the maximum that it is able to make of any of the three products.

Product X is sold in a regulated market and the regulators have set a price of £30 per unit for it.

Required:

(a) State, with supporting workings, the price that must be charged for Products Y and Z, such that the business would find it equally profitable to make and sell any of the three products.

(b) State, with supporting workings, the maximum rate of overtime premium that the business would logically be prepared to pay its skilled workers to work beyond the basic time.

3.8 Intermediate Products Ltd produces four types of water pump. Two of these (A and B) are sold by the business. The other two (C and D) are incorporated, as components, into other products of the business. Neither C nor D is incorporated into A or B. Costings (per unit) for the products are as follows:

	A	B	C	D
	£	£	£	£
Variable materials	15	20	16	17
Variable labour	25	10	10	15
Other variable costs	5	3	2	2
Fixed costs	20	8	8	12
	65	41	36	46
Selling price (per unit)	70	45		

There is an outside supplier who is prepared to supply unlimited quantities of products C and D to the business, charging £40 per unit for product C and £55 per unit for product D.

Next year's estimated demand for the products, from the market (in the case of A and B) and from other production requirements (in the case of C and D) is as follows:

	Units
A	5,000
B	6,000
C	4,000
D	3,000

For strategic reasons, the business wishes to supply a minimum of 50 per cent of the above demand for products A and B.

Manufacture of all four products requires the use of a special machine. The products require time on this machine as follows:

	Hours per unit
A	0.5
B	0.4
C	0.5
D	0.3

Next year there are expected to be a maximum of 6,000 special-machine hours available. There will be no shortage of any other factor of production.

Required:

(a) State, with supporting workings and assumptions, which quantities of which products the business should plan to make next year.

(b) Explain the maximum amount that it would be worth the business paying per hour to rent a second special machine.

(c) Suggest ways, other than renting an additional special machine, that could solve the problem of the shortage of special-machine time.

Chapter 4

FULL COSTING

INTRODUCTION

Full (absorption) costing is a widely used approach that takes account of all of the cost of producing a particular product or service. In this chapter, we shall see how this approach can be used to deduce the cost of some activity, such as making a unit of product (for example, a tin of baked beans), providing a unit of service (for example, a car repair) or creating a facility (for example, building a high speed rail link from London to Birmingham).

The precise approach taken to deducing full cost will depend on whether each product or service is identical to the next or whether each job has its own individual characteristics. It will also depend on whether the business accounts for overheads on a segmental basis. We shall look at how full costing is carried out and we shall also consider its usefulness for management purposes.

This chapter considers the traditional form of full costing, which is known as absorption costing. In Chapter 5 we shall consider activity-based costing, which is a more recently developed approach.

Learning outcomes

When you have completed this chapter, you should be able to:

- Deduce the full (absorption) cost of a cost unit in a single-product and a multi-product environment.

- Discuss the problems of deducing full (absorption) cost in practice.

- Discuss the usefulness of full (absorption) cost information to managers.

- Compare and contrast the full costing and variable costing approaches.

WHAT IS FULL COSTING?

Full cost is the total amount of resources, usually measured in monetary terms, sacrificed to achieve a given objective. Thus, if the objective is to supply a customer with a product or service, all resources sacrificed in order to make the product, or provide the service, are included as part of the full cost. To derive the full cost figure, the various elements of cost incurred are accumulated and then assigned to the particular product or service.

The logic of **full costing** is that the entire cost of running a facility, such as an office or factory, must be regarded as part of the cost of the output that it helps to generate. Take, for example, the rent incurred in running an architect's office. While this may not alter if the architect undertakes one more assignment, there would be nowhere to work unless the office was available. Thus, the office rent must be taken into account when calculating the full cost of providing each architectural assignment.

A **cost unit** is a unit of whatever is having its cost determined, such as an architectural assignment. Usually, it is one unit of output of a particular product or service.

WHY DO MANAGERS WANT TO KNOW THE FULL COST?

We saw in Chapter 1 that the only point in providing management accounting information is to improve the quality of management decisions. There are four main areas where information relating to the full cost of the business's products or services may prove useful. These are:

■ *Pricing and output decisions.* Having full cost information can help managers make decisions on the price to charge customers for the business's products or services. Full cost information, along with relevant information concerning prices, can also be used to determine the number of units of products or services to be produced. We shall consider this aspect in more detail in Chapter 10.

■ *Exercising control.* Determining the full cost of a product or service is often a useful starting point for exercising cost control. Where the reported full cost figure is considered too high, for example, individual elements of full cost may then be examined to see whether there are opportunities for savings. This may lead to re-engineering the production process, finding new sources of supply and so on. We shall pick up this point in later chapters, particularly Chapters 7 and 11.

■ *Assessing relative efficiency.* Full cost information can help compare the cost of carrying out an activity in a particular way, or particular place, with its cost if carried out in a different way, or place. A motor car manufacturer, for example, may wish to compare the cost of building a particular model of car in one manufacturing plant, rather than in another. This could help in deciding where to locate future production.

■ *Assessing performance.* Profit is an important measure of business performance. To measure the profit arising from a particular product or service, the sales revenue that it generates should be compared with the costs consumed in generating that revenue. This can help in assessing past decisions. It can also help in guiding future decisions, such as continuing with, or abandoning, the particular product or service.

Figure 4.1 shows the four uses of full cost information.

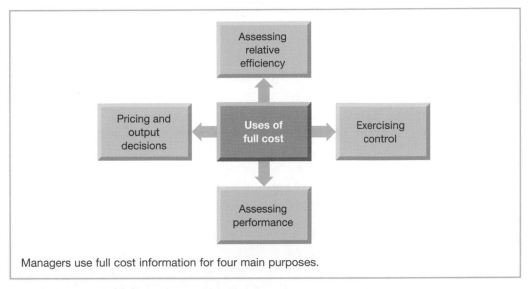

Managers use full cost information for four main purposes.

Figure 4.1 Uses of full cost by managers

Now let us consider **Real World 4.1**.

Real World 4.1

Costing by degrees

The University of Cambridge calculated that, for the academic year 2014/15, the average cost of educating an undergraduate student was £18,000.

This figure represents the full cost of carrying out this activity.

Source: Morgan, J. (2016) Cambridge's 'cost of education' rises to £18K per student' *Times Higher Education Supplement*, 8 September.

When considering the information in Real World 4.1, an important question that arises is 'what does this full cost figure include?' Does it simply include the cost of the salaries earned by academics during the time spent in lectures, seminars and tutorials or does it include other things? If other costs are to be included, what are they? Would they include, for example, a charge for the costs of time spent by academics in:

- preparing materials for lectures;
- editing and updating course materials;
- preparing and marking examination papers;
- invigilation of examinations; and
- organising and visiting placements?

Would there be a charge for administrative staff carrying out teaching support activities such as:

- timetabling;
- preparing prospectuses;
- student counselling; and
- careers' advice?

Would there be a charge for the use of university facilities such as:

- the library;
- lecture halls; and
- laboratories and workshops?

If the cost is not to be included, is the figure of £18,000 potentially misleading? If, on the other hand, the cost of these items is to be included, how can an appropriate charge be determined? Addressing questions such as these is the focus of this chapter and the early part of Chapter 5.

In the sections that follow, we begin by considering how to calculate the full cost of a unit of output for a business providing a single product or service. We then go on to see how the full cost of a unit of output may be calculated for a business providing a range of products or services.

SINGLE-PRODUCT BUSINESSES

The simplest case for determining the full cost per unit of output is where a business produces a single product or service. Here the production process will involve a series of continuous or repetitive activities and the output will consist of identical, or near identical, items. To calculate the full cost per unit of output, we must average the total manufacturing cost over the number of units produced. It is simply a matter of adding up all of the elements of cost of production incurred in a particular period (materials, labour, rent, fuel, power and so on) and dividing this total by the total number of units of output for that period. This approach is referred to as **process costing**.

Activity 4.1

Fruitjuice Ltd began operations at the beginning of May. It has just one product, a sparkling orange drink that is marketed as 'Orange Fizz'. During May the business produced 7,300 litres of the drink. The manufacturing cost incurred was made up as follows:

	£
Ingredients (oranges, sugar, water and so on)	390
Fuel	85
Rent of factory accommodation	350
Depreciation of equipment	75
Labour	852

What is the full cost per litre of producing 'Orange Fizz' in May?

Full cost per litre = Total manufacturing costs/Number of litres produced
= £(390 + 85 + 350 + 75 + 852)/7,300
= 1,752/7,300
= £0.24 per litre

Process-costing problems

Process costing tends to be fairly straightforward as it involves tracking the production of identical, or near identical, items. Nevertheless, problems can still arise when measuring certain elements of manufacturing cost. In the case of Fruitjuice Ltd, for example, how is the cost of depreciation deduced? It can only be an estimate and so its reliability is open to question. The cost of raw materials may also be a problem. Should we use the 'relevant' cost of the raw materials (in this case, almost certainly the replacement cost), or the actual price paid for it (historic cost)? As the cost per litre will presumably be used for decision-making purposes, replacement cost provides the more logical choice. For some reason, however, historic cost seems to be more widely used in practice.

There can also be problems in calculating how much output was produced. If making Orange Fizz is not a very fast process, some of the product will be in the process of being made at any given moment. Partially completed Orange Fizz represents **work in progress** (or work in process) that should be taken into account when calculating the total output, and cost per unit of output, for a period. This can, however, be a little tricky. In Example 4.1 we see why and how we deal with work in progress.

Example 4.1

Gnome Sweet Gnome Ltd began operations on 1 September. It produces a single product, which is a statue of a gnome for use in gardens and patios. During September, the business achieved the following output:

	Units
Completed gnomes	120
Partially completed gnomes at the end of September	15

How do we measure total output for September in a single figure? We cannot simply take the 120 completed gnomes as the measure of total output. To do so would ignore the fact that part of the production effort during September had been expended on partially completed gnomes. Nor can we simply add the 120 completed gnomes to the 15 gnomes that are work in progress. This would ignore the fact that some of the statues are still incomplete. Nevertheless, the partially completed statues must somehow be taken into account when calculating total output.

The approach taken is to calculate the **equivalent units of output** that the work in progress represents. This is the number of completed gnome statues that could have been produced given the material cost and other manufacturing costs incurred. To do this, we must first estimate the degree to which the work in progress has been completed.

Let us assume that the work in progress is estimated to be 80 per cent complete in terms of materials, labour and other costs. The equivalent number of completed gnome statues can then be calculated by multiplying the number of statues that are work in progress by their percentage completion. That is, $15 \times 80\% = 12$ statues.

The total equivalent units of output for the period will, therefore, be $120 + 12 = 132$ statues. This figure represents a weighted average, where the degree of completion provides the weighting.

Take the information in Example 4.1 and assume that the manufacturing cost incurred in producing gnome statues during September was as follows:

	£
Materials (plastic, paint, resin and so on)	1,680
Power for equipment	140
Rent of factory space	1,050
Depreciation of equipment	230
Labour	1,920
Other manufacturing costs	260

What is the full cost per equivalent statue in September?

The costs incurred during September relate to both the completed gnomes and to the work in progress at the end of the month. To derive the full cost per equivalent statue, we must add together all of the elements of manufacturing cost incurred and then divide this amount by the number of equivalent units of completed output. Thus:

Cost per equivalent statue = Total manufacturing cost/Number of equivalent statues produced
= (1,680 + 140 + 1,050 + 230 + 1,920 + 260)/(120 + 12)
= 5,280/132
= £40.00

Total manufacturing cost can now be assigned between completed and partially completed statues in a logical way as follows:

	£
Cost of completed units (120 × £40)	4,800
Cost of partially completed units – work in progress (12* × £40).	480
Total	5,280

* Note that it is the equivalent units of output rather than the actual number of units that is being used.

It is important to be as accurate as possible when estimating the degree of completion. If an overestimate is made, the number of equivalent units of output will be overstated. This, in turn, will lead to an understatement of the full cost per unit of producing each statue during September. If an underestimate is made, the opposite will be true.

Example 4.1 above offers some insight as to how we deal with work in progress; however, further complications can arise. One such complication is where there is work in progress at the beginning, as well as at the end, of the period. Another is where there are varying degrees of completion for work in progress. A product may be, say, 90 per cent complete regarding materials, but 80 per cent complete as far as labour and other costs are concerned. These more technical issues, although not difficult to deal with, are beyond the scope of the book. If you would like to find out more, take a look at the further reading at the end of the chapter.

MULTI-PRODUCT BUSINESSES

Many businesses provide products or services that are distinct rather than identical. In this situation, the process-costing approach that we used with litres of 'Orange Fizz' (Activity 4.1) and garden gnomes (Example 4.1) would be inappropriate. While it may be appropriate to assign an average cost to each *identical* unit of output, this is not the case where units of output are quite different. It would be illogical, for example, to assign the same cost to each car repair carried out by a garage, irrespective of the complexity and size of the repair.

Where a business offers distinct products or services, a **job-costing** approach is normally used. This involves accumulating costs for each individual unit of output in order to determine its full cost. To understand how this can be done, we first need to understand the difference between direct and indirect cost.

Direct and indirect cost

To provide full cost information, the various elements of cost must be accumulated and then assigned to particular cost units on some reasonable basis. Where cost units are not identical, the starting point is to separate cost into two categories: direct cost and indirect cost.

- **Direct cost**. This is a cost that can be identified with specific cost units. That is to say, the cost can be traced to a particular cost unit and can be measured reliably. The main examples of a direct cost are direct materials and direct labour. Thus, in determining the cost of a car repair by a garage, both the cost of spare parts used in the repair and the cost of the mechanic's time would form part of the direct cost of that repair. Collecting elements of direct cost is a simple matter of having a cost-recording system that is capable of capturing the cost of direct materials used on each job and the cost of direct workers.
- **Indirect cost** (or **overheads**). This comprises all other elements of total cost. That is to say those items that cannot be identified with each particular cost unit (job). Thus, the amount paid to rent the garage would be an indirect cost of a particular car repair.

We shall use the terms 'indirect cost' and 'overheads' interchangeably for the remainder of this book.

Real World 4.2 gives some indication of the relative importance of direct and indirect costs in practice.

Counting the cost

A survey of 176 UK businesses operating in various industries, all with an annual turnover of more than £50 million, was conducted by Al-Omiri and Drury. They discovered that the full cost of the businesses' output on average is split between direct and indirect costs as shown in Figure 4.2.

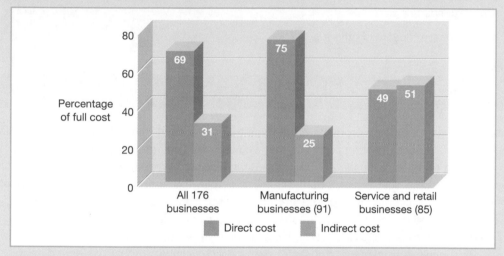

Figure 4.2 Percentage of full cost contributed by direct and indirect cost

For the manufacturers, the 75 per cent direct cost was, on average, made up as follows:

	Percentage
Direct materials	52
Direct labour	14
Other direct costs	9

Source: Al-Omiri, M. and Drury, C. (2007) A survey of factors influencing the choice of product costing systems in UK organizations, *Management Accounting Research*, Vol. 18, pp. 399–424.

Activity 4.4

A garage owner wishes to know the direct cost of each job (car repair) that is carried out. How might the direct cost (labour and materials) information concerning a particular job be collected?

Usually, direct workers are required to record how long was spent on each job. Thus, the mechanic doing the job would record the length of time worked on the car. The pay rates should be available from the human resources department. It is simply then a matter of multiplying the number of hours spent on a job by the relevant rate of pay. The stores staff would normally be required to keep a record of the cost of parts and materials used on each job.

A 'job sheet' will normally be prepared – probably on the computer – for each individual job. The quality of the information generated will rely on staff faithfully recording all elements of direct labour and materials applied to the job.

Job costing

To deduce the full cost of a particular cost unit, we first identify the direct cost of the cost unit, which is usually fairly straightforward. The next step, however, is less straightforward. We have to 'charge' each cost unit with a suitable share of indirect cost (overheads). Put another way, cost units will *absorb* overheads. This term leads to full costing also being called **absorption costing**. The absorption process is shown graphically in Figure 4.3.

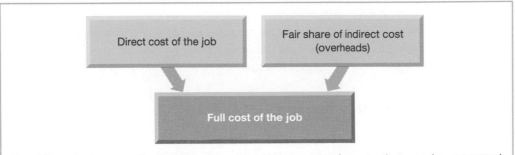

The full cost of any particular job is the sum of those cost elements that can be measured specifically in respect of the job (direct cost) and a share of the cost of creating the environment in which production (of an object or service) can take place, but which do not relate specifically to any particular job (indirect cost).

Figure 4.3 The relationship between direct cost and indirect cost

Activity 4.5

Sparky Ltd is a business that employs a number of electricians. The business undertakes a range of work for its customers, from replacing fuses to installing complete wiring systems in new houses.

In respect of a particular job done by Sparky Ltd, into which category (direct or indirect) would each of the following cost elements fall?

- the wages of the electrician who did the job;
- depreciation of the tools used by the electrician;
- the cost of cable and other materials used on the job;
- rent of the building where Sparky Ltd stores its inventories of cable and other materials.

The electrician's wages earned while working on the particular job and the cost of the materials used on the job are included in direct cost. This is because we can measure how much time was spent on the particular job (and therefore its direct labour cost) and the amount of materials used (and therefore the direct material cost) in the job.

The other cost elements are included in the general cost of running the business and, as such, must form part of the indirect cost of doing the job. They cannot be directly measured in respect of the particular job.

It is important to note that whether a cost is direct or indirect depends on the item being costed – the cost objective. To refer to indirect cost without specifying the cost objective would be wrong.

Broader-reaching cost objectives, such as operating Sparky Ltd for a month, tend to include a higher proportion of direct cost than do more limited ones, such as a particular job done by Sparky Ltd. Costing broader cost objectives is, therefore, more straightforward than costing narrower ones. This is because direct cost is normally easier to deal with than indirect cost.

Before considering full costing in more detail, let us first be clear as to how it differs from the approach discussed in the previous chapter.

Full costing and cost behaviour

We saw in Chapter 3 that the full cost of doing something (or *total cost*, as it is known in the context of marginal analysis) can be analysed between its fixed and variable elements. This is illustrated in Figure 4.4.

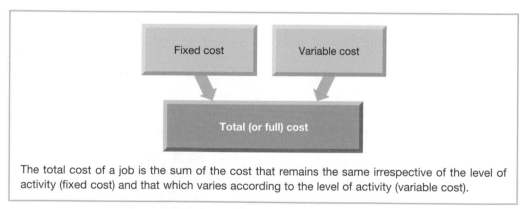

The total cost of a job is the sum of the cost that remains the same irrespective of the level of activity (fixed cost) and that which varies according to the level of activity (variable cost).

Figure 4.4 The relationship between fixed cost, variable cost and total cost

The apparent similarity of what is shown in Figure 4.4 to that shown in Figure 4.3 may create the impression that variable cost and direct cost are the same, and that fixed cost and indirect cost (overheads) are also the same. This, however, is not the case.

Fixed cost and variable cost are defined in terms of **cost behaviour** in the face of changes in the volume of activity. Direct cost and indirect cost, on the other hand, are defined in terms of the extent to which they can be identified with, and measured in respect of, particular cost units (jobs). These two sets of notions are entirely different. While a fixed cost can often be an indirect cost and a variable cost can often be a direct cost, this is far from being a hard and fast rule. Take, for example, most manufactured products. They are likely to have indirect cost, such as power for machinery, which is variable, and direct cost, such as labour, which is fixed. Thus, identifying a cost as being either indirect or direct tells us nothing about whether it is fixed or variable.

The relationship between the reaction of cost to volume changes, on the one hand, and how cost elements must be gathered to deduce the full cost for a particular job, on the other, is shown in Figure 4.5.

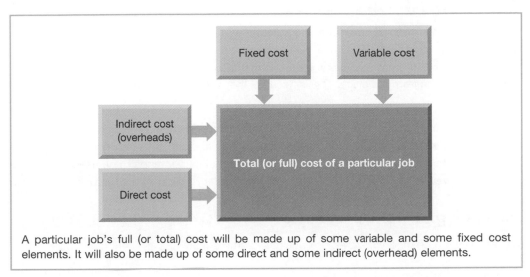

A particular job's full (or total) cost will be made up of some variable and some fixed cost elements. It will also be made up of some direct and some indirect (overhead) elements.

Figure 4.5 The relationship between direct, indirect, variable and fixed costs of a particular job

Total cost is the sum of direct and indirect costs. It is also the sum of fixed and variable costs. We should always bear in mind that these two facts are not connected.

The problem of indirect cost

It is worth emphasising that the distinction between direct and indirect cost is only important in a job-costing environment, that is, where units of output differ. This distinction was of no consequence when costing a litre of 'Orange Fizz' drink (Activity 4.1) as all cost was shared equally between the individual litres of 'Orange Fizz'. Where units of output are not identical, however, this cannot be done if we wish to achieve an appropriate measure of the full cost of a particular job.

Although indirect cost must form part of the full cost of each cost unit, it cannot, by definition, be identified directly with particular cost units. This raises a major practical issue: how can indirect cost be assigned to individual cost units?

OVERHEADS AS SERVICE RENDERERS

Indirect cost (overheads) can be viewed as rendering a service to cost units. Take, for example, a legal case undertaken by a firm of lawyers for a particular client. The legal case can be regarded as receiving a service from the office in which the work is done. It seems reasonable, therefore, to charge each case (cost unit) with a share of the cost of running the office (rent, lighting, heating, cleaning, building maintenance and so on). It also seems reasonable for this charge to be related to the amount of service received from the office.

The next step is the difficult one. How might the cost of running the office, which is a cost incurred for all the work undertaken by the firm, be divided between individual legal cases?

The easiest way would be to share this overhead cost equally between each case handled by the firm within the period. This method, however, has little to commend it.

Where they have not received identical service, we must identify something observable and measurable about the various legal cases that allows us to distinguish between them. In practice, time spent working on each individual case by direct labour tends to be used. It must be stressed, however, that this is not the 'correct' way and it is certainly not the only way.

Job costing: a worked example

To see how job costing works, let us consider Example 4.2.

Example 4.2

Johnson Ltd provides a personal computer maintenance and repair service. It has overheads of £10,000 each month. Each month 1,000 direct labour hours are worked and charged to cost units (jobs carried out by the business). A particular PC repair undertaken by the business used direct materials costing £15. Direct labour worked on the repair was three hours and the wage rate is £16 an hour. Johnson Ltd charges overheads to jobs on a direct labour hour basis. What is the full (absorption) cost of the repair?

Solution

First, let us establish the **overhead absorption (recovery) rate**, that is, the rate at which individual repairs will be charged with overheads. This is £10 (that is, £10,000/1,000) per direct labour hour.

Thus, the full cost of the repair is:

	£
Direct materials	15
Direct labour (3 × £16)	48
	63
Overheads (3 × £10)	30
Full cost of the job	93

Note, in Example 4.2, that the number of labour hours (three hours) appears twice in deducing the full cost: once to deduce the direct labour cost and a second time to deduce the overheads to be charged to the repair. These are really two separate issues, although both are based on the same number of labour hours.

Note also that, if all the jobs undertaken during the month are assigned overheads in a similar manner, all £10,000 of overheads will be charged between the various jobs. Jobs that involve a lot of direct labour will be assigned a large share of overheads. Similarly, jobs that involve little direct labour will be assigned a small share of overheads.

Can you think of reasons why direct labour hours tend to be regarded as the most logical basis for sharing overheads between cost units? Try to think of at least one.

The reasons that occurred to us are as follows:

■ Large jobs should logically attract large amounts of overheads because they are likely to have been rendered more 'service' by the overheads than small ones. The length of time that they are worked on by direct labour may be seen as a rough way of measuring relative size, though other means of doing this may be found – for example, relative physical size, where the cost unit is a physical object, like a manufactured product.

■ Most overheads are related to time. Rent, heating, lighting, non-current asset depreciation and supervisors' and managers' salaries, which are all typical overheads, are all, more or less, time-based. That is, the overheads for one week tend to be about half of those for a similar two-week period. Thus, assigning overheads to jobs on the basis of the time the units of output benefited from the 'service' rendered by the overheads seems logical.

■ Direct labour hours are capable of being measured for each job. They will normally be measured to deduce the direct labour element of cost in any case. Thus, a direct labour hour basis of dealing with overheads is practical to apply in the real world.

It cannot be emphasised enough that there is no 'correct' way to assign overheads to jobs. Overheads cannot, by definition, be easily identified with individual jobs. If, nevertheless, we wish to recognise that overheads are part of the full cost of all jobs, we must find some way of assigning a share of the total overheads to each job. In practice, the direct labour hour method seems to be the most popular way of doing so.

Real World 4.3 describes another approach to assigning overheads to jobs that was used by one well-known organisation.

Real World 4.3

Recovering costs

The UK National Health Service (NHS) calculates the cost of various medical and surgical procedures that it undertakes for its patients. In determining the costs of a procedure requiring time in hospital as an 'in patient', the NHS identifies the full cost of the particular procedure (for example, a knee replacement operation). To this it adds a share of the hospital overheads to cover the cost of the patient's stay in hospital.

Until recently, total ward overheads for a period were absorbed by dividing them by the number of 'bed days' throughout the hospital, to establish a 'bed-day rate'. A bed day is one patient spending one day occupying a bed in the hospital. The total cost of a particular patient's treatment was then calculated as:

the cost of the procedure + (the number of days the patient spent in hospital × the bed day rate)

The direct labour hour basis of absorption was not used. The bed-day rate is, however, an alternative, logical, time-based approach.

The NHS now uses a different form of full costing, which is described in the next chapter.

Source: NHS England (2014) *NHS Better Care Better Value Indicators,* 15 May.

Marine Suppliers Ltd undertakes a range of work, including making sails for small sailing boats on a made-to-measure basis.

The business expects the following to arise during the next month:

Direct labour cost	£60,000
Direct labour time	6,000 hours
Indirect labour cost	£9,000
Depreciation of machinery	£3,000
Rent	£5,000
Heating, lighting and power	£2,000
Machine time	2,000 hours
Indirect materials	£500
Other miscellaneous indirect production cost elements (overheads)	£200
Direct materials cost	£6,000

The business has received an enquiry about a sail. It is estimated that this particular sail will take 12 direct labour hours to make and will require 20 square metres of sailcloth, which costs £10 per square metre.

The business normally uses a direct labour hour basis of charging indirect cost (overheads) to individual jobs.

What is the full (absorption) cost of making the sail?

The direct cost of making the sail can be identified as follows:

	£
Direct materials (20 × £10)	200.00
Direct labour (12 × (£60,000/6,000))	120.00
	320.00

To deduce the indirect cost (overhead) element that must be added to derive the full cost of the sail, we first need to total these cost elements as follows:

	£
Indirect labour	9,000
Depreciation	3,000
Rent	5,000
Heating, lighting and power	2,000
Indirect materials	500
Other miscellaneous indirect production cost (overhead) elements	200
Total indirect cost (overheads)	19,700

Since the business uses a direct labour hour basis of charging indirect cost to jobs, we need to deduce the indirect cost (or overhead) recovery rate per direct labour hour. This is simply:

£19,700/6,000 = £3.28 direct labour hour

Thus, the full cost of the sail is expected to be:

	£
Direct materials (20 × £10)	200.00
Direct labour (12 × (£60,000/6,000))	120.00
Indirect cost (12 × £3.28)	39.36
Full cost	359.36

Figure 4.6 shows the process for applying indirect (overhead) and direct costs to the sail that was the subject of Activity 4.9.

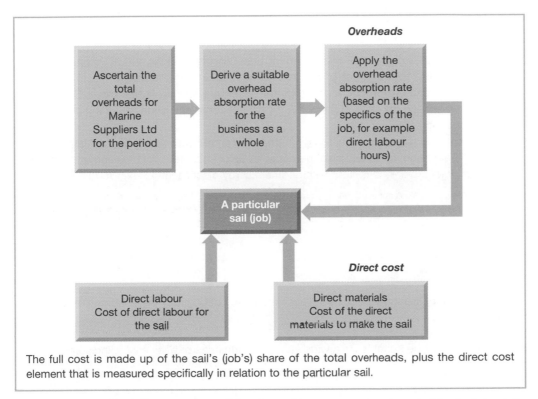

Overheads

Ascertain the total overheads for Marine Suppliers Ltd for the period → Derive a suitable overhead absorption rate for the business as a whole → Apply the overhead absorption rate (based on the specifics of the job, for example direct labour hours)

A particular sail (job)

Direct cost

Direct labour
Cost of direct labour for the sail

Direct materials
Cost of the direct materials to make the sail

The full cost is made up of the sail's (job's) share of the total overheads, plus the direct cost element that is measured specifically in relation to the particular sail.

Figure 4.6 How the full cost is derived for the sail by Marine Suppliers Ltd in Activity 4.9

Activity 4.10

Suppose that Marine Suppliers Ltd (see Activity 4.9) used a machine hour basis of charging overheads to jobs. What would be the cost of the particular job if it was expected to take five machine hours (as well as 12 direct labour hours)?

The total overheads of the business will of course be the same irrespective of the method of charging them to jobs. Thus, the overhead recovery rate, on a machine hour basis, will be:

£19,700/2,000 = £9.85 per machine hour

The full cost of the sail is, therefore, expected to be:

	£
Direct materials (20 × £10)	200.00
Direct labour (12 × (£60,000/6,000))	120.00
Indirect cost (5 × £9.85)	49.25
Full cost	369.25

Real World 4.4 below briefly describes the findings of one study, which reveals differences between larger and smaller businesses in their approach to assigning overheads.

Real World 4.4

Size matters

A questionnaire study of 272 management accountants working in UK manufacturing businesses found that a lower proportion of small and medium size (SME) businesses assigned overheads to product costs than for larger businesses. Furthermore, SMEs that did assign overhead costs used fewer overhead recovery rates when assigning overheads to product costs.

These findings might be expected given the differences between SMEs and larger businesses in resourcing levels and also, perhaps, levels of financial awareness among managers. These findings are consistent with another survey discussed in Real World 4.9.

Source: Brierley, J. (2011) A comparison of the product costing practices of large and small- to medium-sized enterprises: a survey of British manufacturing firms, *International Journal of Management*, Vol. 28, pp. 184–193.

Activity 4.11

Can you think of industries or businesses where job costing may be suitable? Try to think of at least two.

Job costing may be suitable for a wide variety of industries or businesses, including:

- house building;
- civil engineering;
- accounting services;
- film making;
- interior design;
- consultancy; and
- shipbuilding.

You may have thought of others.

Selecting a basis for charging overheads

We saw earlier that there is no single correct way of charging overheads. The final choice is a matter of judgement. It seems reasonable to say, however, that the nature of the overheads should influence the basis for charging them to jobs. Where production is capital-intensive and overheads are primarily machine-based (such as depreciation, machine maintenance, power and so on), machine hours might be preferred. Otherwise direct labour hours might be chosen.

It would be irrational to choose one of these methods in preference to the other simply because it apportions either a higher or a lower amount of overheads to a particular job. The total overheads will be the same irrespective of how they are apportioned between individual jobs and so a method that gives a higher share of overheads to one particular job must give a lower share to the remaining jobs. There is one cake of fixed size: if one person receives a relatively large slice, others must on average receive relatively small slices. To illustrate further this issue of apportioning overheads, consider Example 4.3.

Example 4.3

A business, that provides a service, expects to incur overheads totalling £20,000 next month. The total direct labour time worked is expected to be 1,600 hours and machines are expected to operate for a total of 1,000 hours.

During the next month, the business expects to do just two large jobs. Information concerning each job is as follows:

	Job 1	Job 2
Direct labour hours	800	800
Machine hours	700	300

How much of the total overheads will be charged to each job if overheads are to be charged on:

(a) a direct labour hour basis; and
(b) a machine hour basis?

What do you notice about the two sets of figures that you calculate?

Solution

(a) Direct labour hour basis

Overhead recovery rate = £20,000/1,600 = £12.50 per direct labour hour.

Job 1	£12.50 × 800 = £10,000
Job 2	£12.50 × 800 = £10,000

(b) Machine hour basis

Overhead recovery rate = £20,000/1,000 = £20.00 per machine hour.

Job 1	£20.00 × 700 = £14,000
Job 2	£20.00 × 300 = £6,000

It is clear from these calculations that the total overheads charged to jobs is the same (that is, £20,000) whichever method is used. Whereas the machine hour basis gives Job 1 a higher share of these overheads than the direct labour hour method, the opposite is true for Job 2.

It is not feasible to charge overheads using one method for one job and using the other method for the other job. This would mean either total overheads would not be fully charged to the jobs, or the jobs would be overcharged with overheads. If, for example, the direct labour hour method was used for Job 1 (£10,000) and the machine hour basis was used for Job 2 (£6,000), only £16,000 of a total £20,000 of overheads would be charged to jobs. As a result, the purpose of full (absorption) costing, which is to charge *all* overhead costs to jobs carried out during the period, would not be achieved. Furthermore, if selling prices are based on full cost, there is a risk that the business would not charge high enough prices to cover all its costs.

Figure 4.7 shows the effect of the two different methods of charging overheads to Jobs 1 and 2.

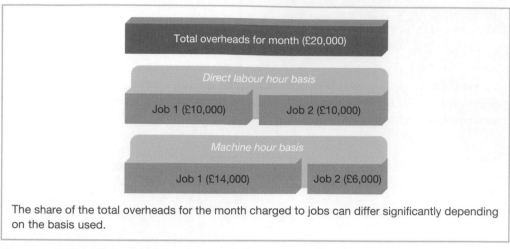

The share of the total overheads for the month charged to jobs can differ significantly depending on the basis used.

Figure 4.7 The effect of different bases of charging overheads to jobs in Example 4.3

Activity 4.12

The point was made above that it would normally be irrational to prefer one basis of charging overheads to jobs simply because it apportions either a higher or a lower amount of overheads to a particular job. This is because the total overheads are the same irrespective of the method of charging the total to individual jobs.

Can you think of any circumstances where it may not be so irrational?

This might occur where a customer has agreed to pay a price for a particular job based on full cost plus an agreed fixed percentage for profit. Here it would be beneficial to the producer for the total cost of the job to be as high as possible. Public sector organisations, such as central and local government, have been known to enter into such **cost-plus pricing** contracts.

These contracts are, however, pretty rare nowadays as they are so open to abuse. Normally, contract prices are agreed in advance, typically in conjunction with competitive tendering.

Real World 4.5 provides some insight into the basis of overhead recovery in practice.

Real World 4.5

Overhead recovery rates in practice

A survey of 129 UK manufacturing businesses showed that the direct labour hour basis (or a close approximation to it) of charging indirect cost (overheads) to cost units was overwhelmingly the most popular. It was used by 72 per cent of the respondents to the survey.

15 per cent of respondents used a 'production-time based overhead rate'. This is presumably something like a machine hour rate.

Although this survey applied only to manufacturing businesses, in the absence of other information it provides some impression of what happens in practice.

Source: Based on information taken from Brierley, J., Cowton, C. and Drury, C. (2007) Product costing practices in different manufacturing industries: a British survey, *International Journal of Management*, Vol. 24, pp. 667–675.

Segmenting the overheads

We have just seen that charging the same overheads to different jobs on different bases is not feasible. It is perfectly feasible, however, to charge one segment of the total overheads on one basis and another segment on another basis.

Activity 4.13

Taking the same business as in Example 4.3, on closer analysis we find that of the overheads that total £20,000 next month, £8,000 relates to machines (depreciation, maintenance, rent of the space occupied by the machines and so on) and the remaining £12,000 to more general overheads. The other information about the business is exactly as it was before.

How much of the total overheads will be charged to each job if the machine-related overheads are to be charged on a machine hour basis and the remaining overheads are charged on a direct labour hour basis?

Direct labour hour basis

        Overhead recovery rate = £12,000/1,600 = £7.50 per direct labour hour

Machine hour basis

        Overhead recovery rate = £8,000/1,000 = £8.00 per machine hour

Overheads charged to jobs

	Job 1 £	Job 2 £
Direct labour hour basis:		
£7.50 × 800	6,000	
£7.50 × 800		6,000
Machine hour basis:		
£8.00 × 700	5,600	
£8.00 × 300		2,400
Total	11,600	8,400

We can see from this that all the overheads of £20,000 have been charged.

Segmenting the overheads in this way is quite common. A business may be divided into separate areas for costing purposes. Overheads can then be charged differently from one area to the next, according to the nature of the work done in each.

Dealing with overheads on a cost centre basis

We saw in Chapter 1 that businesses are often divided into departments, where each department carries out a separate task. Many of these businesses charge overheads to cost units on a department-by-department basis. They do so in the belief that it will give rise to more accurate full costing information. It is probably only in a minority of cases, however, that it leads to any great improvement in accuracy. Although applying overheads on a departmental basis may not be of enormous benefit, it is probably not an expensive exercise. Cost elements are collected department by department for other purposes (particularly control) and so applying overheads on a department-by-department basis may be a fairly straightforward matter.

In Example 4.4 we see how the departmental approach to deriving full cost can be applied in a service-industry context.

The passage of a job through the departments, picking up cost as it goes, can be compared to a snowball being rolled across snow: as it rolls, it picks up more and more snow.

Example 4.4

Autosparkle Ltd offers a motor vehicle paint-respray service. The jobs that it undertakes range from painting a small part of a saloon car, usually following a minor accident, to a complete respray of a double-decker bus.

Each job starts life in the Preparation Department, where it is prepared for the Paintshop. Here, the job is worked on by direct workers, in most cases taking some direct materials from the stores with which to treat the old paintwork and, generally, to render the vehicle ready for respraying. Thus the job will be charged with direct materials, direct labour and a share of the Preparation Department's overheads. The job then passes into the Paintshop Department, already valued at the cost that it picked up in the Preparation Department.

In the Paintshop, the staff draw direct materials (mainly paint) from the stores and direct workers spend time respraying, using sophisticated spraying apparatus as well as working by hand. So, in the Paintshop, the job is charged with direct materials, direct labour and a share of that department's overheads. The job now passes into the Finishing Department, valued at the cost of the materials, labour and overheads that it accumulated in the first two departments.

In the Finishing Department, vehicles are cleaned and polished ready to go back to the customers. Further direct labour and, in some cases, materials are added. All jobs also pick up a share of that department's overheads. The job, now complete, passes back to the customer.

Figure 4.8 shows graphically how this works for a particular job.

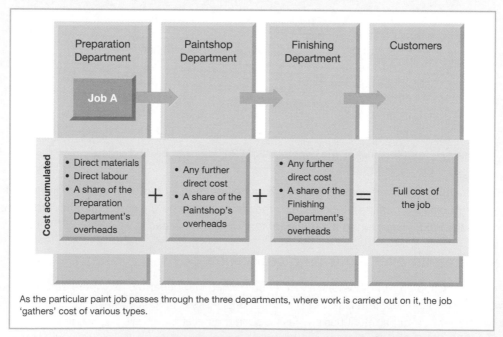

As the particular paint job passes through the three departments, where work is carried out on it, the job 'gathers' cost of various types.

Figure 4.8 A cost unit (Job A) passing through Autosparkle Ltd's process

The approach to charging overheads to jobs (for example, direct labour hours) might be the same for all three departments, or it might be different from one department to another. It is possible that cost elements relating to the spraying apparatus dominate the Paintshop overhead cost, so the Paintshop's overheads might well be charged to jobs on a machine hour basis. The other two departments are probably labour-intensive, so that direct labour hours may be seen as being appropriate there.

Where cost determination is dealt with departmentally, each department is known as a **cost centre**. This can be defined as a particular physical area or some activity or function for which the cost is separately identified. Charging direct cost to jobs in a departmental system is exactly the same as where the whole business is one single cost centre. It is simply a matter of keeping a record of:

■ the number of hours of direct labour worked on the particular job and the grade of labour, where there are different grades with different rates of pay;
■ the cost of the direct materials taken from stores and applied to the job; and
■ any other direct cost elements, for example some subcontracted work, associated with the job.

This record keeping will normally be done cost centre by cost centre.

The total production overheads of the entire business must be broken down on a cost centre basis. That is, they must be divided between the cost centres, so that the sum of the overheads of the individual cost centres equals the overheads for the entire business. By charging all of their overheads to jobs, the cost centres will, between them, charge all of the overheads of the business to jobs.

Real World 4.6 provides an indication of the number of different cost centres that businesses tend to use in practice.

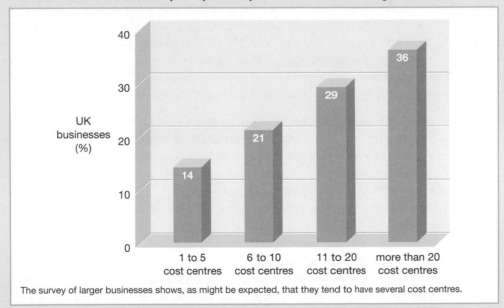

Real World 4.6

Cost centres in practice

It is usual for businesses to have several cost centres. A survey of 186 larger UK businesses involved in various activities by Drury and Tayles showed the following:

The survey of larger businesses shows, as might be expected, that they tend to have several cost centres.

Figure 4.9 Analysis of the number of cost centres within a business

We can see that 86 per cent of businesses surveyed had six or more cost centres and that 36 per cent of businesses had more than 20 cost centres. Although this is not shown in the figure, 3 per cent of businesses surveyed had a single cost centre (that is, there was a business-wide or overall overhead rate used). Clearly, businesses that deal with overheads on a business-wide basis are relatively rare.

Source: Based on information taken from Drury, C. and Tayles, M. (2006) Profitability analysis in UK organisations, *British Accounting Review*, Vol. 38, pp. 405–425.

For cost assignment purposes, we need to distinguish between **product cost centres** and **service cost centres**. Product cost centres are those in which jobs are worked on by direct workers and/or where direct materials are added. In these cost centres, jobs can be charged with a share of their overheads. The Preparation, Paintshop and Finishing Departments, discussed in Example 4.4, are all examples of product cost centres.

Activity 4.14

Can you guess what a service cost centre is? Can you think of an example of a service cost centre for a large manufacturing business?

A service cost centre is one where no direct cost is involved. It renders a service to other cost centres. Examples include:

- Cleaning
- Training
- Stores
- Maintenance
- Human resources
- Catering.

You may have thought of others.

The cost of service cost centres must be charged to product cost centres and become part of the product cost centres' overheads, so that those overheads can, in turn, be charged to jobs. This means all the production overheads of the business will then find their way into the cost of the jobs.

Logically, the cost of a service cost centre should be charged to product cost centres according to the level of service provided to each. Thus, a product cost centre that incurs a higher level of machine maintenance should be charged with a larger share of the maintenance cost centre's (department's) cost.

The process of dividing overheads between cost centres is as follows:

- **Cost allocation**. Allocate indirect cost elements that are specific to particular cost centres. These are items that relate to, and are specifically measurable in respect of, individual cost centres. In other words, they are part of the direct cost of running the cost centre. Examples include:
  - salaries of indirect workers whose activities are wholly within the cost centre, for example the salary of the cost centre manager;
  - rent, where the cost centre is housed in a building for which rent can be separately identified; and
  - electricity, where it is separately metered for each cost centre.
- **Cost apportionment**. Apportion the more general overheads to the cost centres. These are overheads that relate to more than one cost centre, perhaps to all. It would include:
  - rent, where more than one cost centre is housed in the same building;
  - electricity, where it is not separately metered; and
  - salaries of cleaning staff who work in a variety of cost centres.

  These overheads would be apportioned to cost centres on the basis of the extent to which each cost centre benefits from the overheads concerned. For example, the rent cost might be apportioned on the basis of the square metres of floor area occupied by each cost centre. With electricity used to power machinery, the basis of apportionment might be the level of mechanisation of each cost centre. As with charging overheads to individual jobs, there is no single 'correct' basis of apportioning general overheads to cost centres.

- Having allocated and apportioned the overhead cost to all cost centres, the total cost of service cost centres must then be apportioned to product cost centres. Once again, the basis used should reflect the level of service rendered. This time it will reflect the service rendered by the individual service cost centre to the individual production cost centre. With the human resources cost centre (department) cost, for example, the basis of apportionment might be the number of staff in each product cost centre.

Activity 4.15

Can you think why this basis of apportionment of the human resources department may not always be suitable? What does it assume?

It assumes that the number of staff determines the amount of benefit received from the human resources cost centre. Where a particular product cost centre has severe staff problems, it may account for a huge proportion of the human resources department's time even though it employs relatively few people.

The final total for each product cost centre will be charged to jobs as they pass through. The process of applying overheads to cost units on a cost centre (departmental) basis is shown in Figure 4.10.

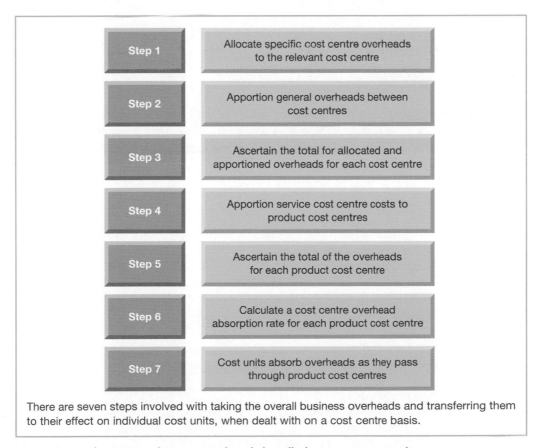

Step 1	Allocate specific cost centre overheads to the relevant cost centre
Step 2	Apportion general overheads between cost centres
Step 3	Ascertain the total for allocated and apportioned overheads for each cost centre
Step 4	Apportion service cost centre costs to product cost centres
Step 5	Ascertain the total of the overheads for each product cost centre
Step 6	Calculate a cost centre overhead absorption rate for each product cost centre
Step 7	Cost units absorb overheads as they pass through product cost centres

There are seven steps involved with taking the overall business overheads and transferring them to their effect on individual cost units, when dealt with on a cost centre basis.

Figure 4.10 The steps in having overheads handled on a cost centre basis

Let us now go on to consider Example 4.5, which deals with overheads on a cost centre (departmental) basis.

A business consists of four cost centres:

- Preparation department
- Machining department
- Finishing department
- Human resources (HR) department.

The first three are product cost centres and the last renders a service to the other three. The level of service rendered is thought to be roughly in proportion to the number of employees in each product cost centre.

Overheads, and other data, for next month are expected to be as follows:

	£000
Rent	10,000
Electricity to power machines	3,000
Electricity for heating and lighting	800
Insurance of building	200
Cleaning	600
Depreciation of machines	2,000
Total monthly salaries of the indirect workers:	
Preparation department	200
Machining department	240
Finishing department	180
HR department	180

The HR department has a staff consisting of only indirect workers (including managers). The other departments have both indirect workers (including managers) and direct workers. There are 100 indirect workers within each of the four departments and none does any 'direct' work.

Each direct worker is expected to work 160 hours next month. The number of direct workers in each department is:

Preparation department	600
Machining department	900
Finishing department	500

Machining department direct workers are paid £12 an hour; other direct workers are paid £10 an hour.

All of the machinery is in the machining department. Machines are expected to operate for 120,000 hours next month.

The floor space (in square metres) occupied by the departments is as follows:

Preparation department	16,000
Machining department	20,000
Finishing department	10,000
HR department	2,000

Deducing the overheads, cost centre by cost centre, can be done, using a schedule, as follows:

	£000	Total £000	Prep'n £000	Mach'g £000	Fin'g £000	HR £000
Allocated cost:						
Machine power		3,000		3,000		
Machine depreciation		2,000		2,000		
Indirect salaries		800	200	240	180	180
Apportioned cost						
Rent	10,000					
Heating and lighting	800					
Insurance of buildings	200					
Cleaning	600					
Apportioned by floor area		11,600	3,867	4,833	2,417	483
Cost centre overheads		17,400	4,067	10,073	2,597	663
Reapportion HR cost by number of staff (including the indirect workers)		–	202	288	173	(663)
		17,400	4,269	10,361	2,770	–

Activity 4.16

Assume that the machining department overheads (in Example 4.5) are to be charged to jobs on a machine hour basis, but that the direct labour hour basis is to be used for the other two departments. What will be the full (absorption) cost of a job with the following characteristics?

	Preparation department	Machining department	Finishing department
Direct labour hours	10	7	5
Machine hours	–	6	–
Direct materials (£)	85	13	6

(*Hint*: This should be tackled as if each cost centre were a separate business, then departmental cost elements are added together for the job so as to arrive at the total full cost.)

First, we need to deduce the indirect (overhead) recovery rates for each cost centre:

Preparation department (direct labour hour based):

$$\frac{£4,269,000}{600 \times 160} = £44.47$$

Machining department (machine hour based):

$$\frac{£10,361,000}{120,000} = £86.34$$

Finishing department (direct labour hour based):

$$\frac{£2,770,000}{500 \times 160} = £34.63$$

The cost of the job is as follows:

	£	£
Direct labour:		
Preparation department (10 × £10)	100.00	
Machining department (7 × £12)	84.00	
Finishing department (5 × £10)	50.00	
		234.00
Direct materials:		
Preparation department	85.00	
Machining department	13.00	
Finishing department	6.00	
		104.00
Overheads:		
Preparation department (10 × £44.47)	444.70	
Machining department (6 × £86.34)	518.04	
Finishing department (5 × £34.63)	173.15	
		1,135.89
Full cost of the job		1,473.89

Activity 4.17

The manufacturing cost for Buccaneers Ltd for next year is expected to be made up as follows:

	£000
Direct materials:	
Forming department	450
Machining department	100
Finishing department	50
Direct labour:	
Forming department	180
Machining department	120
Finishing department	75
Indirect materials:	
Forming department	40
Machining department	30
Finishing department	10
Human resources department	10
Indirect labour:	
Forming department	80
Machining department	70
Finishing department	60
Human resources department	60
Maintenance cost	50
Rent	100
Heating and lighting	20
Building insurance	10
Machinery insurance	10
Depreciation of machinery	120
Total manufacturing cost	1,645

The following additional information is available:

1 Each of the four departments is treated as a separate cost centre.
2 All direct labour is paid £10 an hour for all hours worked.
3 The human resources department renders services to all three of the production departments.
4 The area of the building in which the business manufactures amounts to 50,000 square metres, divided as follows:

	Sq m
Forming department	20,000
Machining department	15,000
Finishing department	10,000
Human resources department	5,000

5 The maintenance employees are expected to divide their time between the production departments as follows:

	%
Forming department	15
Machining department	75
Finishing department	10

6 Machine hours are expected to be as follows:

	Hours
Forming department	5,000
Machining department	15,000
Finishing department	5,000

On the basis of this information:

(a) Allocate and apportion overheads to the three product cost centres.
(b) Deduce overhead recovery rates for each product cost centre using two different bases for each cost centre's overheads.
(c) Calculate the full cost of a job with the following characteristics:

Direct labour hours:	
Forming department	4 hours
Machining department	4 hours
Finishing department	1 hour
Machine hours:	
Forming department	1 hour
Machining department	2 hours
Finishing department	1 hour
Direct materials:	
Forming department	£40
Machining department	£9
Finishing department	£4

Use whichever of the two bases of overhead recovery, deduced in (b), that you consider more appropriate.
(d) Explain why you consider the basis used in (c) to be the more appropriate.

$\rightarrow$

(a) Overheads can be allocated and apportioned as follows:

Cost	Basis of apportionment	Total £000	Forming £000	Machining £000	Finishing £000	HR £000
Indirect materials	Specifically allocated	90	40	30	10	10
Indirect labour	Specifically allocated	270	80	70	60	60
Maintenance	Staff time	50	7.5	37.5	5	–
Rent		100				
Heat and light		20				
Buildings insurance		10				
	Area	130	52	39	26	13
Machine insurance		10				
Machine depreciation		120				
	Machine hours	130	26	78	26	–
		670	205.5	254.5	127	83
HR	Direct labour	–	39.84	26.56	16.6	(83)
		670	245.34	281.06	143.6	–

Note: The direct cost is not included in the above because it is allocated *directly* to jobs.

(b) Overhead recovery rates are as follows:

Basis 1: direct labour hours

$$\text{Forming} = \frac{£245{,}340}{£(180{,}000/10)} = £13.63 \text{ per direct labour hour}$$

$$\text{Machining} = \frac{£281{,}060}{£(120{,}000/10)} = £23.42 \text{ per direct labour hour}$$

$$\text{Finishing} = \frac{£143{,}600}{£(75{,}000/10)} = £19.15 \text{ per direct labour hour}$$

Basis 2: machine hours

$$\text{Forming} = \frac{£245{,}340}{5{,}000} = £49.07 \text{ per machine hour}$$

$$\text{Machining} = \frac{£281{,}060}{15{,}000} = £18.74 \text{ per machine hour}$$

$$\text{Finishing} = \frac{£143{,}600}{5{,}000} = £28.72 \text{ per machine hour}$$

(c) Full cost of job – on direct labour hour basis of overhead recovery:

	£	£
Direct labour cost (9 × £10)		90.00
Direct materials (£40 + £9 + £4)		53.00
Overheads:		
Forming (4 × £13.63)	54.52	
Machining (4 × £23.42)	93.68	
Finishing (1 × £19.15)	19.15	167.35
Full cost		310.35

(d) The reason for using the direct labour hour basis rather than the machine hour basis was that labour is more important, in terms of the number of hours applied to output, than is machine time. Strong arguments could have been made for the use of the alternative basis; certainly, a machine hour basis could have been justified for the machining department.

It may be reasonable to use one basis in respect of one product cost centre's overheads and a different one for those of another. For example, machine hours could have been used for the machining department and a direct labour hours basis for the other two.

From our discussions so far, we can see that assigning overhead costs to products is as much art as science. It is not surprising, therefore, that there have been calls for a more rigorous approach to this problem. We shall examine this point in some detail in the next chapter. In the meantime, however, take a look at **Real World 4.7**.

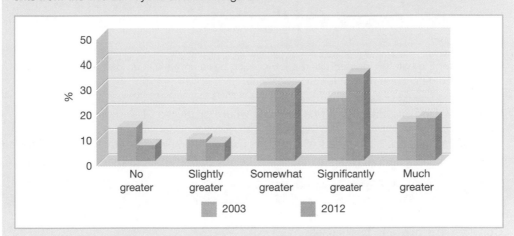
Batch costing

Many types of goods and some services are produced in a batch of identical, or nearly identical, units of output. Each batch produced, however, is distinctly different from other batches. A theatre, for example, may put on a production whose nature and cost is very different from that of other productions. On the other hand, ignoring differences in the desirability of the various types of seating, all of the individual units of output (tickets to see the production) are identical.

In these circumstances, the cost per ticket is calculated using a **batch costing** approach and involves:

■ using a job-costing approach (taking account of direct and indirect costs and so on) to find the cost of mounting the production; and then

■ dividing the cost of mounting the production by the expected number of tickets to be sold to find the cost per ticket.

Figure 4.12 shows the process for deriving the cost of one cost unit (product) in a batch.

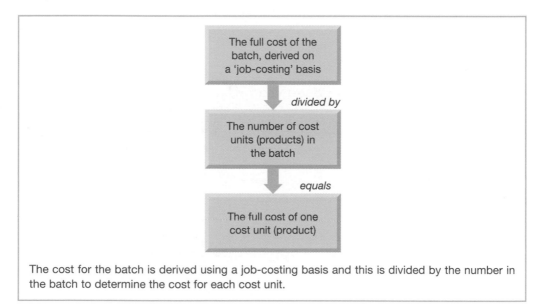

The full cost of the batch, derived on a 'job-costing' basis

divided by

The number of cost units (products) in the batch

equals

The full cost of one cost unit (product)

The cost for the batch is derived using a job-costing basis and this is divided by the number in the batch to determine the cost for each cost unit.

Figure 4.12 Deriving the cost of one cost unit where production is in batches

Batch costing is used in a variety of industries including clothing manufacturing, engineering component manufacturing, tyre manufacturing, bakery goods and footwear manufacturing.

Activity 4.18

Consider the following businesses:

■ a pharmaceutical manufacturer
■ a sugar refiner
■ a picture framer
■ a private hospital

■ a coal-mining business
■ an architect's office
■ a cement manufacturer
■ an antique furniture restorer.

Try to identify for each business which form of full costing (process, job or batch costing) is likely to be most appropriate.

Process costing is likely to be most appropriate for the sugar refiner, the coal-mining business and the cement manufacturer. Each business is normally involved in producing identical, or near identical, items through a series of repetitive activities.

Job costing is likely to be most appropriate for the picture framer, the private hospital, the architect's office and the antique furniture restorer. Each of these businesses is normally involved in producing a customised product, or service, with each item requiring different inputs of labour, materials and so on.

Batch costing is likely to be most appropriate for the pharmaceutical manufacturer. The production process will normally involve making identical products, such as tablets and medicines, in batches, where each batch is different.

Non-manufacturing overheads

An international accounting standard (IAS 2 *Inventories*) requires all inventories, including work in progress, to be valued at full cost. When calculating full cost, only those overheads relating to the manufacturing process should be included. Non-manufacturing overheads do not form part of the full cost calculation. These overheads normally relate to general administration, selling, marketing and distribution and must be charged to the period in which they are incurred. The rules mentioned, however, apply only for external reporting purposes. They need not be applied for internal reporting purposes.

For managerial decision making, non-manufacturing overheads are sometimes included as part of the total cost of goods produced. To do this, an appropriate basis for assigning these overheads to products must be found. This is not an easy task and inappropriate bases are often used. One basis used in practice is direct labour hours, even though its relevance for this purpose is dubious. Another basis used involves adding an amount based on the percentage of total non-manufacturing overheads to total manufacturing costs. (See reference 1 at the end of the chapter.) Thus, if total non-manufacturing overheads were £2.5 million and total manufacturing costs were £10 million, an additional 25 per cent (£2.5m/£10m) loading would be added as part of the total overhead cost.

Activity 4.19

What is the risk of using arbitrary bases for assigning non-manufacturing overheads?

Unless an appropriate share of non-manufacturing overheads is assigned to products, managers will be provided with misleading information.

A final point worth making is that, where the cost of products includes both manufacturing and non-manufacturing costs and things turn out as expected, selling the products at their full cost should cause the business to break even exactly. Thus, whatever profit (in total) is loaded onto full cost to set actual selling prices will result in that level of profit being earned for the period.

Real World 4.8 below describes the findings from a recent study concerning the treatment of non-manufacturing costs.

Real World 4.8

Adding to the cost

A questionnaire-based survey of management accountants in UK manufacturing operations found that the just over half of the operating units included non-manufacturing overheads as part of the total product cost.

Results from 169 of the responses revealed that the smaller the non-manufacturing overheads, as a percentage of either total operating unit costs or total overhead costs, the more likely they were to be included as part of the total cost. This is a surprising result for which the reasons are unclear. The opposite finding might have been expected. That is, the higher the percentage of non-manufacturing overheads, the greater the likelihood that they would be included.

The study also found that other factors, such as the size of the operating units and the level of competition, had no significant effect on the decision to include non-manufacturing overheads as part of the total product cost.

Source: Brierley, J. (2015) An examination of the factors influencing the inclusion of non-manufacturing overhead costs in product costs, *International Journal of Managerial and Financial Accounting*, Vol. 7, pp. 134–150.

Full (absorption) costing and estimation errors

While calculating full cost can be done after the work is completed, it is frequently estimated in advance. This may be because some idea of full cost is needed as a basis for setting a selling price. Estimates, however, rarely turn out to be 100 per cent accurate. Where actual outcomes differ from estimated outcomes, an over-recovery or under-recovery of overheads will normally occur. Example 4.6 illustrates how this over- or under-recovery is calculated.

Example 4.6

Downham Engineering plc produces a standard valve. At the beginning of the year, it was planned that manufacturing the valves would incur £4 million in overheads and would require 400,000 direct labour hours for the year. The business, which uses the direct labour basis of absorbing overheads, set the overhead recovery rate at (£4.0m/400,000) = £10 per direct labour hour.

At the end of the year it was found that, in producing the valves, 450,000 direct labour hours were used in the production process but that the total manufactring overheads were as planned.

The overheads absorbed for the year can be calculated as follows:

Overheads absorbed = overhead recovery rate × actual direct labour hours

As 450,000 direct labour hours were used, the amount charged for overheads would have been:

450,000 × £10 = £4.5 million

By comparing the overheads incurred with the actual overheads absorbed we find that £0.5 million (that is, £4.5m − £4.0m) of overheads were 'over-recovered'.

For external reporting purposes, any under- or over-recovery of overheads is normally adjusted in the income statement. Thus, the over-recovery in Example 4.6 would normally be deducted from the cost of goods sold figure shown in the income statement for that year.

Activity 4.20

Refer to Example 4.6 above. Assume that, at the end of the year, it was found that 380,000 direct labour hours were used during the year in making the valves and that manufacturing overheads incurred were £4.2 million.
What adjustment should be made to the income statement for the year?

The manufacturing overheads recovered will be 380,000 × £10 = £3.8 million. The overheads incurred were £4.2 million. This means that £0.4 million (that is, £4.2m − £3.8m) has been under-recovered. This amount will be added to the cost of goods figure appearing in the income statement for the year.

Real World 4.9 is taken from the results of a survey conducted by the UK Chartered Institute of Management Accountants (CIMA) in July 2009. Broadly, the survey asked management accountants in a wide range of business types and sizes to indicate the extent to which their business used a range of management accounting techniques. 439 management accountants completed the survey. We shall be making reference to this survey on a number of occasions throughout the book. When we do, we shall refer to it as the 'CIMA survey'.

The use of full cost information

The businesses surveyed by CIMA derived full cost information to the following extent:

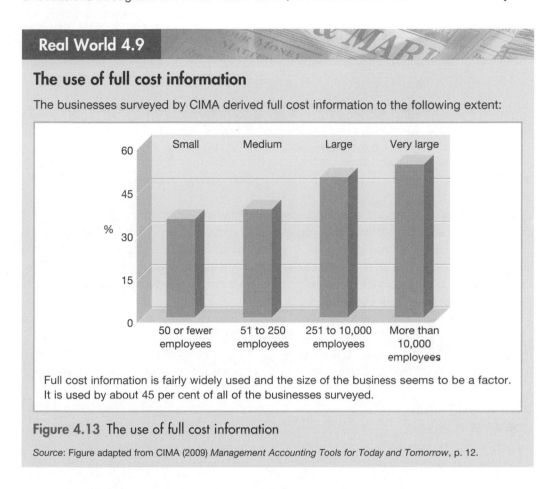

Full cost information is fairly widely used and the size of the business seems to be a factor. It is used by about 45 per cent of all of the businesses surveyed.

Figure 4.13 The use of full cost information

Source: Figure adapted from CIMA (2009) *Management Accounting Tools for Today and Tomorrow*, p. 12.

The CIMA survey reveals that full cost information is more widely used by larger businesses than by smaller ones. The reasons for this are not clear. It may be that larger businesses have greater resources and expertise than smaller ones. This may enable them to employ techniques that are simply not practical for smaller businesses. On the other hand, it may reflect the different types of business within each size category.

Full (absorption) costing and relevant costs

We saw in Chapter 2, that for decision-making purposes relevant costs are future costs that vary with the decision. We have also seen, however, that full costing tends to rely on past cost. Moreover, it focuses on outlay cost and overlooks opportunity costs. This appears to suggest an unbridgeable gap between the relevant cost and the full costing approaches. In which case, the usefulness of full costing for decision making is called into question.

In theory, relevant cost analysis should be used whenever a decision is needed to set a price for a product, to introduce a new product, or to stop producing an existing product. In practice, however, it may not be feasible to do this. Let us assume that a large business makes 300 separate product types. Here the range of possibilities is enormous. In addition to carrying out relevant cost analysis on each product, it could also be carried out on different combinations of two, three, four products and so on. To deal with this tsunami of possible options, full cost information, based on historic cost, can used to act as a filter. It can direct attention to those products or services that would most benefit from relevant cost analysis. By providing an indication of the long-run average cost of each product, managers have some idea of the long-term cash outflows to be incurred. They may then decide to investigate further using relevant cost analysis.

FULL (ABSORPTION) COSTING VERSUS VARIABLE COSTING

An alternative to full (absorption) costing is **variable (marginal) costing** – which we discussed in Chapter 3. We may recall that this approach distinguishes between fixed and variable costs.

Under variable costing, income is measured in a different way to that of full costing. It will include only variable cost (that is, both variable direct and variable indirect cost) as part of the cost of the goods or service produced. Any fixed cost (that is, both fixed direct and fixed indirect cost) will be treated as a cost of the period in which it is incurred. Thus, inventories of finished products, or work in progress, carried from one accounting period to the next, is valued on the basis of their variable cost only.

As we have seen, full costing calculates product cost by taking the direct cost (whether fixed or variable) and an appropriate share of the indirect cost (whether fixed and variable) for the period in which the product is produced.

To illustrate the difference between the two costing approaches, let us consider Example 4.7.

Example 4.7

Lahore Ltd commenced operations on 1 June and makes a single product, which sells for £14 per unit. In the first two months of operations, the following results were achieved:

	June (number of units)	July (number of units)
Production output	6,000	6,000
Sales volume	4,000	5,000
Opening inventories	–	2,000
Closing inventories	2,000	3,000

Manufacturing overhead cost is £18,000 per month and direct manufacturing cost is £5 per unit. There is also a monthly fixed non-manufacturing overhead cost (marketing and administration) of £5,000. There was no work in progress at the end of either June or July. Assume for the sake of simplicity that Lahore Ltd's direct costs are all variable and its overheads are all fixed. (However, this would be very unusual in practice.)

The operating profit for each month is calculated below, first using a variable costing approach and then a full costing approach.

Variable costing

In this case, only the variable costs are charged to the units produced and all the fixed cost (manufacturing and non-manufacturing) is charged to the period. Inventories will be carried forward at their variable cost.

	June		July	
	£	£	£	£
Sales revenue				
(4,000 × £14)		56,000		
(5,000 × £14)				70,000
Opening inventories				
(2,000 × £5)	–		10,000	
Cost of units produced				
(6,000 × £5)	30,000		30,000	
Closing inventories				
(2,000 × £5)	(10,000)	(20,000)		
(3,000 × £5)			(15,000)	(25,000)
Contribution margin		36,000		45,000
Fixed cost:				
Manufacturing	(18,000)		(18,000)	
Non-manufacturing	(5,000)	(23,000)	(5,000)	(23,000)
Operating profit		13,000		22,000

Full costing

In this case, the manufacturing overhead cost becomes part of the product cost and inventories are carried forward to the next period at their full cost – that is, direct (all variable) cost *plus* an appropriate manufacturing overhead (all fixed) cost element. There are 6,000 units produced in each period and the fixed manufacturing overhead cost for each period is £18,000. Hence, the manufacturing overhead cost element per unit is £3 (that is, £18,000/6,000). The full cost per unit will therefore be £8 (that is, £5 + £3).

	June		July	
	£	£	£	£
Sales revenue				
(4,000 × £14)		56,000		
(5,000 × £14)				70,000
Opening inventories	–			
(2,000 × £8)			16,000	
Cost of units produced				
(6,000 × £8)	48,000		48,000	
Closing inventories				
(2,000 × £8)	(16,000)	(32,000)		
(3,000 × £8)			(24,000)	(40,000)
Gross profit		24,000		30,000
Non-manufacturing cost		(5,000)		(5,000)
Operating profit		19,000		25,000

We can see that the total operating profit over the two months is £35,000 (that is, £13,000 + £22,000) when calculated on a variable cost basis. It is £44,000 (that is, £19,000 + £25,000) when calculated on a full cost basis. The difference between the two is £9,000 (that is, £44,000 − £35,000). This difference arises from the way in which the manufacturing overhead (all fixed) cost has been dealt with. On a full cost basis, the cost of inventories at the end of July includes overheads that have yet to be treated as an expense (that is, 3,000 × £3). On a variable cost basis, however, these overheads have already been treated as an expense.

In practice, the choice of costing approach may not have such a dramatic effect on reported profit as shown in Example 4.7. Differences in operating profit shown in this example arise from the changes in inventories levels between periods – from zero at the beginning of June, to 2,000 units at the end of June, to 3,000 units by the end of July. These are significant changes in the context of a monthly output of only 6,000 units. In practice, this would be unusual. Where the same amount of inventories and work in progress are held at reporting-period ends and fixed cost remains unchanged from one reporting period to the next, reported profit will not vary between the two approaches. This is because the same amount of fixed cost will be treated as an expense each period; all of it originating from the current period in the case of variable costing, some of it originating from past periods in the case of full costing.

It is also important to note that, over the entire life of a particular business, total operating profit will be the same whichever costing method has been applied. This is because, ultimately, all fixed costs will be charged as expenses.

Which method is better?

A key difference between the two approaches is that, under the variable costing approach, profit is influenced only by changes in sales. Profit under the full (absorption costing) approach, on the other hand, is influenced by changes in the level of both sales and production.

Activity 4.21

Briefly explain why profit calculated under an absorption costing approach is influenced by changes in the level of production (as well as sales). Take a look at Example 4.7 to help you.

Under a variable costing approach, all fixed production costs are charged to the period in which they are incurred. Under an absorption costing approach, fixed production costs are assigned to inventories and only the fixed production costs linked to those inventories sold during the period are charged against that period's sales revenue.

Where production exceeds sales for a period, some of the fixed production costs incurred during the period will be carried forward in inventories to the next period. The larger the amount of fixed production costs carried forward, the smaller will be the amount charged against profit for the current period. Where sales exceed production, profit for the current period will be charged with fixed production costs brought forward in inventories from the previous period.

It is claimed that, by ignoring the effect of changes in the level of production, the profit calculated under variable costing is a more realistic measure of overall achievement. In a multi-product environment, however, the profitability of each item cannot be determined unless each is assigned an appropriate share of *all* costs. After all, goods and services cannot be provided unless fixed costs are incurred in their production. This suggests that full (absorption) costing provides a more useful measure of profit, item by item.

Variable costing highlights the key relationship between costs, volume of output and profit. This can be very helpful when making a range of management decisions. Full (absorption) costing, on the other hand, tends to obscure this relationship. Under normal reporting procedures, fixed and variable costs are not separated out. It would, however, be quite possible to do this.

We saw in Chapter 3 that variable costing identifies those costs that can be avoided in the short term. This again may be helpful when making a range of management decisions. A powerful counterargument, however, is that, over the long term, all elements of cost can be avoided. For managers to focus solely on those that can be avoided over the short term (the variable costs) may be a bad idea. When making long-term planning decisions, for example, managers need to know the full cost of producing products or services.

In practice, management accountants can prepare internal financial reports using either approach. We have seen, however, that absorption costing must be used for external reporting purposes. Some businesses align their internal reporting procedures with their external reporting procedures. A potential advantage of doing so is that managers will focus on the same numbers as those presented to shareholders and lenders.

Real World 4.10 provides some indication of the extent to which variable costing is used in practice.

Real World 4.10

Variable costing in practice

A survey of 41 UK manufacturing businesses found that 68 per cent of them used a variable costing approach to management reporting.

Many would find this surprising. The requirement is for financial statements in published annual reports to be in full cost terms. It seemed to be widely believed that this has led those businesses to use a full cost approach for management reporting as well. This appears not to be the case, however.

It should be added that many of those that used variable costing quite possibly misused it. For example, three-quarters of those that used it treated labour cost as variable. Possibly in some cases the cost of labour is variable (with the level of activity), but it seems likely that this is not true for most of these businesses. At the same time, most of the 68 per cent treat all overheads as a fixed cost. It seems likely that, for most businesses, overheads would have a variable element.

Source: Dugdale, D., Jones, C. and Green, S. (2005) *Contemporary Management Accounting Practices in UK Manufacturing*, CIMA Research Publication, Vol. 1, Number 13.

Self-assessment question 4.1

Hector and Co. Ltd has been invited to tender for a contract to produce 1,000 clothes hangers. The following information relates to the contract.

■ *Materials:* The clothes hangers are made of metal wire covered with a padded fabric. Each hanger requires two metres of wire and 0.5 square metres of fabric.
■ *Direct labour:* Each hanger requires 10 minutes of skilled labour and five minutes of unskilled labour.

The business already holds sufficient of each of the materials required to complete the contract. Information on the cost of the materials is as follows:

	Metal wire £/m	Fabric £/sq m
Historic cost	2.20	1.00
Current buying-in cost	2.50	1.10
Scrap value	1.70	0.40

The metal wire is in constant use by the business for a range of its products. The fabric has no other use for the business and is scheduled to be scrapped if the present contract does not go ahead.

Unskilled labour, which is paid at the rate of £7.50 an hour, will need to be taken on specifically to undertake the contract. The business is fairly quiet at the moment, which means that a pool of skilled labour exists that will still be employed at full pay of £12.00 an hour to do nothing if the contract does not proceed. The pool of skilled labour is sufficient to complete the contract.

The business charges jobs with overheads on a direct labour hour basis. The production overheads of the entire business for the month in which the contract will be undertaken are estimated at £50,000. The estimated total direct labour hours that will be worked are 12,500. The business tends not to alter the established overhead recovery rate to reflect increases or reductions to estimated total hours arising from new contracts. The total overheads are not expected to increase as a result of undertaking the contract.

The business normally adds 12.5 per cent profit loading to the job cost to arrive at a first estimate of the tender price.

Required:

(a) Price this job on a traditional job-costing basis.
(b) Indicate the minimum price at which the contract could be undertaken such that the business would be neither better nor worse off as a result of doing it.

The solution to this question can be found at the back of the book on p. 515.

SUMMARY

The main points of this chapter may be summarised as follows:

Full (absorption) cost = the total amount of resources sacrificed to achieve a particular objective

Uses of full (absorption) cost information

- Pricing and output decisions.
- Exercising control.
- Assessing relative efficiency.
- Assessing performance.

Single-product businesses – process costing

- Where all units of output are identical, the full cost can be calculated as follows:

$$\text{Cost per unit} = \frac{\text{Total cost of output}}{\text{Number of units produced}}$$

- Where there is work in progress at the end of the period, the equivalent units of output that it represents must be calculated to derive total output and cost per unit of output.

Multi-product businesses – job costing

- Where units of output are not identical, costs are divided into two categories: direct cost and indirect cost (overheads).

- Direct cost = cost that can be identified with, and measured in respect of, specific cost units (for example, labour of a garage mechanic, in relation to a particular car repair).
- Indirect cost (overheads) = cost that cannot be identified with, and measured in respect of, a particular job (for example, the rent of a garage).
- Full (absorption) cost = direct cost + indirect cost.
- Direct/indirect cost is not linked to variable/fixed cost.
- Indirect cost is difficult to assign to individual cost units – different bases are used and there is no single correct approach.
- Traditionally, indirect cost is seen as the cost of providing a 'service' to cost units.
- Time-based methods, such as the direct labour hour method, are often used to assign indirect cost to cost units in practice.

Dealing with indirect cost on a cost centre (departmental) basis

- Indirect cost (overheads) can be segmented – usually on a cost centre basis – each product cost centre has its own overhead recovery rate.
- Cost centres are areas, activities or functions for which costs are separately determined.
- Overheads must be allocated or apportioned to cost centres.
- Service cost centre cost must then be apportioned to product cost centre overheads.
- Product cost centre overheads must then be absorbed by cost units (jobs).

Batch costing

- A variation of job costing where each job consists of a number of identical (or near identical) cost units:

$$\text{Cost per unit} = \frac{\text{Cost of the batch (direct + indirect)}}{\text{Number of units in the batch}}$$

Full cost information and relevant cost

- Full costing does not take account of relevant costs. It focuses on past costs and ignores opportunity costs.
- Relevant cost analysis can be difficult to apply in practice because of the range of possible options.
- Full costing can direct managers' attention to areas that may benefit from relevant cost analysis.

Full (absorption) costing versus variable costing

- With full costing, both fixed and variable costs are included in product cost and treated as expenses when the product is sold.
- With variable costing, only the variable product cost is linked to the products in this way. Fixed cost is treated as an expense of the period in which it was incurred.
- Variable costing tends to be more straightforward and, according to proponents, provides a more realistic measure of overall achievement.
- Proponents of full costing argue, however, that it provides a better measure of profitability, item by item. Manufacturing fixed costs are an essential ingredient of total product cost.

$\rightarrow$

- Variable costing highlights the relationship between cost, volume and profit, which is obscured under a full costing system.

- Variable costing directs managers' attention to those (variable) costs that can be avoided in the short term. However, all costs can be avoided in the long term and it may be a bad idea to focus on the short term.

KEY TERMS

For definitions of these terms, see Appendix A.

Full cost p. 106	**Cost behaviour** p. 114
Full costing p. 106	**Overhead absorption (recovery)**
Cost unit p. 106	**rate** p. 116
Process costing p. 108	**Cost-plus pricing** p. 122
Work in progress p. 109	**Cost centre** p. 125
Equivalent units of output p. 109	**Product cost centre** p. 126
Job costing p. 111	**Service cost centre** p. 126
Direct cost p. 111	**Cost allocation** p. 126
Indirect cost p. 111	**Cost apportionment** p. 126
Overheads p. 111	**Batch costing** p. 134
Absorption costing p. 113	**Variable (marginal) costing** p. 138

REFERENCE

1 Drury, C. and Tayles, M. (1994) Product costing in UK manufacturing organisations, *European Accounting Review*, Vol. 3, no. 3, pp. 443–469.

FURTHER READING

If you would like to explore the topics covered in this chapter in more depth, we recommend the following:

Bhimani, A., Horngren, C., Datar, S. and Rajan, M. (2015) *Management and Cost Accounting*, 6th edn, Pearson, Chapters 3 and 4.

Burns, J., Quinn, M., Warren, L. and Oliveira, J. (2013) *Management Accounting*, McGraw-Hill Education, Chapters 4 and 5.

Drury, C. (2015) *Management and Cost Accounting*, 9th edn, Cengage Learning EMEA, Chapters 2–5.

Hilton, R. and Platt, D. (2014) *Managerial Accounting*, 10th edn, McGraw-Hill Higher Education, Chapters 2 and 3.

REVIEW QUESTIONS

Solutions to these questions can be found at the back of the book on pp. 528–529.

4.1 What problem does the existence of work in progress cause in process costing?

4.2 What is the point of distinguishing direct cost from indirect cost? Why is this not necessary in process-costing environments?

4.3 Are direct cost and variable cost the same thing? Explain your answer.

4.4 It is sometimes claimed that the full cost of a product or service reflects the break-even selling price. Explain what this means.

EXERCISES

Those with **coloured numbers** have solutions given at the back of the book on pp. 541–545.

Basic-level exercises

4.1 Consider this statement:

'In a job costing system, it is necessary to divide up the business into departments. Fixed costs (or overheads) will be collected for each department. Where a particular fixed cost relates to the business as a whole, it must be divided between the departments. Usually this is done on the basis of area of floor space occupied by each department relative to the entire business. When the total fixed costs for each department have been identified, this will be divided by the number of hours that were worked in each department to deduce an overhead recovery rate. Each job that was worked on in a department will have a share of fixed cost allotted to it according to how long it was worked on. The total cost for each job will therefore be the sum of the variable cost of the job and its share of the fixed cost.'

Required:
Prepare a table of two columns. In the first column you should show any phrases or sentences in the above statement with which you do not agree. In the second column you should show your reason for disagreeing with each one.

4.2 Bodgers Ltd, a business that provides a market research service, operates a job costing system. Towards the end of each financial year, the overhead recovery rate (the rate at which indirect cost will be absorbed by jobs) is established for the forthcoming year.

(a) Why does the business bother to predetermine the recovery rate in the way outlined?
(b) What steps will be involved in predetermining the rate?
(c) What problems might arise with using a predetermined rate?

4.3 Pieman Products Ltd makes road trailers to the precise specifications of individual customers. The following are predicted to occur during the forthcoming year, which is about to start:

Direct materials cost	£50,000
Direct labour cost	£160,000
Direct labour time	16,000 hours
Indirect labour cost	£25,000
Depreciation of machine	£8,000
Rent	£10,000
Heating, lighting and power	£5,000
Indirect materials	£2,000
Other indirect cost (overhead) elements	£1,000
Machine time	3,000 hours

All direct labour is paid at the same hourly rate.

A customer has asked the business to build a trailer for transporting a racing motorcycle to race meetings. It is estimated that this will require materials and components that will cost £1,150. It will take 250 direct labour hours to do the job, of which 50 will involve the use of machinery.

Required:

Deduce a logical cost for the job and explain the basis of dealing with overheads that you propose.

Intermediate-level exercises

4.4 Promptprint Ltd, a printing business, has received an enquiry from a potential customer for the quotation of a price for a job. The pricing policy of the business is based on the plans for the next financial year shown below.

	£
Sales revenue (billings to customers)	196,000
Materials (direct)	(38,000)
Labour (direct)	(32,000)
Variable overheads	(2,400)
Maintenance	(3,000)
Depreciation	(27,600)
Rent	(36,000)
Heat and light	(8,000)
Profit	49,000

A first estimate of the direct cost for the particular job is:

	£
Direct materials	4,000
Direct labour	3,600

Required:

(a) Prepare a recommended price for the job based on the plans, commenting on your method, ignoring the information given in the Appendix (below).

(b) Incorporate the effects of the information shown in the Appendix (below) into your estimates of the direct material cost, explaining any changes you consider it necessary to make to the above direct material cost of £4,000.

Appendix to Exercise 4.4

Based on historic cost, direct material cost was computed as follows:

	£
Paper grade 1	1,200
Paper grade 2	2,000
Card (zenith grade)	500
Inks and other miscellaneous items	300
	4,000

Paper grade 1 is regularly used by the business. Enough of this paper to complete the job is currently held. Because it is imported, it is estimated that if it is used for this job, a new purchase order will have to be placed shortly. Sterling has depreciated against the foreign currency by 25 per cent since the last purchase.

Paper grade 2 is purchased from the same source as grade 1. The business holds exactly enough of it for the job, but this was bought in for a special order. This order was cancelled, although the defaulting customer was required to pay £500 towards the cost of the paper. The accountant has offset this against the original cost to arrive at the figure of £2,000 shown above. This paper is rarely used and due to its special chemical coating will be unusable if it is not used on the job in question.

The card is another specialist item currently held by the business. There is no use foreseen and it would cost £750 to replace, if required. However, the inventories controller had planned to spend £130 on overprinting to use the card as a substitute for other materials costing £640.

Inks and other items are in regular use in the print shop.

4.5 Many businesses charge overheads to jobs on a cost centre basis.

Required:

(a) What is the advantage that is claimed for charging overheads to jobs on a cost centre basis and why is it claimed?

(b) What circumstances need to exist for it to make a difference to a particular job whether overheads are charged on a business-wide basis or on a cost centre basis? (Note that the answer to this part of the question is not specifically covered in the chapter. You should, nevertheless, be able to deduce the reason from what you know.)

Advanced-level exercises

4.6 Shown below is an extract from next year's plans for a business manufacturing three products, A, B and C, in three product cost centres.

	A	B	C
Production	4,000 units	3,000 units	6,000 units
Direct material cost	£7 per unit	£4 per unit	£9 per unit
Direct labour requirements:			
Cutting department:			
Skilled operatives	3 hr/unit	5 hr/unit	2 hr/unit
Unskilled operatives	6 hr/unit	1 hr/unit	3 hr/unit
Machining department	½ hr/unit	¼ hr/unit	⅓ hr/unit
Pressing department	2 hr/unit	3 hr/unit	4 hr/unit
Machine requirements:			
Machining department	2 hr/unit	1½ hr/unit	2½ hr/unit

The skilled operatives employed in the cutting department are paid £16 an hour and the unskilled operatives are paid £10 an hour. All the operatives in the machining and pressing departments are paid £12 an hour.

	Product cost centres			Service cost centres	
	Cutting	Machining	Pressing	Engineering	Human resources
Planned total overheads	£154,482	£64,316	£58,452	£56,000	£34,000
Service cost centre					
Cost incurred for the benefit of other cost centres, as follows:					
Engineering services	20%	45%	35%	–	
Human resources services	55%	10%	20%	15%	

The business operates a full absorption costing system.

Required:

Derive the total planned cost of:

(a) One completed unit of product A.

(b) One incomplete unit of product B, which has been processed by the cutting and machining departments but which has not yet been passed into the pressing department.

4.7 Athena Ltd is an engineering business doing work for its customers to their particular requirements and specifications. It determines the full cost of each job taking a 'job-costing' approach, accounting for overheads on a cost centre (departmental) basis. It bases its prices to customers on this full cost figure. The business has two departments (both of which are cost centres): a Machining Department, where each job starts, and a Fitting Department, which completes all of the jobs. Machining Department overheads are charged to jobs on a machine hour basis and those of the Fitting Department on a direct labour hour basis. The budgeted information for next year is as follows:

Heating and lighting	£25,000	(allocated equally between the two departments)
Machine power	£10,000	(all allocated to the Machining Department)
Direct labour	£200,000	(£150,000 allocated to the Fitting Department and £50,000 to the Machining Department; all direct workers are paid £10 an hour)
Indirect labour	£50,000	(apportioned to the departments in proportion to the direct labour cost)
Direct materials	£120,000	(all applied to jobs in the Machining Department)
Depreciation	£30,000	(all relates to the Machining Department)
Machine time	20,000 hours	(all worked in the Machining Department)

Required:

(a) Prepare a statement showing the budgeted overheads for next year, analysed between the two cost centres. This should be in the form of three columns: one for the total figure for each type of overhead and one column each for the two cost centres, where each type of overhead is analysed between the two cost centres. Each column should also show the total of overheads for the year.

(b) Derive the appropriate rate for charging the overheads of each cost centre to jobs (that is, a separate rate for each cost centre).

(c) Athena Ltd has been asked by a customer to specify the price that it will charge for a particular job that will, if the job goes ahead, be undertaken early next year. The job is expected to use direct materials costing Athena Ltd £1,200, to need 50 hours of machining time, 10 hours of Machine Department direct labour and 20 hours of Fitting Department direct labour. Athena Ltd charges a profit loading of 20 per cent to the full cost of jobs to determine the selling price.

Show workings to derive the proposed selling price for this job.

4.8 Bookdon plc manufactures three products, X, Y and Z, in two product cost centres: a machine shop and a fitting section; it also has two service cost centres: a canteen and a machine maintenance section. Shown below are next year's planned production data and manufacturing cost for the business.

	X	Y	Z
Production	4,200 units	6,900 units	1,700 units
Direct materials	£11/unit	£14/unit	£17/unit
Direct labour:			
Machine shop	£6/unit	£4/unit	£2/unit
Fitting section	£12/unit	£3/unit	£21/unit
Machine hours	6 hr/unit	3 hr/unit	4 hr/unit

Planned overheads are as follows:

	Machine shop	Fitting section	Canteen	Machine maintenance section	Total
Allocated overheads	£27,660	£19,470	£16,600	£26,650	£90,380
Rent, heat and light					£17,000
Depreciation and insurance of equipment					£25,000
Additional data:					
Gross carrying amount of equipment	£150,000	£75,000	£30,000	£45,000	
Number of employees	18	14	4	4	
Floor space occupied	3,600 sq m	1,400 sq m	1,000 sq m	800 sq m	

All machining is carried out in the machine shop. It has been estimated that approximately 70 per cent of the machine maintenance section's cost is incurred servicing the machine shop and the remainder servicing the fitting section.

Required:
(a) Calculate the following planned overhead absorption rates:
    (1) A machine hour rate for the machine shop.
    (2) A rate expressed as a percentage of direct wages for the fitting section.
(b) Calculate the planned full cost per unit of product X.

Chapter 5

COSTING AND COST MANAGEMENT IN A COMPETITIVE ENVIRONMENT

INTRODUCTION

We saw in Chapter 1 that major changes have occurred in the business world in recent years. They include more demanding customers, deregulation, privatisation, growing expectations among shareholders and the impact of new technology. These changes have led to a much faster-changing and more competitive environment that has radically altered the way that businesses should be managed. In this chapter we shall consider some of the accounting techniques that have been developed to help businesses maintain their competitiveness in this new era.

We begin this chapter by considering the impact of the competitive environment on the traditional full-costing approach. This approach, which was examined in Chapter 4, has been much criticised for obscuring important information needed to manage costs. Activity-based costing (ABC) is a full-costing approach that offers an alternative to the traditional one. We shall see later how it takes a much more enquiring, much less accepting attitude towards indirect cost (overheads).

To provide goods and services that meet customers' requirements for quality and price, yet deliver an acceptable financial return, businesses are adopting much leaner operations. There is a relentless focus on eliminating waste and spending only on value-creating activities. We end the chapter by exploring the costing and cost management methods developed to support this focus. These new methods often rely on multi-disciplinary teams rather than the traditional management hierarchy in order to deliver change. They also involve much closer scrutiny of business processes.

Learning outcomes

When you have completed this chapter, you should be able to:

- Describe the nature of the modern product costing and pricing environment.
- Discuss the principles and practical aspects of activity-based costing.
- Describe the methods that may be used to manage costs over the life cycle of a product.
- Explain the role of value chain analysis and benchmarking in managing costs.
- Explain the importance of total quality management in the modern environment and identify the main types of quality costs that may be incurred.

Costing and pricing: the traditional way

The traditional, and still widely-used, approach to job costing developed when the notion of trying to determine the cost of industrial production first emerged. This was around the time of the UK Industrial Revolution when industry was characterised by the following:

- *Direct-labour-intensive and direct-labour-paced production.* Labour was at the heart of production. To the extent that machinery was used, it tended to support the efforts of direct labour and the speed of production was dictated by direct labour.
- *A low level of indirect cost relative to direct cost.* Little was spent on power, heat and light, machinery (depreciation charges) and other areas typical of the indirect cost (overheads) of modern businesses.
- *A relatively uncompetitive market.* Transport difficulties, limited industrial production world-wide and a lack of knowledge by customers of competitors' prices meant that businesses could prosper without being too scientific in their costing. Typically they could simply add a margin for profit to full cost to arrive at the selling price (cost-plus pricing). Furthermore, customers would usually accept those products on offer, rather than demand precisely what they wanted.

Since overheads at that time represented a pretty small element of total cost, it was acceptable and practical to deal with them in a fairly arbitrary manner. Not too much effort was devoted to trying to control overheads because the potential rewards of better control were relatively small, certainly when compared with the benefits from firmer control of direct labour and material costs. It was also reasonable to charge overheads to individual jobs on a direct labour hour basis. Most of the overheads were incurred directly in support of direct labour: providing direct workers with a place to work, heating and lighting the workplace, employing people to supervise the direct workers and so on. Direct workers, perhaps aided by machinery, carried out all production.

At that time, service industries were a relatively unimportant part of the economy and would have largely consisted of self-employed individuals. These individuals would probably not have been interested in trying to do more than work out a rough hourly/daily rate for their time and then use this as a basis for pricing.

Costing and pricing: the new environment

In recent years, the world of industrial production has fundamentally changed. Most of it is now characterised by:

- *Capital-intensive and machine-paced production.* Machines are at the heart of much production, including both the manufacture of goods and the provision of services. Most labour supports the efforts of machines, for example, by technically maintaining them. Furthermore, machines often dictate the pace of production. According to evidence provided in Real World 4.2 (page 112), direct labour accounts on average for just 14 per cent of manufacturers' total cost.
- *A high level of indirect cost relative to direct costs.* Modern businesses tend to have very high depreciation, servicing and power costs. There are also high costs of personnel and staff welfare, which were scarcely envisaged in the early days of industrial production. At

the same time, there are very low (sometimes no) direct labour costs. Although direct material cost often remains an important element of total cost, more efficient production methods lead to less waste and, therefore, to a lower total material cost, again tending to make indirect cost (overheads) more dominant. Again, according to Real World 5.2, overheads account for 25 per cent of manufacturers' total cost and 51 per cent of service sector total cost.

■ *A highly competitive international market.* Production, much of it highly sophisticated, is carried out worldwide. Transport, including fast airfreight, is relatively cheap. Fax, telephone and, particularly, the Internet ensure that potential customers can quickly and cheaply find the prices of a range of suppliers. Markets now tend to be highly price-competitive. Customers increasingly demand products custom made to their own requirements. This means that businesses need to know their product costs with greater accuracy. They also have to take a more careful and informed approach to pricing.

■ *Short product life cycles* Technological innovation, greater competition and more demanding customers have forced businesses to quicken the pace of new product development. Technology-based products, for example, are continually updated with improved features and faster processors. This has led to the design stage assuming greater importance and a greater need to manage costs at this stage. It is now widely recognised that the way in which products are designed will largely determine the future costs of production. Shorter product life cycles also create a need for a business to forecast future demand with greater accuracy. This helps to ensure that products are available for sale at the time that customers demand them. Similarly, shorter product life cycles create a need for close tracking of inventories to avoid the costs of obsolescence.

In the UK, as in many developed countries, service industries now dominate the economy, employing the great majority of the workforce and producing most of the value of productive output. Although there are still many self-employed individuals supplying services, many service providers are vast businesses.

Activity 5.1

Can you think of any service providers that are vast businesses? Try to think of at least three.

Some examples that we came up with are:

■ banks
■ restaurant chains
■ insurance businesses
■ airlines
■ hotel chains
■ cinema operators.

You may have thought of others.

For most of these larger service providers, the activities closely resemble modern manufacturing. They too are characterised by high capital intensity, high overheads in relation to direct costs and a competitive international market.

COST MANAGEMENT SYSTEMS

Changes in the competitive environment mean that businesses must now manage costs more effectively. To do this, cost management systems must provide managers with the information needed. Traditional cost management systems have often proved inadequate for this task and so, in recent years, new systems have taken root. We shall look at some of these new systems shortly but, before doing so, let us consider an important reason for their development.

The problem of overheads

In Chapter 4 we considered the traditional approach to job costing (that is, deriving the full cost of a unit of output where each unit of output differs from the others). We may recall that this approach involves collecting the direct costs for each job. These are the costs that can be clearly linked to, and measured in respect of, the particular job. The indirect costs (overheads), which cannot be linked to products in the same way, are allocated, or apportioned, to product cost centres and then charged to individual jobs using appropriate overhead recovery rates.

Activity 5.2

Can you recall the two main methods for charging overheads to individual jobs that were discussed in Chapter 4?

The two main methods are based on direct labour hours and machine hours.

In the past, this approach has worked reasonably well, largely because overhead recovery rates (that is, rates at which overheads are absorbed by jobs) were typically much lower for each direct labour hour than the wage rate paid to direct workers. We have now, however, reached the position where overheads are often far more significant. It is not unusual for overhead recovery rates to be between five and 10 times the hourly wage rate. Where production is dominated by direct labour that is paid, say, £12 an hour, it may be of no great consequence to assign overheads using an overhead recovery rate of, say, £1 an hour. It becomes much more so, however, where the overhead recovery rate is, say, £60 an hour. This can result in very arbitrary product costing. Even a small change in the amount of direct labour worked can have a huge effect on the total cost calculated for a job. This is not because direct labour is highly paid, but rather because of the effect of direct labour hours on the overhead cost loading. In modern manufacturing, direct labour often plays a small part in the production process and overhead costs have little connection to direct labour hours spent on each job. Thus, where a direct labour overhead rate is still being used, it will only add to the arbitrary nature of product costing.

Taking a closer look

The changes in the competitive environment discussed above have led to much closer attention being paid to the issue of overheads, what causes them and how they are charged to jobs. It is increasingly recognised that overheads do not just happen; something must be causing them. To illustrate this point, let us consider Example 5.1.

Example 5.1

Modern Producers Ltd has a storage area within its factory that is set aside for its inventories of finished goods. The cost of running the storage area includes a share of the factory rent and other establishment costs, such as heating and lighting. It also includes the salaries of staff employed to look after the inventories.

The business has two product lines: A and B. Product A tends to be made in small batches and low levels of finished inventories are held. The business prides itself on its ability to instantly supply Product B, in large quantities. As a consequence, most of the space in the storage area is filled with finished Product Bs, ready to be despatched once an order is received.

Traditionally, the whole cost of operating the storage area would have been treated as a part of general overheads and included in the total of overheads charged to jobs, probably on a direct labour hour basis. This means that, when assessing the cost of Products A and B, the cost of operating the storage area would have fallen on them according to the number of direct labour hours worked on manufacturing each one, a factor that has nothing to do with storage. In fact, most of the storage cost should be charged to Product B, since this product causes (and benefits from) the stores' cost much more than Product A.

Failure to account more precisely for the cost of running the storage area is masking the fact that Product B is not as profitable as it seems. It may even be creating losses as a result of the high storage cost that it causes. However, much of this cost is being charged to Product A, even though this product makes much less use of the storage area.

ACTIVITY-BASED COSTING

Activity-based costing (ABC) aims to overcome the kind of problem just described by directly tracing the cost of all activities supporting the production process (that is, the overheads) and linking those costs to particular units of output (of products or services). This is done on the basis that the particular units of output that cause the overheads are linked to them, as we just saw with stores operating costs in Example 5.1. For a manufacturing business, these support activities may include materials ordering, running machines, inspection, processing customer orders and so on. The cost of these support activities goes to make up total overheads cost. The purpose of tracing activity costs in this way is to provide a more realistic, and more finely measured, account of the overhead cost element for a particular unit of output.

To implement a system of ABC, managers must begin by carefully examining the business's operations. They will need to identify:

- each of the various support activities involved in the process of making products or providing services;
- the costs to be assigned to each support activity; and
- the factors that cause a change in the costs of each support activity, that is, the **cost drivers**.

Identifying the cost drivers is a vital element of a successful ABC system. They have a cause-and-effect relationship with activity costs and so are used as a basis for assigning support activity costs to a particular unit of output. This point is now considered in further detail.

Assigning overheads

Once the various support activities, their costs and the factors that drive these costs have been identified, ABC requires three steps:

1 Establishing an overhead **cost pool** for each support activity. There will be just one cost pool for each separate cost driver.
2 Assigning the total cost associated with each support activity to the relevant cost pool.
3 Charging the units of output with the total cost within each pool using the relevant cost driver.

Note that cost pools in ABC are the equivalent of cost centres in the traditional approach, as will be explained shortly.

Step 3, above, involves dividing the amount in each cost pool by the estimated total usage of the cost driver to derive a cost per unit of the cost driver. This unit cost figure is then multiplied by the number of units of the cost driver used by a particular unit of output, to determine the amount of overhead cost to be attached to it (or absorbed by it). Example 5.2 should make this process clear.

Example 5.2

The management accountant at Modern Producers Ltd (see Example 5.1) has estimated that the cost of running the storage area for finished goods for next year will be £90,000. This will be the amount allocated to the 'storage area cost pool'.

It is estimated that each Product A will spend an average of one week in the storage area before being sold. With Product B, the equivalent period is four weeks. Both products are of roughly similar size and have very similar storage needs. It is felt, therefore, that the period spent in the storage area ('product weeks') is the cost driver.

Next year, 50,000 Product As and 25,000 Product Bs are expected to pass through the storage area. The estimated total usage of the cost driver will be the total number of 'product weeks' that the products will be in the storage area. For next year, this will be:

$$\text{Product A } 50,000 \times 1 \text{ week } = \underline{50,000}$$
$$\text{Product B } 25,000 \times 4 \text{ weeks } = \underline{100,000}$$
$$\underline{150,000}$$

The cost per unit of cost driver is the total cost of the storage area divided by the number of 'product weeks', as calculated above. This is:

$$£90,000/150,000 = £0.60$$

To determine the cost to be attached to a particular unit of each product, the figure of £0.60 must be multiplied by the number of 'product weeks' that a product stays in the storage area. Thus, each unit of Product A will be charged with £0.60 (that is, £0.60 × 1) and each Product B with £2.40 (that is, £0.60 × 4).

The nature of support activities and what drives their costs will vary between businesses. In the table below are some examples of support activities that may be found in a manufacturing business, along with their possible cost drivers.

Support activity	Potential cost driver
Purchasing	Number of purchase orders
Setting up machinery	Number of set-ups
Running machinery	Machine hours
Machinery maintenance	Maintenance staff hours
Scheduling production lines	Production schedulers' hours
Product testing	Number of tests conducted
Reworking defective products	Number of defective products

From the table we can see there are two types of cost driver: *activity drivers* and *resource drivers*. The first measures the frequency, or intensity, with which an activity is performed (such as the number of purchase orders) and the second measures the amount of resources consumed to carry out the activity (such as maintenance staff hours).

When identifying relevant cost drivers, a trade-off may need to be made between the level of accuracy required and the costs of collecting the information. Take the example of a large manufacturer making many different products, with each product having several support activities. Here, there may be a vast number of cause-and-effect links between the products and the various support activities. It may, therefore, be possible to identify dozens of cost drivers. The more sophisticated the costing system, however, the more expensive it is to operate. It may be decided, therefore, to limit the number of cost drivers by using the same cost driver for a group of support activities relating to a particular unit of output.

The key steps in the ABC process are shown in diagrammatic form in Figure 5.1.

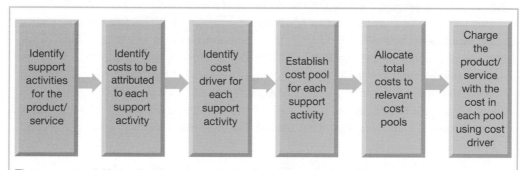

The support activities reflect how resources such as labour and machinery are being deployed. The costs attributed to each cost activity are allocated to a separate cost pool and then charged to products or services using the relevant cost driver.

Figure 5.1 Key steps in the ABC process

ABC and the traditional approach compared

The traditional absorption costing approach and the ABC approach have certain points in common. Both approaches adopt a two-stage allocation process for assigning overhead costs. With the traditional approach, overhead costs are first assigned to product cost centres. The costs accumulated in each cost centre are then charged to units of output using an overhead recovery rate. With the ABC approach, overhead costs are first assigned to cost pools. The costs accumulated are then charged to units of output using the cost driver rate for each activity.

At the first stage of allocation, the cost centre in traditional absorption costing and the cost pool in ABC fulfil similar roles. Both provide a location for assigning overhead costs. However, a cost centre is usually based around a department (see Example 4.5) whereas a cost pool is based around an activity (see Examples 5.1 and 5.2). At the second stage, overhead recovery rates and cost driver rates also fulfil similar roles. Both provide a means of assigning overhead costs to units of output. The two differ, however, in the approach adopted.

We saw in Chapter 4 that overhead recovery rates are typically based on machine hours or, more usually, on direct labour hours. With the traditional approach, it may be appropriate to assign some overhead costs to products using these bases. The cost of running machines (electrical power, oil and so on) will normally vary according to the number of machine hours. Similarly, the cost of supervision may vary according to the number of direct labour hours. Many overhead costs within a modern manufacturing environment, however, do not vary on the basis of either machine hours or direct labour hours. Traditional absorption costing does not recognise this fact whereas ABC does.

Activity 5.3

In a manufacturing business, can you suggest what might drive the cost of:

1 machine testing and calibration; and
2 receiving materials for production?

Potential cost drivers are:

1 the number of tests carried out or the hours spent by maintenance staff testing the machinery; and
2 the number of parts handled or the weight of material received.

You may have thought of others

A particular feature of ABC should be noted when making a comparison with traditional absorption costing. Identifying the various support activities leads to a greater number of cost pools than the number of cost centres typical as the traditional approach. Since each ABC support activity is likely to have its own unique cost driver, this will likely lead to a greater variety of methods for assigning overhead costs to units of output than under the traditional approach. A consequence of these two features is that an ABC system is more complex than the traditional absorption costing system.

The two approaches to dealing with overhead costs are illustrated in Figure 5.2.

ABC and service industries

Much of our discussion of ABC has concentrated on the manufacturing industry, perhaps because early users of ABC were manufacturing businesses. However, ABC may be even more relevant to service industries. In the absence of a direct material element, a service business's total cost is often largely made up of overheads. As we shall see later, there is evidence that ABC has been adopted more widely by businesses that sell services rather than those that make products.

Activity 5.4

What is the difference in the way in which direct costs are accounted for when using ABC compared to the traditional absorption costing approach?

The answer is none at all. Differences between the two approaches are only concerned with the way in which overheads are charged to jobs in order to derive the full cost.

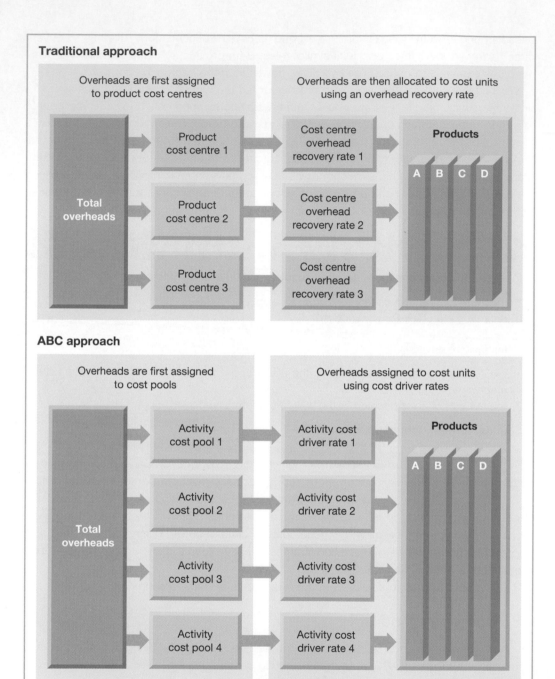

With the traditional approach, overheads are first assigned to product cost centres and then absorbed by cost units based on an overhead recovery rate (using direct labour hours worked on the cost units or some other approach) for each cost centre. With activity-based costing, overheads are assigned to cost pools and then cost units are charged with overheads to the extent that they drive the costs in the various pools.

Source: Adapted from Innes, J. and Mitchell, F. (1990) *Activity Based Costing: A Review with Case Studies*, CIMA Publishing. With kind permission of Elsevier.

Figure 5.2 Traditional versus activity-based costing

Example 5.3 provides an example of activity-based costing and brings together the points that have been raised so far.

Example 5.3

Comma Ltd manufactures two types of Sprizzer – Standard and Deluxe. Each product requires the incorporation of a difficult-to-handle special part (one of them for a Standard and four for a Deluxe). Both of these products are made in batches (large batches for Standards and small ones for Deluxes). Each new batch requires that the production facilities are 'set up'.

Details of the two products are:

	Standard	*Deluxe*
Annual production and sales – units	12,000	12,000
Sales price per unit	£65	£87
Batch size – units	1,000	50
Direct labour time per unit – hours	2	2½
Direct labour rate per hour	£8	£8
Direct material cost per unit	£22	£32
Number of special parts per unit	1	4
Number of set-ups per batch	1	3
Number of separate material issues from stores per batch	1	1
Number of purchase orders issued per year	50	240

In recent months, Comma Ltd has been trying to persuade customers who buy the Standard to purchase the Deluxe instead. An analysis of overhead costs for Comma Ltd has provided the following information:

Overhead cost analysis	*£*	*Cost driver*
Set-up cost	73,200	Number of set-ups
Special part handling cost	60,000	Number of special parts
Purchase order cost	29,000	Number of purchase orders
Material handling cost	63,000	Number of batches
Other overheads	108,000	Labour hours

Required:

(a) Calculate the profit per unit and the return on sales for Standard and Deluxe Sprizzers using both:

   (1) the traditional direct-labour-hour-based absorption of overheads; and

   (2) activity-based costing methods.

(b) Comment on the managerial implications for Comma Ltd of the results in (a) above.

Solution

(a) (1) **Traditional approach**

Using the traditional full (absorption) costing approach that we considered in Chapter 4, the overheads are added together and an overheads recovery rate deduced as follows:

Overheads	*£*
Set-up cost	73,200
Special part handling cost	60,000
Purchase order cost	29,000
Material handling cost	63,000
Other overheads	108,000
	333,200

ACTIVITY-BASED COSTING   **159**

$$\text{Overhead recovery rate} = \frac{\text{Total overheads}}{\text{Number of labour hours}}$$

$$= \frac{333{,}200}{54{,}000 \ [\text{that is, } (12{,}000 \times 2) + (12{,}000 \times 2\frac{1}{2})]}$$

$$= £6.17 \text{ per hour}$$

The total cost per unit of each type of Sprizzer is calculated by adding the direct cost to the overheads cost per unit. The overheads cost per unit is calculated by multiplying the number of direct labour hours spent on the product (2 hours for each Standard and 2½ hours for each Deluxe) by the overheads recovery rate calculated above. Hence:

	Standard £	Deluxe £
Direct costs		
Labour	16.00	20.00
Material	22.00	32.00
Indirect cost		
Overheads (£6.17 per hour)	12.34	15.43
Total cost per unit	50.34	67.43

The return on sales is calculated as follows:

	Standard £ per unit	Deluxe £ per unit
Sales price	65.00	87.00
Total cost (see above)	50.34	67.43
Profit	14.66	19.57
Return on sales [(profit/sales) × 100%]	22.55%	22.49%

(2) **ABC approach**

Using the ABC costing approach, the activity cost driver rates will be calculated as follows:

Overhead cost pool	Driver	(a) Standard driver volume	(b) Deluxe driver volume	(c) Total driver volume (a + b)	(d) Costs £	(e) Driver rate (d/c) £
Set-up	Set-ups per batch	12	720	732	73,200	100
Special part	Special parts per unit	12,000	48,000	60,000	60,000	1
Purchase orders	Purchase orders per year	50	240	290	29,000	100
Material handling	Number of batches	12	240	252	63,000	250
Other overheads	Labour hours	24,000	30,000	54,000	108,000	2

The activity-based costs are derived as follows:

Overhead	(f) Total costs Standard (a × e) £	(g) Total costs Deluxe (b × e) £	Unit costs Standard (f/12,000) £	Unit costs Deluxe (g/12,000) £
Set-up	1,200	72,000	0.10	6.00
Special part	12,000	48,000	1.00	4.00
Purchase orders	5,000	24,000	0.42	2.00
Material handling	3,000	60,000	0.25	5.00
Other overheads	48,000	60,000	4.00	5.00
Total overheads			5.77	22.00

The total cost per unit is calculated as follows:

	Standard £ per unit	Deluxe £ per unit
Direct costs:		
Labour	16.00	20.00
Material	22.00	32.00
Indirect costs		
See above	5.77	22.00
Total cost per unit	43.77	74.00

The return on sales is calculated as follows:

	Standard £ per unit	Deluxe £ per unit
Sales price	65.00	87.00
Total cost (see above)	43.77	74.00
Profit	21.23	13.00
Return on sales [(profit/sales) × 100%]	32.67%	14.94%

(b) The figures show that under the traditional approach the returns on sales for each product are broadly equal. However, the ABC approach shows that the Standard product is far more profitable. Hence, the business should reconsider its policy of trying to persuade customers to switch to the Deluxe product.

Benefits and costs of ABC

By adopting a more forensic approach to assigning overheads, ABC can provide a more accurate cost figure for each unit of output. This should help in assessing product profitability and in making pricing and product mix decisions. ABC can also help managers gain a better understanding of business operations. This, in turn, should help improve performance.

How can ABC help managers' understanding of business operations and how can this lead to an improvement in performance?

Managers gain a deeper insight to the business by identifying the various support activities' costs and what causes them to change. Armed with this deeper insight, managers are better placed to control costs, improve efficiency and make future plans.

Despite its apparent advantages, critics point out that ABC can be a costly exercise. Setting up the costing system, as well as updating it, can consume a great deal of resources. Running an ABC system can also be complex and time-consuming, particularly where business operations involve a large number of activities and cost drivers. Management reports generated from a complex costing system are also likely to be complex. If managers find these reports difficult to understand, the potential benefits of employing ABC may be lost.

Where products or services have similar levels of output involving similar activities and processes, or where overheads form a relatively low proportion of the total costs, the more accurate measurements provided by ABC are unlikely to lead to strikingly different outcomes from those obtained under the traditional approach. As a result, opportunities for better pricing, planning and cost control may be few. If this were the case, switching to an ABC system would be difficult to justify.

Measurement and tracing problems may arise with ABC. Not all costs can be easily traced to a particular activity. Nevertheless, all activity costs have to be assigned to one cost pool or another. To ensure that all these costs are taken into account, some may be assigned to cost pools on an arbitrary basis. Poor quality data on activity costs may also lead to arbitrary cost assignments. A final problem is that the relationship between activity costs and their cost drivers may be difficult to determine. Identifying a cause-and-effect relationship can be difficult where activity costs are fixed and do not change with changes in operating activities.

Finally, ABC is criticised for the same reason that traditional full costing is criticised – it does not provide relevant information for decision making.

Can you recall from Chapter 4 why traditional full costing is criticised for being irrelevant for decision making?

Traditional full costing tends to use past costs and to ignore opportunity costs. Past costs, however, are irrelevant in decision making. Opportunity costs, on the other hand, are relevant and can be significant. For these reasons, some view full costing as an expensive waste of time.

ABC suffers from these same weaknesses. We may also recall from Chapter 4, however, that supporters of full costing claim that it *is* relevant for decision making. It provides an indication of long-run average cost, which, in turn, gives managers some idea of the long-term cash flows to be incurred.

ABC in practice

Real World 5.1 briefly describes how ABC is used at the Royal Mail.

Delivering ABC

Royal Mail processes and delivers around 70 million letters and packages to 28 million addresses each working day. It was in the public sector until 2013, when it became a private sector business. The business operates an ABC system for both internal decision making and for external reporting. Given its size and the range of activities carried out, it is not surprising that the ABC system is very complex. There is a costing manual, which runs to more than 100 pages, to outline the principles and methods employed.

The ABC system operated by Royal Mail employs resource drivers and activity drivers in a two-stage process. Resources used by the business are assigned to activities using resource drivers. The main operational resources consumed and their drivers are as follows:

Resource	Resource driver
Operational staff	Staff hours
Vehicles	Vehicle hours
Machines	Machine hours
Property	Accommodation square metres

The main processes and activities carried out by Royal Mail include the following:

Business process	Description
International Operations	Mail processed for export and despatch for overseas delivery or import mail processed for despatch around the country to other Mail Centres.
Network	Distribution of mail between Mail Centres, International Operations and RDCs (Regional Distribution Centres) moving the mail closer to its final delivery destination.
Inward – Mail Centre	Mail processed for onward despatch to local Delivery Offices.
Local Distribution	Distribution of mail between Mail Centres and Delivery Offices.
Delivery – Indoor	Sorting of the mail to specific delivery routes and then sequenced to the final delivery point in preparation for the actual delivery to individual addresses.
Delivery – Outdoor	Taking the mail from the Delivery Office and delivering to the individual addresses.
Perform Mailroom Management	Provision of mailroom services to businesses where their mail is prepared to meet internal sorting specifications.

These broad processes and activities are broken down into sub-activities for ABC purposes. The costs of these various activities, as calculated through the use of resource drivers, are assigned to products using activity drivers. (As we may imagine, the volume of mail posted by customers is an important basis for activity drivers.) For certain types of activity, however, such as market research and conveyance by couriers, activity drivers are not used. Instead, resource drivers are mapped directly to the activity.

Source: Royal Mail Group Ltd (2015) *ABC Costing Manual 2015–16*, November.

Real World 5.2 provides some indication of the extent to which ABC is used in practice.

Real World 5.2

ABC in practice

A survey of 176 UK businesses operating in various industries, all with annual sales revenue of more than £50 million, was conducted by Al-Omiri and Drury. This indicated that 29 per cent of larger UK businesses use ABC.

The adoption of ABC in the UK varies widely between industries, as is shown in Figure 5.3.

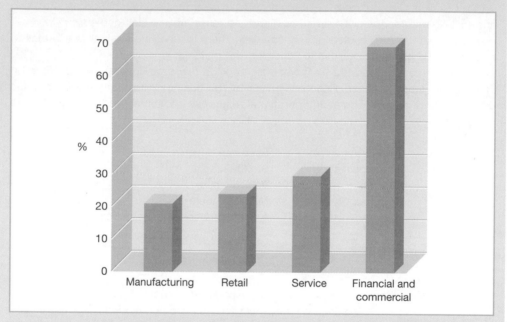

Figure 5.3 The percentage of businesses in different sectors that use ABC

Al-Omiri and Drury took their analysis a step further by looking at the factors that apparently tend to lead a particular business to adopt ABC. They found that businesses that used ABC tended to be:

- large;
- sophisticated, in terms of using advanced management accounting techniques generally;
- in an intensely competitive market for their products; and
- operating in a service industry, particularly in the financial services.

The 2009 CIMA survey emphatically supported the finding that larger businesses tend to use ABC more than smaller ones. It showed that only 22 per cent of businesses with fewer than 50 employees use ABC, whereas 46 per cent of businesses with more than 10,000 employees use the technique.

All of these findings are broadly in line with other recent research evidence involving businesses from around the world.

Sources: Al-Omiri, M. and Drury, C. (2007) A survey of factors influencing the choice of product costing systems in UK organisations, *Management Accounting Research*, Vol. 18, pp. 399–424. CIMA (2009) *Management Accounting Tools for Today and Tomorrow*, p. 12.

MANAGING COSTS OVER THE PRODUCT LIFE CYCLE

In the remainder of this chapter, we shall take a look at further methods that can be used to manage costs in a highly competitive environment. We begin by examining methods that focus on managing costs over the life cycle of a product.

Total life-cycle costing

Total life-cycle costing draws management's attention to the fact that it is not only during the production phase that costs are incurred. Costs begin to accumulate at an earlier point and continue to accumulate after production. Total life-cycle costing is concerned with tracking and reporting all costs relating to a product from the beginning to the end of its life – which could be for a period of 20 years or more. If the revenues generated over the life cycle of the product are also tracked, its profitability can be assessed. This represents a radical departure from traditional management accounting approaches, which are normally concerned with assessing performance over periods of one year or less.

Total life-cycle costing starts from the premise that the life cycle of a product or service has three phases. These are:

1 *The pre-production phase.* This is the period that precedes production of the product or service. During this phase, research and development – both of the product or service and of the market – is conducted. The product or service is designed and so is the means of production. The phase culminates with setting up the necessary production facilities and with advertising and promotion.

2 *The production phase comes next.* During this phase the product is made and sold or the service is provided to customers. This is the phase where traditional absorption costing or ABC usually makes its biggest contribution.

3 *The post-production phase comes last.* During this phase, costs may be incurred to correct faults that arose with products or services sold (after-sales service). Since these costs may start to be incurred before the last product or service is sold, this phase will typically overlap with the production phase. During this phase, costs may also be incurred as a result of closing production at the end of the product's or service's life. Where the risk of environmental damage must be eliminated, these costs can be extremely high.

Activity 5.7

Can you think of two examples where environmental damage, or the risk of it, may have to be dealt with when the production process ends?

Examples include the costs of decommissioning:

- an oil rig;
- a nuclear power station;
- a quarry; and
- a coal mine.

You may have thought of others.

The total life cycle of a product or service is shown in Figure 5.4.

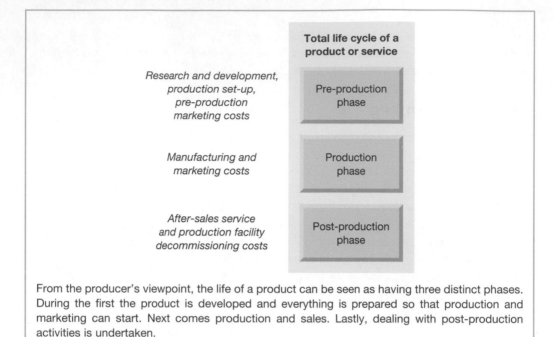

From the producer's viewpoint, the life of a product can be seen as having three distinct phases. During the first the product is developed and everything is prepared so that production and marketing can start. Next comes production and sales. Lastly, dealing with post-production activities is undertaken.

Figure 5.4 The total life cycle of a product or service

For some businesses, particularly those engaged in an advanced manufacturing environment, a very high proportion (perhaps as much as 80 per cent) of the total costs incurred over the life of a particular product are either incurred, or committed, at the pre-production phase. Take the example of a car manufacturer. When designing, developing and setting up production of a new model, a significant proportion of the total life-cycle costs are incurred. In addition, a commitment to incur costs during the production phase is made. This is because the design will incorporate features that lead to particular manufacturing costs. Once the design of the car has been finalised and the manufacturing plant set up, it may be too late to 'design out' a costly feature without incurring another large cost. Decisions made at the pre-production phase can also lead to a commitment to incur costs at the post-production phase. These decisions are, therefore, the most critical as they have the potential for huge cost savings at later points in time.

Activity 5.8

Can you provide an example of a decision made at the pre-production phase of a new car model that will result in costs being incurred after the manufacture of the product?

After-sales service costs may be incurred as a result of some design fault. Once the manufacturing facilities have been established, it may not be economic to revise the design but merely to deal with the problem through after-sales service procedures.

Where the manufacturing plant or production facilities are no longer needed when production ceases there may be decommissioning costs.

To gain competitive advantage, manufacturers may also try to reduce the total life-cycle costs of owning its products. Take, for example, an airplane manufacturer. The total cost of ownership for a passenger airline over its life can be extremely high. Costs include, maintenance, fuel and lost revenues when the airplane is out of service. Steps to reduce these costs for customers must be taken at the pre-production phase through the development of new materials, technology, processes and so on. **Real World 5.3** shows how the total life-cycle costs of ownership influenced Boeing in the design and construction of its new 787 Dreamliner passenger plane.

Real World 5.3

Building a dream

With the 787 Dreamliner, Boeing took greater account of the cost to maintain the airplane structure and systems over their lifetimes. This resulted in the basic 787-8 airplane having 30 per cent lower airframe maintenance costs than any comparable airplane and greater availability for service than any other commercial airplane.

The new life-cycle design philosophy led to significant changes in the way the airplane is built. They include extensive use of composites in the airframe and primary structure, an electric system architecture, a reliable and maintainable design and an improved maintenance programme.

Source: Adapted from Hale, J. (2006) Boeing 787 from the ground up, *Aero Quarterly, Boeing.com Commercial Aeromagazine*, Issue 24, Quarter 4, pp. 17–23.

Total life-cycle costing can be used to manage costs. It was mentioned earlier that, by the start of the production phase, it may be too late to try to manage a large element of the product's or service's total life-cycle cost. With total life-cycle costing, managers will be able to see, at an early stage, the cost consequences of incorporating particular designs or particular elements into products. Where the costs are unacceptable, changes may be made. This may involve assessing the costs of alternative designs. Where a number of equally acceptable designs for a particular product are being considered, knowledge of the total life-cycle costs of each can help decide the final outcome.

Real World 5.4 provides some idea of the extent to which total life-cycle costing is used in practice.

Real World 5.4

Total (whole) life-cycle costing in practice

The 2009 CIMA survey showed that total life-cycle costing is not widely used in practice, as is shown by Figure 5.5. About 14 per cent of all of the businesses surveyed used the approach.

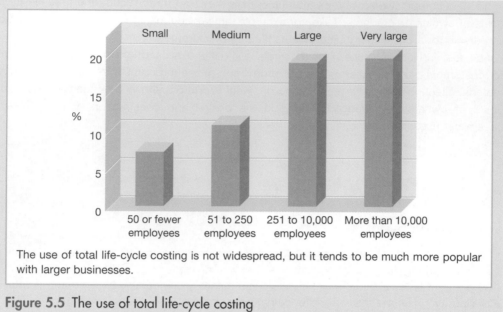

The use of total life-cycle costing is not widespread, but it tends to be much more popular with larger businesses.

Figure 5.5 The use of total life-cycle costing

Source: Adapted from CIMA (2009) *Management Accounting Tools for Today and Tomorrow*, p. 12.

Target costing

We saw in Chapter 4 that businesses may adopt a cost-plus approach to pricing. This involves totalling the costs of providing a product or service and then adding a percentage for profit to derive a selling price. Cost-plus pricing, however, is not normally suitable for businesses that operate in a highly competitive market.

Activity 5.9

Why do you think this is the case?

The cost-plus price figure derived may be unacceptable to potential buyers.

Target costing approaches the pricing decision from the opposite direction to cost-plus pricing. The starting point is to set a target price for a product based on market research, which will normally include an analysis of competitors' prices. The target profit, based on the financial objective of the business, is then deducted from the identified price. The resulting figure is the target cost of the product. Where the target cost is less than the current estimated cost, there will be a 'cost gap'. Efforts must then be made to bridge this gap by making the product, or rendering the service, in a way that meets the target cost.

A team of specialists, drawn from each of the main functional areas, such as design, production, purchasing and marketing, will normally be charged with achieving the target cost. However, stakeholders from outside the business, such as suppliers and customers, may also be invited to join the team. Together they will examine all aspects of the product and the production process to try to eliminate anything that does not add value. This may involve revising the design, developing more efficient means of production, and negotiating with suppliers to provide goods and services more cheaply. The process is often iterative (trial and error) and will continue until total product costs are reduced in line with the target cost figure, or it is found that the target cost figure cannot be achieved. To prevent too much time and resources being consumed in this process, deadlines may be set for reaching the target cost figure.

Target costing is not so much a costing technique as a framework within which various disciplines and techniques may be applied. Thus, some of the techniques covered elsewhere in this chapter, such as activity-based costing, benchmarking and value chain analysis, may be used to help achieve the target cost figure.

The target costing process is summarised in Figure 5.6.

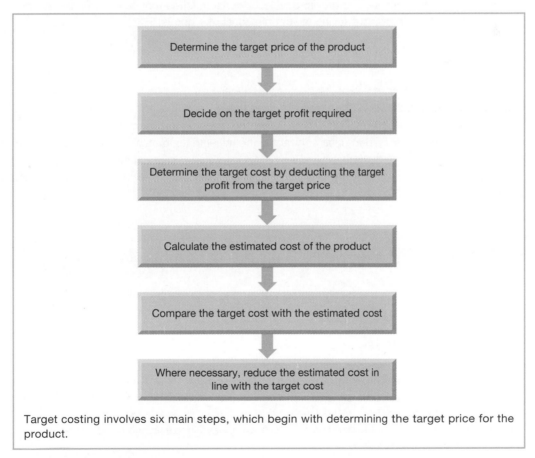

Target costing involves six main steps, which begin with determining the target price for the product.

Figure 5.6 The target costing process

Target costing can be seen as part of total life-cycle costing. As we have seen, a large proportion of the total costs of a product may well be determined at the pre-production phase. Careful planning at this phase of the product's life may prevent future manufacturing costs from becoming 'locked in'. Small changes in design, for example, may reduce the number of components needed or allow standard components rather than specialised components to be used. In the end, these small changes may lead to significant cost savings.

Target costing was developed by Japanese businesses during the 1970s in response to an increasingly competitive environment. It is particularly relevant for manufacturers of products and services with fairly short life cycles.

Activity 5.10

Can you think why target costing is particularly relevant with short-life-cycle products?

It is because cost savings are likely to be greatest where there is a need to make frequent updates to existing products and/or to develop a constant stream of new products – as in, say, the manufacture of fast-moving, electronic consumer goods.

Target costing is less relevant for businesses where product development is not such a significant issue, which will include many service businesses. Nevertheless, opportunities to use this costing approach may still arise. A firm of management consultants, for example, may consider bidding for a particular contract in the belief that a particular price would secure the contract. This price would become the target price and ways would then have to be found to deliver the service to conform to the contract specifications and to the consultancy firm's required financial returns.

Activity 5.11

Although target costing has its enthusiasts, there are potential problems with its use. Try to think of at least two of these.

Potential problems include:

■ Attempts to lower costs can lead to conflict – for example, between the business and its suppliers and between the business and its employees.
■ It can cause considerable stress among employees who are trying to meet target costs that are extremely difficult to achieve.
■ It can be time-consuming, leading to significant delays in the launch of new products.
■ It can be a costly exercise.

You may have thought of others.

Real World 5.5 indicates the level of usage of target costing. This shows quite a low level of usage in the UK. In contrast, other survey evidence shows that target costing is very widely used by Japanese manufacturing businesses.

Target practice

The 2009 CIMA survey showed that target costing is not widely used in practice, as is shown by Figure 5.7.

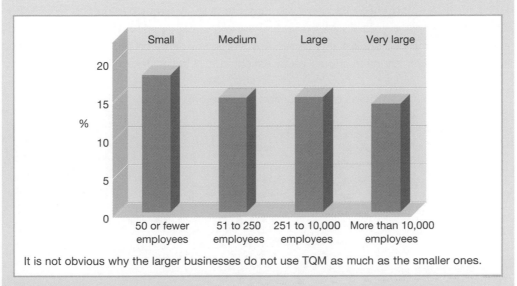

It is not obvious why the larger businesses do not use TQM as much as the smaller ones.

Figure 5.7 The use of target costing

Target costing is used by about 16 per cent of all of the businesses surveyed.

Source: Adapted from CIMA (2009) *Management Accounting Tools for Today and Tomorrow*, p. 12.

Kaizen costing

To ensure long-term competitiveness, businesses may look beyond the use of target costing at the pre-production phase of a product's life. When the production phase is reached, **kaizen costing** may be used to continue the quest for cost savings. The Japanese word 'kaizen' means 'continuous improvement', which can be accomplished through many small steps. Kaizen costing seeks to achieve cost savings through small, incremental changes on a continuous basis rather than, say, through the radical redesign of the production process on a 'one-off' basis. Since the production phase is quite late in the product life cycle (from a cost management point of view) only small cost savings can usually be made. The majority of production-phase cost savings should already have been made through target costing.

To reduce manufacturing costs, the production process is closely examined in the search for improvements. The focus is on the elimination of waste through unnecessary effort and excessive processes. Improvements that may result from a Kaizen approach include:

- eliminating overproduction;
- reducing the number of defective products produced through changes to processes;
- synchronising manufacturing processes and eliminating bottlenecks;

- identifying and eliminating excess inventories;
- reducing waiting times for deliveries through closer links with suppliers; and
- improving storage and handling processes.

When opportunities for small improvements are discovered the results acknowledged by senior management.

Kaizen costing aims to reduce the manufacturing cost of a product to below that incurred during the previous period. This involves target setting. A target percentage reduction in manufacturing cost is set for a period and, at the end of each period, the actual percentage reduction is compared against this target. Any significant deviation between the target and actual percentage reduction should be investigated and action taken if the target has not been reached.

The kaizen costing process is summarised in Figure 5.8.

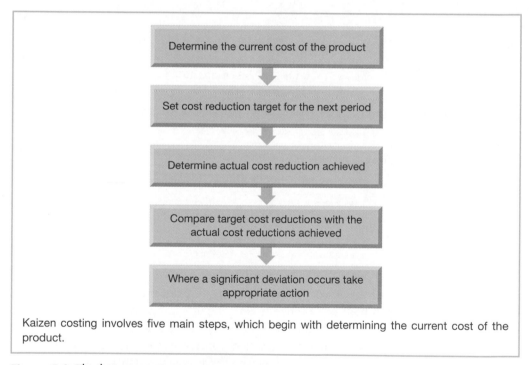

Kaizen costing involves five main steps, which begin with determining the current cost of the product.

Figure 5.8 The kaizen costing process

Kaizen costing is often part of a broader culture of continuous improvement within a business. The underlying philosophy is that no process can ever be perfect and so there is always room for improvement. It involves close scrutiny of every part of the production process with ideas being generated as to how things can be improved. Employees are seen as vital to the success of this approach and are expected to make suggestions for eliminating waste and for improving processes and the quality of output. Unlike traditional cost reduction methods, those working directly on production or rendering the service, for example factory-floor workers, rather than engineers, accountants or managers, are seen as holding the key to improvements.

Why do you think that those on the factory floor hold the key to improvements?

Those closest to production, particularly those with 'hands-on' experience, have a more intimate knowledge of the process. They are, therefore, more likely to spot opportunities for small improvements, such as minimising the time spent going to the stores or changing a sequence of small operations.

A further feature of the Kaizen approach is its focus on good housekeeping. This provides another target for continuous improvement. Close attention is paid to keeping the workplace clean and tidy and efforts are made to improve the safety and comfort of workers. Ensuring that they avoid injury or fatigue is seen as important in strengthening morale and motivation.

Kaizen costing can help to create a more open approach to dealing with issues and problems within a business. It can also help to create a more committed and motivated workforce through team working and employee involvement. There are, however, potential problems associated with this approach. Managers may be sceptical about this new technique and feel undermined by the democratic approach to decision making that it introduces. They may also recoil at the time and effort required to bring about the necessary changes in business culture and operations. A strong commitment by senior management is needed, therefore, to embed Kaizen costing within the business. Finally, there is a risk that employees will suffer stress as a result of continual pressure to reduce costs. We saw earlier that this risk is also present with target costing.

Toyota Materials Handling (Toyota), the Japanese forklift truck maker, is a leading advocate of Kaizen costing and the philosophy of continuous improvement. **Real World 5.6** describes the way in which it operates.

Real World 5.6

Kaizen costing at Toyota

Kaizen is seen by Toyota as a key issue. This implies that all staff members, at all levels of seniority, are consistently, as a matter of daily routine, looking for ways of improving the way that the business operates. All employees are regarded as being equally important in this process. Toyota actively encourages its employees to have a sense of pride in their work and to work efficiently. This involves identifying explicit goals for continuous improvement. In implementing kaizen, Toyota encourages all of its employees to think about the work that they do rather than simply doing their jobs in a mechanical way. Kaizen at Toyota goes well beyond the production process. It extends to all areas including marketing, research and development and administration.

Where employees identify possible areas for improvements, they are encouraged to propose a change in the way things operate. Across the business the kaizen process leads to around 3,000 proposals each year for improvement coming from employees at all levels. These proposals are carefully assessed, each one needing satisfy five criteria, before they are implemented.

Source: Information taken from Kaizen, Toyota Materials Handling, www.toyota-forklifts.eu, Accessed 12 April 2018.

Figure 5.9 shows the phases of the product life cycle covered by the three forms of costing discussed.

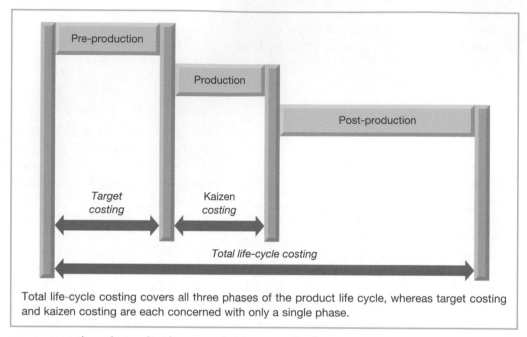

Total life-cycle costing covers all three phases of the product life cycle, whereas target costing and kaizen costing are each concerned with only a single phase.

Figure 5.9 The relationship between the three types of costing

OTHER APPROACHES TO MANAGING COSTS IN THE MODERN ENVIRONMENT

Value chain analysis

To secure competitive advantage, a business must be able to perform key activities more successfully than its competitors. This means that it must either obtain some cost advantage over its competitors, or differentiate itself in some way from them. To help identify particular ways in which competitive advantage may be achieved, it is useful to analyse a business into a sequence of value-creating activities. This sequence is known as the value chain. **Value chain analysis** examines the potential for each link in the chain to add value.

For a manufacturing business, the value-creating sequence begins with the acquisition of inputs, such as raw materials and energy. It ends with the sale of completed goods and after-sales service. Value chain analysis applies equally well to service-providing businesses as to manufacturers. Service providers also have a sequence of activities leading to provision of the service to their customers. For both types of business, analysing these activities in an attempt to identify and eliminate non-value-added activities can reap significant rewards.

Figure 5.10 sets out the main 'links' in the value chain for a manufacturing business. We can see that there are five primary activities and four secondary activities. Primary activities are those involved in producing, selling, storing and distributing the product. Secondary activities provide a support role to the primary activities.

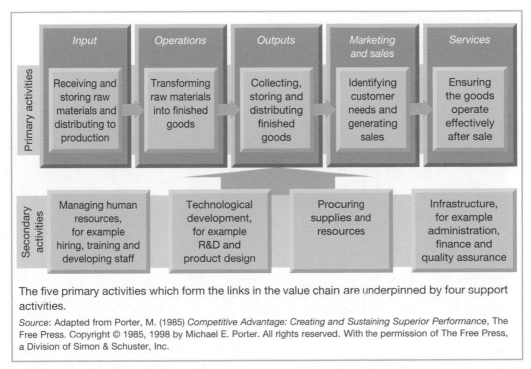

The five primary activities which form the links in the value chain are underpinned by four support activities.

Source: Adapted from Porter, M. (1985) *Competitive Advantage: Creating and Sustaining Superior Performance*, The Free Press. Copyright © 1985, 1998 by Michael E. Porter. All rights reserved. With the permission of The Free Press, a Division of Simon & Schuster, Inc.

Figure 5.10 The main links in the value chain of a manufacturing business

Each link in the value chain represents an activity that will incur costs and affect profits. Ideally, each will add value – that is, the customer will be prepared to pay more for the activity than it costs to carry out. If, however, a business is to outperform its rivals, it must ensure that the value chain is configured in such a way that it leads either to a cost advantage or to differentiation.

To achieve a cost advantage, the costs associated with each link in the chain must be identified and then examined to see whether they can be reduced or eliminated. For example, a non-value-added activity may be identified, such as the inspection of the completed product by a quality controller. The introduction of a 'quality' culture in the business could lead to much greater reliability in output quality. As a result, inspection would no longer be needed and this cost could be eliminated. To achieve differentiation from its rivals, a business must achieve uniqueness in at least one part of the value chain. A large baker, for example, may try to differentiate its products by moving production facilities to its retail shops to ensure that the products are freshly available to customers.

Real World 5.7 provides some impression of the use of value chain analysis in practice.

Value chain analysis

The CIMA survey, mentioned earlier, examined the extent to which value chain analysis is used by businesses of different size. The results are set out in Figure 5.11.

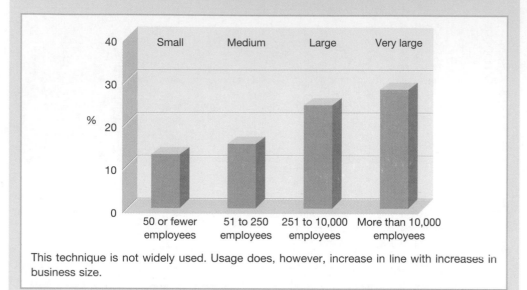

This technique is not widely used. Usage does, however, increase in line with increases in business size.

Figure 5.11 Use of value chain analysis

Source: Adapted from figure in CIMA (2009) *Management Accounting Tools for Today and Tomorrow*, p. 19.

Value chain analysis should help managers gain a clearer view of the strengths and weaknesses of the business and help identify areas for improvement. In some cases, it may result in significant operational changes, such as the introduction of new manufacturing or service-provision technology or the development of new sales policies. In other case, it may result in significant strategic shifts. A manufacturing business, for example, may find that it is unable to match the manufacturing costs achieved by its rivals. At the same time, it may have competitive strengths in the areas of marketing and distribution. In such circumstances, a decision may be made to focus on the business's core competencies. This may lead it to outsource the manufacturing function and to concentrate on the marketing and distribution of the goods.

Benchmarking

Benchmarking is an activity – usually a continuing one – where a business seeks to emulate a business that is 'best-in-class' in order to achieve greater success. The best-in-class business provides a standard, or benchmark, against which a business can compare its own performance. Benchmarking can also provide an insight into how performance can be improved. It can also help to avoid the pitfalls experienced by other businesses. Studying a high-performing business, and discovering the factors that lead to success, may lead to the introduction of new ideas. These could result in improved operational efficiency and greater competitive advantage.

The benchmarking process involves a series of steps, which are set out in Figure 5.12.

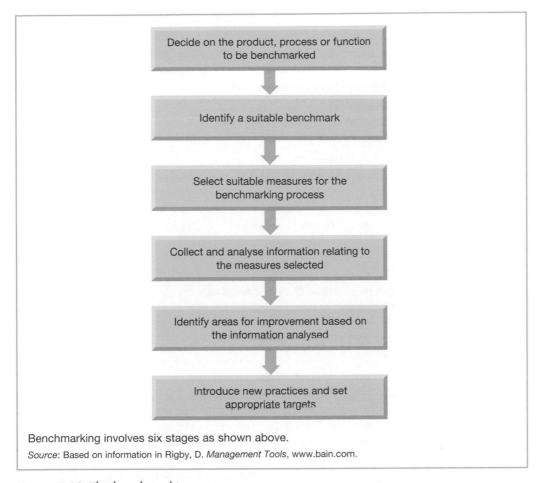

Benchmarking involves six stages as shown above.

Source: Based on information in Rigby, D. *Management Tools*, www.bain.com.

Figure 5.12 The benchmarking process

The benchmarking process has similar features to the kaizen costing process discussed above. It is usually carried out by a team with its members drawn from the various functional areas of the business and will usually continue over time. Furthermore, employees make a vital contribution towards the whole process. This is achieved by offering suggestions for change and by implementing the agreed changes. Finally, some resistance to proposed changes may easily arise and so its successful adoption relies on the strong support of senior management.

Benchmarking can be applied to any products or processes. It can also be applied to business strategies and to strategic decisions. This means that methods of identifying and measuring performance may cover a very wide range. They may include interviews and questionnaires involving managers, employees, suppliers and customers. They may also include the mapping of business processes and statistical analysis as well as using performance indicators based on key factors such as time, quality, income and costs.

Businesses do not have to be benchmarked (that is, be used as a benchmark by another business) and many are understandably reluctant to divulge commercially sensitive information. Thus, a competitor business that is regarded as best-in-class is unlikely to be a willing partner in the benchmarking process. Nevertheless, it may still be possible to glean a lot through an analysis of the competitor's activities using information from other sources. Where a best-in-class business is not a direct competitor, it may be prepared to share information concerning processes or functions carried out by both businesses, such as credit collection and inventories control. It may also be possible for a business to benchmark internally by using a successful division or department as the best-in-class.

In some cases, a database operator can provide information that may be used for benchmarking. An industry association, for example, may collect and disseminate information relating to performance measures submitted by participating businesses. However, the information made available may not identify individual businesses and the data may be aggregated. This kind of benchmarking is not so useful, therefore, when trying to understand why some businesses perform well.

Activity 5.13

Why is this type of benchmarking not so useful for this purpose?

It does not provide access to best-in-class businesses. A deeper understanding of their decisions and processes cannot therefore be gained.

Benchmarking in practice

Real World 5.8 provides an example of how benchmarking may be used to assess the operational efficiency of law firms.

Real World 5.8

Legal fees

The banking group NatWest plc undertook an analysis of the performance of 337 small to medium-sized law firms in the UK. The NatWest report covered law firms with a fee income of up to £27 million during 2012. A variety of measures were used to provide benchmarks against which operational efficiency could be compared. The main measures employed, as well as figures for the upper quartile of law firms for each measure, were:

Performance measure	Calculation of measure	Upper quartile
Fees per equity partner (£000)	Total fees earned/Number of equity (non-salaried) partners	676
Fees per fee earner (£000)	Total fees earned/Number of employees generating fees	193
Profit as a percentage of fees (%)	(Profit/Total fees earned) × 100%	33
Profit per equity partner (£000)	Profit/Number of equity partners	160
Chargeable hours (per year)	Number of hours charged to clients by fee earners	1,198
Recovered rate per hour (£)	Recorded rate per hour by a fee earner × the percentage of time recorded that can be billed	188
Work in progress (days)	The delay from time being recorded for work done to the bill being raised	26
Debtor days (days)	Time taken for clients to pay the bill	27
Total lock-up (days)	The delay from the time being recorded for work done to the cash being received (WIP + Debtor days)	69

For benchmarking purposes, the upper quartile figures can be used as a measure of superior performance and so provide a surrogate for best-in-class.

Source: Adapted from NatWest Bank (2013) 2013 Financial Benchmarking Report – Law firms, nw-businesssense.com.

Try to think of two more measures that could be used as benchmarks against which law firms could measure their operational efficiency. (*Hint:* Think of measures relating to time, income and profit.)

The following measures could also be used:

- year-to-year change in total fees earned;
- year-to-year change in profit per equity partner;
- fee-earning employees as a percentage of total employees;
- percentage of time recorded by fee-earner that is billed to clients;
- profit per employee (both fee-earners and non-fee-earners);
- bad debts as a percentage of total fees earned.

You may have thought of others.

Real World 5.9 provides some indication of the use of and effectiveness of benchmarking among large businesses.

Real World 5.9

Benchmarking

Bain & Company, a large firm of US management consultants, undertakes an annual survey of key management tools. Figure 5.13 shows the results of its 2015 survey, based on the views of 1,067 executives world-wide, looking at levels of usage of, and satisfaction with, benchmarking:

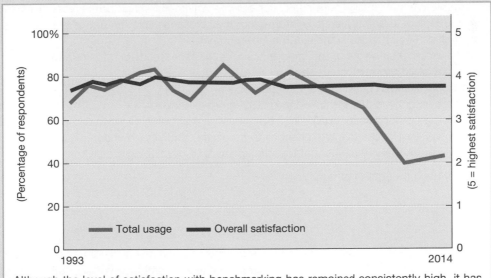

Although the level of satisfaction with benchmarking has remained consistently high, it has not been so widely used in recent years.

Figure 5.13 The use of benchmarking

The chart shows a decline in the level of usage in recent years; however, there has been no decline in the overall level of satisfaction among respondents.

Source: Rigby, D. (2015) *Insights Management Tools, Benchmarking*, Bain & Company, http://www.bain.com, 10 June.

Total quality management

Quality has become a major weapon that businesses deploy when competing against their rivals. As mentioned earlier, customers increasingly demand products (both goods and services) that meet their specific requirements. One of these requirements will be that products should be of a suitable quality. This means that the products should meet customers' needs and be available at a price they are willing to pay.

This emphasis on creating quality products has led to **total quality management (TQM)**. The TQM philosophy is concerned with providing products that meet, or exceed, customers' requirements all of the time. This implies that defective products should never reach the customer. Ideally, there should never be any defective production. TQM has been characterised as 'getting it right first time, every time'. It aims to create a virtuous sequence of events where quality improvements lead to reduced production problems, increased customer satisfaction and increased profits.

Employee involvement at all levels within the business is essential if a quality culture is to be developed. Managers must, therefore, take steps to bring this about.

Activity 5.15

What steps might a business take to ensure a high level of employee involvement in improving quality? Try to think of at least three.

A business may:

- Commit to a high level of communication between management and employees. This will include keeping employees fully informed of the objectives and strategy of the business as well as key changes in the external environment.
- Make employees aware of the importance of a customer focus and the role that quality plays in satisfying customer needs.
- Provide training in quality assurance procedures.
- Provide incentives that are linked to quality improvements.
- Encourage proposals for quality improvements.
- Empower employees to make changes to processes that should improve quality.
- Demonstrate the commitment of top management to developing a quality culture.

You may have thought of others.

As with other techniques discussed in this chapter, TQM is usually seen as a continuous effort rather than a 'one-off' exercise. It requires a detailed investigation of existing processes so that areas for improvement can be identified. To undertake the work needed, teams of employees may be created with members drawn from various business functions. They will be responsible for collecting and analysing data relating to existing processes and for ensuring that new processes are developed and properly monitored. In the quest for quality improvement, a wide range of methods may be used such as benchmarking, employee and customer surveys, statistical analysis and business process mapping.

A systematic approach should be adopted for delivering quality improvements. The main steps to be taken are set out in Figure 5.14.

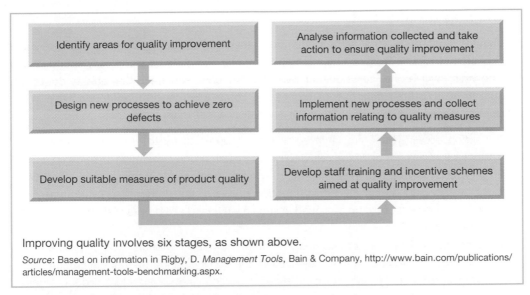

Improving quality involves six stages, as shown above.

Source: Based on information in Rigby, D. *Management Tools*, Bain & Company, http://www.bain.com/publications/articles/management-tools-benchmarking.aspx.

Figure 5.14 Delivering improvements in quality

Real World 5.10 provides some idea of the extent to which TQM is used in practice.

Real World 5.10

Quality practice

Figure 5.15 shows the results of the Bain and Company survey (see Real World 5.9 above) looking at levels of usage of, and satisfaction with, total quality management among respondents.

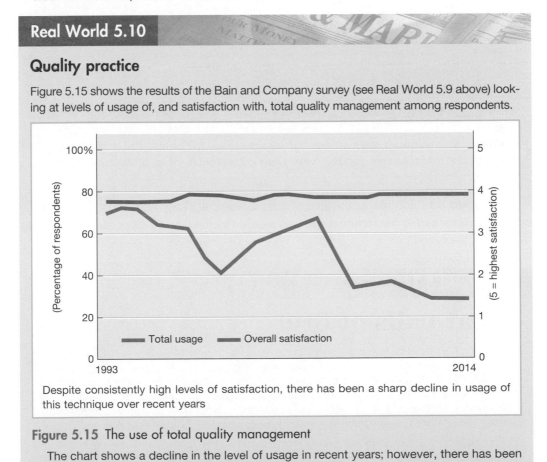

Despite consistently high levels of satisfaction, there has been a sharp decline in usage of this technique over recent years

Figure 5.15 The use of total quality management

The chart shows a decline in the level of usage in recent years; however, there has been no decline in the level of overall satisfaction.

Source: Rigby, D. (2015) *Insights Management Tools, Total Quality Management*, Bain & Company, http://www.bain.com, 10 June.

Managing quality costs

A business must ensure that its products are of the right quality. This means that they must meet customer requirements concerning performance and must be technically sound. Doing this, however, will lead to costs being incurred. It has been estimated that **quality costs** can amount to up to 30 per cent of total processing costs. They tend to be incurred during the production phase of the product life cycle and fall into four main categories:

1 *Prevention costs.* These are involved with procedures to try to prevent products being produced that are not up to the required quality. Such procedures might include staff training on quality issues and investment in new equipment. Some types of prevention costs might be incurred during the *pre-production phase* of the product life cycle, where the production process could be designed in such a way as to avoid potential quality problems with the output.
2 *Appraisal costs.* These are concerned with monitoring raw materials, work in progress and finished products to ensure that they achieve the quality standards that have been set.
3 *Internal failure costs.* These include the costs of rectifying substandard products before they reach the customer as well as the costs of scrap arising from quality failures.
4 *External failure costs.* These include the costs of rectifying quality problems with products that have been passed to the customer. They also include the cost to the business of its lost reputation for quality and reliability.

These four categories of cost together comprise the total quality costs incurred by a business.

Activity 5.16

Which one of the four quality costs identified above is likely to be the most critical? Why?

It is often external failure costs as they can be very costly to correct. They can also lead to lost sales and lost customer goodwill, which may put the entire future of the business at risk.

Real World 5.11 comprises an extracts from a *Financial Times* article that describes the concerns over a well-known product that was recalled by the manufacturer casting a shadow over the entire brand.

Real World 5.11

Great balls of fire!

Samsung's Electronics' suspension of all sales and exchanges of its fire-prone Galaxy Note 7 smartphone has fuelled concerns that the spiralling safety issues and dwindling customer confidence in its flagship device may spread to the company's other consumer products. Analysts warn that damage from the recall fiasco is likely to hit Samsung's reputation as well as sales in coming months, potentially benefiting rivals such as Apple and Google just as their new devices hit the market ahead of the crucial holiday sales season.

The world's largest smartphone maker has stopped all production and sales of the Note 7 as it conducts a thorough investigation into why some replacement models, issued after an initial recall, are also catching fire. The South Korean company urged consumers to stop using the devices and asked all global partners to stop sales and exchanges of the phone during the probe.

However, analysts said it would be difficult for Samsung to regain consumer confidence any time soon, as the second withdrawal of the product in two months highlights the company's struggle to fix the problem. It has also heightened criticism that it was too quick to blame the safety issues on the original battery supplier.

Whatever the cause, the quality issues have raised concerns of "contagion" to other Samsung phones and products if the safety problem relates to components other than the battery. However, there are no signs so far that any other models have issues with overheating, and Samsung's investigation only relates to the affected Galaxy Note 7.

"Samsung's credibility is on the line. Samsung needs to make sure that consumers can trust its brand or else other products [and future products] are at risk," said Bryan Ma, analyst at IDC. Carolina Milanesi, an analyst at Creative Strategies, said Samsung should "kill" the Note product line altogether to prevent the company's broader reputation being tarnished further, with the recall "becoming such a saga". "If Samsung as a brand gets stained, that is what's going to cost them," she said. "The cost of the recall and stopping production is nothing compared to the permanent damage to the brand."

FT *Source*: Extracts from Song, J. and Bradshaw, T. (2016) Samsung recall debacle fuels brand concerns, ft.com, 11 October.

Figure 5.16 summarises the main categories of total quality costs.

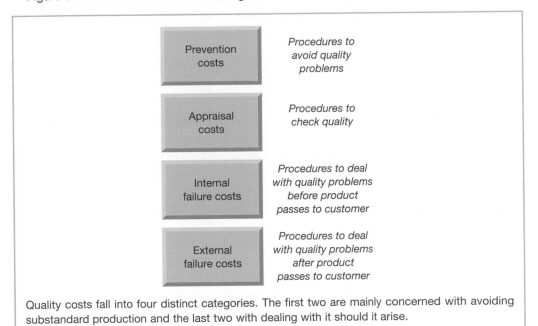

Figure 5.16 The main categories of quality costs

Activity 5.17

Look back at the four categories of quality costs that may be incurred (prevention costs, appraisal costs, internal failure costs and external failure costs), and try to think of at least two examples of specific costs that may be incurred within each category.

■ *Prevention costs* may include those related to quality training sessions, quality improvement meetings, investment in quality-related information systems, statistical quality controls, reviews of product design and projects aimed at product improvement.

→

- *Appraisal costs* may include those related to inspection and testing of the raw materials supplied, reviews of existing processes, quality audits of the final product, checking of testing equipment and reviews of performance standards.
- *Internal failure costs* may include those related to reworking materials, re-testing products, scrapping products and assigning a lower quality grade to products produced (and discounting the selling price).
- *External failure costs* may include those related to dealing with customer complaints, lost future orders, goods returned for reworking, product recalls, reputational loss and legal liability for failure to meet contract specifications.

By identifying, categorising and measuring the various quality costs, we have a basis for managing them. We can see more clearly the returns from investing in quality improvements. Let us say that a business is making products that contain a significant proportion of defects. It may well respond to this problem by increasing inspection costs. However, this may not be enough to eliminate the problem and so internal and external failure costs, such as reworking materials and dealing with customer complaints, may still be incurred. If the business invests in prevention, such as the purchase of new equipment and better staff training, appraisal costs and failure costs may be reduced. In other words, to produce higher quality products, total costs do not have to increase. Indeed, additional costs incurred in prevention may be more than offset by lower appraisal and failure costs leading to significant cost savings.

An alternative view

While the costing methods just described are used and are regarded as useful by many businesses, some believe that they fail to provide the key to successful cost management. It has been suggested that undue emphasis on costing methods, such as total life-cycle costing, is misplaced and what is really needed is for businesses to develop ways of learning and adapting to their changing environment. To manage costs successfully, businesses should continually review them in the face of new threats and pressures rather than relying on particular techniques to provide solutions.

Hopwood (see reference 1 at the end of the chapter) suggests that to transform costs over time to enable them to fit the strategic objectives, businesses do not need very sophisticated techniques or highly bureaucratic systems. Rather, they need to change the ways in which costs are viewed and dealt with. He suggests that the following broad principles should be adopted.

1 Spread the responsibility

Employees throughout the business should share responsibility for managing costs. Thus, design experts, engineers, store managers, sales managers and so on, should all contribute towards managing costs and should see this as part of their job. The involvement of non-accountants is, of course, a feature of target costing and kaizen costing. Thus, this point already appears to be widely accepted.

Hopwood suggests that employees should be provided with a basic understanding of costing ideas, such as fixed and variable costs, relevant costs and so on, to enable them to contribute fully. As cost consciousness permeates the business, and non-accounting employees become more involved in costing issues, the role of accountants will change. They will often facilitate, rather than initiate, cost management proposals and will become part of the multi-skilled teams engaged in creatively managing them.

2 Spread the word

Throughout the business, costs and cost management should become everyday topics for discussion. Managers should seize every opportunity to raise these topics with employees, as talking about costs can often lead to ideas being developed and action being taken to manage costs.

3 Think local

Emphasis should be placed on managing costs within specific sites and settings. Managers of departments, product lines or local offices are more likely to become engaged in managing costs if they are allowed to take initiatives in areas over which they have control. Local managers tend to have local knowledge not possessed by managers at head office. They are more likely to be able to spot cost-saving opportunities than are their more senior colleagues. Where initiatives for cost management have been developed by senior management, and are applied across the whole business, they are unlikely to have the same beneficial effect as local initiatives.

4 Benchmark continually

Benchmarking should be a never-ending journey. There should be regular, as well as special-purpose, reporting of cost information for benchmarking purposes. The costs of competitors may provide a useful basis for comparison, as we saw earlier. In addition, costs that may be expected as a result of moving to new technology or work patterns may be helpful.

5 Focus on managing costs rather than reducing them

Conventional management accounting tends to focus on cost reduction, which is, essentially, taking a short-term perspective on costs. Effective cost management, however, requires that, in some situations, costs should be increased rather than reduced.

Activity 5.18

In what kind of situations might it be a good idea to increase costs? Try to think, in broad terms, of at least one situation.

This may include situations leading to:

- additional revenues being generated;
- lower costs being incurred over the longer term; or
- lower costs being incurred in other areas of the business.

You may have thought of others.

Hopwood argues that these principles, when used in conjunction with overall financial controls, provide the best way to manage costs.

Self-assessment question 5.1

Psilis Ltd makes a product in two qualities, called 'Basic' and 'Super'. The business is able to sell these products at a price that gives a standard profit mark-up of 25 per cent of full cost. Management is concerned by the lack of profit.

Full cost for one unit of a product is calculated by charging overheads to each type of product on the basis of direct labour hours. The costs are as follows:

	Basic £	Super £
Direct labour (all £10/hour)	40	60
Direct material	15	20

The total overheads are £1,000,000.

Based on experience over recent years, in the forthcoming year the business expects to make and sell 40,000 Basics and 10,000 Supers.

Recently, the business's management accountant has undertaken an exercise to try to identify activities and cost drivers in an attempt to be able to deal with the overheads on a more precise basis than had been possible before. This exercise has revealed the following analysis of the annual overheads:

Activity (and cost driver)	Cost £000	Annual number of activities		
		Total	Basic	Super
Number of machine set-ups	280	100	20	80
Number of quality-control inspections	220	2,000	500	1,500
Number of sales orders processed	240	5,000	1,500	3,500
General production (machine hours)	260	500,000	350,000	150,000
Total	1,000			

The management accountant explained the analysis of the £1,000,000 overheads as follows:

- The two products are made in relatively small batches, so that the amount of the finished product held in inventories is negligible. The Supers are made in very small batches because demand for them is relatively low. Each time a new batch is produced, the machines have to be reset by skilled staff. Resetting for Basic production occurs about 20 times a year and for Supers about 80 times: about 100 times in total. The cost of employing the machine-setting staff is about £280,000 a year. It is clear that the more set-ups that occur, the higher the total set-up costs; in other words, the number of set-ups is the factor that drives set-up costs.
- All production has to be inspected for quality, which costs about £220,000 a year. The higher specifications of the Supers mean that there is more chance that there will be quality problems. Thus the Supers are inspected in total 1,500 times annually, whereas the Basics only need about 500 inspections. The number of inspections is the factor that drives these costs.
- Sales order processing (dealing with customers' orders, from receiving the original order to despatching the products) costs about £240,000 a year. Despite the larger amount of Basic production, there are only 1,500 sales orders each year because the Basics are sold to wholesalers in relatively large-sized orders. The Supers are sold mainly direct to the public by mail order, usually in very small-sized orders. It is believed that the number of orders drives the costs of processing orders.

Required:
(a) Deduce the full cost of each of the two products on the basis used at present and, from these, deduce the current selling price.
(b) Deduce the full cost of each product on an ABC basis, taking account of the management accountant's recent investigations.

(c) What conclusions do you draw? What advice would you offer the management of the business?

(d) The managers of the business are concerned that sales order processing is not being carried out efficiently. They have therefore decided to benchmark this function against best practice. Produce a list of measures that might be used by the business as a basis for a benchmarking exercise. (*Hint*: In developing the measures think about the key factors of time, quality, income and cost.)

(e) The benchmarking process will be carried out by a team of staff. Set out the criteria that you feel would be appropriate to use when selecting team members.

The solution to this question can be found at the back of the book on pp. 516–517.

SUMMARY

The main points of this chapter may be summarised as follows:

Activity-based costing (ABC)

- ABC deals with overheads (in full costing) by treating all costs as being caused or 'driven' by activities. It is claimed to be more relevant to the modern commercial environment than is the traditional approach.

- It involves identifying the support activities and their costs (overheads) and then analysing these costs to discover what drives them.

- The costs of each support activity are collected into a cost pool and the relevant cost driver is used to attach an amount of overheads from this pool to each unit of output.

- ABC should provide more accurate costs for each unit of output and should help in better control of overheads.

- ABC is, however, time-consuming and costly, and can suffer from measurement problems. It is unlikely to suit all businesses.

Total (whole) life-cycle costing

- Total life-cycle costing tracks and reports all costs relating to a product from the beginning to the end of its life.

- The life cycle of a product can be broken down into three phases: pre-production, production and post-production.

- A high proportion of costs is incurred and/or committed during the pre-production phase.

Target costing

- Target costing is a market-based approach to managing costs that is used at the pre-production phase.

- It tries to reduce costs so that an acceptable profit can be made at the target price.

- It provides a framework within which various techniques may be used to reduce costs rather than a costing method.

Kaizen costing

- Kaizen costing is concerned with continual and gradual cost reduction at the production phase.

→

- It involves setting targets for reductions in manufacturing costs each period and then comparing actual costs reductions against the targets.

- It is often part of a broader culture of continuous improvement within a business.

Value chain analysis

- Value chain analysis involves examining the various activities in the product life cycle to identify and try to eliminate non-value-added activities.

- Each link in the chain represents an activity that gives rise to costs. Any links in the chain that fail to add value should be evaluated critically and eliminated whenever possible.

Benchmarking

- Benchmarking attempts to emulate a successful operation carried out within, or outside, the business

- It is normally a continuing process aimed at gaining greater operating efficiency and competitive advantage.

- It involves identifying a suitable benchmark measure for a particular product or function, collecting and analysing information relating to the measure, identifying areas for improvement and then introducing new practices and targets.

Managing quality

- The total quality management (TQM) philosophy is concerned with providing products that meet or exceed customers' requirements all of the time.

- Ensuring the quality of output will incur costs, known as *quality costs*. They can be divided into four categories: prevention costs, appraisal costs, internal failure costs and external failure costs.

- If more is spent on prevention costs, cost savings may be made through the reduction of appraisal costs and failure costs.

An alternative view

- Costs may be managed without using sophisticated techniques if:
  - there is a shared responsibility for managing costs;
  - discussion of costs becomes an everyday activity;
  - costs are managed locally;
  - benchmarking is used at regular intervals; and
  - the focus is on managing rather than reducing costs.

KEY TERMS

For definitions of these terms, see Appendix A.

Activity-based costing (ABC) p. 154	**Kaizen costing** p. 170
Cost driver p. 154	**Value chain analysis** p. 174
Cost pool p. 155	**Benchmarking** p. 176
Total life-cycle costing p. 165	**Total quality management (TQM)** p. 180
Target costing p. 168	**Quality costs** p. 182

REFERENCE

1 Hopwood, A. (2002) Costs count in the strategic agenda, ft.com, 13 August.

FURTHER READING

If you would like to explore the topics covered in this chapter in more depth, we recommend the following:

Bhimani, A., Horngren, C., Datar, S. and Rajan, M. (2015) *Management and Cost Accounting*, 6th edn, Pearson, Chapters 11, 12 and 20.

Burns, J., Quinn, M., Warren, L. and Oliveira, J. (2013) *Management Accounting*, McGraw-Hill Education, Chapters 6 and 20.

Drury, C. (2015) *Management and Cost Accounting*, 9th edn, Cengage Learning EMEA, Chapter 21.

Hilton, R. and Platt, D. (2014) *Managerial Accounting*, 10th edn, McGraw-Hill Higher Education, Chapters 3, 5 and 15.

REVIEW QUESTIONS

Solutions to these questions can be found at the back of the book on pp. 529–530.

5.1 How does activity-based costing (ABC) differ from the traditional approach? What is the underlying difference between their philosophies?

5.2 The use of activity-based costing in helping to deduce full costs has been criticised. What has been the basis of this criticism?

5.3 What are the main categories of quality costs that a business may incur and why is it useful to categorise them?

5.4 Identify the main phases of the total life cycle of a product or service and identify the particular phase(s) for which target costing and kaizen costing are particularly appropriate.

EXERCISES

Those with coloured numbers have solutions given at the back of the book on pp. 545–548.

Basic-level exercises

5.1 Comment critically on the following statements that you have overheard:

(a) 'Achieving quality involves additional costs. If you want to improve the quality of products manufactured you have to increase total costs.'

(b) 'TQM and kaizen costing have striking similarities in their philosophy and approach.'

(c) 'Target costing is more relevant for manufacturing businesses than for service businesses.'

5.2 Describe the main similarities and differences in approach between target costing and kaizen costing.

5.3 Saxos plc is planning to adopt benchmarking in order to try to improve the efficiency of its inventory control procedures. It wishes to identify a willing partner that excels in this aspect of operations, wherever the business may be located.

What possible problems may be encountered by Saxos plc when setting up the benchmarking process?

Intermediate-level exercises

5.4 Kaplan plc makes a range of suitcases of various sizes and shapes. There are ten different models of suitcase produced by the business. In order to keep inventories of finished suitcases to a minimum, each model is made in a small batch. Each batch is costed as a separate job and the cost for each suitcase is deduced by dividing the batch cost by the number of suitcases in the batch.

At present, the business derives the cost of each batch using a traditional job-costing approach. Recently, however, a new management accountant was appointed, who is advocating the use of activity-based costing (ABC) to deduce the cost of the batches. The management accountant claims that ABC leads to much more reliable and relevant costs and that it has other benefits.

Required:
(a) Explain how the business deduces the cost of each suitcase at present.
(b) Discuss the purposes to which the knowledge of the cost for each suitcase, deduced on a traditional basis, can be put and how valid the cost is for the purpose concerned.
(c) Explain how ABC could be applied to costing the suitcases, highlighting the differences between ABC and the traditional approach.
(d) Explain what advantages the new management accountant probably believes ABC to have over the traditional approach.

5.5 Jerry's Taxis Ltd operates a taxi service in a large provincial city. All of the taxis are owned by the business and all the drivers are employees rather than owner drivers. The managers wish to benchmark the operating efficiency of the business against another taxi service. A suitable taxi service has been identified and has agreed to the benchmarking exercise. It is highly successful and operates a similar business model in a nearby city of similar size.

Required:
Produce a checklist of *ten* measures of operating efficiency that could be used as the basis for the benchmarking exercise. (*Hint*: When identifying measures, think about the key factors of time, quality, income and costs.)

5.6 Comment critically on the following statements that you have overheard:

(a) 'Direct labour hours are the most appropriate basis to use to charge indirect cost (overheads) to jobs in the modern manufacturing environment where people are so important.'
(b) 'Activity-based costing is a means of more accurately accounting for direct labour cost.'
(c) 'Activity-based costing cannot really be applied to the service sector because the "activities" that it seeks to analyse tend to be related to manufacturing.'
(d) 'Kaizen costing is an approach where great efforts are made to reduce the costs of developing a new product and setting up its production processes.'
(e) 'Benchmarking is an approach to job costing where each direct worker keeps a record of the time spent on each job on his or her workbench before it is passed on to the next direct worker or into finished inventories stores.'

Advanced-level exercises

5.7 Moleskin Ltd manufactures a range of products used in the building industry. Manufacturing is undertaken using one of two processes: the Alpha Process and the Omega process. All of the products are manufactured in batches. The current pricing policy has been to absorb all overheads using direct labour hours to obtain total cost. Price is then calculated as total cost plus a 35 per cent mark-up.

A recent detailed analysis has examined overhead cost; the results are:

	Analysis of overhead costs per month £	Monthly volume
Alpha Process cost	96,000	480 hours
Omega Process cost	44,800	1,280 hours
Set-up cost	42,900	260 set-ups
Handling charges	45,600	380 movements
Other overheads	50,700	See below
	280,000	

There are 4,000 direct labour hours available each month.

Two of Moleskin's products are a joist (JT101) and a girder (GR27). JT101s are produced by the Alpha Process in a simple operation. GR27s are manufactured by the Omega Process, a more complex operation with more production stages. Both products are sold by the metre.

Details for the two products are:

	JT101	GR27
Monthly volume	1,000 metres	500 metres
Batch size	1,000 metres	50 metres
Processing time per batch		
– Alpha	100 hours	–
– Omega	–	25 hours
Set-ups per batch	1	2
Handling charges per batch	1 movement	5 movements
Materials per metre	£16	£15
Direct labour per metre	½ hour	½ hour

Direct labour is paid £16 per hour.

Required:
(a) Calculate the price per metre for both JT101s and GR27s detailed above, using traditional absorption costing based on direct labour hours.
(b) Calculate the price per metre for both JT101s and GR27s using activity-based costing. Assume that 'Other overheads' are allocated using direct labour hours.
(c) Outline the points that you would raise with the management of Moleskin in the light of your answers to (a) and (b).
(d) Outline the practical problems that may be encountered in implementing activity-based techniques and comment on how they may be overcome.

5.8 A business manufactures refrigerators for domestic use. There are three models: Lo, Mid and Hi. The models, their quality and their price are aimed at different markets.

Product costs are computed on a blanket (business-wide) overhead-rate basis using a labour-hour method. Prices as a general rule are set based on cost plus 20 per cent. The following information is provided:

	Lo	Mid	Hi
Material cost (£/unit)	25	62.5	105
Direct labour hours (per unit)	½	1	1
Budget production/sales (units)	20,000	1,000	10,000

The budgeted overheads for the business amount to £4,410,000. Direct labour is costed at £8 an hour.

The business is currently facing increasing competition, especially from imported goods. As a result, the selling price of Lo has been reduced to a level that produces a very low profit margin. To address this problem, an activity-based costing approach has been suggested. The overheads are examined and these are grouped around main business activities of machining (£2,780,000), logistics (£590,000) and establishment (£1,040,000) costs. It is maintained that these costs could be allocated based respectively on cost drivers of machine hours, material orders and space, to reflect the use of resources in each of these areas. After analysis, the following proportionate statistics are available in relation to the total volume of products:

	Lo %	Mid %	Hi %
Machine hours	40	15	45
Material orders	47	6	47
Space	42	18	40

Required:

(a) Calculate for each product the full cost and selling price determined by:
 (1) the original costing method
 (2) the activity-based costing method.
(b) What are the implications of the two systems of costing in the situation given?
(c) What business/strategic options exist for the business in the light of the new information?

Chapter 6

BUDGETING

INTRODUCTION

In its 2016 annual report, Sky plc, the satellite television broadcaster, stated:

> There is a comprehensive budgeting and forecasting process, and the annual budget, which is regularly reviewed and updated, is approved by the board [of directors].

As we shall see, the practice at Sky is typical of businesses of all sizes.

What is a budget? What is it for? How is it prepared? Who prepares it? Why does the board regard it as important enough to consider? We shall be looking at the answers to each of these questions in the course of this chapter.

We shall see that budgets set out short-term plans to help managers run the business. They provide the means to assess whether actual performance was as planned and, if not, the reasons for this. Budgets do not exist in a vacuum; they are an integral part of a planning framework adopted by well-run businesses. To understand fully the nature of budgets we must, therefore, understand the strategic planning framework within which they are set.

The chapter begins with a discussion of the budgeting framework and then goes on to consider detailed aspects of the budgeting process. We shall see that preparing budgets relies on an understanding of many of the issues relating to the behaviour of costs and full costing, topics that we explored in Chapters 4 and 5.

Learning outcomes

When you have completed this chapter, you should be able to:

- Define a budget and show how budgets, strategic objectives and strategic plans are related.
- Explain the budgeting process and the interlinking of the various budgets within the business.
- Identify the uses of budgeting and construct various budgets, including the cash budget, from relevant data.
- Discuss the criticisms that are made of budgeting.

HOW BUDGETS LINK WITH STRATEGIC PLANS AND OBJECTIVES

It is vital that businesses develop plans for the future. Whatever a business is trying to achieve, it is unlikely to happen unless its managers are clear what the future direction of the business is going to be. As we discussed in Chapter 1 (pages 10–11), the development of plans involves five key steps:

1 *Establish mission, vision and objectives*
The mission and vision statements set out the overriding purpose of the business and what it seeks to achieve. The strategic objectives translate these into specific targets for the future and will be used as a basis for evaluating actual performance. You may recall that, in Chapter 1, we met the mission and vision statements of Aggreko plc (page 8).

2 *Undertake a position analysis*
This involves an assessment of where the business is currently placed in relation to where it wants to be, as set out in its mission, vision and strategic objectives.

3 *Identify and assess the strategic options*
The business must explore the various ways in which it might move from where it is now (identified in Step 2) to where it wants to be (identified in Step 1).

4 *Select strategic options and formulate plans*
This involves selecting what seems to be the best of the courses of action, or strategies, (identified in Step 3) and formulating a long-term strategic plan. This strategic plan is then normally broken down into a series of short-term plans, one for each aspect of the business. These plans are the budgets. Thus, a **budget** is a business plan for the short term – typically one year – and is expressed mainly in financial terms. Its role is to convert the strategic plans into actionable blueprints for the immediate future. Budgets will define precise targets concerning such things as:
- cash receipts and payments;
- sales volumes and revenues, broken down into amounts and prices for each of the products or services provided by the business;
- detailed inventories' requirements;
- detailed labour requirements; and
- specific production requirements.

5 *Perform, review and control*
Here the business pursues the budgets derived in Step 4. By comparing the actual outcome with the budgets, managers can see if things are going according to plan. Action must be taken to exercise control where actual performance does not match the budgets.

Activity 6.1

The approach described in Step 3 suggests that managers will systematically collect information and then carefully evaluate all the options available. Do you think this is what managers really do?

In practice, managers may not be as rational and capable as implied.

To develop the point made in the answer to Activity 6.1, managers may find it difficult to handle a large amount of information relating to a wide range of options. To avoid becoming overloaded, they may restrict their range of possible options and/or discard some information. Managers may also adopt simple approaches to evaluating the mass of information provided. These approaches may not, however, lead to the best decisions being made.

From the description of the planning process that we have just met, we can see that the relationship between the mission, vision, strategic objectives, strategic plans and budgets can be summarised as follows:

- the mission and vision set the overall direction and, once set, this is likely to last for quite a long time – perhaps throughout the life of the business;
- the strategic objectives, which are also long-term, will translate the mission and vision into specific, often quantifiable, targets;
- the strategic plans identify how each objective will be pursued; and
- the budgets set out, in detail, the short-term plans and targets necessary to fulfil the strategic objectives.

An analogy might be found in terms of a student enrolling on a course of study. The student's mission might be to have a happy and fulfilling life. A key strategic objective flowing from this mission might be to embark on a career that will be rewarding in various ways. The particular study course might have been identified as the most effective way to work towards this objective. Successfully completing the course would then be the strategic plan. In working towards this strategic plan, passing a particular stage of the course might be identified as the target for the forthcoming year. This short-term target is analogous to the budget. Having achieved the 'budget' for the first year, the student's budget for the second year becomes passing the second stage.

Exercising control

However well planned the activities of a business might be, they will come to nothing unless steps are taken to try to achieve them in practice. The process of making planned events actually occur is known as **control**. This is part of Step 5 (above).

Control can be defined as compelling events to conform to plan. This definition is valid in any context. For example, when we talk about controlling a car, we mean making the car do what we plan that it should do.

In a business context, management accounting has an important role to play in the control process. This is because it is possible to state many plans in financial terms (as budgets). Since it is also possible to state *actual* outcomes in the same terms, making comparison between actual and planned outcomes is a relatively simple matter. Where actual outcomes are at variance with budgets, this variance should be highlighted by financial information. Managers can then take steps to get the business back on track towards the achievement of the budgets. We shall be looking more closely at the control aspect of budgeting in Chapter 7.

Figure 6.1 shows the planning and control process in diagrammatic form.

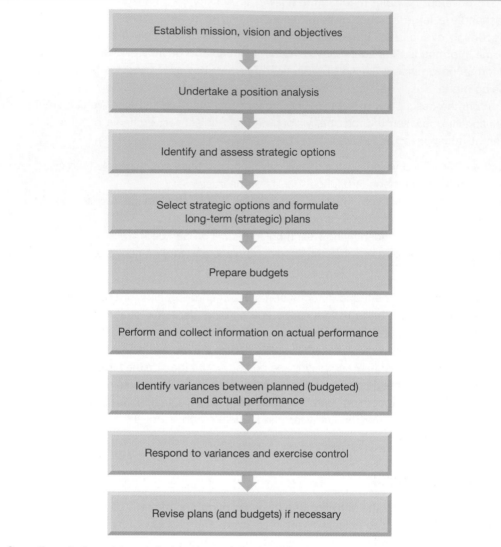

Once the mission, vision and objectives of the business have been determined, the various strategic options available must be considered and evaluated in order to derive a strategic plan. The budget is a short-term financial plan for the business that is prepared within the framework of the strategic plan. Control can be exercised through the comparison of budgeted and actual performance. Where a significant divergence emerges, some form of corrective action should be taken. If the budget figures prove to be based on incorrect assumptions about the future, it might be necessary to revise the budget.

Figure 6.1 The planning and control process

It should be emphasised that planning (including budgeting) is the responsibility of managers rather than accountants. Although accountants play a role in the planning process, by supplying relevant information to managers and by contributing to decision making as part of the management team, they should not dominate the process. In practice, however, this often seems to occur. While accountants may be adept at dealing with financial information, managers are failing in their responsibilities if they allow them to have an excessive influence in the budgeting process.

TIME HORIZON OF PLANS AND BUDGETS

Setting strategic plans is typically a major exercise performed about every five years and budgets are usually set annually for the forthcoming year. These time horizons, however, may vary according to the needs of the particular business. Those businesses involved in certain industries – say, information technology – may feel that five years is too long a planning period since new developments can, and do, occur virtually overnight. Here, a planning horizon of two or three years may be more appropriate. Similarly, a budget need not be set for one year, although this appears to be a widely used time horizon.

One business that keeps its strategic planning under more frequent review is Greene King plc, the brewery, pub and hotel business. **Real World 6.1**, which is an extract from the annual report for the business, explains how strategic planning is a regular annual event.

Real World 6.1

Strategic planning at the pub

According to its annual report, Greene King has the following approach to strategic planning:

> There is a two-day meeting of the board in February each year focusing on strategy, with the business unit managing directors and heads of the main functional areas, namely trading, marketing, HR (Human Resources) and property, attending for part thereof. The strategy sessions include an in-depth review of relevant economic factors and issues affecting the sector and management's projections for the medium term. The board then has the opportunity to agree the strategic plans across all areas for the short and medium term. Following approval of the company's strategy, budgets are prepared for the next financial year, which are reviewed and approved by the board in April. The board also has a programme to review each business unit and main functional area in detail on a regular basis, with particular focus on the achievement of strategic objectives. The relevant managing director or functional head attends such meetings to present and answer questions.

Source: Greene King plc Annual Report 2016, p. 48.

Activity 6.2

Can you think why most businesses prepare detailed budgets for a year ahead, rather than for a shorter or longer period?

The reason is probably that a year represents a long enough time for the budget preparation exercise to be worthwhile, yet short enough into the future for detailed plans to be capable of being made. As we shall see later in this chapter, the process of formulating budgets can be a time-consuming exercise, but there are economies of scale. For example, preparing the budget for the next year would not normally take twice as much time and effort as preparing the budget for the next six months.

An annual budget sets targets for the forthcoming year for all aspects of the business. It is usually broken down into monthly budgets, which define monthly targets. Indeed, in many instances, the annual budget will be built up from monthly figures. The sales staff, for example, may be required to set sales targets for each month of the budget period. These targets may well differ from month to month, particularly where there are seasonal demand variations. Other budgets will be set for each month, as we shall explain shortly. Though, undoubtedly, a year is the standard budgeting period, some would argue that this is too long. Survey evidence suggests that 70 per cent of managers felt that they were unable to plan in detail for more than the next three months, such that annual budgets are obsolete well before the end of the period to which they relate (see reference 1 at the end of the chapter).

BUDGETS AND FORECASTS

A budget may, as we have already seen, be defined as a business plan for the short term. Note particularly that a budget is a *plan*, not a forecast. To talk of a plan suggests an intention or determination to achieve the targets; **forecasts** tend to be predictions of the future state of the environment.

Clearly, forecasts are very helpful to the planner/budget-setter. If, for example, a reputable forecaster has predicted the number of new cars to be purchased in the UK during next year, it will be valuable for a manager in a car manufacturing business to take this into account when setting next year's sales budgets. However, a forecast and a budget are distinctly different.

PERIODIC AND CONTINUAL BUDGETS

Budgeting can be undertaken on a periodic or a continual basis. A **periodic budget** is prepared for a particular period (usually one year). Managers will agree the budget for the year and then allow the budget to run its course. Although it may be necessary to revise the budget on occasions, preparing the periodic budget is, in essence, a one-off exercise during each financial year. A **continual budget**, as the name suggests, is continually updated. We have seen that an annual budget will normally be broken down into smaller time intervals (usually monthly periods) to help control the activities of the business. A continual budget will add a new month to replace the month that has just passed, thereby ensuring that, at all times, a budget for a full planning period is available. A continual budget is also referred to as a **rolling budget**.

Activity 6.3

Which method of budgeting do you think is likely to be more costly and which method is likely to be more beneficial for forward planning?

Periodic budgeting will usually take less time and effort and will, therefore, be less costly. However, as time passes, the budget period shortens and towards the end of the financial year managers will be working to a very short planning period indeed. Continual budgeting, on the other hand, will ensure that managers always have a full year's budget to help them make decisions. It is claimed that continual budgeting ensures that managers plan throughout the year rather than just once each year. In this way it encourages a perpetual forward-looking attitude.

While continual budgeting encourages a forward-looking attitude, there is a danger that budgeting will become a mechanical exercise. Managers may not have time to step back from their other tasks each month and consider the future with sufficient care. Continually taking this forward-looking attitude may be difficult, therefore, to sustain.

Continual budgets do not appear to be very popular in practice. A survey of 340 senior financial staff of small, medium and large businesses in North America revealed that only 9 per cent of businesses use them (see Reference 2 at the end of the chapter). However a 2015 survey suggests that 69 per cent of businesses will adopt a rolling budgeting approach within the next five years. This was a survey involving over 900 finance professionals in businesses of all sizes in more than 50 countries (see Reference 3 at the end of the chapter).

LIMITING FACTORS

Some aspect of the business will, inevitably, stop it achieving its objectives to the maximum extent. This is often a limited ability of the business to sell its products. Sometimes, as we saw in Chapter 3, it is a production shortage (such as labour, materials or plant) that is the **limiting factor**, or, linked to these, a shortage of funds. Often, production shortages can be overcome by an increase in funds – for example, more plant can be bought or leased. This is not always a practical solution, because no amount of money will buy certain labour skills or increase the world supply of some raw material.

Easing an initial limiting factor, for example a plant capacity problem, may be possible. This means that some other factor, perhaps lack of sales demand, will replace the production problem, though at a higher level of output. Ultimately, however, the business will hit a ceiling; some limiting factor will prove impossible to ease.

The limiting factor must be identified. Ultimately, most, if not all, budgets will be affected by the limiting factor. If this can be identified at the outset, all managers can be informed of the restriction early in the process. When preparing budgets, account can then be taken of the limiting factor.

HOW BUDGETS LINK TO ONE ANOTHER

A typical larger business will prepare more than one budget for a particular period. Each budget prepared will relate to a specific aspect of its operations. The ideal situation is probably that there should be a separate operating budget for each person who is in a managerial position, no matter how junior. The contents of each of the individual operating budgets will be summarised in **master budgets**, usually consisting of a budgeted income statement and statement of financial position (balance sheet). The cash budget is considered by some to be a third master budget.

Figure 6.2 illustrates the interrelationship and interlinking of individual operating budgets, in this particular case using a manufacturing business as an example.

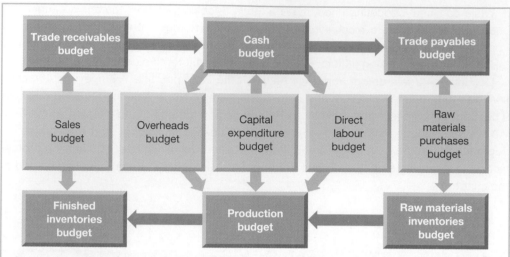

The starting point is usually the sales budget. The expected level of sales normally defines the overall level of activity for the business. The other operating budgets will be drawn up in accordance with this. Thus, the sales budget will largely define the finished inventories requirements and from this we can define the production requirements and so on. This shows the interrelationship of operating budgets for a manufacturing business.

Figure 6.2 The interrelationship of operating budgets

The sales budget is usually the first to be prepared (at the left of Figure 6.2), as the level of sales often determines the overall level of activity for the forthcoming period. This is because sales demand is probably the most common limiting factor. The finished inventories requirement tends to be set by the level of sales, though it would also be dictated by the policy of the business on the level of the finished products inventories that it chooses to hold. The requirement for finished inventories will determine the required production levels, which will, in turn, dictate the requirements of the individual production departments or sections. The demands of manufacturing, in conjunction with the business's policy on how long it holds raw materials before they enter production, define the raw materials inventories budget. The purchases budget will be dictated by the materials inventories budget, which will, in conjunction with the policy of the business on taking credit from suppliers, dictate the trade payables budget. One of the determinants of the cash budget will be the trade payables budget; another will be the trade receivables budget, which itself derives, through the business's policy on settlement periods granted to credit customers, from the sales budget. Cash will also be affected by overheads and direct labour costs (themselves linked to production) and by capital expenditure. Cash will also be affected by new finance and redemption of existing sources. (This is not shown in Figure 6.2 because the diagram focuses only on budgets concerned with operational matters.) The factors that affect policies on matters such as inventories holding, trade receivables collection and trade payables settlement periods will be discussed in some detail in Chapter 12.

A manufacturing business has been used as the example in Figure 6.2 simply because it has all of the types of operating budgets found in practice. Service businesses have similar budgets, but may not have inventories budgets. All of the issues relating to budgets apply equally well to all types of business.

Sales demand is not necessarily the limiting factor. Assuming that the budgeting process takes the order just described, it might be found in practice that there is some constraint other than sales demand. The production capacity of the business may, for example, be incapable of meeting the necessary levels of output to match the sales budget for one or more months. Finding a practical way of overcoming the problem may be possible. As a last resort, it might be necessary to revise the sales budget to a lower level to match the production limitation.

Activity 6.4

Can you think of any ways in which a short-term shortage of production facilities of a manufacturer might be overcome?

We thought of the following:

- Higher production in previous months and increasing inventories ('stockpiling') to meet periods of higher demand.
- Increasing production capacity, perhaps by working overtime and/or acquiring (buying or leasing) additional plant.
- Subcontracting some production.
- Encouraging potential customers to change the timing of their purchases by offering discounts or other special terms during the months that have been identified as quiet.

You might well have thought of other approaches.

There will be the horizontal relationships between budgets, which we have just looked at, but there will usually be vertical ones as well. Breaking down the sales budget into a number of subsidiary budgets, perhaps one for each regional sales manager, is a common approach. The overall sales budget will be a summary of the subsidiary ones. The same may be true of virtually all of the other budgets, most particularly the production budget.

Figure 6.3 shows the vertical relationship of the sales budgets for a business. The business has four geographical sales regions, each one the responsibility of a separate manager. Each regional manager is responsible to the overall sales manager of the business. The overall sales budget is the sum of the budgets for the four sales regions.

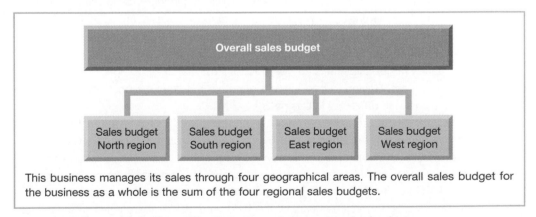

This business manages its sales through four geographical areas. The overall sales budget for the business as a whole is the sum of the four regional sales budgets.

Figure 6.3 The vertical relationship between a business's sales budgets

Although sales are often managed on a geographical basis, and so their budgets reflect this, they may be managed on some other basis. For example, a business that sells a range of products may manage sales on a product-type basis, with a specialist manager responsible for each type of product. Thus, an insurance business may have separate sales managers and, therefore, separate sales budgets, for life insurance, household insurance, motor insurance and so on. Very large businesses may even have separate product-type managers for each geographical region. Each of these managers would have a separate budget, which would combine to form the overall sales budget for the business as a whole.

All of the operating budgets that we have just reviewed must mesh with one another and with the master budgets, that is, the budgeted income statement and statement of financial position.

HOW BUDGETS HELP MANAGERS

Budgets are generally regarded as having five areas of usefulness. These are:

- *Budgets promote forward thinking and the identification of short-term problems.* We have seen that a shortage of production capacity might be identified during the budgeting process. Making this discovery in good time could leave open a number of ways of overcoming the problem. If the potential production problem is picked up early enough, all of the suggestions in the answer to Activity 6.4 and, possibly, other ways of overcoming the problem can be explored. Identifying the problem early gives managers time for calm and rational consideration of the best way of overcoming it. The best solution may only be feasible if action can be taken well in advance.

- *Budgets can help co-ordination between the various sections of the business.* It is crucially important that the activities of the various departments and sections of the business are linked so that the activities of one are complementary to those of another. As we saw when considering Figure 6.2, the activities of the purchasing/procurement department of a manufacturing business, for example, should dovetail with the raw materials needs of the production departments. If they do not, production could run out of raw materials, leading to expensive production stoppages or excessive amounts of raw materials could be bought, leading to large and unnecessary inventories holding costs. We shall see how this co-ordination works in practice later in this chapter.

- *Budgets can motivate managers to better performance.* Having a stated task can motivate managers and staff in their performance. Simply telling managers to do their best is not very motivating, but setting a required level of achievement is more likely to be so. Managers will be better motivated by being able to relate their particular role to the business's overall objectives. Since budgets are directly derived from strategic objectives, budgeting makes this possible. It is not feasible to allow managers to operate in an unconstrained environment. Having to operate in a way that matches the goals of the business is a price of working in an effective business.

- *Budgets can provide a basis for a system of control.* As we saw earlier in the chapter, control is concerned with ensuring that events conform to plans. If managers wish to control and to monitor their own performance, and that of their more junior staff, they need some yardstick against which to measure and assess it. Current performance might be compared with past performance or perhaps with what happens in another business. However, planned performance is usually the best yardstick. If there is information available concerning the actual performance for a period, and this can be compared with the planned performance, then a basis for control will have been established. There is an opportunity to use **management by exception**, an approach where senior managers can spend most of their time dealing with those staff or activities that have failed to achieve the budget (the exceptions). They do not have to spend too much time on those where actual performance conforms to plan. Effective budgets allow all managers to exercise self-control. By knowing what is expected of them and what they have actually achieved, they can assess how well they are performing and take steps to correct matters where they are failing to achieve.

■ *Budgets can provide a system of authorisation for managers to spend up to a particular limit.* Some activities (for example, staff development and research and development) are allocated a fixed amount of funds at the discretion of senior management. This provides the authority to spend.

Figure 6.4 shows the benefits of budgets in diagrammatic form.

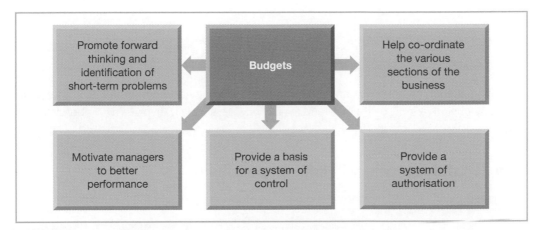

Figure 6.4 Budgets are seen as having five main benefits to the business

The following two activities pick up issues that relate to some of the uses of budgets.

Activity 6.5

The third point on the list of the uses of budgets (motivation) implies that managers are set stated tasks. Do you think there is a danger that requiring managers to work towards such predetermined targets will stifle their skill, flair and enthusiasm?

If the budgets are set in such a way as to offer challenging yet achievable targets, the manager is still required to show skill, flair and enthusiasm. There is the danger, however, that where targets are badly set (either unreasonably demanding or too easy to achieve), they could be demotivating and have a stifling effect.

Activity 6.6

The fourth point on the list of the uses of budgets (control) implies that current management performance is compared with some yardstick. What is wrong with comparing actual performance with past performance, or the performance of others, in an effort to exercise control?

What happened in the past, or is happening elsewhere, does not necessarily represent a sensible target for this year in this business. Considering what happened last year, and in other businesses, may help in the formulation of plans, but past events and the performance of others should not automatically be seen as the target.

The five identified uses of budgets can conflict with one another on occasion. Using the budget as a motivational device may provide an example of this. Some businesses set budget targets at a more demanding level than managers can reasonably be expected to achieve in an attempt to get them to strive harder. For control purposes, however, the budget becomes less useful as a benchmark against which to compare actual performance. Incidentally, there is good reason to doubt the effectiveness of setting excessively demanding targets as a motivational device, as we shall see in Chapter 7.

Where a conflict arises between the different uses of budgets, managers must decide which should be given priority. They must be prepared to trade off the benefits resulting from one particular use for the benefits of another.

THE BUDGET-SETTING PROCESS

Budgeting is such an important area for businesses, and other organisations, that it tends to be approached in a fairly methodical and formal way. This usually involves a number of steps, which we shall now consider.

Step 1: Establish who will take responsibility

Those responsible for the budget-setting process must have real authority within the business.

Activity 6.7

Why should this be the case?

One of the crucial aspects of the process is establishing co-ordination between budgets so that the plans of one department match and are complementary to those of other departments. This usually requires compromise where adjustment of initial budgets must be undertaken. This in turn means that a senior manager has to be closely involved. It is only such a person that is likely to possess the influence and, where needed, formal authority to make departmental managers compromise.

A **budget committee** is usually formed to supervise and take responsibility for the budget-setting process. This committee usually includes a senior representative of most of the functional areas of the business – marketing, production, human resources and so on. Often, a **budget officer** is appointed to carry out the technical tasks of the committee, or to supervise others carrying them out. Not surprisingly, given their technical expertise, accountants are often given this role.

Activity 6.8

As we have just seen, having senior staff involved in the budgeting process enables them to exert authority, should this be needed. Can you suggest another benefit that involvement of senior staff may provide?

Having senior staff involved can help to highlight the importance that they place on budgets and the budgeting process.

Step 2: Communicate budget guidelines to relevant managers

Budgets are intended to be the short-term plans that seek to work towards the achievement of strategic plans and to the overall objectives of the business. It is, therefore, important that, in drawing up budgets, managers are well aware of what the strategic plans are and how the forthcoming budget period is intended to work towards them. Managers also need to be made well aware of the commercial/economic environment in which they will be operating. This may include awareness of market trends, future rates of inflation, forecast changes in technology and so on. It is the budget committee's responsibility to see that managers have all the necessary information.

Step 3: Identify the key, or limiting, factor

As we saw earlier in the chapter, there will be a limiting factor that will restrict the business from achieving its objectives to the maximum extent. Identifying the limiting factor at the earliest stage in the budget-setting process will be helpful.

Step 4: Prepare the budget for the area of the limiting factor

The limiting factor will determine the overall level of activity for the business. The limiting-factor budget will, as we have already seen, usually be the sales budget, since the ability to sell is normally the constraint on future growth. (When discussing the interrelationship of budgets earlier in the chapter, we started with the sales budget for this reason.)

Step 5: Prepare draft budgets for all other areas

The other budgets are prepared, consistent with the budget for the area of the limiting factor. In all budget preparation, the computer has become an indispensable tool. Much of the work of preparing budgets is repetitive and tedious, yet the resultant budget has to be a reliable representation of the plans made. Computers are ideally suited to such tasks and human beings are not. Budgets often have to be redrafted several times because of some minor alteration; computers do this without complaint.

Setting individual budgets may be approached in one of two broad ways. The *top-down approach* is where the senior management of each budget area originates the budget targets, perhaps discussing them with lower levels of management and, as a result, refining them before the final version is produced. With the *bottom-up approach*, the targets are fed upwards from the lowest level. For example, junior sales managers will be asked to set their own sales targets, which then become incorporated into the budgets of higher levels of management until the overall sales budget emerges.

Where the bottom-up approach is adopted, it is usually necessary to haggle and negotiate at different levels of authority to achieve agreement. Perhaps the plans of some departments do not fit in with those of others or the targets set by junior managers are not acceptable to their superiors. The bottom-up approach is less popular in practice than the top-down (see Reference 4 at the end of the chapter).

There will be further discussion of the benefits of participation in target setting in Chapter 7.

Step 6: Review and co-ordinate budgets

The budget committee must, at this stage, review the various budgets and satisfy itself that the budgets are consistent with one another. Where there is a lack of co-ordination, steps must be taken to ensure that the budgets mesh. Since this will require that at least one budget must be revised, this activity normally benefits from a consensual approach. Ultimately, however, the committee may be forced to assert its authority and insist that alterations are made.

Step 7: Prepare the master budgets

The master budgets are the budgeted income statement and budgeted statement of financial position – and, perhaps, a summarised cash budget. The individual operating budgets, that have already been prepared, should provide all of the information required to prepare the master budgets. The budget committee usually undertakes the task of preparing the master budgets.

Step 8: Communicate the budgets to all interested parties

The formally agreed operating budgets are now passed to the individual managers who will be responsible for their implementation. This is, in effect, senior management communicating to the other managers the targets that are expected to be achieved.

Step 9: Monitor performance relative to the budget

Much of the budget-setting activity will have been pointless unless each manager's actual performance is compared with the benchmark of planned performance, which is embodied in the budget. This issue is examined in detail in Chapter 7.

The steps in the budget-setting process are shown in diagrammatic form in Figure 6.5.

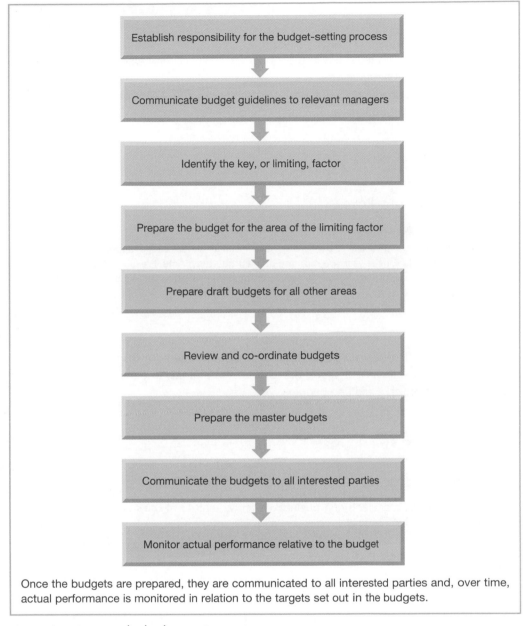

Figure 6.5 Steps in the budget-setting process

Where the established budgets are proving to be unrealistic, it is usually helpful to revise them. They may be proving to be unrealistic because certain assumptions made when the budgets were first set have turned out to be incorrect. This may occur where managers (budget setters) have made poor judgements or where the environment has changed unexpectedly from what was, quite reasonably, assumed. Unrealistic budgets are of little value and revising them may be the only logical approach to take. Nevertheless, revising budgets should be regarded as exceptional and only undertaken after careful consideration.

USING BUDGETS IN PRACTICE

This section provides an indication of how budgets are used, the extent to which they are used and their level of accuracy.

Real World 6.2 shows how Rolls-Royce Holdings plc, the global power and propulsion systems manufacturer, undertakes its budgeting process.

Real World 6.2

Budgeting at Rolls-Royce

According to the annual report of Rolls-Royce:

> The Group has a comprehensive budgeting system with an annual budget approved by the Board. Revised forecasts for the year are reported at least quarterly. Actual results, at both a business and Group level, are reported monthly against budget and variances are kept under scrutiny.

Source: Rolls-Royce Holdings plc, Annual Report 2016, p. 64.

There is quite a lot of survey evidence that reveals the extent to which budgeting is used by businesses in practice. **Real World 6.3** reviews some of this evidence, which shows that most businesses prepare and use budgets.

Real World 6.3

Budgeting in practice

A survey of 41 UK manufacturing businesses found that 40 of the 41 surveyed prepared budgets.

Source: Dugdale, D., Jones, C. and Green, S. (2006) *Contemporary Management Accounting Practices in UK Manufacturing*, CIMA Research Publication, Vol. 1, Number 13.

Another survey of UK businesses, but this time businesses involved in the food and drink sector, found that virtually all of them used budgets.

Source: Abdel-Kader, M. and Luther, R. (2004) *An Empirical Investigation of the Evolution of Management Accounting Practices*, Working paper No. 04/06, University of Essex, October.

A survey of the opinions of senior finance staff at 340 businesses of various sizes and operating in a wide range of industries in North America revealed that 97 per cent of those businesses had a formal budgeting process.

Source: BPM Forum (2008) *Perfect how you project*.

On the other hand, a survey of seven small and four medium-sized UK business found that not all of the small ones had a formal budgeting process, though all of the medium-sized ones did.

Source: Lucas, M., Prowle, M. and Lowth, G. (2013) *Management Accounting Practices of UK Small-Medium-Sized Enterprises*, CIMA, July 2013, p. 6.

Although these four surveys relate to UK and North American businesses, they provide some idea of what is likely also to be the practice elsewhere in the developed world.

Real World 6.4 gives some insight about the accuracy of budgets.

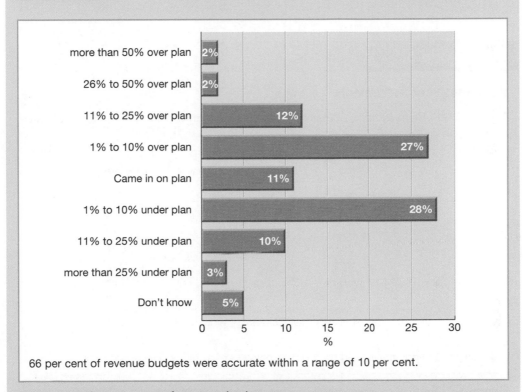
INCREMENTAL AND ZERO-BASE BUDGETING

Budget setting often seems to be done on the basis of what happened last year, with some adjustment for any changes in factors that are expected to affect the forthcoming budget period (for example, inflation). This approach is known as **incremental budgeting** and is often used for **discretionary budgets**, such as research and development and staff training. With this type of budget, the **budget holder** (the manager responsible for the budget) is allocated a sum of money to be spent in the area of activity concerned. Such budgets are referred to as 'discretionary' budgets because the sum allocated is normally at the discretion of senior management.

These budgets are very common in local and central government (and in other public bodies), but are also used in commercial businesses to cover the types of activity just referred to.

Discretionary budgets are often found in areas where there is no clear relationship between inputs (resources applied) and outputs (benefits). Compare this with, say, a raw materials usage budget in a manufacturing business, where the amount of material used and, therefore, the amount of funds involved, are clearly related to the level of production and, ultimately, to sales volumes. Discretionary budgets can easily eat up funds, with no clear benefit being derived. It is often only the proposed periodic increases in these budgets that are closely scrutinised.

Real World 6.5 provides some idea of the extent to which incremental budgeting is used in practice.

Real World 6.5

Budgeting by increments

The 2009 CIMA survey showed that incremental budgeting is quite widely used in practice, as is shown by Figure 6.7.

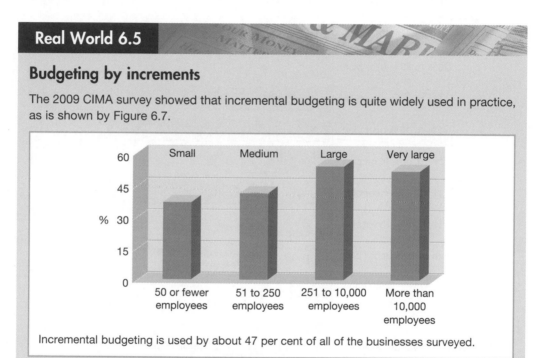

Incremental budgeting is used by about 47 per cent of all of the businesses surveyed.

Figure 6.7 The use of incremental budgeting

It seems reasonable to presume that where businesses use an incremental approach, it is in the context of discretionary budgets.

Source: CIMA (2009) *Management Accounting Tools for Today and Tomorrow*, p. 15.

Zero-base budgeting (ZBB) rests on the philosophy that all spending needs to be justified. Thus, when establishing, say, the training budget each year, it is not automatically accepted that training courses should be financed in the future simply because they were undertaken this year. The training budget will start from a zero base (that is no resources at all) and will only be increased above zero if a good case can be made for the scarce resources of the business to be allocated to this form of activity. Top management will need to be convinced that the proposed activities represent 'value for money'.

ZBB encourages managers to adopt a more questioning approach to their areas of responsibility. To justify the allocation of resources, managers are often forced to think carefully about the particular activities and the ways in which they are undertaken. This questioning approach should result in a more efficient use of business resources. With the increasing computerisation of production, including in the provision of services, there is a progressively larger portion of the total cost of most businesses in areas where the link between outputs and inputs is not always clear. The commitment of resources is, therefore, discretionary rather than demonstrably essential to production. Thus, ZBB is increasingly relevant and seen as an approach to cost management similar to some of the techniques that we discussed in Chapter 5.

Activity 6.10

Can you think of any disadvantages of using ZBB?

The principal problems with ZBB are:

- It is time-consuming and therefore expensive to undertake.
- It can lead to a concentration on cost cutting at the expense of seeing the wider picture.
- Managers whose sphere of responsibility is subjected to ZBB can feel threatened by it.

The benefits of a ZBB approach can be gained to some extent – perhaps at not too great a cost – by using the approach on a selective basis. For example, a particular budget area could be subjected to ZBB-type scrutiny only every third or fourth year. In any case, if ZBB is used more frequently, there is the danger that managers will use the same arguments each year to justify their activities. The process will simply become a mechanical exercise and the benefits will be lost. For a typical business, some areas are likely to benefit from ZBB more than others. As mentioned earlier, the areas most likely to benefit from ZBB involve discretionary spending, such as training, advertising and research and development.

If senior management is aware that their subordinates are likely to feel threatened by the nature of this form of budgeting, care can be taken to apply ZBB with sensitivity. However, in the quest for cost control and value for money, ZBB can result in some tough, but valid, decisions being made.

Real World 6.6 gives some impression of how much ZBB is used in practice.

Real World 6.6

Too low for zero

A significant proportion of UK businesses use ZBB in practice, according to the 2009 CIMA survey. The detail is shown in Figure 6.8.

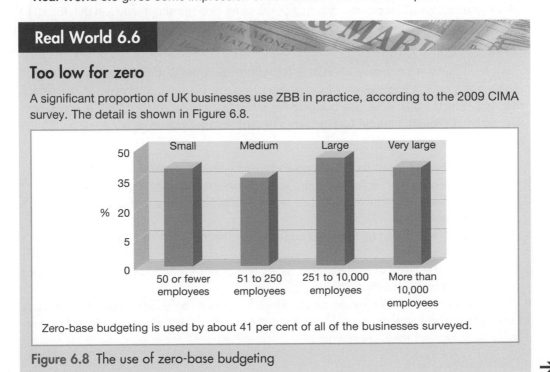

Zero-base budgeting is used by about 41 per cent of all of the businesses surveyed.

Figure 6.8 The use of zero-base budgeting

A separate survey of 406 North American businesses found that, although the popularity of ZBB there had been lower than in the UK, the technique has rapidly grown in popularity recently. The proportion of North American businesses using ZBB jumped from 10 per cent in 2014 to 38 per cent by 2016. Major US food manufacturers seem to have led the way with this increase; Campbell Soup, Kellogg and Kraft Heinz have recently taken up the technique. The growth in the popularity has not been confined to food manufacturers, however.

Sources: CIMA (2009) *Management Accounting Tools for Today and Tomorrow*, p. 15; and McLaughlin, T. (2017), Back to zero: Companies use 1970s budget tool to cut costs as they hunt for growth, *Reuter Business News*, uk. reuter.com, 30 January.

PREPARING BUDGETS

We shall now look in some detail at how the various budgets used by the typical business are prepared, starting with the cash budget and then looking at the others.

The cash budget

It is helpful for us to start with the cash budget because:

- It is a key budget (some people see it as a 'master budget' along with the budgeted income statement and budgeted statement of financial position); most economic aspects of a business are reflected in cash sooner or later. This means that, for a typical business, the cash budget reflects the whole business more comprehensively than any other single budget.
- A very small, unsophisticated business (for example, a corner shop) may feel that full-scale budgeting is not appropriate to its needs, but almost certainly it should prepare a cash budget as a minimum.

Since budgets are normally used only for internal purposes, their format is a matter of management choice and will vary from one business to the next. However, all managers, irrespective of the business, use budgets for similar purposes and so there is some consistency of approach. In most businesses, the cash budget will probably possess the following features:

1 The budget period would be broken down into sub-periods, typically months.
2 The budget would be in columnar form, with one column for each month.
3 Receipts of cash would be identified under various headings and a total for each month's receipts shown.
4 Payments of cash would be identified under various headings and a total for each month's payments shown.
5 The surplus of total cash receipts over payments, or of payments over receipts, for each month would be identified.
6 The running cash balance would be identified. This would be achieved by taking the balance at the end of the previous month and adjusting it for the surplus or deficit of receipts over payments for the current month.

Typically, all of the pieces of information in points 3 to 6 in this list would be useful to management for one reason or another.

Probably the best way to deal with this topic is through an example su as Example 6.1.

Example 6.1

Vierra Popova Ltd is a wholesale business. The budgeted income statements for each of the next six months are as follows:

	Jan £000	Feb £000	Mar £000	Apr £000	May £000	June £000
Sales revenue	52	55	55	60	55	53
Cost of goods sold	(30)	(31)	(31)	(35)	(31)	(32)
Salaries and wages	(10)	(10)	(10)	(10)	(10)	(10)
Electricity	(5)	(5)	(4)	(3)	(3)	(3)
Depreciation	(3)	(3)	(3)	(3)	(3)	(3)
Other overheads	(2)	(2)	(2)	(2)	(2)	(2)
Total expenses	(50)	(51)	(50)	(53)	(49)	(50)
Profit for the month	2	4	5	7	6	3

The business allows all of its customers one month's credit (this means, for example, that cash from sales made during January will be received in February). Sales revenue during December totalled £60,000.

The business plans to maintain inventories at their existing level until March. During that month they are to be reduced by £5,000. Inventories will remain at this lower level indefinitely. Inventories purchases are made on one month's credit. December purchases totalled £30,000. Salaries, wages and 'other overheads' are paid in the month concerned. Electricity is paid quarterly in arrears in March and June. The business plans to buy and pay for a new delivery van in March. This will cost a total of £15,000, but an existing van will be traded in for £4,000 as part of the deal.

The business expects to have £12,000 in cash at the beginning of January.

The cash budget for the six months ending in June will look as follows:

	Jan £000	Feb £000	Mar £000	Apr £000	May £000	June £000
Receipts						
Trade receivables (Note 1)	60	52	55	55	60	55
Payments						
Trade payables (Note 2)	(30)	(30)	(31)	(26)	(35)	(31)
Salaries and wages	(10)	(10)	(10)	(10)	(10)	(10)
Electricity	–	–	(14)	–	–	(9)
Other overheads	(2)	(2)	(2)	(2)	(2)	(2)
Van purchase	–	–	(11)	–	–	–
Total payments	(42)	(42)	(68)	(38)	(47)	(52)
Cash surplus for the month	18	10	(13)	17	13	3
Opening balance (Note 3)	12	30	40	27	44	57
Closing balance	30	40	27	44	57	60

Notes:

1 The cash receipts from trade receivables lag a month behind sales because customers are given a month in which to pay for their purchases. So, December sales will be paid for in January and so on.

2 For inventories to remain constant at the end of each month, the business must replace exactly the amount that has been used. In most months, the purchases of inventories will, therefore, equal the cost of goods sold. During March, however, the business plans to reduce its inventories by £5,000. This means that inventories purchases will be lower than inventories usage in that month. The payments for inventories purchases lag a month behind purchases because the business expects to be allowed a month to pay for what it buys.

3 Each month's cash balance is the previous month's figure plus the cash surplus (or minus the cash deficit) for the current month. The balance at the start of January is £12,000 according to the information provided just before the cash budget (above).

4 Depreciation does not give rise to a cash payment. In the context of profit measurement (in the income statement), depreciation is a very important aspect. Here, however, we are interested only in cash.

Activity 6.11

Looking at the cash budget of Vierra Popova Ltd, what conclusions do you draw and what possible course of action do you recommend regarding the cash balance over the period concerned?

Given the size of the business, there is a fairly large cash balance that seems to be increasing. Management might consider:

■ putting some of the cash into an income-yielding deposit;
■ increasing the investment in non-current (fixed) assets;
■ increasing the investment in current assets;
■ paying a dividend to the owners; and
■ repaying borrowings.

You may have thought of others.

Activity 6.12

Vierra Popova Ltd (Example 6.1) now wishes to prepare its cash budget for the second six months of the year. The budgeted income statements for each month of the second half of the year are as follows:

	July £000	Aug £000	Sept £000	Oct £000	Nov £000	Dec £000
Sales revenue	57	59	62	57	53	51
Cost of goods sold	(32)	(33)	(35)	(32)	(30)	(29)
Salaries and wages	(10)	(10)	(10)	(10)	(10)	(10)
Electricity	(3)	(3)	(4)	(5)	(6)	(6)
Depreciation	(3)	(3)	(3)	(3)	(3)	(3)
Other overheads	(2)	(2)	(2)	(2)	(2)	(2)
Total expenses	(50)	(51)	(54)	(52)	(51)	(50)
Profit for the month	7	8	8	5	2	1

The business will continue to allow all of its customers one month's credit.

It plans to increase inventories from the 30 June level by £1,000 during each month until, and including, September. During the following three months, inventories levels will be decreased by £1,000 each month.

Inventories purchases, which had been made on one month's credit until the June payment, will, starting with the purchases made in June, be made on two months' credit.

Salaries, wages and 'other overheads' will continue to be paid in the month concerned. Electricity is paid quarterly in arrears in September and December.

At the end of December, the business intends to pay off part of some borrowings. This payment is to be such that it will leave the business with a cash balance of £5,000 with which to start next year.

Prepare the cash budget for the six months ending in December. (Remember that any information you need that relates to the first six months of the year, including the cash balance that is expected to be brought forward on 1 July, is given in Example 6.1.)

The cash budget for the six months ended 31 December is:

	July £000	Aug £000	Sept £000	Oct £000	Nov £000	Dec £000
Receipts						
Trade receivables	53	57	59	62	57	53
Payments						
Trade payables (Note 1)	–	(32)	(33)	(34)	(36)	(31)
Salaries and wages	(10)	(10)	(10)	(10)	(10)	(10)
Electricity	–	–	(10)	–	–	(17)
Other overheads	(2)	(2)	(2)	(2)	(2)	(2)
Borrowings repayment (Note 2)	–	–	–	–	–	(131)
Total payments	(12)	(44)	(55)	(46)	(48)	(191)
Cash surplus for the month	41	13	4	16	9	(138)
Opening balance	60	101	114	118	134	143
Closing balance	101	114	118	134	143	5

Notes:

1 There will be no payment to suppliers (trade payables) in July because the June purchases will be made on two months' credit and will therefore be paid in August. The July purchases, which will equal the July cost of sales figure plus the increase in inventories made in July, will be paid for in September and so on.

2 The borrowings repayment is simply the amount that will cause the balance at 31 December to be £5,000.

Preparing other budgets

Although each budget will have its own particular features, many will follow the same sort of pattern as the cash budget. That is, they will show inflows and outflows during each month and the opening and closing balances in each month. Example 6.2 demonstrates the use of some of the other budgets.

Example 6.2

To illustrate these budgets, we shall continue to use the example of Vierra Popova Ltd that we considered in Example 6.1. To the information given there, we need to add the fact that the inventories balance at 1 January was £30,000.

Trade receivables budget

This would normally show the planned amount owed to the business by credit customers at the beginning and at the end of each month, the planned total credit sales revenue for each month and the planned total cash receipts from credit customers (trade receivables). The layout would be something like this:

	Jan £000	Feb £000	Mar £000	Apr £000	May £000	June £000
Opening balance	60	52	55	55	60	55
Sales revenue	52	55	55	60	55	53
Cash receipts	(60)	(52)	(55)	(55)	(60)	(55)
Closing balance	52	55	55	60	55	53

The opening and closing balances represent the amount that the business plans to be owed (in total) by credit customers (trade receivables) at the beginning and end of each month, respectively.

Trade payables budget

Typically this shows the planned amount owed to suppliers by the business at the beginning and at the end of each month, the planned credit purchases for each month and the planned total cash payments to trade payables. The layout would be something like this:

	Jan £000	Feb £000	Mar £000	Apr £000	May £000	June £000
Opening balance	30	30	31	26	35	31
Purchases	30	31	26	35	31	32
Cash payment	(30)	(30)	(31)	(26)	(35)	(31)
Closing balance	30	31	26	35	31	32

The opening and closing balances represent the amount planned to be owed (in total) by the business to suppliers (trade payables), at the beginning and end of each month respectively.

Inventories budget

This would normally show the planned amount of inventories to be held by the business at the beginning and at the end of each month, the planned total inventories purchases for each month and the planned total monthly inventories usage. The layout would be something like this:

	Jan £000	Feb £000	Mar £000	Apr £000	May £000	June £000
Opening balance	30	30	30	25	25	25
Purchases	30	31	26	35	31	32
Inventories used	(30)	(31)	(31)	(35)	(31)	(32)
Closing balance	30	30	25	25	25	25

The opening and closing balances represent the amount of inventories, at cost, planned to be held by the business at the beginning and end of each month respectively.

A *raw materials inventories budget*, for a manufacturing business, would follow a similar pattern, with the 'inventories usage' being the cost of the inventories put into production. A *finished inventories budget* for a manufacturer would also be similar to the one shown above, except that 'inventories manufactured' would replace 'purchases'. A manufacturing business would normally prepare both a raw materials inventories budget and a finished inventories budget. Both of these would typically be based on the full cost of the inventories (that is, including overheads). There is no reason, however, why the inventories should not be valued on a variable cost, or direct cost, basis if this would provide more useful information.

The inventories budget will normally be expressed in financial terms, but may also be expressed in physical terms (for example, kilograms or metres) for individual inventories' items.

Note how the trade receivables, trade payables and inventories budgets in Example 6.2 link to one another, and to the cash budget for the same business shown in Example 6.1. Note particularly that:

- the purchases figures in the trade payables budget and in the inventories budget are identical;
- the cash payments figures in the trade payables budget and the trade payables figures in the cash budget are identical;
- the cash receipts figures in the trade receivables budget and the trade receivables figures in the cash budget are identical.

Other values would link different budgets in a similar way. For example, the row of sales revenue figures in the trade receivables budget would be identical to the sales revenue figures that will be found in the sales budget. This is how the linking (co-ordination), which was discussed earlier in this chapter, is achieved.

Activity 6.13

Have a go at preparing the trade receivables budget for Vierra Popova Ltd for the six months from July to December (see Activity 6.12).

The trade receivables budget for the six months ended 31 December is:

	July £000	Aug £000	Sep £000	Oct £000	Nov £000	Dec £000
Opening balance (Note 1)	53	57	59	62	57	53
Sales revenue (Note 2)	57	59	62	57	53	51
Cash receipts (Note 3)	(53)	(57)	(59)	(62)	(57)	(53)
Closing balance (Note 4)	57	59	62	57	53	51

Notes:
1 The opening trade receivables figure is the previous month's sales revenue figure (sales are on one month's credit).
2 The sales revenue is the current month's figure.
3 The cash received each month is equal to the previous month's sales revenue figure.
4 The closing balance is equal to the current month's sales revenue figure.

Note that if we knew any three of the four figures each month, we could deduce the fourth.

This budget could be set out in any manner that would have given the sort of information that management would require in respect of planned levels of trade receivables and associated transactions.

Activity 6.14

Have a go at preparing the trade payables budget for Vierra Popova Ltd for the six months from July to December (see Activity 6.12). (Hint: Remember that the trade payables settlement period alters from the June purchases onwards.)

→

The trade payables budget for the six months ended 31 December is:

	July £000	Aug £000	Sept £000	Oct £000	Nov £000	Dec £000
Opening balance	32	65	67	70	67	60
Purchases	33	34	36	31	29	28
Cash payments	–	(32)	(33)	(34)	(36)	(31)
Closing balance	65	67	70	67	60	57

This, again, could be set out in any manner that would have given the sort of information that management would require in respect of planned levels of trade payables and associated transactions.

ACTIVITY-BASED BUDGETING

Activity-based budgeting (ABB) extends the principles of activity-based costing, which we discussed in Chapter 5, to the budgeting process. Under a system of ABB, the first step is usually to determine the sales budget. This is, of course, the same starting point as under conventional budgeting. The next step is to identify the activities needed to achieve the budgeted sales, along with their cost drivers. For each activity, a budgeted cost driver rate is established, which is then multiplied by the estimated usage of the cost driver (as determined by the sales budget). This final calculation provides the activity budget for the period. The various steps in the process are shown in diagrammatic form in Figure 6.9 below.

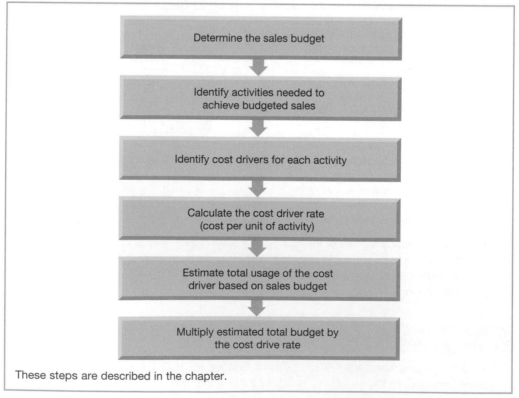

These steps are described in the chapter.

Figure 6.9 Main steps in the ABB process

Example 6.3 should help to make the ABB process clear.

Example 6.3

Danube Ltd produces two products, the Gamma and the Delta. The sales budget for next year shows that 60,000 units of Gamma and 80,000 units of Delta are expected to be sold. Each type of product spends time in the finished goods stores, which has been identified as a cost-driving activity.

Both products are of roughly similar size and have very similar storage needs. It is felt, therefore, that the period spent in the stores ('product weeks') is the cost driver. It is estimated that Product Gamma will spend an average of two weeks in the stores before being sold; for Product Delta, the average period is five weeks.

To derive the activity budget for the finished goods stores, the estimated total usage of the cost driver must be calculated. This will be the total number of 'product weeks' that the products are in store.

Product		Product weeks
Delta	60,000 × 2 weeks =	120,000
Gamma	80,000 × 5 weeks =	400,000
		520,000

The budgeted rate for the cost driver, based on figure calculated using ABC, has been set at £1.50 per product week.

The number of product weeks will then be multiplied by the budgeted rate for the cost driver to derive the activity budget figure. That is:

$$520,000 \times £1.50 = £780,000$$

A similar process will be carried out for the other cost-driving activities identified.

Note that budgets are prepared based on the various activities carried out. (In the case of Example 6.3 above, it was finished goods stores.) They are not prepared according to function, as occurs with under the conventional approach. Under ABB, each activity has a cost pool and there is a separate budget for each cost pool.

Through the application of ABC principles, the factors that cause costs are known and there is a direct linking of costs with output. This means that ABB should provide a better understanding of future resource needs and more accurate budgets. It should also provide a better understanding of the effect on budgeted costs of changes in the usage of the cost driver because of the explicit relationship between cost drivers, activities and costs.

Control should be improved within an ABB environment for two reasons:

- By developing more accurate budgets, managers can be provided with demanding yet realistic targets.
- ABB should ensure that costs are closely linked to responsibilities. Managers who have control over particular cost drivers will become accountable for the costs that are caused. An important principle of effective budgeting is that those responsible for meeting a particular budget (budget holders) should have control over the events that affect performance in their area.

As with ABC, a system of ABB can be costly to implement and to run. A careful weighing of costs and benefits should therefore be carried out before considering its adoption. Furthermore, it is only feasible to adopt ABB if the business is also adopting a system of ABC. ABB and traditional absorption costing will not blend together.

Real World 6.7 provides some indication of the extent to which ABB is used in practice.

Real World 6.7

Quite a lot of activity

The 2009 CIMA survey showed that ABB is used by a significant proportion of businesses in practice, as shown in Figure 6.10.

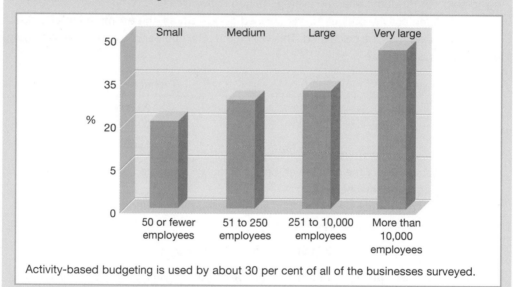

Activity-based budgeting is used by about 30 per cent of all of the businesses surveyed.

Figure 6.10 The use of activity-based budgeting

Unsurprisingly, the percentages that use ABB almost precisely match the proportion of the same survey sample that use activity-based costing. It is logical that businesses that use an activity-based approach to deriving their costs should also apply the same approach to holding managers responsible for the costs that are incurred, through the budgets.

Source: CIMA (2009) *Management Accounting Tools for Today and Tomorrow*, p. 15.

NON-FINANCIAL MEASURES IN BUDGETING

The efficiency of internal operations and customer satisfaction levels have become of critical importance to businesses striving to survive in an increasingly competitive environment. As we shall see in Chapter 10, non-financial performance indicators have an important role to play in assessing performance in such key areas as customer/supplier delivery times, set-up times, defect levels and customer satisfaction levels.

There is no reason why budgeting needs to be confined to financial targets and measures. Non-financial measures can also be used as the basis for targets and can be brought into the budgeting process. They can then be reported alongside the financial targets for the business.

BUDGETS AND MANAGEMENT BEHAVIOUR

All accounting reports are intended to affect human behaviour. In the case of budgets, it is the behaviour of managers that is the focus of interest. We have seen that budgets try to encourage managers to work towards the business's objectives and to do this in a co-ordinated manner.

Whether budgets are effective is of crucial importance to a business. We shall examine this topic in detail in Chapter 7, after considering how budgets help managers to exercise control.

WHO NEEDS BUDGETS?

Until relatively recently it would have been a heresy to suggest that budgeting was not of central importance to any business. The benefits of budgeting, mentioned earlier in this chapter, have been widely recognised and the vast majority of businesses prepare annual budgets (see Real World 6.3 on page 208). However, there is increasing concern that, in today's highly dynamic and competitive environment, budgets may actually be harmful to the achievement of business objectives. This has led a small number of businesses to abandon traditional budgets as a tool of planning and control.

Various criticisms have been made of the conventional budgeting process. It is claimed, for example, that:

- Budgets cannot deal with a fast-changing environment and they are often out of date before the start of the budget period.
- They focus too much management attention on the achievement of short-term financial targets. Instead, managers should focus on the things that create value for the business (for example, innovation, building brand loyalty, responding quickly to competitive threats and so on).
- They reinforce a 'command and control' structure that concentrates power in the hands of senior managers and prevents junior managers from exercising autonomy. This is particularly true where a top-down approach that allocates budgets to managers is being used. Where managers feel constrained, attempts to retain and recruit able managers can be difficult.
- Budgeting takes up an enormous amount of management time that could be better used. In practice, budgeting can be a lengthy process that may involve much negotiation, reworking and updating. However, this may add little to the achievement of business objectives.
- Budgets are based around business functions (sales, marketing, production and so on). To achieve the business's objectives, however, the focus should be on business processes that cut across functional boundaries and reflect the needs of the customer.
- They encourage incremental thinking by employing a 'last year plus *x* per cent' approach to planning. This can inhibit the development of 'break out' strategies that may be necessary in a fast-changing environment.
- They can protect costs rather than lower costs, particularly in the area of discretionary budgets. In some cases, a fixed budget for an activity, such as research and development, is allocated to a manager. If the amount is not spent, the budget may be taken away and, in future periods, the budget for this activity may be either reduced or eliminated. Such a response to unused budget allocations may encourage managers to spend the whole of the budget, irrespective of need, in order to protect the allocations they receive.

- They promote 'sharp' practice among managers. In order to meet budget targets, managers may try to negotiate lower sales targets or higher cost allocations than they feel is really necessary. This helps them to build some 'slack' into the budgets and so meeting the budget becomes easier (see Reference 5 at the end of the chapter).

Figure 6.11 summarises the common criticisms of traditional budgeting.

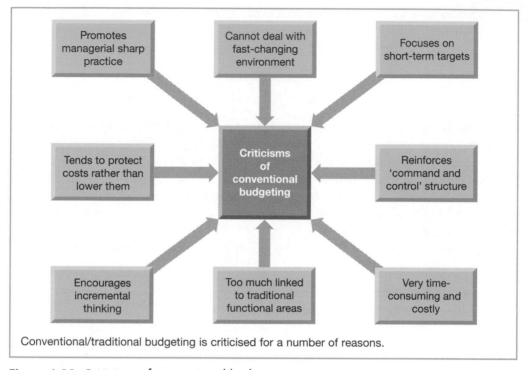

Figure 6.11 Criticisms of conventional budgeting

Although some believe that many of the problems identified can be solved by better budgeting systems such as activity-based budgeting and zero-base budgeting and by taking a more flexible approach, others believe that a more radical solution is required.

Real World 6.8 is taken from a question and answer column written by John Timpson. He was the chief executive of a very successful high street shoe-repairing and key-cutting business with over 800 branches (and expanding) throughout the UK. His answer to a question about budgeting echoes some of the criticisms of conventional budgeting that we have just considered. The answer appeared in the *Daily Telegraph*.

Real World 6.8

Cobblers

A long time ago I learnt that having a lot of figures doesn't mean you are better informed – it just makes life more complicated.

In the 1980s, we set budget sales figures for every shop every week, our Finance Director insisting that individual shop numbers added up to his company budget. It was a tortuous process that took weeks of area management time and although head office hoped the plan would provide the perfect incentive, it made no difference to our performance. Sales never seemed to follow our forecast – our customers clearly didn't know how much they were expected to spend! I scrapped the budgetary process and for the last 20 years we have compared branch performance with last year – it has saved us a lot of bother.

Life at Timpson has little to do with budgets and we don't have KPIs (key performance indicators). We have bought several loss making companies and found that every one of them was monitoring minute detail from Head Office – Sketchley, the dry cleaners, were keen on keeping a count of their 'supercrease' sales; Max Spielmann, the photo chain, kept an eye on the average price of picture frames; and shoe repairers Mr Minit was controlling costs so closely that they recorded every shop's expenditure on postage stamps. While management concentrated on the detail they seemed to miss out on the big picture. Instead of studying their computers they should have visited more shops to talk to the colleagues who met their customers.

Of the few figures I receive, the most important is the bank balance compared with the same day last year. It gives me a daily health check on our business. I get a daily report on all the new shops we have opened in the last three months and a weekly sales report for the company, in total, and by department. We revise our profit forecast every week and produce management accounts every month, but I seldom look beyond the front page summary.

The only time I ask for detail is when we are introducing a new service – like our current growth in portraits, locksmith work and complicated car keys. If you know which shops are successful you can pass their secret around the rest of the business.

With little to look at it is easy to see how the company is doing and I have plenty of time left to visit our branches and discover what is really going on.

Source: John Timpson (2011), The management column, *Daily Telegraph* Business, 5 June.

BEYOND CONVENTIONAL BUDGETING

In recent years, a few businesses have abandoned budgeting, although they still recognise the need for forward planning. No one seriously doubts that there must be appropriate systems in place to steer a business towards its objectives. It is claimed, however, that the systems adopted should reflect a broader, more integrated approach to planning. The new systems that have been implemented are often based around a 'leaner' financial planning process that is more closely linked to other measurement and reward systems. Emphasis is placed on the use of rolling forecasts and key performance indicators (such as market share, customer satisfaction and innovations) that identify both monetary and non-monetary targets to be achieved both over the long term and in the short term. These are often very demanding ('stretch') targets, based on benchmarks that have been set by world-class businesses.

The new 'beyond budgeting' model promotes a more decentralised, participative approach to managing the business. It is claimed that the traditional hierarchical management structure, where decision making is concentrated at the higher levels of the hierarchy, encourages a culture of dependency where meeting the budget targets set by senior managers is the key to managerial success. This traditional structure is replaced by a network structure where decision making is devolved to 'front-line' managers. A more open, questioning attitude among employees is encouraged by the new structure. There is a sharing of knowledge and best practice; protective behaviour by managers is discouraged. In addition, rewards are linked to targets based on improvement in relative performance rather than to meeting the budget. It is claimed that this new approach allows greater adaptability to changing conditions, increases performance and increases motivation among staff.

Figure 6.12 sets out the main differences between the traditional and 'beyond budgeting' planning models.

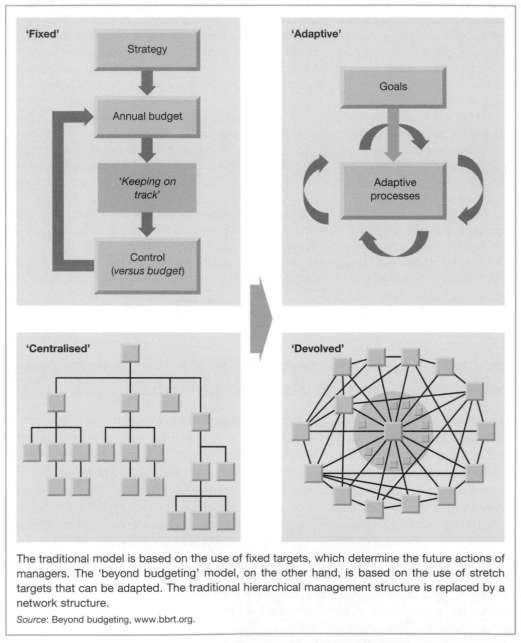

The traditional model is based on the use of fixed targets, which determine the future actions of managers. The 'beyond budgeting' model, on the other hand, is based on the use of stretch targets that can be adapted. The traditional hierarchical management structure is replaced by a network structure.

Source: Beyond budgeting, www.bbrt.org.

Figure 6.12 The traditional planning model versus the 'beyond budgeting' planning model

Real World 6.9 looks at the management planning systems at Toyota, the well-known Japanese motor vehicle business. Toyota does not use conventional budgets.

Steering Toyota

The Beyond Budgeting Institute (BBI) is at the forefront of those who argue that budgeting systems have an adverse effect on the ability of businesses to compete effectively. The following is an outline of Toyota's planning and control systems, published by BBI:

> Despite incurring its first loss in many decades (not even Toyota can make a profit when the market suddenly collapses by over 30 per cent) Toyota remains the best managed manufacturing company in the world. Its Toyota Production System is legendary and spawned the lean manufacturing movement. The management focus is on continuously improving systems and meeting internal and external customers' needs. Everyone has a voice and is expected to contribute to the continuous improvement of their work. Medium-term operational goals aimed at best practice are set at every level. Planning takes place at the plant/team level and happens monthly within a clear strategic framework (12 month rolling forecasts support capacity planning). Knowledge about current performance is visual and immediate (e.g. throughput, downtime, inventory levels). Resources are made available just-in-time to meet each customer order. There are no fixed targets, no annual budget contracts and people are trusted with information to make the right decisions.

Source: BBI, *Toyota – A World Class manufacturing model*, www.bbrt.org/beyond-budgeting, accessed 13 April 2017.

Whether the trickle of businesses that now seek an alternative to budgets will turn into a flood remains to be seen. However, it is clear that in today's highly competitive environment a business must be flexible and responsive to changing conditions. Management systems that in any way hinder these attributes will not survive.

LONG LIVE BUDGETS!

Despite the criticisms, budgeting remains a very widely used technique and Real World 6.3 provides supporting evidence. Furthermore, **Real World 6.10** suggests that things are unlikely to change much in the near future. It contains an account of a round table discussion at a Better Budgeting forum. Although the discussion took place some time ago, the points made still seem relevant and are well put.

Alive and kicking

A Better Budgeting forum was attended by representatives of 32 large organisations, including BAA (the airport operator), the BBC, Ford Motors, Sainsbury (the supermarket business) and Unilever (the household goods group).
The report of the forum discussions said:

> If you were to believe all that has been written in recent years, you'd be forgiven for thinking that budgeting is on its way to becoming extinct. Various research reports allude to the widespread dissatisfaction with the bureaucratic exercise in cost cutting that budgeting is accused of having become. Budgets are pilloried as being out of touch with the needs of modern business and accused of taking too long, costing too much and encouraging all sorts of perverse behaviour.

Yet if there was one conclusion to emerge from the day's discussions it was that budgets are in fact alive and well. Not only did all the organisations present operate a formal budget but all bar two had no interest in getting rid of it. Quite the opposite – although aware of the problems it can cause, the participants by and large regarded the budgeting system and the accompanying processes as indispensable.

Later in the report, in what could have been a reference to the use of 'rolling forecasts' among businesses that claim to have abandoned budgeting (see Real World 6.9, relating to Toyota), it said:

It quickly became obvious that, as one participant put it, 'one man's budget is another man's rolling forecast'. What people refer to when they talk about budgeting could in reality be very different things.

This presumably meant that businesses that abandon 'budgets' reintroduce them under another name.

Source: The Chartered Institute of Management Accountants and The Faculty of Finance and Management, Institute of Chartered Accountants in England and Wales (2004) *Better Budgeting*, March.

Activity 6.15

John Timpson (see Real World 6.8) denies having a budgetary process for his business. From what he says, do you agree?

Although Timpson may no longer have a full budgeting system in place, there are still benchmarks and targets. It can be argued that these constitute a rudimentary budgeting system. He compares branch performance with the previous year and the bank balance with the same day in the previous year. This is presumably because he sees last year's figures as some sort of benchmark or budget. Furthermore, he mentions 'profit forecasts', which may well suggest a target, or budget, to be achieved.

Real World 6.11 provides survey evidence of senior finance staff that indicates considerable support for budgets. Nevertheless, many recognise that budgeting is not always well managed and acknowledge some of the criticisms of budgets mentioned earlier.

Real World 6.11

Problems with budgets

The survey of the opinions of senior finance staff at 340 businesses of various sizes and operating in a wide range of industries in North America that was mentioned earlier (see Real World 6.3) showed that 86 per cent of those surveyed regarded the budget process as either 'essential' or 'very important'. However,

- 66 per cent thought that budgeting in their business was not agile or flexible enough;
- 59 per cent were not very confident that budget targets would be met in the following year;
- 67 per cent felt that their business devoted inappropriate amounts of time to budgeting (51 per cent felt it was too much and 16 per cent too little);
- 76 per cent felt that their businesses used inappropriate software in the budgeting process (generally using a spreadsheet rather than custom-designed software).

Source: BPM Forum (2008) *Perfect how you project*.

Despite the undoubted problems with budgeting, and the way in which it is often carried out, the 'beyond budgeting' approach is not popular in practice, as revealed by **Real World 6.12**.

Not going into the beyond

The 2009 CIMA survey showed that the 'beyond budgeting' philosophy is little followed in practice, as is shown by Figure 6.13.

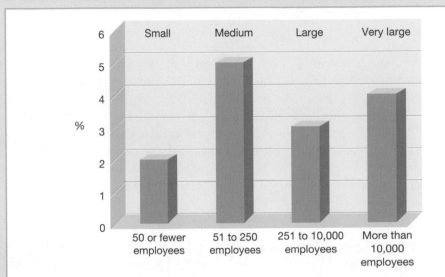

The 'beyond budgeting' philosophy is followed by only about 3 per cent of all of the businesses surveyed.

Source: CIMA (2009) *Management Accounting Tools for Today and Tomorrow*, p. 15.

Figure 6.13 The use of the 'beyond budgeting' philosophy

A survey of 588 management accountants working in Canada and the USA, working in businesses of a large range of sizes and activities, indicated that budgets are overwhelmingly regarded as key tools in management. The results may be summarised as follows:

Percentage of businesses where the budget was regarded as:

'more helpful than harmful'	28
'good value'	27
'very good value'	20
'excellent value'	7

Thus, 82 per cent of businesses regarded budgeting as broadly beneficial.

Only 5 per cent of management accountants surveyed worked in organisations where managers were considering abandoning budgeting. The survey revealed that steps had recently been taken or were to be taken to overcome some of the criticisms identified by the 'beyond budgeting' advocates.

Source: Libby, T. and Lindsay, R. (2010) Beyond budgeting or budgeting reconsidered? A survey of North-American budgeting practice, *Management Accounting Research*, Vol. 21, Issue 1, pp. 56–75.

A survey of 40 managers in UK businesses showed that all of their businesses used budgets, with only 5 per cent expressing serious doubt about their usefulness. Like the survey of Canadian and US management accountants, this study showed that the nature of budgeting was changing to overcome perceived problems.

Source: Dugdale, D. and Lyne, S. (2010) Budgeting practice and organisational structure, Chartered Institute of Management Accountants, *Research*, Volume 6, Issue 4, April.

Do you think that the continuing popularity of traditional budgeting is the result of habit and an unwillingness to try a different approach?

It might be true that businesses are simply following the traditional approach without giving serious consideration to an alternative approach. This, however, does not seem likely, particularly for large, well-managed, businesses. A great deal of thought has probably been given to the alternative but it has been concluded that the traditional approach has more to commend it.

Maintaining a system of budgeting is very costly, yet in this era where there is acute consciousness of the need to control costs, budgeting remains very popular. It is very unlikely that businesses like BSkyB, Greene King, Rolls-Royce, Ford Motors, Sainsbury and Unilever, all mentioned in the chapter, would blindly continue with such a costly activity unless they were confident that it was worth it. The senior managements of major businesses, must have asked the question: is budgeting economically beneficial? Their deliberations must have assured them that it is.

Self-assessment question 6.1 pulls together the points made in this chapter about preparing budgets.

Antonio Ltd, which makes and sells one standard product, has planned production and sales for the next nine months as follows:

	Production Units	Sales Units
May	350	350
June	400	400
July	500	400
August	600	500
September	600	600
October	700	650
November	750	700
December	750	800
January	750	750

During the period, the business plans to advertise so as to generate these increases in sales. Payments for advertising of £1,000 and £1,500 will be made in July and October respectively.

The selling price per unit will be £20 throughout the period. Forty per cent of sales are normally made on two months' credit. The other 60 per cent are settled within the month of the sale.

Raw materials will be held for one month before they are taken into production. Purchases of raw materials will be on one month's credit (buy one month, pay the next). The cost of raw materials is £8 per unit of production.

Other direct production expenses, including labour, are £6 per unit of production. These will be paid in the month concerned.

Various production overheads, which at present are £1,800 a month and are expected to continue at that level until the end of June, are expected to rise to £2,000 each month from

1 July to 31 October. They are expected to rise again from 1 November to £2,400 a month and to remain at that level for the foreseeable future. These overheads include a steady £400 each month for depreciation. Overheads are planned to be paid 80 per cent in the month of production and 20 per cent in the following month.

To help to meet the planned increased production, a new item of plant will be bought and delivered in August. The cost of this item is £6,600; the contract with the supplier will specify that this will be paid in three equal amounts in September, October and November.

The raw materials inventories level is planned to be enough for 500 units of production on 1 July. The balance at the bank on the same day is planned to be £7,500.

Required:

(a) Draw up the following for the six months ending 31 December:
   (1) A raw materials inventories budget, showing both physical quantities and financial values.
   (2) A trade payables budget.
   (3) A cash budget.
(b) The cash budget reveals a potential cash deficiency during October and November. Can you suggest any ways in which a modification of plans could overcome this problem?

The solution to this question can be found at the back of the book on pp. 517–519.

SUMMARY

The main points of this chapter may be summarised as follows:

A budget is a short-term business plan, expressed in financial or in physical terms.

- Budgets are the short-term means of working towards the business's objectives.
- They are usually prepared for a one-year period with sub-periods of a month.
- There is usually a separate budget for each key area.

Periodic and continual budgets

- Periodic budgets are prepared for a particular period (usually one year).
- Continual (rolling) budgets are continually updated, thereby ensuring, that there are budgets for a full planning period.

Uses of budgets

- Promote forward thinking.
- Help coordinate the various aspects of the business.
- Motivate performance.
- Provide the basis of a system of control.
- Provide a system of authorisation.

The budget-setting process

- Establish who will take responsibility.
- Communicate guidelines.

→

- Identify key factor.
- Prepare budget for key factor area.
- Prepare draft budgets for all other areas.
- Review and coordinate.
- Prepare master budgets (income statement and statement of financial position).
- Communicate the budgets to interested parties.
- Monitor performance relative to budget.

Incremental budgeting and zero-base budgeting (ZBB)

- Incremental budgets are often based on those of previous periods, with some adjustment for factors affecting the forthcoming period.
- ZBB rests on the philosophy that all spending must be justified.
- ZBB promotes a more questioning approach in order to achieve a more efficient use of resources.

Preparing budgets

- There is no standard style – practicality and usefulness are the key issues.
- They are usually prepared in columnar form, with a column for each month (or similarly short period).
- Each budget must link (co-ordinate) with others.

Activity-based budgeting (ABB)

- ABB extends the principles of ABC to budgeting.
- Budgets are based on the cost-driving activity rather than a business function.
- Can result in more accurate budgets and closer links between costs and management responsibilities.

Criticisms of budgets

- Cannot deal with rapid change.
- Focus on short-term financial targets, rather than value creation.
- Encourage a 'top-down' management style.
- Can be time-consuming.
- Based around traditional business functions and do not cross boundaries.
- Encourage incremental thinking (last year's figure, plus x per cent).
- Protect rather than lower costs.
- Promote 'sharp' practice among managers.
- Budgeting is still widely regarded as useful and extensively practised despite the criticisms and the costliness of a traditional budgeting system.
- Even businesses that claim to have abandoned budgets use planning and control devices that appear to be budgets by another name.

REFERENCES

1 BPM Forum (2008) Perfect how you project.

2 O'Mahoney, J. and Lyon, J. (2015) Planning, budgeting and forecasting: An eye to the future, KPMG/ACCA.

3 PWC (2010) *Breaking the cycle; The case for eliminating the budget*, PWC.

4 Durfee, D. (2006) Alternative budgeting, *CFO Magazine*, June.

5 Teach, E. (2014) No time for budgets, *CFO Magazine*, 27 May.

FURTHER READING

If you would like to explore the topics covered in this chapter in more depth, we recommend the following:

Atkinson, A., Kaplan, R., Matsumura, E. and Young, S.M. (2013) *Management Accounting*, 6th edn, Pearson, Chapter 10.

Bhimani, A. Horngren, C., Datar, S. and Rajan, M. (2015), *Management and Cost Accounting*, 6th edn, Pearson, Chapter 14.

Drury, C. (2015) *Management and Cost Accounting*, 9th edn, Cengage Learning EMEA, Chapter 15.

Hilton, R. and Platt, D. (2014) *Managerial Accounting*, McGraw-Hill Higher Education, Chapter 9.

REVIEW QUESTIONS

Solutions to these questions can be found at the back of the book on p. 530

6.1 Define a budget. How is a budget different from a forecast?

6.2 What were the five uses of budgets that were identified in the chapter?

6.3 What do budgets have to do with control?

6.4 What is a budget committee? What purpose does it serve?

Exercises with coloured numbers have solutions given at the back of the book on pp. 549–553.

Basic-level exercises

6.1 Prolog Ltd is a small wholesaler of high-specification personal computers. It has in recent months been selling 50 machines a month at a price of £2,000 each. These machines cost £1,600 each. A new model has just been launched and this is expected to offer greatly enhanced performance. Its selling price and cost will be the same as for the old model. From the beginning of January, sales are planned to increase at a rate of 20 machines each month until the end of June, when sales will amount to 170 units a month. Sales are planned to continue at that level thereafter. Operating costs including depreciation of £2,000 a month are planned as follows:

	Jan	Feb	Mar	Apr	May	June
Operating costs (£000)	6	8	10	12	12	12

Prolog expects to receive no credit for operating costs. Additional shelving for storage will be bought, installed and paid for in April, costing £12,000. Tax of £25,000 is due at the end of March. Prolog anticipates that trade receivables will amount to two months' sales revenue. To give its customers a good level of service, Prolog plans to hold enough inventories at the end of each month to fulfil anticipated demand from customers in the following month. The computer manufacturer, however, grants one month's credit to Prolog. Prolog Ltd's statement of financial position is:

Statement of financial position at 31 December

	£000
ASSETS	
Non-current assets	80
Current assets	
Inventories	112
Trade receivables	200
Cash	–
	312
Total assets	392
Equity and liabilities	
Equity	
Share capital (25p ordinary shares)	10
Retained profit	177
	187
Current liabilities	
Trade payables	112
Taxation	25
Overdraft	68
	205
Total equity and liabilities	392

Required:

(a) Prepare a cash budget for Prolog Ltd showing the cash balance or required overdraft for the six months ending 30 June.

(b) State briefly what further information a banker would require from Prolog Ltd before granting additional overdraft facilities for the anticipated expansion of sales.

6.2 You have overheard the following statements:

(a) 'A budget is a forecast of what is expected to happen in a business during the next year.'

(b) 'Monthly budgets must be prepared with a column for each month so that you can see the whole year at a glance, month by month.'

(c) 'Budgets are OK but they stifle all initiative. No manager worth employing would work for a business that seeks to control through budgets.'

(d) 'Activity-based budgeting is an approach that takes account of the planned volume of activity in order to deduce the figures to go into the budget.'

(e) 'Any sensible person would start with the sales budget and build up the other budgets from there.'

Required:

Critically discuss these statements, explaining any technical terms.

Intermediate-level exercises

6.3 A nursing home, which is linked to a large hospital, has been examining its budgetary control procedures, with particular reference to overhead costs.

The level of activity in the facility is measured by the number of patients treated in the budget period. For the current year, the budget stands at 6,000 patients and this is expected to be met.

For months 1 to 6 of this year (assume 12 months of equal length), 2,700 patients were treated. The actual variable overhead costs incurred during this six-month period are as follows:

Expense	£
Staffing	59,400
Power	27,000
Supplies	54,000
Other	8,100
Total	148,500

The hospital accountant believes that the variable overhead costs will be incurred at the same rate during months 7 to 12 of the year.

Fixed overheads are budgeted for the whole year as follows:

Expense	£
Supervision	120,000
Depreciation/financing	187,200
Other	64,800
Total	372,000

Required:

(a) Present an overheads budget for the six-month period ending the year (one budget). You should show each expense. What is the total overhead cost for each patient that would be incorporated into any statistics?

(b) The nursing home actually treated 3,800 patients during months 7 to 12, the actual variable overheads were £203,300 and the actual fixed overheads were £190,000. In summary form, examine how well the home exercised control over its overheads.

(c) Interpret your analysis and point out any limitations or assumptions.

6.4 Linpet Ltd is to be incorporated on 1 June. The opening statement of financial position of the business will then be as follows:

	£
Assets	
Cash at bank	60,000
Share capital	
£1 ordinary shares	60,000

During June, the business intends to make payments of £40,000 for a leasehold property, £10,000 for equipment and £6,000 for a motor vehicle. The business will also purchase initial trading inventories costing £22,000 on credit.

The business has produced the following estimates:

1 Sales revenue for June will be £8,000 and will increase at the rate of £3,000 a month until, and including, September. In October, sales revenue will rise to £22,000, and in subsequent months it will be maintained at this figure.

2 The gross profit percentage (that is, (gross profit/sales) ×100) on goods sold will be 25 per cent.

3 There is a risk that supplies of trading inventories will be interrupted towards the end of the accounting year. The business therefore intends to build up its initial level of inventories (£22,000) by purchasing £1,000 of inventories each month in addition to the monthly purchases necessary to satisfy monthly sales requirements. All purchases of inventories (including the initial inventories) will be on one month's credit.

4 Sales revenue will be divided equally between cash and credit sales. Credit customers are expected to pay two months after the sale is agreed.

5 Wages and salaries will be £900 a month. Other overheads will be £500 a month for the first four months and £650 a month thereafter. Both types of expense will be payable when incurred.

6 80 per cent of sales revenue will be generated by salespeople who will receive 5 per cent commission on sales revenue. The commission is payable one month after the sale is agreed.

7 The business intends to purchase further equipment in November for £7,000 cash.

8 Depreciation will be provided at the rate of 5 per cent a year on property and 20 per cent a year on equipment. (Depreciation has not been included in the overheads mentioned in point 5 above.)

Required:
(a) State why a cash budget is required for a business.
(b) Prepare a cash budget for Linpet Ltd for the six-month period to 30 November.

6.5 Lewisham Ltd manufactures one product line – the Zenith. Plans over the next few months are as follows:

1 *Sales demand*

	Units
July	180,000
August	240,000
September	200,000
October	180,000

Each Zenith will sell for £3.

2 *Receipts from sales.* Payments from credit customers are expected to be 70 per cent during the month of sale, and 28 per cent during the following month. The remaining trade receivables are expected to go bad (that is, to be uncollectable).

Credit customers who pay in the month of sale are entitled to deduct a 2 per cent discount from the invoice price.

3 *Finished goods inventories.* These are expected to be 40,000 units at 1 July. The business's policy is that, in future, the inventories at the end of each month should equal 20 per cent of the following month's planned sales requirements.

4 *Raw materials inventories.* These are expected to be 40,000 kg on 1 July. The business's policy is that, in future, the inventories at the end of each month should equal 50 per cent of the following month's planned production requirements. Each Zenith

requires 0.5 kg of the raw material, which costs £1.50/kg. Raw materials purchases are paid in the month after purchase.

5 *Labour and overheads.* The direct labour cost of each Zenith is £0.50. The variable overhead element of each Zenith is £0.30. Fixed overheads, including depreciation of £25,000, total £47,000 a month. All labour and overheads are paid during the month in which they arise.

6 *Cash in hand.* At 1 August the business plans to have a bank balance (in funds) of £20,000.

Required:
Prepare the following budgets:

(a) Finished inventories budget (expressed in units of Zenith) for each of the three months July, August and September.
(b) Raw materials inventories budget (expressed in kilograms of the raw material) for the two months July and August.
(c) Cash budget for August and September.

Advanced-level exercises

6.6 Daniel Chu Ltd, a new business, will start production on 1 April, but sales will not start until 1 May. Planned sales for the next nine months are as follows:

	Sales Units
May	500
June	600
July	700
August	800
September	900
October	900
November	900
December	800
January	700

The selling price of a unit will be a consistent £100 and all sales will be made on one month's credit. It is planned that sufficient finished goods inventories for each month's sales should be available at the end of the previous month.

Raw materials purchases will be such that there will be sufficient raw materials inventories available at the end of each month precisely to meet the following month's planned production. This planned policy will operate from the end of April. Purchases of raw materials will be on one month's credit. The cost of raw material is £40 a unit of finished product.

The direct labour cost, which is variable with the level of production, is planned to be £20 a unit of finished production. Production overheads are planned to be £20,000 each month, including £3,000 for depreciation. Non-production overheads are planned to be £11,000 a month, of which £1,000 will be depreciation.

Various non-current (fixed) assets costing £250,000 will be bought and paid for during April.

Except where specified, assume that all payments take place in the same month as the cost is incurred.

The business will raise £300,000 in cash from a share issue in April.

Required:
Draw up the following for the six months ending 30 September:

(a) A finished inventories budget, showing just physical quantities.
(b) A raw materials inventories budget showing both physical quantities and financial values.

(c) A trade payables budget.

(d) A trade receivables budget.

(e) A cash budget.

6.7 Newtake Records Ltd owns a small chain of shops selling rare classical and jazz recordings. At the beginning of June the business had an overdraft of £35,000 and the bank had asked for this to be eliminated by the end of November. As a result, the directors have recently decided to review their plans for the next six months.

The following plans were prepared for the business some months earlier:

	May £000	June £000	July £000	Aug £000	Sept £000	Oct £000	Nov £000
Sales revenue	180	230	320	250	140	120	110
Purchases	135	180	142	94	75	66	57
Administration expenses	52	55	56	53	48	46	45
Selling expenses	22	24	28	26	21	19	18
Taxation payment	–	–	–	22	–	–	–
Finance payments	5	5	5	5	5	5	5
Shop refurbishment	–	–	14	18	6	–	–

Notes:

1 The inventories level at 1 June was £112,000. The business believes it is preferable to maintain a minimum inventories level of £40,000 of goods over the period to 30 November.

2 Suppliers allow one month's credit. The first three months' purchases are subject to a contractual agreement, which must be honoured.

3 The gross profit margin, that is (gross profit/sales) × 100%, is 40 per cent.

4 Cash from all sales is received in the month of sale. However, 50 per cent of customers pay with a credit card. The charge made by the credit card business to Newtake Records Ltd is 3 per cent of the sales revenue value. These charges are in addition to the selling expenses identified in the table immediately preceding these notes. The credit card business pays Newtake Records Ltd in the month of sale.

5 The business has a bank loan, which it is paying off in monthly instalments of £5,000. The interest element represents 20 per cent of each instalment.

6 Administration expenses are paid when incurred. This item includes a charge of £15,000 each month in respect of depreciation.

7 Selling expenses are payable in the following month.

Required (working to the nearest £1,000):

(a) Prepare a cash budget for the six months ending 30 November which shows the cash balance at the end of each month.

(b) Prepare the inventories budget for the six months to 30 November which shows the inventories position at the end of each month.

(c) Prepare a budgeted income statement for the whole of the six-month period ending 30 November. (A monthly breakdown of profit is *not* required.)

(d) What problems is Newtake Records Ltd likely to face in the next six months? Can you suggest how the business might deal with these problems?

6.8 Brown and Jeffreys, a West Midlands business, makes one standard product for use in the motor trade. The product, known as the Fuel Miser, for which the business holds the patent, when fitted to the fuel system of production model cars has the effect of reducing petrol consumption.

Part of the production is sold direct to a local car manufacturer, which fits the Fuel Miser as an optional extra to several of its models. The rest of the production is sold through various retail outlets, garages and so on.

Brown and Jeffreys assemble the Fuel Miser, but all three components are manufactured by local engineering businesses. The three components are codenamed A, B and C. One Fuel Miser consists of one of each component.

The planned sales for the first seven months of the forthcoming accounting period, by channels of distribution and in terms of Fuel Miser units, are as follows:

	Jan	Feb	Mar	Apr	May	June	July
Manufacturers	4,000	4,000	4,500	4,500	4,500	4,500	4,500
Retail and so on	2,000	2,700	3,200	3,000	2,700	2,500	2,400
	6,000	6,700	7,700	7,500	7,200	7,000	6,900

The following further information is available:

1 There will be inventories of finished units at 1 January of 7,000 Fuel Misers.
2 The inventories of raw materials at 1 January will be:
   A 10,000 units
   B 16,500 units
   C 7,200 units
3 The selling price of Fuel Misers is to be £10 each to the motor manufacturer and £12 each to retail outlets.
4 The maximum production capacity of the business is 7,000 units a month. There is no possibility of increasing this.
5 Assembly of each Fuel Miser will take 5 minutes of direct labour. Direct labour is paid at the rate of £14.40 an hour during the month of production.
6 The components are each expected to cost the following:
   A £2.50
   B £1.30
   C £0.80
7 Indirect costs are to be paid at a regular rate of £32,000 each month.
8 The cash at the bank at 1 January will be £2,620.

The planned sales volumes must be met and the business intends to pursue the following policies *for as many months as possible*, consistent with meeting the sales targets:

■ Finished inventories at the end of each month are to equal the following month's total sales to retail outlets and half the total of the following month's sales to the motor manufacturer.
■ Raw materials at the end of each month are to be sufficient to cover production requirements for the following month. The production for July will be 6,800 units.
■ Suppliers of raw materials are to be paid during the month following purchase. The payment for January will be £21,250.
■ Customers will pay in the month of sale, in the case of sales to the motor manufacturer, and the month after sale, in the case of retail sales. Retail sales during December were 2,000 units at £12 each.

Required:
Prepare the following budgets in monthly columnar form, both in terms of money and units (where relevant), for the six months of January to June inclusive:

(a) Sales budget.*
(b) Finished inventories budget (valued at direct cost).†

(c) Raw materials inventories budget (one budget for each component).[†]

(d) Production budget (direct costs only).[*]

(e) Trade receivables budget.[†]

(f) Trade payables budget.[†]

(g) Cash budget.[†]

Notes:

[*] The sales and production budgets should merely state each month's sales or production in units and in money terms.

[†] The other budgets should all seek to reconcile the opening balance of inventories, trade receivables, trade payables or cash with the closing balance through movements of the relevant factors over the month.

Chapter 7

ACCOUNTING FOR CONTROL

INTRODUCTION

Associated British Foods Group plc, the food processor (including Ovaltine and Ryvita) and retailer (Primark), states in its 2016 annual report (p. 62):

> All operations prepare annual operating plans and budgets which are updated regularly. Performance against budget is monitored at operational level and centrally, with variances being reported promptly. The cash position at group and operational level is monitored constantly and variances from expected levels are investigated thoroughly.

This raises important issues such as the way in which performance is monitored, the nature of variances, why the business should identify them, how they should be reported and what action the business should take where variances occur. These issues provide the focus for the chapter. We shall see that the procedures at Associated British Foods are widely adopted throughout the business world.

This chapter develops some of the themes that were discussed in Chapter 6. We shall see how a budget can be used to help control a business and how, by collecting information on actual performance and comparing it with the budget, it is possible to identify those activities that are in control and those that are not.

We shall take a look at standard costing and its relationship with budgeting. We shall see that a budget is often constructed from standards. Like budgets, standards provide targets against which actual performance can be measured. Finally, we shall explore the behavioural aspects of budgets and standards. We shall assess their value as a motivational device and consider the ways in which managers may use them in practice.

Learning outcomes

When you have completed this chapter, you should be able to:

- Discuss the role and limitations of budgets for performance evaluation and control.
- Undertake variance analysis and discuss possible reasons for the variances calculated.
- Explain the nature, role and limitations of standard costing.
- Discuss the issues that should be taken into account when designing an effective system of budgetary control.

BUDGETING FOR CONTROL

In Chapter 6, we saw that budgets provide a useful basis for exercising control over a business. Control involves making events conform to a plan and, since a budget is a short-term plan, making events conform to it is an obvious way to try to control the business. We also saw that, for most businesses, the routine is as shown in Figure 7.1.

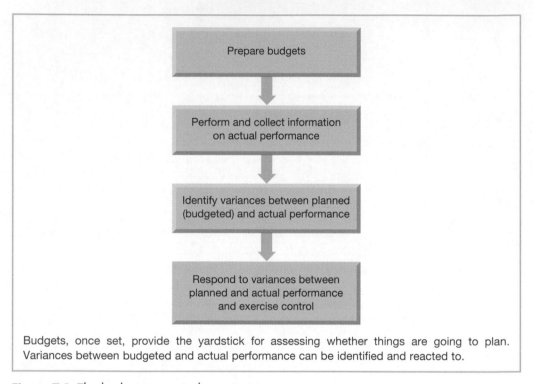

Budgets, once set, provide the yardstick for assessing whether things are going to plan. Variances between budgeted and actual performance can be identified and reacted to.

Figure 7.1 The budgetary control process

If plans are drawn up sensibly, we have a basis for exercising control over the business. We must, however, measure actual performance in the same terms as those in which the budget is stated. If they are not in the same terms, proper comparison will not be possible.

Exercising control involves finding out where and why things did not go according to plan and then seeking ways to put them right for the future. One reason why things may not have gone according to plan is that the budget targets were unachievable. In this case, it may be necessary to revise the budgets for future periods.

This last point does not imply that budget targets can simply be ignored if the going gets tough. Rather, it means that they should be adaptable. Unrealistic budgets cannot form a basis for exercising control and little can be gained by sticking with them.

Real World 7.1 discusses how one budget, which was revised in the light of cost overruns, was still too ambitious.

Digging itself out of a hole

DiamondCorp plc owns, and was developing, the Lace diamond mine in South Africa. An update on progress by the business revealed that the tunnelling budget had been revised upwards. Despite this, tunnelling costs were exceeding even the revised budget. According to the business, the costs of developing the tunnel were averaging Rand 39,135 per metre whereas the revised budget allowed only Rand 37,000. Management felt that actions taken to reduce costs, such as fitting chains to the tyres of some of the machinery used in the tunnelling process, were starting to effect cost savings. Overall, the cost of developing the mine was within budget.

Source: Information taken from DiamondCorp plc (2014), Lace Diamond mine Project Update, www.24hgold.com, 30 October.

Providing there is an adequate system of budgetary control, decision making and responsibility can be delegated to junior management. However, senior management can still retain control by using the system to discover which junior managers are meeting budget targets. This enables a *management-by-exception* environment to be created where senior management can focus on areas where things are *not* going according to plan (the exceptions – it is to be hoped). Junior managers who are performing to budget can be left to get on with their jobs.

TYPES OF CONTROL

The control process just outlined is known as **feedback control**. Its main feature is that steps are taken to get operations back on track as soon as there is a signal that they have gone wrong. This is similar to the thermostatic control that is a feature of most central heating systems. The thermostat incorporates a thermometer that senses when the temperature has fallen below a pre-set level (analogous to the budget). The thermostat then takes action to correct matters by activating the heating device that restores the required minimum temperature. Figure 7.2 depicts the stages in a feedback control system using budgets.

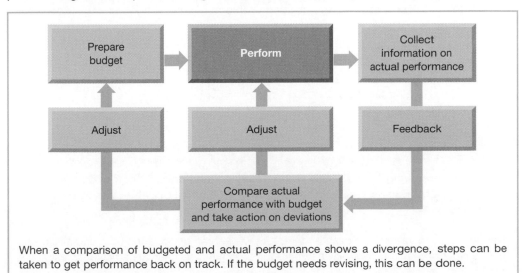

When a comparison of budgeted and actual performance shows a divergence, steps can be taken to get performance back on track. If the budget needs revising, this can be done.

Figure 7.2 Feedback control

There is an alternative type of control, known as **feedforward control**. Here predictions are made as to what can go wrong and steps are then taken to avoid any undesirable outcome. Budgets can also be used to exert this type of control. It involves preparing a budget and then comparing it with a forecast of actual outcomes in order to identify potential problems. For example, a cash budget may be compared with a forecast of actual cash flows. Where significant deviations from budget are revealed, corrective action may be taken before the problems arise. Figure 7.3 depicts the stages in a feedforward control system using budgets.

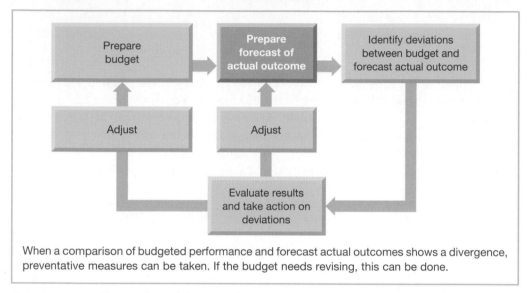

Figure 7.3 Feedforward control

Feedforward controls are proactive and try to anticipate problems beforehand, whereas feedback controls react to existing problems. To put it another way, feedforward controls are preventative, whereas feedback controls are remedial. As it is better to avoid problems rather than have to solve them, feedforward controls are preferable. However, they require timely and accurate predictions of actual outcomes, which are not always available.

Activity 7.1

The act of preparing budgets may lead directly to feedforward control. Can you think how preparing budgets may help to anticipate problems? Use the cash budget as an example.

During the preparation of a cash budget, it may become obvious that it is unrealistic and needs amendment. It may reveal that there will be insufficient cash at particular times during the budget period. By anticipating the cash shortage, there may be an opportunity to revise the spending commitments in the budget.

We saw in Chapter 1 that the key financial objective of a business is to increase the wealth of its owners (shareholders). Since profit is the net increase in wealth from business operations, the most important budget target to meet is the profit target. We shall therefore take this as our starting point when comparing the budget with the actual results. Example 7.1 shows the budgeted and actual income statements for Baxter Ltd for the month of May.

Example 7.1

The following are the budgeted and actual outcomes for Baxter Ltd, a manufacturing business, for the month of May:

	Budget	Actual
Output (production and sales)	1,000 units	900 units
	£	£
Sales revenue	100,000	92,000
Raw materials	(40,000) (40,000 metres)	(36,900) (37,000 metres)
Labour	(20,000) (2,500 hours)	(17,500) (2,150 hours)
Fixed overheads	(20,000)	(20,700)
Operating profit	20,000	16,900

From these figures, it is clear that the budgeted profit was not achieved. As far as May is concerned, this is a matter of history. However, the business (or one or more aspects of it) is out of control. Senior management must discover where things went wrong during May and try to ensure that these mistakes are not repeated in later months. It is not enough to know that things went wrong overall. We need to know precisely where and why. To achieve this, we must compare the budgeted and actual figures for the various items (sales revenue, raw materials and so on) in the statement shown above.

Activity 7.2

Can you see any problems in comparing the various items (sales revenue, raw materials and so on) for the budget with the actual performance of Baxter Ltd in an attempt to draw conclusions as to which aspects were out of control?

The problem is that the actual level of output was not as budgeted. In fact it was 10 per cent lower than budget. This means that we cannot, for example, say that there was a labour cost saving of £2,500 (that is, £20,000 − £17,500) and conclude that all is well in that area.

Flexing the budget

One practical way to overcome our difficulty is to 'flex' the budget to what it would have been had the planned level of output been 900 units rather than 1,000 units. **Flexing a budget** simply means revising it, assuming a different volume of output.

To flex the budget, we need to know which revenues and costs are fixed and which are variable relative to the volume of output. Once we know this, flexing is a simple operation.

We shall assume that sales revenue, materials cost and labour cost vary strictly with volume. Fixed overheads, by definition, will not. Whether, in real life, labour cost does vary with the volume of output is not so certain, but it will serve well enough as an assumption for our purposes. If labour cost is actually fixed, we can simply take this into account in the flexing process.

On the basis of our assumptions regarding the behaviour of revenues and costs, the flexed budget would be as follows:

	Flexed budget
Output (production and sales)	900 units
	£
Sales revenue	90,000
Raw materials	(36,000) (36,000 metres)
Labour	(18,000) (2,250 hours)
Fixed overheads	(20,000)
Operating profit	16,000

This is simply the original budget, with the sales revenue, raw materials and labour cost figures scaled down by 10 per cent (the same factor as the actual output fell short of the budgeted one).

Putting the original budget, the flexed budget and the actual outcome for May together gives us the following:

	Original budget	Flexed budget	Actual
Output (production and sales)	1,000 units	900 units	900 units
	£	£	£
Sales revenue	100,000	90,000	92,000
Raw materials	(40,000)	(36,000) (36,000 m)	(36,900) (37,000 m)
Labour	(20,000)	(18,000) (2,250 hr)	(17,500) (2,150 hr)
Fixed overheads	(20,000)	(20,000)	(20,700)
Operating profit	20,000	16,000	16,900

Flexible budgets allow us to make a more valid comparison between the budget (using the flexed figures) and the actual results. Key differences, or variances, between budgeted and actual results for each aspect of the business's activities can be calculated. In the rest of this section we consider some of these variances.

Sales volume variance

Let us begin by dealing with the shortfall in sales volume. By flexing the budget, as we just did, it may seem as if we are saying that it does not matter that the business failed to achieve the budgeted sales volume. We simply revise the budget and carry on as if all is well. However, losing sales volume clearly does matter. A sales volume shortfall normally means losing profit. The first point we must pick up, therefore, is the profit shortfall arising from the loss of sales of 100 units of the product.

Activity 7.3

What will be the loss of profit arising from the sales volume shortfall, assuming that everything except sales volume was as planned?

The answer is simply the difference between the original and flexed budget profit figures. The only difference between these two profit figures is the volume of sales; everything else was the same. (That is to say that the flexing was carried out assuming that the per-unit sales revenue, raw material cost and labour cost were all as originally budgeted.) This means that the figure for the loss of profit due to the volume shortfall, taken alone, is £4,000 (that is, £20,000 − £16,000).

When we considered the relationship between cost, volume and profit in Chapter 3, we saw that selling one unit less will result in one less unit contribution to profit. The contribution is sales revenue less variable cost. We can see from the original budget that the unit sales revenue is £100 (that is, £100,000/1,000), raw material cost is £40 a unit (that is, £40,000/1,000) and labour cost is £20 a unit (that is, £20,000/1,000). Thus the contribution is £40 a unit (that is, £100 − (£40 + £20)).

If 100 units of sales are lost, £4,000 (that is, 100 × £40) of contributions and, therefore, profit are forgone. Incidentally, this would be an alternative means of finding the sales volume variance, instead of taking the difference between the original and flexed budget profit figures. Once we have produced the flexed budget, however, it is generally easier to compare the two profit figures.

The difference between the original and flexed budget profit figures is called the **sales volume variance**.

In this case, it is an **adverse variance** because, taken alone, it has the effect of making the actual profit lower than the budgeted profit. A variance that has the effect of increasing profit beyond the budgeted profit is known as a **favourable variance**. We can therefore say that a **variance** is the effect of one factor (taken alone) on the budgeted profit. Shortly we shall consider other forms of variance, some of which may be favourable and some adverse. The difference between the sum of all the various favourable and adverse variances will represent the difference between the budgeted and actual profit. This is shown in Figure 7.4.

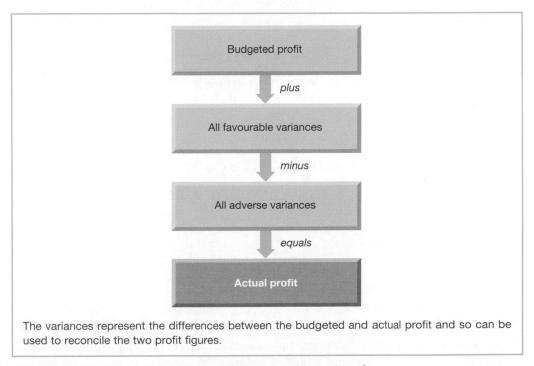

The variances represent the differences between the budgeted and actual profit and so can be used to reconcile the two profit figures.

Figure 7.4 Relationship between the budgeted and actual profit

When calculating a particular variance, such as that for sales volume, we assume that all other factors went according to plan.

Activity 7.4

What else do the relevant managers of Baxter Ltd need to know about the May sales volume variance?

They need to know why the volume of sales fell below the budgeted figure. Only by discovering this information will they be in a position to try to ensure that it does not occur again.

Who should be held accountable for this sales volume variance? The answer is probably the sales manager, who should know precisely why this has occurred. This is not the same as saying, however, that it was the sales manager's fault. The problem may have been that the business failed to produce the budgeted quantities so that not enough items were available to sell. Nevertheless, the sales manager should know the reason for the problem.

The budget and actual figures for Baxter Ltd for June are given in Activity 7.5 and will be used as the basis for a series of activities that provide an opportunity to calculate and assess the variances. We shall continue to use the May figures for explaining the variances.

Note that the business had budgeted for a higher level of output for June than it did for May.

Activity 7.5

	Budget for June	Actual for June
Output (production and sales)	1,100 units	1,150 units
	£	£
Sales revenue	110,000	113,500
Raw materials	(44,000) (44,000 metres)	(46,300) (46,300 metres)
Labour	(22,000) (2,750 hours)	(23,200) (2,960 hours)
Fixed overheads	(20,000)	(19,300)
Operating profit	24,000	24,700

Try flexing the June budget, comparing it with the original June budget and so find the sales volume variance.

	Flexed budget
Output (production and sales)	1,150 units
	£
Sales revenue	115,000
Raw materials	(46,000) (46,000 metres)
Labour	(23,000) (2,875 hours)
Fixed overheads	(20,000)
Operating profit	26,000

The sales volume variance is £2,000 (favourable) (that is, £26,000 − £24,000). It is favourable because the original budget profit was lower than the flexed budget profit. This arises from more sales actually being made than were budgeted.

For the month of May, we have already identified one reason why the budgeted profit of £20,000 was not achieved and that the actual profit was only £16,900. This was the £4,000 loss of profit (adverse variance) that arose from the sales volume shortfall. Now that the budget is flexed, we can compare the other factors, like with like, and reach further conclusions about May's trading.

We can see that May's sales revenue, raw materials, labour and fixed overheads figures all differ between the flexed budget and the actual results. This means that the adverse sales volume variance was not the only problem area. To gain further information relating to each of the revenue and cost items mentioned, we need to calculate further variances. We shall now do this.

Sales price variance

Starting with the sales revenue figure, we can see that, for May, there is a difference of £2,000 (favourable) between the flexed budget and the actual figures. This can only arise from higher prices being charged than were envisaged in the original budget, because any variance arising from the volume difference has already been 'stripped out' in the flexing process. This price difference is known as the **sales price variance**. Higher sales prices will, all other things being equal, mean more profit. So there is a favourable variance.

When senior management is trying to identify the reason for a sales price variance, it would normally be the sales manager who should be able to offer an explanation. As we shall see later in the chapter, favourable variances of significant size will normally be investigated.

Activity 7.6

Using the figures in Activity 7.5, what is the sales price variance for June?

The sales price variance for June is £1,500 (adverse) (that is, £115,000 − £113,500). Actual sales prices, on average, must have been lower than those budgeted. The actual price averaged £98.70 (that is, £113,500/1,150) whereas the budgeted price was £100. Selling output at a lower price than that budgeted will have an adverse effect on profit, hence an adverse variance.

The sales variances are summarised in Figure 7.5.

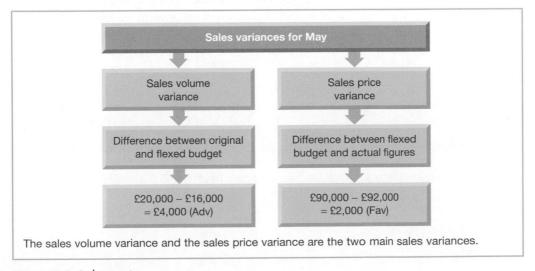

Figure 7.5 Sales variances

Let us now move on to look at the cost variances, starting with materials variances.

Materials variances

In May, there was an overall or **total direct materials variance** of £900 (adverse) (that is, £36,900 − £36,000). It is adverse because the actual material cost was higher than the budgeted one, which has an adverse effect on operating profit.

Who should be held accountable for this variance? The answer depends on whether the difference arises from excess usage of the raw material, in which case it is the production manager, or whether it is a higher-than-budgeted cost per metre being paid, in which case it is the responsibility of the buying manager. Fortunately, we can go beyond this total variance to examine the effect of changes in both usage and cost.

We can see from the figures that in May there was a 1,000 metre excess usage of the raw material (that is, 37,000 metres − 36,000 metres). All other things being equal, this alone would have led to a profit shortfall of £1,000, since clearly the budgeted cost per metre is £1. The £1,000 (adverse) variance is known as the **direct materials usage variance**. Normally, this variance would be the responsibility of the production manager.

Activity 7.7

Using the figures in Activity 7.5, what was the direct material usage variance for June?

The direct material usage variance for June was £300 (adverse) (that is, (46,300 metres − 46,000 metres) × £1). It is adverse because more material was used than was budgeted, for an output of 1,150 units. Excess usage of material will tend to reduce profit.

The other aspect of direct materials is their cost. The **direct materials price variance** simply takes the actual cost of materials used and compares it with the budgeted cost, given the quantity used. In May the actual cost of direct materials used was £36,900, whereas the budgeted cost of the 37,000 metres was £37,000. Thus we have a favourable variance of £100. Paying less than the budgeted cost will have a favourable effect on profit, hence a favourable variance.

Activity 7.8

Using the figures in Activity 7.5, what was the direct materials price variance for June?

The direct materials price variance for June was zero (that is, £46,300 − (46,300 × £1)).

As we have just seen, the total direct materials variance is the sum of the usage variance and the price variance. The relationship between the direct materials variances for May is shown in Figure 7.6.

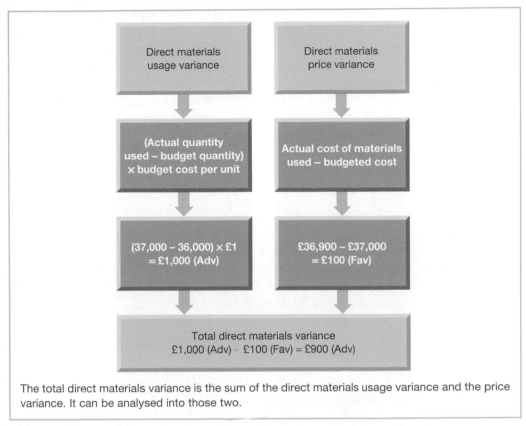

The total direct materials variance is the sum of the direct materials usage variance and the price variance. It can be analysed into those two.

Figure 7.6 Total, usage and price variances for direct materials for May

Labour variances

Direct labour variances are similar in form to those for direct materials. The **total direct labour variance** for May was £500 (favourable) (that is, £18,000 − £17,500). It is favourable because £500 less was spent on labour than was budgeted for the actual level of output achieved.

Again, this total variance is not particularly helpful and needs to be analysed further into its usage and cost elements. We should bear in mind that the number of hours used to complete a particular quantity of output is the responsibility of the production manager, whereas the responsibility for the rate of pay lies primarily with the human resources manager.

The **direct labour efficiency variance** compares the number of hours budgeted for the achieved level of production with the actual number of hours taken. It then costs this difference at the budgeted hourly rate. For May, the budgeted hourly rate is £8 as the original budget shows that 2,500 hours were budgeted to cost £20,000. Thus, the variance is (2,250 hours − 2,150 hours) × £8 = £800 (favourable). It is favourable because fewer hours were worked than budgeted for the actual level of output. Working more quickly tends to increase profit.

Activity 7.9

Using the figures in Activity 7.5, what was the direct labour efficiency variance for June?

The direct labour efficiency variance for June was £680 (adverse) (that is, (2,960 hours − 2,875 hours) × £8). It is adverse because the work took longer than the budget allowed and so will have an adverse effect on profit.

The **direct labour rate variance** compares the actual cost of the hours worked with their budgeted cost. For 2,150 hours worked in May, the budgeted cost would be £17,200 (that is, 2,150 × £8). So, the direct labour rate variance is £300 (adverse) (that is, £17,500 − £17,200).

The relationship between the direct labour variances for May is shown in Figure 7.7.

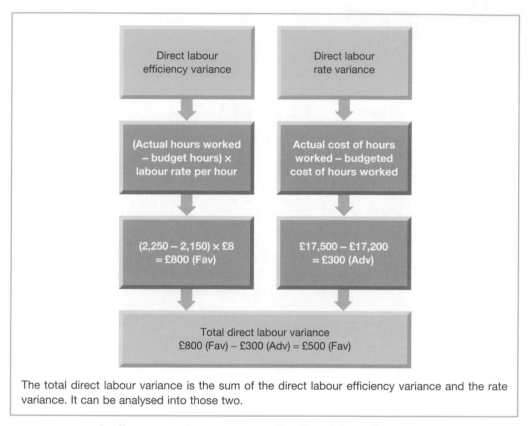

The total direct labour variance is the sum of the direct labour efficiency variance and the rate variance. It can be analysed into those two.

Figure 7.7 Total, efficiency and rate variances for direct labour for May

Activity 7.10

Using the figures in Activity 7.5, what was the direct labour rate variance for June?

The direct labour rate variance for June was £480 (favourable) (that is, (2,960 × £8) − £23,200). It is favourable because a lower rate was paid than budgeted. Paying a lower wage rate will have a favourable effect on profit.

Fixed overhead variance

The final area is that of overheads. In our example, we have assumed that all of the overheads are fixed. Variable overheads certainly exist in practice, but they have been omitted here simply to restrict the amount of detail. Variances involving variable overheads are similar in style to labour and material variances.

The **fixed overhead spending variance** is simply the difference between the flexed (or original – they will be the same) budget and the actual figures. For May, this was £700 (adverse) (that is, £20,700 – £20,000). It is adverse because more overheads cost was actually incurred than was budgeted. This will lead to less profit. In theory, this is the responsibility of whoever controls overheads expenditure.

In practice, overheads can be a very slippery area and one that is notoriously difficult to control. Overheads, both fixed and variable, are made up of more than one type of cost. Typically, they include such things as rent, administrative costs, management salaries, cleaning, electricity and so on. Each item mentioned could be separately budgeted and the actual figures recorded. Individual spending variances can then be identified for each overhead item to reveal problem areas.

Activity 7.11

Using the figures in Activity 7.5, what was the fixed overhead spending variance for June?

The fixed overhead spending variance for June was £700 (favourable) (that is, £20,000 – £19,300). It was favourable because less was spent on overheads than budgeted, thereby having a favourable effect on profit.

RECONCILING THE BUDGETED PROFIT WITH THE ACTUAL PROFIT

We are now in a position to reconcile the original May budgeted operating profit with the actual operating profit, as follows:

	£	£
Budgeted operating profit		20,000
Favourable variances		
Sales price	2,000	
Direct materials price	100	
Direct labour efficiency	800	2,900
Adverse variances		
Sales volume	(4,000)	
Direct materials usage	(1,000)	
Direct labour rate	(300)	
Fixed overhead spending	(700)	(6,000)
Actual operating profit		16,900

Activity 7.12

If you were the chief executive of Baxter Ltd, what attitude would you take to the overall difference between the budgeted profit and the actual one?
  How would you react to the individual variances shown above?

You would probably be concerned about how large the variances are and their direction (favourable or adverse). In particular you may have thought of the following:

- The overall adverse profit variance is £3,100 (that is £20,000 − £16,900). This represents 15.5 per cent of the budgeted profit (that is £3,100/£20,000 × 100%) and you (as chief executive) would almost certainly see it as significant and worrying.
- The £4,000 adverse sales volume variance represents 20 per cent of budgeted profit and would be a particular cause of concern.
- The £2,000 favourable sales price variance represents 10 per cent of budgeted profit. Since this is favourable it might be seen as a cause for celebration rather than concern. On the other hand, it means that Baxter Ltd's output was, on average, sold at prices 10 per cent above the planned price. This could have been the cause of the worrying adverse sales volume variance. The business may have sold fewer units because it charged higher prices.
- The £100 favourable direct materials price variance is very small in relation to budgeted profit – only 0.5 per cent. It would be unrealistic to expect the actual figures to hit the precise budgeted figures each month and so this is unlikely to be regarded as significant. The direct materials usage variance, however, represents 5 per cent of the budgeted profit. The chief executive may feel this is cause for concern.
- The £800 favourable direct labour efficiency variance represents 4 per cent of budgeted profit. Although it is a favourable variance, the reasons for it may be worth investigating. The £300 adverse direct labour rate variance represents only 1.5 per cent of the budgeted profit and may not be regarded as significant.
- The £700 fixed overhead adverse variance represents 3.5 per cent of budgeted profit. The chief executive may feel that this is too low to cause real concern.

The chief executive will now need to ask some questions as to why things went so badly wrong in several areas and what can be done to improve future performance.

We shall shortly come back to the dilemma as to which variances to investigate and which to accept.

Activity 7.13

Using the figures in Activity 7.5, reconcile the original operating profit figure for June with the actual June figure.

	£	£
Budgeted operating profit		24,000
Favourable variances		
Sales volume	2,000	
Direct labour rate	480	
Fixed overhead spending	700	3,180
Adverse variances		
Sales price	(1,500)	
Direct materials usage	(300)	
Direct labour efficiency	(680)	(2,480)
Actual operating profit		24,700

The following are the budgeted and actual income statements for Baxter Ltd for the month of July:

	Budget	Actual
Output (production and sales)	1,000 units	1,050 units
	£	£
Sales revenue	100,000	104,300
Raw materials	(40,000) (40,000 metres)	(41,200) (40,500 metres)
Labour	(20,000) (2,500 hours)	(21,300) (2,600 hours)
Fixed overheads	(20,000)	(19,400)
Operating profit	20,000	22,400

Produce a reconciliation of the budgeted and actual operating profit, going into as much detail as possible with the variance analysis.

The original budget, the flexed budget and the actual outcome are as follows:

	Original budget	Flexed budget	Actual
Output (production and sales)	1,000 units	1,050 units	1,050 units
	£	£	£
Sales revenue	100,000	105,000	104,300
Raw materials	(40,000)	(42,000) (42,000 m)	(41,200) (40,500 m)
Labour	(20,000)	(21,000) (2,625 hr)	(21,300) (2,600 hr)
Fixed overheads	(20,000)	(20,000)	(19,400)
Operating profit	20,000	22,000	22,400

Reconciliation of the budgeted and actual operating profits for July

	£	£
Budgeted operating profit		20,000
Favourable variances:		
Sales volume (22,000 − 20,000)	2,000	
Direct materials usage ((42,000 − 40,500) × £1)	1,500	
Direct labour efficiency ((2,625 − 2,600) × £8)	200	
Fixed overhead spending (20,000 − 19,400)	600	4,300
Adverse variances:		
Sales price (105,000 − 104,300)	(700)	
Direct materials price ((40,500 × £1) − 41,200)	(700)	
Direct labour rate ((2,600 × £8) − 21,300)	(500)	(1,900)
Actual operating profit		22,400

Real World 7.2 shows how a well-known UK-based business, Tate and Lyle plc, uses variance analysis to exercise control over its operations. Many businesses explain in their annual reports how they operate systems of budgetary control.

Refined controls

Tate and Lyle plc makes it clear that it too uses budgets and variance analysis to help keep control over its activities. The 2015 annual report states that there is:

A comprehensive planning and budgeting system for all items of expenditure with an annual budget approved by the Board. Performance is reported monthly against budget and prior year results; significant variances are investigated.

The board of directors of this business will not seek explanations of variances arising at each department, but they will be looking at figures for the business as a whole or the results for major divisions of it.

Equally certainly, department managers will receive a monthly (or perhaps more frequent) report of variances arising within their area of responsibility alone.

Source: Tate & Lyle plc Annual Report 2015, p. 51.

Real World 7.3 gives some indication of the importance of flexible budgeting in practice.

Flexing the budgets

A survey of the UK food and drinks industry provides us with an indication of the importance attached by management accountants to flexible budgeting. The survey asked those in charge of the management accounting function to rate the importance of flexible budgeting by selecting one of three possible categories – 'not important', 'moderately important' or 'important'. Figure 7.8 sets out the results, from the sample of 117 respondents.

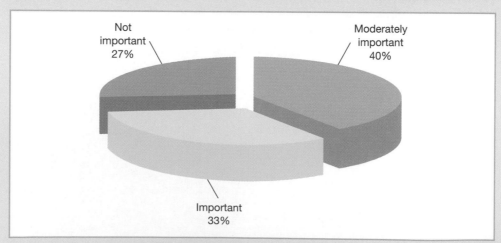

Figure 7.8 Degree of importance attached to flexible budgeting

Respondents were also asked to state the frequency with which flexible budgeting was used within the business, using a five-point scale ranging from 1 (never) through to 5 (very often). Figure 7.9 sets out these results.

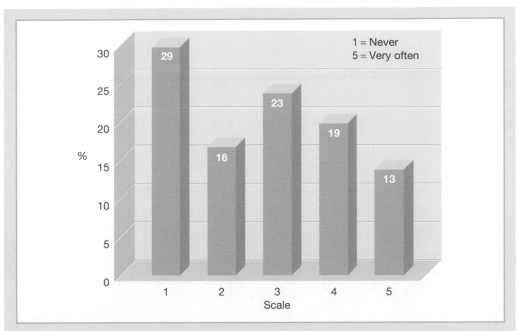

Figure 7.9 Frequency of use of flexible budgets

We can see that, while flexible budgeting is regarded as important by a significant proportion of management accountants and is being used in practice, not all businesses use it.

Source. Taken from information appearing in Abdel-Kader, M. and Luther, R. (2004) *An Empirical Investigation of the Evolution of Management Accounting Practices*, Working paper No. 04/06, University of Essex, October.

REASONS FOR ADVERSE VARIANCES

Adverse variances may occur simply because the budgets against which performance is being measured are unachievable. If this is the case, budgets will not provide a useful means of exercising control. There are other reasons, however, that may lead to actual performance deviating from budgeted performance.

Activity 7.15

The variances that we have considered are:

- sales volume;
- sales price;
- direct materials usage;
- direct materials price;
- direct labour efficiency;
- direct labour rate; and
- fixed overhead spending.

Assuming that the budget targets are reasonable, jot down possible reasons for *adverse* variances arising for each of the above.

The reasons that we thought of included the following:

Sales volume

- Poor performance by sales staff.
- Deterioration in market conditions between the time the budget was set and the actual event.
- Lack of goods or services to sell as a result of some production problem.

Sales price

- Poor performance by sales staff.
- Deterioration in market conditions between the time the budget was set and the actual event.

Direct materials usage

- Poor performance by production department staff, leading to high rates of scrap.
- Substandard materials, leading to high rates of scrap.
- Faulty machinery, causing high rates of scrap.

Direct materials price

- Poor performance by the buying department staff.
- Using higher quality material than was planned.
- Change in market conditions between the time when the budget was set and the actual event.

Labour efficiency

- Poor supervision.
- A low skill grade of worker taking longer to do the work than envisaged for a higher skill grade.
- Low-grade materials, leading to high levels of scrap and wasted labour time.
- Problems with a customer for whom a service is being rendered.
- Problems with machinery, leading to labour time being wasted.
- Dislocation of materials supply, leading to workers being unable to proceed with production.

Labour rate

- Poor performance by the human resources department.
- Using a higher grade of worker than planned.
- Change in labour market conditions between the time budget was set and the actual event.

Fixed overheads

- Poor supervision of overheads.
- General increase in costs of overheads not taken into account in the budget.

Note that different variances may have the same underlying cause. For example, the purchase of low quality, cheaper materials may result in an unfavourable direct materials usage variance, a favourable direct materials price variance and an unfavourable direct labour efficiency variance.

VARIANCE ANALYSIS IN SERVICE INDUSTRIES

Although we have used the example of a manufacturing business to explain variance analysis, this does not imply that variance analysis is irrelevant for service sector businesses. It is simply that manufacturing businesses usually have all of the variances found in practice. Service businesses, for example, may not have material variances.

According to the business's 2016 annual report, Next plc, the well-known retailer, uses budgets and variance analysis to help manage its business. It is probably the case that most major service sector businesses use some form of variance reporting to help them manage their affairs.

NON-OPERATING-PROFIT VARIANCES

There are many areas of business where a budget will be used, but where any variances will not have a direct effect on operating profit. The variances will often, however, have an indirect effect and, sometimes, a profound one. The cash budget, for example, sets out planned receipts, payments and the resultant cash balance for the period. If this budget turns out to be wrong because of, say, unforeseen expenditures, there may be unplanned cash shortages and accompanying costs. These costs may be limited to interest incurred on borrowing. If, however, borrowing cannot cover the cash shortage, the consequences could be more serious, such as lost profits from projects that are abandoned due to lack of funds.

Control must, therefore, be exercised over areas such as cash management, to try to avoid adverse **non-operating-profit variances**.

INVESTIGATING VARIANCES

It is unreasonable to expect budget targets to be met precisely each month and so variances will usually arise. Discovering the reasons for these variances can be costly. Information will usually have to be produced and examined and discussions with appropriate members of staff carried out. Sometimes, activities may have to be brought to a halt to discover what went wrong. Since small variances are almost inevitable, and investigating variances can be expensive, managers need some guiding principle concerning which variances to investigate and which to accept.

Activity 7.16

What principle do you feel should guide managers when deciding whether to spend money investigating a particular variance? (*Hint*: Think back to Chapter 1)

When deciding whether to produce accounting information, there should be a consideration of both benefit and cost. The benefit likely to be gained from knowing why a variance arose needs to be weighed against the cost of obtaining that knowledge.

There are difficulties in implementing this principle, however, as both the value of the benefit and the cost of investigation may be difficult to assess in advance of the investigation.

The following practical guidelines for investigating variances, which try to take some account of benefit and cost, may be adopted by managers:

- Significant *adverse* variances should normally be investigated, as a continuation of the underlying problem could be very costly. Managers must decide what 'significant' means and, ultimately, this will be a matter of managerial judgement. It may be decided, for example, that variances above a threshold of a percentage of the budgeted figure (say, 5 per cent) or a fixed financial amount (say, £1,000) are considered significant.
- Significant *favourable* variances should probably be investigated. Although they may not cause such immediate concern as adverse variances, they still indicate that things are not going according to plan. If actual performance is significantly better than planned, it may mean that the budget target is unrealistically low.
- Insignificant variances, though not triggering immediate investigation, should be kept under review. For each aspect of operations, the cumulative sum of variances, over a series of control periods, should be zero, with small adverse variances in some periods being compensated for by small favourable ones in others. This is because small variances caused by random factors will not necessarily recur and they are as likely to be favourable as adverse. Where a variance is caused by systemic (non-random) factors, which recur over time, the cumulative sum of the periodic variances will not be zero but an increasing figure. Even though the individual variances may be insignificant, the cumulative effect of these variances may not. Thus, an investigation may well be worthwhile, particularly if the variances are adverse. Example 7.2 below looks at this review process.

While these guidelines may be of some help, managers must be flexible. They may, for example, decide against investigating a significant variance where the cost of correcting the potential causes is expected to be very high. They may calculate that it would be cheaper to live with the problem and so adjust the budget.

Where a variance is caused by systemic (non-random) factors, which recur over time, the cumulative sum of the periodic variances will not be zero but an increasing figure. Even though the individual variances may be insignificant, the cumulative effect of these variances may not. Thus, an investigation may well be worthwhile, particularly if the variances are adverse.

To illustrate the cumulative effect of relatively small systemic variances, let us consider Example 7.2.

Example 7.2

Indisurers Ltd finds that the variances for direct labour efficiency for processing motor insurance claims, since the beginning of the year, are as follows:

	£		£
January	250 (adverse)	July	200 (adverse)
February	150 (favourable)	August	150 (favourable)
March	50 (favourable)	September	230 (adverse)
April	200 (adverse)	October	150 (favourable)
May	220 (adverse)	November	50 (favourable)
June	80 (favourable)	December	260 (adverse)

The average total cost of labour performing this task is about £12,000 a month. Management believes that none of these variances, taken alone, is significant given the monthly labour cost. The question is, are they significant when taken together? If we add them together, taking account of the signs, we find that we have a net adverse variance for the year of £730. Of itself this, too, is probably not significant, but we should expect the cumulative total to be close to zero where the variances are random. We might feel that a pattern is developing and, given long enough, a net adverse variance of significant size might build up.

Investigating the labour efficiency might be worth doing. Finding the cause of the variance would put management in a position to correct a systemic fault, which could lead to future cost savings. (Note that 12 periods are probably not enough to reach a statistically sound conclusion on whether the variances are random or not, but it provides an illustration of the point.)

Plotting the cumulative variances, from month to month, as in Figure 7.10, makes it clear what is happening as time proceeds.

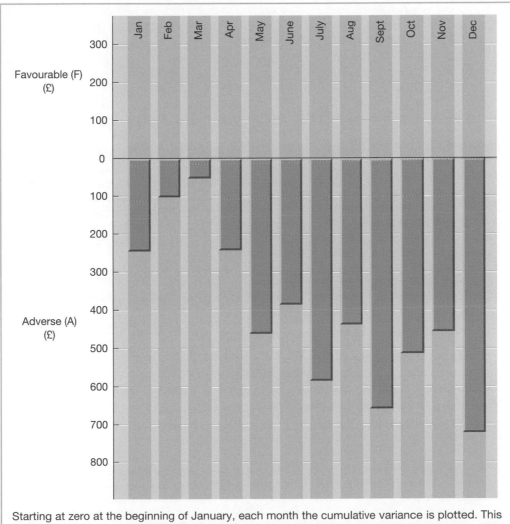

Starting at zero at the beginning of January, each month the cumulative variance is plotted. This is the sum taking account of positive and negative signs. The January figure is £250 (A). The February one is £100 (A) (that is £250 (A) plus £150 (F)) and so on. The graph seems to show an overall trend of adverse variances, but with several favourable variances involved.

Figure 7.10 The cumulative variances for labour efficiency in motor insurance claim handling at Indisurers Ltd

VARIANCE ANALYSIS IN PRACTICE

Real World 7.4 provides some evidence concerning the use of variance analysis.

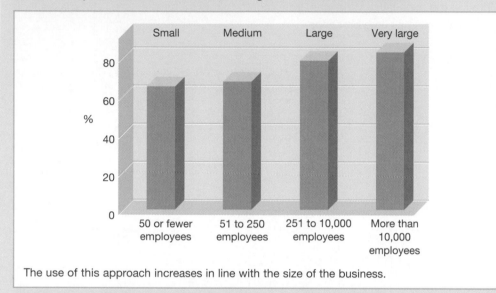
COMPENSATING VARIANCES

There may be superficial appeal in the idea of **compensating variances**. These are linked favourable and adverse variances, which are traded off against each other. A sales manager, for example, may suggest that more of a particular service could be sold if prices were lowered, and that, overall, this would result in increased profits. This suggestion would lead to a favourable sales volume variance, but also to an adverse sales price variance. On the face of it, provided that the former is greater than the latter, all would be well.

Can you think of a reason why the sales manager should not go ahead with the price reduction?

The change in policy will have ramifications for other areas of the business, including

- the need to supply more of the service: staff and other resources may not be available to accommodate this increase; and
- the need to provide more finance: increased levels of activity will lead to an increased need for funds to pay, for example, additional staff costs.

Trading off variances in this way is, therefore, not normally acceptable without a more far-reaching consultation and revision of plans.

STANDARD QUANTITIES AND COSTS

We have already seen that a budget is a business plan for the short term – typically one year – that is expressed mainly in financial terms. A budget is typically constructed from standards. **Standard quantities and costs** (or revenues) are those planned for an individual unit of input or output and provide the building blocks for budgets.

We can say about Baxter Ltd's operations (see Example 7.1 on page 243) that:

- the standard selling price is £100 for one unit of output;
- the standard marginal cost for one manufactured unit is £60;
- the standard raw materials cost is £40 for one unit of output;
- the standard raw materials usage is 40 metres for one unit of output;
- the standard raw materials price is £1 a metre (that is, for one unit of input);
- the standard labour cost is £20 for one unit of output;
- the standard labour time is 2.50 hours for one unit of output; and
- the standard labour rate is £8 an hour (that is, for one unit of input).

Standards, like the budgets to which they are linked, represent targets against which actual performance can be measured. They also provide the basis for variance analysis, which, as we have seen, helps managers to identify where deviations from planned, or standard, performance have occurred and the extent of those deviations. To maintain their usefulness for planning and control purposes, they should be subject to frequent review and, where necessary, revision.

Real World 7.5 provides some evidence on the frequency of updating standards in practice.

Keeping up standards

KPMG, the accountancy firm, conducted interviews with senior financial officers of 12 large international manufacturing businesses covering pharmaceuticals, industrials and consumer goods. A key finding was that increasing economic volatility was leading to more frequent updates of standards. Most of the businesses updated standards annually. However, one updated on a quarterly basis and one had not updated for two years because of the costs and time involved.

Source: KPMG (2010) *Standard costing: insights from leading companies*, February.

Standards may be applied to a wide variety of products or services. A firm of accountants, for example, may set standard costs per hour for each grade of staff (audit manager, audit senior, trainee and so on). When planning a particular audit of a client business, it can decide the standard hours that each grade of staff should spend on the audit and, using the standard cost per hour for each grade, it can derive a standard cost or 'budget' for the job as a whole. These standards can subsequently be compared with the actual hours and hourly rates.

SETTING STANDARDS

When setting standards various points have to be considered. We shall now explore some of the more important of these.

Who sets the standards?

Standards often result from the collective effort of various individuals including management accountants, industrial engineers, human resource managers, production managers and other employees. The manager responsible for achieving a particular standard will usually have some involvement and may provide specialised knowledge. This involvement, however, provides the risk that 'slack' may be built into the standard in order to make it easier to achieve.

How is information gathered?

Setting standards involves gathering information concerning how much material should be used, how much machine time should be required, how much direct labour time should be spent and so on. Two possible ways of collecting information for standard setting are available.

Activity 7.18

Can you think what these possible ways are?

The first is to examine the particular processes and tasks involved in producing the product or service and to develop suitable estimates. Standards concerning material usage, machine time and direct labour hours may be established by carrying out dummy production runs, time-and-motion studies and so on. This will require close collaboration between the management accountant, industrial engineers and those involved in the production process.

The second approach is to collect information relating to past costs, times and usage for the same, or similar, products and to use this information as a basis for predicting the future. This information may have to be adjusted to reflect changes in price, changes in the production process and so on.

Where the product or service is entirely new or involves entirely new processes, the first approach will probably have to be used, even though it is usually more costly.

What kind of standards should be used?

There are basically two types of standards that may be used: **ideal standards** and **practical standards**. Ideal standards, as the name suggests, assume perfect operating conditions where there is no inefficiency due to lost production time, defects and so on. The objective of setting ideal standards, which are attainable in theory at least, is to encourage employees to strive towards excellence. Practical standards, also as the name suggests, do not assume ideal operating conditions. Although they demand a high level of efficiency, account is taken of possible lost production time, defects and so on. They are designed to be challenging yet achievable.

There are two major difficulties with using ideal standards.

- They do not provide a useful basis for exercising control. Unless the standards set are realistic, any variances computed are extremely difficult to interpret.
- They may not achieve their intended purpose of motivating managers: indeed, the opposite may occur. As we shall see a little later, the evidence suggests that where managers regard a target as beyond their grasp, it is likely to have a demotivating effect.

Given these problems, it is not surprising that practical standards seem to enjoy more widespread support than ideal standards. Nevertheless, by taking account of wastage, lost production time and so on, there is a risk that they will entrench operating inefficiencies.

THE LEARNING-CURVE EFFECT

Where an activity undertaken by direct workers has been unchanged for some time, and the workers are experienced at performing it, the standard labour time will normally stay unchanged. However, where a new activity is introduced, or new workers are involved with performing an existing activity, a **learning-curve** effect will normally occur. This is shown in Figure 7.12.

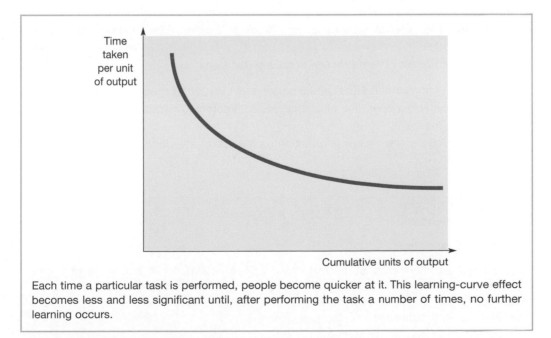

Each time a particular task is performed, people become quicker at it. This learning-curve effect becomes less and less significant until, after performing the task a number of times, no further learning occurs.

Figure 7.12 The learning-curve effect

The first unit of output takes a relatively long time to produce. As experience is gained, the worker takes less time to produce each successive unit of output. The rate of reduction in the time taken will, however, decrease as experience is gained. Thus, for example, the reduction in time taken between the first and second unit produced will be much bigger than the reduction between, say, the ninth and the tenth. Eventually, the rate of reduction in time taken will reduce to zero so that each unit will take as long as the preceding one. At this point, where the curve in Figure 7.12 becomes horizontal (the bottom right of the graph), the learning-curve effect will have been eliminated and a steady, long-term standard time for the activity will have been established.

The learning-curve effect seems to have little to do with whether workers are skilled or unskilled; if they are unfamiliar with the task, the learning-curve effect will arise. Practical experience shows that learning curves show remarkable regularity and, therefore, predictability from one activity to another.

The learning-curve effect applies equally well to activities involved with providing a service (such as dealing with an insurance claim, in an insurance business) as to manufacturing-type activities (like upholstering an armchair by hand, in a furniture-making business).

Clearly, the learning-curve effect must be taken into account when setting standards, and when interpreting any adverse labour efficiency variances, where a new process and/or new staff are involved.

OTHER USES FOR STANDARD COSTING

We have already seen that standards can play a valuable role in performance evaluation and control. However, standards relating to costs, usages, selling prices and so on may also be used for other purposes such as:

- measuring operating efficiency;
- product-sourcing decisions;
- determining the cost of inventories and work in progress for income measurement purposes; and
- determining the cost of items for use in pricing decisions.

This does not mean that standards should be seen as the primary measure in all cases. When making decisions about operating efficiency, product sourcing or pricing, they may be used as a secondary measure.

Real World 7.6 provides some information on the use of standards for decision making.

Real World 7.6

Standard practice

The KPMG survey, mentioned in Real World 7.5 (page 261), found that some of the 12 manufacturing businesses in the study had moved away from using standard costing as the key measure of operating effectiveness and for product-sourcing decisions. Instead, they relied on other operating and financial measures.

Source: KPMG (2010) *Standard costing: insights from leading companies*, February.

SOME PROBLEMS . . .

Although standards and variances may be useful for decision-making purposes, they have limited application. Many business and commercial activities do not have direct relationships between inputs and outputs, as is the case with, say, the number of direct labour hours worked and the number of products manufactured. Many expenses of modern business are in areas such as human resource development, advertising, maintenance of equipment and research and development, where the expense is discretionary and there is no direct link to the level of output.

There are also potential problems when applying standard costing techniques. These include the following:

- Standards can quickly become out of date as a result of both changes in the production process and price changes. When standards become outdated, performance can be adversely affected. For example, a human resources manager who recognises that it is impossible to meet targets on rates of pay for labour, because of general labour cost rises, may have less incentive to minimise costs.
- Factors may affect a variance for which a particular manager is accountable but over which the manager has no control. When assessing the manager's performance, these uncontrollable factors should be taken into account, but there is always a risk that they will not.
- In practice, creating clear lines of demarcation between the areas of responsibility of various managers may be difficult. In this case, one of the prerequisites of effective standard costing is lost.
- Once a standard has been met, there is no incentive for employees to improve the quality or quantity of output further. There are usually no additional rewards for doing so, only additional work. Indeed, employees may have a disincentive for exceeding a standard as it may then be viewed by managers as too loose and therefore in need of tightening. However, simply achieving a standard, and no more, may not be enough in highly competitive and fast-changing markets. To compete effectively, a business may need to strive for continuous improvement and standard costing techniques may impede this process.
- Standard costing may create incentives for managers and employees to act in undesirable ways. It may, for example, encourage the build-up of excess inventories, leading to significant storage and financing costs. This problem can arise where there are opportunities for discounts on bulk purchases of materials, which the purchasing manager then exploits to achieve a favourable direct materials price variance. One way to avoid this problem might be to impose limits on the level of inventories held.

Activity 7.19

Can you think of another example of how a manager may achieve a favourable direct materials price variance but in doing so would create problems for a business?

A manager may buy cheaper, but lower quality, materials. Although this may lead to a favourable price variance, it may also lead to additional inspection and reworking costs and, perhaps, lost sales.

To avoid this problem, the manager may be required to buy material of a particular quality or from particular sources.

A final example of the perverse incentives created by standard costing relates to labour efficiency variances. Where these variances are calculated for individual employees, and form the basis for their rewards, there is little incentive for them to work co-operatively. Co-operative working may, however, be in the best interests of the business. To avoid this problem, some businesses calculate labour efficiency variances for groups of employees rather than individual employees. This, however, creates the risk that some individuals will become 'free riders' and will rely on the more conscientious employees to carry the load.

Activity 7.20

How might the business try to eliminate the 'free-rider' problem just mentioned?

One way would be to carry out an evaluation, perhaps by the group members themselves, of individual contributions to group output, as well as evaluating group output as a whole.

Real World 7.7 indicates that, despite the problems mentioned above, standard costing is used by businesses.

Real World 7.7

Standard usage

The CIMA survey, mentioned previously, examined the extent to which the use of standard costing varies with business size. Figure 7.13 shows the results.

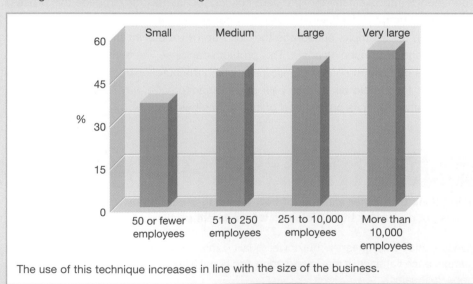

The use of this technique increases in line with the size of the business.

Figure 7.13 Standard costing and business size

Source: Figure adapted from CIMA (2009) *Management Accounting Tools for Today and Tomorrow*, p. 12.

The traditional standard costing approach was developed during an era when business operations were characterised by few product lines, long production runs and heavy reliance on direct labour. More recently, the increasingly competitive environment and the onward march of technology have changed the business landscape. Now, many business operations are characterised by a wide range of different products, shorter product life cycles (leading to shorter production runs) and automated production processes. The effect of these changes has resulted in:

- a need for more frequent development of standards to deal with frequent changes to the product range;
- a change in the focus for control – where manufacturing systems are automated, for example, direct labour becomes less important than direct materials; and
- a decline in the importance of monitoring cost and usage variances – where manufacturing systems are automated, deviations from standards relating to costs and usage become less frequent and less significant.

Thus, where a business has highly automated production systems, traditional standard costing, with its emphasis on costs and usage, is likely to take on less importance. Other elements of the production process such as quality, production levels, product cycle times, delivery times and the need for continuous improvement become the focus of attention.

This does not mean, however, that a standards-based approach is not useful for the new manufacturing environment. It can still provide valuable control information and there is no reason why standard costing systems cannot be redesigned to reflect a concern for some of the elements mentioned earlier. Nevertheless, other measures, including non-financial ones, may help to augment the information provided by the standard costing system.

Real World 7.8 indicates the extent to which particular standard costing variances are calculated.

Maintaining standards

Senior financial managers of 33 UK businesses were asked about their costing systems. It emerged that standard costing was used by 30 of the businesses concerned, which represented most of the businesses that might be expected to use this method. The popularity among these businesses of standards for each of the main cost items is set out in Figure 7.14.

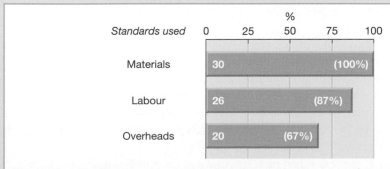

Standards for materials were used by all businesses in the survey that used standard costing. Standards for labour were used by nearly all businesses.

Figure 7.14 The popularity of standards in practice

Despite the popularity of materials standards, the study found that four businesses calculated the total direct materials variance only and that only two-thirds of businesses calculated both the direct materials price and usage variances. For labour standards, the variance analysis is even less complete. The study found that 15 businesses calculated the total direct labour variance only and just one-third of businesses calculated both the direct labour and efficiency variances. It seems, therefore, that standard costing was not extensively employed by the businesses.

Source: Figure based on information in Dugdale, D., Jones, C. and Green, S. (2006) *Contemporary Management Accounting Practices in UK Manufacturing*, CIMA Research Publication, Vol. 1, Number 13.

MAKING BUDGETARY CONTROL EFFECTIVE

It should be clear from what we have seen of **budgetary control** that a system, or a set of routines, must be put in place to enable the potential benefits to be gained. Most businesses that operate successful budgetary control and standard costing systems tend to share common features. These include the following:

- *A serious attitude taken to the system.* This should apply to all levels of management, right from the very top. For example, senior managers need to make clear to subordinates that they take notice of the monthly variance reports and base some of their actions and decisions upon them.
- *Clear demarcation between areas of managerial responsibility.* It needs to be made clear which manager is responsible for each business area. In this way, accountability can be ascribed for an area that seems to be going out of control.
- *Budget targets that are challenging yet achievable.* Setting unachievable targets is likely to have a demotivating effect. Managers may be permitted to participate in establishing their own targets to help create a sense of ownership. This, in turn, may increase levels of commitment and motivation. We shall consider this in more detail shortly.
- *Established data collection, analysis and reporting routines.* These should take the actual results and the budget figures and use them to calculate and report the variances. This should be part of the business's regular accounting information system, so that the required reports are automatically produced each month.
- *Reports aimed at individual managers, rather than general-purpose documents.* This avoids managers having to read through many pages of reports to find the part that is relevant to them.
- *Fairly short reporting periods.* These would typically be one month long, so that things cannot go too far wrong before they are picked up.
- *Timely variance reports.* Reports should be produced and made available to managers shortly after the end of the relevant reporting period. If it is not until the end of June that a manager is informed that the performance in May was below the budgeted level, it is quite likely that the performance for June will be below target as well. Reports on the performance in May ideally need to emerge in early June.
- *Action being taken to get operations back under control if they are shown to be out of control.* The report will not change things by itself. Managers need to take action to try to ensure that the reporting of significant adverse variances leads to action to put things right for the future.

Budgets are prepared with the objective of affecting the attitudes and behaviour of managers. The point was made in Chapter 6 that budgets are intended to motivate managers; research evidence generally shows that budgets can be effective in achieving this. More specifically, the research shows:

■ The existence of budgets can improve job satisfaction and performance. Where a manager's role might otherwise be ill-defined or ambiguous, budgets can bring structure and certainty. Budgets provide clear, quantifiable, targets to be pursued. This can be reassuring to managers and can increase their level of commitment.

■ Demanding, yet achievable, budget targets tend to motivate better than less demanding targets. It seems that setting the most demanding targets that are acceptable to managers is a very effective way to motivate them.

■ Unrealistically demanding targets tend to have an adverse effect on managers' performance. Once managers begin to view the budget targets as being too difficult to achieve, their level of motivation and performance declines. The relationship between the level of performance and the perceived degree of budget difficulty is shown in Figure 7.15.

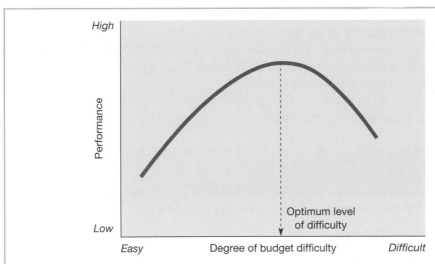

At a low level of budget difficulty, performance also tends to be low as managers do not find the targets sufficiently motivating. However, as the degree of difficulty starts to increase, managers rise to the challenge and improve their performance. Beyond a certain point, managers see the budgets as being too difficult to achieve and so motivation and performance decline.

Figure 7.15 Relationship between the level of performance and the perceived degree of budget difficulty

■ The participation of managers in setting their targets tends to improve motivation and performance. This is probably because those managers feel a sense of commitment to the targets and a moral obligation to achieve them.

It has been suggested that allowing managers to set their own targets will lead to slack (that is, easily achievable) targets being introduced. This would make achievement of the target that much easier. On the other hand, in an effort to impress, a manager may select a target that is not really achievable. These points imply that care must be taken over the extent to which managers have unfettered choice of their own targets.

Conflict can occur in the budget-setting process, as different groups may well have different agendas. For example, junior managers may be keen to build slack into their budgets while their senior managers may seek to impose unrealistically demanding budget targets. Sometimes, such conflict can be constructive and can result in better decisions being made. To resolve the conflict over budget targets, negotiations may have to take place and other options may have to be explored. This may lead to a better understanding by all parties of the issues involved and final agreement may result in demanding, yet achievable, targets.

The impact of management style

There has been a great deal of discussion among experts on the way in which managers use information generated by the budgeting system and the impact of its use on the attitudes and behaviour of subordinates (staff). A pioneering study by Hopwood (see reference 1 at the end of the chapter) examined the way that managers, working within a manufacturing environment, used budget information to evaluate the performance of subordinates. He argued that three distinct styles of management could be observed. These are:

- *Budget-constrained style.* This management style focuses rigidly on the ability of subordinates to meet the budget. Other factors relating to the performance of subordinates are not given serious consideration even though they might include improving the long-term effectiveness of the area for which the subordinate has responsibility.
- *Profit-conscious style.* This management style uses budget information in a more flexible way and often in conjunction with other data. The main focus is on the ability of each subordinate to improve long-term effectiveness.
- *Non-accounting style.* In this case, budget information plays no significant role in the evaluation of a subordinate's performance.

Activity 7.21

How might a manager respond to information that indicates a subordinate has not met the budget targets for the period, assuming the manager adopts

(a) a budget-constrained style?
(b) a profit-conscious style?
(c) a non-accounting style?

(a) A manager adopting a budget-constrained style is likely to take the budget information very seriously. This may result in criticism of the subordinate and, perhaps, some form of sanction.
(b) A manager adopting a profit-conscious style is likely to take a broader view when examining the budget information and so will take other factors into consideration (for example, factors that could not have been anticipated at the time of preparing the budgets), before deciding whether criticism or sanction is justified.
(c) A manager adopting a non-accounting style will regard the failure to meet the budget as being relatively unimportant and so no action may be taken.

Hopwood found that subordinates working for a manager who adopts a budget-constrained style had unpleasant experiences. They suffered higher levels of job-related stress and had poorer working relationships, with both their colleagues and their manager, than those whose manager adopted one of the other two styles. Hopwood also found that the subordinates of a budget-constrained style of manager were more likely to manipulate the budget figures, or to take other undesirable actions, to ensure the budgets were met.

Reservations about the Hopwood study

Although Hopwood's findings are interesting, subsequent studies have cast doubt on their universal applicability. Later studies confirm that human attitudes and behaviour are complex and can vary according to the particular situation. For example, it has been found that the impact of different management styles on such factors as job-related stress and the manipulation of budget figures seems to vary. It is likely to depend on such factors as the level of independence enjoyed by the subordinates and the level of uncertainty associated with the tasks to be undertaken.

It seems that where there is a high level of interdependence between business divisions, subordinate managers are more likely to feel that they have less control over their performance. This is because the performance of staff in other divisions could be an important influence on the final outcome. In such a situation, rigid application of the budget could be viewed as being unfair and may lead to undesirable behaviour. However, where managers have a high degree of independence, the application of budgets as a measure of performance is likely to be more acceptable. In this case, the managers are likely to feel that the final outcome is much less dependent on the performance of others.

Later studies have also shown that where a subordinate is undertaking a task that has a high degree of uncertainty concerning the outcome (for example, developing a new product), budget targets are unlikely to be an adequate measure of performance. In such a situation, other factors and measures should be taken into account in order to derive a more complete assessment of performance. However, where a task has a low degree of uncertainty concerning the outcome (for example, producing a standard product using standard equipment and an experienced workforce), budget measures may be regarded as more reliable indicators of performance. Thus, it appears that a budget-constrained style is more likely to work where subordinates enjoy a fair amount of independence and where the tasks set have a low level of uncertainty concerning their outcomes.

Failing to meet the budget

The existence of budgets gives senior managers a ready means to assess the performance of their subordinates (that is, junior managers). If a subordinate fails to meet a budget, the relevant senior manager must handle this carefully. Adverse variances may imply that the subordinate needs help. If this is the case, a harsh, critical approach would have a demotivating effect and would be counterproductive.

Real World 7.9 gives some indication of the effects of the **behavioural aspects of budgetary control** in practice.

Real World 7.9

Behavioural problems

A survey indicated that there is a large degree of participation in setting budgets by those expected to perform to the budget (the budget holders).

The survey also showed that senior managers have greater influence in setting the targets than their junior manager budget holders. Where there is a conflict between the cost estimates submitted by the budget holders and their senior managers, in 40 per cent of respondent businesses the senior manager's view would prevail without negotiation. In nearly 60 per cent of cases, however, a reduction would be negotiated between the budget holder and the senior manager. The general view of those that responded to the survey, regarding budget holders influencing the setting of their own budgets, is:

- 23 per cent of respondents believe that budget holders should not have too much influence since they will seek to obtain easy budgets (build in slack);
- 69 per cent of respondents take an opposite view.

The general view on how senior managers should judge their subordinates is:

- 46 per cent of respondents think that senior managers should judge junior managers mainly on their ability to achieve the budget;
- 40 per cent think otherwise.

Although this research is not very recent (1993), in the absence of more recent evidence it provides some feel for budget setting in practice.

Source: Drury, C., Braund, S., Osborne, P. and Tayles, M. (1993) *A Survey of Management Accounting Practices in UK Manufacturing Companies*, Chartered Association of Certified Accountants.

Budgets and innovation

We saw in Chapter 6 that budgets are often criticised for reinforcing a 'command and control' structure that concentrates power in the hands of senior managers and prevents junior managers from exercising autonomy. It has been argued that this can deter innovation and can leave subordinates feeling constrained and frustrated. There is not compelling evidence, however, to support this view. **Real World 7.10** discusses some research that explored the possible tension between budgetary control and innovative behaviour.

Real World 7.10

Not guilty

A research project was carried out within a large multinational business, which is referred to as 'Astoria' by researchers to preserve its anonymity. The business employs a broadly traditional budgeting system even though it is subject to rapid technological change and operates within a highly competitive environment. Interviews with 25 managers, drawn from different functional areas, were conducted to see whether the budgeting process stifled innovation in any way. The researchers concluded:

> . . . we found little evidence to suggest that managers at Astoria were deterred from engaging in innovative activities simply because they had budget responsibilities. Of course, the amount of resources available to them may have presented a sort of boundary, but they didn't see the presence of budgetary targets as a constraint. The closest we came to finding any suggestion that budgets might inhibit innovation was a comment from one manager who remarked that 'everybody has a sandpit to play in. My sandpit financially is my control plan. If I stay within it, I'm free to play.' More generally, managers considered that, if they felt restricted in pursuing innovation, it was the degree of general empowerment they had that mattered. One manager went so far as to say that he felt 'constrained in some ways by not having enough hours in the day'. Our findings suggest that, although much of the accounting literature argues that budgets may deter innovation, this seems far from the truth.

Source: Marginson, D. and Ogden, S. (2005) Budgeting and innovation, *Financial Management*, April, pp. 29–31.

Toscanini Ltd makes a standard product, which is budgeted to sell at £4.00 a unit, in a competitive market. It is made by taking a budgeted 0.4 kg of material, budgeted to cost £2.40/kg, and having it worked on by hand by an employee, paid a budgeted £8.00/hour, for a budgeted 6 minutes. Monthly fixed overheads are budgeted at £4,800. The output for May was budgeted at 4,000 units.

The actual results for May were as follows:

	£
Sales revenue (3,500 units)	13,820
Materials (1,425 kg)	(3,420)
Labour (345 hours)	(2,690)
Fixed overheads	(4,900)
Actual operating profit	2,810

No inventories of any description were held at the beginning or end of the month.

Required:

(a) Deduce the budgeted profit for May and reconcile it, through variances, with the actual profit in as much detail as the information provided will allow.

(b) State which manager should be held accountable, in the first instance, for each variance calculated.

(c) Assuming that the budget was well set and achievable, suggest at least one feasible reason for each of the variances that you identified in (a), given what you know about the business's performance for May.

(d) If it were discovered that the actual total world market demand for the business's product was 10 per cent lower than estimated when the May budget was set, explain how and why the variances that you identified in (a) could be revised to provide information that would be potentially more useful.

The solution to this question can be found at the back of the book on pp. 519–520.

SUMMARY

The main points of this chapter may be summarised as follows:

Controlling through budgets

- Budgets can act as a system of both feedback and feedforward control.
- To exercise control, budgets can be flexed to match actual volume of output.

Variance analysis

- Variances may be favourable or adverse according to whether they result in an increase to, or a decrease from, the budgeted profit figure.
- Budgeted profit plus all favourable variances less all adverse variances equals actual profit.
- Commonly calculated variances:
  - Sales volume variance = difference between the original budget and the flexed budget profit figures.
  - Sales price variance = difference between actual sales revenue and actual volume at the standard sales price.

- Total direct materials variance = difference between the actual direct materials cost and the direct materials cost according to the flexed budget.
- Direct materials usage variance = difference between actual usage and budgeted usage, for the actual volume of output, multiplied by the standard materials cost.
- Direct materials price variance = difference between the actual materials cost and the actual usage multiplied by the standard materials cost.
- Total direct labour variance = difference between the actual direct labour cost and the direct labour cost according to the flexed budget.
- Direct labour efficiency variance = difference between actual labour time and budgeted time, for the actual volume of output, multiplied by the standard labour rate.
- Direct labour rate variance = difference between the actual labour cost and the actual labour time multiplied by the standard labour rate.
- Fixed overhead spending variance = difference between the actual and budgeted spending on fixed overheads.

- Significant and/or persistent variances should normally be investigated to establish their cause. However, the costs and benefits of investigating variances must be considered.

- Trading off favourable variances against linked adverse variances should not be automatically acceptable.

- Not all activities can usefully be controlled through traditional variance analysis.

Standard costing

- Standards are budgeted physical quantities and financial values for one unit of inputs and outputs.

- There are two types of standards: ideal standards and practical standards.

- Information necessary for developing standards can be gathered by analysing the task or by using past data.

- There tends to be a learning-curve effect: routine tasks are performed more quickly with experience.

- Standards can be useful in providing data for income measurement, pricing decisions, product sourcing and efficiency measurement.

- Standards have their limitations, particularly in modern manufacturing environments; however, they are still widely used.

Effective budgetary control

- Good budgetary control requires establishing systems and routines to ensure such things as a clear distinction between individual managers' areas of responsibility; prompt, frequent and relevant variance reporting; and senior management commitment.

- There are behavioural aspects of control relating to management style, participation in budget setting and the failure to meet budget targets that should be taken into account by senior managers.

- The view that budgetary control stifles initiative is not well supported by the evidence.

REFERENCE

1 Hopwood, A.G. (1972) An empirical study of the role of accounting data in performance evaluation, *Empirical Research in Accounting*, a supplement to the *Journal of Accounting Research*, pp. 15–82.

FURTHER READING

If you would like to explore the topics covered in this chapter in more depth, we recommend the following:

Atkinson, A., Kaplan, R., Matsamura, E. and Young, S.M. (2013) *Management Accounting: Information for Decision Making and Strategy Execution*, 6th edn, Pearson, Chapters 9 and 11.

Bhimani, A., Horngren, C., Datar, S. and Rajan, M. (2015) *Management and Cost Accounting*, 6th edn, Pearson, Chapters 14–16.

Drury, C. (2015) *Management and Cost Accounting*, 9th edn, Cengage Learning EMEA, Chapters 16–18.

Hilton, R. and Platt, D. (2014) *Managerial Accounting*, McGraw-Hill Higher Education, Chapters 10 and 11.

REVIEW QUESTIONS

Solutions to these questions can be found at the end of the book on pp. 530–531.

7.1 Explain what is meant by feedforward control and distinguish it from feedback control.

7.2 What is meant by a variance? What is the point in analysing variances?

7.3 What is the point in flexing the budget in the context of variance analysis? Does flexing imply that differences between budget and actual in the volume of output are ignored in variance analysis?

7.4 Should all variances be investigated to find their cause? Explain your answer.

Exercises with **coloured numbers** have solutions given at the back of the book on pp. 553–556.

Basic-level exercises

7.1 You have recently overheard the following remarks:

(a) 'A favourable direct labour rate variance can only be caused by staff working more efficiently than budgeted.'

(b) 'Selling more units than budgeted, because the units were sold at less than standard price, automatically leads to a favourable sales volume variance.'

(c) 'Using below-standard materials will tend to lead to adverse materials usage variances but cannot affect labour variances.'

(d) 'Higher-than-budgeted sales could not possibly affect the labour rate variance.'

(e) 'An adverse sales price variance can only arise from selling a product at less than standard price.'

Required:
Critically assess these remarks, explaining any technical terms.

7.2 You have recently overheard the following remarks:

(a) 'When calculating variances, we ignore differences of volume of output, between original budget and actual, by flexing the budget. If there were a volume difference, it is water under the bridge by the time that the variances come to be calculated.'

(b) 'It is very valuable to calculate variances because they will tell you what went wrong.'

(c) 'All variances should be investigated to find their cause.'

(d) 'Research evidence shows that the more demanding the target, the more motivated the manager.'

(e) 'Most businesses do not have feedforward controls of any type, just feedback controls through budgets.'

Required:
Critically assess these remarks, explaining any technical terms.

Intermediate-level exercises

7.3 Pilot Ltd makes a standard product, which is budgeted to sell at £5.00 a unit. It is made by taking a budgeted 0.5 kg of material, budgeted to cost £3.00 a kilogram, and having it worked on by hand by an employee, paid a budgeted £10.00 an hour, for a budgeted $7^{1}/_{2}$ minutes. Monthly fixed overheads are budgeted at £6,000. The output for March was budgeted at 5,000 units.

The actual results for March were as follows:

	£
Sales revenue (5,400 units)	26,460
Materials (2,830 kg)	(8,770)
Labour (650 hours)	(6,885)
Fixed overheads	(6,350)
Actual operating profit	4,455

No inventories existed at the start or end of March.

Required:
(a) Deduce the budgeted profit for March and reconcile it with the actual profit in as much detail as the information provided will allow.

(b) State which manager should be held accountable, in the first instance, for each variance calculated.

7.4 Antonio plc makes Product X, the standard costs of which are:

	£
Sales revenue	31
Direct labour (1 hour)	(11)
Direct materials (1 kg)	(10)
Fixed overheads	(3)
Standard profit	7

The budgeted output for March was 1,000 units of Product X; the actual output was 1,100 units, which was sold for £34,950. There were no inventories at the start or end of March.

The actual production costs were:

	£
Direct labour (1,075 hours)	12,210
Direct materials (1,170 kg)	11,630
Fixed overheads	3,200

Required:

Calculate the variances for March as fully as you are able from the available information and use them to reconcile the budgeted and actual profit figures.

Advanced-level exercises

7.5 Bradley-Allen Ltd makes one standard product. Its budgeted operating statement for May is as follows:

		£	£
Sales (volume and revenue):	800 units		64,000
Direct materials:	Type A	(12,000)	
	Type B	(16,000)	
Direct labour:	Skilled	(4,000)	
	Unskilled	(10,000)	
Fixed overheads:		(12,000)	
			(54,000)
Budgeted operating profit			10,000

The standard costs were as follows:

Direct materials:	Type A	£50/kg
	Type B	£20/m
Direct labour:	Skilled	£10/hour
	Unskilled	£8/hour

During May, the following occurred:

1 950 units were sold for a total of £73,000.
2 310 kg (costing £15,200) of type A material were used in production.
3 920 metres (costing £18,900) of type B material were used in production.
4 Skilled workers were paid £4,628 for 445 hours.
5 Unskilled workers were paid £11,275 for 1,375 hours.
6 Fixed overheads cost £11,960.

There were no inventories of finished production or of work in progress at either the beginning or end of May.

Required:

(a) Prepare a statement that reconciles the budgeted to the actual profit of the business for May, through variances. Your statement should analyse the difference between the two profit figures in as much detail as possible.

(b) Explain how the statement in (a) might be helpful to managers.

7.6 Mowbray Ltd makes and sells one product, the standard costs of which are as follows:

	£
Direct materials (3 kg at £2.50/kg)	(7.50)
Direct labour (15 minutes at £9.00/hr)	(2.25)
Fixed overheads	(3.60)
	(13.35)
Selling price	20.00
Standard profit margin	6.65

The monthly production and sales are planned to be 1,200 units.

The actual results for May were as follows:

	£	
Sales revenue	18,000	
Direct materials	(7,400)	(2,800 kg)
Direct labour	(2,300)	(255 hr)
Fixed overheads	(4,100)	
Operating profit	4,200	

There were no inventories at the start or end of May. As a result of poor sales demand during May, the business reduced the price of all sales by 10 per cent.

Required:

Calculate the budgeted profit for May and reconcile it to the actual profit through variances, going into as much detail as is possible from the information available.

7.7 Brive plc has the following standards for its only product:

Selling price:	£110/unit
Direct labour:	1 hour at £10.50/hour
Direct material:	3 kg at £14.00/kg
Fixed overheads:	£27.00/unit, based on a budgeted output of 800 units/month

During May, there was an actual output of 850 units and the operating statement for the month was as follows:

	£
Sales revenue	92,930
Direct labour (890 hours)	(9,665)
Direct materials (2,410 kg)	(33,258)
Fixed overheads	(21,365)
Operating profit	28,642

There were no inventories of any description at the beginning and end of May.

Required:

Prepare the original budget and a budget flexed to the actual volume. Use these to compare the budgeted and actual profits of the business for the month, going into as much detail with your analysis as the information given will allow.

7.8 Varne Chemprocessors is a business that specialises in plastics. It uses a standard costing system to monitor and report its purchases and usage of materials. During the most recent month, accounting period six, the purchase and usage of chemical UK194 were as follows:

$$\text{Purchases/usage:} \quad 28{,}100 \text{ litres}$$
$$\text{Total price:} \quad £51{,}704$$

Because of fire risk and the danger to health, no inventories are held by the business.

UK194 is used solely in the manufacture of a product called Varnelyne. The standard cost specification shows that, for the production of 5,000 litres of Varnelyne, 200 litres of UK194 are needed at a total standard cost of £392. During period six, 637,500 litres of Varnelyne were produced.

Price variances, over recent periods, for two other raw materials used by the business are:

Period	UK500 £		UK800 £	
1	301	F	298	F
2	251	A	203	F
3	102	F	52	A
4	202	A	98	A
5	153	F	150	A
6	103	A	201	A

where F = favourable variance and A = adverse variance.

Required:

(a) Calculate the price and usage variances for UK194 for period six.

(b) The following comment was made by the production manager:

'I knew at the beginning of period six that UK194 would be cheaper than the standard cost specification, so I used rather more of it than normal; this saved £4,900 on other chemicals.' What changes do you need to make in your analysis for (a) as a result of this comment?

(c) Calculate, for both UK500 and UK800, the cumulative price variances and comment briefly on the results.

Chapter 8

MAKING CAPITAL INVESTMENT DECISIONS

INTRODUCTION

This chapter looks at how businesses should assess proposed investments in new plant, machinery, buildings and other long-term assets. This is a very important area; expensive and far-reaching consequences can flow from bad investment decisions.

We shall also consider some of the practical aspects that should be taken into account when evaluating investment proposals. Finally, we shall discuss the ways that managers can oversee capital investment projects and how control may be exercised throughout the life of a project.

Learning outcomes

When you have completed this chapter, you should be able to:

- Explain the nature and importance of investment decision making.
- Identify and evaluate the four main investment appraisal methods found in practice.
- Discuss the popularity and use of the four main investment appraisal methods in practice.
- Explain the methods used to monitor and control investment projects.

THE NATURE OF INVESTMENT DECISIONS

The essential feature of investment decisions is *time*. Investment involves making an outlay of something of economic value, usually cash, at one point in time, which is expected to yield economic benefits to the investor at some other point in time. Usually, the outlay precedes the benefits. Furthermore, the outlay is typically a single large amount while the benefits arrive as a series of smaller amounts over a fairly protracted period.

Investment decisions tend to be of profound importance to the business because:

- *Large amounts of resources are often involved.* Many investments made by businesses involve laying out a significant proportion of their total resources (see **Real World 8.2**). If mistakes are made with the decision, the effects on the businesses could be significant, if not catastrophic.
- *Relatively long timescales tend to be involved.* There is usually more time for things to go wrong between the decision being made and the end of the project, in comparison with many business decisions.
- *It is often difficult and/or expensive to bail out of an investment once it has been undertaken.* Investments made by a business are often specific to its needs. A hotel business, for example, may invest in a new, custom-designed hotel complex. If the business found, after having made the investment, that room occupancy rates were significantly lower than projected, the only course of action might be to sell the complex. The specialist nature of the complex may, however, lead to it having a rather limited resale value. This could mean that the amount recouped from the investment is much less than it had originally cost.

Real World 8.1 gives an illustration of a major investment by a well-known business operating in the UK.

Real World 8.1

Brittany Ferries launches an investment

Brittany Ferries, the cross-Channel ferry operator, is having an additional ferry built. The ferry is costing the business an amount thought to be well in excess of £200 million and will be used on the Portsmouth to Caen route from 2019. Although Brittany Ferries is a substantial business, this level of expenditure is significant. Clearly, the business believes that acquiring the new ferry will be profitable for it, but how would it have reached this conclusion? Presumably the anticipated future benefits from carrying passengers and freight as well as the costs of labour, fuel and maintenance will have been major inputs to the decision.

Source: www.brittany-ferries.co.uk.

The issues raised by Brittany Ferries' investment will be the main subject of this chapter.

Real World 8.2 indicates the level of annual net investment for a number of randomly selected, well-known UK businesses. We can see that the scale of investment varies from one business to another. (It also tends to vary from one year to another for a particular business.) In nearly all of these businesses the scale of investment was significant, despite the fact that many businesses were cutting back on investment during the economic recession.

The scale of investment by UK businesses

	Expenditure on additional non-current assets as a percentage of:	
	Annual sales revenue	End-of-year non-current assets
British Sky Broadcasting plc (television)	8.9	8.3
Go-Ahead Group plc (transport)	3.4	25.7
J D Wetherspoon plc (pub operator)	7.8	14.9
Marks and Spencer plc (stores)	5.8	8.7
Ryanair Holdings plc (airline)	18.6	19.0
Severn Trent Water plc (water and sewerage)	23.5	5.4
Vodafone plc (telecommunications)	29.2	11.3
Wm Morrison Supermarkets plc (supermarkets)	2.3	4.6

Source: Annual reports of the businesses concerned for the financial year ending in 2016.

Real World 8.2 considers only expenditure on non-current assets, but business investment typically requires a significant outlay on current assets to support it (additional inventories, for example). This suggests that the real scale of investment is even greater than indicated above.

Activity 8.1

When managers are making decisions involving capital investments, what should the decision seek to achieve?

Investment decisions must be consistent with the objectives of the particular organisation. For a private sector business, maximising the wealth of the owners (shareholders) is normally assumed to be the key financial objective.

INVESTMENT APPRAISAL METHODS

Given the importance of investment decisions, it is essential that proper screening of investment proposals takes place. An important part of this screening process is to ensure that appropriate methods of evaluation are used. Research shows that there are basically four methods used by businesses to evaluate investment opportunities:

- accounting rate of return (ARR);
- payback period (PP);
- net present value (NPV); and
- internal rate of return (IRR).

It is possible to find businesses that use variants of these four methods. It is also possible to find businesses, particularly smaller ones, that do not use any formal appraisal method but rely instead on the 'gut feeling' of their managers. Most businesses, however, seem to use one (or more) of these four methods.

We will examine the effectiveness of each of these methods, but we shall see that only one of them (NPV) offers a wholly logical approach. The others all have flaws. To help us examine each method, it might be useful to see how each would cope with a particular investment opportunity. Let us consider Example 8.1.

Example 8.1

Billingsgate Battery Company has carried out some research that shows there is a market for a standard service that it has recently developed.

Provision of the service would require investment in a machine that would cost £100,000, payable immediately. Sales of the service would take place throughout the next five years. At the end of that time, it is estimated that the machine could be sold for £20,000.

Inflows and outflows from sales of the service would be expected to be:

Time		£000
Immediately	Cost of machine	(100)
1 year's time	Operating profit before depreciation	20
2 years' time	Operating profit before depreciation	40
3 years' time	Operating profit before depreciation	60
4 years' time	Operating profit before depreciation	60
5 years' time	Operating profit before depreciation	20
5 years' time	Disposal proceeds from the machine	20

Note that, broadly speaking, the operating profit before deducting depreciation (that is, before non-cash items) equals the net amount of cash flowing into the business. Broadly, apart from depreciation, all of this business's expenses cause cash to flow out of the business. Sales revenues tend to lead to cash flowing in. Expenses tend to lead to it flowing out. For the time being, we shall assume that working capital – which is made up of inventories, trade receivables and trade payables – remains constant. This means that operating profit before depreciation will tend to equal the net cash inflow.

To simplify matters, we shall assume that the cash from sales and for the expenses of providing the service are received and paid, respectively, at the end of each year. This is clearly unlikely to be true in real life. Money will have to be paid to employees (for salaries and wages) on a weekly or a monthly basis. Customers will pay within a month or two of buying the service. On the other hand, making the assumption probably does not lead to a serious distortion. It is a simplifying assumption, that is often made in real life, and it will make things more straightforward for us now. We should be clear, however, that there is nothing about any of the four methods that *demands* that this assumption is made.

Having set up the example, we shall now go on to consider how each of the appraisal methods works.

ACCOUNTING RATE OF RETURN (ARR)

The first of the four methods that we shall consider is the **accounting rate of return (ARR)**. This method takes the average accounting operating profit that the investment will generate and expresses it as a percentage of the average investment made over the life of the project. In other words:

$$\text{ARR} = \frac{\text{Average annual operating profit}}{\text{Average investment to earn that profit}} \times 100\%$$

We can see from the equation that, to calculate the ARR, we need two pieces of information about the particular project:

- the annual average operating profit; and
- the average investment.

In our example, the average annual operating profit *before depreciation* over the five years is £40,000 (that is, £000(20 + 40 + 60 + 60 + 20)/5). Assuming 'straight-line' depreciation (that is, equal annual amounts), the annual depreciation charge will be £16,000 (that is, £(100,000 − 20,000)/5). Therefore, the average annual operating profit *after depreciation* is £24,000 (that is, £40,000 − £16,000).

The average investment over the five years can be calculated as follows:

$$\text{Average investment} = \frac{\text{Cost of machine} + \text{Disposal value}^*}{2}$$

$$= \frac{£100,000 + £20,000}{2}$$

$$= £60,000$$

*Note: To find the average investment we are simply adding the value of the amount invested at the beginning and end of the investment period together and dividing by two.

The ARR of the investment, therefore, is:

$$\text{ARR} = \frac{£24,000}{£60,000} \times 100\% = 40\%$$

The following decision rules apply when using ARR:

- For any project to be acceptable, it must achieve a target ARR as a minimum.
- Where there are competing projects that all seem capable of exceeding this minimum rate (that is, where the business must choose between more than one project), the one with the higher (or highest) ARR should be selected.

To decide whether the 40 per cent return is acceptable, we need to compare this percentage return with the minimum rate required by the business.

Chaotic Industries is considering an investment in a fleet of 10 delivery vans to take its products to customers. The vans will cost £15,000 each to buy, payable immediately. The annual running costs are expected to total £50,000 for each van (including the driver's salary). The vans are expected to operate successfully for six years, at the end of which period they will all be sold, with disposal proceeds expected to be about £3,000 a van. At present, the business outsources transport, for all of its deliveries, to a commercial carrier. It is expected that this carrier will charge a total of £530,000 each year for the next six years to undertake the deliveries.

What is the ARR of buying the vans? (Note that cost savings are as relevant a benefit from an investment as are net cash inflows.)

The vans will save the business £30,000 a year (that is, £530,000 − (£50,000 × 10)), before depreciation, in total. Therefore, the inflows and outflows will be:

Time		£000
Immediately	Cost of vans (10 × £15,000)	(150)
1 year's time	Saving before depreciation	30
2 years' time	Saving before depreciation	30
3 years' time	Saving before depreciation	30
4 years' time	Saving before depreciation	30
5 years' time	Saving before depreciation	30
6 years' time	Saving before depreciation	30
6 years' time	Disposal proceeds from the vans (10 × £3,000)	30

The total annual depreciation expense (assuming a straight-line method) will be £20,000 (that is, (£150,000 − £30,000)/6). Therefore, the average annual saving, *after depreciation*, is £10,000 (that is, £30,000 − £20,000).

The average investment will be

$$\text{Average investment} = \frac{£150,000 + £30,000}{2}$$

$$= £90,000$$

and the ARR of the investment is

$$\text{ARR} = \frac{£10,000}{£90,000} \times 100\%$$

$$= 11.1\%$$

ARR and ROCE

Return on capital employed (ROCE) is a widely-used measure of economic performance. It expresses the business's operating profit as a percentage of the value of the assets used to generate it. Both ROCE and ARR take the same approach to measuring business performance. Both relate operating profit to the cost of assets used to generate that profit. ROCE, however, assesses the performance of the entire business *after* it has performed, while ARR assesses the performance of a particular investment *before* it has performed.

We saw that investments are required to achieve a minimum target ARR. Given the link between the two measures, this target could be based on overall ROCE previously achieved. It could also be based on the industry-average ROCE.

The link between ARR and ROCE may be used to build a case for adopting ARR as the appropriate method of investment appraisal. As already mentioned, ROCE is a widely-used measure of performance. Furthermore, some businesses express their financial objective in terms of a target ROCE. It may seem sensible, therefore, to use a method of investment appraisal that is consistent with this overall measure. A secondary point in support of ARR is that it provides a result expressed percentage terms, which many managers seem to prefer.

Problems with ARR

ARR suffers from a major defect as a means of assessing investment opportunities. To illustrate this defect, consider Activity 8.3 below.

Activity 8.3

A business is evaluating three competing projects whose profits are shown below. All three involve investment in a machine that is expected to have no residual value at the end of the five years. Note that all the projects have the same total operating profits after depreciation over the five years.

Time		Project A £000	Project B £000	Project C £000
Immediately	Cost of machine	(160)	(160)	(160)
1 year's time	Operating profit after depreciation	20	10	160
2 years' time	Operating profit after depreciation	40	10	10
3 years' time	Operating profit after depreciation	60	10	10
4 years' time	Operating profit after depreciation	60	10	10
5 years' time	Operating profit after depreciation	20	160	10

What defect in the ARR method would prevent it from distinguishing between these competing projects? (*Hint*: The defect is not concerned with the ability of the decision maker to forecast future events, though this too can be a problem. Try to remember the essential feature of investment decisions, which we identified at the beginning of this chapter.)

In this example, each project has the same total operating profit over the five years (£200,000) and the same average investment of £80,000 (that is, £160,000/2). This means that each project will give rise to the same ARR of 50 per cent (that is, £40,000/£80,000).

ARR, therefore, fails to distinguish between them even though they are not of equal merit. This is because ARR ignores the time factor and, therefore, the cost of financing the project.

To maximise the wealth of the owners, a manager faced with a choice between the three projects set out in Activity 8.3 should select Project C. This is because most of the benefits arise within 12 months of making the initial investment. Project A would rank second and Project B would be a poor third. Any appraisal technique that is not capable of distinguishing between these three situations is seriously flawed. We shall look at why timing is so important later in the chapter.

There are further problems associated with the ARR method, which we shall now discuss.

Use of average investment

Using the average investment in calculating ARR can lead to daft results. Example 8.2 illustrates the kind of problem that can arise.

George put forward an investment proposal to his boss. The business uses ARR to assess investment proposals using a minimum 'hurdle' rate of 27 per cent. Details of the proposal were:

Cost of equipment	£200,000
Estimated residual value of equipment	£40,000
Average annual operating profit before depreciation	£48,000
Estimated life of project	10 years
Annual straight-line depreciation charge	£16,000 (that is, (£200,000 – £40,000)/10)

The ARR of the project will be:

$$ARR = \frac{48,000 - 16,000}{(200,000 + 40,000)/2} \times 100\% = 26.7\%$$

The boss rejected George's proposal because it failed to achieve an ARR of at least 27 per cent. Although George was disappointed, he realised that there was still hope. In fact, all that the business had to do was to give away the piece of equipment at the end of its useful life rather than sell it. The residual value of the equipment then became zero and the annual depreciation charge became ([£200,000 – £0]/10) = £20,000 a year. The revised ARR calculation was then:

$$ARR = \frac{48,000 - 20,000}{(200,000 + 0)/2} \times 100\% = 28\%$$

Use of accounting profit

We have seen that ARR is based on accounting profit. When measuring performance over the whole life of a project, however, it is cash flows rather than accounting profits that are important. Cash is the ultimate measure of the economic wealth generated by an investment. This is because it is cash that is used to acquire resources and for distribution to owners. Accounting profit is more appropriate for reporting achievement on a periodic basis. It is a useful measure of productive effort for a relatively short period, such as a year or half year. It is really a question of 'horses for courses'.

Target ARR

We saw earlier a target ARR against which to assess investment opportunities must be chosen. This cannot be objectively determined and so will depend on the judgement of managers. The target ARR may therefore vary both over time and between businesses.

Competing investments

The ARR method can create problems when considering competing investments of different size. Consider Activity 8.4.

Activity 8.4

Sinclair Wholesalers plc is currently considering opening a new sales outlet in Coventry. Two possible sites have been identified for the new outlet. Site A has an area of 30,000 square metres. It will require an average investment of £6 million and will produce an average operating profit of £600,000 a year. Site B has an area of 20,000 square metres. It will require an average investment of £4 million and will produce an average operating profit of £500,000 a year.

What is the ARR of each investment opportunity? Which site would you select and why?

The ARR of Site A is £600,000/£6m = 10 per cent. The ARR of Site B is £500,000/£4m = 12.5 per cent. Site B, therefore has the higher ARR. In terms of the absolute operating profit generated, however, Site A is the more attractive. If the ultimate objective is to increase the wealth of the shareholders of Sinclair Wholesalers plc, it would be better to choose Site A even though the percentage return is lower. It is the absolute size of the return rather than the relative (percentage) that is important. This is a general problem of using comparative measures, such as percentages, when the objective is measured in absolute terms, such as an amount of money.

Real World 8.3 illustrates how using percentage measures can lead to confusion.

Real World 8.3

Increasing road capacity by sleight of hand

During the 1970s, the Mexican government wanted to increase the capacity of a major four-lane road. It came up with the idea of repainting the lane markings so that there were six narrower lanes occupying the same space as four wider ones had previously done. This increased the capacity of the road by 50 per cent (that is, $\frac{2}{4} \times 100$). A tragic outcome of the narrower lanes was an increase in deaths from road accidents. A year later-the Mexican government had the six narrower lanes changed back to the original four wider ones. This reduced the capacity of the road by 33 per cent (that is, $\frac{2}{6} \times 100$). The Mexican government reported that, overall, it had increased the capacity of the road by 17 per cent (that is, 50% − 33%), despite the fact that its real capacity was identical to that which it had been originally. The confusion arose because each of the two percentages (50 per cent and 33 per cent) is based on different bases (four and six).

Source: Gigerenzer, G., *Reckoning with Risk,* Penguin, 2003.

According to its 2016 annual report, Next plc, the fashion and household retailer, uses ARR in assessing its investments in new retail space.

PAYBACK PERIOD (PP)

The second approach to appraising possible investments is the **payback period (PP)**. This is the time taken for an initial investment to be repaid out of the net cash inflows from a project. As the PP method takes time into account and it deals with cash, rather than accounting profit, it appears, at first glance, to overcome two key weaknesses of the ARR method.

Let us consider PP in the context of the Billingsgate Battery Company example. We should recall that the project's cash flows are:

Time		£000
Immediately	Cost of machine	(100)
1 year's time	Operating profit before depreciation	20
2 years' time	Operating profit before depreciation	40
3 years' time	Operating profit before depreciation	60
4 years' time	Operating profit before depreciation	60
5 years' time	Operating profit before depreciation	20
5 years' time	Disposal proceeds	20

Note that all of these figures are amounts of cash to be paid or received (we saw earlier that operating profit before depreciation is a rough measure of the cash flows from the project).

The payback period can be derived by calculating the cumulative cash flows as follows:

Time		Net cash flows £000	Cumulative net cash flows £000	
Immediately	Cost of machine	(100)	(100)	
1 year's time	Operating profit before depreciation	20	(80)	(−100 + 20)
2 years' time	Operating profit before depreciation	40	(40)	(−80 + 40)
3 years' time	Operating profit before depreciation	60	20	(−40 + 60)
4 years' time	Operating profit before depreciation	60	80	(20 + 60)
5 years' time	Operating profit before depreciation	20	100	(80 + 20)
5 years' time	Disposal proceeds	20	120	(100 + 20)

We can see that the cumulative cash flows become positive at the end of the third year. Had the cash flows arisen evenly over the year, the precise payback period would be:

$$2 \text{ years} + (^{40}/_{60}) \text{ years} = 2\tfrac{2}{3} \text{ years}$$

where the top part of the fraction (40) represents the cash flow needed at the beginning of the third year to repay the initial outlay and the bottom part (60) represents the projected cash flow during the third year.

The following decision rules apply when using PP:

- For a project to be acceptable it should have a payback period no longer than a maximum payback period set by the business.
- If there were two (or more) competing projects whose payback periods were all shorter than the maximum payback period requirement, the project with the shorter (or shortest) payback period should be selected.

Thus, if the Billingsgate Battery Company had a maximum acceptable payback period of four years, the project would be undertaken. A project with a payback period longer than four years would not be acceptable.

What is the payback period of the Chaotic Industries project from Activity 8.2?

The inflows and outflows are expected to be:

Time		Net cash flows £000	Cumulative net cash flows £000	
Immediately	Cost of vans	(150)	(150)	
1 year's time	Saving before depreciation	30	(120)	(−150 + 30)
2 years' time	Saving before depreciation	30	(90)	(−120 + 30)
3 years' time	Saving before depreciation	30	(60)	(−90 + 30)
4 years' time	Saving before depreciation	30	(30)	(−60 + 30)
5 years' time	Saving before depreciation	30	0	(−30 + 30)
6 years' time	Saving before depreciation	30	30	(0 + 30)
6 years' time	Disposal proceeds from the vans	30	60	(30 + 30)

The payback period here is five years; that is, it is not until the end of the fifth year that the vans will pay for themselves out of the savings that they are expected to generate.

The PP method views projects that can recoup their cost quickly as preferable to those that cannot. In other words, it emphasises liquidity.

Problems with PP

The PP method takes more account of the timing of the cash flows than the ARR method. It is not, however, a complete answer to the problem. To understand why this is the case, consider the following cash flows arising from three competing projects.

Time		Project 1 £000	Project 2 £000	Project 3 £000
Immediately	Cost of machine	(200)	(200)	(200)
1 year's time	Operating profit before depreciation	70	20	70
2 years' time	Operating profit before depreciation	60	20	100
3 years' time	Operating profit before depreciation	70	160	30
4 years' time	Operating profit before depreciation	80	30	200
5 years' time	Operating profit before depreciation	50	20	440
5 years' time	Disposal proceeds	40	10	20

Can you see from the above why PP is not a complete answer to the problem concerning the timing of cash flows?

The PP for each project is three years and so all three projects would be regarded as equally acceptable. This conclusion does not, however, take full account of the timing of cash flows. It does not distinguish between those projects that pay back a significant amount early within the three-year payback period and those that do not.

The PP method also ignores cash flows after the payback period. Managers concerned with increasing owners' wealth would prefer Project 3 because the cash inflows are received earlier. Most of the initial cost of making the investment has been repaid by the end of the second year. Furthermore, the cash inflows are greater in total.

The cumulative cash flows of each project in Activity 8.6 are set out in Figure 8.1.

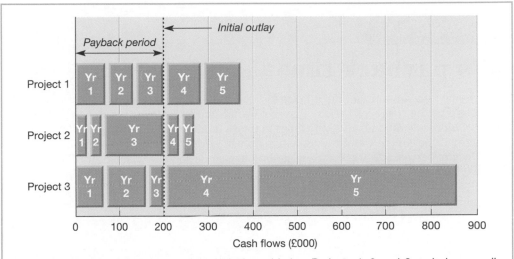

The payback method of investment appraisal would view Projects 1, 2 and 3 as being equally attractive. In doing so, the method completely ignores the fact that Project 3 provides most of the payback cash earlier in the three-year period and goes on to generate large benefits in later years.

Figure 8.1 The cumulative cash flows of each project in Activity 8.6

Some additional points concerning the PP method are now considered.

Relevant information

We saw earlier that the PP method is simply concerned with how quickly the initial investment can be recouped. While this neatly avoids the practical problems of forecasting cash flows over a long period, it means that not all relevant information may be taken into account. Cash flows arising beyond the payback period are ignored.

Risk

By favouring projects with a short payback period, the PP method provides a way of dealing with risk. However, it offers a fairly crude approach to the problem. It deals only with the risk that the project will end earlier than expected. This is only one of many risk areas. For example, what about the risk that the demand for the product may be less than expected? More systematic approaches to dealing with risk are available and we shall discuss these in Chapter 9.

Wealth maximisation

Although the PP method takes some note of the timing of project costs and benefits, it is not concerned with maximising the wealth of the business owners. Rather, it favours projects that pay for themselves quickly.

Required payback period

Managers must select a maximum acceptable payback period. When doing so, they confront a similar problem to the one arising when setting a target ARR. No objective basis can be used to determine this period: it is simply a matter of judgement.

Real World 8.4 is a short extract from a *Financial Times* article that discusses the increasing use of robots by Chinese manufacturers and the rapid decline in their payback period.

Real World 8.4

It's payback time

Every year, the amount of time it takes for a company's investment in a robot to pay off — known as the "payback period" — is narrowing sharply, making it more attractive for small Chinese companies and workshops to invest in automation. The payback period for a welding robot in the Chinese automotive industry, for instance, dropped from 5.3 years to 1.7 years between 2010 and 2015, according to calculations by analysts at Citi. By 2017, the payback period is forecast to shrink to just 1.3 years.

 Source: Bland, B. (2016) China's robot revolution, ft.com, 6 June.

NET PRESENT VALUE (NPV)

From what we have seen so far, it seems that to make sensible investment decisions, we need a method of appraisal that both:

- considers *all* of the costs and benefits of each investment opportunity; and
- makes a logical allowance for the *timing* of those costs and benefits.

The third of the four methods of investment appraisal, the **net present value (NPV)** method provides us with exactly this.

Consider the Billingsgate Battery example's cash flows, which we should recall are:

Time		£000
Immediately	Cost of machine	(100)
1 year's time	Operating profit before depreciation	20
2 years' time	Operating profit before depreciation	40
3 years' time	Operating profit before depreciation	60
4 years' time	Operating profit before depreciation	60
5 years' time	Operating profit before depreciation	20
5 years' time	Disposal proceeds	20

Given a financial objective of maximising owners' wealth, it would be easy to assess this investment if all cash inflows and outflows were to occur immediately. It would then simply be a matter of adding up the cash inflows (total £220,000) and comparing them with the cash outflows (£100,000). This would lead us to conclude that the project should go ahead because the owners would be better off by £120,000. It is, of course, not as easy as this because time is involved. The cash outflow will occur immediately, whereas the cash inflows will arise at different points in the future.

Why does time matter?

Time is an important issue because people do not normally see an amount paid out now as equivalent in value to the same amount being received in a year's time. Thus, if we were offered £100 in one year's time in exchange for paying out £100 now, we would not be interested, unless we wished to do someone a favour.

Activity 8.7

Why would you see £100 to be received in a year's time as not equal in value to £100 to be paid immediately? (There are basically three reasons.)

The reasons are:

- interest lost;
- risk; and
- inflation.

We shall now take a closer look at these three reasons in turn.

Interest lost

If we are to be deprived of the opportunity to spend our money for a year, we could equally well be deprived of its use by placing it on deposit in a bank or building society. By doing this, we could have our money back at the end of the year along with some interest earned. This interest, which is forgone by not placing our money on deposit, represents an *opportunity cost*. As we saw in Chapter 2, an opportunity cost occurs where one course of action deprives us of the opportunity to derive benefit from an alternative action.

An investment must exceed the opportunity cost of the funds invested if it is to be worthwhile. Therefore, if Billingsgate Battery Company sees putting the money in the bank on deposit as the alternative to investment in the machine, the return from investing in the machine must be better than that from investing in the bank. If this is not the case, there is no reason to buy the machine.

Risk

All investments expose their investors to risk. Thus, when Billingsgate Battery Company buys a machine on the strength of estimates made before its purchase, it must accept that things may not turn out as expected.

Can you identify the kind of risks that the business may face?

We have come up with the following:

■ The machine might not work as well as expected; it might break down, leading to loss of the business's ability to provide the service.
■ Sales of the service may not be as buoyant as expected.
■ Labour costs may prove to be higher than expected.
■ The sale proceeds of the machine could prove to be less than were estimated.

You may have thought of others.

It is important to remember that the purchase decision must be taken *before* any of these things are known. It is only after the machine has been purchased that we find out whether, say, the forecast level of sales is going to be achieved. We can study reports and analyses of the market. We can commission sophisticated market surveys and advertise widely to promote sales. All these may give us more confidence in the likely outcome. Ultimately, however, we must decide whether to accept the risk that things will not turn out as expected in exchange for the opportunity to generate profits.

We saw in Chapter 1 that people normally expect greater returns in exchange for taking on greater risk. So, when considering the Billingsgate Battery Company's investment opportunity, it is not enough to say that this business should buy the machine providing the expected returns are higher than the bank deposit interest rate because of the much higher risk involved. The logical equivalent of investing in the machine would be an investment of similar risk.

Determining how risky a particular project is and, therefore, the size of the the **risk premium** is a difficult task. We shall consider this in more detail in the next chapter.

Inflation

If we are to be deprived of £100 for a year, when we come to spend that money it will not buy the same amount of goods and services as it would have done a year earlier. Generally, we shall not be able to buy as many tins of baked beans or pairs of jeans or bus tickets as before. This is because of the loss in the purchasing power of money, or **inflation**, which tends to occur over time. Investors will expect to be compensated for this loss of purchasing power. This will be on top of a return that takes account of what could be gained from an alternative investment of similar risk.

In practice, interest rates observable in the market tend to take inflation into account. This means that rates offered to building society and bank depositors normally include an allowance for the expected rate of inflation.

What should managers do?

To summarise, managers seeking to increase the wealth of the business owners should only invest where the owners will be adequately compensated for the loss of interest, for the loss in the purchasing power of money invested and for the risk that the expected returns may not materialise. This normally involves investigating whether the proposed investment will yield a return greater than the basic rate of interest (which will normally include an allowance for inflation) plus an appropriate risk premium.

These three factors (interest lost, risk and inflation) are set out in Figure 8.2.

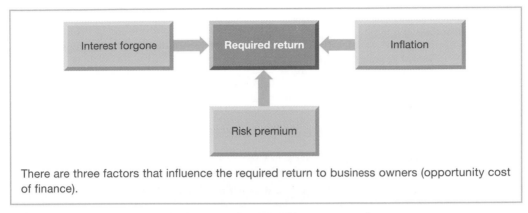

There are three factors that influence the required return to business owners (opportunity cost of finance).

Figure 8.2 Factors influencing the return required by investors from a project

Dealing with the time value of money

We saw above that money has a time value. That is, £100 received today is not regarded as equivalent in value to £100 received at some future date. We cannot, therefore, simply compare the cash inflows with cash outflows for an investment where they arise at different points in time. Each of these cash flows must be expressed in similar terms. Only then can a direct comparison be made.

To illustrate how this can be done, let us now return to the Billingsgate Battery Company example. We should recall that the cash flows expected from this investment are:

Time		£000
Immediately	Cost of machine	(100)
1 year's time	Operating profit before depreciation	20
2 years' time	Operating profit before depreciation	40
3 years' time	Operating profit before depreciation	60
4 years' time	Operating profit before depreciation	60
5 years' time	Operating profit before depreciation	20
5 years' time	Disposal proceeds	20

Let us assume that, instead of making this investment, the business could make an alternative investment with similar risk and obtain a return of 20 per cent a year.

Activity 8.9

Given that the Billingsgate Battery Company could invest its money at a rate of 20 per cent a year, what is the present (immediate) value of the expected first year receipt of £20,000? In other words, if instead of having to wait a year for the £20,000 and, therefore, being deprived of the opportunity to invest it at 20 per cent, the business could have some money now, what sum would be equivalent to getting £20,000 in one year's time?

The business should be happy to accept a lower amount if it could get this amount immediately rather than waiting a year. This is because it could invest this amount at 20 per cent (in the alternative project). Logically, it should be prepared to accept an amount that, with a year's income, will grow to £20,000. If we call this amount PV (for present value), we can say:

$$PV + (PV \times 20\%) = £20{,}000$$

that is, the amount plus income from investing the amount for the year equals the £20,000. If we rearrange this equation, we find:

$$PV \times (1 + 0.2) = £20{,}000$$

(Note that 0.2 is the same as 20 per cent, but expressed as a decimal.) Further rearranging gives:

$$PV = £20{,}000/(1 + 0.2) = £16{,}667$$

Thus, the managers of Billingsgate Battery Company who have the opportunity to invest at 20 per cent a year would not mind whether they have £16,667 now or £20,000 in a year's time. In other words, £16,667 represents the *present value* of £20,000 received in one year's time.

We can make a more general statement about the PV of a particular cash flow. It is:

PV of the cash flow of year n = actual cash flow of year n divided by $(1 + r)^n$

where n is the year of the cash flow (that is, how many years into the future) and r is the opportunity financing cost expressed as a decimal (instead of as a percentage).

If we derive the present value (PV) of each of the cash flows associated with Billingsgate's machine investment, we can easily make the direct comparison between the cost of making the investment (£100,000) and the subsequent benefits to be derived in years 1 to 5.

We have already seen how this works for the £20,000 inflow for year 1. For year 2, the calculation would be:

$$\text{PV of year 2 cash flow (that is, £40,000)} = £40{,}000/(1 + 0.2)^2 = £40{,}000/(1.2)^2$$
$$= £40{,}000/1.44 = £27{,}778$$

Thus, the present value of the £40,000 to be received in two years' time is £27,778.

Activity 8.10

See whether you can show that Billingsgate Battery Company would find £27,778, receivable now, as equally acceptable to receiving £40,000 in two years' time, assuming that there is a 20 per cent investment opportunity.

To answer this activity, we simply apply the principles of *compounding*. Income earned is reinvested and then added to the initial investment to derive the future value. Thus:

	£
Amount available for immediate investment	27,778
Income for year 1 (20% × 27,778)	5,556
	33,334
Income for year 2 (20% × 33,334)	6,667
	40,001

(The extra £1 is only a rounding error.)

Since the business can turn £27,778 into £40,000 in two years, these amounts are equivalent. We can say that £27,778 is the present value of £40,000 receivable after two years (given a 20 per cent cost of finance).

The act of reducing the value of a cash flow, to take account of the period between the present time and the time that the cash flow is expected, is known as **discounting**. Discounting, in effect, charges the project with the cost of financing it. Ignoring this financing cost would be to overlook a significant cost of undertaking the project.

Calculating the net present value

Now let us calculate the present values of all of the cash flows associated with the Billingsgate machine project and, from them, the *net present value (NPV)* of the project as a whole.

The relevant cash flows and calculations are:

Time	Cash flow £000	Calculation of PV	PV £000
Immediately (time 0)	(100)	$(100)/(1 + 0.2)^0$	(100.00)
1 year's time	20	$20/(1 + 0.2)^1$	16.67
2 years' time	40	$40/(1 + 0.2)^2$	27.78
3 years' time	60	$60/(1 + 0.2)^3$	34.72
4 years' time	60	$60/(1 + 0.2)^4$	28.94
5 years' time	20	$20/(1 + 0.2)^5$	8.04
5 years' time	20	$20/(1 + 0.2)^5$	8.04
Net present value (NPV)			24.19

Note that $(1 + 0.2)^0 = 1$.

Once again, we must decide whether the machine project is acceptable to the business. To help us, the following decision rules for NPV should be applied:

- If the NPV is positive the project should be accepted; if it is negative the project should be rejected.
- If there are two (or more) competing projects that have positive NPVs, the project with the higher (or highest) NPV should be selected.

In this case, the NPV is positive, so we should accept the project and buy the machine. The reasoning behind this decision rule is quite straightforward. Investing in the machine will make the business, and its owners, £24,190 better off than they would be by taking up the next best available opportunity. The total benefits from investing in this machine are worth a total of £124,190 today. Since the business can 'buy' these benefits for just £100,000 today, the investment should be made. If, however, the present value of the benefits were below £100,000, it would be less than the cost of 'buying' those benefits and the opportunity should, therefore, be rejected.

Activity 8.11

What is the *maximum* the Billingsgate Battery Company should be prepared to pay for the machine, given the potential benefits of owning it?

The business would logically be prepared to pay up to £124,190 since the wealth of the owners of the business would be increased up to this price – although the business would prefer to pay as little as possible.

Using present value tables

To deduce each PV in the Billingsgate Battery Company project, we took the relevant cash flow and multiplied it by $1/(1 + r)^n$. There is a slightly different way to do this. Tables exist that show values of this **discount factor** for a range of values of r and n. Such a table appears in at the end of this book in Appendix E on pages 575–576. Take a look at it.

Look at the column for 20 per cent and the row for one year. We find that the factor is 0.833. This means that the PV of a cash flow of £1 receivable in one year is £0.833. So the present value of a cash flow of £20,000 receivable in one year's time is £16,660 (that is, 0.833 × £20,000). This is the same result, ignoring rounding errors, as we found earlier by using the equation.

Activity 8.12

What is the NPV of the Chaotic Industries project from Activity 8.2, assuming a 15 per cent opportunity cost of finance (discount rate)? (Use the present value table in Appendix E, page 575.)

Remember that the net cash inflows and outflow are expected to be:

Time		£000
Immediately	Cost of vans	(150)
1 year's time	Saving before depreciation	30
2 years' time	Saving before depreciation	30
3 years' time	Saving before depreciation	30
4 years' time	Saving before depreciation	30
5 years' time	Saving before depreciation	30
6 years' time	Saving before depreciation	30
6 years' time	Disposal proceeds from the vans	30

The calculation of the NPV of the project is as follows:

Time	Cash flows £000	Discount factor (15%)	Present value £000
Immediately	(150)	1.000	(150.00)
1 year's time	30	0.870	26.10
2 years' time	30	0.756	22.68
3 years' time	30	0.658	19.74
4 years' time	30	0.572	17.16
5 years' time	30	0.497	14.91
6 years' time	30	0.432	12.96
6 years' time	30	0.432	12.96
			NPV = (23.49)

Activity 8.13

How would you interpret this result?

The project has a negative NPV. This means that the present values of the benefits from the investment are worth less than the initial outlay. Any amount up to £126,510 (the present value of the benefits) would be worth paying, but not £150,000.

The table in Appendix E shows how the value of £1 diminishes as its receipt goes further into the future. Assuming an opportunity cost of finance of 20 per cent a year, £1 to be received immediately, obviously, has a present value of £1. However, as the time before it is to be received increases, the present value diminishes significantly, as is shown in Figure 8.3.

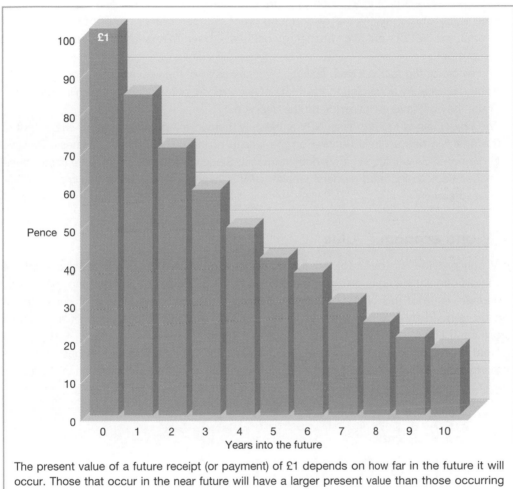

The present value of a future receipt (or payment) of £1 depends on how far in the future it will occur. Those that occur in the near future will have a larger present value than those occurring at a more distant point in time.

Figure 8.3 Present value of £1 receivable at various times in the future, assuming an annual financing cost of 20 per cent

The discount rate and the cost of capital

We have seen that the appropriate discount rate to use in NPV assessments is the opportunity cost of finance. This is, in effect, the cost to the business of the finance needed to fund the investment. It will normally be the cost of a mixture of funds (shareholders' funds and borrowings) employed by the business and is often referred to as the **cost of capital**. We shall refer to it as cost of capital from now on.

WHY NPV IS BETTER

From what we have seen, NPV offers a better approach to appraising investment opportunities than either ARR or PP. This is because it fully takes account of each of the following:

- *The timing of the cash flows.* By discounting the various cash flows associated with each project according to when they are expected to arise, NPV takes account of the time value of money. As the discounting process incorporates the opportunity cost of capital, the net benefit *after* financing costs have been met is identified (as the NPV of the project).
- *The whole of the relevant cash flows.* NPV includes *all* of the relevant cash flows. They are treated differently according to their date of occurrence, but they are all taken into account. Thus, they all have an influence on the decision.
- *The objectives of the business.* NPV is the only method of appraisal in which the output of the analysis has a direct bearing on the wealth of the owners of the business. Positive NPVs enhance wealth; negative ones reduce it. Since we assume that private sector businesses seek to increase owners' wealth, NPV is superior to the other two methods discussed earlier.

NPV and economic value

NPV can provide the basis for valuing an economic asset. This is any asset capable of yielding financial benefits and will include such things as equity shares and loans. The *economic value* of this type of asset will depend on the net benefits that it generates. It can be derived by adding together the discounted (present) values of all of the asset's future cash flows.

Real World 8.5 comprises extracts from a *Financial Times* article that discusses a telecoms takeover in New Zealand where the NPV has been used to assess its financial viability.

Real World 8.5

Reaching for the Sky

Flight of the Conchords, a sitcom about Kiwis adrift among New Yorkers ignorant of their nation, spawned the wry slogan: "New Zealand: it's not part of Australia". Nor is New Zealand's Sky Network Television part of the UK's Sky, mentioned above. But the group is set to become a subsidiary of deal-hungry telecoms group Vodafone through a NZ$3.4 billion merger, which, for readability, we'll convert to US$2.4bn.

British companies have been hanging back from mergers and acquisitions ahead of the Brexit vote. Vodafone is going ahead with this deal, though in a place about as far as you can get from Nigel Farage without boarding a spaceship.

Telephone air time is increasingly commodified. There is fierce competition in pay TV. The combination of SNT and Voda's New Zealand operations is expected to yield cost and capital expenditure synergies with a net present value of $295 million.

 Source: Extract from Guthrie, J. (2016) Kiwi combo, Lombard, ft.com, 9 June.

INTERNAL RATE OF RETURN (IRR)

This is the last of the four major methods of investment appraisal found in practice. It is closely related to the NPV method in that both involve discounting future cash flows. The **internal rate of return (IRR)** of an investment is the discount rate that, when applied to its future cash flows, will produce an NPV of precisely zero. In essence, it represents the yield from a particular investment opportunity.

Activity 8.14

We should recall that, when we discounted the cash flows of the Billingsgate Battery Company machine project at 20 per cent, we found that the NPV was a positive figure of £24,190 (see page 297). What does the NPV of the machine project tell us about the rate of return that the investment will yield for the business (that is, the project's IRR)?

As the NPV is positive when discounting at 20 per cent, it implies that the project's rate of return is more than 20 per cent. The fact that the NPV is pretty large implies that the actual rate of return is quite a lot above 20 per cent. Normally, we should expect increasing the discount rate to reduce NPV, because the higher the discount rate the lower the discounted figure.

IRR cannot usually be calculated directly. Iteration (trial and error) is the approach normally adopted. Doing this manually, however, is fairly laborious. Fortunately, computer spreadsheet packages can do this with ease.

Despite it being laborious, we shall now derive the IRR for the Billingsgate project manually. We shall increase the size of the discount rate to reduce NPV, because a higher discount rate gives a lower discounted figure.

Let us try a higher rate, say, 30 per cent and see what happens.

Time	Cash flow £000	Discount factor 30%	PV £000
Immediately (time 0)	(100)	1.000	(100.00)
1 year's time	20	0.769	15.38
2 years' time	40	0.592	23.68
3 years' time	60	0.455	27.30
4 years' time	60	0.350	21.00
5 years' time	20	0.269	5.38
5 years' time	20	0.269	5.38
			NPV = (1.88)

By increasing the discount rate from 20 per cent to 30 per cent, we have reduced the NPV from £24,190 (positive) to £1,880 (negative). Since the IRR is the discount rate that will give us an NPV of exactly zero, we can conclude that the IRR of Billingsgate Battery Company's machine project is very slightly below 30 per cent. Further trials could lead us to the exact rate, but there is probably not much point, given the likely inaccuracy of the cash flow estimates. For most practical purposes, it is good enough to say that the IRR is about 30 per cent.

The relationship between the NPV and the IRR is shown graphically in Figure 8.4 using the information relating to the Billingsgate Battery Company.

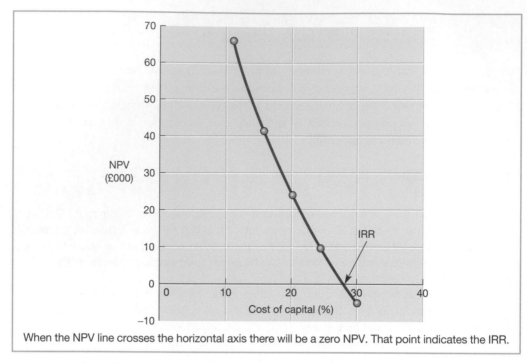

When the NPV line crosses the horizontal axis there will be a zero NPV. That point indicates the IRR.

Figure 8.4 The relationship between the NPV and IRR methods

In Figure 8.4, if the discount rate is equal to zero, the NPV will be the sum of the net cash flows. In other words, no account is taken of the time value of money. However, as the discount rate increases there is a corresponding decrease in the NPV of the project. When the NPV line crosses the horizontal axis there will be a zero NPV. That point represents the IRR.

Activity 8.15

What is the internal rate of return of the Chaotic Industries project from Activity 8.2?
(*Hint*: Remember that you already know the NPV of this project at 15 per cent (from Activity 8.12).)

Since we know that, at a 15 per cent discount rate, the NPV is a relatively large negative figure, our next trial should use a lower discount rate, say 10 per cent:

Time	Cash flows £000	Discount factor (10% – from the table)	Present value £000
Immediately	(150)	1.000	(150.00)
1 year's time	30	0.909	27.27
2 years' time	30	0.826	24.78
3 years' time	30	0.751	22.53
4 years' time	30	0.683	20.49
5 years' time	30	0.621	18.63
6 years' time	30	0.564	16.92
6 years' time	30	0.564	16.92
			NPV = (2.46)

This figure is close to zero NPV. However, the NPV is still negative and so the precise IRR will be a little below 10 per cent.

We could undertake further trials to derive the precise IRR. If done manually, this can be quite time-consuming. We can, however, get an acceptable approximation to the answer fairly quickly by first calculating the change in NPV arising from a 1 per cent change in the discount rate. This is achieved by taking the difference between the two trials (that is, 15 per cent and 10 per cent) that have already been carried out (in Activities 8.12 and 8.15):

Trial	Discount factor	Net present value
	%	£000
1	15	(23.49)
2	10	(2.46)
Difference	5	21.03

The change in NPV for every 1 per cent change in the discount rate will be:

$$(21.03/5) = 4.21$$

The amount by which the IRR would need to fall below the 10 per cent discount rate, in order to achieve a zero NPV would therefore be:

$$(2.46/4.21) \times 1\% = 0.58\%$$

The IRR is therefore:

$$(10.00 - 0.58) = 9.42\%$$

To say that the IRR is about 9 or 10 per cent, however, is near enough for most purposes.

Note that this approach to obtaining a more accurate figure for IRR assumes a straight-line relationship between the discount rate and NPV. We can see from Figure 8.4 that this assumption is not strictly correct. Over a relatively short range, however, this simplifying assumption is not usually a problem and so we can still arrive at a reasonable approximation using the approach taken. As most businesses have software packages to derive a project's IRR, it is not usually necessary to make the calculations just described.

The following decision rules are applied when using IRR:

- For any project to be acceptable, it must meet a minimum IRR requirement. This is often referred to as the *hurdle rate* and, logically, this should be the opportunity cost of capital.
- Where there are competing projects, the one with the higher (or highest) IRR should be selected.

Activity 8.16

Assume that a project has an IRR that exceeds the business's cost of capital. Why might it be helpful to consider how much it exceeds it by?

It may help us to make some judgement about the riskiness of the project, as far as the projected cost of capital is concerned. We should be able to see how far this figure could rise in practice before the project would become unfavourable (assuming all of the other inputs to the project appraisal turned out to be as expected).

Real World 8.6 illustrates how the French energy business, EDF, used IRR in assessing a deal to build a nuclear power station in the UK.

Real World 8.7 gives some examples of IRRs sought in practice.

return of 5.3 per cent. This figure is the real return (that is, ignoring inflation). It would probably be fair to add at least 3 per cent to compare it with the targets for the businesses listed above. Also, the targets for five of the businesses are probably pre-tax (the businesses do not specify, except Rentokil Initial). In that case, it is probably reasonable to add about a third to the average Stock Exchange returns. This would give us around 11 per cent per year. This would be roughly in line with the Marks and Spencer target. The targets for the other businesses, however, seem rather ambitious – particularly ambitious in the case of Rentokil Initial, given that it's an after-tax rate. Their rate is for takeover targets, which they may regard as being particularly risky. Next's target is also high, though it relates to advertising campaigns.

Sources: GlaxoSmithKline plc, Annual Report 2015, p. 24; Next plc, Annual Report 2016, p. 13; Carillion plc, Annual Report 2014, p. 26; Rentokil Initial plc, www.rentokil-initial.com, accessed 23 September 2016; Gresham House plc, www.greshamhouse.com; accessed 23 September 2016; Press release on 2012 annual results, Marks and Spencer plc, 22 May 2012; Dimson, E., Marsh, P. and Staunton, M. (2015) *Credit Suisse Global Investments Returns Yearbook*.

Problems with IRR

IRR has certain key attributes in common with NPV. All cash flows are taken into account and their timing is logically handled. The main problem of IRR, however, is that it does not directly address the question of wealth generation. It can, therefore, lead to the wrong decision being made. This is because the IRR approach will always rank a project with, for example, an IRR of 25 per cent above that of a project with an IRR of 20 per cent. Although accepting the project with the higher percentage return will often generate more wealth, this may not always be the case. This is because IRR completely ignores the *scale of investment*.

With a 15 per cent cost of capital, £15 million invested at 20 per cent for one year will make us wealthier by £0.75 million (that is, $15 \times (20 - 15)\% = 0.75$). With the same cost of capital, £5 million invested at 25 per cent for one year will make us only £0.5 million (that is, $5 \times (25 - 15)\% = 0.50$). IRR does not recognise this point.

Activity 8.17

Which other investment appraisal method ignores the scale of investment?

We saw earlier that the ARR method suffers from this problem.

Competing projects do not usually show such large differences in scale and so IRR and NPV normally give the same signal. However, as NPV will always give the correct signal, it is difficult to see why any other method should be used.

A further problem with the IRR method is that it has difficulty handling projects with unconventional cash flows. In the examples studied so far, each project has a negative cash flow arising at the start of its life and then positive cash flows thereafter. In some cases, however, a project may have both positive and negative cash flows at future points in its life. Such a pattern of cash flows can result in there being more than one IRR, or even no IRR at all. This can make the IRR method difficult to use, although it should be said that this problem is also quite rare in practice.

SOME PRACTICAL POINTS

When undertaking an investment appraisal, there are several practical points to bear in mind:

- *Past costs.* As with all decisions, we should take account only of relevant costs in our analysis. Only costs that vary with the decision should be considered, as we discussed in Chapter 2. This means that all past costs should be ignored, as they cannot vary with the decision. A business may incur costs (such as development costs and market research costs) *before* the evaluation of an opportunity to launch a new product. As those costs have already been incurred, they should be disregarded, even though the amounts may be substantial and relate directly to the project. Costs that have already been committed but not yet paid should also be disregarded. Where a business has entered into a binding contract to incur a particular cost, it becomes in effect a past cost even though payment may not be due until some point in the future.

- *Common future costs.* It is not only past costs that do not vary with the decision; some future costs may also be the same. For example, the cost of raw materials may not vary with the decision whether to invest in a new piece of manufacturing plant or to continue to use existing plant.

- *Opportunity costs.* Opportunity costs arising from benefits forgone must be taken into account. For example, when considering a decision concerning whether to continue to use a machine already owned by the business, the realisable value of the machine might be an important opportunity cost.

- *Taxation.* Owners will be interested in the after-tax returns generated from the business. Profits from the project will be taxed, the capital investment may attract tax relief and so on. As the rate of tax is often significant, taxation becomes an important consideration when making investment decisions. Unless tax is formally taken into account, the wrong decision could easily be made. This means that both the amount and the timing of tax outflows should be reflected in the cash flows for the project.

- *Cash flows not profit flows.* We have seen that for the NPV, IRR and PP methods, it is cash flows rather than profit flows that are relevant to the assessment of investment projects. Nevertheless, some proposals may only contain data relating to profits over the investment period. These will need to be adjusted in order to derive the cash flows. As mentioned earlier, operating profit *before* non-cash items (such as depreciation) provides an approximation to the cash flows for the period. We should, therefore, work back to this figure.

    When the data are expressed in profit rather than cash flow terms, some adjustment for changes in working capital may also be needed. Launching a new product, for example, may give rise to an increase in the net investment made in working capital (trade receivables and inventories less trade payables). This would normally require an immediate outlay of cash, which should be shown as a cash outflow in the NPV calculations. However, at the end of the life of the project, the additional working capital will be released. This divestment results in an effective inflow of cash at the end of the project. This should be shown in the NPV calculations at the point at which it is received.

- *Year-end assumption.* In the examples and activities considered so far, we have assumed that cash flows arise at the end of the relevant year. This simplifying assumption is used to make the calculations easier. As we saw earlier, this assumption is unrealistic, as money will have to be paid to employees on a weekly or monthly basis, credit customers will pay within a month or two of the sale and so on. Nevertheless, it is probably not a serious distortion. It is perfectly possible to deal more precisely with the timing of the cash flows.

■ *Interest payments.* When using discounted cash flow techniques (NPV and IRR), interest payments should not be taken into account in deriving cash flows for the period. Discounting already takes account of the costs of financing. To include interest charges in deriving cash flows for the period would therefore be double counting.

■ *Other factors.* Investment decision making must not be viewed as simply a mechanical exercise. The results derived from a particular investment appraisal method will be only one input to the decision-making process. There may be broader issues connected to the decision that have to be taken into account but which may be difficult or impossible to quantify.

The reliability of the forecasts and the validity of the assumptions used in the evaluation will also have a bearing on the final decision.

Activity 8.18

The directors of Manuff (Steel) Ltd are considering closing one of the business's factories. There has been a reduction in the demand for the products made at the factory in recent years. The directors are not optimistic about the long-term prospects for these products. The factory is situated in an area where unemployment is high.

The factory is leased with four years of the lease remaining. The directors are uncertain whether the factory should be closed immediately or at the end of the period of the lease. Another business has offered to sublease the premises from Manuff (Steel) Ltd at a rental of £40,000 a year for the remainder of the lease period.

The machinery and equipment at the factory cost £1,500,000. The value at which they appear in the statement of financial position is £400,000. In the event of immediate closure, the machinery and equipment could be sold for £220,000. The working capital at the factory is £420,000. It could be liquidated for that amount immediately, if required. Alternatively, the working capital can be liquidated in full at the end of the lease period. Immediate closure would result in redundancy payments to employees of £180,000.

If the factory continues in operation until the end of the lease period, the following operating profits (losses) are expected:

	Year 1 £000	Year 2 £000	Year 3 £000	Year 4 £000
Operating profit (loss)	160	(40)	30	20

These figures are derived after deducting a charge of £90,000 a year for depreciation of machinery and equipment. The residual value of the machinery and equipment at the end of the lease period is estimated at £40,000.

Redundancy payments are expected to be £150,000 at the end of the lease period if the factory continues in operation. The business has an annual cost of capital of 12 per cent. Ignore taxation.

(a) Determine the relevant cash flows arising from a decision to continue operations until the end of the lease period rather than to close immediately.
(b) Calculate the net present value of continuing operations until the end of the lease period, rather than closing immediately.
(c) What other factors might the directors take into account before making a final decision on the timing of the factory closure?
(d) State, with reasons, whether or not the business should continue to operate the factory until the end of the lease period.

→

Your answer should be:

(a) Relevant cash flows

	Years				
	0	1	2	3	4
	£000	£000	£000	£000	£000
Operating cash flows (Note 1)		250	50	120	110
Sale of machinery (Note 2)	(220)				40
Redundancy costs (Note 3)	180				(150)
Sublease rentals (Note 4)		(40)	(40)	(40)	(40)
Working capital invested (Note 5)	(420)				420
Cash flows	(460)	210	10	80	380

Notes:

1 Each year's operating cash flows are calculated by adding back the depreciation charge for the year to the operating profit for the year. In the case of the operating loss, the depreciation charge is deducted.
2 In the event of closure, machinery could be sold immediately. As a result, an opportunity cost of £220,000 is incurred if operations continue.
3 By continuing operations, there will be a saving in immediate redundancy costs of £180,000. However, redundancy costs of £150,000 will be paid in four years' time.
4 By continuing operations, the opportunity to sublease the factory will be foregone.
5 Immediate closure would mean that working capital could be liquidated. By continuing operations, this opportunity is forgone. However, working capital can be liquidated in four years' time.

(b)

	Years				
	0	1	2	3	4
Discount rate 12 per cent	1.000	0.893	0.797	0.712	0.636
Present value	(460.0)	187.5	8.0	57.0	241.7
Net present value	34.2				

(c) Other factors that may influence the decision include:
- *The overall strategy of the business.* The business may need to set the decision within a broader context. It may be necessary to manufacture the products at the factory because they are an integral part of the business's product range. The business may wish to avoid redundancies in an area of high unemployment for as long as possible.
- *Flexibility.* A decision to close the factory is probably irreversible. If the factory continues, however, there may be a chance that the prospects for the factory will brighten in the future.
- *Creditworthiness of sub-lessee.* The business should investigate the creditworthiness of the sub-lessee. Failure to receive the expected sublease payments would make the closure option far less attractive.
- *Accuracy of forecasts.* The forecasts made by the business should be examined carefully. Inaccuracies in the forecasts or any underlying assumptions may change

(d) The NPV of the decision to continue operations rather than close immediately is positive. Hence, shareholders would be better off if the directors took this course of action. The factory should therefore continue in operation rather than close down. This decision is likely to be welcomed by employees and would allow the business to maintain its flexibility.

The main methods of investment appraisal are summarised in Figure 8.5.

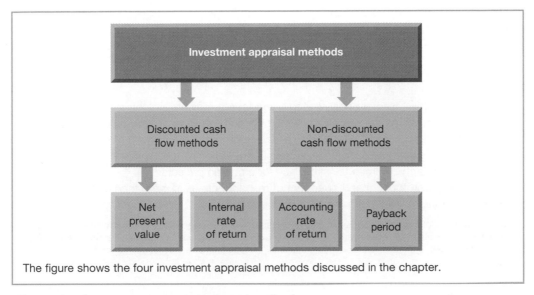

The figure shows the four investment appraisal methods discussed in the chapter.

Figure 8.5 The main investment appraisal methods

INVESTMENT APPRAISAL IN PRACTICE

Many surveys have been conducted in the UK, and elsewhere in the world, into the methods of investment appraisal used by businesses. They have shown the following features:

- Businesses tend to use more than one method to assess each investment decision.
- The discounting methods (NPV and IRR) have become increasingly popular over time. NPV and IRR are now the most popular of the four methods.
- PP continues to be popular and, to a lesser extent, so does ARR. This is despite the severe theoretical shortcomings of both of these methods.
- Larger businesses tend to rely more heavily on discounting methods than smaller businesses and tend to use more of the four methods.

Real World 8.8 shows the results of a survey of a number of UK manufacturing businesses concerning their use of investment appraisal methods.

Real World 8.8

A survey of UK business practice

Senior financial managers at 83 of the UK's largest manufacturing businesses were asked about the investment appraisal methods used to evaluate both 'strategic' and 'non-strategic' projects. Strategic projects are broadly defined as those that aim to increase or change the competitive capabilities of a business, such as introducing a new manufacturing process. Non-strategic decisions tend to be less far-reaching, like replacing an item of plant in an existing and continuing activity.

Method	Non-strategic projects Mean score	Strategic projects Mean score
Net present value	3.6829	3.9759
Internal rate of return	3.3293	3.7073
Accounting rate of return	1.9867	2.2667
Payback	3.4268	3.6098

Response scale 1 = never, 2 = rarely, 3 = often, 4 = mostly, 5 = always

We can see that, for both non-strategic and for strategic investments, the NPV method is the most popular. As the sample consists of large businesses (nearly all with annual total sales revenue in excess of £100 million), a fairly sophisticated approach to evaluation might be expected. Nevertheless, for non-strategic investments, the payback method comes second in popularity. It drops to third place for strategic projects.

The survey also found that 98 per cent of respondents used more than one method and 88 per cent used all four methods of investment appraisal.

Source: Based on information in Alkaraan, F. and Northcott, D. (2006) Strategic capital investment decision-making: A role for emergent analysis tools? A study of practice in large UK manufacturing companies, *The British Accounting Review*, 38, p. 159.

A survey of large businesses in five leading industrialised countries, including the UK, also shows considerable support for the NPV and IRR methods. There is less support for the payback method but, nevertheless, it still seems to be fairly widely used. **Real World 8.9** sets out some key findings.

Real World 8.9

A multinational survey of business practice

A survey of investment and financing practices in five different countries was carried out by Cohen and Yagil. This survey, based on a sample of the largest 300 businesses in each country, revealed the following concerning the popularity of three of the investment appraisal methods discussed in this chapter.

Frequency of the use of investment appraisal techniques

	USA	UK	Germany	Canada	Japan	Average
IRR	4.00	4.16	4.08	4.15	3.29	3.93
NPV	3.88	4.00	3.50	4.09	3.57	3.80
PP	3.46	3.89	3.33	3.57	3.52	3.55

Response scale 1 = never, 2 = rarely, 3 = often, 4 = mostly, 5 = always

Key findings of the survey include the following:

- IRR is more popular than NPV in all countries, except Japan. The difference between the two methods, however, is not statistically significant.
- Managers of UK businesses use investment appraisal techniques the most, while managers of Japanese businesses use them the least. This may be related to business traditions within each country.
- There is a positive relationship between business size and the popularity of the IRR and NPV methods. This may be related to the greater experience and understanding of financial

theory of managers of larger businesses. A more recent survey (by Lucas, Prowle and Lowth) of some much smaller UK businesses indicated that none of them carried out any investment appraisal. This adds emphasis to the size/sophistication relationship in this context.

Source: Cohen, G. and Yagil, J. (2004) *A multinational survey of corporate financial policies*, Working Paper, Haifa University; Lucas, M., Prowle, M. and Lowth, G. (2013) *Management Accounting Practices of UK Small-medium-sized Enterprises*, CIMA, July.

Activity 8.19

Earlier in the chapter, we discussed the limitations of the PP method. Can you explain why it is still a reasonably popular method of investment appraisal among managers?

There seem to be several possible reasons:

- PP is easy to understand and use.
- It can avoid the problems of forecasting far into the future.
- It gives weight to early cash flows when there is greater certainty concerning the accuracy of their predicted value.
- It emphasises the importance of liquidity. Where a business has liquidity problems, a short payback period for a project is likely to appear attractive.

The popularity of PP may suggest a lack of sophistication by managers, concerning investment appraisal. This criticism is most often made against managers of smaller businesses. This point is borne out by both of the surveys discussed in Real World 8.9 which have found that smaller businesses are much less likely to use discounted cash flow methods (NPV and IRR) than larger ones. Other surveys have tended to reach a similar conclusion.

IRR may be popular because it expresses outcomes in percentage terms rather than in absolute terms. This form of expression seems to be preferred by managers, despite the problems of percentage measures that we discussed earlier. This may be because managers are used to percentage figures as targets (for example, return on capital employed).

Real World 8.10 shows extracts from the 2016 annual report of Rolls-Royce plc, a global technology company focused on power and propulsion systems.

Real World 8.10

The use of NPV at Rolls-Royce

In its 2016 annual report and accounts, Rolls-Royce plc stated that:

> The Group subjects all major investments and capital expenditure to a rigorous examination of risks and future cash flows to ensure that they create shareholder value. All major investments, including the launch of major programmes, require Board approval.
>
> The Group has a portfolio of projects at different stages of their life cycles. Discounted cash flow analysis of the remaining life of projects is performed on a regular basis.

Source: Rolls-Royce Holdings plc Annual Report 2016, p. 185.

Rolls-Royce indicates that it uses NPV (the report refers to creating shareholder value and to discounted cash flow, which strongly imply NPV). It is interesting to note that Rolls-Royce not only assesses new projects but also reassesses existing ones. This must be a sensible commercial approach. Businesses should not continue with existing projects unless those projects have a positive NPV based on future cash flows. Just because a project seemed to have a positive NPV before it started, and at early stages in its life, does not mean that this will persist, in the light of changing circumstances. Activity 8.18 (pages 307–308) considered a decision to close down a project.

INVESTMENT APPRAISAL AND STRATEGIC PLANNING

So far, we have tended to view investment opportunities as unconnected, independent, events. In practice, however, successful businesses are those that set out a clear strategic framework for the selection of investment projects in the way described in Chapter 1. Unless this framework is in place, it may be difficult to identify those projects that are likely to generate a positive NPV. The best investment projects are usually those that match the business's internal strengths (for example, skills, experience, access to finance) with the opportunities available. In areas where this match does not exist, other businesses, for which the match does exist, are likely to have a distinct competitive advantage. This means that they can provide the product or service at a better price and/or quality.

Setting out the framework just described is an essential part of *strategic planning.* In practice, strategic plans often have a time span of around five years. It involves asking 'where do we want our business to be in five years' time and how can we get there?' It will set the appropriate direction in terms of products, markets, financing and so on, to ensure that the business is best placed to generate profitable investment opportunities.

Real World 8.11 shows how one large business made an investment that fitted its strategic objectives.

MANAGING INVESTMENT PROJECTS

So far, we have been concerned with the process of carrying out calculations to help choose among already identified investment opportunities. While this is important, it is only *part* of the process of investment decision making. There are other important aspects that managers must also consider.

It is possible to see the investment process as a sequence of five stages, each of which managers must consider. These are set out in Figure 8.6 below.

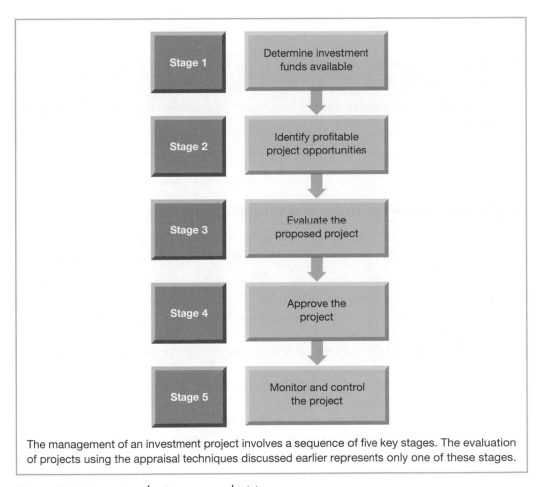

The management of an investment project involves a sequence of five key stages. The evaluation of projects using the appraisal techniques discussed earlier represents only one of these stages.

Figure 8.6 Managing the investment decision

Stage 1: Determine investment funds available

The amount of funds available for investment may be limited by the external market for funds or by internal management. In practice, it is the business's own senior managers that are more likely to impose limits, perhaps because they lack confidence in the business's ability to handle higher levels of investment. In either case, however, it may mean that the funds will not be sufficient to finance all of the potentially profitable investment opportunities available. This shortage of investment funds is known as **capital rationing.** When it arises, managers are faced with the task of deciding on the most profitable use of those funds available.

Stage 2: Identify profitable project opportunities

A vital part of the investment process is the search for profitable investment opportunities. The business should adopt a systematic approach to identifying feasible projects. To maintain a competitive edge, this should be a normal part of the planning process. The search process will usually involve scanning the environment for changes in technology, customer demand, market conditions and so on. Gathering the information needed may take some time, particularly for unusual or non-routine investment opportunities.

To help identify good investment opportunities, some businesses provide financial incentives to members of staff who come forward with good investment proposals. Even unrefined proposals may be welcome. Resources can then be invested to help develop the proposals to a point where formal submission can be made.

Activity 8.20

It can be argued that the sequence of these first two stages can be reversed. Can you figure out why?

In theory, finance can always be found for profitable investment opportunities.

Stage 3: Evaluate the proposed project

If management is to agree to the investment of funds in a project, that project's proposal must be rigorously screened. For larger projects, this will involve providing answers to a number of questions, including:

- What are the nature and purpose of the project?
- Does the project align with the overall strategy and objectives of the business?
- How much finance is required?
- What other resources (such as expertise, work space and so on) are required for successful completion of the project?
- How long will the project last and what are its key stages?
- What is the expected pattern of cash flows?
- What are the major problems associated with the project and how can they be overcome?
- What is the NPV of the project? If capital is rationed, how does the NPV of this project compare with that of other opportunities available?
- Have risk and inflation been taken into account in the appraisal process and, if so, what are the results?

The ability and commitment of those responsible for proposing and managing the project will be vital to its success. This means that, when evaluating a new project, one consideration will be the quality of those proposing it. Senior managers may decide not to support a project that appears profitable on paper if they lack confidence in the ability of key managers to see it through to completion.

Stage 4: Approve the project

Once the managers responsible for investment decision making are satisfied that the project should be undertaken, formal approval can be given. However, a decision on a project may be postponed if senior managers need more information from those proposing the project, or if revisions are required to the proposal. Proposals may be rejected if they are considered unprofitable or likely to fail. Before rejecting a proposal, however, the implications of not pursuing the project must be carefully considered. Failure to pursue a particular project may impact such areas as market share, staff morale and existing business operations.

Approval may be authorised at different levels of the management hierarchy according to the nature of the investment and the amount of finance needed. For example, a plant manager may be given authority to invest in new equipment up to a maximum of, say, £500,000. For amounts above this figure, authority may be required from more senior management.

Stage 5: Monitor and control the project

Making a decision to invest does not automatically cause the investment to be made or mean that things will progress smoothly. Managers will need to manage the project actively through to completion. This, in turn, will require further information gathering.

Much of the control of a project would be through the routine budgetary control procedures that we met in Chapters 6 and 7. Management should also receive progress reports at regular intervals concerning the project. These should provide information relating to the actual cash flows for each stage of the project, which can then be compared against the forecast figures. Reasons for significant variations should be ascertained and corrective action taken where possible. Any changes in the expected completion date of the project or any expected variations in future cash flows from budget should be reported immediately. In extreme cases, managers may even abandon the project if circumstances appear to have changed dramatically for the worse.

Key non-financial measures may also be used to monitor performance. Measures may include wastage rates, physical output, customer satisfaction scores and so on. Certain types of projects, such as construction and civil engineering projects, may have 'milestones' (that is particular stages of completion) to be reached by certain dates. Progress towards each milestone should be monitored carefully and early warning should be given of any problems that may thwart their achievement. Project management techniques (for example, critical path analysis) should be employed wherever possible and their effectiveness monitored.

An important part of the control process is a **post-completion audit** of the project. This is, in essence, a review of the project performance to see if it lived up to expectations and whether any lessons can be learned. In addition to an evaluation of financial costs and benefits, non-financial measures of performance such as the ability to meet deadlines and levels of quality achieved will often be examined.

Adopting post-completion audits should encourage the use of more realistic estimates at the initial planning stage. Where over-optimistic estimates are used in an attempt to secure project approval, the managers responsible should be held accountable at the post-completion stage. **Real World 8.12** provides some evidence of a need for greater realism.

Real World 8.12

Looking on the bright side

McKinsey and Co, the management consultants, surveyed 2,500 senior managers worldwide. The managers were asked their opinions on investments made by their businesses in the previous three years. The general opinion was that estimates for the investment decision inputs had been too optimistic. For example, sales levels had been overestimated in about 50 per cent of cases, but underestimated in less than 20 per cent of cases. It is not clear whether the estimates were sufficiently inaccurate to call into question the decision that had been made.

The survey went on to ask about the extent to which investments made seemed, in the light of the actual outcomes, to have been mistakes. Managers felt that 19 per cent of investments that had been made should not have gone ahead. On the other hand, they felt that 31 per cent of rejected projects should have been taken up. Managers also felt that 'good money was thrown after bad' in that existing investments that were not performing well were continuing to be supported in a significant number of cases.

Source: Based on information in 'How companies spend their money', A McKinsey Global Survey, www.theglobalmarketer.com, 2007.

Other studies confirm a tendency among managers to use over-optimistic estimates when preparing investment proposals (see reference 1 at the end of the chapter).

Activity 8.21

Can you think of any drawbacks to the use of a post-completion audit? Could it have an adverse effect on management behaviour?

One potential problem is that it will inhibit managers from proposing and supporting high-risk projects. If things go wrong, they could be blamed. This may result in only low-risk projects being submitted for approval. A further potential problem is that managers will feel threatened by the post-completion audit investigation and so will not cooperate fully with the audit team.

The behaviour of managers is likely to be influenced by the way in which a post-completion audit is conducted. If it is simply used as a device to apportion blame, then the problems mentioned in Activity 8.21 may easily occur. But if it is used in a constructive way, these problems may be avoided. It should be seen as a tool for learning and should take full account of the degree of risk associated with a project.

Post-completion audits can be costly and time-consuming and so the potential benefits must be weighed against the costs involved. This may result in only larger projects being audited. However, a random sample of smaller projects may also be audited.

Real World 8.13 provides some indication of the extent to which post-completion audits are used by businesses.

Real World 8.13

Looking back

The CIMA survey, mentioned in earlier chapters, examined the extent to which post-completion audits are used in practice. The results for all businesses surveyed, as well as for very large businesses (that is, with more than 10,000 employees), are set out in Figure 8.7.

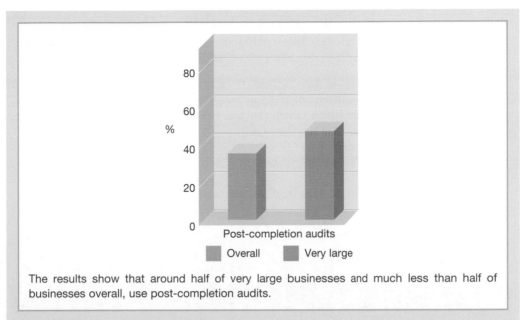

The results show that around half of very large businesses and much less than half of businesses overall, use post-completion audits.

Figure 8.7 Post-completion audits

We can see that larger businesses are more likely to use this technique. These businesses are likely to undertake more and bigger investment projects and have more finance staff to monitor business performance and so the results are not surprising.

Source: Adapted from figure in CIMA (2009) *Management Accounting Tools for Today and Tomorrow*, CIMA, July, p. 18.

Real World 8.14 describes how one large retailer, Kingfisher plc, goes about monitoring and controlling its investment projects. Kingfisher sells do-it-yourself goods notably through the B&Q chain of stores.

Real World 8.14

Getting a grip

The 2016 annual report of Kingfisher plc reveals that the business invested £333 million during the year 2015/16. According to the report, to monitor and control this high level of expenditure, the following procedures are adopted:

> The Group has a rigorous approach to capital allocation and authorisation, including an annual strategic planning and capital allocation process, an annual budget process, a project by project capital approval process and a bi-annual post-investment review process.

This approach is in line with the processes that Kingfisher previously carried out which included:

■ Strategic planning every year which was to look ahead to the next three years and inform key decisions for allocation of capital upon review by the board;

■ Approval by the capital expenditure committee which would review significant capital investment in projects, such as those above £0.75 million;

→

- At a higher level where projects exceed £15 million these needed approval by the board;
- Criteria for investment including their own KEP (Kingfisher economic profit - now discontinued) as well as NPV. They also would challenge IRR and discounted payback hurdle rates;
- A full assessment or review post-investment of all projects above £0.75 million. This would happen annually and include projects completed in the last two to four years. The Board and capital expenditure committee use this exercise to inform future project proposals
- An assessment of efficiency and profitability by store to bring improvements across their stores, including strengthening returns from weaker stores by applying lessons learnt from more successful stores.

Source: Adapted from Kingfisher plc Annual Report 2015/16, p. 28 (www.kingfisher.co.uk).

Self-assessment question 8.1

Beacon Chemicals plc is considering buying some equipment to produce a chemical named X14. The new equipment's capital cost is estimated at £100 million. If its purchase is approved now, the equipment can be bought and production can commence by the end of this year. £50 million has already been spent on research and development work. Estimates of revenues and costs arising from the operation of the new equipment are:

	Year 1	Year 2	Year 3	Year 4	Year 5
Sales price (£/litre)	100	120	120	100	80
Sales volume (million litres)	0.8	1.0	1.2	1.0	0.8
Variable cost (£/litre)	50	50	40	30	40
Fixed cost (£m)	30	30	30	30	30

If the equipment is bought, sales of some existing products will be lost resulting in a loss of contribution of £15 million a year, over the life of the equipment.

The accountant has informed you that the fixed cost includes depreciation of £20 million a year on the new equipment. It also includes an allocation of £10 million for fixed overheads. A separate study has indicated that if the new equipment were bought, additional overheads, excluding depreciation, arising from producing the chemical would be £8 million a year. Production would require additional working capital of £30 million.

For the purposes of your initial calculations ignore taxation.

Required:

(a) Deduce the relevant annual cash flows associated with buying the equipment.
(b) Deduce the payback period.
(c) Calculate the net present value using a discount rate of 8 per cent.
(d) How sensitive is the NPV calculated in (c) to the estimate of the annual loss of contribution from the existing products? Comment on the sensitivity.

(*Hint*: You should deal with the investment in working capital by treating it as a cash outflow at the start of the project and an inflow at the end.)

The solution to this question can be found at the end of the book on pp. 520–521.

SUMMARY

The main points of this chapter may be summarised as follows:

Accounting rate of return (ARR) is the average accounting profit from the project expressed as a percentage of the average investment.

- Decision rule – projects with an ARR above a defined minimum are acceptable; the greater the ARR, the more attractive the project becomes.
- Conclusion on ARR:
    - does not relate directly to shareholders' wealth – can lead to illogical conclusions;
    - takes almost no account of the timing of cash flows;
    - ignores some relevant information and may take account of some irrelevant;
    - relatively simple to use;
    - much inferior to NPV.

Payback period (PP) is the length of time that it takes for the cash outflow for the initial investment to be repaid out of resulting cash inflows.

- Decision rule – projects with a PP up to a defined maximum period are acceptable; the shorter the PP, the more attractive the project.
- Conclusion on PP:
    - does not relate to shareholders' wealth;
    - ignores inflows after the payback date;
    - takes little account of the timing of cash flows;
    - ignores much relevant information;
    - does not always provide clear signals and can be impractical to use;
    - much inferior to NPV, but it is easy to understand and can offer a liquidity insight, which might be the reason for its widespread use.

Net present value (NPV) is the sum of the discounted values of the net cash flows from the investment.

- Money has a time value.
- Decision rule – all positive NPV investments enhance shareholders' wealth; the greater the NPV, the greater the enhancement and the greater the attractiveness of the project.
- PV of a cash flow = cash flow $\times 1/(1 + r)^n$, assuming a constant discount rate.
- Discounting brings cash flows at different points in time to a common valuation basis (their present value), which enables them to be directly compared.
- Conclusion on NPV:
    - relates directly to shareholders' wealth objective;
    - takes account of the timing of cash flows;
    - takes all relevant information into account;
    - provides clear signals and is practical to use.

Internal rate of return (IRR) is the discount rate that, when applied to the cash flows of a project, causes it to have a zero NPV.

- Represents the average percentage return on the investment, taking account of the fact that cash may be flowing in and out of the project at various points in its life.

- Decision rule – projects that have an IRR greater than the cost of capital are acceptable; the greater the IRR, the more attractive the project.
- Cannot normally be calculated directly; a trial and error approach is usually necessary.
- Conclusion on IRR:
  - does not relate directly to shareholders' wealth. Usually gives the same signals as NPV but can mislead where there are competing projects of different size;
  - takes account of the timing of cash flows;
  - takes all relevant information into account;
  - problems of multiple IRRs when there are unconventional cash flows;
  - inferior to NPV.

Use of appraisal methods in practice:

- all four methods identified are widely used;
- the discounting methods (NPV and IRR) show a steady increase in usage over time;
- many businesses use more than one method;
- larger businesses seem to be more sophisticated in their choice and use of appraisal methods than smaller ones.

Investment appraisal and strategic planning

- It is important that businesses invest in a strategic way so as to play to their strengths.

Managing investment projects

- Determine investment funds available – dealing, if necessary, with capital rationing problems.
- Identify profitable project opportunities.
- Evaluate the proposed project.
- Approve the project.
- Monitor and control the project – using a post-completion audit approach.

KEY TERMS

For definitions of these terms, see Appendix A.

Accounting rate of return (ARR) p. 284	**Inflation** p. 294
Return on capital employed (ROCE) p. 285	**Discounting** p. 297
	Discount factor p. 298
Payback period (PP) p. 288	**Cost of capital** p. 299
Net present value (NPV) p. 292	**Internal rate of return (IRR)** p. 301
Risk premium p. 294	**Capital rationing** p. 313
	Post-completion audit p. 315

REFERENCE

1 Linder, S. (2005) *Fifty Years of Research on Accuracy of Capital Expenditure Project Estimates: A Review of the Findings and Their Validity*, Otto Beisham Graduate School of Management, April.

FURTHER READING

If you would like to explore the topics covered in this chapter in more depth, we recommend the following:

Arnold, G. (2013) *Corporate Financial Management*, 5th edn, Pearson, Chapters 2–4.

Drury, C. (2015) *Management and Cost Accounting*, 9th edn, South Western Cengage Learning, Chapters 13 and 14.

McLaney, E. (2017) *Business Finance: Theory and Practice*, 11th edn, Pearson, Chapters 4–6.

Pike, R., Neale, B. and Linsley, P. (2015) *Corporate Finance and Investment*, 8th edn, Pearson, Chapters 3–7.

REVIEW QUESTIONS

Solutions to these questions can be found at the back of the book on pp. 531–532.

8.1 Why is the net present value method of investment appraisal considered to be theoretically superior to other methods that are found in practice?

8.2 The payback period method has been criticised for not taking the time value of money into account. Could this limitation be overcome? If so, would this method then be preferable to the NPV method?

8.3 Research indicates that the IRR method is extremely popular even though it has short-comings when compared to the NPV method. Why might managers prefer to use IRR rather than NPV when carrying out discounted cash flow evaluations?

8.4 Why are cash flows rather than profit flows used in the IRR, NPV and PP methods of investment appraisal?

EXERCISES

Exercises with coloured numbers have solutions given at the back of the book on pp. 557–560.

Basic-level exercises

8.1 The directors of Mylo Ltd are currently considering two mutually exclusive investment projects. Both projects are concerned with the purchase of new plant. The following data are available for each project:

	Project 1 £000	Project 2 £000
Cost (immediate outlay)	100	60
Expected annual operating profit (loss):		
Year 1	29	18
2	(1)	(2)
3	2	4
Estimated residual value of the plant after 3 years	7	6

The business has an estimated cost of capital of 10 per cent. It uses the straight-line method of depreciation for all non-current (fixed) assets when calculating operating profit. Neither project would increase the working capital of the business. The business has sufficient funds to meet all investment expenditure requirements.

Required:

(a) Calculate for each project:
 (1) The net present value.
 (2) The approximate internal rate of return.
 (3) The payback period.
(b) State, with reasons, which, if any, of the two investment projects the directors of Mylo Ltd should accept.

8.2 Arkwright Mills plc is considering expanding its production of a new yarn, code name X15. The plant is expected to cost £1 million and have a life of five years and a nil residual value. It will be bought, paid for and ready for operation on 31 December Year 0. £500,000 has already been spent on development costs of the product; this has been charged in the income statement in the year it was incurred.

The following results are projected for the new yarn:

	Year 1 £m	Year 2 £m	Year 3 £m	Year 4 £m	Year 5 £m
Sales revenue	1.2	1.4	1.4	1.4	1.4
Costs, including depreciation	(1.0)	(1.1)	(1.1)	(1.1)	(1.1)
Profit before tax	0.2	0.3	0.3	0.3	0.3

Tax is charged at 20 per cent on annual profits (before tax and after depreciation) and paid one year in arrears. Depreciation of the plant has been calculated on a straight-line basis. Additional working capital of £0.6 million will be required at the beginning of the project and released at the end of Year 5. You should assume that all cash flows occur at the end of the year in which they arise.

Required:

(a) Prepare a statement showing the incremental cash flows of the project relevant to a decision concerning whether or not to proceed with the construction of the new plant.
(b) Compute the net present value of the project using a 10 per cent discount rate.
(c) Compute the payback period to the nearest year. Explain the meaning of this term.

Intermediate-level exercises

8.3 Newton Electronics Ltd has incurred expenditure of £5 million over the past three years researching and developing a miniature hearing aid. The hearing aid is now fully developed. The directors are considering which of three mutually exclusive options should be taken to exploit the potential of the new product. The options are:

1 The business could manufacture the hearing aid itself. This would be a new departure, since the business has so far concentrated on research and development projects. However, the business has manufacturing space available that it currently rents to another business for £100,000 a year. This space will not continue to be leased if the decision is not to manufacture. The business would have to purchase plant and equipment costing £9 million and invest £3 million in working capital immediately for production to begin.

A market research report, for which the business paid £50,000, indicates that the new product has an expected life of five years. Sales of the product during this period are predicted as:

	Predicted sales for the year ended 30 November				
	Year 1	Year 2	Year 3	Year 4	Year 5
Number of units (000s)	800	1,400	1,800	1,200	500

The selling price per unit will be £30 in the first year but will fall to £22 in the following three years. In the final year of the product's life, the selling price will fall to £20. Variable production costs are predicted to be £14 a unit. Fixed production costs (including depreciation) will be £2.4 million a year. Marketing costs will be £2 million a year.

The business intends to depreciate the plant and equipment using the straight-line method and based on an estimated residual value at the end of the five years of £1 million. The business has a cost of capital of 10 per cent a year.

2 Newton Electronics Ltd could agree to another business manufacturing and marketing the product under licence. A multinational business, Faraday Electricals plc, has offered to undertake the manufacture and marketing of the product. In return, it will make a royalty payment to Newton Electronics Ltd of £5 per unit. It has been estimated that the annual number of sales of the hearing aid will be 10 per cent higher if the multinational business, rather than Newton Electronics Ltd, manufactures and markets the product.

3 Newton Electronics Ltd could sell the patent rights to Faraday Electricals plc for £24 million, payable in two equal instalments. The first instalment would be payable immediately and the second at the end of two years. This option would give Faraday Electricals the exclusive right to manufacture and market the new product.

Required:
Ignoring taxation.

(a) Calculate the net present value (as at the beginning of Year 1) of each of the options available to Newton Electronics Ltd.
(b) Identify and discuss any other factors that Newton Electronics Ltd should consider before arriving at a decision.
(c) State, with reasons, what you consider to be the most suitable option.

8.4 Dirk plc has recently created a new male fragrance 'Sirocco' at a total development cost of £0.4 million. The business is now considering producing the fragrance, which will require an immediate outlay for new equipment of £10.5 million. Estimates relating to production of the fragrance are:

	Year 1	Year 2	Year 3	Year 4
Sales price (£/per bottle)	9.0	8.0	6.0	6.0
Sales volume (bottles)	1.0m	1.2m	1.2m	0.5m
Variable cost (£/per bottle)	1.0	1.0	1.0	1.4
Fixed cost (£)	4.5m	4.5m	4.5m	4.5m

The fixed cost includes depreciation of £2.5 million a year for the new equipment needed. This equipment will be sold at the end of the four years of production, and the sales proceeds will reflect the residual value. Fixed cost also includes an allocation of £0.3 million to represent a 'fair share' of general business overheads.

If the project goes ahead, sales of an existing male fragrance, 'Mistral', will decline, resulting in a loss of contribution of £0.8 million per year for the next three years.

Producing the new fragrance will require an immediate outlay for working capital of £1.8 million, which can be released at the end of the production period.

Dirk plc has a cost of capital of 8 per cent.

Required:
(a) Calculate for the investment project:
   (1) the net present value
   (2) the approximate internal rate of return.
(b) Briefly comment on the results of your calculations in (a).

8.5 C. George (Controls) Ltd manufactures a thermostat that can be used in a range of kitchen appliances. The manufacturing process is, at present, semi-automated. The equipment used cost £540,000 and has a carrying amount (as shown on the statement of financial position) of £300,000. Demand for the product has been fairly stable at 50,000 units a year in recent years.

The following data, based on the current level of output, have been prepared in respect of the product:

	Per unit	
	£	£
Selling price		12.40
Labour	(3.30)	
Materials	(3.65)	
Overheads: Variable	(1.58)	
Fixed	(1.60)	
		(10.13)
Operating profit		2.27

Although the existing equipment is expected to last for a further four years before it is sold for an estimated £40,000, the business has recently been considering purchasing new equipment that would completely automate much of the production process. The new equipment would cost £670,000 and would have an expected life of four years, at the end of which it would be sold for an estimated £70,000. If the new equipment is purchased, the old equipment could be sold for £150,000 immediately.

The assistant to the business's accountant has prepared a report to help assess the viability of the proposed change, which includes the following data:

	Per unit	
	£	£
Selling price		12.40
Labour	(1.20)	
Materials	(3.20)	
Overheads: Variable	(1.40)	
Fixed	(3.30)	
		(9.10)
Operating profit		3.30

Depreciation charges will increase by £85,000 a year as a result of purchasing the new machinery; however, other fixed costs are not expected to change.

In the report the assistant wrote:

The figures shown above that relate to the proposed change are based on the current level of output and take account of a depreciation charge of £150,000 a year in respect of the new equipment. The effect of purchasing the new equipment will be to increase the operating profit to sales revenue ratio from 18.3 per cent to 26.6 per cent. In addition, the purchase of the new equipment will enable us to reduce our inventories level immediately by £130,000.

In view of these facts, I recommend purchase of the new equipment.

The business has a cost of capital of 12 per cent. Ignore taxation.

Required:

(a) Prepare a statement of the incremental cash flows arising from the purchase of the new equipment.

(b) Calculate the net present value of the proposed purchase of new equipment.

(c) State, with reasons, whether the business should purchase the new equipment.

(d) Explain why cash flow, rather than profit, projections are used to assess the viability of proposed capital expenditure projects.

Advanced-level exercises

8.6 The accountant of your business has recently been taken ill through overwork. In his absence, his assistant has prepared some calculations of the profitability of a project, which are to be discussed soon at the board meeting of your business. His workings, which are set out below, include some errors of principle. You can assume that there are no arithmetical errors.

Year	0	1	2	3	4	5
	£000	£000	£000	£000	£000	£000
Sales revenue		450	470	470	470	470
Less Costs						
Materials		126	132	132	132	132
Labour		90	94	94	94	94
Overheads		45	47	47	47	47
Depreciation		120	120	120	120	120
Working capital	180					
Interest on working capital		27	27	27	27	27
Write-off of development costs	—	30	30	30	—	—
Total costs	180	438	450	450	420	420
Operating profit/(loss)	(180)	12	20	20	50	50

$$\frac{\text{Total profit (loss)}}{\text{Cost of equipment}} = \frac{(£28,000)}{£600,000} = \text{Return on investment (4.7\%)}$$

You ascertain the following additional information:

1 The cost of equipment includes £100,000, being the carrying value of an old machine. If it were not used for this project, it would be scrapped with a zero net realisable value. New equipment costing £500,000 will be purchased on 31 December Year 0. You should assume that all other cash flows occur at the end of the year to which they relate.

2 The development costs of £90,000 have already been spent.

3 Overheads have been costed at 50 per cent of direct labour, which is the business's normal practice. An independent assessment has suggested that incremental overheads are likely to amount to £30,000 a year.

4 The business's cost of capital is 12 per cent.

Required:
Ignore taxation.

(a) Prepare a corrected statement of the incremental cash flows arising from the project. Where you have altered the assistant's figures you should attach a brief note explaining your alterations.

(b) Calculate:
   (1) The project's payback period.
   (2) The project's net present value as at 31 December Year 0.

(c) Write a memo to the board advising on the acceptance or rejection of the project.

8.7 Chesterfield Wanderers is a professional football club that has enjoyed considerable success in league competitions in recent years. As a result, the club has accumulated £10 million to spend on its further development. The board of directors is currently considering two mutually exclusive options for spending the funds available.

The first option is to acquire another player. The team manager has expressed a keen interest in acquiring Basil ('Bazza') Ramsey, a central defender, who currently plays for a rival club. The rival club has agreed to release the player immediately for £10 million if required. A decision to acquire 'Bazza' Ramsey would mean that the existing central defender, Vinnie Smith, could be sold to another club. Chesterfield Wanderers has recently received an offer of £2.2 million for this player. This offer is still open but will only be accepted if 'Bazza' Ramsey joins Chesterfield Wanderers. If this does not happen, Vinnie Smith will be expected to stay on with the club until the end of his playing career in five years' time. During this period, Vinnie will receive an annual salary of £400,000 and a loyalty bonus of £200,000 at the end of his five-year period with the club.

Assuming 'Bazza' Ramsey is acquired, the team manager estimates that gate receipts will increase by £2.5 million in the first year and £1.3 million in each of the four following years. There will also be an increase in advertising and sponsorship revenues of £1.2 million for each of the next five years if the player is acquired. At the end of five years, the player can be sold to a club in a lower division and Chesterfield Wanderers will expect to receive £1 million as a transfer fee. During his period at the club, 'Bazza' will receive an annual salary of £800,000 and a loyalty bonus of £400,000 after five years.

The second option is for the club to improve its ground facilities. The west stand could be extended and executive boxes could be built for businesses wishing to offer corporate hospitality to clients. These improvements would also cost £10 million and would take one year to complete. During this period, the west stand would be closed, resulting in a reduction of gate receipts of £1.8 million. However, gate receipts for each of the following four years would be £4.4 million higher than current receipts. In five years' time, the club has plans to sell the existing grounds and to move to a new stadium nearby. Improving the ground facilities is not expected to affect the ground's value when it comes to be sold. Payment for the improvements will be made when the work has been completed at the end of the first year. Whichever option is chosen, the board of directors has decided to take on additional ground staff. The additional wages bill is expected to be £350,000 a year over the next five years.

The club has a cost of capital of 10 per cent. Ignore taxation.

Required:

(a) Calculate the incremental cash flows arising from each of the options available to the club.
(b) Calculate the net present value of each of the options.
(c) On the basis of the calculations made in (b) above, which of the two options would you choose and why?
(d) Discuss the validity of using the net present value method in making investment decisions for a professional football club.

8.8 One of the most successful products of Dallan plc, over recent years, is an electric motor known commercially as the 'Powermite'. This motor is believed by management to have only a limited future market and should be superseded by a more modern one. Such a motor has been developed for the business by an independent consultancy business at a cost of £300,000, which is due to be paid on 31 December 20X0. A decision now needs to be made on producing and marketing the new motor which, if it is marketed, will be sold under the name 'Dynamotor'. The basic proposal is to cease production and marketing of the Powermite at the end of 20X0 and to replace it with the Dynamotor.

The directors have agreed to base their decision on a net present value analysis of the possibilities.

Manufacture of the Dynamotor would take place using new, substantially automated plant. This plant would cost £1.2 million, payable when the plant would be installed on 31 December 20X0.

Assuming that the Powermite is phased out at the end of 20X0, sales of the Dynamotor are expected to be as follows:

Year	Units
20X1	10,000
20X2	15,000
20X3	20,000
20X4	15,000
20X5	10,000

A selling price of £100 per unit is expected for the Dynamotor. Variable manufacturing costs are expected to be £40 per unit and incremental fixed costs £250,000 per annum.

If the Powermite is phased out at the end of 20X0, redundancies among production staff will take place on 31 December 20X0. The business will make redundancy payments totalling £120,000 on that date.

Management believes that, if the Dynamotor were not introduced, there would be a continuing demand for the Powermite until 20X3, assuming an £80 per unit price, as follows:

Year	Units
20X1	4,000
20X2	3,000
20X3	2,000

The Powermite has an estimated £45 per unit variable cost element and has avoidable (incremental) fixed costs of £70,000 per annum.

If the Dynamotor is not introduced, and the Powermite retained, redundancy payments would be:

		£
At 31 December	20X0	80,000
	20X1	30,000
	20X2	10,000

Plant currently used in Powermite manufacture is now fairly old and, whenever it is to be disposed of, would have a market value at, or close to, zero.

The directors estimate that the cost of capital will be 15 per cent per year for the foreseeable future.

Required:
On the basis of NPV, provide calculations that indicate whether the business should introduce the Dynamotor and discontinue the Powermite or continue Powermite production and not introduce the Dynamotor.

Chapter 9

MANAGING RISK

INTRODUCTION

Decisions, by their nature, relate to the future. The only thing certain about the future, however, is that we do not know what is going to happen. All decision making is, therefore, risky.

In this chapter we shall see that, when making management decisions, potential risks must be considered. This involves assessing the likelihood and extent that benefits and costs relating to a proposed course of action will not turn out as predicted. Failure to carefully weigh relevant benefits and costs, along with the risks associated with each, is likely to result in poor decisions being made.

Learning outcomes

When you have completed this chapter, you should be able to:

- Explain the nature of risk and the importance of considering risk when making decisions.

- Identify and evaluate the most popular approaches to risk assessment found in practice.

- Explain how the outcomes from assessing risk can be used.

- Discuss the popularity and use of the various approaches to risk assessment found in practice.

DEALING WITH RISK

All business activities are risky. This means that consideration of **risk** is an important aspect of management decision making. Risk, in this context, is the extent and likelihood that what is projected to occur will not actually happen. Although we shall discuss risk mainly in the context of investment decision making, its importance is just as great when making shorter-term decisions like those considered in Chapters 2 and 3. The approaches to dealing with risk that we are about to consider are equally applicable to shorter-term decisions. Risk is, however, a particularly important issue in the context of investment decisions, because of:

1 *The relatively long timescales involved.* There tends to be more time for things to go wrong between the decision being made and the completion of the project compared to other business decisions.
2 *The scale of funds involved.* Many investment projects involve very large amounts of finance. If things go wrong, the impact can be both significant and lasting.

Various approaches to dealing with risk have been proposed. They fall into two categories: assessing the level of risk and reacting to the level of risk. We shall now consider formal methods of dealing with risk that fall within each category.

ASSESSING THE LEVEL OF RISK

Sensitivity analysis

A popular way of assessing the level of risk is to carry out **sensitivity analysis** on the proposed project. This involves an examination of the key input values affecting the project to see how changes in each input might individually influence the viability of the project.

The starting point is to appraise the investment using the best estimates for each of the input factors (for example, labour cost, material cost and so on). Assuming the assessment is positive, each input value is then examined to see how far the estimated figure could change before the project becomes unviable for that reason alone. Let us suppose that the NPV for an investment in a machine, which provides a particular service, has a positive value. If we were to carry out sensitivity analysis on this proposed investment, we should consider each of the key input factors, in turn:

- initial outlay for the machine;
- sales volume and selling price;
- relevant operating costs;
- life of the project; and
- cost of capital (to be used as the discount rate).

We should try to find the value that each input could have before the NPV figure becomes negative (that is, the value for the input at which NPV would be zero). The difference between the value for that input factor at which the NPV would equal zero and its estimated value represents the margin of safety for that input. The factors influencing the NPV of the investment in the machine project are set out in Figure 9.1.

A computer spreadsheet model of the project can be extremely valuable for this exercise. It then becomes a very simple matter to try various values for the input data and to see the

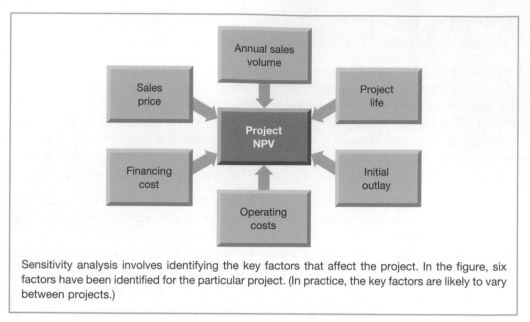

Sensitivity analysis involves identifying the key factors that affect the project. In the figure, six factors have been identified for the particular project. (In practice, the key factors are likely to vary between projects.)

Figure 9.1 Factors affecting the sensitivity of NPV calculations

effect of each. By carrying out sensitivity analysis, the decision maker is able to get a 'feel' for the project, which otherwise might not be possible.

Example 9.1, which illustrates sensitivity analysis, is straightforward and can be undertaken without recourse to a spreadsheet.

Example 9.1

S. Saluja (Property Developers) Ltd intends to bid at an auction, to be held today, for a large house that has fallen into disrepair. The auctioneer believes that the house will be sold for about £450,000. The business wishes to renovate the property and to divide it into studio flats, to be sold individually. The renovation will be in two stages and will cover a two-year period. Stage 1 will cover the first year of the project. It will cost £500,000 and the six flats completed during this stage are expected to be sold for a total of £900,000 at the end of the first year. Stage 2 will cover the second year of the project. It will cost £300,000 and the three remaining flats are expected to be sold at the end of the second year for a total of £450,000. The cost of renovation will be the subject of a binding contract with local builders, if the property is bought. There is, however, some uncertainty over the remaining input values. The business estimates its cost of capital at 12 per cent a year.

Required

(a) What is the NPV of the proposed project?

(b) Assuming none of the other inputs deviates from the best estimates provided:

   (1) What auction price would have to be paid for the house to cause the project to have a zero NPV?
   (2) What cost of capital would cause the project to have a zero NPV?
   (3) What is the sale price of each of the flats that would cause the project to have a zero NPV? (Each flat is projected to be sold for the same price: £150,000.)

Solution

(a) The NPV of the proposed project is as follows:

	Cash flows £	Discount factor 12%	Present value £
Year 1 (£900,000 – £500,000)	400,000	0.893	357,200
Year 2 (£450,000 – £300,000)	150,000	0.797	119,550
Initial outlay			(450,000)
Net present value			26,750

(b) (1) To lead to a zero NPV, the auction price would have to be £26,750 higher than the current estimate – that is, a total price of £476,750. This is about 6 per cent above the current estimated price.

(2) As there is a positive NPV, the cost of capital that would cause the project to have a zero NPV must be higher than 12 per cent. Let us try 20 per cent.

	Cash flows £	Discount factor 20%	Present value £
Year 1 (£900,000 – £500,000)	400,000	0.833	333,200
Year 2 (£450,000 – £300,000)	150,000	0.694	104,100
Initial outlay			(450,000)
Net present value			(12,700)

As the NPV using a 20 per cent discount rate is negative, the 'break-even' cost of capital lies somewhere between 12 per cent and 20 per cent. A reasonable approximation is obtained as follows:

	Discount rate %	Net present value £
	12	26,750
	20	(12,700)
Difference	8	39,450

The change in NPV for every 1 per cent change in the discount rate will be:

$$39,450/8 = £4,931$$

The reduction in the 20 per cent discount rate required to achieve a zero NPV would therefore be:

$$12,700/4,931 = 2.6\%$$

The cost of capital (that is, the discount rate) would, therefore, have to be approximately 17.4 per cent (20.0 – 2.6) for the project to have a zero NPV.

This calculation is, of course, the same as that used in Chapter 8, when calculating the IRR of the project. In other words, 17.4 per cent is the IRR of the project.

(3) To obtain a zero NPV, the sale price of each flat must be reduced so that the NPV is reduced by £26,750. In year 1, six flats are sold and in year 2, three flats are sold.

The discount factor at the 12 per cent rate for year 1 is 0.893 and for year 2 is 0.797. We can derive the fall in price per flat (Y) to give a zero NPV by using the equation:

$$(6Y \times 0.893) + (3Y \times 0.797) = £26,750$$
$$Y = £3,452$$

The sale price of each flat necessary to obtain a zero NPV is therefore:

$$£150,000 - £3,452 = £146,548$$

This represents a fall in the estimated price of 2.3 per cent.

Activity 9.1

How would you assess the sensitivities of the three factors that were calculated in Example 9.1? Taken individually, do they make this a risky project?

The calculations indicate that the auction price would have to be about 6 per cent above the estimated price before a zero NPV is obtained. The margin of safety is, therefore, not very high for this factor. In practice, this should not represent a real risk because the business could withdraw from the bidding if the price rises to an unacceptable level.

The other two factors represent more real risks. Only after the project is at a very late stage can the business be sure as to what actual price per flat will prevail. The same may be true for the cost of capital, though it may be possible to raise finance for the project at a rate fixed before the auction of the house. It would be unusual to be able to have fixed contracts for sale of all of the flats before the auction.

The calculations reveal that the price of the flats would have to fall by only 2.3 per cent from the estimated price before the NPV is reduced to zero. Hence, the margin of safety for this factor is very small. However, even if the funding arrangements cannot be fixed in advance, the cost of capital is less sensitive to changes and there would have to be an increase from 12 per cent to 17.4 per cent before the project produced a zero NPV. It seems from the calculations that the sale price of the flats is the key sensitive factor to consider.

In the light of the conclusion from Activity 9.1, it would be sensible to carefully re-examine the potential market value of the flats before a final decision is made.

The steps in the process of undertaking a sensitivity analysis are set out in Figure 9.2.

A slightly different form of sensitivity analysis than the one just described is to pose a series of 'what if?' questions. This can help to see how possible changes to each input factor will affect the viability of the investment project. Thus, when considering sales relating to the machine investment described earlier, the following 'what if?' questions may be asked:

- What if sales volume is 5 per cent higher than expected?
- What if sales volume is 10 per cent lower than expected?
- What if sales price is reduced by 15 per cent?
- What if sales price could be increased by 20 per cent?

While this form of sensitivity analysis also examines the effect of changes in each key factor, it does not seek to find the point at which a change makes the project no longer viable.

Real World 9.1 describes a feasibility study of a silver mining project. It incorporated sensitivity analysis to test the robustness of the estimated NPV of the project.

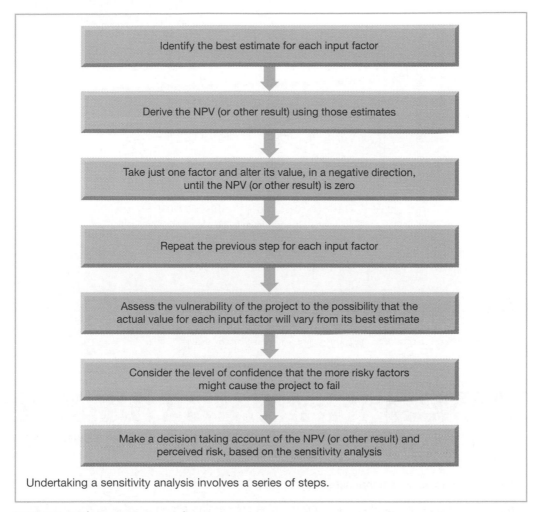

Undertaking a sensitivity analysis involves a series of steps.

Figure 9.2 The sensitivity analysis process

A sensitive subject

In 2016, Silver Bear Resources Inc released the findings of a feasibility study for the Vertikalny Central deposit of the Mangazeisky Silver Project in the Republic of Sakha (Yakutia), Russia. As part of the study, sensitivity analysis was carried out, based on an NPV discount rate of 5 per cent. This revealed that the silver price was the most sensitive variable, followed by the exchange rate, operating costs and capital expenditure costs.

Figure 9.3 below shows the sensitivity of each of these key variables in a diagrammatic form. The NPV of the project is shown on the vertical axis and the percentage change in the base case (most likely outcome) is shown on the horizontal axis.

We can see from the figure, for example, that a fall in the silver price of 30 per cent would take the NPV of the project close to zero whereas a 30 per cent rise in the price would almost double the NPV of the project, when compared to the base case.

Presenting the sensitivity analysis in this way may make it more accessible to those who lack a good grasp of finance.

→

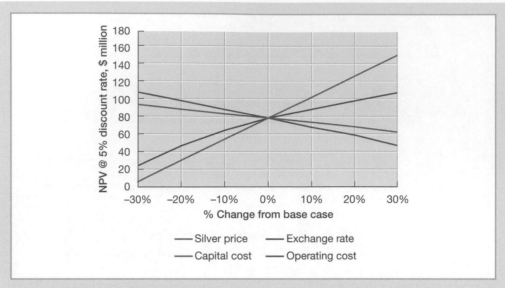

Figure 9.3 NPV sensitivity analysis of the Mangazeisky Silver Project

Source: Silver Bear Resources Inc (2016) *Silver bear announces completion of positive feasibility study at the mangazeisky silver project yakutia russia* www.silverbearresources.com, 9 June.

Activity 9.2

There are major drawbacks with the use of sensitivity analysis. Can you suggest what they are? There are generally considered to be three of them.

The main drawbacks are that sensitivity analysis:

■ Does not give managers clear decision rules concerning acceptance or rejection of the project and so they must rely on their own judgement.
■ Does not provide any indication of the likelihood that a particular change to an input factor will actually occur.
■ Is a static form of analysis. Only one input is considered at a time, while the rest are held constant. In practice, however, it is likely that more than one input value will differ from the best estimates provided.

Scenario analysis

Picking up the last point in the answer to Activity 9.2, a slightly different approach, which overcomes the problem of dealing with a single variable at a time, is **scenario analysis**, sometimes known as *scenario building*. Here, a number of variables are changed simultaneously so as to provide a particular 'state of the world', or scenario. A number of internally consistent 'states of the world' can be presented to managers, with each drawing attention to variables that are vital to a project's success. A popular form of scenario analysis in practice is to provide:

■ an optimistic view of likely future events;
■ a pessimistic view of likely future events; and
■ a 'most likely' view of future events.

This approach has been criticised because it does not indicate the likelihood of each scenario occurring, nor does it identify other possible scenarios that might occur. Nevertheless, the portrayal of optimistic and pessimistic scenarios may be useful in providing managers with some feel for the 'downside' risk and 'upside' potential associated with a project.

Real World 9.2 sets out an example of how a business created alternative scenarios to provide some idea of the risks involved in a proposed mining project.

Real World 9.2

Making a scene

In July 2014, Minco plc, a mining business, announced the completion of a preliminary economic assessment of a project to mine for electrolytic manganese metal (EMM) in Woodstock, Canada. This assessment considered four possible scenarios. The main features of each include the likely output from the mine and the prices achieved and are described below.

Base (most likely) case:	3,000 tonnes per day (t/d)) operation, with a sulphuric acid plant, importing sulphur to produce sulphuric acid on site, producing on average 80,104 tonnes per year (t/a) EMM, Pricing based on 50/50 average three-year trailing average of US and European prices to March 31, 2014
Alternate case A:	1,500 t/d operation, with a sulphuric acid plant, importing sulphur to produce sulphuric acid on site, producing on average 41,062 t/a EMM, pricing based on three-year trailing average of US and European prices to March 31, 2014
Alternate case B:	3,000 t/d operation, without a sulphuric acid plant, importing sulphuric acid, producing on average 80,104 t/a EMM, pricing based on 50/50 average three-year trailing average of US and European prices to March 31, 2014
Alternate case C:	1,500 t/d operation, without a sulphuric acid plant, importing sulphuric acid, producing on average 41,062 t/a EMM, pricing based on three-year trailing average of US prices to March 31, 2014

The key estimates and outcomes (expressed both in US and Canadian dollars) of the base case scenario are as follows:

Project life	• 40-year project life • Years 1 to 13 production from open pit mining • Years 14 to 40 production from stockpiles
Operating costs	• US$0.64/lb EMM average operating costs for Years 1 to 20 • US$0.68/lb EMM average operating costs for life of project
EMM pricing	• US$1.38/lb EMM calculated based on an average of 50% of the North American and 50% of the European three-year trailing averages to March 31, 2014 • US$139.04/t of 62% iron ore fines calculated based upon three-year trailing average to March 31, 2014
IRR	• Pre-tax IRR of 17.97% with a 5.56 year payback • Post-tax IRR of 14.40% with a 6.94 year payback

→

NPV	• CDN\$846 million pre-tax NPV (8% discount rate)
	• CDN\$461 million post-tax NPV (8% discount rate)
Cashflow	• CDN\$131 million average annual pre-tax cashflow
	• CDN\$4.416 billion life of project pre-tax cashflow
	• CDN\$92 million average annual post-tax cashflow
	• CDN\$2.890 billion life of project post-tax cashflow
Capital expenditure	• CDN\$864 million pre-production capital
	• CDN\$317 million sustaining capital over 40-year life of project
Mill production	• 3,000 t/d or 1,050,000 tonnes processed per year (t/a)
	• Average of 80,104 tonnes of EMM per year over life of project
	• Average of 23,214 tonnes of 62% iron ore fines per year over life of project
Grade to mill	• Average of 11.70% manganese (Mn) in Years 1 to 20
	• Average of 9.86% Mn over life of project
Community Benefit	• 223 jobs in Years 1 to 13
	• 110 jobs from Years 14 to 40
Provincial benefit	• CDN\$932 million in taxes and royalties to New Brunswick Government over life of project

It is interesting to note that the benefits identified are not simply confined to the business. They also include benefits accruing to the local community and to the province.

Source: Minco Plc (2014) *Woodstock Mn–New Brunswick*, www.mincoplc.com, 10 July.

Expected values

Another means of assessing risk is through the use of statistical probabilities. It may be possible to identify a range of feasible values for each of the items of input data and to assign a probability of occurrence to each of these values. Using this information, we can derive an **expected value**, which is, in effect, a weighted average of the possible outcomes where the probabilities are used as weights. Where we derive the expected value for an investment project, the output of the calculation is known as the **expected net present value (ENPV)**. To illustrate this method, let us consider Example 9.2.

Example 9.2

C. Piperis (Properties) Ltd has the opportunity to acquire a lease on a block of flats that has only two years remaining before it expires. The cost of the lease would be £100,000. The occupancy rate of the block of flats is currently around 70 per cent and the flats are let almost exclusively to naval personnel. There is a large naval base located nearby, but there is little other demand for the flats. The occupancy rate of the flats will change in the remaining two years of the lease, depending on the outcome of a defence review. The navy is currently considering three options for the naval base. These are:

■ *Option 1.* Increase the size of the base by closing one in another region and transferring the personnel to the one located near the flats.
■ *Option 2.* Close the naval base near to the flats and leave only a skeleton staff there for maintenance purposes. The personnel would be moved to a base in another region.
■ *Option 3.* Leave the base open but reduce staffing levels by 20 per cent.

The directors of Piperis have estimated the following net cash flows for each of the two years under each option and the probability of their occurrence:

	£	Probability
Option 1	80,000	0.6
Option 2	12,000	0.1
Option 3	40,000	0.3
		1.0

Note that the sum of the probabilities is 1.0 (in other words, it is certain that one of the possible options will arise). The business has a cost of capital of 10 per cent.

Should the business purchase the lease on the block of flats?

Solution

To calculate the expected NPV of the proposed investment, we must first calculate the weighted average of the expected outcomes for each year where the probabilities are used as weights, by multiplying each cash flow by its probability of occurrence. Thus, the expected annual net cash flows will be:

	Cash flows £ (a)	Probability (b)	Expected cash flows £ (a × b)
Option 1	80,000	0.6	48,000
Option 2	12,000	0.1	1,200
Option 3	40,000	0.3	12,000
Expected cash flows in each year			61,200

Having derived the expected annual cash flows, we can now discount these using a rate of 10 per cent to reflect the cost of capital:

Year	Expected cash flows £	Discount factor at 10%	Expected present value £
1	61,200	0.909	55,631
2	61,200	0.826	50,551
			106,182
Initial investment			(100,000)
Expected NPV			6,182

We can see that the expected NPV is positive. Hence, the wealth of shareholders is expected to increase by purchasing the lease.

The ENPV approach has the advantage of producing a single numerical outcome and of having a clear decision rule to apply. If the ENPV is positive, we should invest; if it is negative, we should not.

However, the approach produces an average figure that may not be capable of occurring. This point was illustrated in Example 9.1 where the expected annual cash flow (£61,200) does not correspond to any of the stated possibilities.

Perhaps more importantly, using an average figure can obscure the underlying risk associated with the project. Simply deriving the ENPV, as in Example 9.1, can be misleading. Without some idea of the individual possible outcomes and their probability of occurring, managers are in the dark. In Example 9.1, both Option 2 and Option 3 provide an outcome that would be wealth destroying. As it is 40 per cent probable that one of these two options will occur, this is a significant risk. Only Option 1 (60 per cent probable) provides an outcome that enhances owners' (shareholders') wealth. In advance of making the investment, of course, it is not known which option will actually occur.

None of this implies that the investment in the flats should not be made. It simply means that managers are better placed to make a decision where information on all the possible outcomes is available. Activity 9.3 further illustrates this point.

Activity 9.3

Qingdao Manufacturing Ltd is considering two competing projects. Details are as follows:

- Project A has a 0.9 probability of producing a negative NPV of £200,000 and a 0.1 probability of producing a positive NPV of £3.8m.
- Project B has a 0.6 probability of producing a positive NPV of £100,000 and a 0.4 probability of producing a positive NPV of £350,000.

What is the expected net present value of each project?

The expected NPV of Project A is:

$$[(0.1 \times £3.8 \text{ m}) - (0.9 \times £200,000)] = £200,000$$

The expected NPV of Project B is:

$$[(0.6 \times £100,000) + (0.4 \times £350,000)] = £200,000$$

Although the expected NPV of each project in Activity 9.3 is identical, this does not mean that the business will be indifferent about which project to undertake. We can see from the information provided that Project A has a high probability of making a loss whereas Project B is not expected to make a loss under either possible outcome. If we assume that the owners (shareholders) dislike risk – which is usually the case – they would prefer the business to take on Project B. It provides the same expected return as Project A but has a lower level of risk.

It can be argued that the problem identified above may not be significant where the business is engaged in several similar projects. This is because a worse than expected outcome on one project may well be balanced by a better than expected outcome on another project. In practice, however, investment projects may be unique events and this argument will not then apply. Also, where the project is large in relation to other projects undertaken, the argument loses its force. One final point, a factor that causes one project to have an adverse outcome may also cause other projects to have an adverse outcome. For example, a large, unexpected increase in the price of oil may have a simultaneous adverse effect on all of the investment projects of a particular business.

Event tree diagrams

Where the expected NPV approach is being used, it is probably a good idea to make known to managers the different possible outcomes and the probability attached to each outcome. By so doing, managers will be able to gain an insight to the *downside risk* attached to the project. The information relating to each outcome can be presented in the form of a diagram if required. The construction of such a diagram is illustrated in Example 9.3.

This information can be displayed in the form of a diagram (Figure 9.4).

Example 9.3

Zeta Computing Services Ltd has recently produced some software for a client organisation. The software has a life of two years and will then become obsolete. The cost of producing the software was £60,000. The client has agreed to pay a licence fee of £80,000 a year for the software, if it is used in only one of its two divisions, and £120,000 a year, if it is used in both of its divisions. The client may use the software for either one or two years in either division but will definitely use it in at least one division in each of the two years.

Zeta believes there is a 0.6 chance that the licence fee received in any one year will be £80,000 and a 0.4 chance that it will be £120,000. There are, therefore, four possible outcomes attached to this project (where p denotes probability):

- *Outcome 1.* Year 1 cash flow £80,000 ($p = 0.6$) and Year 2 cash flow £80,000 ($p = 0.6$). The probability of both years having cash flows of £80,000 will be:

$$0.6 \times 0.6 = 0.36$$

- *Outcome 2.* Year 1 cash flow £120,000 ($p = 0.4$) and Year 2 cash flow £120,000 ($p = 0.4$). The probability of both years having cash flows of £120,000 will be:

$$0.4 \times 0.4 = 0.16$$

- *Outcome 3.* Year 1 cash flow £120,000 ($p = 0.4$) and Year 2 cash flow £80,000 ($p = 0.6$). The probability of this sequence of cash flows occurring will be:

$$0.4 \times 0.6 = 0.24$$

- *Outcome 4.* Year 1 cash flow £80,000 ($p - 0.6$) and Year 2 cash flow £120,000 ($p = 0.4$). The probability of this sequence of cash flows occurring will be:

$$0.6 \times 0.4 = 0.24$$

The source of probabilities

As we might expect, assigning probabilities to possible outcomes can often be a problem. There may be many possible outcomes arising from a particular investment project. To identify each outcome and then assign a probability to it may prove to be an impossible task. When assigning probabilities to possible outcomes, an objective or a subjective approach may be used.

Objective probabilities are based on verifiable evidence, usually information gathered from past experience. For example, the transport manager of a business operating a fleet of motor vans may be able to provide information concerning the possible life of a new motor van purchased based on the record of similar vans acquired in the past. From the information available, probabilities may be developed for different possible lifespans. However, the past may not always be a reliable guide to the future, particularly during a period of rapid change. With motor vans, for example, changes in design and technology or changes in the purpose for which the vans are being used may undermine the validity of past data.

Subjective probabilities are based on opinion and will be used where past data are either inappropriate or unavailable. The opinions of independent experts may provide a useful basis for developing subjective probabilities, though even these may contain bias, which will affect the reliability of the judgements made.

Despite the problems associated with assigning probabilities, we should not be dismissive of its potential usefulness. Assigning probabilities can help to make explicit some of the risks associated with a project and should help decision makers to appreciate the uncertainties that have to be faced.

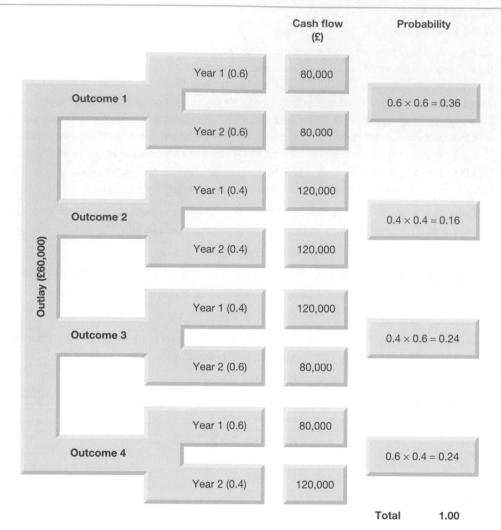

		Cash flow (£)	Probability

Outcome 1
- Year 1 (0.6) — 80,000
- Year 2 (0.6) — 80,000
- 0.6 × 0.6 = 0.36

Outcome 2
- Year 1 (0.4) — 120,000
- Year 2 (0.4) — 120,000
- 0.4 × 0.4 = 0.16

Outcome 3
- Year 1 (0.4) — 120,000
- Year 2 (0.6) — 80,000
- 0.4 × 0.6 = 0.24

Outcome 4
- Year 1 (0.6) — 80,000
- Year 2 (0.4) — 120,000
- 0.6 × 0.4 = 0.24

Outlay (£60,000)

Total 1.00

There are four different possible outcomes associated with the project, each with its own probability of occurrence. The sum of the probabilities attached to each outcome must equal 1.00; in other words, it is certain that one of the possible outcomes will occur. For example, outcome 1 would occur where only one division uses the software in each year.

Figure 9.4 The different possible project outcomes for the Zeta project (Example 9.2)

Activity 9.4

Devonia (Laboratories) Ltd has recently carried out successful clinical trials on a new type of skin cream that has been developed to reduce the effects of ageing. Research and development costs incurred relating to the new product amounted to £160,000. To gauge the market potential of the new product, independent market research consultants were hired at a cost of £45,000. The market research report submitted by the consultants indicates that the skin cream is likely to have a product life of four years and could be sold to retail chemists and large department stores at a price of £20 per 100 ml container. For each of the four years of the new product's life, sales demand has been estimated as follows:

Number of 100 ml containers sold	Probability of occurrence
11,000	0.3
14,000	0.6
16,000	0.1

If the business decides to launch the new product, it is possible for production to begin at once. The equipment necessary to produce it is already owned by the business and originally cost £150,000. At the end of the new product's life, it is estimated that the equipment could be sold for £35,000. If the business decides against launching the new product, the equipment will be sold immediately for £85,000, as it will be of no further use.

The new product will require one hour's labour for each 100 ml container produced. The cost of labour is £8.00 an hour. Additional workers will have to be recruited to produce the new product. At the end of the product's life, the workers are unlikely to be offered further work with the business and total redundancy costs of £10,000 are expected. The cost of the ingredients for each 100 ml container is £6.00. Additional overheads arising from production of the new product are expected to be £15,000 a year.

The new skin cream has attracted the interest of the business's competitors. If the business decides not to produce and sell the skin cream, it can sell the patent rights to a major competitor immediately for £125,000.

Devonia has a cost of capital of 12 per cent. Ignore taxation.

Required:
(a) Calculate the expected net present value (ENPV) of the new product.
(b) State, with reasons, whether or not Devonia should launch the new product.

Your answer should be as follows:

(a) Expected sales volume per year = $(11{,}000 \times 0.3) + (14{,}000 \times 0.6) + (16{,}000 \times 0.1)$
$\qquad\qquad\qquad\qquad\qquad\quad$ = 13,300 units

Expected annual sales revenue = 13,300 × £20
$\qquad\qquad\qquad\qquad\qquad\quad$ = £266,000

Annual labour $\qquad\qquad\qquad$ = 13,300 × £8
$\qquad\qquad\qquad\qquad\qquad\quad$ = £106,400

Annual ingredient costs $\qquad$ = 13,300 × £6
$\qquad\qquad\qquad\qquad\qquad\quad$ = £79,800

Incremental cash flows:

	Years				
	0	1	2	3	4
	£	£	£	£	£
Sale of patent rights	(125.0)				
Sale of equipment	(85.0)				35.0
Sales revenue		266.0	266.0	266.0	266.0
Cost of ingredients		(79.8)	(79.8)	(79.8)	(79.8)
Labour costs		(106.4)	(106.4)	(106.4)	(106.4)
Redundancy					(10.0)
Additional overheads	–	(15.0)	(15.0)	(15.0)	(15.0)
	(210.0)	64.8	64.8	64.8	89.8
Discount factor (12%)	1.000	0.893	0.797	0.712	0.636
	(210.0)	57.9	51.6	46.1	57.1
ENPV	2.7				

(b) The ENPV of the project is positive. This may be seen as a signal that the project should be undertaken. However, the ENPV is very low in relation to the size of the project and careful checking of the key estimates and assumptions would be advisable. A relatively small downward revision of sales (volume and/or price) or upward revision of costs could make the project ENPV negative.

Note, incidentally, that we could have derived an individual NPV for each of the three levels of sales demand and then calculated an ENPV by applying the relevant probability to each of the three NPVs. This would give the same ENPV as in the solution to Activity 9.4.

With decisions involving probabilities, like the one in Activity 9.4, it would be helpful to derive the NPV for each of the possible outcomes regarding sales levels. This would enable the decision maker to have a clearer view of the risk involved with the investment.

Activity 9.5

How would knowing the NPVs of each outcome help Devonia's managers in Activity 9.4?

It would be helpful because the managers would be able to see the NPV that would arise with each of the three possible outcomes, together with each one's likelihood (probability) of actually occurring.

In a simple case, like that in Activity 9.4 (Devonia), deriving the NPV for each possible outcome is quite straightforward. With a typical real-world decision, however, there are very many variables, each with a large number of possible outcomes. This could lead to literally millions of different possible outcomes for the decision as a whole. Here, the only practical approach may be to find the expected value for each of the inputs and then use these values to calculate the expected value for the decision as a whole.

Reacting to the level of risk

Demanding a higher rate of return is the logical reaction to a risky project. Clear, observable evidence shows that there is a relationship between risk and the return required by investors. For example, a bank would normally ask for a higher rate of interest on a loan where it perceives the borrower to be less likely to be able to repay the amount borrowed.

When assessing investment projects, it is normal to increase the discount rate in the face of increased risk – that is, to demand a risk premium: the higher the level of risk, the higher the risk premium that will be demanded. The risk premium is added to the 'risk-free' rate of return to derive the total return required (the **risk-adjusted discount rate**). The risk-free rate is normally taken to be equivalent to the rate of return from government loan notes.

In practice, a business may divide projects into low-risk, medium-risk and high-risk categories and then assign a **risk premium** to each category. The cash flows from a particular project will then be discounted using a rate based on the risk-free rate plus the appropriate risk premium. Since all investments are risky to some extent, all projects will have a risk premium linked to them.

The relationship between risk and return is illustrated in Figure 9.5.

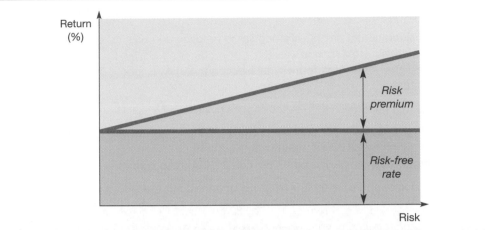

It is logical to take account of the riskiness of projects by changing the discount rate. A risk premium is added to the risk-free rate to derive the appropriate discount rate. A higher return will normally be expected from projects where the risks are higher; thus, the riskier the project, the higher the risk premium.

Figure 9.5 Relationship between risk and return

RISK MANAGEMENT IN PRACTICE

Evidence shows that assessing risk and taking account of the riskiness of decisions is widely practised by managers in real life. **Real World 9.3** looks at some survey evidence on the use of various approaches to risk.

The evidence seems to suggest that:

- formal consideration of risk is very popular in practice and has increased in popularity over recent decades (A&N); and
- some of the businesses that formally take account of risk use more than one approach. (A&N and C&Y).

Two of the main approaches to assessing the riskiness of projects are:

1. sensitivity analysis/scenario analysis, used by 89 per cent of A&N respondents and 'frequently' used by C&Y respondents; and
2. use of probabilities, employed by 77 per cent of A&N respondents.

There are also two main reactions to being faced with risky projects:

1. raising the required rate of return, used by 82 per cent of A&N respondents; and
2. shortening the required payback period, used by 75 per cent of A&N respondents.

Sources: Alkaraan, F. and Northcott, D. (2006) Strategic capital investment decision-making: a role for emergent analysis tools? A study of practice in large UK manufacturing companies, *British Accounting Review*, Vol. 38, pp. 149–173;

Cohen, G. and Yagil, J. (2010) Sectoral differences in corporate financial behaviour: an international survey, *The European Journal of Finance*, Vol. 16, pp. 245–262.

Self-assessment question 9.1

Simtex Ltd has invested £120,000 to date in developing a new type of shaving foam. The shaving foam is now ready for production and it has been estimated that the business will sell 160,000 cans a year of the new product over the next four years. At the end of four years, the product will be discontinued and probably replaced by a new product.

The shaving foam is expected to sell at £6 a can and the variable cost is estimated at £4 per can. Fixed cost (excluding depreciation) is expected to be £300,000 a year. (This figure includes £130,000 of the existing general overheads of the business that will be apportioned to this new product.)

To manufacture and package the new product, equipment costing £480,000 must be acquired immediately. The estimated value of this equipment in four years' time is £100,000. The business calculates depreciation using the straight-line method (equal amounts each year). It has an estimated cost of capital of 12 per cent.

Required:

(a) Deduce the net present value of the new product.

(b) Calculate by how much each of the following must change before the new product is no longer profitable:
    (1) the discount rate;
    (2) the initial outlay on new equipment;
    (3) the net operating cash flows; and
    (4) the residual value of the equipment.

(c) Should the business produce the new product?

The solution to this question can be found at the back of the book on pp. 521–522.

SUMMARY

The main points of this chapter may be summarised as follows:

Dealing with risk

- All decision making has an element of risk, often a large element.
- Investment decisions are particularly risk because:
  - they are relatively long term; and
  - involve large amounts.

Sensitivity analysis

- Sensitivity analysis is an assessment, taking each input factor in turn, of how much each one can vary from estimate before a project is not viable.
- It provides useful insights to projects.
- It does not give a clear decision rule, but provides an impression.
- It is rather static, but scenario analysis can solve this problem by setting up a number of realistic scenarios, enabling decision makers to assess each one.

Expected value

- Expected value is the weighted average of the various values, weighted by the probability of occurrence.
- Expected net present value (ENPV) is the weighted average of the possible outcomes for an investment project, based on probabilities for each of the inputs.
- Expected value provides a single value and a clear decision rule.
- The single ENPV figure can hide the real risk.
- The ENPV figure should be supported by information on the range and dispersion of possible outcomes.
- Probabilities may be subjective (based on opinion) or objective (based on evidence).

Reacting to the level of risk

- Logically, high risk should lead to high returns.
- Using a risk-adjusted discount rate, where a risk premium is added to the risk-free rate, is a logical response to risk.

Risk management in practice

- Formal risk assessment is popular and increasingly so.
- Some businesses apply more than one approach to risk.
- Sensitivity analysis is very popular.
- Use of probabilities is also widely adopted.
- The popular reactions to perceived riskiness are increasing the required rate of return (discount rate) and shortening the required payback period.

FURTHER READING

If you would like to explore the topics covered in this chapter in more depth, we recommend the following:

Arnold, G. (2013) *Corporate Financial Management*, 5th edn, Pearson, Chapter 6.

Drury, C. (2015) *Management and Cost Accounting*, 9th edn, South Western Cengage Learning, Chapter 14.

McLaney, E. (2017) *Business Finance: Theory and Practice*, 11th edn, Pearson, Chapter 6.

Pike, R., Neale, B. and Linsley, P. (2015) *Corporate Finance and Investment*, 8th edn, Pearson, Chapter 7.

REVIEW QUESTIONS

Solutions to these questions can be found at the back of the book on p. 532.

9.1 What are the limitations of the results of a sensitivity analysis such as the one carried out in Example 9.1 (Saluja)?

9.2 When deducing the expected NPV of a project, you can:

(a) identify all possible outcomes (and their individual NPVs) and deduce the expected NPV from them; or

(b) deduce the expected value of each of the inputs and use these to deduce the expected NPV directly.

What are the advantages and disadvantages of each of these two approaches?

9.3 Is there reason to believe that objective probabilities are more reliable than subjective ones?

9.4 In what way are 'expected' values misnamed?

EXERCISES

Exercises with coloured numbers have solutions given at the back of the book on pp. 561–564

Basic-level exercises

9.1 The management of Parklife Ltd, a small business, has just undertaken the appraisal of a major investment in a new production facility. As an independent consultant on business, the management has asked you to go through the calculations and give your opinion on whether the data, assumptions, approach and calculations used in the appraisal seem reasonable.

You discover that the appraisal was based on net present value (NPV) assessment, using best estimates of all of the input figures. You are satisfied that everything else about the appraisal is reasonable. You note that the appraisal shows a comfortable positive NPV.

When you asked the management what they had done about risk, you were told that it had been ignored because no one in the business knew how to deal with it. You have now been asked to draw up some briefing notes for the management that identify possible approaches that could be taken to dealing with risk.

Required:
Draw up the briefing note requested. This should identify all possible approaches that the management could adopt to take risk into account. The strengths and weaknesses of each approach, in the context of this particular decision, should be highlighted.

9.2 Easton Ltd needs to purchase a machine to manufacture a new product. The choice lies between two machines (A and B). Each machine has an estimated life of three years with no expected scrap value.

Machine A will cost £15,000 and Machine B will cost £20,000, payable immediately in each case. The total variable costs of manufacture of each unit are £1 if made on Machine A, but only £0.50 if made on Machine B. This is because Machine B is more sophisticated and requires less labour to operate it.

The product will sell for £4 per unit. The demand for the product is uncertain but is estimated at 2,000 units for each year, 3,000 units for each year or 5,000 units for each year. (Note that whatever sales volume level actually occurs, that level will apply to each of the three years.)

The sales manager has placed probabilities on the level of demand as follows:

Annual demand	Probability of occurrence
2,000	0.2
3,000	0.6
5,000	0.2

Assume that both taxation and fixed costs will be unaffected by any decision made.
Easton Ltd's cost of capital is 6 per cent per year.

Required:
(a) Calculate the NPV for each of the three activity levels for each machine, A and B, and, using those results, calculate the expected NPV for each machine.
(b) What advice would you give the business in selecting between the two machines?

Intermediate-level exercises

9.3 In Exercise 9.2, assume that the 2,000 level is the 'best estimate' of annual demand. Also assume that only Machine A is available.

Required:
(a) Should the business acquire Machine A on the basis of its NPV?
(b) Carry out a sensitivity analysis on the decision recommended in (a) to the best estimates of the following factors:
  • Annual demand;
  • Selling price per unit;
  • Variable cost per unit; and
  • Initial investment.

9.4 Plaything plc has just developed a new mechanical toy, the Nipper. The development costs totalled £300,000. To assess the commercial viability of the Nipper, a market survey has been undertaken at a cost of £35,000. The survey suggests that the Nipper will have a market life of four years and can be sold by Plaything plc for £20 per Nipper. Demand for the Nipper for each of the four years has been estimated as follows:

Number of Nippers	Probability of occurrence
11,000	0.3
14,000	0.6
16,000	0.1

If the decision is made to go ahead with the Nipper, production and sales will begin immediately. Production will require the use of machinery that the business already owns, having bought it for £200,000 three years ago. If Nipper production does not go ahead, the machinery will be sold for £85,000, there being no other use for it. If it is used in Nipper production, the machinery will be sold for an estimated £35,000 at the end of the fourth year. Each Nipper will take one hour's labour of employees who will be taken on specifically for the work at a rate of £8.00 per hour. The business will incur an estimated £10,000 in redundancy costs relating to these employees at the end of the four years.

Materials will cost an estimated £6.00 per Nipper. Nipper production will give rise to an additional fixed cost of £15,000 per year.

It is believed that if Plaything plc decides not to go ahead with producing the Nipper, the rights to the product could be sold to another business for £125,000, receivable immediately.

Plaything plc has a cost of capital of 12 per cent per year.

Required:

(a) On the basis of the expected net present value (ENPV), should the business go ahead with production and sales of the Nipper? (Ignore taxation and inflation.)

(b) Assess the ENPV approach to investment decision making.

9.5 Kernow Cleaning Services Ltd provides street-cleaning services for local councils in the far south west of England. The work is currently labour-intensive and few machines are used. However, the business has recently been considering the purchase of a fleet of street-cleaning vehicles at a total cost of £540,000. The vehicles have a life of four years and are likely to result in a considerable saving of labour costs. Estimates of the likely labour savings and their probability of occurrence are set out below:

	Estimated savings £	Probability of occurrence
Year 1	80,000	0.3
	160,000	0.5
	200,000	0.2
Year 2	140,000	0.4
	220,000	0.4
	250,000	0.2
Year 3	140,000	0.4
	200,000	0.3
	230,000	0.3
Year 4	100,000	0.3
	170,000	0.6
	200,000	0.1

Estimates for each year are independent of other years. The business has a cost of capital of 10 per cent.

Required:

(a) Calculate the expected net present value (ENPV) of the street-cleaning machines.

(b) Calculate the net present value (NPV) of the worst possible outcome and the probability of its occurrence.

Advanced-level exercises

9.6 Computer Tuition Ltd (CT) specialises in providing courses for computer users, often tailoring its courses to meet the specific needs of particular clients. CT's primary financial objective is to maximise the wealth of its shareholders.

CT has been asked by the Small Business Skills Agency (SBSA), a UK government sponsored organisation, to run a series of two-day computer users' induction courses, in various parts of the UK, over a three-year period starting in January 20X4. The courses are part of the implementation of SBSA's policy of actively encouraging the use of computers in small businesses.

SBSA will make suitable premises available to CT, rent free, at various locations, during the three years. It has also undertaken to publicise the courses in a newsletter that it publishes for small businesses. SBSA insists that CT must charge £50 per place on a two-day course.

CT has commissioned a market survey to assess the likely demand. The market research survey cost £5,000. This has yet to be paid by CT. The survey reveals that, without advertising, other than in the SBSA newsletter, there is a 0.6 probability of selling 12,000 places, a 0.2 probability of selling 14,000 and a 0.2 probability of selling 16,000 during 20X4. Left unadvertised, the demand for places in 20X5 and 20X6 is expected to remain at the same level as actually occurs in 20X4. The market researchers point out that, should the lowest level of demand occur in 20X4, it would almost certainly be as a result of the publicity in the newsletter being overlooked by businesses. The market researchers are very confident that a direct mailing, to all businesses that might buy places on courses, would raise demand from 12,000 to 14,000 places per year for the remainder of the three years. The market researchers believe that, at either the 14,000 or the 16,000 level of demand, there would be no prospect of improving demand by any means.

A direct mailing would cost £140,000. It is only feasible to undertake a direct mailing in late December. One could be undertaken in December 20X3. Alternatively, one could be made in December 20X4.

Instructors will be recruited for the duration of the project and paid a total of £350,000 per annum. They will be responsible for managing the project locally. CT will pay their travelling and subsistence expenses, estimated at a total of £100,000 per year for each of the three years.

The project would require CT to provide personal computers to be used by participants on the courses. CT has suitable hardware available from another project which is coming to an end in December 20X3. The computers were bought in May 20X4 for £400,000. If they are not used in this project, they will be sold on 31 December 20X3 for an estimated £250,000, receivable on that date. It is estimated that at the end of the SBSA project the computers would be disposed of for a zero net realisable value, probably by donating them to a school.

It is estimated that the variable costs, for documentation and disks, will amount to an estimated £5 per place sold.

CT's finance cost is estimated at 12 per cent per year.

There are not thought to be any incremental costs associated with the project, other than those to which reference has already been made.

It is estimated that the working capital associated with the SBSA project will be negligible.

Required:

(a) State, with supporting workings, when, if at all, the direct mailing should be undertaken.

(b) Provide a schedule of expected cash flows relevant to the project and use this to recommend, with supporting calculations, whether or not CT should undertake the project.

9.7 Hi Fido plc manufactures high fidelity sound reproduction equipment for the household market. It has recently spent £500,000 developing a new loudspeaker, called the Tracker. A decision now needs to be taken as to whether to go ahead with producing and marketing Trackers. This is to be based on the expected net present value (ENPV) of the relevant cash flows, discounted at the business's estimate of the 20X0 cost of capital of 8 per cent per year. Management believes that a three-year planning horizon is appropriate for this decision, so it will be assumed that sales will not continue beyond 20X3.

Manufacture of Trackers would require acquisition of some plant costing £1 million, payable on installation, on 31 December 20X0. For the purposes of assessing the viability of the Tracker, it will be assumed that the plant would not have any disposal value on 31 December 20X3.

The first sales of Trackers would be expected to be made during the year ending 31 December 20X1. There is uncertainty as to the level of sales that could be expected, so a market survey has been undertaken at a cost of £100,000. The survey suggests that, at the target price of £200 per pair of Trackers, there would be a 60 per cent chance of selling 10,000 pairs and a 40 per cent chance of selling 12,000 pairs during 20X1. If the 20X1 volume of sales were to be at the lower level, 20X2 sales would be either 8,000 pairs of Trackers (30 per cent chance) or 10,000 pairs (70 per cent chance). If the 20X1 volume of sales were to be at the higher level, 20X2 sales would be estimated at 12,000 pairs of Trackers (50 per cent chance) or 15,000 pairs (50 per cent chance). In 20X3 the volume of sales would be expected to be 50 per cent of whatever level of sales actually occur in 20X2.

Sales of Trackers would be expected to have an adverse effect on sales of Repros, a less sophisticated loudspeaker, also produced by the business, to the extent that for each two pairs of Trackers sold, one fewer pairs of Repros would be sold. This effect would be expected to continue throughout the three years.

Materials and components would be bought in at a cost of £70 per pair of Trackers. Manufacture of each pair of Trackers would require three hours of labour. This labour would come from staff released by the lost Repro production. To the extent that this would provide insufficient hours, staff would work overtime, paid at £9 an hour.

The Repro has the following cost structure:

	Per pair £
Selling price	100
Materials	20
Labour (4 hours)	36
Fixed overheads (on a labour-hour basis)	33

The management team currently employed would be able to manage the Tracker project, except that, should the project go ahead, four managers, who had accepted voluntary redundancy from the business, would be asked to stay on until the end of 20X3. These managers were due to leave the business on 31 December 20X0 and to receive lump sums of £30,000 each at that time. They were also due to receive an annual fee of £8,000 each for consultancy work which the business would require of them from time to time. If they were to agree to stay on, they would receive an annual salary of £20,000 each, to include the consultancy fee. They would also receive lump sums of £35,000 each on 31 December 20X3. It is envisaged that the managers would be able to fit any consultancy requirements around their work managing the Tracker project. These payments would all be borne by the business.

Tracker production and sales would not be expected to give rise to any additional operating costs beyond those mentioned above.

Working capital to support both Tracker and Repro production and sales would be expected to run at a rate of 15 per cent of the sales value. The working capital would need to be in place by the beginning of each year concerned.

Sales should be assumed to occur on the last day of the relevant calendar year.

Required:
On the basis of ENPV, should Hi Fido plc go ahead with the Tracker project?

9.8 Tufty plc produces a small range of industrial pumps using automated methods. The business is now considering production of a new model of pump, starting on 1 January 20X3. The business wishes to assess the new pump over a four-year timescale.

Production of the new pump will require the use of automated production equipment. This production equipment could be bought new, on 31 December 20X2, for a cost of £1 million. As an alternative to buying new production equipment, the business could use some equipment that it already owns. This is proving surplus to requirements, owing to a recent downturn in demand for another of the business's products. This downturn is expected to continue for the foreseeable future.

The surplus production equipment could be sold for an estimated £400,000 on 1 January 20X3. It was bought new in 20X0 for £1 million. If it were used on production of the new pumps, it would be expected to have a zero market value by 31 December 20X6.

If the equipment for the new pumps were to be bought new in 20X2, it would be disposed of on 1 January 20X7. It is expected to have a total realisable value of £400,000 on that date.

Fixed annual incremental costs, excluding depreciation, of producing the new pump would total £80,000. Variable annual costs would be £200,000 if the new production equipment is to be used, but £300,000 if the existing production equipment is to be used, since the existing production equipment is less automated and would require a higher labour input.

Sales of the new pumps would be expected to generate revenues of £600,000 for each of the four years.

Production of the new pump is expected to give rise to an additional working capital requirement of 10 per cent of annual revenues. These amounts will need to be in place by 1 January of the relevant year and will be released on 31 December 20X6.

It is not expected that any other incremental costs would be involved with the decision to produce the new pump.

The cost of capital for the business is 10 per cent per year.

All revenues and expenses should be treated as if they occurred on the last day of the relevant calendar year, except where the date is specifically stated.

Required:

(a) Prepare a schedule that derives the annual net relevant cash flows arising from producing the new pump and use this to assess the decision on the basis of net present value (NPV). You should make clear whether the surplus production equipment should be sold or used on production of the new pump on 1 January 20X3.

(b) Assess, and comment on, the sensitivity of the estimate of the fixed annual incremental costs of producing the new pump to the decision reached in (a).

STRATEGIC MANAGEMENT ACCOUNTING: PERFORMANCE EVALUATION AND PRICING IN A COMPETITIVE ENVIRONMENT

INTRODUCTION

We begin the chapter by considering strategic management accounting. We shall discuss the nature of this aspect of management accounting and then go on to examine some of the techniques that fall within its scope. This will include an examination of the balanced scorecard, which seeks to integrate financial and non-financial measures into a framework for the achievement of business objectives.

We shall also explore the idea of shareholder value, which has been a 'hot' issue among managers in recent years. Many leading businesses claim that the quest for shareholder value is the driving force behind strategic and operational decisions. We shall consider what the term 'shareholder value' means and examine one of the main methods of measuring shareholder value.

We end the chapter by looking at the key issues surrounding pricing decisions. Managers must approach pricing decisions with care because of the impact they can have on the profitability of a business. We shall consider the way in which prices are set, both in theory and in practice, within a competitive environment.

Learning outcomes

When you have completed this chapter, you should be able to:

- Discuss the nature of strategic management accounting and describe its role in providing information about competitors and customers.

- Discuss the role of non-financial measures of performance in management accounting and describe how the balanced scorecard attempts to integrate both financial and non-financial measures.

- Explain the term 'shareholder value' and describe the role of EVA® in measuring and delivering shareholder value.

- Explain the theoretical underpinning of pricing decisions and discuss the practical issues involved in determining an appropriate selling price for the output of a business.

WHAT IS STRATEGIC MANAGEMENT ACCOUNTING?

Businesses are increasingly being managed along strategic lines. By this we mean that strategies adopted by a business are increasingly providing the basis for both long-term and short-term decisions. If management accounting is to help guide decision making within a strategic framework, the reports provided and techniques used must align closely with the framework that has been put in place. Conventional management accounting has been criticised, however, for failing to address fully the strategic aspects of managing a business. This does not mean that the techniques discussed so far are obsolete. It does mean, however, that management accounting must continue to develop if it is to retain its position at the heart of business decision making.

Strategic management accounting is concerned with providing information that will support the strategic plans and decisions made within a business. We saw in Chapter 1 that strategic planning involves five steps:

1 Establishing the mission, vision and objectives of a business.
2 Undertaking a position analysis, such as a SWOT (strengths, weaknesses, opportunities and threats) analysis, to establish how the business is placed in relation to its environment.
3 Identifying and assessing the possible strategic options that will lead the business from its present position to the achievement of its objectives.
4 Selecting the most appropriate strategic options and formulating long- and short-term plans to pursue them.
5 Reviewing business performance and exercising control by assessing actual performance against planned performance.

To some extent, conventional management accounting already supports this strategic process. We saw in Chapter 7, for example, how budgets are an integral part of the strategic planning framework. We also saw in Chapter 8 the role of investment appraisal techniques in evaluating long-term plans. Nevertheless, there is scope for further development. If management accounting is fully to support the strategic planning process, there is a need for further development in three broad areas:

■ *It must become more outward-looking.* The conventional approach to management accounting does not give enough consideration to external factors affecting the business. These factors, however, are vitally important to strategic planning and decision making. Managers need to understand, for example, the external environment within which the business operates when undertaking a position analysis or when formulating future plans. Management accounting can play a useful role here by providing information relating to the environment, such as the performance of the business's competitors and the profitability of its customers.
■ *There must be greater concern for developing and implementing methods through which a business can outperform the competition.* In a competitive environment, a business must gain an advantage over its rivals to survive and prosper over the longer term. Competitive advantage can be gained in various ways and one important way is through cost leadership: that is, the ability to produce products or services at a lower cost than that of other businesses. Although conventional management accounting provides a number of cost determination and control techniques to help a business operate more efficiently, these techniques are not always enough. Rather than seeking simply to count and control the costs incurred, costs and cost structures may need to be transformed. Thus, management

accounting has a role to play in helping to shape the costs of the business to fit the strategic agenda.

■ *There must be a concern for monitoring the strategies of the business and for bringing these strategies to a successful conclusion.* Management accounting must place greater emphasis on long-term planning issues and act as the guardian of business strategy. This involves developing a comprehensive range of performance measures to help ensure that the objectives of the business are being met. As these objectives are often couched in both financial and non-financial terms, the measures developed must reflect this fact.

Let us now turn our attention to the ways in which management accounting can help in each of the three areas identified.

FACING OUTWARDS

If a business is to thrive and prosper, its managers must develop a good understanding of the environment within which it operates. Management accounting can contribute to this understanding by providing information concerning the product markets within which the business competes.

Activity 10.1

What kind of information might be helpful to managers seeking to understand a particular product market? Try to think of at least two kinds of information.

Information may include:

■ the total size of the market for the product or service provided by the business;
■ the business's percentage share of that total market;
■ the business's percentage share of the various segments (for example, geographical) of that market;
■ likely future changes in the nature of that market; and
■ trends over time in that market's size.

The kind of information identified above should help managers when making pricing decisions. We shall consider product markets and pricing decisions in more detail later in the chapter.

Managers of a business should also have a good understanding of the threat posed by its competitors and the benefits obtained from its customers. There is a strong case for incorporating key information concerning both competitors and customers as part of the routine management reports. This should help managers to respond more quickly to any opportunities and threats that may arise. Let us now turn our attention to the kind of information that may be provided about these two groups.

Competitor analysis

To compete effectively, a business should gain a sound knowledge of its main competitors. By undertaking **competitor analysis**, it may acquire a source of competitive advantage. This may help in strategic planning as well as product pricing and business acquisition decisions. **Real World 10.1** indicates, however, that many businesses do not monitor their competitors and so fail to gain this advantage.

Two methods of undertaking competitor analysis are **competitor array** and **competitor profiling**. We shall now discuss both of these.

Competitor array

This involves identifying the key success factors for the industry and ranking the business and its competitors according to these factors. The competitor array process is illustrated in Example 10.1.

Example 10.1

Alba plc is a 'no-frills' airline that has two main competitors, Badox plc and Corta plc. To gain an understanding of the business's relative competitive position, the managers of Alba plc have identified five key success factors relating to its market.

To analyse competitive position, each success factor is given a weight, based on its relative importance, and the sum of these weights is equal to 1.0. The managers award their own business and each of its competitors a score, out of a maximum of 10, for each factor. A weighted score for each factor is then calculated along with an overall score for each of the three businesses.

$\rightarrow$

The following table indicates the scores awarded for each business:

Success factor	Weight	Alba plc		Competitor 1 Badox plc		Competitor 2 Corta plc	
		Score	Weighted score	Score	Weighted score	Score	Weighted score
Low fares	0.4	7	2.8	5	2.0	6	2.4
Quality of route network	0.2	4	0.8	8	1.6	7	1.4
Operational efficiency	0.2	6	1.2	8	1.6	5	1.0
Customer service standards	0.1	7	0.7	8	0.8	2	0.2
Internet sales capability	0.1	8	0.8	9	0.9	9	0.9
Total	1.0		6.3		6.9		5.9

We can see that this kind of analysis relies heavily on subjective judgement. Nevertheless, it can help to identify the relative strengths and weaknesses of each business, which can be used as a basis for both offensive and defensive strategies.

Competitor profiling

This involves an examination of the aims, intentions and capabilities of competitors. To illustrate the benefits of competitor profiling, let us assume that a business proposes to reduce its sales prices by 10 per cent. What would be the reaction of competitors? Would this reduction be matched by them and thereby cancel out any advantage to be gained? Would it lead to a price war where sales prices follow a downward spiral? If competitors could not match the price reduction, would they be able to continue to supply, given the likely sales volume reduction that they would suffer? The proposal to reduce prices cannot be fully evaluated until competitors' likely reaction to the proposal is known.

To find out what drives a competitor and how it might act in the future, four key aspects of its business should be analysed. These are:

1 *Mission and objectives.* Where is the competitor going? In particular, what are its profit objectives, what rate of sales growth is it trying to achieve, what market share does it seek?
2 *Strategies.* How does the competitor expect to achieve its mission and objectives? What investments are being made in new technology? What alliances and joint ventures are being created? What new products or services are to be launched? What mergers and acquisitions are planned? What cost reduction strategies are being developed?
3 *Assumptions.* How do the competitor's managers view the world? What assumptions are held about:
   ■ future trends within the industry;
   ■ the competitive strengths of other businesses; and
   ■ the feasibility of launching into new markets?
4 *Resources and capabilities.* How serious is the potential threat? What is the competitor's scale and size? Does it have superior technology? Is it profitable? Does it have a strong liquidity position? What is its cost structure? What is the quality of its management? What is the reputation and quality of its products? How good is its marketing and distribution network?

These four aspects provide the framework for analysing competitors, as shown in Figure 10.1.

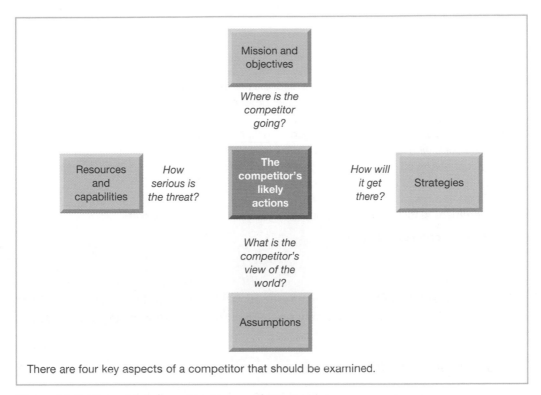

There are four key aspects of a competitor that should be examined.

Figure 10.1 Framework for competitor analysis

Sources of information

Gathering information to answer the questions posed above is not always easy. Businesses are understandably reluctant to release information that may damage their competitive position. Nevertheless, there are sources of information available that can be used.

A useful starting point is to examine a competitor's annual report. In the UK, all limited companies are obliged to provide information about their business in an annual report that is available to the public. Similar provisions relate to limited companies in most countries in the world. The annual report will contain an income statement, statement of cash flows and statement of financial position. When taken together, these statements provide a useful picture of financial health. In addition, the annual report will often contain a significant amount of non-financial information, which may reveal much about the aims, strategy, management and values of a business.

There are other sources of both published and unpublished information that may also be employed.

Activity 10.2

What sources of published and unpublished information might a business use to gain an understanding of a competitor? Try to think of at least four sources.

The potential sources are many and varied and include:

- announcements made by the competitor;
- press coverage of the competitor's business;
- statements by managers made at conferences or on the competitor's website;
- house journals, brochures and catalogues produced by the competitor;
- market share data and discussions with financial analysts;
- discussions with customers who trade both with the business and with the competitor;
- discussions with suppliers to both the business and its competitor;
- physical observation, such as insights from 'mystery shopping';
- detailed inspection of the competitor's products and prices;
- industry reports; and
- government statistics on such matters as the total size of the market.

You may have thought of others.

It is worth mentioning that specialist agencies can be employed to provide a profile of competitors. These agencies often rely on the kind of information sources described in Activity 10.2.

Customer profitability analysis

Businesses seek to attract and retain customers that produce profitable sales orders. It is, therefore, important to know whether a particular customer, or type of customer, generates profits for the business. Modern businesses are likely to find that much of the cost incurred is not related to the cost of products sold but to the associated selling and distribution cost. This has led to a shift in emphasis from product profitability to customer profitability.

Customer profitability analysis (CPA) assesses the profitability of each customer or type of customer. In order for CPA to be undertaken, the total costs associated with selling and distributing goods or services to particular customers must be identified. These include the cost of:

- *Handling the customer's order.* This covers costs involved with receiving the order and other activities up to the point where the goods are despatched, or the service provided. This will include the costs of raising invoices, recording sales and other accounting tasks.
- *Visiting the customer.* Many businesses have sales employees that carry out visits to customers. This may be done to take orders as well as to keep the customer informed of changes to the business's product range.
- *Delivering the customer's goods.* A business may use either a delivery service or its own transport. The distances involved as well as the size and nature of the goods will determine the cost incurred.
- *Holding inventories.* Customers tend to require inventories to be held by the business. This might be particularly the case where, for example, a customer operates a 'just-in-time' raw material delivery policy. This can require deliveries to be made frequently and at short notice, normally putting pressure on the supplier to hold higher inventories levels. (We shall discuss 'just-in-time' inventories management in more detail in Chapter 12.)
- *Granting credit.* The business will have to finance any credit allowed to its customers. This may vary from customer to customer, depending on how promptly they pay.
- *After-sales support.* Technical assistance or servicing may be offered as part of the sales agreement.

The typical customer related costs are summarised in Figure 10.2

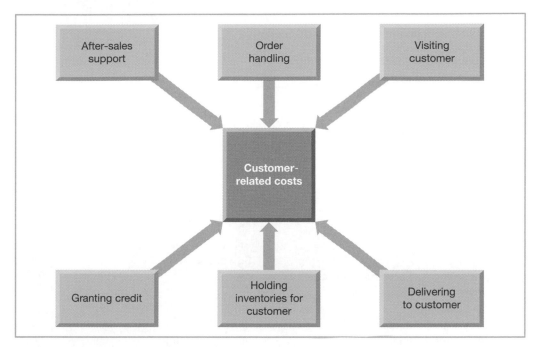

Figure 10.2 Customer-related costs

These customer-related costs are probably best determined using an activity-based costing approach to cost allocation. This means that, once customer-related costs are identified, cost drivers must be established and appropriate cost driver rates deduced.

Activity 10.3

Imat plc identified the following costs relating to its customers:

- Order handling
- Invoicing and collection
- Shipment processing
- Sales visits
- After-sales service.

Suggest a possible cost driver for each of the items identified.

We thought of the following:

Customer-related cost	Possible cost driver
Order handling	Number of orders placed
Invoicing and collection	Number of invoices sent
Shipment processing	Number of shipments made
Sales visits	Number of sales visits made
After-sales service	Number of technical support visits made

These are only suggestions. Other factors may be found that drive each cost.

Once customer-related costs are derived, a CPA statement, which is essentially a summary income statement, can be produced for each customer and/or type of customer. The CPA statement will show:

- the relevant sales revenue;
- the basic cost of creating or buying in the goods or services supplied (that is, cost of goods sold);

- any general selling and administration costs of the business; and
- the customer-related costs identified above.

Example 10.2 illustrates a CPA statement.

Example 10.2

Imat plc – CPA statement for December

	Customer			
	A plc £000	B plc £000	C plc £000	D plc £000
Sales revenue	125	75	80	145
Cost of goods sold	(87)	(52)	(56)	(101)
Gross profit	38	23	24	44
General selling and administrative costs	(19)	(11)	(12)	(22)
Customer-related costs:				
Order handling	(4)	(2)	(2)	(4)
Invoicing and collection	(4)	(2)	(2)	(4)
Shipment processing	(6)	(4)	(4)	(8)
Sales visits	(7)	(1)	(1)	(2)
After-sales service	(6)	–	(1)	–
Profit/(loss) for the month	(8)	3	2	4

Where all customers are charged the same price for products, the top part of the CPA statement, which is concerned with deducing the gross profit, may be viewed as relating to product profitability. The bottom part of the CPA statement, which is the part below the gross profit figure, may be viewed as relating to customer profitability. To analyse customer profitability, we can express each of the costs found in this bottom part as a percentage of gross profit.

Example 10.3 provides the results.

Example 10.3

Imat plc – Customer profitability analysis

	Customer			
	A plc %	B plc %	C plc %	D plc %
Gross profit	100.0	100.0	100.0	100.0
General selling and administrative costs	50.0	47.8	50.0	50.0
Customer-related costs:				
Order handling	10.5	8.7	8.3	9.1
Invoicing and collection	10.5	8.7	8.3	9.1
Shipment processing	15.8	17.4	16.7	18.2
Sales visits	18.4	4.3	4.2	4.5
After-sales service	15.8	–	4.2	–
Profit/(loss) for the month	(21.0)	13.1	8.3	9.1
	100.0	100.0	100.0	100.0

The information generated shows that one customer, A plc, is generating a loss. To find out whether this is a persistent problem, trend analysis can be undertaken which plots the customer-related costs as a percentage of gross profit over time. An example of a trend analysis for A plc is shown in Figure 10.3.

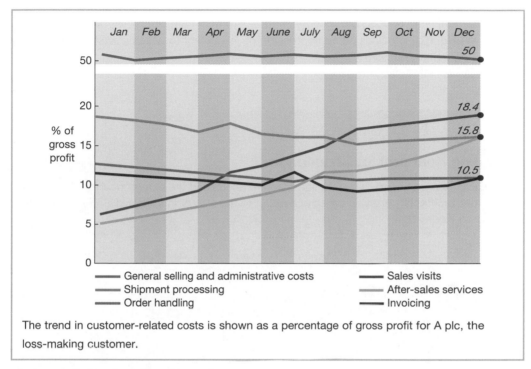

The trend in customer-related costs is shown as a percentage of gross profit for A plc, the loss-making customer.

Figure 10.3 Trend analysis for A plc

In practice, a small proportion of customers often generate a large proportion of total profit. Where this occurs, the business may focus its marketing and customer support efforts on these customers. The less profitable customers may then be targeted for price increases or, perhaps, reduced customer support, as we saw in Activity 10.4.

Where a business has many customers, the analysis of individual customers' profitability may not be feasible. In such a situation, it may be better to categorise customers according to particular attributes and then to assess the profitability of each category.

The support services division of one large computer business, for example, divides its customers into three categories based on:

- technical capabilities;
- how they use the product; and
- the type of service contract they have. (See reference 1 at the end of the chapter.)

However, identifying appropriate categories for customers can sometimes be difficult.

Real World 10.2 provides some impression of the extent to which customer profitability analysis is used in practice.

Real World 10.2

Profiting from profitability analysis

The CIMA survey, mentioned in earlier chapters, examined the extent to which the use of customer profitability analysis varies according to the size of the business. The results are set out in Figure 10.4.

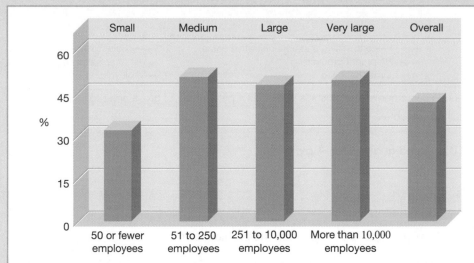

CPA is fairly widely used with more than half of medium-size, large and very large businesses using this technique. The survey also found that in Europe (excluding the UK) 61 per cent of businesses employed CPA; this compared with 36 to 47 per cent of businesses in other regions.

Figure 10.4 Use of customer profitability analysis

Source: Adapted from figure in CIMA (2009) *Management Accounting Tools for Today and Tomorrow*, p. 17.

COMPETITIVE ADVANTAGE THROUGH COST LEADERSHIP

Many businesses try to compete on price: that is, they try to provide goods or services at prices that compare favourably with those of their competitors. To do this successfully over time, they must also compete on costs; lower prices can only normally be sustained by lower costs. A strategic commitment to competitive pricing must therefore be accompanied by a strategic commitment to managing the cost base. In the past, managing costs was often cyclical in nature. It took on importance during tough economic times but, when things improved, some easing back would occur. In today's more competitive environment, however, it has become a continuous process.

Real World 10.3 sets out the results of a recent survey of 210 senior executives from some of the largest US businesses. The survey carried out by Deloitte, an international accounting and consulting firm, confirms that bearing down on costs is a high priority for many large US businesses. Deloitte argues, however, that significant cost improvements can only be achieved by adopting a strategic approach.

Real World 10.3

Missing the target

The 2016 Deloitte survey of 210 senior executives of US-based Fortune 1000 companies found that, irrespective of whether sales revenues were increasing or decreasing, businesses regarded delivering cost improvements as a high priority. Furthermore, by 2016 a clear majority of business surveyed were pursuing cost reduction targets of 10 per cent or more and a third were pursuing targets of more than 20 per cent. The survey found, however, that the outcomes from cost improvement initiatives were often disappointing. In 2016, the majority of cost reduction initiatives failed to meet their targets. Figures 10.5 and 10.6 set out the key findings.

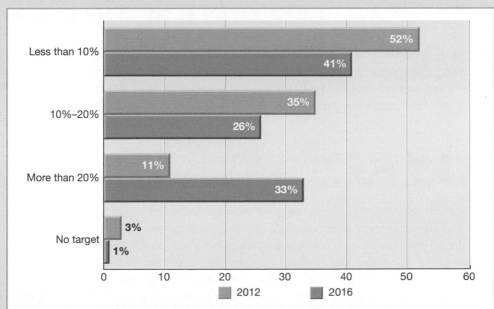

Nearly 60 per cent of businesses had a cost reduction target of 10 per cent or more. 33 per cent of businesses have set aggressive targets of more than 20 per cent.

Figure 10.5 Annual cost reduction targets

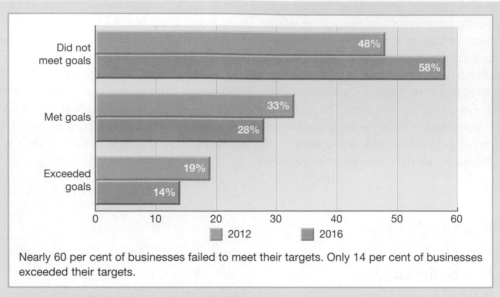

Nearly 60 per cent of businesses failed to meet their targets. Only 14 per cent of businesses exceeded their targets.

Figure 10.6 Success in meeting cost targets

According to Deloitte, an important cause of failure in meeting cost reduction targets is the use of tactical approaches, which focus on business processes. To achieve significant cost reductions, so it was argued, a strategic approach should be adopted. This involves focusing on initiatives such as reconfiguring operations, centralising functions, outsourcing and offshore operations.

Source: Deloitte (2016) *Thriving in Uncertainty: Cost improvement practices and trends in the Fortune 1000*, www2.Deloitte.com, April.

In Chapter 5 we saw that, to manage costs in an active way, new forms of costing and cost management have been devised. Some of the methods discussed, such as total life-cycle costing, reflect a clear concern for long-term cost reduction. They, fall therefore within the scope of strategic cost management.

NON-FINANCIAL MEASURES OF PERFORMANCE

Financial measures have long been seen as the most important ones for a business. They provide a valuable means of summarising and evaluating business achievement. Furthermore, the continued importance of financial measures is in no real doubt. Nevertheless, there has been increasing recognition that financial measures alone will not provide managers with sufficient information to manage a business effectively. Non-financial measures are also needed to help gain a deeper understanding of the business and to help achieve its objectives, including financial objectives.

Financial measures portray various aspects of business achievement (for example, sales revenues, profits and return on capital employed) that can help managers determine whether the business is increasing the wealth of its owners. These measures are vitally important but, in an increasingly competitive environment, managers also need to understand what *drives* the creation of wealth. These **value drivers** may be such things as employee satisfaction, customer loyalty and the level of product innovation. Often they do not lend themselves to financial measurement. Non-financial measures, however, may provide some means of assessment.

Activity 10.5

How might we measure

(a) employee satisfaction?
(b) customer loyalty?
(c) the level of product innovation?

(a) Employee satisfaction may be measured through the use of an employee survey. This could examine attitudes towards various aspects of the job, the degree of autonomy that is permitted, the level of recognition and reward received, the level of participation in decision making, the degree of support received in carrying out tasks and so on. Less direct measures of satisfaction may include employee turnover rates and employee productivity. However, other factors may have a significant influence on these measures.

(b) Customer loyalty may be measured through the proportion of total sales generated from existing customers, the number of repeat sales made to customers, the percentage of customers renewing subscriptions or other contracts and so on.

(c) The level of product innovation may be measured through the number of innovations during a period compared to those of competitors, the percentage of sales attributable to recent product innovations, the number of innovations that are brought successfully to market and so on.

Financial measures tend to be 'lag' indicators, in that they tell us about outcomes. In other words, they measure the consequences arising from past management decisions. Non-financial measures can also act as 'lag indicators' but can, perhaps more usefully, be used as 'lead' indicators. This is because they tend to focus on those things that drive performance. If we measure changes in these value drivers, we may be able to predict changes in future financial performance. A business may find from experience, for example, that a 10 per cent decline in the level of product innovation during one period tends to lead to a 20 per cent reduction in sales revenues over the next three periods. In this case, the level of product innovation can be regarded as a lead indicator. It can tell managers that a future decline in sales is likely, unless corrective action is taken. Thus, by using this lead indicator, managers can identify key changes at an early stage and can respond quickly.

The balanced scorecard

One of the most impressive attempts to integrate the use of financial and non-financial measures has been the **balanced scorecard**, developed by Robert Kaplan and David Norton (see reference 2 at the end of the chapter). The balanced scorecard is both a management system and a measurement system. In essence, it provides a framework that translates the aims and objectives of a business into a series of key performance measures and targets. This framework is intended to make the strategy of the business more coherent by tightly linking it to particular targets and initiatives. As a result, managers should be able to see more clearly whether the objectives that have been set have actually been achieved.

The balanced scorecard approach involves setting objectives and developing appropriate measures and targets in four main areas:

1 *Financial.* This area will specify the financial returns required by shareholders and may involve the use of financial measures such as:

- return on capital employed;
- operating profit margin; and
- percentage sales revenue growth.

2 *Customer.* This area will specify the kind of customer and/or markets that the business wishes to service and will establish appropriate measures such as:

- customer satisfaction; and
- new customer growth levels.

3 *Internal business process.* This area will specify those business processes (for example, innovation, types of operation and after-sales service) that are important to the success of the business. It will also establish appropriate measures, such as:

- percentage of sales from new products;
- time to market for new products;
- product cycle times; and
- speed of response to customer complaints.

4 *Learning and growth.* This area will specify the kind of people, the systems and the procedures that are necessary to deliver long-term business growth. This area is often the most difficult for the development of appropriate measures. However, examples of measures may include:

- employee motivation;
- employee skills profiles; and
- information systems' capabilities.

These four areas are shown in Figure 10.7.

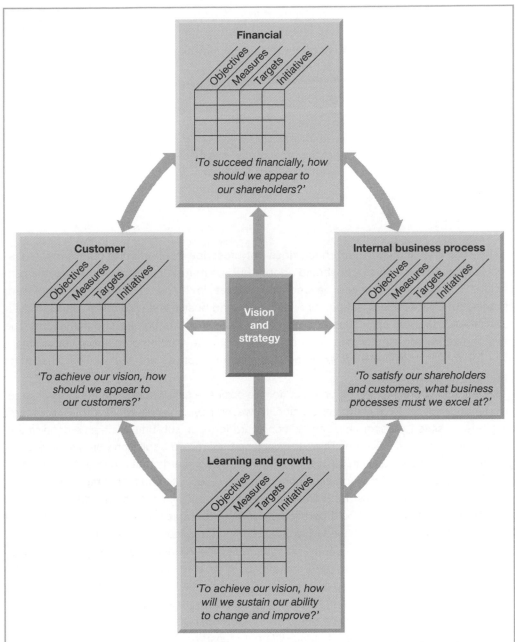

There are four main areas covered by the balanced scorecard. Note that, for each area, a fundamental question must be addressed. By answering these questions, managers should be able to develop the key objectives of the business. Once this has been done, suitable measures and targets can be developed that are relevant to those objectives. Finally, appropriate management initiatives will be developed to achieve the targets set.

Source: Kaplan, R. and Norton, D. (1996) *The Balanced Scorecard*, Harvard Business School Press. Copyright © 1996 by the Harvard Business School Publishing Corporation. All rights reserved. Reprinted by permission of Harvard Business School Press.

Figure 10.7 The balanced scorecard – for translating a strategy into operational processes

The balanced scorecard approach does not prescribe the particular objectives, measures or targets that a business should adopt; this is a matter for the individual business to decide. There are differences between businesses in terms of technology employed, organisational structure, management philosophy and business environment, so each business should develop objectives and measures that reflect its unique circumstances. The balanced scorecard simply sets out the framework for developing a coherent set of objectives for the business and for ensuring that these objectives are then linked to specific targets and initiatives.

A balanced scorecard will be prepared for the business as a whole or, in the case of large, diverse businesses, for each major division. However, having prepared an overall scorecard, it is then possible to prepare a balanced scorecard for each sub-unit, such as a department, within the business or division. Thus, the balanced scorecard approach can cascade down the business and can result in a pyramid of balanced scorecards that are linked to the 'master' balanced scorecard through an alignment of the objectives and measures employed.

Although many measures, both financial and non-financial, could be used in a balanced scorecard, only a handful should be used. According to Kaplan and Norton, a maximum of 20 measures will normally be needed to capture the factors that are critical to the success of the business. (If a business has come up with more than 20 measures, it is usually because the managers have not thought hard enough about what the key measures really are.) The key measures developed should be a mix of lagging indicators (those relating to outcomes) and lead indicators (those relating to the things that drive performance). Interestingly, Tesco plc, the UK supermarket business, operated for a number of years with a version of the balanced scorecard that had more than 40 different measures. This was abandoned in 2015 in favour of a balance scorecard with a much more limited number of measures. The business's new CEO, Dave Lewis, felt that the older version was too complex for staff to handle.

Although the balanced scorecard employs measures across a wide range of business activity, it does not seek to dilute the importance of financial measures and objectives. In fact, the opposite is true. Kaplan and Norton insist that a balanced scorecard must reflect a concern for the financial objectives of the business. This means that measures and objectives in the other three areas identified must ultimately be related back to the financial objectives. There must be a cause-and-effect relationship. So, for example, an investment in staff development (in the learning and growth area) may lead to improved levels of after-sales service (internal business process area) which, in turn, may lead to higher levels of customer satisfaction (customer area) and, ultimately, higher sales revenues and profits (financial area). At first, cause-and-effect relationships may not be very clearly identified. However, by gathering information over time, the business can improve its understanding of the linkages and thereby improve the effectiveness of the scorecard.

Figure 10.8 shows the cause-and-effect relationship between the investment in staff development and the business's financial objectives.

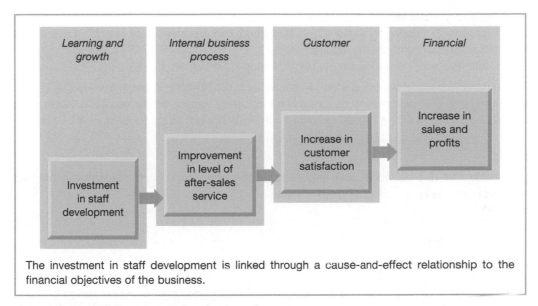

The investment in staff development is linked through a cause-and-effect relationship to the financial objectives of the business.

Figure 10.8 The cause-and-effect relationship

Activity 10.7

Do you think the approach illustrated in Figure 10.8 is a rather cynical way of dealing with staff development? Should staff development have to be justified in terms of the financial results achieved?

This approach may seem rather cynical. However, Kaplan and Norton argue that unless this kind of link between staff development and increased financial returns can be demonstrated, managers are likely to become sceptical about the benefits of staff development and so the result may be that there will be no investment in staff.

Why is this framework referred to as a *balanced* scorecard? According to Kaplan and Norton, there are various reasons. It is because it aims to strike a balance between:

■ *external* measures, relating to customers and shareholders, and *internal* measures, relating to business process, learning and growth;
■ the measures that reflect *outcomes* (lag indicators) and measures that help *predict future performance* (lead indicators); and
■ *hard* financial measures and *soft* non-financial measures.

It is possible to adapt the balanced scorecard to fit the needs of the particular business. Barclays plc, the UK bank has done this as **Real World 10.4** explains.

Real World 10.4

Bank balance

Barclays has developed a version of the balance scorecard that covers five key areas, namely:

1. Customer and client – dealing with bank/customer relationships
2. Colleague – covering staff development and relations
3. Citizenship – relating to the bank's relationships with the communities in which it operates
4. Conduct – focusing on the bank's integrity
5. Company – concentrating on the bank's financial performance

The bank has just eight key performance indicators (KPIs) within these five areas.

The bank's annual reports devote a large amount of space to discussing its balanced scorecard and reporting its performance for the year against target for each of the KPIs.

Source: www.home.barclays, accessed 16 March 2017.

Real World 10.5 provides some impression of the extent to which the balanced scorecard is used in practice.

Real World 10.5

A question of balance

Bain & Company, a firm of management consultants, undertakes a regular survey of key management tools. Figure 10.9 shows the results of its 2015 survey, based on a database of more than 13,000 executives worldwide, looking at levels of usage as, and satisfaction with, the balanced scorecard.

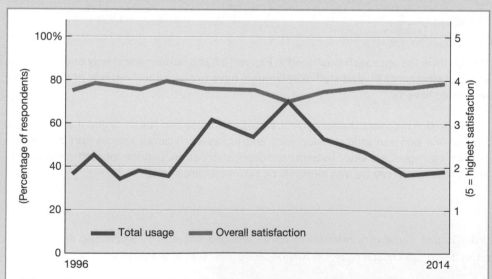

Although the level of satisfaction with this technique has been consistently high, the level of usage has varied over time.

Figure 10.9 Use of (and satisfaction with) the balanced scorecard

We can see that the level of usage has risen and then fallen over the period 1996 to 2014. The level of satisfaction with this management tool, however, has been consistently high.

Source: Rigby, D. (2015) *Insights Management Tools, Balanced Scorecard*, Bain and Company, http://www.bain.com/publications/articles/management-tools-balanced-scorecard.aspx, 10 June, used with permission from Bain & Company.

Real World 10.6 provides an interesting analogy with aeroplane pilots limiting themselves to just one control device.

This story makes the point that concentrating on only a few areas of performance may lead to other important areas being ignored. Too narrow a focus can adversely affect behaviour and distort performance. This may, in turn, mean that the business fails to meet its strategic objectives. Perhaps we should bear in mind another apocryphal story concerning a factory in Russia which, under the former communist regime, produced nails. The factory had its output measured according only to the weight of nails manufactured. For one financial period, it achieved its output target by producing one very large nail!

Scorecard problems

Not all attempts to embed the balanced scorecard approach within a business are successful. Why do things go wrong? It has been suggested that often too many measures are used, thereby making the scorecard too complex and unwieldy. We saw earlier that Tesco revised its version of the scorecard for this reason. It has also been suggested that managers are confronted with trade-off decisions between the four different dimensions. They struggle with this because they lack a clear compass. Imagine a manager who has a limited budget and therefore has to decide whether to invest in staff training or product innovation. If both add value to the business, which choice will be optimal for the business?

While such problems exist, David Norton believes that there are two main reasons why the balanced scorecard fails to take root within a business, as **Real World 10.7** explains.

Norton's last point in Real World 10.7, relating to linking performance as measured by scorecard targets to management pay, has been taken up by Barclays (Real World 10.3). At Barclays, part of senior management remuneration is directly dependent on scorecard performance.

MEASURING SHAREHOLDER VALUE

Traditional measures of financial performance have been subject to much criticism in recent years. As a result, new measures that help to guide and assess strategic management decisions have been advocated. These new measures are based on the idea of increasing shareholder value. In this section, we shall consider one of the more popular of these measures. Before doing so, however, we shall see why increasing shareholder value is regarded as the ultimate financial objective of a business.

The quest for shareholder value

For some years, shareholder value has been a 'hot' issue among managers. Many leading businesses now claim that the quest for shareholder value is the driving force behind their strategic and operational decisions. Let us begin, therefore, by considering what is meant by the term 'shareholder value'.

In simple terms, 'shareholder value' is about putting the needs of shareholders at the heart of management decisions. It is argued that shareholders invest in a business with a view to maximising their financial returns in relation to the risks that they are prepared to take. Since shareholders appoint managers to act on their behalf, management decisions and actions should reflect a concern for maximising shareholder returns. Although the business may have other 'stakeholder' groups, such as employees, customers and suppliers, it is the shareholders that should be seen as the most important group.

This, of course, is not a new idea. As we discussed in Chapter 1, maximising shareholder wealth is assumed to be the key objective of a business. However, not everyone accepts this. Some believe that a balance must be struck between the competing claims of the various stakeholders. A debate concerning the merits of each viewpoint is beyond the scope of this book; however, it is worth pointing out that, in recent years, the business environment has radically changed.

In the past, shareholders have been accused of being too passive and of accepting too readily the profits and dividends that managers have delivered. However, this has changed. Shareholders are now much more assertive and, as owners of the business, are in a position to insist that their needs are given priority. Since the 1980s we have witnessed the deregulation and globalisation of business, as well as enormous changes in technology. The effect has been to create a much more competitive world. This has meant not only competition for products and services but also competition for funds. Businesses must now compete more strongly for shareholder funds and so must offer competitive rates of return.

Thus, self-interest may be the most powerful reason for managers to make every effort to maximise shareholder returns. If they do not, there is a risk that shareholders will either replace them with managers who will, or allow the business to be taken over by another business with managers who are dedicated to maximising shareholder returns.

How can shareholder value be created?

Creating shareholder value can be viewed as a four-stage process:

- *Stage 1:* Set objectives for the business that reflect the central importance of maximising shareholder returns. This will set a clear direction for the business.

- *Stage 2:* Establish an appropriate means of measuring the returns, or value, that have been generated for shareholders. For reasons that we shall discuss later, the traditional methods of measuring returns to shareholders are inadequate for this purpose.

- *Stage 3:* Manage the business in such a manner as to promote shareholder returns maximisation. This means setting demanding targets and then achieving them through the best possible use of resources, the use of incentive systems and the embedding of a shareholder value culture throughout the business.

- *Stage 4:* Measure the shareholder returns over a period of time to see whether the objectives have actually been achieved.

Figure 10.10 shows the shareholder value creation process.

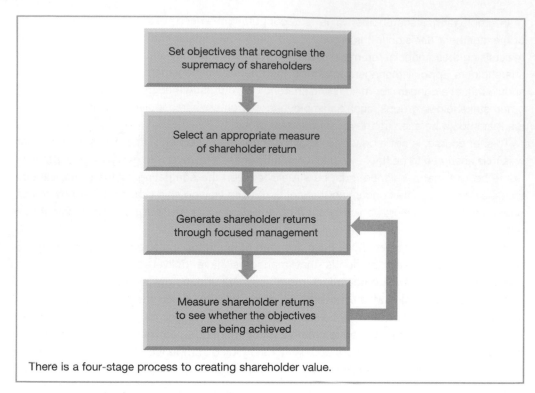

Set objectives that recognise the supremacy of shareholders

↓

Select an appropriate measure of shareholder return

↓

Generate shareholder returns through focused management

↓

Measure shareholder returns to see whether the objectives are being achieved

There is a four-stage process to creating shareholder value.

Figure 10.10 The four-stage process for creating shareholder value

The need for new measures

Given a commitment to maximise shareholder returns, we must select an appropriate measure that will help us assess the returns to shareholders over time. It is argued that the traditional methods for measuring shareholder returns are seriously flawed and so should not be used for this purpose.

Activity 10.8

What are the traditional methods of measuring shareholder returns?

The traditional approach is to use accounting profit or some ratio that is based on accounting profit, such as return on shareholders' funds or earnings per share.

There are broadly four problems with using accounting profit, or a ratio based on profit, to assess shareholder returns. These are:

■ *Profit is measured over a relatively short period of time (usually one year).* However, when we talk about maximising shareholder returns, we are concerned with maximising returns over the *long term*. Using profit as the key measure runs the risk that managers will take decisions that improve performance in the short term, but have an adverse effect on performance in the long term. For example, profits may be increased in the short term by cutting back on staff training and research expenditure. However, this type of expenditure may be vital to long-term survival.

- *Risk is ignored.* A fundamental business reality is that there is a clear relationship between the level of returns achieved and the level of risk that must be taken to achieve those returns. It is often the case that the higher the level of returns required, the higher the level of risk that must be taken. A management strategy that produces an increase in profits can reduce shareholder value if the increase in profits achieved is not commensurate with the increase in the level of risk. Thus, profit alone is not enough.

- *Accounting profit does not take account of all of the costs of the capital invested by the business.* The conventional approach to measuring profit deducts the cost of borrowing (that is, interest charges) in arriving at profit for the period, but there is no similar deduction for the cost of shareholder funds. Critics of the conventional approach point out that a business will not make a profit, in an economic sense, unless it covers the cost of all capital invested, including shareholder funds. Unless the business achieves this, it will operate at a loss and so shareholder value will be reduced.

- *Accounting profit reported by a business can vary according to the particular accounting policies that have been adopted.* The way that accounting profit is measured can vary from one business to another. Some businesses adopt a very conservative approach, which finds expression in particular accounting policies. This might include immediately treating some intangible assets (for example, research and development and goodwill) as expenses ('writing them off') rather than retaining them on the statement of financial position as assets. Similarly, the use of the reducing-balance method of depreciation (which means high depreciation charges in the early years) reduces profit in those early years.

Businesses that adopt less conservative accounting policies would report higher profits in the early years of owning depreciating assets. Writing off intangible assets over a long time period (or, perhaps, not writing off intangible assets at all) will have this effect. So will the use of the straight-line method of depreciation. There may also be some businesses that indulge in 'creative accounting'. This is adopting particular accounting policies, or carrying out particular transactions, in a way that paints a picture of financial health that is in line with what managers would like shareholders and others to see, rather than what is a true and fair view of financial performance and position. This often involves artificially increasing the revenue figures or reducing the expense figures for a period in order to inflate profits. Creative accounting has been a major problem for accounting rule makers and for society generally.

Economic value added (EVA®)

Economic value added (EVA®) has been developed and trademarked by a US management consultancy firm, Stern Stewart. However, EVA® is based on the idea of economic profit, an idea that has been around for many years. The measure reflects the point made earlier that, for a business to be profitable in an economic sense, it must generate returns that exceed the required returns of investors. It is not enough simply to make an accounting profit, because this measure does not take full account of the returns required by investors.

EVA® indicates whether or not the returns generated exceed the required returns by investors. The formula is as follows:

$$\text{EVA}^® = \text{NOPAT} - (R \times C)$$

where

NOPAT = net operating profit after tax

R = required returns of investors

C = capital invested (that is, the net assets of the business).

Only when EVA® is positive can we say that the business is increasing shareholder wealth. To maximise shareholder wealth, managers must increase EVA® by as much as possible.

Activity 10.9

Can you suggest what managers might do in order to increase EVA®? (*Hint*: Use the formula shown above as your starting point.)

The formula suggests that in order to increase EVA® managers may try to:

- increase NOPAT. This may be done either by reducing expenses or by increasing sales revenue; and/or
- reduce capital invested by using assets more efficiently. This means selling off any assets that are not generating adequate returns and investing in assets that generate a satisfactory NOPAT; and/or
- reduce the required rates of return for investors. This may be achieved by changing the capital structure in favour of borrowing (which tends to be cheaper to service than share capital). However, this strategy can create problems.

EVA® relies on conventional financial statements (income statement and statement of financial position) to measure the wealth created for shareholders. However, the NOPAT and capital figures shown on these statements are used only as a starting point. They have to be adjusted because of the problems and limitations of conventional measures. According to Stern Stewart, the major problem is that both profit and capital tend to be understated because of the conservative bias in accounting measurement.

Profit is understated as a result of judgemental write-offs (such as goodwill written off or research and development expenditure written off) and as a result of excessive provisions being created (such as an allowance for trade receivables). Both of these stem from taking an unrealistically pessimistic view of the value of some of the business's assets.

Capital can also be understated because assets are reported at their original cost (less amounts written off for depreciation and so on), which can, in some cases, produce figures considerably below current market values. In addition, certain assets, such as internally generated goodwill and brand names, are omitted from the financial statements because no external transactions have occurred.

Stern Stewart has identified more than a hundred adjustments that could be made to the conventional financial statements in order to eliminate the conservative bias. However, it is believed that, in practice, only a handful of adjustments will usually have to be made to the accounting figures of any particular business. Unless an adjustment is going to have a significant effect on the calculation of EVA®, it is really not worth making. The adjustments made should reflect the nature of the particular business. Each business is unique and so must customise the calculation of EVA® to its particular circumstances. (This aspect of EVA® can be seen either as indicating flexibility or as being open to manipulation depending on whether or not you support this measure.)

Common adjustments that have to be made include:

1 *Research and development (R&D) costs and marketing costs.* Logically, these costs should be treated as an expense over the period that they benefit. Following standard accounting practice, however, tends to mean that they are often written off in the period in which they are incurred. This means that any amounts written off immediately should be added back to the assets on the statement of financial position. This will increase the figure for invested capital to be written off over time. It will also increase operating profit.

2 *Restructuring costs.* This item can be viewed as an investment in the future rather than an expense to be written off. Supporters of EVA® argue that by restructuring, the business is better placed to meet future challenges and so any amounts incurred should be added back to assets. This too will increase operating profit, where such costs are charged in deriving operating profit.

3 *Marketable investments.* Investment in shares and loan notes of other businesses are not included as part of the capital invested in the business. This is because the income from marketable investments is not included in the calculation of operating profit. (Income from this source will be added in the income statement *after* operating profit has been calculated.)

In addition to these accounting adjustments, the tax charge must be adjusted so that it is based on the operating profits for the year. This means that it should not take account of the tax charge on non-operating income, such as income from investments, or the tax allowance on interest payable.

Example 10.4 is a simple demonstration of how EVA® may be calculated.

Example 10.4

Scorpio plc was established two years ago and has produced the following statement of financial position and income statement at the end of the second year of trading.

Statement of financial position as at the end of the second year

	£m
ASSETS	
Non-current assets	
Plant and equipment	80.0
Motor vehicles	12.4
Marketable investments	6.6
	99.0
Current assets	
Inventories	34.5
Trade receivables	29.3
Cash	2.1
	65.9
Total assets	164.9

EQUITY AND LIABILITIES

Equity

Share capital	60.0
Retained earnings	23.7
	83.7

Non-current liabilities

Loan notes	50.0

Current liabilities

Trade payables	30.3
Taxation	0.9
	31.2
Total equity and liabilities	164.9

Income statement for the second year

	£m
Sales revenue	148.6
Cost of sales	(76.2)
Gross profit	72.4
Wages	(24.6)
Depreciation of plant and equipment	(12.8)
Marketing expenses	(22.5)
Allowances for trade receivables	(4.5)
Operating profit	8.0
Income from investments	0.4
	8.4
Interest payable	(0.5)
Ordinary profit before taxation	7.9
Restructuring costs	(1.9)
Profit before taxation	6.0
Tax	(1.5)
Profit for the year	4.5

Discussions with the chief financial officer reveal the following:

1 Marketing costs relate to the launch of a new product. The benefits of the marketing campaign are expected to last for three years (including this most recent year).

2 The allowance for trade receivables was created this year and the amount is considered to be very high. A more realistic figure for the allowance would be £2.0 million.

3 Restructuring costs were incurred as a result of a collapse in a particular product market. As a result of the business restructuring, benefits are expected to flow for an infinite period.

4 The business has a 10 per cent required rate of return for investors.

5 The rate of tax on profits is 25 per cent.

The first step in calculating EVA® is to adjust the net operating profit after tax to take account of the various points revealed by the discussion with the chief financial officer. The revised figure is calculated as follows:

NOPAT adjustment

	£m	£m
Operating profit		8.0
Tax (Note 1)		(2.0)
		6.0

EVA® adjustments (to be added back to profit)

	£m	£m
Marketing costs (⅔ × 22.5)	15.0	
Excess allowance	2.5	17.5
Adjusted NOPAT		23.5

The next step is to adjust the net assets (as represented by equity and loan notes) to take account of the points revealed.

Adjusted net assets (or capital invested)

	£m	£m
Net assets (from the statement of financial position)		133.7
Marketing costs (Note 2)	15.0	
Allowance for trade receivables	2.5	
Restructuring costs (Note 3)	1.9	19.4
		153.1
Marketable investments (Note 4)		(6.6)
Adjusted net assets		146.5

Notes:

1 Tax is based on 25% of the operating profits (£8.0m × 25% = £2.0m). (Tax complications, such as the difference between the tax allowance for non-current assets and the accounting charge for depreciation have been ignored.)
2 The marketing costs represent two years' benefits added back (⅔ × £22.5m).
3 The restructuring costs are added back to the net assets as they provide benefits over an infinite period. (Note that they were not added back to the operating profit as these costs were deducted after arriving at operating profit in the income statement.)
4 The marketable investments do not form part of the operating assets of the business. The income from these investments is not, therefore, part of the operating income.

Activity 10.10

Can you work out the EVA® for the second year of Scorpio plc in Example 10.4?

EVA® can be calculated as follows:

$$EVA® = NOPAT - (R \times C)$$
$$= £23.5m - (10\% \times £146.5m)$$
$$= £8.9m \text{ (to one decimal place}$$

We can see that EVA® is positive and so the business increased shareholder wealth during the year.

Real World 10.8 reveals the economic value added over time for one well-known US soft drinks business.

Real World 10.8

Losing its fizz

Economic value added, along with its key components, is set out below for Coca Cola.

	2016	2015	2014	2013	2012
Net operating profit after taxes (NOPAT) ($m)	5,782	7,572	7,253	9,244	9,631
Cost of capital (%)	8.32	8.46	8.44	8.50	8.66
Invested capital ($m)	79,169	77,538	76,173	75,127	68,944
Economic value added	**(802)**	**1,016**	**821**	**2,861**	**3,658**

We can see that NOPAT decreased over the three-year period to 31 December 2014. Though the cost of capital decreased slightly over the same period, the invested capital increased significantly. The end result was a significant decrease in EVA® over time.

In the year to 31 December 2015, an increase in NOPAT more than compensated for the increase in the cost of capital and capital invested. As a result, EVA® increased. During 2016, a much lower operating profit led to a loss of economic value.

Source: Stock Analysis on Net, www.stock-analysis-on-net.com, accessed 16 March 2017.

Although EVA® is used by many large businesses, both in the USA and Europe, it tends to be used for management purposes only: few businesses report this measure to shareholders. One business that does, however, is Whole Foods Market, a leading retailer of natural and organic foods, which operates more than 460 stores in the USA and the UK. **Real World 10.9** describes the way in which the business uses EVA® and the results of doing so.

Real World 10.9

The Whole picture

Whole Foods Market aims to improve its operations by achieving improvements to EVA®. To encourage managers along this path, an incentive plan has been introduced. The plan embraces senior executives, regional managers and store managers and the bonuses awarded form a significant part of their total remuneration. To make the incentive plan work, measures of EVA® based on the whole business, the regional level, the store level and the team level are calculated.

EVA® is also used to evaluate capital investment decisions such as the acquisition of new stores and the refurbishment of existing stores. Unless there is clear evidence that value will be added, investment proposals are rejected. EVA® is also used to improve operational efficiency. It was mentioned earlier that one way in which EVA® can be increased is through an improvement in NOPAT. The business is, therefore, continually seeking ways to improve sales and profit margins and to bear down on costs.

Source: Based on information in www.wholefoodsmarket.com, accessed 25 October 2016.

An important advantage of the EVA® measure is the discipline to which managers are subjected as a result of the charge for capital that has been invested. Before any increase in shareholder wealth can be recognised, an appropriate deduction is made for the use of business resources. Thus, EVA® encourages managers to use these resources efficiently. Where managers are focused simply on increasing profits, there is a danger that the resources used to achieve any increase in profits will not be taken into proper account.

Shareholder value-based management in practice

The extent to which shareholder value-based management is applied in practice is picked up in **Real World 10.10**.

Real World 10.10

Practice management

Shareholder value-based management, probably the main example of which is EVA®, or variants of it, seems to be fairly widely used by larger businesses in practice. Ernst and Young undertook a major survey of management accounting practices in US businesses. The survey tended to be of larger businesses. It showed that 52 per cent of the businesses were, in 2003, using some shareholder value-based approach to management, with a further 40 per cent considering adopting such an approach in the future.

Ryan and Trahan examined the performances over the first five years of 84 US businesses that had adopted a shareholder value-based approach during the period 1984 to 1997. They found that the businesses that had adopted it significantly improved their economic performances, relative to similar businesses that had not. This improvement persisted throughout the five years that were assessed and was more marked among smaller businesses than larger ones.

There appears not to be similar information on the position in the UK or elsewhere. However, there is no reason to believe that the UK position differs greatly from the US one.

Sources: Ernst and Young (2003) *Survey of Management Accounting*, Ernst and Young; Ryan, H. and Trahan, E. (2007) Corporate financial control mechanisms and firm performance: the case of value based management systems, *Journal of Business Finance and Accounting* Vol. 34, pp. 111–138.

JUST ANOTHER FAD?

The techniques described in this chapter are all potentially valuable to a business, but their successful implementation is far from certain. According to one source, failure rates are as high as 60 per cent (see reference 3 at the end of the chapter). A depressingly common scenario is that a new technique will be enthusiastically adopted but, within a short while, disillusionment will set in. Managers decide that the technique does not meet their requirements and so it is abandoned. In some businesses, a pattern of adoption, disillusionment and abandonment of new techniques may develop. Where this occurs, employees are likely to become sceptical and to dismiss any newly-adopted technique as simply a passing fad.

Introducing a new technique is likely to be costly and can cause considerable upheaval. Managers must, therefore, tread carefully. They must try to identify the potential problems, as well as the benefits, that may accrue from its adoption. The main problems that lie in wait are:

- the excessive optimism that managers often have in their ability to implement a new technique that will quickly yield good results;
- the assumption that others will share the enthusiasm felt for a new technique; and
- the failure to acknowledge that there will be losers as well as winners when a new technique is implemented (see reference 3 at the end of the chapter).

Managers must be realistic about what can be achieved from a new technique and must accept that resistance to its introduction is likely. They must not underestimate what it will take to ensure a successful outcome.

PRICING

As we saw earlier in this chapter, pricing the business's output is usually a crucial matter. In this section, we shall take a closer look at pricing. We shall begin by considering some theoretical aspects of the subject before going on to look at more practical issues, particularly the role of management accounting information in pricing decisions.

Economic theory

In most market conditions, the price charged by a business will determine the number of units sold. This is shown graphically in Figure 10.11.

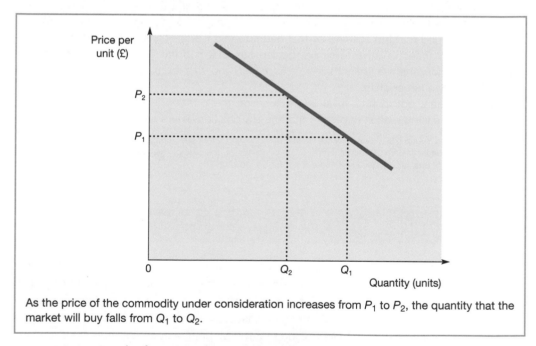

As the price of the commodity under consideration increases from P_1 to P_2, the quantity that the market will buy falls from Q_1 to Q_2.

Figure 10.11 Graph of quantity demanded against price for Commodity A

This figure indicates the number of units of output that the market would demand at various prices. As price increases, people are less willing to buy the commodity (call it Commodity A). Note that the commodity might be a physical product or a service. At a relatively low price per unit (P_1), the quantity of units demanded by the market (Q_1) is fairly high. When the price is increased to P_2, the demand decreases to Q_2. The graph shows a linear (straight-line) relationship between the price and demand. In practice, the relationship, though broadly similar, may not be quite so straightforward.

Not all commodities show exactly the same slope of line. Figure 10.12 shows the demand/price relationship for Commodity B, a different commodity from the one depicted in Figure 10.11.

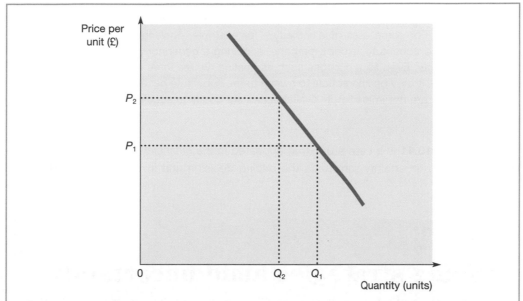

As the price of the commodity increases from P_1 to P_2, the quantity that the market will buy falls from Q_1 to Q_2. This fall in demand is less than was the case for Commodity A, which has the greater elasticity of demand.

Figure 10.12 Graph of quantity demanded against price for Commodity B

Although a rise in price of Commodity B, from P_1 to P_2, causes a fall in demand, the fall in demand is much smaller than is the case for Commodity A with a similar rise in price. As a result, we say that Commodity A has a higher **elasticity of demand** than Commodity B. Demand for A reacts much more dramatically to price changes (stretches more) than does demand for B. Elastic demand tends to be associated with commodities that are not essential, perhaps because there is a ready substitute.

It is very helpful for those involved with pricing decisions to have some feel for the elasticity of demand of the commodity that will be the subject of a decision. The sensitivity of the demand to the pricing decision is obviously much greater (and the pricing decision more crucial) with commodities whose demand is elastic than with commodities whose demand is relatively inelastic.

Activity 10.11

Which would have the more elastic demand – a particular brand of chocolate bar or mains electricity supply? Explain your response.

A branded chocolate bar seems likely to have a fairly *elastic* demand. This is for several reasons, including the following:

- Few buyers of the bar would feel that chocolate bars are essentials.
- Other chocolate bars, probably quite similar to the one in question, will be easily available.

Mains electricity probably has a relatively *inelastic* demand. This is because:

- Many users of electricity would find it very difficult to manage without fuel of some description.

- For neither household nor business users of electricity is there an immediate, practical substitute. For some uses of electricity – for example, powering machinery – there is probably no substitute, except, perhaps, acquiring a generator and ceasing to use the mains supply. Even for a purpose such as heating, where there are substitutes such as gas and oil, it may be impractical to switch to the substitute because gas and oil heating appliances are not immediately available and are costly to acquire.

Real World 10.11 is a case study that appeared in the *Financial Times*. It reveals how, in practice, much uncertainty surrounds the pricing decision and in gauging the elasticity of demand.

Real World 10.11

Pricing strategies amid uncertainty

The story. By 2001, the online community Craigslist had disrupted the whole North American newspaper classified advertising market. On Craigslist community sites in a number of cities, users could look for free for jobs, housing, personal items, other services, items for sale and community topics such as volunteering. Mr Newmark's vision was of an online community that was accessible to anyone with a computer, regardless of the user's ability to pay. Craigslist also had a culture of no commercialisation or outside investors.

The challenge. When the Internet bubble burst in 2001, the site's sole reliance on job postings at $75 per insertion began to pose difficulties. By then, Craigslist had 40,000 or so paid-for job listings a year and all other listings were free. The recession posed a serious threat to this annual operating revenue of $3 million. Mr Newmark and his team needed to work out how to replace $1 million in projected lost revenue while keeping the organisation's culture and brand.

The strategy. The team identified and analysed a variety of new pricing alternatives that might make up the projected shortfall.

- **Charge more for job listings.** This seemed the most obvious option as Craigslist's rivals often charged more than double its fees. But they also had better products, such as graphic display, levels of search and so on. Also, with weak demand due to the downturn, raising prices might be poorly received.
- **Fundraise through a virtual tip jar.** This idea, a pop-up onscreen suggestion of a donation, is best analysed by adjusting levers such as possible amounts and percentage of people who might donate – a sensitivity analysis. To achieve $1 million, Craigslist judged it would need 10 per cent of users to donate $10 per transaction on average. The team thought this wildly optimistic as use of the site had been free.
- **Charge fees for services listings.** This raised the issue of elasticity of demand: if Craigslist charged for listings, the numbers would drop – but by how much? Mature businesses often have transaction records from which they can derive the demand curve, but it is common for an Internet business to begin as a free site. Without any data or experience as a commercial site, Craigslist had no practical way to predict the effect. One alternative, market research, would be a less than ideal way to obtain limited data and information on consumers' willingness to pay. The team estimated that, based on $40 per listing and an assumption that 50 per cent of users would be retained, Craigslist would easily reach the $1 million goal. But the wider damage to the brand, even with a small testing of the waters, could be substantial.
- **Charge for ads for autos, personal items or services, and house rentals.** At just $20 per listing for autos, for example, the team worked out Craigslist would achieve $1 million, even with a 50 per cent drop in listings. The team concluded Craigslist could make

much more than its goal if it chose and then stuck to a relatively high price per listing, even if demand fell.

What happened. Overall, the team felt the various pricing options would hurt the brand and culture – with the possible exception of charging for auto advertisements since sellers would be gaining a large sum of money in one lump. In fact, the effect of the 2001 downturn on hiring was less harsh than feared, so Craigslist escaped making any big changes to its pricing strategy. It stayed true to the founder's vision and today Craigslist still charges $75 for job listings and everything else on its site remains free.

The lessons. The Craigslist team recognised two important issues. First, when consumers are used to a website being free or cheap, they may be resistant to the introduction of fees or price increases. Second, there was a danger that not only would the revenue raised be insufficient, but introducing a commercialised approach could have serious negative ramifications for the brand and culture that were so vital to Craiglist's success.

FT *Source*: Robinson, D. (2012) Pricing strategies amid uncertainty, ft.com, 30 July.
© The Financial Times Limited 2012. All Rights Reserved. Used with permission of the author.

To enhance the wealth of shareholders, managers may seek to maximise profits – that is, to create the largest possible difference between total cost (the lower amount) and total revenue. Prices are then set so as to achieve this effect. To do this, managers need some insight concerning the way in which cost and price relate to volume of output.

Figure 10.13 depicts the relationship between cost and volume of output, which we have already met in Chapter 3.

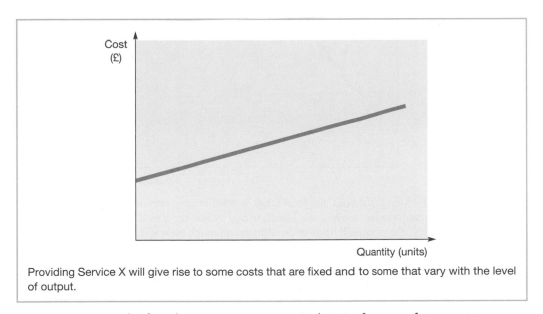

Providing Service X will give rise to some costs that are fixed and to some that vary with the level of output.

Figure 10.13 Graph of total cost against quantity (volume) of output of Service X

The figure shows that the total cost of providing a particular commodity (Service X) increases as the quantity of output increases. It is shown here as a straight line. In practice, it may be curved, either curving upwards (tending to become closer to the vertical) or flattening out (tending to become closer to the horizontal). The figure assumes that the marginal cost of each unit is constant over the range shown, hence the straight line.

Figure 10.14 shows the total sales revenue against quantity of Service X sold. The total sales revenue increases as the quantity of output increases, but often at a decreasing rate.

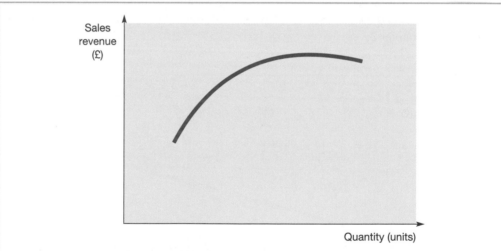

As more units of Service X are sold, the total sales revenue initially increases, but at a declining rate. This is because, in order to persuade people to buy increasing quantities, the price must be reduced. Eventually, the price will have to be reduced so much (to encourage additional sales) that the total sales revenue will fall as the number of units sold increases.

Figure 10.14 Graph of total sales revenue against quantity (volume) sold of Service X

Figure 10.14 implies that there will come a point where, to make increased sales, prices will have to be reduced so much that total sales revenue will not increase by much for each additional sale.

When examining break-even analysis in Chapter 3, we assumed a constant price per unit over a range of output. Now we are saying that, in practice, it does not work like this. How can these two positions be reconciled? The answer is that, when using break-even analysis, we normally consider only a relatively small range of output, namely the relevant range (see page 83). It may well be that over a small range, particularly at low levels of output, a constant sales price per unit is a reasonable assumption. This is to say that, to the left of the curve in Figure 10.14, there may be a straight line from zero up to the start of the curve.

Figure 10.15 combines information about total sales revenue and total cost for Service X over a range of output levels.

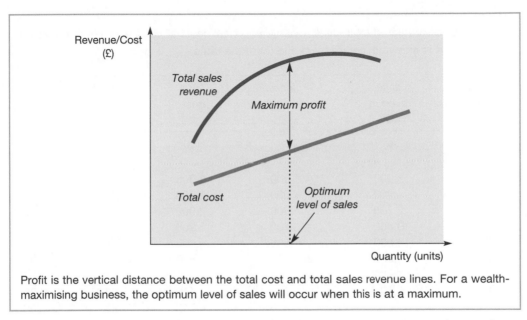

Profit is the vertical distance between the total cost and total sales revenue lines. For a wealth-maximising business, the optimum level of sales will occur when this is at a maximum.

Figure 10.15 Graph of total sales revenue and total cost against quantity (volume) of output of Service X

The total sales revenue increases, but at a decreasing rate, and the total cost of production increases as the quantity of output increases. The maximum profit is made where the total sales revenue and total cost lines are vertically furthest apart. At the left-hand end of the graph, we are clearly above break-even point because the total sales revenue line has already gone above the total cost line. At the lower levels of volume of sales and output, the total sales revenue line is climbing more steeply than the total cost line. The business will wish to keep expanding output as long as this continues to be the case, because profit is the vertical distance between the two lines. A point will be reached where the total sales revenue line will become only as steep as the total cost line. After this, it will become less steep; expanding further will reduce overall profit, because in this area of the graph the marginal cost is greater than the marginal revenue.

The point at which profit is maximised is where the two lines stop diverging, that is, the point at which the two lines are climbing at exactly the same rate. Thus we can say that profit is maximised at the point where:

> **Marginal sales revenue = Marginal cost of production**

– that is,

$$
\begin{bmatrix}
\text{Increase in total sales} \\
\text{revenue from selling} \\
\text{one more unit}
\end{bmatrix}
=
\begin{bmatrix}
\text{Increase in total costs} \\
\text{that will result from} \\
\text{selling one more unit}
\end{bmatrix}
$$

To see how this approach can be applied, consider Example 10.5.

Example 10.5

A schedule of predicted total sales revenue and total costs at various levels of provision for Service Y is shown in columns (a) and (c) of the table.

Quantity of output (units)	Total sales revenue £	Marginal sales revenue £	Total cost £	Marginal cost £	Profit/ (loss) £
	(a)	(b)	(c)	(d)	(e)
0	0		0		0
1	1,000	1,000	2,300	2,300	(1,300)
2	1,900	900	2,600	300	(700)
3	2,700	800	2,900	300	(200)
4	3,400	700	3,200	300	200
5	4,000	600	3,500	300	500
6	4,500	500	3,800	300	700
7	4,900	400	4,100	300	800
8	5,200	300	4,400	300	800
9	5,400	200	4,700	300	700
10	5,500	100	5,000	300	500

Column (b) is deduced by taking the total sales revenue for one fewer unit sold from the total sales revenue at the sales level under consideration (column (a)). For example, the marginal sales revenue of the fifth unit of the service sold (£600) is deduced by taking the total sales revenue for four units sold (£3,400) away from the total sales revenue for five units sold (£4,000).

Column (d) is deduced similarly, but using total cost figures from column (c). Column (e) is found by deducting column (c) from column (a).

It can be seen by looking at the profit/(loss) column that the maximum profit (£800) occurs with an output of seven or eight units. Thus the maximum output should be eight units of the service. This is the point where marginal cost and marginal revenue are equal (at £300).

Figure 10.16 shows the total cost and total revenue for Service Y in Example 10.5.

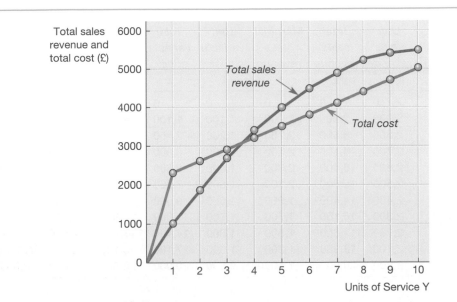

The profit (or loss) at any particular level of activity (sales of the service) is the difference between the total sales revenue and the total cost. On the graph, the vertical distance between the two curves gives this. Note that the highest profit occurs where the marginal cost equals the marginal sales revenue, that is, where the two curves run parallel to one another.

Figure 10.16 Total cost and total revenue for Service Y

Output (number of machines)	Unit sales revenue £	Total sales revenue £	Marginal sales revenue £	Unit variable cost £	Total variable cost £	Total cost £	Marginal cost £	Profit/ (loss) £
0	0	0	0	0	0	3,000	3,000	(3,000)
1	2,900	2,900	2,900	1,100	1,100	4,100	1,100	(1,200)
2	2,800	5,600	2,700	1,200	2,400	5,400	1,300	200
3	2,700	8,100	2,500	1,300	3,900	6,900	1,500	1,200
4	2,600	10,400	2,300	1,400	5,600	8,600	1,700	1,800
5	2,500	12,500	2,100	1,500	7,500	10,500	1,900	2,000
6	2,400	14,400	1,900	1,600	9,600	12,600	2,100	1,800
7	2,300	16,100	1,700	1,700	11,900	14,900	2,300	1,200
8	2,200	17,600	1,500	1,800	14,400	17,400	2,500	200
9	2,100	18,900	1,300	1,900	17,100	20,100	2,700	(1,200)
10	2,000	20,000	1,100	2,000	20,000	23,000	2,900	(3,000)

An output of five machines each week will maximise profit at £2,000 a week.

The additional cost of producing the fifth machine compared with the cost of producing the first four (£1,900) is just below the marginal revenue (the amount by which the total revenue from five machines exceeds that from selling four (£2,100)).

The additional cost of producing the sixth machine compared with the cost of producing the first five (£2,100) is just above the marginal revenue (the amount by which the total revenue from six machines exceeds that from selling five (£1,900)).

Some practical considerations

Despite the analysis in Activity 10.14, an output of five machines a week may not prove to be the best decision. This might be for one or more practical reasons:

- Demand is notoriously difficult to predict, even assuming no changes in the environment.
- The effect of sales of the new machine on the business's other products may mean that the machine cannot be considered in isolation. Five machines a week may be the optimum level of output if sales were being taken from a rival business or a new market were being created, but possibly not in other circumstances.
- Costs are difficult to estimate.
- Since labour is in short supply, the relevant labour cost should probably include an element for opportunity cost. This is because staff may have to be taken away from some other profitable activity to put them onto production of this new machine.
- The optimum level of sales volume is derived on the assumption that short-run profit maximisation is the goal of the business. Unless this is consistent with wealth enhancement in the longer term, it may not be in the business's best interests.

These points highlight some of the weaknesses of the theoretical approaches to pricing, particularly the fact that costs and demands are difficult to predict. It would be wrong, however, to dismiss the theory. The fact that the theory does not work perfectly in practice does not mean that it cannot offer helpful insights concerning the nature of markets, how profit relates to volume and the notion of an optimum level of output.

Full cost (cost-plus) pricing

We saw in Chapter 4 that one of the reasons that some businesses deduce full costs is to base selling prices on them. This may seem a perfectly logical approach. If a business charges the full cost (including non-manufacturing cost) of its output as a selling price, the business will, in theory, break even. This is because the sales revenue will exactly cover all of the costs. Charging an additional amount above full cost will yield a profit.

An obvious problem with cost-plus pricing is that the market may not agree with the price. That is, cost-plus pricing takes no account of the market demand function (the relationship between price and quantity demanded, which we considered above). A business may calculate the full cost of a product and then add a profit loading, only to find that a rival supplier is offering a similar product for a much lower price, or that the market simply will not buy at the cost-plus price.

Where a **full cost (or cost-plus) pricing** approach is to be used, the required profit from each unit sold must be determined. This should be based on the total profit required for the period. In practice, this required profit is often set in relation to the amount of capital invested in the business. In other words, businesses seek to generate a target return on capital employed. If this is the case, the profit loading on full cost should reflect the business's target profit, which is based on a target return on capital employed.

Activity 10.15

A business has just completed a service job whose full cost has been calculated at £112. For the current period, the total costs (direct and indirect) are estimated at £250,000. The profit target for the period is £100,000.
Suggest a selling price for the job.

If the profit is to be earned by jobs in proportion to their full cost, then the profit for each pound of full cost must be £0.40 (that is, £100,000/250,000). Thus, the target profit on the job must be:

$$£0.40 \times 112 = £44.80$$

This means that the target price for the job must be:

$$£112 + £44.80 = £156.80$$

Other bases could be found for apportioning a share of profit to jobs – for example, direct labour or machine hours. These may be preferred where they are believed to provide a fairer measure of resources consumed.

Cost-plus pricing implies that the seller sets the price, which is then accepted by the customer. In some cases, however, the price is not finalised until after the product or service has been completed. This may occur with a car repair or with work carried out by a firm of accountants.

Real World 10.12 provides some impression of how much cost-plus pricing is used in practice.

Counting the cost plus

Guilding and others conducted a survey of 267 large UK and Australian businesses and found the following:

- Cost plus is regarded as important in determining selling prices by most of the businesses, but many businesses only use it for a small percentage of their total sales.
- Retailers base most of their sales prices on their costs. This is not surprising; we might expect that retailers add a mark-up on their cost prices to arrive at selling prices.
- Retailers and service businesses (both financial services and others) attach more importance to cost-plus pricing than do manufacturers and others.
- Cost-plus pricing tends to be more important in industries where competition is most intense. This is perhaps surprising, because we might have expected fewer 'price makers' in more competitive markets.
- The extent of the importance of cost-plus pricing seems to have nothing to do with the size of the business. We might have imagined that larger businesses would have more power in the market and be more likely to be price makers, but the evidence does not support this. The reason could be that many larger businesses are, in effect, groups of smaller businesses. These smaller subsidiaries may not be bigger players in their markets than are small independent businesses. Also, cost-plus pricing tends to be particularly important in retailing and service businesses, where many businesses are quite small.

The CIMA survey also showed that larger businesses are just as likely to use cost-plus pricing as smaller ones, with about 60 per cent of the businesses surveyed using that approach. This survey also showed that manufacturing businesses tend to use cost-plus pricing (76 per cent) more than was the case with service providers (57 per cent).

Sources: Guilding, C., Drury, C. and Tayles, M. (2005) An empirical investigation of the importance of cost-plus pricing, *Management Auditing Journal*, Vol. 20, No. 2, pp. 125–137; CIMA (2009) *Management Accounting Tools for Today and Tomorrow*, p. 13.

Full cost pricing in the public sector

With public sector contracts, a price is usually determined by competitive tendering. Here, each potential supplier offers a price for which it will perform the subject of the contract. The supplier offering the lowest price is then selected, subject to quality safeguards. In some cases, however, particularly where only one supplier is capable of doing the work, a fixed cost-plus approach will be used. The problem is that, under these circumstances, cost plus pricing can be abused.

Activity 10.16

We discussed this problem in Chapter 4. Can you recall how this abuse may arise?

When using a cost-plus approach, the higher the cost, the greater the profit loading. It would, therefore, be beneficial for the contractor (who enjoys a monopoly position) to report as high a cost as possible. This may be achieved by using overhead recovery rates that assign a higher proportion of total costs to the public sector contract than to other contracts being undertaken.

Cost-plus pricing may also be used where monopoly suppliers of public utility services are negotiating with a government-appointed regulator the prices to be charged to customers. UK mains water suppliers, for example, when agreeing customer prices, argue their case with Ofwat, the water industry regulator, on the basis of cost-plus information.

Price makers and price takers

Businesses are *price makers* where they can dictate prices for their products or services. This may arise because they enjoy a monopoly, or near monopoly position, within a market or because the product or service supplied is unique. The vast majority of businesses, however, are *price takers*. They operate within a competitive market and their products or services are not unique. They must accept the price offered by the market in order to sell their products or services.

Real World 10.13 discusses the profit implications of three mining businesses (Glencore plc, Lonmin plc and Anglo American plc) miners that are price takers.

Real World 10.13

On the take

Lonmin, Anglo and Glencore are all price takers, which means they have to accept the market price for commodities produced. So cost-cutting and asset sales can only boost earnings by so much, ultimately higher profits require higher commodity prices. And as the markets for many commodities remain oversupplied, it could be a long time before supply/demand fundamentals fall back in line and prices start to move higher again.

Source: Extract from The Motley Fool (2016) Can Glencore plc, Lonmin plc and Anglo American plc double again by the end of 2016?, www.fool.co.uk, 13 April.

Businesses that are price makers can adopt a cost-plus pricing policy. For businesses that are price takers, however, cost-plus pricing has less relevance. Nevertheless, it may still help in deciding whether to enter a market. A business may find that the market selling price for a particular product or service does not cover its current cost, plus an acceptable profit. This information may be used to bear down on costs in an effort to arrive at a cost-plus price that will be accepted by the market. Here, the market is providing the target price. If this target price cannot be achieved, the business should stay away from the market.

Activity 10.17

Which costing method should be suitable to help the business reach the target price? (*Hint*: Think back to Chapter 5).

Target costing should be suitable to close the 'cost gap'. This gap is the difference between the target cost and the current cost of producing the product or service.

Pricing on the basis of marginal cost

The marginal cost approach reveals the minimum price that a business can offer a product for sale. This minimum price will result in the business being as well off as a result of making the sale as it would have been had it not done so. We saw in Chapter 3 that **marginal cost**

pricing is based on the assumption that fixed costs are not affected by the decision to produce and, therefore, only variable costs need be considered.

A marginal cost approach would only normally be used where there is not the opportunity to sell at a price that will cover the full cost. The business can sell at any price above the marginal cost and still be better off, simply because it happens to find itself in the position that certain costs will be incurred in any case.

Activity 10.18

A commercial aircraft is due to take off in one hour's time with 20 seats unsold. What is the minimum price at which these seats could be sold such that the airline would be no worse off as a result?

The answer is that any price above the additional cost of carrying one more passenger would represent an acceptable minimum. If there are no such costs, the minimum price is zero.

The answer to Activity 10.18 should not be taken to imply that the airline will seek to charge the minimum price; it will presumably try to get the highest price that the market will bear. The fact that the market will not bear the full cost, plus a profit margin, should not, in principle, be sufficient for the airline to refuse to sell seats, where there is spare passenger capacity.

In practice, airlines are major users of marginal cost pricing. They often offer low-priced tickets for off-peak travel, where there are not sufficient customers willing to pay 'normal' prices. By insisting on a Saturday stopover for return tickets, they tend to exclude business travellers, who are probably forced to travel, but for whom a Saturday stopover may be unattractive. UK train operators often offer substantial discounts for off-peak travel. Similarly, hotels often charge very low rates for off-peak rooms. A hotel mainly used by business travellers will often offer very low room rates for Friday and Saturday occupancy.

Marginal pricing must be regarded as a short-term or limited approach that can be adopted because a business has spare capacity, such as having empty aircraft seats. Ultimately, if the business is to be profitable, all costs must be covered by sales revenue.

Activity 10.19

When we considered marginal cost pricing in Chapter 3, we identified three problems with its use. Can you remember what these problems are?

The three problems are as follows:

■ The possibility that spare capacity will be 'sold off' cheaply when there is another potential customer who will offer a higher price but, by the time they do so, the capacity will be fully committed. It is a matter of commercial judgement as to how likely this will be. In the circumstances of Activity 10.18, for example, would an hour before take-off be sufficiently close for the airline to be fairly confident that no 'normal' passenger will come forward to buy a seat?
■ The problem that selling the same product but at different prices could lead to a loss of customer goodwill. Would a 'normal' passenger be happy to be told by another passenger that the latter had bought his or her ticket very cheaply, compared with the normal price?

- If the business is going to suffer continually from being unable to sell its full production potential at the 'regular' price, it might be better, in the long run, to reduce capacity and make fixed-cost savings. Using the spare capacity to produce marginal benefits may lead to the business failing to address this issue. Would it be better for the airline to operate smaller aircraft or to have fewer flights, either of these leading to fixed-cost savings, than to sell off surplus seats at marginal prices?

Real World 10.14 provides an unusual example where humanitarian issues are the driving force for adopting marginal pricing.

Real World 10.14

Drug prices in developing countries

Large pharmaceutical businesses have recently been under considerable pressure to provide cheap drugs to developing countries. It has been suggested that life-saving therapeutic drugs should be sold to these countries at a price that is close to their marginal cost. Indeed, the UK Department for International Development would like to see HIV drugs sold at marginal cost in the poorest countries. However, a number of obstacles to such a pricing policy have been identified:

1. It may lead to customer revolts in the West [the 'loss of customer goodwill' referred to above].
2. There is a concern that the drugs may not reach their intended patients and could be re-exported to Western countries. A major cost of producing a new drug is the research and development costs incurred. Marginal costs of production, however, are usually very low. Thus, a selling price based on marginal cost is likely to be considerably lower than the normal (full cost) selling price in the West. This, it is feared, may lead to the cheap drugs provided leaking back into the West. Acquiring drugs at a price near to their marginal cost and reselling them at a figure close to the selling price in the West offers unscrupulous individuals an opportunity to make huge profits.
3. Compensation for any adverse consequences that may arise from the drugs sold will be sought in courts in the West, thereby creating the risk of huge payouts. This would make the risk to the pharmaceutical businesses of selling the drugs out of proportion to the benefits to them, in terms of the prices that would be charged.

GlaxoSmithKline plc, the UK-based pharmaceuticals giant, has experimented with selling at lower prices in poorer countries. Their experience is that obstacles 1 and 2 (above) are not significant problems in practice. The result of this is that GlaxoSmithKline significantly cut the prices of its medicines in emerging economies in 2010 and again in 2016.

Source: Based on information from Jack, A. (2009) GSK to slash drug prices for developing countries, ft.com, 30 November; Kollewe, J. (2016) GlaxoSmithKline to lower drug prices in poorer countries, www.guardian.com, 31 March.

Target pricing

We saw in Chapter 5 that, as the starting point of the target-costing approach to cost management, a target selling price must be identified. Using market research and so on, a target unit selling price and a planned sales volume are set. This is the combination of price and quantity demanded that the business would derive from its estimation of the product's demand function (see pages 168–170). The target price reflects the likely market price that the business seeks to meet, while being able to make an acceptable profit.

Pricing strategies

Cost and the market-demand function are not the only determinants of price. Businesses may employ pricing strategies that, in the short term, do not seek to maximise profit. The intention is rather to maximise profits over the long term. An example of such a strategy is **penetration pricing**. Here, a new product is sold relatively cheaply in order to sell in large quantity and to dissuade competitors from entering the market. Once the product is established as the market leader, prices are then raised to more profitable levels.

Activity 10.20

What is the risk associated with applying a penetration pricing strategy? Why might it prove difficult to eventually raise prices?

Customers may become accustomed to low prices and may develop expectations as to what amount should be paid. They may, therefore, resist higher prices.

Products may have to be offered at a low price for some time before the price can eventually be raised. Where this is the case, the business must ensure that it has the financial resources to sustain a period of low prices.

Real World 10.15 provides some idea of the extent to which penetration pricing is used in practice.

Real World 10.15

Not much penetration

The CIMA survey showed that penetration pricing is not widely used in practice, as is shown by Figure 10.17.

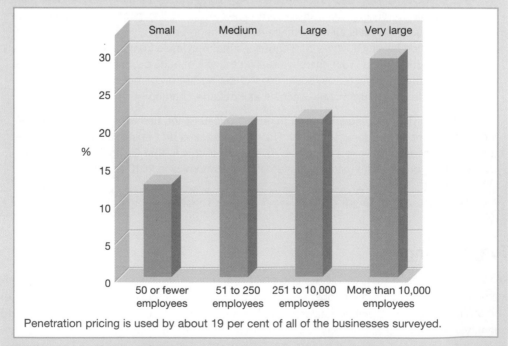

Penetration pricing is used by about 19 per cent of all of the businesses surveyed.

Figure 10.17 The use of penetration pricing

It should be noted that relatively few businesses operate in markets where penetration pricing could beneficially be used. In that context, the survey may be seen to indicate that penetration pricing is quite popular in suitable markets.

Source: Adapted from CIMA (2009) *Management Accounting Tools for Today and Tomorrow*, p. 13.

Price skimming is almost the opposite of penetration pricing. It seeks to exploit the notion that the market can be stratified according to resistance to price. Here, a new product is initially priced highly and sold only to those buyers in the stratum that are insensitive to high prices. Once this stratum of the market is saturated, the price is lowered to attract the next stratum. The price is gradually lowered as each stratum is saturated. This pricing strategy can generate high profit margins which, in turn, can encourage competitors to enter the market. It therefore works best where there are significant barriers to entry, such as patent protection.

A price skimming strategy will only usually be employed where demand for the product is inelastic.

Activity 10.21

Why do you think a business would only apply a price skimming strategy where this is the case?

If demand were elastic, the high prices set when the product is first launched would have a very damaging effect on sales.

Price skimming is often used for consumer electronic products. DVD players provide a good example. When they first entered the market in the 1990s, DVD players would typically cost over £400. They can now be bought for less than £20. Advancing technology, economies of scale and increasing competition have all contributed to this price fall, but price skimming was also a major factor. Certain customers regarded a DVD player as a 'must-have' product. These 'early adopters' were therefore prepared to pay a high price to have one. Once the early adopters had bought their DVD player, the price was gradually reduced, until we reached today's price. Televisions, CD players, home computers and mobile telephones are further examples of where a price-skimming strategy has been used.

When adopting a price skimming strategy, a business should bear in mind two points. First, it should avoid lowering the price of a new product too quickly after its initial launch. This can upset early adopters, who may feel that they have been overcharged. Second, the business should avoid *price discrimination*, which involves selling the same product to different customers for different prices. This can be illegal. In some cases, slight changes to the product characteristics are made to sidestep potential legal problems. However, the boundary line between price skimming and price discrimination is not always easy to identify.

Real World 10.16 provides some idea of the extent to which price skimming is used in practice.

Just skimming the surface

The CIMA survey showed that price skimming is not widely used in practice, as is shown by Figure 10.18.

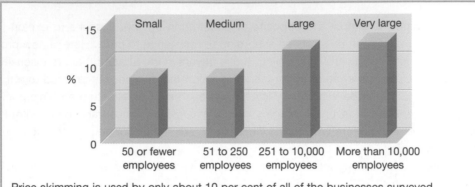

Price skimming is used by only about 10 per cent of all of the businesses surveyed.

Figure 10.18 The use of price skimming

As with penetration pricing, few businesses operate in markets where price skimming could be used.

Source: Adapted from CIMA (2009) *Management Accounting Tools for Today and Tomorrow*, p. 13.

Self-assessment question 10.1

Peverell plc reported the following income in its second year of operations.

Income statement for the second year

	£m
Sales revenue	420.0
Cost of sales	(250.0)
Gross profit	170.0
Wages	(65.0)
Depreciation of plant and equipment	(17.0)
Marketing expenses	(40.0)
Allowances for trade receivables	(10.0)
Operating profit	38.0
Income from investments	7.0
	45.0
Interest payable	(10.0)
Ordinary profit before taxation	35.0
Restructuring costs	(25.0)
Profit before taxation	10.0
Tax	(2.0)
Profit for the year	8.0

The following information is also available:

1 Marketing costs relate to the launch of Product 753Y. The benefits of the marketing campaign are expected to last for five years (including this most recent year).

2 The allowance for trade receivables was created this year and the amount is considered to be very high. A more realistic figure for the allowance would be £2.0 million.

3 Restructuring costs were incurred as a result of a collapse in a particular product market. By restructuring the business, benefits are expected to flow for an infinite period.

4 The business has a 12 per cent required rate of return for investors.

5 The rate of tax on profits is 20 per cent.

6 The figure for capital invested (net assets) for the period (after relevant adjustments) is £150 million.

Required:

(a) Calculate for the second year of operations:
   (1) Adjusted net operating profit after tax
   (2) EVA®.
   (Workings should be in £m to one decimal place.)

(b) Identify three major differences between the cost-plus approach and the target costing approach to pricing.

(c) A business that makes and sells laptop computers is seeking to adopt three non-financial measures that will act as lead indicators concerning its internal business processes. Can you suggest three measures not mentioned in the chapter that may be suitable?

(d) The shareholder value approach to managing businesses takes a different approach from the stakeholder approach to managing businesses. In the latter case, the different stakeholders of the business (employees, customers, suppliers and so on) are considered of equal importance and so the interests of shareholders will not dominate. Is it possible for these two approaches to managing businesses to coexist in harmony within a particular economy?

(e) It has been argued that many businesses are overcapitalised. If this is true, what may be the reasons for businesses having too much capital and how can EVA® help avoid this problem?

The solution to this question can be found at the back of the book on pp. 522–523.

SUMMARY

The main points of this chapter may be summarised as follows:

Strategic management accounting (SMA)

- It is concerned with providing information to support strategic plans and decisions.

- It is more outward looking, more concerned with outperforming the competition and more concerned with monitoring progress towards strategic objectives than conventional management accounting.

Facing outwards

- Competitor analysis examines the objectives, strategies, assumptions and resource capabilities of competitors. The purpose is to gain a source of competitive advantage.

- Customer profitability analysis assesses the profitability of each customer or type of customer to the business. It recognises that much of the cost incurred by businesses is not related to the cost of products sold but to the cost of selling and distribution.

Competitive advantage through cost leadership

■ New costing and cost management techniques, such as total life-cycle costing, target costing and kaizen costing, reflect a concern for long-term cost management. As a result, they fall within the scope of strategic management accounting.

Translating strategies into action

■ Non-financial measures are increasingly being used to manage the business.

■ The balanced scorecard is a management tool that uses financial and non-financial measures to assess progress towards objectives.

■ It has four aspects: financial, customer, internal business process and learning and growth.

■ It encourages a balanced approach to managing the business.

Measuring shareholder value

■ Shareholder value is seen as the key objective of most businesses.

■ One approach used to measure shareholder value is economic value added (EVA®).

■ Economic value added is a means of measuring whether the returns generated by the business exceed the required returns of investors.

$$EVA^® = NOPAT - (R \times C)$$

where

NOPAT = net operating profit after tax
R = required returns from investors
C = capital invested (that is, the net assets of the business).

Pricing output

■ In theory, profit is maximised where the price is such that

Marginal sales revenue = Marginal cost of production

■ Elasticity of demand indicates the sensitivity of demand to price changes.

■ Full cost (cost-plus) pricing takes the full cost and adds a mark-up for profit.

■ The market may not accept the price (most businesses are 'price takers').

■ It can provide a useful benchmark.

■ Marginal cost pricing takes the marginal cost and adds a mark-up for profit. It can be useful in the short term, but in the longer term all costs must be covered.

■ Target sales prices are those established as the first step in the target costing process. They indicate the likely market price and, in turn, help managers to deduce the cost ceiling that would ensure an acceptable profit.

■ Penetration pricing is concerned with obtaining a large market share in order to maximise profit over the longer term.

■ Price skimming attempts to exploit the various market strata according to resistance to price. It can only normally be used where other suppliers are facing barriers to entry.

REFERENCES

1 Crawford, D. and Baveja, S. (2006) In search of new value for the support operation, ft.com, 27 July.

2 Kaplan, R. and Norton, D. (1996) *The Balanced Scorecard*, Harvard Business School Press.

3 Bruce, R. (2006) Tread a careful path between creative hope and blind faith, ft.com, 2 February.

FURTHER READING

If you would like to explore topics covered in this chapter in more depth, we recommend the following:

Bhimani, A., Horngren, C., Datar, S. and Rajan, M. (2015) *Management and Cost Accounting*, 6th edn, Pearson, Chapter 12.

Drury, C. (2015) *Management and Cost Accounting*, 9th edn, Cengage Learning, Chapters 10 and 22.

Kaplan, R. and Norton, D. (1996) *The Balanced Scorecard*, Harvard Business School Press.

Stewart, B. (2013) *Best-Practice EVA: The Definitive Guide to Measuring and Maximizing Shareholder Value*, Wiley Finance.

REVIEW QUESTIONS

Solutions to these questions can be found at the back of the book on pp. 532–533.

10.1 Both A Ltd and B Ltd buy 1,000 units of a business's service each year, paying the same price per unit. Suggest possible reasons why the business may regard A Ltd as a more desirable customer than B Ltd.

10.2 What are the four main areas on which the balanced scorecard is based?

10.3 What is meant by elasticity of demand? How does knowledge of the elasticity of demand affect pricing decisions?

10.4 According to economic theory, at what point is profit maximised? Why is it at this point?

Exercises with coloured numbers have solutions given at the back of the book on pp. 565–567.

Basic-level exercises

10.1 Research evidence suggests that, in practice, a cost-plus approach influences many pricing decisions.

Required:
What is meant by cost-plus pricing and what are the problems of using this approach?

10.2 Woodner Ltd provides a standard service. It is able to provide a maximum of 100 units of this service each week. Experience shows that at a price of £100, no units of the service would be sold. For every £5 below this price, the business is able to sell 10 more units. For example, at a price of £95, 10 units would be sold, at £90, 20 units would be sold and so on. The business's fixed costs total £2,500 a week. Variable costs are £20 per unit over the entire range of possible output. The market is such that it is not feasible to charge different prices to different customers.

Required:
What is the most profitable level of output of the service?

10.3 Sharma plc makes one standard product for which it charges the same basic price of £20 a unit, though discounts are allowed to certain customers. The business is in the process of carrying out a profitability analysis of all of its customers during the financial year just ended.

Information about Lopez Ltd, one of Sharma's customers, is as follows:

Discount on sales price	5%
Number of units sold	40,000
Manufacturing cost	£12 a unit
Number of sales orders	22
Number of deliveries	22
Distance travelled to deliver	120 miles
Number of sales visits from Sharma's staff	30

Sharma uses an activity-based approach to ascribing costs to customers, as follows:

Cost pool	Cost driver	Rate
Order handling	Number of orders	£75 an order
Delivery costs	Miles travelled	£1.50 a mile
Customer sales visits	Number of visits	£230 a visit

Lopez Ltd usually takes two months' credit, of which the cost to Sharma is estimated at 2 per cent per month.

Required:
Calculate the profit that Sharma plc derived from sales to Lopez Ltd during last year.

Intermediate-level exercises

10.4 Virgo plc is considering introducing a system of EVA® and wants its managers to focus on the longer term rather than simply focus on the year-to-year EVA® results. The business is seeking your advice as to how a management bonus system could be arranged so as to ensure that the longer term is taken into account. The business is also unclear as to how much of the managers' pay should be paid in the form of a bonus and when such bonuses should be paid. Finally, the business is unclear as to where the balance between individual performance and corporate performance should be struck within any bonus system.

The chief financial officer has recently produced figures that show that if Virgo plc had used EVA® over the past three years, the results would have been as follows:

Year 1	£25 million (profit)
Year 2	£20 million (loss)
Year 3	£10 million (profit)

Required:

Set out your recommendations for a suitable bonus system for the divisional managers of the business. (This topic was not directly covered in the chapter, but try to use the broad principles that you have learned to answer the question. There is no single correct answer.)

10.5 You have overheard the following statements:
   (a) 'To maximise profit you need to sell your output at the highest price.'
   (b) 'Elasticity of demand deals with the extent to which costs increase as demand increases.'
   (c) 'Provided that the price is large enough to cover the marginal cost of production, the sale should be made.'
   (d) 'According to economic theory, profit is maximised where total cost equals total revenue.'
   (e) 'Price skimming is charging low prices for the output until you have a good share of the market and then putting up your prices.'

Required:

Comment critically on each of these statements, clearly explaining all technical terms.

Advanced-level exercises

10.6 Sillycon Ltd is a business engaged in the development of new products in the electronics industry. Subtotals on the spreadsheet of planned overheads reveal:

	Electronics department	Testing department	Service department
Overheads: variable (£000)	1,200	600	700
fixed (£000)	2,000	500	800
Planned activity: Direct labour hours (000)	800	600	

The three departments are cost centres.

For the purposes of reallocation of the service department's overheads, it is agreed that variable overhead costs vary with the direct labour hours worked in each cost centre. Fixed overheads of the service cost centre are to be reallocated on the basis of maximum practical capacity of the two product cost centres, which is the same for each. Direct labour is a variable cost.

The business has a long-standing practice of marking up full manufacturing costs by between 25 per cent and 35 per cent in order to establish selling prices.

It is hoped that one new product, which is in a final development stage, will offer some improvement over competitors' products, which are currently marketed at between £90 and £110 each. Product development engineers have determined that the direct material content is £7 a unit. The product will take 2 labour hours in the electronics department and 1½ hours in testing. Hourly labour rates are £20 and £12, respectively.

Management estimates that the fixed costs that would be specifically incurred in relation to the product are: supervision £13,000, depreciation of a recently acquired machine £100,000 and advertising £37,000 a year. These fixed costs are included in the table above.

Market research indicates that the business could expect to obtain and hold about 25 per cent of the market or, optimistically, 30 per cent. The total market is estimated at 20,000 units.

Note: It may be assumed that the existing plan has been prepared to cater for a range of products and no single product decision will cause the business to amend it.

Required:

(a) Prepare a summary of information that would help with the pricing decision for the new product. Such information should include marginal cost and full cost implications after allocation of service department overheads.

(b) Explain and elaborate on the information prepared.

10.7 Pisces plc produced the following statement of financial position (balance sheet) and income statement at the end of the third year of trading:

Statement of financial position as at the end of the third year

	£m
ASSETS	
Non-current assets	
Property	40.0
Machinery and equipment	80.0
Motor vans	18.6
Marketable investments	9.0
	147.6
Current assets	
Inventories	45.8
Trade receivables	64.6
Cash	1.0
	111.4
Total assets	259.0
EQUITY AND LIABILITIES	
Equity	
Share capital	80.0
Reserves	36.5
	116.5
Non-current liabilities	
Loan notes	80.0
Current liabilities	
Trade payables	62.5
Total equity and liabilities	259.0

Income statement for the third year

	£m
Sales revenue	231.5
Cost of sales	(143.2)
Gross profit	88.3
Wages	(43.5)
Depreciation of machinery and equipment	(14.8)
R&D costs	(40.0)
Allowance for trade receivables	(10.5)
Operating loss	(20.5)
Income from investments	0.6
	(19.9)
Interest payable	(0.8)
Ordinary loss before taxation	(20.7)
Restructuring costs	(6.0)
Loss before taxation	(26.7)
Tax	–
Loss for the year	(26.7)

An analysis of the underlying records reveals the following:

1 R&D costs relate to the development of a new product in the previous year. These costs are being written off over a two-year period (starting last year). However, this is a prudent approach and the benefits are expected to last for 16 years.

2 The allowance for trade receivables (bad debts) was created this year and the amount of the provision is very high. A more realistic figure for the allowance would be £4 million.

3 Restructuring costs were incurred at the beginning of the year and are expected to provide benefits for an infinite period.

4 The business has a 7 per cent required rate of return for investors.

Required:
Calculate the EVA® for the business for the third year of trading.

10.8 The GB Company manufactures a variety of electric motors. The business is currently operating at about 70 per cent of capacity and is earning a satisfactory return on investment.

International Industries (II) has approached the management of GB with an offer to buy 120,000 units of an electric motor. II manufactures a motor that is almost identical to GB's motor, but a fire at the II plant has shut down its manufacturing operations. II needs the 120,000 motors over the next four months to meet commitments to its regular customers; II is prepared to pay £19 each for the motors, which it will collect from the GB plant.

GB's product cost, based on current planned cost for the motor, is:

	£
Direct materials	5.00
Direct labour (variable)	6.00
Manufacturing overheads	9.00
Total	20.00

Manufacturing overheads are applied to production at the rate of £18.00 a direct labour hour. This overheads rate is made up of the following components:

	£
Variable factory overhead	6.00
Fixed factory overhead – direct	8.00
– allocated	4.00
Applied manufacturing overhead rate	18.00

Additional costs usually incurred in connection with sales of electric motors include sales commissions of 5 per cent and freight expense of £1.00 a unit.

In determining selling prices, GB adds a 40 per cent mark-up to the product cost. This provides a suggested selling price of £28 for the motor. The marketing department, however, has set the current selling price at £27.00 to maintain market share. The order would require additional fixed factory overheads of £15,000 a month in the form of supervision and clerical costs. If management accepts the order, 30,000 motors will be manufactured and delivered to II each month for the next four months.

Required:

(a) Prepare a financial evaluation showing the impact of accepting the II order. What is the minimum unit price that the business's management could accept without reducing its operating profit?

(b) State clearly any assumptions contained in the analysis of (a) above and discuss any other organisational or strategic factors that GB should consider.

Chapter 11

MEASURING DIVISIONAL PERFORMANCE

INTRODUCTION

While small businesses can be managed as a single unit, most large businesses are divided into operating units or divisions. We saw in Chapter 1 that large businesses may work more effectively towards their strategic objectives if managed in this way. Where a divisional structure is in place, selecting appropriate measures to assess divisional performance becomes an important issue. In this chapter, we consider the strengths and weaknesses of the main measures that are used.

A particular operating division may supply products or services to other divisions within the same business. When this occurs, the problem of measuring divisional performance can be more difficult. This is because the price at which goods and services are transferred between divisions has an important influence on key performance indicators such as sales revenue and profits. We shall discuss the possible approaches that can be used to set transfer prices and we shall identify the guiding principle to be followed.

Finally, we examine the role of non-financial measures in helping to assess divisional performance. We shall see why they are important and how they can improve the quality of management decisions.

Throughout this chapter, we shall be picking up some of the points made in earlier chapters, particularly Chapters 3, 5, 8 and 10.

Learning outcomes

When you have completed this chapter, you should be able to:

■ Discuss the potential advantages and disadvantages for a business of adopting a divisional structure.

■ Identify the major methods of measuring the performance of operating divisions and divisional managers and assess the usefulness of such methods.

■ Describe the problems of determining transfer prices between divisions, and outline the methods used in practice.

■ Explain the increasing importance of non-financial measures in managing a business and how they may be used for decision-making purposes.

Why do businesses divisionalise?

Many large businesses have operations that are extremely complex. This may be due to the nature of their output. They often supply a huge number of products and services, many of which may be technically intricate. It may also be due, however, to the fact that they have operating units located throughout the world. Where business operations are complex, there is often a need for an extended management hierarchy. This allows decisions concerning operating units to be devolved from senior managers to those further down the hierarchy. It is simply not feasible for senior managers to know everything that is going on within the various operating units. Thus, it is impractical for them to make all the decisions relating to these units. By creating separate **divisions** with some autonomy, a large business should be able to operate more effectively.

Devolving decisions

Managers must be given discretion over the operations for which they are responsible. This can be done by treating each department or division as a separate **responsibility centre**. The degree of responsibility and discretion allowed to the centres' managers, however, can vary. In practice, responsibility centres tend to fall into three broad categories:

1 *Cost centres.* These are responsibility centres where the managers have responsibility for, and control over, the costs incurred. These managers have no responsibility, however, for revenues or for the deployment of investment funds. You may recall that cost centres were discussed in Chapter 4 when calculating the full (or absorption) cost of producing a unit of output.
2 *Profit centres.* The manager of a **profit centre** has responsibility for production and sales performance. The manager is assigned non-current assets and working capital and is expected to generate profits through their effective use. The delegated authority therefore encompasses such matters as pricing, marketing, volume of output, sources of supply and sales mix. Any additional investment for the centre would, however, require the agreement of senior managers.
3 *Investment centres.* The manager of an **investment centre** has responsibility for investment and working capital decisions as well as production and sales performance. Thus, an investment centre is a profit centre with added responsibility for investment decisions. It is, in many respects, a business within a business.

The various forms of responsibility centre can be viewed as a progression where each higher form incorporates the previous form(s). Thus, the responsibilities of profit centre managers include those of cost centre managers and the responsibilities of investment centre managers include those of profit centre managers. Divisions typically operate either as profit or investment centres.

There are no hard and fast rules concerning the form of responsibility centre to be adopted by a particular division. Profit centres may be preferred over cost centres where divisional managers have greater knowledge than senior managers about local conditions. This gives them an advantage when making decisions concerning prices, output and so on. Profit centres may also be preferred over cost centres where few benefits are to be gained by separate divisions working together.

Can you think why profit centres may be preferred in these circumstances?

Under these circumstances, little may be gained from senior managers coordinating divisional operations centrally. They may therefore decide to give the divisions greater autonomy.

Investment centres may be preferred over profit centres where divisional operations are capital intensive and where senior managers are not in a position to identify the best investment strategy for the division.

A business may well have responsibility centres of all three types operating at the same time. A large division of a business may, for example, operate as an investment centre and so have responsibility for all aspects of its operations. Within that division, there may be profit centres, perhaps one for each product manufactured. Within each profit centre, there may be manufacturing areas that are treated as cost centres.

Breaking the business down into responsibility centres can help to plan and control its operations. Each manager of a responsibility centre will receive financial information relating to performance and must act upon it. They will then be held accountable for their actions. Providing managers of responsibility centres with relevant financial information is referred to as **responsibility accounting**.

Real World 11.1 provides an example of a business, Timpson Ltd, in which decision making has become highly devolved. In effect, each separate store is treated as a responsibility centre, even though most of the stores are quite small.

Real World 11.1

Devolving resoling

Timpsons is a highly successful retail service provider with over 1,300 stores throughout the UK and Ireland. Its stores provide a range of services, including shoe repairs, engraving and key cutting. There are 32 area management teams, each responsible for about 40 stores, but stores staff have an unusually high level of autonomy. According to the business's website:

> The Timpson ethos is to provide great customer service and to do this we operate an 'Upside Down' management style. We believe the best way to give great customer service is to give freedom to the colleagues that serve customers. The management teams delegate authority but retain responsibility and we have only 2 rules:

- Look the part
- Put the money in the till

Source: Timpson, About Timpson, www.timpson.co.uk/about-timpson, accessed 16 March 2017.

Activity 11.2

What sort of financial information will usually be provided to managers of responsibility centres? (*Hint*: Think back to Chapters 6 and 7.)

This will usually take the form of budgets, along with feedback on actual performance for each budget period. Variances from budget will also be reported.

Divisional structures

A business may be divided into divisions in any way that top management considers appropriate. We saw in Chapter 1, however, that divisions are usually organised according to

- the services provided or the products made; and/or
- the geographical location.

Within each division, departments are often created and organised along functional lines. However, certain functions, which provide support across the various divisions, may be undertaken at head office to avoid duplication.

Real World 11.2 sets out the organisational chart for Savills plc, which provides real estate services worldwide (estate agency and so on) through several operating divisions. The business generates sales revenue of around £900 million per year.

Real World 11.2

Real estate operations

Savills plc is divided into five operating divisions as set out in Figure 11.1. The operating divisions are primarily based on geography.

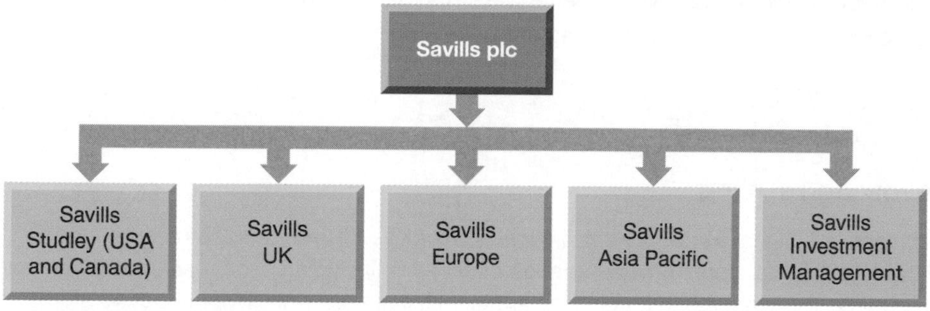

The business has five operating divisions, with each specialising in a particular geographical area or type of activity.

Figure 11.1 The organisational chart for Savills plc

Savills said of its organisational structure:

We use a flat management structure to ensure an efficient decision-making process, enabling us to maintain our flexible, responsive approach to delivering the highest levels of client service. This is an innovative structure for a company our size.

Source: Savills plc, savills.co.uk, accessed 26 October 2016.

Is divisionalisation a good idea?

There are several advantages claimed for dividing business operations into divisions and for allowing divisional managers a measure of autonomy.

Try to identify and briefly explain at least three advantages that may accrue to a business that decides to divisionalise. (We have already touched on some possible advantages.)

The following reasons occurred to us:

■ *Market information.* Divisional managers will gather an enormous amount of information concerning customers, markets, sources of supply and so on, which may be difficult and costly to transmit to senior managers. In some cases, they might find it impossible to pass on all of the knowledge and experience gathered. Furthermore, as divisional managers are 'in the front line' they can often use this information to the best advantage.

■ *Management motivation.* Divisional managers are likely to display greater commitment if they feel they have a significant influence over divisional decisions. Research evidence suggests that participation in decision making encourages a sense of responsibility towards seeing those decisions through. There is a danger that divisional managers will simply lose motivation if decisions concerning the division are made by senior managers and then imposed on them.

■ *Management development.* Allowing divisional managers a degree of autonomy should help in their development. They will become exposed to marketing, production, financial issues and so on. This should help them to gain valuable specialist skills. In addition, the opportunity to run a division more or less as a separate business should develop their ability to think in strategic terms. This can be of great benefit to the business when it is looking for successors to the current generation of senior managers.

■ *Specialist knowledge.* Where a business offers a wide range of products and services, senior managers cannot be expected to have the expertise to make operating decisions concerning each product and service. It is more practical to give divisional managers, who possess this detailed knowledge, responsibility for such matters.

■ *Allowing a strategic role for senior managers.* If senior managers were required to take detailed responsibility for the day-to-day operations of each division, they would become bogged down with making a huge number of relatively minor decisions. Even if they were capable of making better operating decisions than the divisional managers, this is unlikely to be the best use of their time. Managers operating at a senior level should develop a strategic role. They must look to the future to identify the opportunities and threats facing the business and make appropriate plans. By taking a broader view of the business and plotting a course to be followed, senior managers will be making the most valuable use of their time.

■ *Timely decisions.* If information concerning a local division has to be gathered, shaped into a report and then passed up the hierarchy before a decision is made, it is unlikely that the business will be able to act quickly when dealing with changing conditions or emerging issues. In a highly competitive or turbulent environment, the speed of response to market changes can be critical. Divisional managers can usually formulate a response much more quickly than senior managers.

The potential advantages of divisionalisation that have been identified are summarised in Figure 11.2.

Real World 11.3 sets out Associated British Foods plc's attitude to its divisional structure. The business has five operating divisions (or 'segments'): sugar production, agriculture, retail (including Primark), grocery products (including Kingsmill, Ovaltine and Ryvita) and ingredients (including yeast and enzymes).

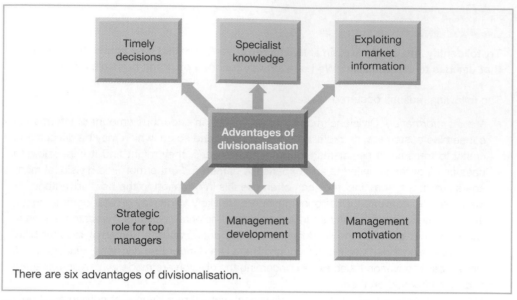

There are six advantages of divisionalisation.

Figure 11.2 Advantages of divisionalisation

Although most large businesses have separate operating divisions, there are problems that may arise as a result of adopting this type of structure. These include:

■ *Goal conflict.* The goals of the operating division may be inconsistent with those of either the business as a whole or of other divisions. For example, an operating division of a business may be unable to sell computer equipment to the UK government because another operating division within the business is selling military equipment to a hostile government. Overall profits of the business, however, may be increased if the military equipment sales cease, allowing a new market to develop for the computing equipment sold by the other division.

■ *Risk avoidance.* Where managers of a division are faced with a large project involving a high level of risk, they may decide against the project despite its potential high returns. The prospect of losing their jobs if things go wrong may be at the forefront of their minds. However, the business's owners (shareholders) may prefer to take the risks involved because they see the project as just one of a number undertaken by the business. While each particular project will have its risks, owners may believe that, overall, the expected returns will compensate for the risks involved. Divisional managers may not take such a detached view because they lack a diversified portfolio of projects to offset the effect of things going badly wrong.

- *Management 'perks'.* If divisional managers are allowed autonomy, there is a danger that they will award themselves substantial perquisites or 'perks'. These perks may include such things as a generous expense allowance, elegant offices and a chauffeur. These additional benefits may mean that divisional managers receive a far better remuneration package than the market requires for their services. The obvious way to avoid this is to monitor divisional managers' behaviour. The costs of monitoring, however, may outweigh any benefits arising from identifying and reducing these perks.

- *Increasing costs.* Additional costs may be borne by the business as a result of adopting a divisional structure. For example, each division may have its own market research department, which may duplicate the efforts of market research departments in other divisions. By organising into smaller operating units, the business may also be unable to take advantage of its size in order to reduce costs. It may, for example, be unable to negotiate quantity discounts with suppliers, as each division will decide which supplier to use and will only purchase quantities that are appropriate for its needs.

- *Competition.* Divisions within the same business that offer similar or substitute products may find themselves in competition with one another. Where this competition is intense, prices may be reduced which may, in turn, reduce profits of the business as a whole. For this reason, divisionalisation works best where the divisions do not offer closely related products or services, or where they operate in separate geographical regions.

The potential disadvantages of divisionalisation that have been identified are summarised in Figure 11.3.

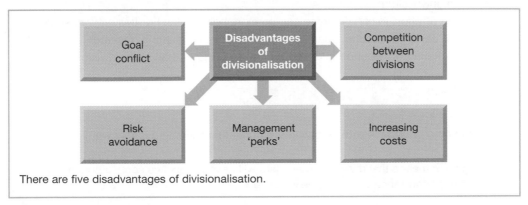

There are five disadvantages of divisionalisation.

Figure 11.3 Disadvantages of divisionalisation

We have seen that divisionalisation is not without its problems. While it may not be possible to eliminate these completely, it may be possible to reduce their severity. An important task of senior managers is to devise a structure that reaps the benefits of divisionalisation but somehow minimises the difficulties that it brings.

The problems of goal conflict and competition may be dealt with by regulating the behaviour of divisional managers. They must be prevented from making decisions that result in an increase in profits for their particular division, but which reduce the profits of the business as a whole.

Activity 11.4

Can you see a drawback with regulating the behaviour of divisional managers in this way?

Such a policy would cut across the autonomy of divisional managers.

It is important for divisional managers to appreciate, however, that they are not operating completely independent units and that they also have responsibilities towards the business as a whole.

The problem of risk avoidance by management is a complex one that may be difficult to deal with in practice. It might be possible, however, to encourage divisional managers to take on more risk if the rewards offered reflect the higher levels of risk involved. Observation of real life tells us that individuals are often prepared to take on greater risk providing they receive compensation through higher rewards.

If things start to go wrong, it may also be possible for the business, through the use of budget variance reports, to distinguish between those variances that are outside the control of the divisional manager and those that are within the manager's control. Divisional managers would then be accountable only for the variances within their control. It is not always easy, however, to obtain unbiased information for preparing budgets from divisional managers when they know that such information will be used to evaluate their performance.

Management perks may be controlled by senior managers by setting out clear rules as to what is acceptable. To some extent, observing the behaviour and actions of divisional managers can reveal any transgressions. Many perks, such as luxury cars, chauffeurs and elegant offices, are highly visible.

Duplication of effort in certain areas can be extremely costly. For this reason, some businesses prefer certain functions, such as administration, accounting, research and development and marketing, to be undertaken by central staff rather than at the divisional level.

Activity 11.5

Can you see a drawback with resolving the duplication problem in this way?

Once again, it means that divisional managers will have to sacrifice some autonomy for the sake of the performance of the business overall.

It is clear that divisionalisation poses a major challenge for senior managers. While seeking to promote divisional autonomy they must also ensure that divisional objectives mesh with overall strategic objectives. This calls for sound judgement, as no techniques or models are available to solve this problem.

A further challenge for senior managers is to identify valid and reliable performance measures that can help assess a division and its managers. It is to this challenge that we now turn.

MEASURING DIVISIONAL PROFIT

Businesses operate with the objective of increasing owners' (shareholders) wealth which, on a short-term basis, translates into making a profit. Thus, profit and profitability are crucially important in measuring the performance of both operating divisions and their managers. There are various measures of performance available. When deciding on the appropriate measure, it is important to be clear about the purpose for which it is to be used.

To help understand the issues involved, let us consider the following divisional income statement. We can see that it incorporates various measures of profit that can be used to assess performance.

Household Appliances
Divisional Income Statement for last year

	£m
Sales revenue	980
Variable expenses	(490)
Contribution	490
Controllable divisional fixed expenses	(130)
Controllable profit	360
Non-controllable divisional fixed expenses	(150)
Divisional profit before common expenses	210
Apportioned cost of common expenses	(80)
Divisional profit for the period	130

Before looking at the various measures of profit, we should be clear that the words 'controllable' and 'non-controllable' in this income statement refer to the ability of the divisional manager to exert an influence over particular expenses. Thus, an expense authorised by a senior manager is not under the control of the divisional manager, even though it may relate to the division. An expense authorised by the divisional manager, on the other hand, is within the manager's control.

We can see from the income statement that there are four measures of profit that could be used to assess performance. These are

- contribution;
- controllable profit;
- divisional profit before common expenses; and
- divisional profit for the period.

Let us now consider each of these in turn.

Contribution

The first measure of profit is the *contribution*, which represents the difference between the total sales revenue of the division and the variable expenses incurred. We considered this measure at length in Chapter 3. There we saw that it can be a useful measure for gaining an insight into the relationship between costs, output levels and profit.

Activity 11.6

Assume that you are the chief executive of a divisionalised business. Would you use contribution as a primary measure of divisional performance? Why?

Contribution would probably not be used. It has its drawbacks for this purpose. The most important drawback is that it only takes account of variable expenses and ignores any fixed expenses incurred. This means that not all aspects of operating performance are considered.

As variable expenses are taken into account in this measure and fixed expenses are ignored, it would be tempting to arrange things so that fixed expenses rather than variable expenses are incurred wherever possible. In this way, the contribution will be maximised. For example, you may decide, as divisional manager, to employ less casual labour and to use machines to do the work instead (even though this may be a more expensive option).

Controllable profit

The second measure of profit is the *controllable profit*, which takes account of all expenses that are within the control of divisional managers. Many view this as the best measure of performance for divisional managers, as they will be in a position to determine the level of expenses incurred. However, in practice, it may be difficult to categorise costs as being either **controllable costs** or **non-controllable costs**.

There may be some expenses that can be influenced by divisional managers, yet are not entirely under their control. A depreciation charge may provide one example. A divisional manager may be required to purchase a particular type of computer hardware to ensure the information systems of the division are compatible with those used throughout the business. The manager may, however, have some discretion over the frequency with which the hardware is replaced, as well as over the purchase of particular hardware models that perform beyond the minimum standards needed for the business. Depending on how this discretion is exercised, the depreciation charge for the period may differ significantly from the charge that would arise if the manager stuck to the minimum standards laid down by senior managers.

Divisional profit before common expenses

The third measure of profit is *divisional profit before common expenses*, which takes account of all divisional expenses (controllable and non-controllable) that are incurred by the division. This provides us with a measure of how the division contributes to the overall profits of the business.

It can be argued that the performance of divisional managers should be judged on the basis of those things that are within their control. Hence, the controllable profit would be the most appropriate measure to use. The contribution measure does not take account of all the expenses that are controllable by divisional managers, while the divisional profit before common expenses takes account of some expenses that are not under the control of divisional managers. The divisional profit, however, may be appropriate for evaluating the performance of the division, as it deducts all divisional expenses from the divisional revenues earned. It is a fairly comprehensive measure of divisional achievement.

Divisional profit for the period

The final measure of profit is *divisional profit for the period*, which is derived after deducting a proportion of the common expenses incurred for the period. The expenses assigned to each division will usually represent what senior managers believe is a fair share of the total common expenses incurred. These expenses will typically include such things as marketing, human resource management, accounting, planning, information technology and research and development expenses.

In practice, the way in which these are assigned between divisions can be extremely contentious. Some divisional managers may be convinced that they have been assigned an unfair share of the common expenses. They may also believe that the divisions are being loaded with expenses over which they have little control. As a result, the divisional profit figure does not truly reflect the achievements of the division. These problems may, therefore, prevent senior managers from assigning common expenses to the various divisions.

Activity 11.9

Can you think of any arguments *for* apportioning common expenses to divisions? Try to think of at least one.

The business as a whole will only make a profit after all common expenses have been covered. Apportioning these expenses to the divisions should help make divisional managers more aware of this fact. In addition, senior managers may wish to compare the results of the division with the results of similar businesses in the same industry that are operating as independent entities. By apportioning common expenses to the divisions, a more valid basis for comparison is provided. Independent businesses will have to bear these kinds of expenses before arriving at their profit for the period. The effect of apportioning common expenses may also help to impose an element of control over these expenses. Divisional managers may put pressure on senior managers to keep common expenses low so as to minimise the adverse effect on divisional profits.

Real World 11.4 sheds some light on the amount of common expenses assigned to divisions.

Real World 11.4

Something in common

Drury and El-Shishini conducted a survey of 124 senior financial managers of divisionalised businesses within the manufacturing sector. They found that nearly all managers (95 per cent) stated that the divisions used common resources such as marketing, human resource management, accounting and so on. The survey asked those managers to state the approximate cost of using these resources as a percentage of annual divisional sales revenue. Figure 11.4 sets out the findings.

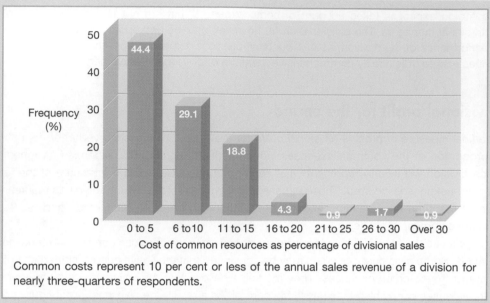

Common costs represent 10 per cent or less of the annual sales revenue of a division for nearly three-quarters of respondents.

Figure 11.4 Common costs as a percentage of divisional annual sales revenue

We can see that the costs of using common resources tend to be fairly low. The reasons for this are not entirely clear. One possible explanation is that highly decentralised businesses tend to have divisions that are self reliant. Hence, the level of dependence on common resources will be low. Another possible explanation is that businesses with a large number of divisions have a greater opportunity to spread the costs of common resources among the various divisions. The study found, however, little or no evidence to support these explanations.

Source: Drury, C. and El-Shishini, E. (2005) *Divisional Performance Measurement: An Examination of Potential Explanatory Factors*, CIMA Research Report, August, p. 32.

DIVISIONAL PERFORMANCE MEASURES

Divisional profit, by itself, is an inadequate measure of divisional performance. Some account must be taken of the investment in assets required to generate that profit. Two measures of divisional performance that do this are

■ return on investment (ROI), and
■ residual income (RI).

We shall now deal with each of these measures in turn.

Return on investment (ROI)

Return on investment (ROI) is a popular method of assessing the profitability of divisions. The ratio is calculated as follows:

$$\text{ROI} = \frac{\text{Divisional profit}}{\text{Divisional investment (assets employed)}} \times 100\%$$

The definition of divisional profit for this ratio will depend on the purpose for which it is being used.

Activity 11.10

Which definition of profit is likely to be appropriate when assessing the performance of:

(a) a divisional manager
(b) a division.

We saw earlier that, when evaluating the performance of a divisional manager, controllable profit may be more appropriate. When evaluating the performance of a division, divisional profit for the period may be more appropriate.

Various definitions can also be used for the divisional investment figure in the ratio. Total assets (non-current assets plus current assets) or net assets (non-current assets plus current assets less current liabilities) may be used. In addition, non-current assets may be measured using their historic cost, or their historic cost less accumulated depreciation, or on some other basis, such as current market value. It can be argued that a market-based value is the most valid approach as it would provide a more realistic measure of achievement.

Whichever definitions of divisional profit and divisional investment are used, they must be consistently applied. It could be very misleading, for example, to compare the ROIs of two divisions where no common definitions are employed.

The ROI ratio can be broken down into two main elements as shown in Figure 11.5. The first ratio is the divisional profit expressed as a percentage of sales revenue. The second is the sales revenue expressed as a percentage of the divisional investment base.

The RI ratio can be divided into two elements: divisional profit to divisional sales revenues and divisional sales revenue to divisional investment. By analysing RI in this way, we can see the influence of both profitability and efficiency.

Figure 11.5 The main elements of the RI ratio

This separation into the two main elements highlights the fact that ROI is determined by both the profit margin on each £ of sales revenue and the ability to generate a high level of sales revenue in relation to the investment base. In other words, it is determined by both profitability and efficiency in the use of assets.

The following data relate to the performance and position of two operating divisions that sell similar products:

	Kuala Lumpur Division	Singapore Division
	£m	£m
Sales revenue	300	750
Divisional profit	30	25
Divisional investment	600	500

What observations can you make about the performance of each division?

Firstly, the ROIs for both divisions are identical at 5 per cent a year (that is, 30/600 and 25/500). The information shows, however, that the divisions appear to be pursuing different strategies. The profit margins for the Kuala Lumpur and Singapore Divisions are 10 per cent (that is, 30/300) and 3.3 per cent (that is, 25/750) respectively. The sales revenue to divisional investment ratios for the Kuala Lumpur and Singapore Divisions are 50 per cent (that is, 300/600) and 150 per cent (that is, 750/500) respectively. Thus, we can see that the Kuala Lumpur Division sells goods at a higher profit margin than the Singapore Division, resulting in lower sales revenue to assets employed.

ROI is a measure of *profitability*, as it relates profits to the size of the investment made in the division. This relative measure allows comparisons between divisions of different sizes. However, ROI has its drawbacks. Where it is used as the primary measure of performance for divisional managers, there is a danger that it will lead to behaviour that is not really consistent with the interests of the business overall.

Russell Francis plc has two divisions, both selling similar products but operating in different geographical areas. The Wessex Division reported a £20m controllable profit from a divisional investment of £100m and the Sussex Division a £15m controllable profit from a divisional investment of £50m.

The divisional manager of each division has the opportunity to invest £20m in the development of a new product line that will boost controllable profit by £5m. The minimum acceptable ROI for each division is 16 per cent a year.

Which operating division has been the more successful? How might each divisional manager react to the new opportunity?

Although the Wessex Division has achieved a higher profit in absolute terms, it has a lower ROI than the Sussex Division. The ROI for Wessex is 20 per cent a year (that is, £20m /£100m) compared with 30 per cent (that is, £15m/£50m) for the Sussex Division. Using ROI as the measure of performance, the Sussex Division is therefore the better-performing division.

The ROI from the new investment is 25 per cent a year (that is, £5m/£20m). Thus, by taking on this investment, the divisional manager of Wessex will increase the ROI of the division, which currently stands at 20 per cent a year. However, the divisional manager of Sussex will reduce the ROI of the division by taking this opportunity. The ROI of the investment is below the overall ROI of 30 per cent a year for the division.

If ROI is used as the primary measure of divisional performance, the divisional manager of Sussex may decline the opportunity for fear that a reduction in divisional ROI will reflect poorly on performance. However, the return from the opportunity of 25 per cent a year comfortably exceeds the minimum ROI of 16 per cent a year. Thus, failure to exploit the opportunity will mean the profit potential of the division is not fully realised.

Activity 11.12 illustrates the problems that can arise when using comparative measures such as percentages.

A further disincentive to invest can result where the divisional non-current assets are measured in terms of the original cost less any accumulated depreciation to date (that is, written-down value). Where depreciation is being charged each year, the written-down value of the divisional investment will be reduced. Provided that profit stays at the same level, this means that ROI will climb during the lifetime of the depreciating assets.

To illustrate this point consider Example 11.1.

Example 11.1

The following are the profits and investment for a division over a four-year period:

Year	Divisional profit £m	Divisional investment £m	ROI at written down value %
1	30	200	15.0
2	30	180	16.7
3	30	160	18.8
4	30	140	21.4

The investment is plant and equipment that cost £200m at the beginning of year 1. It is being depreciated at the rate of 10 per cent of cost each year.

We can see that the ROI increases over time simply because the investment base is shrinking. This is despite the fact that it is the same plant and equipment, generating as much profit. We have just seen that divisional managers may be discouraged from investing in further assets where the ROI is below the existing ROI for the division. In this example, the divisional manager would probably be reluctant to replace the plant and equipment and return the division to a 15 per cent ROI. This would be the case even though the need for new investment will increase as the existing equipment becomes fully depreciated.

Activity 11.13

How might the problem caused by ROI being boosted simply through a reduction in the investment base, as in Example 11.1, be resolved? Try to think of one solution.

One way around the problem would be to keep the investment in assets at original cost and not to deduct depreciation for purposes of calculating ROI. However, non-current assets normally lose their productive capacity over time, and this fact should really be recognised. Another way around the problem is to use some measure of current market value, such as replacement cost, for the investment in assets. However, there may be problems in establishing current values for some assets.

Residual income (RI)

The weaknesses of the ROI method, particularly the fact that it ignores the cost of financing a division, has led some businesses to search for a more appropriate measure of divisional performance. An alternative measure is that of **residual income (RI)**. RI is the amount of income, or profit, generated by a division, which exceeds the minimum acceptable level of income. If we assume that the objective of the business is to increase owners' (shareholders') wealth, the minimum acceptable level of income to be generated is the amount necessary to cover the cost of capital.

Taking the divisional profit figure and then deducting an imputed charge for the capital invested will give the RI. Thus:

Divisional profit − Charge for capital invested = Residual income

Example 11.2 should make the process clear.

Example 11.2

A division produced a profit of £100m and there was a divisional investment of £600m with a cost of financing this investment of 15 per cent a year. The residual income would be as follows:

	£m
Divisional profit	100
Charge for capital invested (15% × £600m)	(90)
Residual income	10

A positive RI, as in Example 11.2, means that the division is generating returns in excess of the minimum requirements of the business. The higher the excess returns, the better the performance of the division.

Activity 11.14

Does this measure seem familiar to you? Where have we discussed a similar measure to this earlier in the book?

This measure is based on the same idea as the EVA® measure that we discussed in Chapter 10. We shall consider this point in more detail a little later in the chapter.

Activity 11.15

Simonson Pharmaceuticals plc operates the Helena Beauty Care Division, which has reported the following results for last year:

Divisional investment	£200m
Divisional profit	£30m

The division has the opportunity to invest in a new product. This will require an additional investment in non-current assets of £40m and is expected to generate additional profits of £5m a year. This business has a cost of capital of 10 per cent a year.

Calculate the residual income of the division for last year. Do you believe that the division should produce the new product? How might the divisional manager react to the new product opportunity if ROI were used as the means of evaluating performance?

The residual income for last year is:

	£m
Divisional profit	30
Charge for capital invested (10% × £200)	(20)
Residual income	10

The residual income expected from the new product is:

	£m
Additional divisional profit	5
Charge for additional capital (10% × £40m)	(4)
Residual income	1

The residual income is positive and, therefore, it would be worthwhile to produce the new product. It would cover all of the costs involved, including the cost of financing the investment.

The ROI of the division for last year was 15 per cent a year (that is, £30m/£200m). However, the new product is only expected to produce an ROI of 12.5 per cent a year (that is, £5m/£40m). The effect of producing the new product will be to reduce the overall ROI of the division (assuming similar results from the existing activities next year). The divisional manager may, therefore, reject the new investment opportunity, despite the fact that acceptance would enhance the owners' (shareholders') wealth.

Looking to the longer term

A problem with both ROI and RI is that divisional managers may focus on short-term divisional performance at the expense of the longer term. There is a danger that investment opportunities will be rejected because they reduce short-term ROI and RI, even though over the longer term they have a positive NPV. This is illustrated in Example 11.3.

Example 11.3

A division is faced with an investment opportunity that will require an initial investment of £90,000 and produce the following operating cash flows over the next five years:

Year	£
1	18,000
2	18,000
3	25,000
4	50,000
5	60,000

Assuming a cost of capital of 16 per cent a year, the NPV of the project will be:

Year	Cash flows	Discount factor @ 16%	Present value
	£		£
1	18,000	0.862	15,516
2	18,000	0.743	13,374
3	25,000	0.641	16,025
4	50,000	0.552	27,600
5	60,000	0.476	28,560
			101,075
Initial investment			(90,000)
Net present value			11,075

This indicates that the NPV is positive and, therefore, it would be in the shareholders' interests to undertake the project.

To calculate ROI and RI, we need to derive the divisional profit for each year (that is, deduct a charge for depreciation from the operating cash flows shown above). This assumes that the annual cash flows broadly equal the profit before charging depreciation. Assuming also that depreciation is charged equally over the life of the assets acquired and there is no residual value for the assets, the annual depreciation charge will be £18,000 (that is, £90,000/5).

After deducting an annual depreciation charge, the divisional profit for each year will be as follows:

Year	£
1	zero
2	zero
3	7,000
4	32,000
5	42,000

Activity 11.16

Calculate the ROI and RI for each of the five years of the project's life. (Base the ROI calculation on the cost of the assets concerned.)

The ROI for the project will be as follows:

Year	£	ROI
		%
1	zero/90,000	zero
2	zero/90,000	zero
3	7,000/90,000	7.8
4	32,000/90,000	35.6
5	42,000/90,000	46.7

The RI will be as follows:

Year	Divisional profit £	Capital charge £	RI £
1	zero	14,400*	(14,400)
2	zero	14,400	(14,400)
3	7,000	14,400	(7,400)
4	32,000	14,400	17,600
5	42,000	14,400	27,600
			9,000

* The capital charge is 16% × £90,000 = £14,400.

Activity 11.17

What do you deduce from the calculations resulting from Activity 11.16?

We can see that, in the early years, the ROI and RI calculations do not produce good results, though the situation is reversed in later years. For the first two years the ROI is zero and for the first three years the RI is negative. Divisional managers may, therefore, be discouraged from making investments if they feel that central management would view the results in the early years unfavourably. Given the results of the NPV analysis, however, the managers would not be acting in the owners' (shareholders) best interests by rejecting the proposal.

Note, however, that the RI of the project overall is positive and so provides a result that is consistent with the NPV result, over the five years.

Various approaches have been proposed in an attempt to avoid the kind of problem described in the solution to Activity 11.17. It has been suggested, for example, that for the purpose of calculating divisional ROI and RI, the assets employed in the project should not be included in the divisional investment base until the project is fully established and generating good returns.

Comparing performance

Assessing divisional performance requires some benchmark against which we can compare the chosen measure(s). There are various bases for comparison available, including:

- *Other divisions within the business.* Comparing different divisions within the same business, however, may not be very useful where the divisions operate in different industries. Different types of industries have different levels of risk and this in turn produces different expectations concerning acceptable levels of return. (See Chapter 9.)
- *Previous performance of the division.* It is possible to compare current performance with previous performance to see whether there has been any improvement or deterioration. However, we often need to compare performance against some external standard in order to bring to light operating inefficiencies within the division. Furthermore, the economic environment in past periods may be quite different from the current environment, which can invalidate comparisons.
- *Similar businesses within the same industry.* The performance of similar divisions of other businesses, or whole businesses operating within the same industry, may provide a useful

basis for comparison. However, there are often problems associated with this basis. (We shall come back to this in Activity 11.18.)

- *Budgeted (target) performance.* This is the best basis for comparison because achievement of the budget should lead the division, and the business as a whole, towards its strategic objectives. In setting the budget, performances elsewhere in the business, previous levels of performance by the division and the performance of competitors may well be considered. Ultimately, however, it is against what the division has planned that its actual performance should be assessed.

Activity 11.18

What problems are we likely to come across, in practice, when seeking to compare the performance of a particular division with a similar division of another business, or a whole business entity? Try to think of at least two problems.

We may encounter a number of problems such as:

- *Obtaining the information required.* This is particularly true for a division within another business. This information may not be available to those outside the business.
- *Differences in accounting policies.* Different approaches to such matters as depreciation methods and inventories valuation methods may result in different measures of profit.
- *Differences in asset structure.* The different age of non-current assets employed, the decision to rent rather than buy particular assets and so on, may result in differences in the measures derived.

EVA® REVISITED

We saw in Chapter 10 that EVA® measures the amount of wealth that has been created for the owners (shareholders). We may recall that it is based on the following formula:

$$EVA^® = NOPAT - (R \times C)$$

where

NOPAT = net operating profit after tax
R = required returns of investors (that is, cost of financing)
C = capital invested (that is, the net assets).

This measure, though not specifically designed for assessing divisional performance, may nevertheless be used for this purpose.

There are clear similarities between EVA® and RI. Both recognise that, in economic terms, profit can only arise after all costs, including financing costs, have been taken into account. Hence, a charge for capital invested is employed. When comparing the two measures, it may seem that there is no real difference between them. However, EVA® is a more rigorous measure. The various elements in the EVA® equation (net operating profit after tax, required returns of investors and net assets) are defined more clearly and in such a way that there is an unambiguous link between EVA® and wealth creation. This is not the case with RI. Thus, EVA® should prevail over RI when assessing divisional performance.

Real World 11.5 provides some insights as to what senior managers consider important when evaluating the performance of divisional managers. It seems that, whatever the theoretical appeal of EVA®, it is not widely used for this purpose.

Ranking the measures

In their survey of senior financial managers of 124 divisionalised businesses within the manufacturing sector, referred to in Real World 11.4, Drury and El-Shishini asked the managers to rank in order of importance the three measures that they considered most important for evaluating managerial performance. The results are:

Financial measure	Ranked most important by number of managers	Percentage of respondents	Ranked second most important by number of managers	Percentage of respondents	Ranked third most important by number of managers	Percentage of respondents
Achievement of a target rate of return on capital employed (ROI)	9	7.3	21	18.1	41	41.0
A target profit after charging interest on capital employed (RI)	18	14.5	11	9.5	5	5.0
A target profit before charging interest on capital employed	68	54.8	23	19.8	5	5.0
A target economic value added (EVA®) figure	11	8.9	8	6.9	10	10.0
A target cash flow figure	10	8.1	45	38.8	27	27.0
Other	8	6.4	8	6.9	12	12.0
	124	100.0	116	100.0	100	100.0

We can see that target profit *before* charging interest on capital employed was by far the most popular measure. Although ROI and RI are well-known measures, neither was frequently cited as the most important measure by senior financial managers. The limited support for target EVA® may be partially due to the fact that it was a relatively new measure at the time.

Source: Drury, C. and El-Shishini, E. (2005) *Divisional Performance Measurement: An Examination of Potential Explanatory Factors*, CIMA Research Report, August, p. 30.

TRANSFER PRICING

A division may sell goods or services to another division within the same business. A brick-manufacturing division, for example, may sell its products to a house-building division. The price at which transfers between divisions are made is an important issue. Setting prices for inter-divisional trading is known as **transfer pricing**. For the division providing the goods or service, transfers represent part, or possibly all, of its output. If the performance of the division is to be measured in a meaningful way, the division should be credited with 'sales revenue' for the goods or services transferred. Failure to do so would mean that it must bear the expenses of creating the goods or service, but will receive no credit. Similarly, the receiving (buying) division must be charged with the expense of using the goods or service transferred if its performance is to be measured in a meaningful way.

Where inter-divisional transfers represent a large part of the total sales or purchases of a division, transfer pricing becomes a very important issue. Small changes in the transfer price of goods or services can result in large changes in profits for the division concerned. As divisional managers are often assessed (and partially remunerated) according to the profits generated by their division, setting transfer prices may well be a sensitive issue between divisional managers.

While the transfer prices used will affect the profits of individual divisions, the profits of the business as a whole should not be *directly* affected. An increase in the transfer price of goods or services will lead to an increase in the profits of the selling division, which is normally cancelled out by the decrease in profits of the buying division. However, the transfer prices set between divisions can *indirectly* lead to a loss of profits to the business as a whole. This is because the level at which they are set may encourage a divisional manager to take actions that would benefit the division but not the business as a whole. For example a divisional manager may choose to buy a particular product or service from an outside supplier because it is cheaper than the established internal transfer price. In such a situation, the profits of the business as a whole may be adversely affected.

Activity 11.19

Under what circumstances would the business as a whole not be worse off if one of its divisions chooses to buy goods from an external source rather than from another division?

If the division supplying the goods is able to sell them to the external market, at the same, or a higher, price, the business as a whole would not suffer any loss.

The objectives of transfer pricing

Transfer pricing may help achieve various objectives. In particular, transfer prices may help to promote:

- *The independence of divisions.* If divisional managers are allowed to set their own transfer prices, and other divisions are allowed to decide whether to trade at the prices quoted, the autonomy of individual divisions is encouraged. This, in turn, should help motivate divisional managers.
- *The assessment of divisional performance.* Inter-divisional sales will contribute to total revenues for a division, which in turn influence divisional profit. Setting an appropriate transfer price is, therefore, important in deriving a valid measure of divisional profit. This should be of value in helping to establish incentives for, and promoting accountability of, divisional managers.
- *The optimisation of profits for the business.* Transfer prices may be set at a level that promotes the optimisation of profits for the business as a whole. Thus, a division may be prevented from quoting a transfer price for goods that encourages buying divisions to seek cheaper sources of supply from outside the business.
- *The allocation of divisional resources.* Transfer prices are important in determining the level of output for particular goods and services. The transfer price will influence the level of return from inter-divisional sales which, in turn, will influence the level of output and investment for a particular product, or group of products.

■ *Tax minimisation.* Where a business has operations in various countries, it may be benefi-cial to set transfer prices such that the bulk of profits are reported in divisions where the host country has low tax rates. However, tax laws operating in many countries seek to prevent this kind of profit manipulation.

These objectives for transfer pricing are summarised in Figure 11.6.

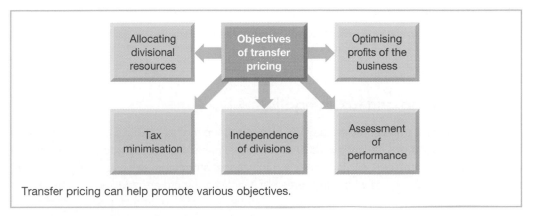

Transfer pricing can help promote various objectives.

Figure 11.6 Objectives of transfer pricing

Activity 11.20

Is there a conflict between any of these transfer-pricing objectives? If so, can a single transfer price help achieve all these objectives?

It is quite possible for there to be a conflict between the objectives identified. Thus, a single transfer price is unlikely to achieve all the stated objectives. To optimise the profits for the business as a whole, for example, transfer prices may have to be imposed centrally, which would undermine the autonomy of divisions. In addition, a centrally imposed transfer price may result in inter-divisional sales at artificially low prices, which would disadvantage par-ticular divisions. It may also result in reported profit figures in both the buying and selling divisions becoming meaningless as measures of achievement.

Real World 11.6 reveals that, in practice, setting transfer prices tends to be highly centralised.

Real World 11.6

Setting transfer prices

Tang surveyed 95 very large US businesses that were all listed in the Fortune 1000 group of businesses. Of those businesses, 88 per cent used transfer pricing for both domestic and international transfers between divisions. Tang reported that most businesses saw interna-tional transfer pricing as one of the most important functions of the business, which was vital to business profits, tax compliance and divisional evaluation. It is, perhaps, not surpris-ing therefore that divisions do not usually set transfer prices. The survey produced the fol-lowing results:

	%	%
Transfer prices set centrally		59
– In consultation with divisions	43	
– Without consultation with divisions	16	
Transfer prices set by divisions		22
		81

The remaining respondents stated that government regulations constrain their ability to determine transfer prices.

Source: Tang, R. (2002) *Current Trends and Corporate Cases in Transfer Pricing*, Quorum Books.

Transfer pricing and tax mitigation

We saw earlier that transfer prices may be used to reduce the tax liabilities of businesses with international operations. It is claimed that many of these businesses adopt novel transfer pricing policies, combined with complex organisational structures, to ensure that profits are reported in those countries where tax rates are low. Where there are doubts over the legality of these complicated manoeuvres, the tax authorities must try to unravel them.

Real World 11.7 comprises extracts from an Institute for Fiscal Studies paper on how tax authorities around the world are finding it increasingly difficult to deal with the transfer pricing policies that businesses adopt.

Real World 11.7

Try googling 'transfer pricing'

Corporate tax has rarely excited the imagination of the public as much as in recent years. This week Google has become the latest company to attract widespread anger over the amount of tax it has paid in the UK. The sense that there are some big, profitable companies paying relatively little in corporate tax has led many to try to allocate blame. Are multinationals simply behaving badly? Is HMRC (the UK tax authority) cutting sweetheart deals with favoured companies? Have politicians failed in their task of writing the tax rules?

The most important question relates to what we're trying to tax. The current tax rules are *not* designed to tax the profits from UK sales. They're certainly not designed to tax either revenue or sales generated in the UK. They are instead designed to tax that part of a firm's profit that arises from value created in the UK. That is the principle underlying all corporate tax regimes across the OECD. The trouble is that calculating how much profit arises from value added in any individual country can be very tricky, and is often open to honest dispute.

Multinationals operate across tax jurisdictions and create profits from activities in many countries. Working out how to allocate profits to different jurisdictions is difficult. In practice, countries have long agreed to divvy up profits according to where the underlying value was created. But there is often no single 'correct' answer to how much profit should be taxed in the UK. For example: if a worker in the UK and a worker in Ireland collaborate in arranging and concluding a sale, or in designing a new product, or writing a piece of software, how much of resulting income should be attributed to UK activities?

The tax rules seek to provide an answer to this. Transfer pricing rules dictate the prices that a firm can charge for a transaction – including payments for services or for the use of ideas – that happens between two parts of the same firm that are located in different tax jurisdictions. These are the rules that determine taxable profit allocation. Yet the rules can never be detailed enough to set out what the outcome should be in every possible case. This creates room for disagreement over what the tax rules mean. This is why HMRC is often engaged with multinationals about how much tax they pay: not because they are busy cutting special deals, but because they are trying to apply the tax rules in a consistent manner.

Multinationals are in a good position to be able to employ hordes of tax advisors that help them to conclude any uncertainty in way that leads to lower tax bills, and to take advantage of any loopholes to avoid tax. Some of those loopholes are well known and many exist in other countries' tax regimes. For example, the well documented "Double Irish" refers to differences between Irish and US tax laws that allow US multinationals to shift profits out of Ireland to tax havens such as Bermuda. These kinds of gaps in tax systems can create opportunities for tax avoidance on a grand scale. There is literally nothing the UK government can do unilaterally about some of these loopholes.

Source: Extracts from Miller, H. and Pope, T. (2016) *What does the row over Google's tax bill tell us about the corporate tax systems*, Institute for Fiscal Studies, 26 January.

Tax authorities in various countries are trying to stamp out transfer pricing abuses. Investigations of transfer pricing policies of individual businesses are becoming more common and cross-border co-operation between tax authorities has increased. Information is exchanged and treaties are signed which set out transfer pricing rules that businesses are expected to follow. Not all tax authorities, however, have the resources and expertise to investigate what can be complex and opaque practices. Those in emerging economies often find it hard to mount a serious challenge to transfer pricing abuses. Nevertheless, the recent difficult economic climate has prompted many governments to try to boost tax revenues by greater regulation and surveillance of transfer pricing methods.

Real World 11.8 sets out evidence from a recent survey by EY, an international firm of tax advisors and consultants, which shows how concerned businesses have become about the close scrutiny of transfer pricing by tax-seeking governments.

Real World 11.8

The tax man cometh

EY's 2016 survey of 623 transfer pricing executives in 36 jurisdictions across 17 industries finds that respondents are encountering significantly more transfer pricing disputes in more jurisdictions than in the past. And, perhaps more significantly for the months and years to come, respondents are anticipating an expanding swathe of conflict spanning a wider range of geographies across a broader range of issues. The field of play since our last survey has shifted so dramatically that the number of firms indicating "tax risk management" as their top transfer pricing priority has surged to 75%, up from 66% in our 2013 survey; in 2007 and 2010, that proportion was just 50%. The increased risk aversion found in this year's survey was prevalent across all industries, although it reached 88% for the banking and capital markets and wealth and asset management sectors. EY Global Transfer Pricing Leader Peter Griffin explains that across all industries, "managing tax risk is becoming far and away the highest priority within transfer pricing."

Though industry findings are relatively consistent, there are some geography-based variances. For example, only 65% of respondents from the Americas indicate that tax risk management is their top transfer pricing priority. On the other end of the spectrum, some 81% of Japanese-based businesses identified risk management as their top priority. Europe (75%), Australia and New Zealand (75%), and the rest of the Asia-Pacific region (72%) were broadly in line with the global results.

In recent years, transfer pricing has attracted the attention of the news media, politicians and social justice groups that suspect multinational corporations use transfer pricing to pay less than a "fair share" of tax. Largely as a product of this heightened visibility, tax authorities are under pressure to implement greater and unprecedented demands for transparency. As of October 2016, 44 countries have implemented all or some of the BEPS [Base Erosion and Profit Shifting] recommendations. In all, more than 80 countries globally are committed to implementation. This compels more disclosure about a business's transfer pricing activities in the aggregate, and how this aligns to the operating model. But it also necessitates a shift from a reactive stance to a proactive review of policies, procedures and operations so that any inevitable disclosures contain nothing untoward. Companies today must increasingly demonstrate that they are following not only the letter but also the spirit of the tax and transfer pricing rules — as should any responsible corporate citizen.

Source: Extracts from *In the spotlight: a new era of transparency and risk for transfer pricing 2016*, EY Transfer Pricing Survey Series, www.ey.com, pp. 3 and 4.

There is evidence that the use of, perhaps, manipulated transfer prices to lessen the business's overall tax burden is on the decline. The attention paid to this issue by the various national tax authorities may well be the reason for this.

Transfer pricing policies

There are various approaches to setting a transfer price for goods and services between divisions. In this section, we explore some of the most common approaches. Before doing this, however, it is worth identifying the principle that *the best transfer price is one based closely on the opportunity cost of the goods or services concerned*. The opportunity cost represents the best alternative forgone. Thus, when examining the various approaches, the extent to which they reflect the opportunity cost of the goods or services should be the appropriate benchmark against which they are measured.

Market prices

Market prices are the prices that exist in the 'outside' market (that is, outside the business whose divisions are involved in the transfer). Intuition may tell us that market prices should be the appropriate method of setting transfer prices. Using this approach, the transfer price is an objective, verifiable amount that has real economic credibility. Where there is a competitive and active market for the products, the market price will represent the opportunity cost of goods and services. For the selling division, it is the revenue lost by selling to another division rather than to an outside customer. For the buying division, it is the best purchase price available.

The market price, however, may not always be appropriate. Activity 11.21 illustrates why.

Wolf Industries plc has an operating division that produces microwave ovens. The ovens are normally sold to retailers for £120. The division is currently producing 3,000 ovens a month (which uses only about 50 per cent of the division's manufacturing capacity). The ovens have the following cost structure:

	Cost for one oven
	£
Variable cost	70
Fixed cost apportionment	20
Total cost	**90**

Another division of the business has offered to buy 2,000 ovens for £75 each. How would you respond to such an offer if you were manager of the division making the microwave ovens?

Since the division is operating below capacity, basing the transfer price on market prices may lead to lost sales. Other divisions within the business have no price incentive to buy their ovens internally. This may lead them to buy from outside sources rather than from the selling division and this loss of sales will not be made good by sales to outside customers.

We saw in Chapter 3 that businesses may base selling prices on the variable cost of the goods or services, rather than on the market price, where there is a short-term problem of excess capacity. Provided that the selling price exceeds the variable cost of the goods or service, a contribution will be made towards the profits of the business. This principle can equally be applied to divisions of businesses. Thus, in such circumstances, a selling price somewhere between the variable cost of the product (£70) and the market price (£120) may be the best price for divisional transfers.

Senior management could intervene to insist that the microwave ovens are bought internally, but this would undermine divisional autonomy and the right of divisions to make their own decisions.

A final point to consider when making inter-divisional transfers at market prices is that the selling division may benefit from lower selling and distribution costs. Where this occurs, part of these benefits may be passed on to the buying division in the form of lower prices. Thus, an adjustment may be made to the market price of the goods transferred.

Apart from the problems just considered, there is another, more fundamental, problem with using market prices that we may encounter in practice. Can you think what it may be?

An external market may simply not exist. It may not be possible for the potential buying division to identify external suppliers, and therefore an external price, for the particular goods or services. Alternatively, and more likely, there may be no potential external customers for the selling division's output. The goods or services may be so tailored to the needs of the buying division that it is the only market available.

Variable cost

We have just seen that using *variable cost* is appropriate where the division is operating below capacity. In these particular circumstances, the opportunity cost to the supplying division is not the market price. The division will not have to stop selling to the market in order to supply another division since there is a capacity to do both. In these circumstances, the opportunity cost is equal to the variable cost of producing the good or service. However, this represents an absolute minimum transfer price and a figure above the variable cost is required for a contribution to be made towards fixed costs and profit. Where the division is operating at full capacity and external customers are prepared to pay above the variable cost, an internal transfer price based on variable cost would mean that inter-divisional sales are less profitable than sales to external customers. Managers of the selling division would therefore have no incentive to agree transfer prices on a strictly variable cost basis (even though the business as a whole may benefit). If senior managers impose this pricing method, divisional autonomy will be undermined.

Full cost

Transfers can be made at *full cost*. In such circumstances, the selling division will make no profit on the transactions. This can hinder an evaluation of divisional performance. It would also lead to difficulties in making resource allocation decisions concerning the level of output, product mix and investment levels within the division.

Activity 11.23

Can you think why using full cost may lead to resource allocation difficulties?

Full cost means that no profit is made by the selling division and, therefore, a valuable measure of efficiency is lost.

It is possible to add a mark-up to the full cost of the goods or services to ensure that the selling division makes a profit. However, the amount of the mark-up must be justified in some way or it will become a contentious issue between buying and selling divisions.

A cost-based approach (with or without the use of a mark-up) does not provide an incentive for managers of a selling division to bear down on costs. They can simply pass the costs on to the buying division. By so doing, any operating inefficiencies within selling divisions will be transferred to buying divisions. Where the mark-up is based on a percentage of cost, the selling division's profit will be higher if it incurs higher costs. If, however, buying divisions can go to outside suppliers, pressure can be exerted on the selling divisions to control their costs. Although the full cost approach can be found in practice, it has little to commend it since it is not linked to opportunity cost.

Transferring goods or services between divisions can be based on either a standard (budgeted) cost or an actual cost approach. The case for using standard costs appears to be the stronger.

What are the arguments in favour of using standard (budgeted) costs rather than actual costs?

Information relating to actual costs may not be available until after the transfer has taken place, which can create planning problems for the buying division. If standard (budgeted) costs are used, this problem is overcome. It may also help impose some discipline on the selling division as adverse variances cannot simply be passed on to the buying division. These arguments apply whether variable or full costs are being used as the transfer price.

The way in which standards are set, however, must be closely monitored to prevent transfer prices becoming a contentious issue. The manager of the buying division may be quick to point out that there is no incentive for the selling division to develop tight standards. Indeed, the opposite is true. Loose standards will make it easier to generate favourable variances.

Negotiated prices

It is possible to adopt an approach that allows the divisional managers to arrive at **negotiated prices** for inter-divisional transfers. However, this can lead to serious disputes. Where divisional managers are unable to agree a price, senior management will be required to arbitrate. This can be a time-consuming process and may deflect senior management from its more strategic role. Furthermore, divisional managers may resent the decisions made by senior managers and see these as undermining the autonomy of their divisions.

Negotiated transfer prices probably work best where there is an external market for the goods supplied by the buying and selling divisions and where divisional managers are free to accept or reject offers made by other divisions. Under such circumstances, the negotiated price is likely to be closely related to the external market price of the products. In other circumstances, the negotiated prices may be artificial and misleading. Where, for example, a division sells the whole of its output to another division, the latter division may find itself in a weak bargaining position. As a result, the agreed transfer price may not provide a valid measure of divisional performance. Negotiated prices are likely to be influenced by the negotiating skills of managers, which can be a problem where this largely determines the outcome.

Figure 11.7 summarises the various approaches to transfer pricing that have been discussed.

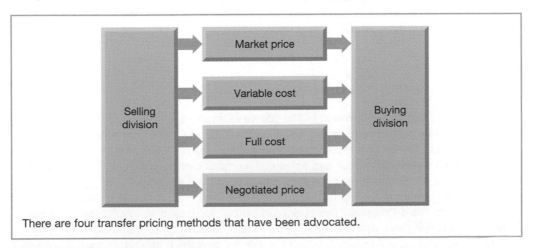

There are four transfer pricing methods that have been advocated.

Figure 11.7 Transfer pricing methods

Divisions with mixed sales

A division may sell part of its output to another division within the same business and part to outside customers. For a business with only two divisions, the position will be as set out in Figure 11.8.

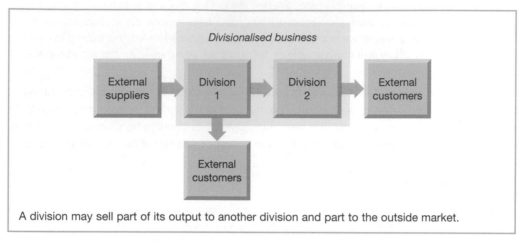

A division may sell part of its output to another division and part to the outside market.

Figure 11.8 Relationship between divisions and the external market

Activity 11.25 requires you to calculate the budgeted divisional profits for a business with divisions that have mixed sales.

Activity 11.25

Dorset Ltd has two operating divisions: Cornwall and Devon. Cornwall produces a very high quality fabric that is used in making curtains. The budgeted cost of a square metre of the fabric is made up as follows:

	£
Variable cost	
Labour	4
Material	7
	11
Fixed cost	
Overheads	13
Total cost	24

The budgeted output for Cornwall is 300,000 sq m each year.

Devon makes curtains and uses 1.1 sq m of this fabric to make 1 sq m of curtains. The management of Dorset Ltd insists that Cornwall must sell to Devon as much of the fabric as is required to meet its needs and any surplus output can then be sold to outside businesses at the market price for the fabric, which is £30 per sq m.

The management of Dorset Ltd also insists that Devon must buy all its requirements for this fabric from Cornwall. The budgeted output for Devon is 200,000 sq m of curtains. Devon sells its output for £75 per sq m and, in addition to the cost of the fabric, incurs fixed and variable costs totalling £35 per sq m at the budgeted output. What will be the budgeted profit for each operating division, assuming a transfer pricing policy based on:

- variable cost;
- full cost; and
- market price?

Comment on your findings.

For Cornwall, the budgeted profit under each transfer pricing policy will be:

	Variable cost £000	Full cost £000	Market price £000
Revenue			
Devon (200,000 × 1.1):			
× £11	2,420		
× £24		5,280	
× £30			6,600
External market ((300,000 − (200,000 × 1.1)) × £30)	2,400	2,400	2,400
	4,820	7,680	9,000
Costs			
Variable (300,000 × £11)	(3,300)	(3,300)	(3,300)
Fixed (300,000 × £13)	(3,900)	(3,900)	(3,900)
Budgeted profit (loss)	(2,380)	480	1,800

For Devon, the budgeted profit under each transfer pricing policy will be:

	Variable cost £000	Full cost £000	Market price £000
Revenue			
200,000 × £75	15,000	15,000	15,000
Costs			
Fabric (200,000 × 1.1):			
× £11	(2,420)		
× £24		(5,280)	
× £30			(6,600)
Other costs (200,000 × £35)	(7,000)	(7,000)	(7,000)
Budgeted profit	5,580	2,720	1,400

We can see that Cornwall will make a significant loss under the variable cost policy. Most of the division's output must be sold to Devon and, while the surplus sold to the external market makes a contribution, it is not enough to cover the fixed cost. Cornwall manages to make a small profit under the full cost policy, which is entirely due to the sales to the outside market. If there were no external sales, the division would simply break even. When, however, transfer prices are set at market price, Cornwall makes a significant profit.

For Devon, the situation is reversed. It makes a significant profit under the variable cost policy but, when fabric prices are increased under the full cost policy, and then further increased under the market price policy, so the budgeted profit declines. Devon's profits, of course, are unaffected by Cornwall's sales to outside businesses.

Note that the same total profit (£3,200) will be made by Dorset Ltd, irrespective of which transfer price is used.

Differential transfer prices

There is no reason why, for a particular inter-divisional transaction, there cannot be two transfer prices. By setting the buying price, for the buying division, at one value and the selling price, for the selling division, at a different value, both divisions may be encouraged to act in the best interests of the business as a whole. This would mean that the overall profit for the business would not equal the sum of the profits of the individual divisions (as was the case in Activity 11.25). However, this is not necessarily a problem.

Real World 11.9 sets out transfer pricing guidelines for businesses operating in the water industry.

Real World 11.9

Thinking water

To protect the interests of customers, the UK government regulates the activities of water and sewerage businesses. Many of these businesses are part of large groups with diversified operations, some of which are not regulated. The government regulator, Ofwat, must therefore be assured that any transactions between the regulated water and sewerage activities, on the one hand, and other unregulated businesses, on the other, are not to the disadvantage of customers of the regulated activities. If, for example, water or sewerage services were charged to other unregulated businesses at a price below cost, or services bought in from other businesses were charged at a price above their market value, customers of the regulated water and sewerage services might have to bear an unfair share of the costs of the business as a whole.

To prevent this problem from occurring, the following transfer pricing guidelines are in place:

■ transfer prices for goods and services transferred in either direction should be fair; and
■ transfer prices for goods and services transferred in either direction should be based on market price, unless no market exists, when they should be based on cost.

Source: Ofwat (2015) *Guidelines for transfer pricing in the water and sewerage sectors: Regulatory accounting guideline 5.06*, ofwat.gov.uk, February, accessed 27 October 2016.

Real World 11.10 provides detail about the use of transfer pricing in US businesses.

Real World 11.10

Transfer pricing in practice

The Tang survey mentioned in Real World 11.6 (p. 428) found that the popularity of transfer pricing methods differed according to whether they were domestic transfers or international transfers. For domestic transfers, the results were as follows:

	%	%
Cost-based transfer prices		
– Full production cost	33	
– Full production cost plus mark-up	16	
– Other cost-based methods	4	53
Market-based transfer prices		26
Negotiated transfer prices		17
Other methods		4
		100

For international transfers, the results were:

	%	%
Cost-based transfer prices		
– Full production cost	14	
– Full production cost plus mark-up	28	
– Other cost-based methods	1	43
Market-based transfer prices		35
Negotiated transfer prices		14
Other methods		8
		100

We can see that there is greater reliance on methods that allow discretion in determining divisional profits when making international transfers.

Source: Tang, R. (2002) *Current Trends and Corporate Cases in Transfer Pricing*, Quorum Books.

Transfer pricing and service industries

There is no reason why a transfer between divisions need take the form of a physical object. A water utility business, for example, may have separate divisions for services such as IT, scientific testing and customer relations. These services may be bought by other divisions within the business providing water services. The transfer pricing issues raised earlier apply equally for these circumstances.

NON-FINANCIAL MEASURES OF PERFORMANCE

Individual divisions and businesses overall employ non-financial measures to evaluate performance. These measures can help managers cope with an uncertain environment: the greater the uncertainty of the environment, the greater the need for non-financial measures. They contribute to a broader and more complete range of information for managers, which should, in turn, contribute to a more balanced assessment of performance. It is not surprising, therefore, that these measures have taken on increasing importance in recent years.

The reporting of non-financial measures can provide a useful counterweight to the reporting of financial information. It is often the case that 'the things that count are the things that get counted'. That is, the degree of importance given to items will depend on whether they are readily measurable (as are revenue, profit and so on), irrespective of their real significance. Thus, where managers receive reports based exclusively on short-term financial performance measures, these become the main focus of attention. This can result in decisions that enhance these performance measures while other aspects of business performance are ignored. In an effort to increase annual profit, for example, a decision may be made to cut back on research and development costs. This, however, may seriously undermine the long-term viability of the business. To mitigate this risk, the reporting of non-financial measures concerning the quality and success of research and development can help provide a more complete picture.

Non-financial measures can also provide managers with insights that are difficult or impossible to gain with purely financial ones. For example, customer satisfaction is difficult to assess simply on the basis of financial values.

We saw in Chapter 10 that financial measures are normally 'lag indicators' that tell us about the outcomes of management decisions. Sales revenues and profits earned, for example, are both examples of lag indicators. Some non-financial measures are also lag indicators, but others may be 'lead indicators' that provide an insight into the elements that drive performance such as product quality, delivery times and innovation levels. It is, therefore, important to identify and measure the non-financial factors that are critical to future success. **Real World 11.11** is an article written by a senior executive of Enterprise Rent-a-Car, the car hire business. It provides an example of a non-financial measure that is used by Enterprise. This measure not only serves as a useful measure of customer satisfaction, but also is a vital lead indicator.

Real World 11.11

Is everybody happy?

"Completely satisfied" are two words every company wants to hear from its customers. It's a simple but effective performance yardstick.

This is the measure that Enterprise Rent-A-Car has used over the past 20 years to assess the quality of customer care offered by branch employees. It telephone surveys 100,000 customers every year just in the UK and measures how many say they are "completely satisfied" with the service they received. This is then rolled into a score – the Enterprise Service Quality Index or ESQi – which drives much of Enterprise's decision making.

ESQi helps the company go a step further. For rental branches, customer service measures are *the* performance measure. Employees cannot seek promotion unless their branch ESQi is at or above the average for the company. This ethos stems from company founder Jack Taylor, who believed that if you look after your customers, the profits will look after themselves.

The real value of ESQi as a management tool is that the data is collected at each individual branch. Branch managers have nowhere to hide if their customer service is not up to scratch. ESQi results – specifically the number of customers who were "completely satisfied" – are included in the branch's profit and loss statements. Customer service figures are important as any other result.

One of the most important lessons ESQi has taught Enterprise is that "completely satisfied" customers are three times more likely to be loyal customers or to recommend Enterprise to their friends than those who were only "somewhat satisfied".

Ultimately, customer satisfaction is more than just something for a company to be proud of. It is a key component of business success. In this way, ESQi became more than just supplementary data. It keeps managers focussed and reinforces the company message that customer satisfaction is a cornerstone of the business model. Profit on its own is not enough.

This focus on customer satisfaction continues to determine the sort of person that gets ahead at Enterprise. ESQi scores follow employees from one job to the next. Managers won't get promoted without a consistently high ESQi score. It simply doesn't matter how high your sales and profit is. Without a good record of demonstrable passion for excellent customer service, reward and promotion will not come.

Source: Extracts from Swallow, B. (2014) *ESQi: Why is a 20-year-old service measure still so influential*? http://www.mycustomer.com/service/management/esqi-why-is-a-20-year-old-service-measure-still-so-influential, May.

What is measured?

Some of the main areas covered by non-financial measures include:

■ *Research and development (R&D) achievement.* For some businesses, R&D is vital to long-term success. Developing suitable measures relating to the quality and success of R&D outcomes may therefore be useful. These might include the number of innovations successfully launched, the percentage of total sales revenue arising from new products, and the time taken to bring a new product to market.

■ *Staff training and morale.* It is a modern-day mantra that the employees are the most valuable assets of a business. If this is the case, it is useful to know how the managers are cultivating this resource. Staff training may be measured directly by such means as the number of training days per employee, or indirectly through measures of customer satisfaction. Staff morale may be revealed by staff turnover, absenteeism levels and attitude surveys.

■ *Product/service quality.* In a competitive environment, the quality of the products and services offered is of vital importance. Measures such as number of product defects, percentage of scrap, number of warranty claims and number of customer complaints may be important.

■ *Market share.* The percentage share of total sales generated within a particular market can help to assess the success of the product range.

■ *Environmental and social concerns.* In highly industrialised societies, there is increasing pressure on businesses to acknowledge their responsibility towards the environment and to assess the impact of their activities on the communities in which they are based. An assessment of the policies on such matters as pollution, wildlife protection and employment of minorities can be carried out to see whether the business is being a good 'corporate citizen'.

Although this is not an exhaustive list of areas, it nevertheless provides a flavour of what non-financial measures can cover.

Activity 11.26

Bling plc operates a chain of high street shops selling costume jewellery to those in the 18 to 30 age range. The business aims to sell products that are both highly fashionable and of good quality, and tries to ensure that customers are provided with a wide range from which to choose.

Suggest *four* non-financial measures that may help the business to assess its performance in achieving these aims.

Possible non-financial measures include:

■ the percentage of new products that were 'first to market';
■ the percentage of sales revenue from new products;
■ the percentage of returned items;
■ the number of customer complaints concerning quality;
■ customer satisfaction scores;
■ the number of different types of product available for sale;
■ the percentage of items unable to be supplied due to insufficient inventories;
■ the average inventories turnover period; and
■ the percentage share of the market in which the business competes.

You may have thought of others.

Real World 11.12 provides some impression of the kind of non-financial measures that are regarded as important by management accountants in manufacturing businesses.

Real World 11.12

Rank-and-file measures

A study by Abdel-Maksoud and others asked management accountants employed in 313 UK manufacturing businesses to assess the importance of 19 'shop floor' non-financial measures. The accountants were asked to rank the measures on a scale ranging from 1 (low) to 7 (high). The mean importance accorded to each of the 19 measures is set out in Figure 11.9.

% of businesses using measure	Measure	Mean importance
92	On-time delivery	6.4
95	Number of complaints from customers	6.2
91	Number of customer returns	5.9
90	Efficiency (std hrs produced/worked)	5.8
87	Defects (% of total production)	5.8
90	Scrap (% of total production)	5.7
97	Absenteeism	5.5
70	Number of warranty claims	5.5
62	Manufacturing cycle efficiency	5.3
86	Activity (std hrs produced/budgeted std hrs)	5.3
84	Capacity utilisation (hrs worked/budgeted hrs)	5.3
92	Proportion of overtime worked	5.3
68	% schedule adherence	5.2
76	% on-time production	5.2
84	Rework (% of total production)	5.2
90	Employee lateness	4.9
89	Staff turnover	4.6
63	Employee attitudes	4.5
56	Batches (% adjusted)	4.1

We can see that the degree of importance attached to the 19 'shop floor' financial measures identified varies, but all are located at the upper end of the scale.

Figure 11.9 Importance attached to various non-financial measures by management accountants

We can see that the first three measures relate to customers. This is followed by four measures relating to cost control and the efficiency of processes.

Source: Abdel-Maksoud, A., Dugdale, D. and Luther, R. (2005) Non-financial performance measurement in manufacturing companies, The British Accounting Review, Vol. 37, Issue 3, pp. 261–297.

Choosing non-financial measures

There is an almost infinite number of non-financial measures that may be reported; however, it would not be sensible to report too many. Managers may become overloaded, which would undermine rather than improve the quality of decision making. It would also add significantly to the costs of gathering and reporting information. Choices must be made and the measures chosen must reflect some logic and coherence. What is needed is a set of non-financial measures that deal with the things that really matter and fit into a logical framework.

Activity 11.27

Can you suggest how this might be done? (*Hint*: Think back to a particular approach that we discussed in Chapter 10.)

A useful approach would be to employ the balanced scorecard. We may recall that this provides a coherent framework and attempts to translate the aims and objectives of the business into a series of key performance measures and targets. In this way, strategy is linked more closely to particular measures. The choice of measure (either financial or non-financial) would then be determined according to its value in achieving the agreed strategy.

Real World 11.13 provides some evidence of the popularity of the balanced scorecard among UK divisionalised businesses.

Real World 11.13

A balanced measure

The study by Drury and El-Shishini mentioned earlier asked senior financial managers of divisionalised businesses about the approaches used to incorporate non-financial measures. Of the 97 respondents, 55 per cent adopted the balanced scorecard approach for the business as a whole; 43 per cent also used this approach to evaluate divisional performance.

Source: Drury, C. and El-Shishini, E. (2005) *Divisional Performance Measurement: An Examination of Potential Explanatory Factors*, CIMA Research Report, August, p. 31.

Who should report?

We saw in Chapter 1 that management accounting assesses performance through both financial and non-financial measures. Indeed, reporting non-financial measures, such as budgeted units of production, can be traced back to the early years of the development of the subject. However, the scale and importance of non-financial measures have increased dramatically in recent years and this has raised questions as to whether it should be the management accountant's responsibility to report such measures. Although many see it as a natural development of the management accountant's role, some believe that it will lead to unbalanced reports. There is a fear that financial measures will dominate, resulting in an emphasis on lag indicators rather than lead indicators.

Real World 11.14 provides some evidence to support the view that management accountants consider financial measures to be more important than non-financial measures.

Finance matters

The study by Drury and El-Shishini mentioned earlier asked senior financial managers about the relative importance of financial and non-financial measures for assessing divisional performance. To do this, a seven-point scale was used where 1 represented the view that financial measures were considerably more important than non-financial measures, 7 represented the view that non-financial measures were considerably more important than financial ones, and 4 represented a midpoint which reflected the view that they were of about the same importance. The managers' scores were as follows:

	%
Financial measures more important (scores 1 to 3)	71
Financial and non-financial measures of equal importance (score 4)	18
Non-financial measures more important (scores 5 to 7)	11
	100

Source: Drury, C. and El-Shishini, E. (2005) *Divisional Performance Measurement: An Examination of Potential Explanatory Factors*, CIMA Research Report, August, pp. 31 and 32.

Despite the above, it is worth remembering, however, that, over time, management accountants have strengthened their position at the heart of decision making. This could only have been achieved by responding to the changing needs of business. We should not, therefore, assume that they are unwilling or unable to take on new challenges.

Self-assessment question 11.1

Andromeda International plc has two operating divisions, the managers of which are given considerable autonomy. To assess the performance of divisional managers, senior management uses ROI. For the purposes of this measure the assets employed include both non-current and current assets. The business has a minimum acceptable ROI of 15 per cent a year and uses the straight-line method of depreciation for external reporting purposes.

Extracts from the budgets for each of the two divisions for next year are as follows:

	Jupiter division	Mars division
	£000	£000
Divisional profit	260	50
Non-current assets at cost	940	1,200
Current assets	390	180

Since the budgets were prepared, two investment opportunities have been brought to the attention of the relevant divisional managers. These are as follows:

1 Senior management would like to see the productivity of the Mars division improve. To help achieve this, they have authorised the divisional manager to buy some new equipment costing £300,000. This will have a life of five years and will lead to operating savings of £90,000 each year.

2 A new product can be sold by the Jupiter division. This will increase sales revenue by £250,000 each year over the next five years. It will be necessary to increase marketing costs by £60,000 a year and inventories held will increase by £90,000. The contribution margin ratio (that is, contribution to sales revenue × 100%) for the new product will be 30 per cent.

Required:

(a) Calculate the expected ROI for each division assuming:

    (1) the investment opportunities are not taken up; and

    (2) the investment opportunities are taken up.

(b) Comment on the results obtained in (a) and state how the divisional managers and senior managers might view the investment opportunities.

(c) Discuss the implications of using net book value (that is, cost after accumulated depreciation) rather than gross book value (that is, before accumulated depreciation) as a basis for valuing non-current assets when calculating ROI.

(d) A product sold by Jupiter division requires a component that it currently buys from an outside supplier. There are plans that next year the Mars division should make the required components and 'sell' them to Jupiter. This will give rise to managers having to set an internal transfer price for the components.

    Outline what objective an effective transfer price should achieve, what (in theory) an ideal transfer price should be based on and what (in this particular case) is likely to be the basis of the transfer price.

The solution to this question can be found at the back of the book on pp. 523–524.

SUMMARY

The main points of this chapter may be summarised as follows:

Divisionalisation

- Businesses tend to operate through responsibility centres.
- Responsibility centres are typically
  - cost centres, which have responsibility for managing costs;
  - profit centres, which have responsibility for managing revenues and costs; and
  - investment centres, which have responsibility for managing most aspects including investment.
- Responsibility centres allow responsibility accounting (that is, managers being held accountable for their particular area) to be carried out.
- Most large businesses operate through divisions.
- Divisions tend to be either profit centres or investment centres.
- Divisionalisation is usually made according to
  - product or service, or
  - geographical location.
- Benefits of divisionalisation are said to include
  - better access to market information;
  - motivating middle and junior managers;
  - developing managers through experience;
  - better use of specialised knowledge;
  - allowing senior managers to deal with strategic issues; and
  - enabling timely decision making.

- Problems of divisionalisation are said to include
  - goal conflict between divisions;
  - excessive avoidance of risky courses of action;
  - excessive management 'perks';
  - costly duplication of facilities and other losses of economies of scale; and
  - divisions competing with each other to the detriment of the business as a whole.

Divisional performance measurement

- Various measures of divisional profit exist. The most suitable measure will depend on the purpose for which it will be used.
- Return on investment (ROI) = (divisional profit/divisional investment) × 100%.
  - Can be broken down into a profit margin and an asset turnover element.
  - Definitions of the divisional profit and divisional investment can vary – whatever definitions are used need to be consistent.
- ROI is a comparative (percentage) measure that can mislead.
  - Can lead to the rejection of beneficial activities because they lower the ROI despite generating wealth.
  - Tends to focus on the short term.
- Residual income (RI) = divisional profit less a capital charge (investment × cost of capital).
  - Relates to wealth generated.
  - An absolute measure (£s), not a percentage.
  - Tends to focus on the short term.
- RI is generally considered a better performance indicator than ROI.
- Assessing divisional performance requires some basis for comparison, such as:
  - other divisions of the same business;
  - previous performance of the same division;
  - performance of businesses within the same industry as the division; and
  - budgeted (planned) performance – probably the best basis of comparison.
- EVA® may also be used to measure divisional performance.

Transfer pricing

- Involves setting prices for transfers (sales and purchases) between divisions of the same business.
- An important issue because transfer prices have a direct effect on divisional profit and therefore on ROI and RI.
- Transfer pricing has the following objectives:
  - promoting divisional independence;
  - providing a basis for measuring effectiveness;
  - promoting the objectives of the business as a whole;
  - allocating resources provided for individual divisions; and
  - minimising tax charges.
- The best transfer prices are based on the opportunity cost for both divisions.

- In practice, the following are found:

  - Market prices – usually best because they tend to represent the opportunity cost; however, a market may not exist in practice.
  - Variable cost – represents the opportunity cost to a supplying division with spare capacity.
  - Full cost, usually plus a profit loading – rarely reflects the opportunity cost and tends to pass on inefficiencies.
  - Negotiated prices – enable the divisions to act as independent businesses but can be unfair.

Non-financial measures

- Non-financial measures have increased in importance due to environmental uncertainty.
- Possible areas for measurement include:

  - research and development;
  - staff training and morale;
  - product/service quality;
  - market share; and
  - environmental and social concerns.

- Non-financial measures should be integrated with financial measures into a logical framework, such as the balanced scorecard.
- Management accountants often take responsibility for reporting non-financial measures,

KEY TERMS

For definitions of these terms, see Appendix A.

Division p. 408	**Non-controllable cost** p. 416
Responsibility centre p. 408	**Return on investment (ROI)** p. 418
Profit centre p. 408	**Residual income (RI)** p. 422
Investment centre p. 408	**Transfer pricing** p. 427
Responsibility accounting p. 409	**Market price** p. 432
Controllable cost p. 416	**Negotiated price** p. 435

FURTHER READING

If you would like to explore the topics covered in this chapter in more depth, we recommend the following:

Bhimani, A., Horngren, C., Datar, S. and Rajan, M. (2015) *Management and Cost Accounting*, 6th edn, Pearson, Chapter 18.

Burns, J., Quinn, M., Warren, L. and Oliveira, J. (2013) *Management Accounting*, McGraw-Hill Education, Chapter 18.

Drury, C. (2015) *Management and Cost Accounting*, 9th edn, Cengage Learning EMEA, Chapters 19 and 20.

Hilton, R. and Platt, D. (2014) *Managerial Accounting*, McGraw-Hill Higher Education, Chapter 13.

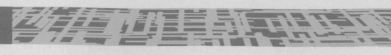
Solutions to these questions can be found at the back of the book on p. 533.

11.1 What problems might be encountered when a business attempts to incorporate non-financial measures into its management reports?

11.2 Westcott Supplies Ltd has an operating division that produces a single product. In addition to the conventional RI and ROI measures, central management wishes to use other methods of measuring performance and productivity to help assess the division.

Identify four possible measures (financial or non-financial) that top management may decide to use.

11.3 Jerry and Co. is a large computer consultancy business that has a division specialising in robotics. Can you identify three *non-financial measures* that might be used to help assess the performance of this division?

11.4 A UK survey of decentralised businesses revealed that negotiated prices are the most popular form of transfer pricing method.

Is this necessarily the best approach in theory? Why?

EXERCISES

Exercises with coloured numbers have solutions given at the back of the book on pp. 568–571.

Basic-level exercises

11.1 'In divisionalised organisations, complete autonomy of action is impossible when a substantial level of inter-divisional transfers take place.'

Required:
(a) In this context, explain what is meant by 'divisionalised organisation' and 'autonomy of action'.
(b) What are the benefits of this autonomy?
(c) Are there any dangers from permitting autonomy of action and in what ways do inter-divisional transfers make complete autonomy impossible?

11.2 Measures are required to assess the performance of divisions and of divisional managers. Three financial measures are:

- contribution;
- controllable profit; and
- return on investment (ROI).

Required:
(a) For each of the these measures explain:
- the way in which each measure is calculated;
- for what purpose they are most suitably applied; and
- the weaknesses of each method.
(b) Suggest three different non-financial measures of performance that may be appropriate to an operating division and consider how such measures, in general, offer improvements when used in conjunction with financial measures.

11.3 You have recently taken a management post in a large divisionalised business. A substantial proportion of the business of your division is undertaken through inter-divisional transfers.

Required:
(a) What are the objectives of a system of transfer pricing?
(b) Describe the use of, and problems associated with, transfer prices based on
- variable cost; and
- full cost.

(c) Where an external market exists, to what extent is market price an improvement on cost?

Intermediate-level exercises

11.4 The following information applies to the planned operations of Division A of ABC Corporation for next year:

	£
Sales revenue (100,000 units at £12)	1,200,000
Variable cost (100,000 units at £8)	800,000
Fixed cost (including depreciation)	250,000
Division A investment (at original cost)	500,000

The minimum desired rate of return on investment is the cost of capital of 20 per cent a year.

The business is highly profit-conscious and delegates a considerable level of autonomy to divisional managers. As part of a procedure to review planned operations of Division A, a meeting has been convened to consider two options:

Option X
Division A may sell a further 20,000 units at £11 to customers outside ABC Corporation. Variable costs per unit will be the same as budgeted but, to enable capacity to increase by 20,000 units, one extra piece of equipment will be required costing £80,000. The equipment will have a four-year life and the business depreciates assets on a straight-line basis. No extra fixed costs will occur.

Option Y
Included in the current plan of operations of Division A is the sale of 20,000 units to Division B also within ABC Corporation. A competitor of Division A, from outside ABC Corporation, has offered to supply Division B at £10 per unit. Division A intends to adopt a strategy of matching the price quoted from outside ABC Corporation to retain the order.

Required:

(a) Calculate Division A's residual income based on:
(1) the original planned operation;
(2) Option X only added to the original plan; and
(3) Option Y only added to the original plan
and briefly interpret the results of the options as they affect Division A.
(b) Assess the implications for Division A, Division B and the ABC Corporation as a whole of Option Y, bearing in mind that if Division A does not compete on price, it will lose the 20,000 units order from Division B. Make any recommendations you consider appropriate.

11.5 The following information applies to the budgeted operations of the Goodman division of the Telling Company:

	£
Sales revenue (50,000 units at £8)	400,000
Variable cost (50,000 units at £6)	(300,000)
Contribution	100,000
Fixed cost	(75,000)
Divisional profit for the period	25,000
Divisional investment	150,000

The minimum desired return on investment is the cost of capital of 20 per cent a year.

Required:

(a) (1) Calculate the divisional expected ROI (return on investment).
  (2) Calculate the division's expected RI (residual income).
  (3) Comment on the results of (1) and (2).

(b) The division has the opportunity to sell an additional 10,000 units at £7.50. Variable cost per unit would be the same as budgeted, but fixed costs would increase by £5,000. Additional investment of £20,000 would be required. If the manager accepted this opportunity, by how much and in what direction would the residual income change?

(c) Goodman expects to sell 10,000 units of its budgeted volume of 50,000 units to Sharp, another division of the Telling Company. An outside business has promised to supply the 10,000 units to Sharp at £7.20. If Goodman does not meet the £7.20 price, Sharp will buy from the outside business. Goodman will not save any part of the fixed cost if the work goes outside, but the variable cost will be avoided completely.

  (1) Show the effect on the total profit of the Telling Company if Goodman meets the £7.20 price.
  (2) Show the effect on the total profit of the Telling Company if Goodman does not meet the price and the work goes outside.

11.6 Glasnost plc is a large business organised on divisional lines. Two typical divisions are East and West. They are engaged in broadly similar activities and, therefore, central management compares their results to help it to make judgements on managerial performance. Both divisions are regarded as investment centres.

A summary of last year's financial results of the two divisions is as follows:

	West		East	
	£000	£000	£000	£000
Capital employed		2,500		500
Sales revenue		1,000		400
Manufacturing cost:				
Direct	(300)		(212)	
Indirect	(220)		(48)	
Selling and distribution cost	(180)	(700)	(40)	(300)
Divisional profit		300		100
Apportionment of uncontrollable common overhead costs		(50)		(20)
Profit for the period		250		80

At the beginning of last year, West division incurred substantial expenditure on automated production lines and new equipment. East has quite old plant. Approximately 50 per cent of the sales revenue of East comes from internal transfers to other divisions within the business. These transfers are based on an unadjusted prevailing market price. The inter-divisional transfers of West are minimal.

Management of the business focuses on return on investment as a major performance indicator. The required minimum rate of return is the business's cost of capital of 10 per cent a year.

Required:

(a) Compute any ratios (or other measures) that you consider will help in an assessment of the costs and performance of the two divisions.

(b) Comment on this performance, making reference to any matters that give cause for concern when comparing the divisions or in divisional performance generally.

Advanced-level exercises

11.7 The University of Devonport consists of six faculties and an administration unit. Under the university's management philosophy, each faculty is treated, as far as is reasonable, as an independent entity. Each faculty is responsible for its own budget and financial decision making.

A new course in the Faculty of Geography (FG) requires some input from a member of staff of the Faculty of Modern Languages (FML).

The two faculties are in dispute about the 'price' that FG should pay FML for each hour of the staff member's time. FML argues that the hourly rate should be £175. This is based on the FML budget for this year, which in broad outline is as follows:

	£000
Academic staff salaries (25 staff)	1,062
Faculty overheads (nearly all fixed costs)	903
	1,965

Each academic is expected to teach on average for 15 hours a week for 33 weeks a year.

FML wishes to charge FG an hourly rate which will cover the appropriate proportion of the member of staff's salary plus a 'fair' share of the overheads plus 10 per cent for a small surplus.

FG is refusing to pay this rate. One of FG's arguments is that it should not have to bear any other cost than the appropriate share of the salary. FG also argues that it could find a lecturer who works at the nearby University of Tavistock and is prepared to do the work for £50 an hour, as an additional, spare-time activity.

FML argues that it has deliberately staffed itself at a level which will enable it to cover FG's requirements and that the price must therefore cover the costs.

The university's Vice-Chancellor (its most senior manager) has been asked to resolve the dispute. You are the university's finance manager.

Required:

Make notes in preparation for a meeting with the Vice-Chancellor, where you will discuss the problem with her. The Vice-Chancellor is a historian by background and is not familiar with financial matters. Your notes will therefore need to be expressed in language that an intelligent layperson can understand.

Your notes should deal both with the objectives of effective transfer prices and with the specifics of this case. You should raise any issues that you think might be relevant.

11.8 AB Ltd operates retail stores throughout the country. The business is divisionalised. Included in its business are Divisions A and B. A centralised and automated warehouse that replenishes inventories using computer-based systems supports the work of these divisions.

For many years AB Ltd has given considerable autonomy to divisional managers and has emphasised return on investment (ROI) as a composite performance measure. This is calculated after apportionment of all actual costs and assets of the business and 'its appropriate service facilities', which includes the costs and assets of the warehouse.

The following information is available for last year:

	Division A		Division B	
	Actual £m	Budget £m	Actual £m	Budget £m
Sales revenue	30.0	50.0	110.0	96.0
Assets employed	20.0		48.0	
Operating profit	4.3		14.7	

These actual figures do not include the apportioned costs or assets of the automated warehouse shared by the two divisions. The data available for the warehouse facility for last year are:

	Warehouse	
	Actual £m	Budget £m
Despatches (that is, sales revenue)	140.0	146.0
Assets employed at book value	8.0	8.0
Operating cost:		
Depreciation	1.6	1.6
Other elements of fixed cost	1.1	0.9
Variable storage cost	0.6	0.5
Variable handling cost	1.3	1.1
Total operating cost	4.6	4.1

When the warehouse investment was authorised it was agreed that the assets employed and the actual expenses were to be apportioned between the divisions concerned in the proportions originally agreed (50 per cent each). However, it was also pointed out that in the future the situation could be redesigned and there was no need for one single basis to apply. For example, the space occupied by inventories of the two divisions is now A 40 per cent and B 60 per cent. This information could be used in the apportionment of assets and expenses.

Required:

(a) (1) Calculate the actual return on investment (ROI) for Divisions A and B after incorporating the warehouse assets and actual costs apportioned on an equal basis as originally agreed.

(2) What basis of apportionment of assets and actual costs would the manager of Division A argue for, in order to maximise the reported ROI of the division? How would you anticipate that the manager of Division B might react?

(b) It has been pointed out that a combination of bases of apportionment may be used instead of just one, such as the space occupied by inventories (A 40 per cent, B 60 per cent) or the level of actual or budgeted sales revenue. If you were given the freedom to revise the calculation, what bases of apportionment would you recommend in the circumstances? Discuss your approach and recalculate the ROI of Division A on your recommended basis.

Work to two places of decimals only.

Chapter 12

MANAGING WORKING CAPITAL

INTRODUCTION

This chapter considers the factors to be taken into account when managing the working capital of a business. Each element of working capital will be identified and the major issues surrounding them will be discussed. Working capital represents a significant investment for many businesses and so its proper management and control can be vital. We saw in Chapter 8 that an investment in working capital is typically an important aspect of many new investment proposals.

Learning outcomes

When you have completed this chapter, you should be able to:

- Identify the main elements of working capital.
- Discuss the purpose of working capital and the nature of the working capital cycle.
- Explain the importance of establishing policies for the control of working capital.
- Explain the factors that have to be taken into account when managing each element of working capital.

WHAT IS WORKING CAPITAL?

Working capital is usually defined as current assets less current liabilities. The major elements of current assets are:

■ inventories;
■ trade receivables; and
■ cash (in hand and at bank).

The major elements of current liabilities are:

■ trade payables; and
■ bank overdrafts.

The size and composition of working capital can vary between industries. For some types of business, the investment in working capital can be substantial. A manufacturing business, for example, will often invest heavily in raw material, work in progress and finished goods. It will also normally sell its goods on credit, giving rise to trade receivables. A retailer, meanwhile, holds only one form of inventories (finished goods) and will normally sell its goods for cash rather than on credit. Many service businesses hold no inventories.

Most businesses buy goods and/or services on credit, giving rise to trade payables. Few, if any, businesses operate without a cash balance. In some cases, however, it is a negative one (a bank overdraft).

Working capital represents a net investment in short-term assets. These assets are continually flowing into and out of the business and are essential for day-to-day operations. The various elements of working capital are interrelated and can be seen as part of a short-term cycle. For a manufacturing business, the working capital cycle can be depicted as shown in Figure 12.1.

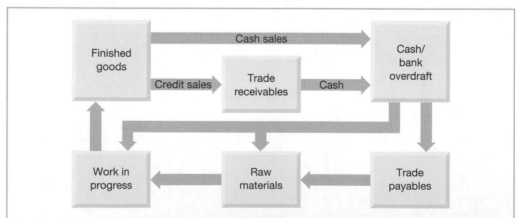

Cash is used to pay trade payables for raw materials, or raw materials are bought for immediate cash settlement. Cash is also spent on labour and other items that turn raw materials into work in progress and, finally, into finished goods. The finished goods are sold to customers either for cash or on credit. In the case of credit customers, there will be a delay before the cash is received from the sales. Receipt of cash completes the cycle.

Figure 12.1 The working capital cycle

For a retailer, the situation would be as in Figure 12.1 except that there will be only inventories of finished goods. There will be no work in progress or raw materials. For a purely service business, the working capital cycle would also be similar to that depicted in

Figure 12.1 except that there would be no inventories of finished goods or raw materials. There may well be work in progress, however, since many forms of service take time to complete. A case handled by a firm of solicitors, for example, may take several months. During this period, costs will build up before the client is billed for them.

MANAGING WORKING CAPITAL

The management of working capital is an essential part of the business's short-term planning process. Management must decide how much of each element should be held. As we shall see later, there are costs associated with holding either too much or too little of each element. Management must be aware of these costs, which include opportunity costs, in order to manage working capital effectively. Potential benefits must then be weighed against likely costs and so achieve the optimum investment.

The working capital needs of a business are likely to vary over time as a result of changes in the business environment. Managers must monitor these changes to ensure that the business retains an appropriate level of investment in working capital.

Activity 12.1

What kinds of changes in the business environment might lead to a decision to change the level of investment in working capital? Try to identify four possible changes that could affect the working capital needs of a business.

These may include the following:

- changes in interest rates;
- changes in market demand for the business's output;
- changes in the seasons; and
- changes in the state of the economy.

You may have thought of others.

Changes arising within the business could also alter working capital needs. These internal changes might include using different production methods (resulting, perhaps, in a need to hold a lower level of inventories) and changes in the level of risk that managers are prepared to take.

THE SCALE OF WORKING CAPITAL

It is tempting to think that, compared with the scale of investment in non-current assets, the amounts invested in working capital are trivial. However, this is not the case. For many businesses, the scale of investment in working capital is vast.

Real World 12.1 gives some impression of the working capital investment for five UK businesses that are either very well known by name, or whose products are everyday commodities for most of us. These businesses were randomly selected, except that each one is high profile and from a different industry. For each business, the major items appearing on the statement of financial position are expressed as a percentage of the total investment by the providers of long-term finance (equity and non-current liabilities).

A summary of the statements of financial position of five UK businesses

Business:	Next plc	Ryanair Holdings plc	Babcock In. Group plc	Tesco plc	Severn Trent plc
Statement of financial position date:	30.1.16	31.3.16	31.3.16	27.2.16	31.3.16
Non-current assets	59	82	106	120	102
Current assets					
Inventories	42	–	3	10	–
Trade and other receivables	91	1	18	7	7
Other current assets	3	44	1	31	2
Cash and near cash	6	16	4	13	1
	142	61	26	61	10
Total assets	201	143	132	181	112
Equity and non-current liabilities	100	100	100	100	100
Current liabilities					
Trade and other payables	58	30	28	35	7
Other short-term liabilities	13	13	1	34	1
Overdrafts and short-term borrowings	30	–	3	12	4
	101	43	32	81	12
Total equity and non-current liabilities	201	143	132	181	112

The non-current assets, current assets and current liabilities are expressed as a percentage of the total long-term investment (equity plus non-current liabilities) of the business concerned. Next plc is a major retail and home shopping business. Ryanair is a leading airline. Babcock International Group plc is a large engineering and support business. Tesco plc is one of the UK's leading supermarkets. Severn Trent plc is an important supplier of water, sewerage services and waste management, mainly in the UK.

Source: Table constructed from information appearing in the financial statements for the year ended during 2016 for each of the five businesses concerned.

Real World 12.1 reveals quite striking differences in the make-up of the statement of financial position from one business to the next. Take, for example, the current assets and current liabilities. Although the totals for current assets are pretty large when compared with the total long-term investment, these percentages vary considerably between businesses. When looking at the mix of current assets, we can see that only Next, Babcock and Tesco, which produce and/or sell goods, hold some inventories. The other two businesses are service providers and so inventories are an insignificant item. We can also see that very few of the sales of Tesco, Ryanair and Severn Trent are on credit, as they have relatively little invested in trade receivables.

Note that Tesco's trade payables are much higher than its inventories. Since trade payables represent amounts due to suppliers of inventories, it means that Tesco receives the cash from a typical trolley load of groceries well in advance of paying for them. The relatively large 'Other current assets' and 'Other short-term liabilities' for Tesco arises from advances to and deposits from customers, respectively, that arise from the business's involvement in banking.

In the sections that follow, we shall consider each element of working capital separately and how they might be properly managed. Before doing so, however, it is worth looking at **Real World 12.2**, which suggests that there is considerable scope for improving working capital management among European businesses.

Working capital not working hard enough

According to a survey of 1,000 of Europe's largest businesses (excluding financial and auto manufacturing businesses), working capital is not as well managed as it could be. The survey, conducted in 2015 by Ernst and Young, suggests that larger European businesses had, in total, between €280 billion and €480 billion tied up in working capital that could be released through better management of inventories, trade receivables and trade payables. The potential for savings represents between 11 per cent and 19 per cent of the total working capital invested and between 4 per cent and 7 per cent of total sales. The lower figure of each range is calculated by comparing the results for each business with the results for the average for the industry, and the higher figure is calculated by comparing the results for each business with the upper quartile (that is the best performing 25 per cent of businesses) of the industry within which that business operates.

The report suggests that the higher figure for each range probably represents an ambitious target for savings as, across Europe, there are wide variations in payment terms, customer types, discount practices and so on.

The average investment (in days) for each of the five years to 2015, by the largest 1,000 European businesses, for each of the main elements of working capital is set out in Figure 12.2. As the figure shows, the working capital performance of businesses has not altered very much over the period. Within each average, however, some businesses have improved and some have deteriorated.

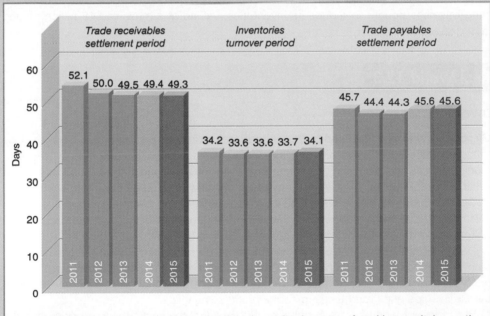

The figure shows very little change, overall, in the main elements of working capital over the five-year period.

Figure 12.2 Average investment (in days) for the main working capital elements

The survey results also revealed that there are slightly lower levels of working capital held by large US businesses than by their European counterparts.

Source: Compiled from information in *All Tied Up: Working Capital Management Report 2016 and 2015*, Ernst and Young, www.ey.com.

Real World 12.2 focuses on the working capital problems of large businesses. For smaller businesses, however, these problems may be even more acute.

Activity 12.2

Why might smaller businesses carry more excess working capital than larger ones?

Smaller businesses are less well resourced in terms of people, expertise and technology. This can lead to difficulties in controlling the level of working capital.

MANAGING INVENTORIES

A business may hold inventories for various reasons, the most common of which is to meet the immediate day-to-day requirements of customers and production. However, a business may hold more than is necessary for this purpose where there is a risk that future supplies may be interrupted or scarce. Similarly, if there is a risk that the cost of inventories will increase in the future, a business may decide to buy in large quantities.

Mining businesses and businesses that trade in commodities, such as precious metals, oil, coffee and so on, can benefit by holding large amounts of inventories when commodity prices are rising. When prices are falling, however, large inventories' holdings can be a burden. **Real World 12.3** is an extract from an article that describes how one commodities' trading and mining business sought to reduce its inventories, valued at a massive $18 billion, during a recent downturn.

Real World 12.3

Inventories overload

Glencore plc has been battered by the global downturn in commodities prices. Sources close to the company say it is also reducing its vast trading inventories. "If you look at where commodities prices are today and how the market conditions changed in the past six months - it is fair to say that the only way for inventories is to go down," a source close to Glencore said.

Despite the steep fall in commodities prices since last year, the total value of Glencore's inventories have barely budged, another way of saying that the volume of hydrocarbons, metals and other commodities the business is holding has ballooned in size.

Under the conditions in place at the start of 2015, traders expected the price of oil to recover from last year's steep falls. The cost of buying and storing it was lower than the price for contracts to deliver it in future months. Traders responded by storing millions of barrels in ships and inland tanks to earn a profit selling it later.

But in recent months, with a global oil glut growing, the cost of storage rising and the market now expecting low prices to persist longer, future prices for many commodities have fallen closer to, or lower than, spot (immediate) prices. That means there is less to be earned from holding inventories.

Hence traders ranging from BP to Vitol have been reducing inventories. When Glencore presents investors with an update it will most likely show a cut in inventories of billions of dollars.

Source: Extracts from McFarlane, S. and Zhdannikov, D. (2015) Glencore shrinking its $18 bn commodity inventory mountain, www.reuters.com, 29 October.

For some types of business, inventories held may represent a substantial proportion of total assets held. For example, a car dealership that rents its premises may have nearly all of its total assets in the form of inventories. Manufacturers also tend to invest heavily in inventories, as they typically need to hold three kinds of inventories: raw materials, work in progress and finished goods. Each form of inventories represents a particular stage in the production cycle.

For businesses with seasonal demand, the level of inventories held may vary substantially over the year. One such example might be greetings card manufacturers. For those businesses with fairly stable demand, the level of inventories held may vary little from one month to the next.

Businesses that hold inventories simply to meet the day-to-day requirements of their customers, and for production, will normally seek to minimise the amount of inventories held. This is because there are significant costs associated with holding inventories. These costs include:

- storage and handling costs;
- the cost of financing the inventories;
- the cost of pilferage and obsolescence; and
- the cost of opportunities forgone in tying up funds in this form of asset.

To gain some impression of the cost involved in holding inventories, **Real World 12.4** estimates the *financing* cost of inventories for five large businesses.

Real World 12.4

Inventories financing cost

The financing cost of inventories for each of five large businesses, based on their respective opportunity costs of capital, is calculated below.

Business	Type of operations	Cost of capital (a) %	Average inventories held* (b) £m	Financing cost of holding inventories (a) × (b) £m	Operating profit £m	Financing cost as a % of operating profit/(loss) %
Associated British Foods plc	Food producer	12.2	1,729	210	947	22.2
Babcock International Group plc	Engineering and business support	9.1	147.2	13.4	352.5	3.8
Go-ahead Group plc	Transport operator	8.8	18.1	1.6	117.4	1.4
Kingfisher plc	DIY retailer	7.4	1989	147.2	526	30.0
J Sainsbury plc	Supermarket	9.0	982.5	88.4	707	12.5

* Based on opening and closing inventories for the relevant financial period.

We can see that for three of the five businesses, inventories financing costs are significant in relation to their operating profits. The nature of their businesses requires Associated British Foods, Kingfisher and Sainsbury to invest heavily in inventories. Sainsbury, however, is likely to turn over its inventories more quickly than the other three. For Go-ahead inventories

→

financing costs are not significant. This is because it is a service provider with a much lower investment in inventories.

These figures do not take account of other costs of inventories' holding mentioned earlier, such as the cost of providing secure storage. As these other costs may easily outweigh the costs of finance, the total cost of maintaining inventories may be very high in relation to operating profits.

The five businesses were not selected because they have particularly high inventories' costs but simply because they are among the relatively few that publish their costs of capital.

Source: Annual reports of the businesses for the years ended during 2015 and 2016.

Given the potentially high cost of holding inventories, it may be tempting to think that a business should seek to hold few or no inventories. There are, however, costs that may arise when the level of inventories is too low.

Activity 12.3

What costs might a business incur as a result of holding too low a level of inventories? Try to jot down at least three types of cost.

In answering this activity you may have thought of the following costs:

- loss of sales, from being unable to provide the goods required immediately;
- loss of customer goodwill, for being unable to satisfy customer demand;
- purchasing inventories at a higher price than might otherwise have been necessary to replenish inventories quickly;
- high transport costs incurred to ensure that inventories are replenished quickly;
- lost production due to shortage of raw materials; and
- inefficient production scheduling due to shortages of raw materials.

To help manage inventories, a number of procedures and techniques may be employed. We shall now consider the more important of these.

Budgeting future demand

Preparing appropriate budgets is one of the best ways to ensure that inventories will be available to meet future production and sales requirements. These budgets should deal with each inventories item that the business buys, makes and/or sells. It is important that they are realistic, as they will determine future ordering and production levels. The budgets may be derived in various ways. They may be developed using statistical techniques, such as time series analysis, or may be based on the judgement of sales and marketing staff. We discussed budgets and budgeting, at some length, in Chapter 6.

Financial ratios

One ratio that can be used to help monitor inventories levels is the **average inventories turnover period ratio**. This ratio is calculated as follows:

$$\text{Average inventories turnover period} = \frac{\text{Average inventories held}}{\text{Cost of sales}} \times 365$$

The ratio provides a picture of the average period for which inventories are held. This can be useful as a basis for comparison. The average inventories turnover period can be calculated for individual product lines, and for particular categories of inventories, as well as for inventories as a whole.

Recording and reordering systems

A sound system of recording inventories movements is a key element in managing inventories. There should be proper procedures for recording inventories purchases and usages. Periodic checks should be made to ensure that the amount of physical inventories held corresponds with what is indicated by the inventories' records.

There should also be clear procedures for the reordering of inventories. Authorisation for both the purchase and the issue of inventories should be confined to a few nominated members of staff. This should avoid problems of duplication and lack of co-ordination. To determine the point at which inventories should be reordered, information will be required concerning the **lead time** (that is, the time between the placing of an order and the receipt of the goods) and the likely level of demand.

Activity 12.4

An electrical wholesaler sells a particular type of light switch. The annual demand for the light switch is 10,400 units and the lead time for orders is four weeks. Demand for the light switch is even throughout the year. At what level of inventories of the light switch should the business reorder, assuming that it is confident of the information given above?

The average weekly demand for the switch is 10,400/52 = 200 units. During the time between ordering new switches and receiving them, the quantity sold will be 4 × 200 units = 800 units. So the business should reorder no later than when the level held reaches 800 units. This should avoid running out of inventories.

For most businesses, there will be some uncertainty surrounding the level of demand, pattern of demand and lead time. To avoid the risk of running out of inventories, a buffer, or safety, inventories level may be maintained. The amount of buffer inventories is a matter of judgement. In forming this judgement, the following should be taken into account:

- the degree of uncertainty concerning the above factors;
- the likely costs of running out of the item concerned; and
- the cost of holding the buffer inventories.

The effect of holding a buffer will be to raise the inventories level at which an order for new inventories is placed (the reorder point).

Activity 12.5

Assume the same facts as in Activity 16.4, except that the business wishes to maintain buffer inventories of 300 units. At what level should the business reorder?

Reorder point = expected level of demand during the lead time *plus* the level of buffer inventories

= 800 + 300

= 1,100 units

Carrying buffer inventories will increase the cost of holding inventories. This must, however, be weighed against the cost of running out of inventories, in terms of lost sales, production problems and so on.

Activity 12.6

Hora plc holds inventories of a particular type of motor car tyre, which is ordered in batches of 1,200 units. The supply lead times and usage rates for the tyres are:

	Maximum	Most likely	Minimum
Supply lead times	25 days	15 days	8 days
Daily usage	30 units	20 units	12 units

The business wishes to avoid the risk of running out of inventories.

At what minimum level of inventories should Hora plc place a new order, such that it can guarantee not to run out?

What is the size of the buffer inventories based on the most likely lead times and usages?

If Hora plc were to place an order based on the maximum lead time and usage, but only the minimum lead time and usage were actually to occur, what would be the level of inventories immediately following the delivery of the new inventories? What does this inventories figure represent?

To be certain of avoiding running out of inventories, the business must assume a reorder point based on the maximum usage and lead time. This is 750 units (that is, 30 × 25).

The most likely usage during the lead time will be only 300 units (that is, 20 × 15). Thus, the buffer inventories based on most likely usage and lead time is 450 units (that is, 750 − 300).

The level of inventories when a new order of 1,200 units is received, immediately following the minimum supply lead time and minimum daily usage during the lead time, is 1,854 units (that is, 1,200 + 750 − (8 × 12)). This should represent the maximum inventories holding for the business.

Levels of control

Deciding on the appropriate level of inventories control to adopt requires a careful weighing of costs and benefits. This may lead to the implementation of different levels of control according to the nature of the inventories held. The **ABC system of inventories control** is based on the idea of selective levels of control. A business may find it possible to divide its inventories into three broad categories: A, B and C. Each category will be based on the value of inventories held, as illustrated in Example 12.1.

Example 12.1

Alascan Products plc makes door handles and door fittings. It makes them in brass, in steel and in plastic. The business finds that brass fittings account for 10 per cent of the physical volume of the finished inventories that it holds, but these represent 65 per cent of the total value. These are treated as Category A inventories. There are sophisticated recording procedures, tight control is exerted over inventories movements and there is a high level of security where the brass inventories are stored. This is economically viable because these inventories represent a relatively small proportion of the total volume.

The business finds that steel fittings account for 30 per cent of the total volume of finished inventories and represent 25 per cent of the total value. These are treated as Category B inventories, with a lower level of recording and management control being applied.

The remaining 60 per cent of the volume of inventories is plastic fittings, which represent the least valuable items, accounting for only 10 per cent of the total value of finished inventories held. These are treated as Category C inventories, so the level of recording and management control would be lower still. Applying to these inventories the level of control that is applied to Category A or even Category B inventories would be uneconomic.

Categorising inventories in this way helps to direct management effort to the most important areas. It also helps to ensure that the costs of controlling inventories are proportionate to their value.

Figure 12.3 provides a graphical depiction of the ABC approach to inventories control.

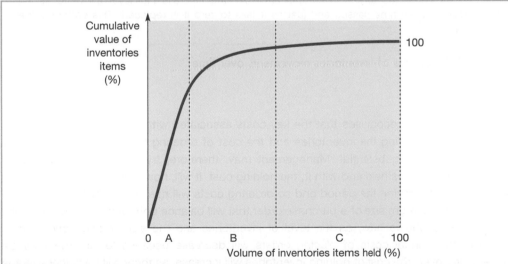

Category A contains inventories that, though relatively few in quantity, account for a large proportion of the total value. Category B inventories consists of those items that are less valuable but more numerous. Category C comprises those inventories items that are very numerous but relatively low in value. Different inventories' control rules would be applied to each category. For example, only Category A inventories would attract the more expensive and sophisticated controls.

Figure 12.3 ABC method of analysing and controlling inventories

Inventories management models

Economic order quantity

Decision models may be used to help manage inventories. The **economic order quantity (EOQ)** model is concerned with determining the quantity of a particular inventories item that should be ordered each time. In its simplest form, the EOQ model assumes that demand is constant. This implies that inventories will be depleted evenly over time to be replenished just at the point that they run out. These assumptions would lead to a 'saw-tooth' pattern to represent inventories movements, as shown in Figure 12.4.

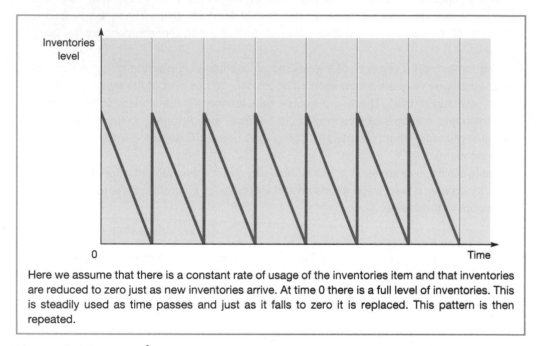

Here we assume that there is a constant rate of usage of the inventories item and that inventories are reduced to zero just as new inventories arrive. At time 0 there is a full level of inventories. This is steadily used as time passes and just as it falls to zero it is replaced. This pattern is then repeated.

Figure 12.4 Patterns of inventories movements over time

The EOQ model recognises that the key costs associated with inventories' management are the cost of holding the inventories and the cost of ordering them. The cost of holding inventories can be substantial. Management may, therefore, try to minimise the average amount of inventories held and with it, the holding cost. It will, however, increase the number of orders placed during the period and so ordering costs will rise. The EOQ model seeks to calculate the optimum size of a purchase order that will balance both of these cost elements.

Figure 12.5 shows how, as the level of inventories and the size of inventories orders increase, the annual costs of placing orders will decrease because fewer orders will be placed. However, the cost of holding inventories will increase, as there will be higher average inventories levels. The total costs curve, which is based on the sum of holding costs and ordering costs, will fall until the point E, which represents the minimum total cost. Thereafter, total costs begin to rise. The EOQ model seeks to identify point E, at which total costs are minimised. This will represent half of the optimum amount that should be ordered on each occasion. Assuming, as we are doing, that inventories are used evenly over time and that they fall to zero before being replaced, the average inventories level equals half of the order size.

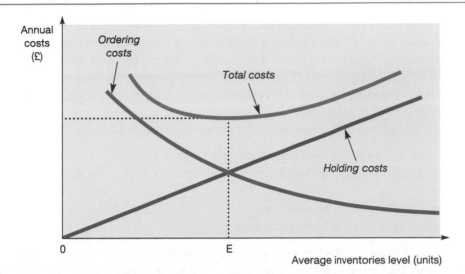

Small inventories levels imply frequent reordering and high annual ordering costs. Small inventories levels also imply relatively low inventories holding costs. High inventories levels imply exactly the opposite. There is, in theory, an optimum order size that will lead to the sum of ordering and holding costs (total costs) being at a minimum.

Figure 12.5 Inventories holding and order costs

The EOQ model, which can be used to derive the most economic order quantity, is:

$$EOQ = \sqrt{\frac{2DC}{H}}$$

where
D = the annual demand for the inventories item (expressed in units of the inventories item);
C = the cost of placing an order;
H = the cost of holding one unit of the inventories item for one year.

Activity 12.7

HLA Ltd sells 2,000 bags of cement each year. It has been estimated that the cost of holding one bag of cement for a year is £4. The cost of placing an order for new inventories is estimated at £250.
   Calculate the EOQ for bags of cement.

Your answer to this activity should be as follows:

$$EOQ = \sqrt{\frac{2 \times 2,000 \times 250}{4}} = 500 \text{ bags}$$

This will mean that the business will have to order bags of cement four times each year (that is 2,000/500) in batches of 500 bags so that sales demand can be met.

Note that the cost of inventories, which is the price paid to the supplier, does not directly affect the EOQ model. It is concerned only with the administrative costs of placing and handling each order and the costs of holding the inventories. However, more expensive inventories items tend to have greater holding costs. This may be because an ABC system of inventories control is in place or because they tie up more finance than less expensive inventories, or both. Therefore the cost of inventories may have an indirect influence on the economic order size that is calculated.

The basic EOQ model has a number of limiting assumptions. In particular, it assumes that:

- demand for an inventories item can be predicted with accuracy;
- demand is constant over the period and does not fluctuate through seasonality or for other reasons;
- no 'buffer' inventories are required; and
- there are no discounts for bulk purchasing.

The model can be modified, however, to overcome each of these limiting assumptions. Many businesses use this model (or a development of it) to help in the management of inventories.

Activity 12.8

Petrov plc sells 10,000 tonnes of sand each year and demand is constant over time. The purchase cost of each tonne is £15 and the cost of placing and handling an order is estimated to be £32. The cost of holding 1 tonne of sand for one year is estimated to be £4. The business uses the EOQ model to determine the appropriate order quantity and holds no buffer inventories.

Calculate the total annual cost of trading in this product.

The total annual cost will be made up of three elements:

- the cost of purchases;
- the cost of ordering; and
- the cost of holding this item in inventories.

The *annual cost of purchases* is 10,000 × £15 = £150,000.
The *annual cost of ordering* is calculated as follows:
The EOQ is:

$$EOQ = \sqrt{\frac{2 \times 10,000 \times 32}{4}} = 400 \text{ tonnes}$$

This will mean that 10,000/400 = 25 orders will be placed each year. The *annual cost of ordering* is therefore 25 × £32 = £800.

The *annual cost of holding inventories* is calculated as follows:
The average quantity of inventories held will be half the optimum order size, as mentioned earlier. That is, 400/2 = 200 tonnes. The *annual holding cost* is therefore 200 × £4 = £800

The *total annual cost of trading in this product* is therefore:

$$£150,000 + £800 + £800 = £151,600*$$

*Note that the annual ordering cost and annual holding cost are the same. This is no coincidence. If we look back at Figure 12.5 we can see that the economic order quantity represents the point at which total costs are minimised. At this point, annual order costs and annual holding costs are equal.

Enterprise resource planning systems

Enterprise resource planning (ERP) systems provide an automated and integrated approach to managing a business. They consist of a suite of software applications (modules) that record, report, analyse and interpret data for a range of business operations, including production, marketing, human resources, accounting and inventories management. These integrated software applications are supported by a common database, which is operated on a real-time (or near real-time) basis and which can be accessed remotely.

An ERP software application for the management of inventories will carry out a wide range of tasks such as:

- forecasting demand using statistical formulae;
- making reorder decisions based on forecast future demand;
- ordering the transfer of goods between locations;
- tracking and reporting inventories according to type, serial numbers and so on;
- providing real-time information concerning shipping costs, trends in inventories holdings, on-time deliveries and so on;
- allocating warehouse space for where goods are to be stored;
- helping inventories audits by setting tolerance levels for variations between actual and reported inventories held; and
- pricing inventories being shipped, to take account of required profit margins, bulk discounts and so on.

The software application will normally embed best practice within a particular industry, but may be customised to meet the needs of an individual business.

ERP inventories' management applications greatly enhance the quality, range and timeliness of information to managers. This can be of enormous benefit in driving efficiencies and in responding to changing circumstances. These applications can, however, be costly to introduce.

Activity 12.9

Try to identify at least *three* types of cost that may be incurred when adopting an ERP inventories' management application.

These include:

- initial outlay cost;
- customising the application;
- staff training and development;
- converting existing files to fit the application;
- testing; and
- re-engineering business processes to accommodate the application.

You may have thought of others.

Just-in-time inventories management

In recent years, many businesses have tried to eliminate the need to hold inventories by adopting **just-in-time (JIT) inventories management**. This approach was originally used in the US defence industry during the Second World War, but was first used on a wide scale by

Japanese manufacturing businesses. The essence of JIT is, as the name suggests, to have supplies delivered to the business just in time for them to be used in the production process or in a sale. By adopting this approach, the inventories holding cost can move from the business itself to the suppliers. On the other hand, a well-managed JIT system should lead to significantly lower inventories levels for all parties, leading to significant overall cost savings. A failure by a particular supplier to deliver on time, however, could cause enormous problems and costs to the business. Thus JIT may save cost, but it tends to increase risk.

For JIT to be successful, there needs to be a close relationship between a business and its suppliers. It is important that a business informs suppliers of its inventories' requirements in advance so that suppliers can schedule their own production to that of the business. Suppliers must then deliver materials of the right quality at the agreed times. Any delivery failures could lead to a dislocation of production and could be very costly. Successful JIT tends to require that suppliers are geographically near to the business.

Activity 12.10

Superlec plc makes electrical appliances. One of its major component suppliers is Technicalities Ltd. The two businesses have recently established a comprehensive JIT relationship.

Would you expect that the inventories of Technicalites Ltd to:

- increase,
- reduce, or
- stay the same

as a result of the change of relationship?

The introduction of JIT by Superlec Ltd will pass the inventories holding problem to Technicalities Ltd. As a result, Technicalities inventories' holdings could increase. However, the close working relationship that a JIT relationship requires should lead to a reduction in the total amount of inventories that would, otherwise, be held by the supplier. Knowing Superlec's inventories' requirements in advance should help Technicalities to schedule its own production and inventories to those requirements. It may encourage Technicalites to introduce a system of JIT from its own suppliers.

Adopting JIT will usually require re-engineering a business's production process in order to avoid the risk that production will be brought to a halt for any reason. Changes may, therefore, be made to the production layout and to working practices. To ensure that orders are quickly fulfilled, the production process must be flexible and responsive. Production flows may be redesigned and employees may be given greater responsibility to deal with unanticipated problems. Information systems must also be installed that both monitor and facilitate an uninterrupted production flow.

Although a business that applies JIT will not have to hold inventories, there may be other costs associated with this approach. For example, the close relationship necessary between the business and its suppliers may prevent the business from taking advantage of cheaper sources of supply that become available. Furthermore, where a supplier needs to hold inventories for the customer, it may try to recoup this additional cost through increased prices.

JIT is widely viewed as more than simply an inventories control system. The philosophy underpinning this approach is that of *total quality management*. This is concerned with eliminating waste and striving for excellence. There is an expectation that suppliers will always deliver inventories on time and that there will be no defects in the items supplied. There is also an expectation that, for manufacturers, the production process will operate at maximum efficiency. This means that there will be no production breakdowns and the queuing and storage times of products manufactured will be eliminated, as only time spent directly on processing the products is seen as adding value. While these expectations may be impossible to achieve, they can help to create a culture that is dedicated to the pursuit of excellence and quality.

Activity 12.11

Bantam Blinds Ltd manufactures blinds and awnings for offices and homes. The business has recently introduced a JIT inventories management system. As the management accountant of the business, you have been asked to recommend measures to help monitor its effectiveness in improving delivery and production flows.

Try to identify at least three measures that may be used by managers on a regular basis for this purpose.

Measures that may be used include:

- on-time deliveries made by suppliers as a percentage of total deliveries;
- production breakdowns per period;
- defective parts received from suppliers as a percentage of total parts delivered; and
- machine-time availability as a percentage of planned availability.

You may have thought of others.

A final point worth making is that successful implementation of a JIT system rests with the workforce. A more streamlined and efficient production flow will only be achieved if workers are well trained and fully committed to the pursuit of quality. They must be prepared to operate as part of a team and to adapt to changes in both the nature and pace of working practices. They must also be prepared to show initiative in dealing with problems arising in the production process.

Real World 12.5 shows how a very well-known businesses operating in the UK uses JIT to advantage.

Real World 12.5

JIT at Nissan

Nissan Motors UK limited, the UK manufacturing arm of the world-famous Japanese car business, has a plant in Sunderland in the north east of England. Here it operates a fairly well-developed JIT system. For example, Calsonic Kansei supplies car exhausts from a factory close to the Nissan plant. It makes deliveries to Nissan once every 30 minutes on average, so as to arrive exactly as the exhausts are needed in production. This is fairly typical of all of the 200 suppliers of components and materials to the Nissan plant.

Nissan used to have a comprehensive JIT system. More recently, however, Nissan has drawn back from its total adherence to JIT. By using only local suppliers, it had cut itself off from the opportunity to exploit low-cost suppliers, particularly those located in China. A change in policy has led the business to hold buffer inventories for certain items to guard against disruption of supply arising from sourcing parts from the Far East.

Sources: Information taken from Tighe, C. (2006) Nissan reviews just-in-time parts policy, *Financial Times*, 23 October; Ludwig, C. (2014) Local logistics and Engineering partnership at Nissan Europe, *Automotive Logistics*, 5 February.

XYZ inventories management

XYZ inventories management classifies inventories into three categories according to variability of customer demand. Category X items are those that display relatively little variation in demand over time. In other words, sales follow a fairly steady path. This pattern of sales demand makes it possible to produce forecasts with a high degree of accuracy. Category Y items display greater variability in demand. Sales of these items may be affected by seasonal factors, changes in the competitive environment, changes in interest rates and so on. Nevertheless, it is still possible to identify and to predict, to some degree, the impact of these factors. It should, therefore, be possible to forecast sales demand with reasonable accuracy. Category Z items display a high level of variability in demand. Sales may fluctuate dramatically from one period to the next. The underlying reasons for these fluctuations may be difficult to identify and, even where this can be done, their impact may be difficult to predict. Under these conditions, accurate sales forecasting becomes impossible.

Possible patterns of demand for each of the three categories of inventories are shown in Figure 12.6 below.

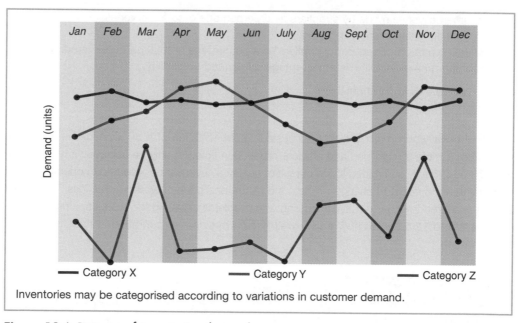

Inventories may be categorised according to variations in customer demand.

Figure 12.6 Patterns of inventories demand

By classifying inventories according to their variability in demand, a business can manage them more effectively. Demand for Category X items can be forecast with a high degree of accuracy, which means that automated ordering and processing systems can be implemented. It also means that there is no need to keep significant buffer inventories in case of unexpected surges in demand. Demand for Category Y items is less easy to predict, which makes complete automation of ordering and processing inventories more difficult. Some manual involvement is likely to be needed. Furthermore, the higher risk of error in forecasting demand means that a higher level of buffer inventories should be maintained. Demand for Category Z items is unpredictable, which makes accurate forecasting impossible. As a result, automated ordering and processing systems cannot be employed. Raising purchase orders, setting buffer inventories' levels and so on must, therefore, be carried out manually. In some cases it may be necessary to hold significant buffer inventories. However, where sales fluctuate dramatically and product life cycles are short, this can lead to high costs of obsolescence. It may be better to have no buffer inventories and to raise purchase orders only after customer orders have been received.

Some businesses combine the ABC inventories control approach discussed earlier with the XYZ approach. When this occurs, both the value of the inventories held and their variation in demand are taken into account. This can help in clarifying how particular inventories should be treated. Let us say, for example, a batch of inventories is categorised as AX – that is, A (high value) and X (steady demand). This will mean that they should be monitored closely, that ordering can be fully automated and that only low buffer inventories are needed. These inventories may also be suitable for the implementation of a JIT system.

MANAGING TRADE RECEIVABLES

Selling goods or services on credit will result in costs being incurred by a business. These costs include the costs of credit administration, of bad debts and of opportunities forgone to use the funds for other purposes. However, these costs must be weighed against the benefits of increased sales revenue resulting from the opportunity for customers to delay payment.

Selling on credit is the norm outside the retail industry. When a business offers to sell its goods or services on credit, it must have clear policies concerning:

- which customers should receive credit;
- how much credit should be offered;
- what length of credit it is prepared to offer;
- whether discounts will be offered for prompt payment;
- what collection policies should be adopted; and
- how the risk of non-payment can be reduced.

In this section, we consider each of these issues.

Which customers should receive credit and how much should they be offered?

A business offering credit runs the risk of not receiving payment for goods or services supplied. Therefore, care must be taken over the type of customer to whom credit facilities are offered and how much credit is allowed. When considering a proposal from a customer for the supply of goods or services on credit, a business should take into account a number of factors. The following **five Cs of credit** provide a useful checklist:

- *Capital.* The customer must appear to be financially sound before any credit is extended. Where the customer is a business, its financial statements should be examined. Particular regard should be given to the customer's likely future profitability and liquidity. In addition, any major financial commitments (such as outstanding borrowings, capital expenditure commitments and contracts with suppliers) should be taken into account.

- *Capacity.* The customer must appear to have the capacity to pay for the goods acquired on credit. The customer's payment record to date should be examined to provide important clues. To help further assess capacity, the type of business and the amount of credit required in relation to the customer's total financial resources should be taken into account.

- *Collateral.* On occasions, it may be necessary to ask for some kind of security for goods supplied on credit. When this occurs, the business must be convinced that the customer is able to offer a satisfactory form of security.

- *Conditions.* The state of the industry in which the customer operates, as well as the general economic conditions of the particular region or country, should be taken into account. The sensitivity of the customer's business to changes in economic conditions can also have an important influence on the ability of the customer to pay on time.

- *Character.* It is important to make some assessment of the customer's character. The willingness to pay will depend on the honesty and integrity of the individual with whom the business is dealing. Where the customer is a business, this will mean assessing the characters of its senior managers as well as their reputation within the industry. The selling business must feel confident that the customer will make every effort to pay any amounts owing.

To help assess the above factors, various sources of information are available. They include:

- *Trade references.* Some businesses ask potential customers to provide references from other suppliers that have extended credit to them. This can be extremely useful as long as the references provided are truly representative of the opinions of all the customer's suppliers. There is a danger that a potential customer will be selective when giving details of other suppliers, in an attempt to create a more favourable impression than is deserved.

- *Bank references.* It is possible to ask the potential customer for a bank reference. Although banks are usually prepared to supply references, their contents are not always very informative. The bank will usually charge a fee for providing a reference.

- *Published financial statements.* A limited company is obliged by law to file a copy of its annual financial statements with the Registrar of Companies. These are available for public inspection and can provide a useful insight into performance and financial position. Many companies also publish their annual financial statements on their websites or on computer-based information systems. A problem with the publicly-available financial statements is that they are often quite out of date by the time that they can first be examined by the potential supplier of credit.

- *The customer.* Interviews with the directors of the customer business and visits to its premises may be carried out to gain an impression of the way that the customer conducts its business. Where a significant amount of credit is required, the business may ask the customer for access to internal forecasts and other unpublished financial information to help assess the level of risk involved.

- *Credit agencies.* Specialist agencies exist to provide information that can be used to assess the creditworthiness of a potential customer. The information that a credit agency supplies may be gleaned from various sources, including the customer's financial statements and news items relating to the customer from both published and unpublished sources. The credit agencies may also provide a credit rating for the business. Agencies will charge a fee for their services.
- *Register of County Court Judgments.* Any money judgments given against the business or an individual in a county court will be maintained on the register for six years. This register is available for inspection by any member of the public for a small fee.
- *Other suppliers.* Similar businesses will often be prepared to exchange information concerning slow payers or defaulting customers through an industry credit circle. This can be a reliable and relatively cheap way of obtaining information.

Activity 12.13

It was mentioned above that, although banks are usually prepared to supply references, their contents are not always very informative. Why might this be the case?

If a bank's customer is in financial difficulties, the bank may be unwilling to add to its problems by supplying a poor reference. It is worth remembering that the bank's loyalty is likely to be with its customer rather than the enquirer.

Once a customer is considered creditworthy, credit limits should be established. When doing so, the business must take account of its own financial resources and risk appetite. Unfortunately, there are no theories or models to guide a business when deciding on the appropriate credit limit to adopt; it is really a matter of judgement. Some businesses adopt simple 'rule of thumb' methods based on the amount of sales made to the customer (say, twice the monthly sales figure for the customer) or the maximum the business is prepared to be owed (say, a maximum of 20 per cent of its working capital) by all of its customers.

Length of credit period

A business must determine what credit terms it is prepared to offer its customers. The length of credit offered to customers can vary significantly between businesses. It may be influenced by such factors as:

- the typical credit terms operating within the industry;
- the degree of competition within the industry;
- the bargaining power of particular customers;
- the risk of non-payment;
- the capacity of the business to offer credit; and
- the marketing strategy of the business.

The last point may require some explanation. Credit policy can be a basis on which a business may compete for custom with its competitors. So if, for example, a business wishes to increase its market share, it may decide to be more generous in its credit policy in an attempt to stimulate sales. Potential customers may be attracted by the offer of a longer credit period. However, any such change in policy must take account of the likely costs and benefits arising. To illustrate this point, consider Example 12.2.

Example 12.2

Torrance Ltd produces a new type of golf putter. The business sells the putter to whole-salers and retailers and has an annual sales revenue of £600,000. The following data relate to each putter produced:

	£
Selling price	40
Variable cost	(20)
Fixed cost apportionment	(6)
Profit	14

The business's cost of capital is estimated at 10 per cent a year.

Torrance Ltd wishes to expand the sales volume of the new putter. It believes that offering a longer credit period can achieve this. The business's average trade receivables settlement period is currently 30 days. It is considering three options in an attempt to increase sales revenue. These are as follows:

	Option		
	1	2	3
Increase in average settlement period (days)	10	20	30
Increase in sales revenue (£)	30,000	45,000	50,000

To help the business to decide on the best option, the benefits of the various options should be weighed against their respective costs. Benefits will be represented by the increase in profit from the sale of additional putters. From the information supplied, we can see that the contribution to profit (that is, selling price (£40) less variable costs (£20)) is £20 a putter. This represents 50 per cent of the selling price. So, whatever increase occurs in sales revenue, the additional contribution to profit will be half of that figure. The fixed cost can be ignored in our calculations, as it will remain the same whichever option is chosen.

The increase in contribution under each option will therefore be:

	Option		
	1	2	3
50% of the increase in sales revenue (£)	15,000	22,500	25,000

The increase in trade receivables under each option will be as follows:

	Option		
	1	2	3
	£	£	£
Projected level of trade receivables:			
40 × £630,000/365 (Note 1)	69,041		
50 × £645,000/365 (Note 2)		88,356	
60 × £650,000/365			106,849
Current level of trade receivables:			
30 × £600,000/365	(49,315)	(49,315)	(49,315)
Increase in trade receivables	19,726	39,041	57,534

The increase in receivables that results from each option will mean an additional finance cost to the business.

The net increase in the business's profit arising from the projected change is:

	Option		
	1	*2*	*3*
	£	£	£
Increase in contribution (see above)	15,000	22,500	25,000
Increase in finance cost (Note 3)	(1,973)	(3,904)	(5,753)
Net increase in profits	13,027	18,596	19,247

The calculations show that Option 3 will be the most profitable one.

Notes:

1 If the annual sales revenue totals £630,000 and 40 days' credit is allowed (both of which will apply under Option 1), the average amount that will be owed to the business by its customers, at any point during the year, will be the daily sales revenue (that is, £630,000/365) multiplied by the number of days that the customers take to pay (that is 40). Exactly the same logic applies to Options 2 and 3 and to the current level of trade receivables.

2 The increase in the finance cost for Option 1 will be the increase in trade receivables (£19,726) × 10 per cent. The equivalent figures for the other options are derived in a similar way.

Example 12.2 illustrates the broad approach that a business should take when assessing changes in credit terms. However, by extending the length of credit, other costs may be incurred. These may include bad debts and additional collections costs, which should also be taken into account in the calculations.

Real World 12.6 is an article that discusses how supermarkets have often been guilty of extending the credit period granted by its suppliers.

Real World 12.6

Credit where it's due

Supermarkets are still routinely mistreating suppliers by paying bills late, despite government pressure for grocers to clean up their act, a study has revealed. An analysis of thousands of invoices from small and medium-sized suppliers found that almost 70 per cent of payments made by supermarkets were late in 2015.

On average, supermarkets settled bills 7.24 days beyond contractually agreed terms last year, according to research conducted by MarketInvoice, an online invoice finance company. The sector's payment performance was markedly worse than technology companies, banks and the broader FTSE 350 average. Banks paid supplier invoices only 0.3 days late.

The continued poor performance of large grocers comes despite the creation of the Groceries Code Adjudicator in 2013 to improve the treatment of suppliers. Anil Stocker, a co-founder of MarketInvoice, said: "That these bad payment practices are clearly sector-wide is a sign that something is very wrong in the supermarket industry."

Ian Cass, managing director of the Forum of Private Business, said: "Supermarkets get paid pretty much immediately for their products, so there is no excuse for paying late . . . I never thought I would hear myself state that anyone should follow the example of banks, but it is clear that is precisely what supermarkets should do."

MarketInvoice analysed almost 15,000 invoices during 2015, including 1,000 supermarket invoices. It also analysed more than 5,000 invoices filed between 2010 and 2014. It said that 14 per cent of invoices to supermarkets were paid more than two weeks later than agreed terms, and 7 per cent were more than a month late. This was on top of grocers' standard contractual payment terms, which can mean suppliers wait three months or more to be paid.

Source: Hurley, J. (2016) Suppliers 'routinely kept waiting by supermarkets', www.thetimes.co.uk, 25 January.

An alternative approach to evaluating the credit decision

It is possible to view the credit decision as a capital investment decision. Granting trade credit involves an opportunity outlay of resources in the form of cash (which has been temporarily forgone) in the expectation that future cash flows will be increased (through higher sales) as a result. A business will usually have choices concerning the level of investment to be made in credit sales and the period over which credit is granted. These choices will result in different returns and different levels of risk. There is no reason in principle why the NPV investment appraisal method, which we considered in Chapter 8, should not be used to evaluate these choices. The NPV method takes into account both the time value of money and the level of risk involved.

Approaching the problem as an NPV assessment is not different in principle from the way that we dealt with the decision in Example 12.2. In both approaches, the time value of money is considered, but in Example 12.2 we did it by charging a financing cost on the outstanding trade receivables.

Cash discounts

To encourage prompt payment from its credit customers, a business may offer a **cash discount** (or discount for prompt payment). The size of any discount will be an important influence on whether a customer decides to pay promptly.

From the business's viewpoint, the cost of offering discounts must be weighed against the likely benefits in the form of a reduction both in the cost of financing trade receivables and in the amount of bad debts. Example 12.3 shows how this may be done.

Example 12.3

Williams Wholesalers Ltd currently asks its credit customers to pay by the end of the month after the month of delivery. In practice, customers take rather longer to pay – on average 70 days. Sales revenue amounts to £4 million a year and bad debts to £20,000 a year.

It is planned to offer customers a cash discount of 2 per cent for payment within 30 days. Williams estimates that 50 per cent of customers will accept this facility but that the remaining customers, who tend to be slow payers, will not pay until 80 days after the sale. At present, the business has an overdraft facility at an interest rate of 13 per cent a year. If the plan goes ahead, bad debts will be reduced to £10,000 a year and there will be savings in credit administration expenses of £6,000 a year.

Should Williams Wholesalers Ltd offer the new credit terms to customers?

Solution

The first step is to determine the reduction in trade receivables arising from the new policy.

		£	£
Existing level of trade receivables	(£4m × 70/365)		767,123
New level of trade receivables:	£2m × 80/365	438,356	
	£2m × 30/365	164,384	(602,740)
Reduction in trade receivables			164,383

The costs and benefits of offering the discount can be set out as follows:

	£	£
Cost and benefits of policy		
Cost of discount (£2m × 2%)		40,000
Less		
Interest saved on the reduction in trade receivables		
(£164,383* × 13%)	21,370	
Administration cost saving	6,000	
Cost of bad debts saved (20,000 − 10,000)	10,000	(37,370)
Net cost of policy		2,630

These calculations show that the business will be worse off by offering the new credit terms.

*It could be argued that the interest should be based on the amount expected to be received; that is the value of the trade receivables *after* taking account of the discount. Basing it on the expected receipt figure would not, however, alter the conclusion that the business should not offer the new credit terms.

Activity 12.14

In practice, there is always the danger that a customer may be slow to pay and yet may still take the discount offered. Where the customer is important to the business, it may be difficult to insist on full payment. How might a business overcome this problem?

Instead of allowing customers to deduct a discount, customers who pay promptly can be rewarded separately, say on a three-monthly basis. The reward could be a cash payment to the customer or, perhaps, a credit note. The value of the reward would be equal to the cash discounts earned by each customer during the three months.

Debt factoring and invoice discounting

Trade receivables can, in effect, be turned into cash by either factoring them or having sales invoices discounted. Both are forms of asset-based finance, which involves a financial institution providing a business with an advance up to 80 per cent of the value of the trade receivables outstanding. These methods are fairly popular approaches to managing receivables.

Credit insurance

It is often possible for a supplier to insure its entire trade receivables, individual customer accounts or the outstanding balance relating to a particular transaction.

Collection policies

A business offering credit must ensure that receivables are collected as quickly as possible so that non-payment risk is minimised and operating cash flows are maximised. Various steps can be taken to achieve this, including the following.

Develop customer relationships

For major customers, it is often useful to cultivate a relationship with the key staff responsible for paying sales invoices. By so doing, the chances of prompt payment may be increased.

For less important customers, the business should at least identify the key members of staff responsible for paying invoices, who can be contacted in the event of a payment problem.

Publicise credit terms

The credit terms of the business should be made clear in all relevant correspondence, such as order acknowledgements, invoices and statements. In early negotiations with the prospective customer, credit terms should be openly discussed and an agreement reached.

Issue invoices promptly

An efficient collection policy requires an efficient accounting system. Invoices (bills) must be sent out promptly to customers, as must monthly statements. Reminders must also be despatched promptly to customers who are late in paying. If a customer fails to respond to a reminder, the accounting system should alert managers so that a stop can be placed on further deliveries.

Use financial ratios to monitor outstanding receivables

Managers can monitor the effectiveness of collection through the use of ratios. They can, for example, calculate the **average settlement period for trade receivables** ratio. This ratio is calculated as follows:

$$\text{Average settlement period for trade receivables} = \frac{\text{Average trade receivables}}{\text{Credit sales}} \times 365$$

Although this ratio can be useful, it is important to remember that it produces an *average* figure for the number of days for which debts are outstanding. This average may be badly distorted by a few large customers who are very slow, or very fast, payers.

A further ratio that may be of assistance is the **trade receivables to sales ratio**. This ratio is calculated as follows:

$$\text{Trade receivables to sales} = \frac{\text{Trade receivables outstanding at end of the period}}{\text{Sales revenue for the period}}$$

In practice, this ratio is normally calculated on a monthly basis and can be used to detect trends. Since it uses the month-end figure, as the numerator, it has a little more immediacy than a ratio calculated on an annual basis, as the average settlement period for trade receivables ratio (above) tends to be. Where, for example, the ratio is increasing each month, it means that trade receivables are growing faster than sales revenue.

Activity 12.15

Why might this trend be a cause of concern?

It suggests that the business is slow in collecting its receivables, which may signal future cash flow problems.

Where trade receivables exceed the current monthly sales revenue, the ratio will be greater than one. Calculating this ratio for seasonal businesses can be tricky as the ratio will tend to increase or decrease as the seasons change. Thus, making comparisons with similar months in previous years may be more useful in detecting trends.

Produce an ageing schedule of trade receivables

A more detailed and informative approach to monitoring receivables may be to produce an **ageing schedule of trade receivables**. Receivables are divided into categories according to the length of time they have been outstanding. An ageing schedule can be produced, on a regular basis, to help managers see the pattern of outstanding receivables. An example of an ageing schedule is set out in Example 12.4.

Example 12.4

Ageing schedule of trade receivables at 31 December

Customer	Days outstanding				Total
	1 to 30 days	31 to 60 days	61 to 90 days	More than 90 days	
	£	£	£	£	£
A Ltd	12,000	13,000	14,000	18,000	57,000
B Ltd	20,000	10,000	–	–	30,000
C Ltd	–	24,000	–	–	24,000
Total	32,000	47,000	14,000	18,000	111,000

This shows a business's trade receivables figure at 31 December, which totals £111,000. Each customer's balance is analysed according to how long the amount has been outstanding. (This business has just three credit customers.) To help focus management attention, accounts may be listed in order of size, with the largest debts first.

We can see from the schedule, for example, that A Ltd still has £14,000 outstanding for between 61 and 90 days (that is, arising from sales during October) and £18,000 outstanding for more than 90 days (that is, arising from sales during September or even before). This information can be very useful for credit control purposes.

Usually accounting software includes this ageing schedule as one of the routine reports available to managers. Such packages often have the facility to put customers 'on hold' when they reach their credit limits. Putting a customer on hold means that no further credit sales will be made to that customer until amounts owing from past sales have been settled.

Real World 12.7 sets out the ageing schedule of receivables published by Sky plc, the satellite broadcaster.

Real World 12.7

Analysing receivables

Sky plc publishes an analysis of its trade receivables each year according to how long they are overdue. Figures for the previous year are also published for comparison purposes.

The ageing of the group's net trade receivables which are past due date but not impaired is as follows:

	2016	2015
	£m	£m
Up to 30 days past due date	61	27
30 to 60 days past due date	14	8
60 to 120 days past due date	4	4
120+ days past due	3	1
	82	40

76 per cent of Sky's unimpaired trade receivables were still within due date (30 days) at the business's 2016 year-end.

Source: Sky plc Annual Report 2016, p. 100.

Identify the pattern of receipts

A slightly different approach to exercising control over receivables is to identify the pattern of receipts from credit sales on a monthly basis. This involves monitoring the percentage of credit sales that are paid in the month of sale and the percentage that is paid in subsequent months. To do this, credit sales for each month must be examined separately. Example 12.5 illustrates this.

Example 12.5

A business made credit sales of £250,000 in June. It received 30 per cent of that amount during June, 40 per cent during July, 20 per cent during August and 10 per cent during September. The pattern of credit sales receipts and amounts owing is:

Pattern of credit sales receipts

	Receipts from June credit sales	Amounts received	Amount outstanding from June sales at month-end	Amount outstanding
	£	%	£	%
June	75,000	30	175,000	70
July	100,000	40	75,000	30
August	50,000	20	25,000	10
September	25,000	10	0	0

This information can be used as a basis for control. Targets may be established for the pattern of cash received from credit sales. The actual pattern can then be compared with the target pattern of receipts to see whether there is any significant deviation (see Figure 12.7). Where this is the case, managers should consider corrective action.

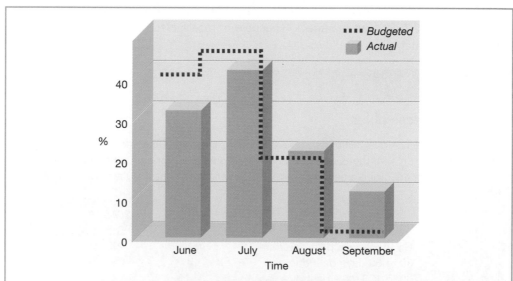

It can be seen that 30 per cent of the sales income for June is received in that month; the remainder is received in the following three months. The expected (target) pattern of cash receipts for June sales, which has been assumed, is also depicted. By comparing the actual and expected pattern of receipts, it is possible to see whether credit sales are being properly controlled and to decide whether corrective action is required.

Figure 12.7 Comparison of actual and expected (target) receipts over time for Example 12.5

Answer queries quickly

It is important for relevant staff to deal with customer queries on goods and services supplied quickly and efficiently. Payment is unlikely to be made by customers until their queries have been dealt with.

Deal with slow payers

A business making significant sales on credit will, almost inevitably, be faced with customers who do not pay. When this occurs, there should be established procedures for dealing with the problem. There should be a timetable for sending out reminders and for adding customers to a 'stop list' for future supplies. The timetable may also specify the point at which the unpaid amount is passed to a collection agency for recovery. These agencies often work on a 'no collection – no fee' basis. Charges for their services vary but can be up to 15 per cent of the amounts collected.

Legal action may also be considered against delinquent credit customers. The cost of such action, however, must be weighed against likely returns. There is little point, for example, in incurring large legal expenses to try to recoup amounts owing if there is evidence that the customer has no money. Where possible, an estimate of the cost of bad debts should be taken into account when setting prices for products or services.

As a footnote to our consideration of managing receivables, **Real World 12.8** outlines some of the excuses that long-suffering credit managers must listen to when chasing payment for outstanding debts.

Real World 12.8

It's in the post

It's been reported that businesses in the UK regularly experience late payment. A recent survey shows that the type of excuses given for this have changed little over the years despite the advance of online payment. Here are some of the most frequent excuses given:

1. We can't pay you until we have been paid by others ourselves
2. Our cheque is in the post to you
3. We have a dispute on the account so we can't pay you yet
4. We haven't received your invoice
5. We think there's an error in your invoice so can't make payment
6. We only pay by cheque and unfortunately our manager is away so the cheque can't be written

These are by no means the only excuses. others regularly used include bereavement, the fact that there's nobody in the office at the moment, and that the company is changing bank accounts.

Source: Adapted from https://debtadvocate.co.uk/the-uk-top-10-excuses-for-late-payment/.

Reducing the risk of non-payment

Efficient collection policies are important in reducing the risk of non-payment. There are, however, other ways in which a business can reduce this type of risk. Possibilities include:

- requiring customers to pay part of their sale value in advance of the goods being sent;
- agreeing to offset amounts owed for the purchase of goods against amounts due for goods supplied to the same business;

- requiring a third-party guarantee from a financially sound business such as a bank or parent company;
- making it a condition of sale that the legal title to the goods is not passed to the customer until the goods are paid for; and/or
- taking out insurance to cover the cost of any legal expenses incurred in recovering the amount owed. (Some customers may refuse to pay if they feel the business does not have the resources to pursue the debt through the courts.)

MANAGING CASH

Why hold cash?

Most businesses hold a certain amount of cash. There are broadly three reasons why they do so.

Activity 12.16

Can you think what these reasons may be? Try to think of at least one.

The three reasons are:

1 *To meet day-to-day commitments.* A business needs a certain amount of cash to pay for wages, overhead expenses, goods purchased and so on, when they fall due. Cash has been described as the lifeblood of a business. Unless it circulates through the business and is available to meet maturing obligations, the survival of the business will be put at risk. Simply being profitable is not enough to ensure survival.
2 *For precautionary purposes.* If future cash flows are uncertain, it would be prudent to hold a balance of cash. For example, a major customer that owes a large sum to the business may be in financial difficulties. This could lead to an expected large receipt not arriving. By holding cash, the business could retain its capacity to meet its obligations. Similarly, if there is some uncertainty concerning future outlays, a cash balance will be needed.
3 *To exploit opportunities.* A business may decide to hold cash to put itself in a position to exploit profitable opportunities as and when they arise. For example, it may enable the acquisition of a competitor business that suddenly becomes available at an attractive price.

How much cash should be held?

The amount of cash held tends to vary considerably between businesses. The decision as to how much cash a business should hold is a difficult one. Various factors can influence the final decision.

Try to think of four possible factors that might influence the amount of cash that a business holds.

You may have thought of the following:

- *The nature of the business.* Some businesses, such as utilities (for example, water, electricity and gas suppliers), have cash flows that are both predictable and reasonably certain. This will enable them to hold lower cash balances. For some businesses, cash balances may vary greatly according to the time of year. A seasonal business may accumulate cash during the high season to enable it to meet commitments during the low season.
- *The opportunity cost of holding cash.* Where there are profitable opportunities in which to invest, it may not be wise to hold a large cash balance.
- *The level of inflation.* Holding cash during a period of rising prices will lead to a loss of purchasing power. The higher the level of inflation, the greater will be this loss.
- *The availability of near-liquid assets.* If a business has marketable securities or inventories that may easily be liquidated, high cash balances may not be necessary.
- *The availability of borrowing.* If a business can borrow easily (and quickly) there is less need to hold cash.
- *The cost of borrowing.* When interest rates are high, the option of borrowing becomes less attractive.
- *Economic conditions.* When the economy is in recession, businesses may prefer to hold cash so that they can be well placed to invest when the economy improves. In addition, during a recession, businesses may experience difficulties in collecting trade receivables. They may therefore hold higher cash balances than usual in order to meet commitments.
- *Relationships with suppliers.* Too little cash may hinder the ability of the business to pay suppliers promptly. This can lead to a loss of goodwill. It may also lead to discounts being forgone.

Controlling the cash balance

Several models have been developed to help control the cash balance of the business. One such model proposes the use of upper and lower control limits for cash balances and the use of a target cash balance. The model assumes that the business will invest in marketable investments that can easily be liquidated. These investments will be purchased or sold, as necessary, in order to keep the cash balance within the control limits.

The model proposes two upper and two lower control limits (see Figure 12.8). If the business exceeds either of the *outer* limits, the managers must decide whether, over the next few days, the cash balance is likely to return to a point within the *inner* control limits set. If this seems likely, then no action is required. If, however, it does not seem likely, managers should change the cash position by either buying or selling marketable investments. In Figure 12.8, we can see that the lower outer control limit has been breached for four days. If a four-day period is unacceptable, managers should sell marketable investments to replenish the cash balance.

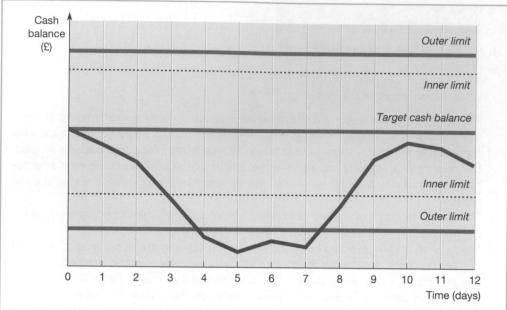

Management sets the upper and lower limits for the business's cash balance. When the balance goes beyond either of these limits, unless it is clear that the balance will return fairly quickly to within the limit, action will need to be taken. If the upper limit is breached, some cash will be placed on deposit or used to buy some marketable investments. If the lower limit is breached, the business will need to borrow some cash or sell some securities.

Figure 12.8 Controlling the cash balance

The model relies heavily on management judgement to determine where the control limits are set and the length of the period within which breaches of the control limits are acceptable. Past experience may be useful in helping managers decide on these issues. There are other models, however, that do not rely on management judgement. Instead, these use quantitative techniques to determine an optimal cash policy. One model proposed is the cash equivalent of the inventories economic order quantity model, discussed earlier in the chapter.

Cash budgets and managing cash

To manage cash effectively, it is useful for a business to prepare a cash budget. This is a very important tool for both planning and control purposes. Cash budgets were considered in Chapter 6 and so we shall not consider them again in detail. However, it is worth repeating that these statements enable managers to see how planned events are expected to affect the cash balance. The cash budget will identify periods when cash surpluses and cash deficits are expected.

When a cash surplus is expected to arise, managers must decide on the best use of the surplus funds. When a cash deficit is expected, managers must make adequate provision by borrowing, liquidating assets or rescheduling cash payments or receipts to deal with this. Cash budgets can help to control the cash held. Actual cash flows can be compared with the planned cash flows for the period. If there is a significant divergence between the planned cash flows and the actual cash flows, explanations must be sought and corrective action taken where necessary.

To refresh your memory on cash budgets it would probably be worth looking back at Chapter 6, pages 193 to 238.

Operating cash cycle

When managing cash, it is important to be aware of the **operating cash cycle (OCC)** of the business. For a business that purchases goods on credit for subsequent resale on credit, such as a wholesaler, it represents the period between the outlay of cash for the purchase of inventories and the ultimate receipt of cash from their sale. The OCC for this type of business is as shown in Figure 12.9.

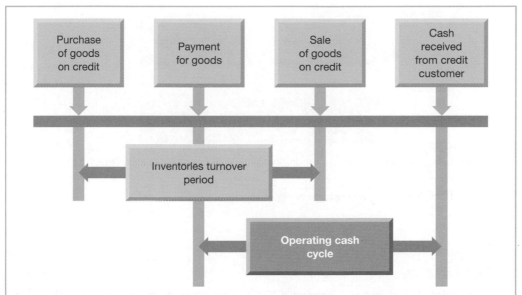

The OCC is the time lapse between paying for goods and receiving the cash from the sale of those goods. The length of the OCC has a significant impact on the amount of funds that the business needs to apply to working capital.

Figure 12.9 The operating cash cycle

Figure 12.9 shows that payment for inventories acquired on credit occurs some time after those inventories have been purchased. Therefore, no immediate cash outflow arises from the purchase. Similarly, cash receipts from credit customers will occur some time after the sale is made. There will be no immediate cash inflow as a result of the sale. The OCC is the period between the payment made to the supplier, for the goods concerned, and the cash received from the credit customer. Although Figure 12.9 depicts the position for a wholesaling business, the precise definition of the OCC can easily be adapted for other types of business.

The OCC is important because it has a significant influence on the financing requirements of the business. Broadly, the longer the cycle, the greater will be the financing requirements and the greater financial risks. The business may therefore wish to reduce the OCC to the minimum period possible. A business with a short OCC is said to have 'good (or strong) cash flow'.

For businesses that buy and sell goods on credit, the OCC can be deduced from their financial statements through the use of certain ratios. The calculations required are as shown in Figure 12.10.

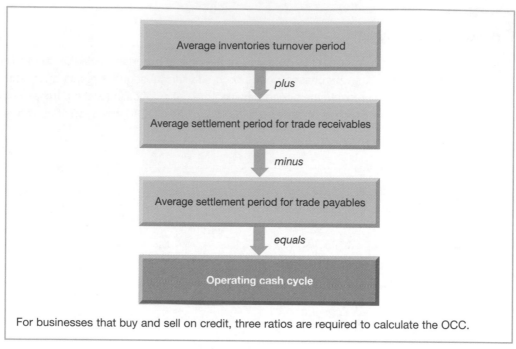

Figure 12.10 Calculating the operating cash cycle

Activity 12.18

The financial statements of Freezeqwik Ltd, a distributor of frozen foods, for the year ended 31 December last year are:

Income statement for the year ended 31 December last year

	£000	£000
Sales revenue		820
Cost of sales		
Opening inventories	142	
Purchases	568	
	710	
Closing inventories	(166)	(544)
Gross profit		276
Administration expenses		(120)
Distribution expenses		(95)
Operating profit		61
Financial expenses		(32)
Profit before taxation		29
Taxation		(7)
Profit for the year		22

Statement of financial position as at 31 December last year

	£000
ASSETS	
Non-current assets	
Property, plant and equipment	364
Current assets	
Inventories	166
Trade receivables	264
Cash	24
	454
Total assets	818
EQUITY AND LIABILITIES	
Equity	
Ordinary share capital	300
Retained earnings	352
	652
Current liabilities	
Trade payables	159
Taxation	7
	166
Total equity and liabilities	818

All purchases and sales are on credit. There has been no change in the level of trade receivables or payables over the period.

Calculate the length of the OCC for the business.

The OCC may be calculated as follows:

Number of days

Average inventories turnover period:

$$\frac{\text{(Opening inventories + Closing inventories)}/2}{\text{Cost of sales}} \times 365 = \frac{(142 + 166)/2}{544} \times 365 \qquad 103$$

Average settlement period for trade receivables:

$$\frac{\text{Trade receivables}}{\text{Credit sales}} \times 365 = \frac{264}{820} \times 365 \qquad 118$$

Average settlement period for trade payables:

$$\frac{\text{Trade payables}}{\text{Credit purchases}} \times 365 = \frac{159}{568} \times 365 \qquad (102)$$

OCC   119

We can see from the formula above that if a business wishes to reduce the OCC, it should do one or more of the following:

- reduce the average inventories turnover period;
- reduce the average settlement period for trade receivables; and/or
- increase the average settlement period for trade payables.

Assume that Freezeqwik Ltd (Activity 12.18) wishes to reduce its OCC by 30 days. Evaluate each of the options available to this business.

The average inventories turnover period for the business represents more than three months' sales requirements. Similarly, the average settlement period for trade receivables represents nearly four months' sales. Both periods seem quite long. It is possible that both could be reduced through greater operating efficiency. Improving inventories control and credit control procedures may achieve the required reduction in OCC without any adverse effect on future sales. If so, this may offer the best way forward.

The average settlement period for trade payables represents more than three months' purchases. Any decision to extend this period, however, must be given very careful consideration. It is quite long and may already be breaching the payment terms required by suppliers.

There is no reason why the 30 days reduction in the OCC could not come from a combination of altering all three of the periods involved (inventories, trade receivables and trade payables).

Before a final decision is made, full account must be taken of current trading conditions.

It seems to be quite common, in practice, for businesses to try to maintain the OCC at a particular target level. However, not all days in the OCC are of equal value. In Activity 12.18, for example, the operating cash cycle is 119 days. If the average settlement period for both trade receivables and trade payables were increased by seven days, the OCC would remain at 119 days. The amount tied up in working capital, however, would not remain the same. Trade receivables would increase by £15,726 (that is, 7 × £820,000/365) and trade payables would increase by £10,893 (that is, 7 × £568,000/365). This means that there would be a net increase of £4,833 in working capital.

Real World 12.9 shows the average operating cash cycle for large US and European businesses.

Real World 12.9

Cycling along

The survey of working capital by Ernst and Young (see Real World 12.2, page 457) calculated the average operating cash cycle for the top 1,000 European businesses (excluding financial and auto manufacturing businesses). The results for the period 2002 to 2014 are set out in Figure 12.11.

The average operating cash cycle has reduced by 21 per cent over the twelve years between 2002 and 2014, with each element of working capital making a contribution to this. The inventories holding period fell by 3 per cent and the trade

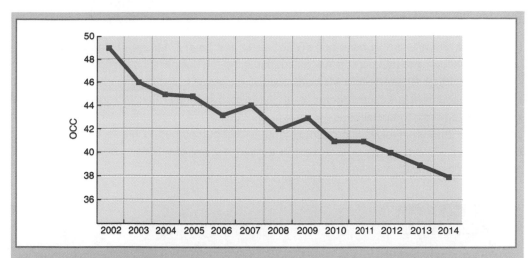

Figure 12.11 The average OCC of large European businesses for 2002 to 2014

receivables settlement period fell by 11 per cent, while the trade payables settlement period increased by 7 per cent.

Source: Adapted from Table 2 in Ernst and Young (2014) All Tied Up: Working Capital Management Report 2014, p. 6, www.ey.com.

Cash transmission

A business will normally wish to benefit from receipts from customers at the earliest opportunity. Where cash is received, the benefit is immediate. Where payment is made by cheque, however, there may be a delay before it is cleared through the banking system. The business must therefore wait before it can benefit from the amount paid in. In recent years, the CHAPS (Clearing House Automated Payments) system has helped to reduce the time that cheques spend in the banking system. It is now possible for cheques to be fast tracked so that they reach the recipient's bank account on the same day. Payment by cheque, however, is in decline. Increasingly, customers prefer to instruct their bank to make a direct transfer of the amount owed to the business's bank account. The transfer may be completed within hours and provides a more efficient form of cash transmission for both parties.

Transfers between a customer's bank account and the business bank account may also be carried out by setting up a standing order or a direct debit. In both cases, the transfer will then take place on an agreed date. Businesses providing services over time, such as insurance, satellite television and mobile phone services, often rely on this method of payment.

A final way in which a business may be paid promptly is through the use of a debit card. This allows the customer's bank account to be charged (debited) and the seller's bank account to be simultaneously increased (credited) with the sale price of the item. Many types of business, including retailers and restaurants, use this method. It is operated through computerised cash tills and is referred to as electronic funds transfer at point of sale (EFTPOS).

Bank overdrafts

Bank overdrafts are simply bank current accounts that have a negative balance. They are a type of bank loan and can be a useful tool in managing the business's cash flow requirements.

Real World 12.10 shows how Mears Group plc managed to improve its cash flows through better management practices. Mears is an AIM-listed business that provides maintenance and improvements to social housing, as well as other support services. Most of its work is small scale (that is, involves lots of small jobs) and is outsourced to Mears by public-sector organisations. The businesses took part in a major survey of working capital management undertaken by REL Consulting.

Real World 12.10

Putting cash to work

The nature of the work undertaken by Mears tends to lead to the business undertaking thousands of relatively small value jobs. This leads to potential problems in managing working capital, particularly in the area of management and collection of trade receivables (debts). The business's finance director, Andrew Smith, makes the point that, for such a business, failure to manage trade receivables effectively could easily lead to the collapse of the business. Despite the difficulties, Mears proved to be one of the best performers in this area, as shown by the 2015 REL Working Capital Survey, having massively reduced the length of its operating cash cycle from its previous years results.

Mears attributed its improvement in trade receivables management to the introduction of a new IT system, in the design of which, accountants had been heavily involved. The business has managed to promote a 'cash culture' where a particular job is only viewed as being completed once the cash for it has been received.

Source: Information taken from Crump, R., (2015) 'Debt is king: REL working capital survey 2015, *Financial Director*, 20 August.

MANAGING TRADE PAYABLES

Most businesses buy their goods and services on credit. Trade payables are the other side of the coin from trade receivables. In a trade credit transaction, one business's trade payable is another one's trade receivable. Trade payables are an important source of finance for most businesses. They have been described as a 'spontaneous' source, as they tend to increase in line with the increase in the level of activity achieved by a business.

There are potential costs associated with taking trade credit. A business that buys supplies on credit may incur additional administration and accounting costs resulting from the scrutiny and payment of invoices, maintaining and updating payables accounts, and so on. Furthermore, customers who take credit may not be as well treated as those who pay immediately. When goods are in short supply, they may be given lower priority. They may also be less favoured in terms of delivery dates or in gaining access to technical support. Where credit is required, customers may even have to pay more. In most industries, however, trade credit is the norm. As a result, these disadvantages do not normally apply unless, perhaps, the credit facilities are being abused.

The benefits to be gained from taking credit usually outweigh any costs involved. In effect, it is an interest-free loan from suppliers. It can also provide a more convenient way of paying for goods and services than paying by cash. Furthermore, during a period of inflation, there is an economic gain from paying later rather than sooner for goods and services supplied.

Activity 12.20

Why might a supplier prefer a customer to take a period of credit rather than pay for the goods or services on delivery? (There are probably two reasons.)

1 Paying on delivery may not be administratively convenient for the seller. Most customers will take a period of credit, so the systems of the seller will be geared up to receive payment after a reasonable period of credit.
2 A credit period can allow any problems with the goods or service supplied to be resolved before payment is made. This might avoid the seller having to make refunds.

Delaying payment to suppliers may be a sign of financial problems. It may also, however, reflect an imbalance in bargaining power. It is not unusual for large businesses to delay payment to small suppliers, which are reliant on them for continuing trade. The UK government has encouraged large businesses to sign up to a 'Prompt Payment Code' to help small suppliers. This achieved only limited success, however. As a result, the Code was strengthened in 2017.

Taking advantage of cash discounts

Where a supplier offers a discount for prompt payment, the business should give careful consideration to the possibility of paying within the discount period. Example 12.6 illustrates the cost of forgoing possible discounts.

Example 12.6

Hassan Ltd takes 70 days to pay for goods from its supplier. To encourage prompt payment, the supplier has offered the business a 2 per cent discount if payment for goods is made within 30 days. Hassan Ltd is not sure, however, whether it is worth taking the discount offered.

If the discount is taken, payment could be made on the last day of the discount period (that is, the 30th day). However, if the discount is not taken, payment will be made after 70 days. This means that, by not taking the discount, the business will receive an extra 40 days' (that is, 70 – 30) credit. The cost of this extra credit to the business will be the 2 per cent discount forgone. If we annualise the cost of this discount forgone, we have:

$$365/40 \times 2\% = 18.3\%^*$$

We can see that the annual cost of forgoing the discount is very high. It may, therefore, be profitable for the business to pay the supplier within the discount period, even if it means that it will have to borrow to enable it to do so.

* This is an approximate annual rate. For the more mathematically minded, the precise rate is:

$$\{[(1 + 2/98)^{9.125}] - 1\} \times 100\% = 20.2\%$$

The key difference is that, in this calculation, compound interest is used, whereas in the first calculation, simple interest is used, which is not strictly correct.

Controlling trade payables

To help monitor the level of trade credit taken, management can calculate the **average settlement period for trade payables ratio**. This ratio is:

$$\text{Average settlement period for trade payables} = \frac{\text{Average trade payables}}{\text{Credit purchases}} \times 365$$

Once again, this provides an average figure, which could be misleading. A more informative approach would be to produce an ageing schedule for payables. This would look much the same as the ageing schedule for receivables described earlier in Example 12.4.

Managing working capital

As a footnote to our discussion about the management of working capital, we draw on the experience of two firms of management consultants. **Real World 12.11** is an extract from an article that makes the point that many businesses do not pay as much attention to it as they should since the rewards in liberating funds tied up are often huge. The article was written by two consultants with the international management consultants, McKinsey and Company.

Real World 12.11

Uncovering cash

Managing a company's working capital isn't the sexiest task. It's often painstakingly technical. It's hard to know how well a company is doing, even relative to peers; published financial data are too high level for precise benchmarking. And because working capital doesn't appear on the income statement, it doesn't directly affect earnings or operating profit—the measures that most commonly influence compensation (salaries, bonuses and so on). Although working capital management has long been a business-school staple, our research shows that performance is surprisingly variable, even among companies in the same industry.

That's quite a missed opportunity—and it has implications beyond the finance department. Working capital can amount to as much as several months' worth of revenues, which isn't trivial. Improving its management can be a quick way to free up cash. We routinely see companies generate tens or even hundreds of millions of dollars of cash impact within 60 to 90 days, without increasing sales or cutting costs. And the rewards for persistence and dedication to continuous improvement can be lucrative.

The global aluminum company Alcoa made working capital a priority in 2009 in response to the financial crisis and global economic downturn, and it recently celebrated its 17th straight quarter of year-on-year reduction in net working capital. Over that time, the company has reduced its net working capital cycle—the amount of time it takes to turn assets and liabilities into cash—by 23 days and unlocked $1.4 billion in cash. For distressed companies, that kind of improvement can be a lifeline. For healthy companies, the windfall can often be reinvested in ways that more directly affect value creation, such as growth initiatives or increased balance-sheet flexibility. Moreover, the process of improving working capital can also highlight opportunities in other areas, such as operations, supply-chain management, procurement, sales, and finance.

Of course, not all reductions in working capital are beneficial. Too little inventory can disrupt operations. Stretching supplier payment terms can leak back in the form of higher prices, if not negotiated carefully, or unwittingly send a signal of distress to the market. But managers who are mindful of such pitfalls can still improve working capital by setting incentives that ensure visibility, collecting the right data, defining meaningful targets, and managing ongoing performance.

Working capital is often undermanaged simply because of lack of awareness or attention. It may not be tracked or published in a way that is transparent and relevant to employees, or it may not be communicated as a priority. In particular, working capital is often underemphasized when the performance of a business—and of its managers—is evaluated primarily on income-statement measures such as earnings before interest, taxes, depreciation, and amortization (EBITDA) or earnings per share, which don't reflect changes in working capital.

What actions should managers take, beyond communicating that working capital is important? In our experience, the selection of metrics (measurements) to manage the business and measure performance is especially important, because different metrics will lead to different outcomes. For one manufacturing company, switching from EBITDA (earnings before interest, taxes, depreciation and amortisation) to free cash flow as a primary measure of performance had an immediate effect; managers began to measure cash flow at the plant level and then distributed inventory metrics to frontline supervisors. As a result, inventories quickly fell as managers, for the first time, identified and debated issues such as the right level of inventories and coordination among plants.

Source: Extract from Davies, R. and Merin, D. (2014) *Uncovering Cash and Insights From Working Capital;* McKinsey and Company, www.mckinsey.com, July.

Real World 12.12 sets out a 'health check' for businesses concerning the management of working capital. It was devised by REL Consulting, a firm of management consultants specialising in working capital management issues.

Real World 12.12

Working out whether working capital is working

The diagnostic check below takes the form of a series of questions, each with five possible answers. These answers attract a score from 0 to 4 according to the maturity level of the working capital management process: the higher the score, the more mature it is. The questions contain a few differences in terminology to that used in the chapter. These differences are as follows:

DSO (Days sales outstanding) = Settlement period for trade receivables
DIO (Days inventory turnover) = Inventory turnover period
DPO (Days payables outstanding) = Settlement period for trade payables
CCC (Cash conversion cycle) = Operating cash cycle

What are the strengths and weaknesses of your current working capital processes?

1. How quickly do you collect cash?
   __ Less than 30 days (4)
   __ 31–45 days (3)
   __ 46–60 days (2)
   __ More than 61 days (1)
   __ Don't know (0)

2. What per cent of payments do you receive after the due date?
   __ Less than 5% (4)
   __ 6–10% (3)
   __ 11–20% (2)
   __ 21%+ (1)
   __ Don't know (0)

3. How quickly do you pay supplier invoices?
   __ Don't know (0)
   __ Less than 30 days (1)
   __ 31–45 days (2)
   __ 46–60 days (3)
   __ More than 61 days (4)

4. What proportion of supplier invoices are paid after the due date?
   __ 0–5% (4)
   __ 6–10% (3)
   __ 11–20% (2)
   __ 21%+ (1)
   __ Don't know (0)

→

5. How much inventory do you hold in days?
__ Up to 30 days (4)
__ 31–60 days (3)
__ 61–90 days (2)
__ More than 91 (1)
__ Don't know (0)

6. What per cent of orders are delivered on time?
__ 98–100% (4)
__ 95–97% (3)
__ 90–94% (2)
__ Less than 90% (1)
__ Don't know (0)

7. How quickly after month-end do you report the metrics of DSO, DIO, DPO & CCC?
__ Within 5 days (4)
__ 6–10 days (3)
__ 11–15 days (2)
__ >16 days (1)
__ Do not report at all (0)

8. How standardised are your working capital metrics across the different reporting units?
__ Fully standardised (4)
__ Partly standardised (3)
__ Only standard at Group level (2)
__ Not at all standardised (1)
__ Do not report at all (0)

9. How well trained are employees in working capital management?
__ Fully trained with regular updates (4)
__ Trained at least once (3)
__ Ad hoc training (2)
__ Access to relevant WC training materials on company intranet (1)
__ No specific WC training (0)

10. Are the functional and individual responsibilities for working capital management documented and clearly assigned across the organisation?
__ Fully documented and assigned for all levels in the organisation (4)
__ Partially documented and assigned at C-suite (3)
__ Partially documented and assigned within functional roles (2)
__ Not documented but assigned on ad hoc basis (1)
__ Not considered (0)

Source: REL Consulting, *The Working Capitalist – Spring 2016*, p. 8, www.relconsultancy.com.

Self-assessment question 12.1

Town Mills Ltd is a wholesale business. Extracts from the business's most recent financial statements are as follows:

Income statement for the year ended 31 May

	£000
Sales	903
Cost of sales	(652)
Gross profit	251
Other operating expenses	(109)
Operating profit	142
Interest	(11)
Profit before taxation	131
Taxation	(38)
Profit for the year	93

Statement of financial position as at 31 May

	£000
ASSETS	
Non-current assets	
Property, plant and equipment at cost	714
Accumulated depreciation	(295)
	419
Current assets	
Inventories	192
Trade receivables	202
	394
Total assets	813
EQUITY AND LIABILITIES	
Equity	
Ordinary share capital	200
Retained earnings	246
	446
Current liabilities	
Trade payables	260
Borrowings (all bank overdraft)	107
	367
Total equity and liabilities	813

The levels of trade receivables and trade payables increased by 10 per cent, by value, during the year ended 31 May. Inventories levels remained the same. The chief financial officer believes that inventories levels are too high and should be reduced.

Required:
(a) Calculate the average operating cash cycle (in days) during the year ended 31 May and explain to what use this value can be put and what limitations it has.
(b) Discuss whether there is evidence that the business has a liquidity problem.
(c) Explain the types of risk and cost that might be reduced by following the chief financial officer's proposal to reduce inventories levels.

The answer to this question can be found at the back of the book on pp. 524–525.

SUMMARY

The main points of this chapter may be summarised as follows.

Working capital

- Is the difference between current assets and current liabilities.

- That is, working capital = inventories + trade receivables + cash – trade payables – bank overdrafts.

- An investment in working capital cannot be avoided in practice – typically large amounts are involved.

Inventories

- There are costs of holding inventories, which include:
  - lost interest;
  - storage cost;
  - insurance cost; and
  - obsolescence.
- There are also costs of not holding sufficient inventories, which include:
  - loss of sales and customer goodwill;
  - production dislocation;
  - loss of flexibility – cannot take advantage of opportunities; and
  - reorder costs – low inventories imply more frequent ordering.
- Practical points on inventories management include:
  - implement selective levels of control based on value (ABC);
  - identify optimum order size – models can help with this;
  - set inventories reorder levels;
  - use budgets;
  - keep reliable inventories records;
  - use accounting ratios (for example, inventories turnover period ratio);
  - establish systems for security of inventories and authorisation;
  - employ ERP applications to automate and integrate the recording and management of inventories;
  - implement just-in-time (JIT) inventories management; and
  - categorise inventories based on variations in demand (XYZ).

Trade receivables

- When assessing which customers should receive credit, the five Cs of credit can be used:
  - capital;
  - capacity;
  - collateral;
  - condition; and
  - character.
- The costs of allowing credit include:
  - lost interest;
  - lost purchasing power;
  - costs of assessing customer creditworthiness;
  - administration cost;
  - bad debts; and
  - cash discounts (for prompt payment).
- The costs of denying credit include loss of customer goodwill.
- Practical points on receivables management:
  - establish a policy;
  - assess and monitor customer creditworthiness;
  - establish effective administration of receivables;

- establish a policy on bad debts;
- consider cash discounts;
- use financial ratios (for example, average settlement period for trade receivables ratio); and
- use ageing summaries.

Cash

- The costs of holding cash include:
  - lost interest; and
  - lost purchasing power.
- The costs of holding insufficient cash include:
  - loss of supplier goodwill if unable to meet commitments on time;
  - loss of opportunities;
  - inability to claim cash discounts; and
  - costs of borrowing (should an obligation need to be met at short notice).
- Practical points on cash management:
  - establish a policy;
  - plan cash flows;
  - make judicious use of bank overdraft finance – it can be cheap and flexible;
  - use short-term cash surpluses profitably;
  - bank frequently;
  - transmit cash promptly;
  - operating cash cycle (for a wholesaler) = average inventories' turnover period + average settlement period for trade receivables – average settlement period for trade payables.
- An objective of working capital management is to limit the length of the operating cash cycle (OCC), subject to any risks that this may cause.

Trade payables

- The costs of taking credit include:
  - higher price than purchases for immediate cash settlement;
  - administrative costs; and
  - restrictions imposed by seller.
- The costs of not taking credit include:
  - lost interest-free borrowing;
  - lost purchasing power; and
  - inconvenience – paying at the time of purchase can be inconvenient.
- Practical points on payables management:
  - establish a policy;
  - exploit free credit as far as possible; and
  - use accounting ratios (for example, average settlement period for trade payables ratio).

FURTHER READING

If you would like to explore the topics covered in this chapter in more depth, we recommend the following:

Sagner, J. (2014) *Working Capital Management: Applications and Case Studies*, Wiley Corporate F&A, Chapters 2–8.

Brigham, E. and Ehrdhart, M. (2016) *Financial Management: Theory and Practice*, 15th edn, Cengage Learning Custom Publishing, Chapters 16 and 28.

Hillier, D., Clacher, I., Ross, S., Westerfield, R. and Jordan, B. (2014) *Fundamentals of Corporate Finance*, 2nd European edn, McGraw-Hill Education, Chapter 17.

McLaney, E. (2017) *Business Finance: Theory and practice*, 11th edn, Pearson, Chapters 8, 9, 11 and 12.

Pike, R., Neale, B. and Linsley, P. (2015) *Corporate Finance and Investment*, 8th edn, Pearson, Chapters 13 and 14.

REVIEW QUESTIONS

Solutions to these questions can be found at the back of the book on p. 534.

12.1 Tariq is the credit manager of Heltex plc. He is concerned that the pattern of monthly cash receipts from credit sales shows that credit collection is poor compared with budget. Heltex's sales director believes that Tariq is to blame for this situation, but Tariq insists that he is not. Why might Tariq not be to blame for the deterioration in the credit collection period?

12.2 How might each of the following affect the level of inventories held by a business?

(a) An increase in the number of production bottlenecks experienced by the business.
(b) A rise in the business's cost of capital.
(c) A decision to offer customers a narrower range of products in the future.
(d) A switch of suppliers from an overseas business to a local business.
(e) A deterioration in the quality and reliability of bought-in components.

12.3 What are the reasons for holding inventories? Are these reasons different from the reasons for holding cash?

12.4 Identify the costs of holding:

(a) too little cash`
(b) too much cash.

EXERCISES

Exercises with coloured numbers have solutions given at the back of the book on pp. 571–574.

Basic-level exercises

12.1 The chief executive officer of Sparkrite Ltd, a trading business, has just received summary sets of financial statements for last year and this year:

Income statements for years ended 30 September

	Last year		This year	
	£000	£000	£000	£000
Sales revenue		1,800		1,920
Cost of sales				
Opening inventories	160		200	
Purchases	1,120		1,175	
	1,280		1,375	
Closing inventories	(200)	(1,080)	(250)	(1,125)
Gross profit		720		795
Expenses		(680)		(750)
Profit for the year		40		45

Statements of financial position as at 30 September

	Last year £000	This year £000
ASSETS		
Non-current assets	950	930
Current assets		
Inventories	200	250
Trade receivables	375	480
Cash at bank	4	2
	579	732
Total assets	1,529	1,662
EQUITY AND LIABILITIES		
Equity		
Fully paid £1 ordinary shares	825	883
Retained earnings	509	554
	1,334	1,437
Current liabilities	195	225
Total equity and liabilities	1,529	1,662

The chief financial officer has expressed concern at the increase in inventories and trade receivables levels.

Required:

(a) Show, by using the data given, how you would calculate ratios that could be used to measure inventories and trade receivables levels during last year and this year.

(b) Discuss the ways in which the management of Sparkrite Ltd could exercise control over the levels of:
   (i)   inventories
   (ii) trade receivables.

12.2 Hercules Wholesalers Ltd has been particularly concerned with its liquidity position in recent months. The most recent income statement and statement of financial position of the business are as follows:

Income statement for the year ended 31 December last year

	£000	£000
Sales revenue		452
Cost of sales		
Opening inventories	125	
Purchases	341	
	466	
Closing inventories	(143)	(323)
Gross profit		129
Expenses		(132)
Loss for the year		(3)

Statement of financial position as at 31 December last year

	£000
ASSETS	
Non-current assets	
Property, plant and equipment	357
Current assets	
Inventories	143
Trade receivables	163
	306
Total assets	663
EQUITY AND LIABILITIES	
Equity	
Ordinary share capital	100
Retained earnings	158
	258
Non-current liabilities	
Borrowings – loans	120
Current liabilities	
Trade payables	145
Borrowings – bank overdraft	140
	285
Total equity and liabilities	663

The trade receivables and payables were maintained at a constant level throughout the year.

Required:

(a) Explain why Hercules Wholesalers Ltd is concerned about its liquidity position.

(b) Calculate the operating cash cycle for Hercules Wholesalers Ltd.

(c) State what steps may be taken to improve the operating cash cycle of the business.

Intermediate-level exercises

12.3 International Electric plc at present offers its customers 30 days' credit. Half of the customers, by value, pay on time. The other half takes an average of 70 days to pay. The business is considering offering a cash discount of 2 per cent to its customers for payment within 30 days.

The credit controller anticipates that half of the customers who now take an average of 70 days to pay (that is, a quarter of all customers) will pay in 30 days. The other half (the final quarter) will still take an average of 70 days to pay. The scheme will also reduce bad debts by £300,000 a year.

Annual sales revenue of £365 million is made evenly throughout the year. At present the business has a large overdraft (£60 million) with its bank at an interest cost of 12 per cent a year.

Required:

(a) Calculate the approximate equivalent annual percentage cost of a discount of 2 per cent, which reduces the time taken by credit customers to pay from 70 days to 30 days. (*Hint*: This part can be answered without reference to the narrative above.)

(b) Calculate the value of trade receivables outstanding under both the old and new schemes.

(c) How much will the scheme cost the business in discounts?

(d) Should the business go ahead with the scheme? State what other factors, if any, should be taken into account.

12.4 Your superior, the general manager of Plastics Manufacturers Limited, has recently been talking to the chief buyer of Plastic Toys Limited, which manufactures a wide range of toys for young children. At present, Plastic Toys is considering changing its supplier of plastic granules and has offered to buy its entire requirement of 2,000 kg a month from you at the going market rate, provided that you will grant it three months' credit on its purchases. The following information is available:

1 Plastic granules sell for £10 a kg, variable costs are £7 a kg and fixed costs £2 a kg.
2 Your own business is financially strong and has sales revenue of £15 million a year. For the foreseeable future it will have surplus capacity and it is actively looking for new outlets.
3 Extracts from Plastic Toys' financial statements:

	Year 1 £000	Year 2 £000	Year 3 £000
Sales revenue	800	980	640
Operating profit (Profit before interest and tax)	100	110	(150)
Capital employed	600	650	575
Current assets			
Inventories	200	220	320
Trade receivables	140	160	160
	340	380	480
Current liabilities			
Trade payables	180	190	220
Overdraft	100	150	310
	280	340	530
Working capital	60	40	(50)

Required:

Advise your general manager on the acceptability of the proposal. You should give your reasons and do any calculations you consider necessary.

12.5 Delphi plc has recently decided to enter the expanding market for digital radios. The business will manufacture the radios and sell them to small TV and hi-fi specialists, medium-sized music stores and large retail chain stores. The new product will be launched next February and predicted sales revenue for the product from each customer group for February and the expected rate of growth for subsequent months are as follows:

Customer type	February sales revenue £000	Monthly compound sales revenue growth %	Credit sales (Months)
TV and hi-fi specialists	20	4	1
Music stores	30	6	2
Retail chain stores	40	8	3

The business is concerned about the financing implications of launching the new product, as it is already experiencing liquidity problems. In addition, it is concerned that the credit control department will find it difficult to cope. This is a new market for the business and there are likely to be many new customers who will have to be investigated for creditworthiness.

Workings should be in £000 and calculations made to one decimal place only.

Required:

(a) Prepare an ageing schedule of the monthly trade receivables balance relating to the new product for each of the first four months of the new product's life, and comment on the results. The schedule should analyse the trade receivables outstanding according to customer type. It should also indicate, for each customer type, the relevant percentage outstanding in relation to the total amount outstanding for each month.

(b) Identify and discuss the factors that should be taken into account when evaluating the creditworthiness of the new business customers.

Advanced-level exercises

12.6 Mayo Computers Ltd has annual sales of £20 million. Bad debts amount to £100,000 a year. All sales made by the business are on credit and, at present, credit terms are negotiable by the customer. On average, the settlement period for trade receivables is 60 days. Trade receivables are financed by an overdraft bearing a 14 per cent rate of interest per year. The business is currently reviewing its credit policies to see whether more efficient and profitable methods could be employed. Only one proposal has so far been put forward concerning the management of trade credit.

The credit control department has proposed that customers should be given a 2.5 per cent discount if they pay within 30 days. For those who do not pay within this period, a maximum of 50 days' credit should be given. The credit department believes that 60 per cent of customers will take advantage of the discount by paying at the end of the discount period. The remainder will pay at the end of 50 days. The credit department believes that bad debts can be effectively eliminated by adopting the proposed policies and by employing stricter credit investigation procedures, which will cost an additional £20,000 a year. The credit department is confident that these new policies will not result in any reduction in sales revenue.

Required:

Calculate the net annual cost (savings) to the business of abandoning its existing credit policies and adopting the proposals of the credit control department. (*Hint*: To answer this question you must weigh the costs of administration and cash discounts against the savings in bad debts and interest charges.)

12.7 Boswell Enterprises Ltd is reviewing its trade credit policy. The business, which sells all of its goods on credit, has estimated that sales revenue for the forthcoming year will be £3 million under the existing policy. Credit customers representing 30 per cent of trade receivables are expected to pay one month after being invoiced and 70 per cent are expected to pay two months after being invoiced. These estimates are in line with previous years' figures.

At present, no cash discounts are offered to customers. However, to encourage prompt payment, the business is considering giving a 2.5 per cent cash discount to credit customers who pay in one month or less. Given this incentive, the business expects credit customers accounting for 60 per cent of trade receivables to pay one month after being invoiced and those accounting for 40 per cent of trade receivables to pay two months after being invoiced. The business believes that the introduction of a cash discount policy will prove attractive to some customers and will lead to a 5 per cent increase in total sales revenue.

Irrespective of the trade credit policy adopted, the gross profit margin of the business will be 20 per cent for the forthcoming year and three months' inventories will be held. Fixed monthly expenses of £15,000 and variable expenses (excluding discounts), equivalent to 10 per cent of sales revenue, will be incurred and will be paid one month in arrears. Trade payables will be paid in arrears and will be equal to two months' cost of sales. The business will hold a fixed cash balance of £140,000 throughout the year, whichever trade credit policy is adopted. Ignore taxation.

Required:
(a) Calculate the investment in working capital at the end of the forthcoming year under:
   (1) the existing policy
   (2) the proposed policy.
(b) Calculate the expected profit for the forthcoming year under:
   (1) the existing policy
   (2) the proposed policy.
(c) Advise the business as to whether it should implement the proposed policy.
(*Hint*: The investment in working capital will be made up of inventories, trade receivables and cash, *less* trade payables and any unpaid expenses at the year end.)

12.8 Goliath plc is a food wholesaler. The most recent financial statements of the business are as follows:

Income statement for the year to 31 May

	£000	£000
Sales revenue		2,400.0
Cost of sales		
Opening inventories	550.0	
Purchases	1,450.0	
	2,000.0	
Closing inventories	(560.0)	(1,440.0)
Gross profit		960.0
Administration expenses		(300.0)
Selling expenses		(436.0)
Operating profit		224.0
Interest payable		(40.0)
Profit before taxation		184.0
Taxation (25%)		(46.0)
Profit for the period		138.0

Statement of financial position as at 31 May

	£000
Non-current assets	
Property, plant and equipment	456.4
Current assets	
Inventories	560.0
Trade receivables	565.0
Cash at bank	36.4
	1,161.4
Total assets	1,617.8
Equity	
£1 ordinary shares	200.0
Retained earnings	520.8
	720.8
Non-current liabilities	
Borrowings – loan notes	400.0
Current liabilities	
Trade payables	451.0
Taxation	46.0
	497.0
Total equity and liabilities	1,617.8

All sales and purchases are made on credit.

The business is considering whether to grant extended credit facilities to its customers. It has been estimated that increasing the settlement period for trade receivables by a further 20 days will increase the sales revenue of the business by 10 per cent. However, inventories will have to be increased by 15 per cent to cope with the increased demand. It is estimated that purchases will have to rise to £1,668,000 during the next year as a result of these changes. To finance the increase in inventories and trade receivables, the business will increase the settlement period taken from suppliers by 15 days and use a loan facility bearing a 10 per cent rate of interest for the remaining balance.

If the policy is implemented, bad debts are likely to increase by £120,000 a year and administration costs will rise by 15 per cent.

Required:

(a) Calculate the increase or decrease to each of the following that will occur in the forthcoming year if the proposed policy is implemented:

(i) operating cash cycle (based on year-end figures)

(ii) net investment in inventories, trade receivables and trade payables

(iii) profit for the period.

(b) Should the business implement the proposed policy? Give reasons for your conclusion.

Appendix A
GLOSSARY OF KEY TERMS

ABC system of inventories control A method of applying different levels of inventories control, based on the value of each category of inventory. *p. 461*

Absorption costing A method of costing in which a 'fair share' of the total manufacturing/ service provision overhead cost is included when calculating the cost of a particular product or service. *p. 113*

Accounting rate of return (ARR) The average profit from an investment, expressed as a percentage of the average investment made. *p. 284*

Activity-based budgeting (ABB) A system of budgeting based on the philosophy of activity-based costing (ABC). *p. 218*

Activity-based costing (ABC) A technique for relating overheads to specific production or provision of a service. It is based on acceptance of the fact that overheads do not just occur but are caused by activities, such as holding products in stores, which 'drive' the costs. *p. 154*

Adverse variance A difference between planned and actual performance, usually where the difference will cause the actual profit to be lower than the budgeted one. *p. 245*

Ageing schedule of trade receivables A report analysing trade receivables into categories, according to the length of time outstanding. *p. 477*

Average inventories turnover period ratio The average time that inventories are held by the business. *p. 459*

Average settlement period for trade payables ratio The average time taken for a business to pay its trade payables (suppliers). *p. 491*

Average settlement period for trade receivables ratio The average time taken for trade receivables (credit customers) to pay the amounts owing to the business. *p. 477*

Balanced scorecard A framework for translating the aims and objectives of a business into a series of key performance measures and targets. *p. 364*

Batch costing A technique for identifying full cost, where the production of many types of goods and services, particularly goods, involves producing a batch of identical or nearly identical units of output, but where each batch is distinctly different from other batches. *p. 133*

Behavioural aspects of budgetary control The effect on people's attitudes and behaviour of the various aspects of using budgets as the basis for planning and controlling a business or other organisation. *p. 271*

Benchmarking Identifying a successful business, or part of a business, and measuring the efficiency and effectiveness of one's own business by comparison with this standard. *p. 176*

Benefit An outcome, resulting from a course of action, that helps a business to achieve its objectives. *p. 41*

Big data The huge volume of data that businesses collect relating to its environment. The data are varied, often generated at great velocity and collected from multiple sources. *p. 30*

Break-even (BE) analysis The activity of deducing the break-even point of some activity by analysing the relationship between cost, volume and revenue. *p. 70*

Break-even chart A graphical representation of the cost and sales revenue of some activity, at various levels, which enables the break-even point to be identified. *p. 71*

Break-even point (BEP) A level of activity where revenue will exactly equal total cost, so there is neither profit nor loss. *p. 72*

Budget A financial plan for the short term, typically one year or less. *p. 194*

Budget committee A group of managers formed to supervise and take responsibility for the budget-setting process. *p. 204*

Budget holder An individual responsible for a particular budget. *p. 209*

Budget officer An individual, often an accountant, appointed to carry out, or take immediate responsibility for having carried out, the tasks of the budget committee. *p. 204*

Budgetary control Using the budget as a yardstick against which the effectiveness of actual performance may be assessed. *p. 268*

Business cycle The expansion and contraction of business activity occurring within an economy over time. *p. 83*

Capital rationing Where a business has more viable investment opportunities than it has funds to finance them. *p. 313*

Cash discount A reduction in the amount due for goods or services sold on credit in return for prompt payment. *p. 475*

Committed cost A cost incurred that has not yet been paid, but which must, under some existing contract or obligation, be paid. *p. 46*

Comparability The requirement that similar items should be treated in the same manner for measurement and reporting purposes. *p. 19*

Compensating variance The situation where two variances, one adverse and the other favourable, are of equal size, and therefore cancel each other out. *p. 260*

Competitor analysis The process of gaining a sound knowledge of a competitor's business in order to gain competitive advantage. *p. 353*

Competitor array The process of identifying the key success factors for the industry and ranking the business and its competitors according to these factors. *p. 354*

Competitor profiling An examination of information relating to competitors to find out what strategies and plans they have developed, how they may react to the plans that the business has developed, and whether they have the capability to pose a serious threat. *p. 354*

Continual (or rolling) budget A budgeting system that continually updates budgets so that there is always a budget for a full planning period. *p. 198*

Contribution margin ratio The contribution from an activity expressed as a percentage of the sales revenue. *p. 76*

Contribution per unit Sales revenue per unit less variable cost per unit. *p. 75*

Control Compelling events to conform to plan. *p. 195*

Controllable cost A cost that is the responsibility of a specific manager. *p. 415*

Cost Amount of resources, usually measured in monetary terms, sacrificed to achieve a particular objective. *p. 41*

Cost allocation Assigning cost to cost centres according to the amount of cost that has been incurred in each centre. *p. 126*

Cost apportionment Dividing cost between cost centres on a basis that is considered to reflect fairly the cost incurred in each centre. *p. 126*

Cost behaviour The manner in which cost alters with changes in the level of activity. *p. 114*

Cost–benefit analysis Systematically weighing the cost of pursuing some objective against the benefits that it is likely to generate to enable a decision to be made as to whether to proceed. *p. 41*

Cost centre Some area, object, person or activity for which elements of cost are separately collected. In the context of responsibility accounting, it is an aspect of a business where management is responsible for the costs incurred. *p. 125*

Cost driver An activity that causes, or 'drives', a cost. *p. 154*

Cost of capital The cost to a business of the finance needed to fund an investment. *p. 299*

Cost-plus (or full cost) pricing Pricing output on the basis of its full cost, normally with a loading for profit. *p. 122*

Cost pool The sum of the overhead costs that are seen as being caused by the same cost driver. *p. 155*

Cost unit The objective for which a cost is being deduced, usually a product or service. *p. 106*

Customer profitability analysis (CPA) An assessment of the profitability to the business of individual customers, or types of customer. *p. 357*

Direct cost A cost that can be identified with a specific cost unit, to the extent that the effect of the cost can be measured in respect of that cost unit. *p. 111*

Direct labour efficiency variance The difference between the actual direct labour hours worked and the number of direct labour hours according to the flexed budget (budgeted direct labour hours for the actual output). This figure is multiplied by the budgeted direct labour rate for one hour. *p. 249*

Direct labour rate variance The difference between the actual cost of the direct labour hours worked and the direct labour cost allowed (actual direct labour hours worked at the budgeted labour rate). *p. 250*

Direct materials price variance The difference between the actual cost of the direct material used and the direct materials cost allowed (actual quantity of material used at the budgeted direct material cost). *p. 248*

Direct materials usage variance The difference between the actual quantity of direct materials used and the quantity of direct materials according to the flexed budget (budgeted usage for actual output). This quantity is multiplied by the budgeted direct materials cost for one unit of the direct materials. *p. 248*

Discount factor The rate applied to future cash flows to derive the present value of those cash flows. *p. 298*

Discounting Applying a discount factor to the cash flows of a project to take account of the time period involved and the cost of capital. It is, in effect, charging the project with the cost of financing it. *p 297*

Discretionary budget A budget based on a sum allocated at the discretion of senior management. *p. 209*

Division Business segment, often organised along geographical and/or product lines, through which large businesses are managed. *p. 407*

Economic order quantity (EOQ) The quantity of inventories that should be bought with each order so as to minimise total inventories ordering and carrying costs. *p. 463*

Economic value added (EVA®) A measure of business performance that concentrates on wealth generation. It is based on economic profit rather than accounting profit and takes full account of the cost of financing. *p. 374*

Economies of scale Cost savings per unit that result from undertaking a large volume of activities; they are due to factors such as division and specialisation of labour and discounts from bulk buying. *p. 82*

Elasticity of demand The extent to which the level of demand alters with changes in price. *p. 382*

Enterprise resource planning (ERP) system A system for automating and integrating business operations. *p. 466*

Equivalent units of output The number of completed units of output that could have been produced given the material cost and other manufacturing costs incurred. *p. 109*

Expected net present value (ENPV) A weighted average of the possible present value outcomes, where the probabilities associated with each outcome are used as weights. *p. 336*

Expected value A weighted average of the possible outcomes, where the probabilities associated with each outcome are used as weights. *p. 336*

Faithful representation The quality that ensures that information represents what it is supposed to represent. *p. 18*

Favourable variance A difference between planned and actual performance, usually where the difference will cause the actual profit to be higher than the budgeted profit. *p. 245*

Feedback control A control device where actual performance is compared with planned and where action is taken to deal with possible future divergences between these. *p. 241*

Feedforward control A control device where forecast future performance is compared with planned performance, and where action is taken to deal with divergences between these. *p. 242*

Financial accounting The measuring and reporting of accounting information for external users (those users other than the managers of the business). *p. 33*

Five Cs of credit A checklist of factors to be taken into account when assessing the creditworthiness of a customer. *p. 471*

Fixed cost A cost that stays the same when changes occur to the volume of activity. *p. 65*

Fixed overhead spending variance The difference between the actual fixed overhead cost and the fixed overhead cost, according to the flexed (and the original) budget. *p. 251*

Flexible budget A budget that is adjusted to reflect the actual level of output achieved. *p. 244*

Flexing a budget Revising a budget to what it would have been had the planned level of output been different. *p. 243*

Forecast Prediction of future outcomes or of the future states of the environment. *p. 198*

Full cost The total of direct and indirect cost of pursuing some activity or objective (such as providing a particular product or service). *p. 106*

Full cost pricing *See* Cost-plus pricing. *p. 390*

Full costing Deducing the total direct and indirect (overhead) costs of pursuing some activity or objective. *p. 106*

High-low method An approach to distinguishing between the fixed and variable elements of a cost by looking at just two sets of past data. *p. 69*

Historic cost What was paid for an asset when it was originally acquired. *p. 42*

Ideal standards Standards that assumes perfect operating conditions where there is no inefficiency due to lost production time, defects and so on. The objective of setting an ideal standard is to encourage employees to strive towards excellence. *p. 262*

Incremental budgeting Constructing budgets on the basis of what happened in the previous period, with some adjustment for expected changes in the forthcoming budget period. *p. 209*

Indirect cost (or overheads) The element of cost that cannot be directly measured in respect of a particular cost unit – that is, all cost except direct cost. *p. 111*

Inflation An increase in the general price of goods and services resulting in a corresponding decline in the purchasing power of money. *p. 294*

Internal rate of return (IRR) The discount rate for an investment that will have the effect of producing a zero NPV. *p. 301*

Investment centre Some area or activity whose manager is responsible and accountable for the profit generated and capital invested. *p. 407*

Irrelevant cost A cost that is not relevant to a particular decision. *p. 43*

Job costing A technique for identifying the full cost per cost unit, where each cost unit is not identical to other cost units produced. *p. 111*

Just-in-time (JIT) inventories management A system of inventories management that aims to have supplies delivered to production or sales just in time for their required use. *p. 466*

Kaizen costing An approach to cost control where an attempt is made to control cost by trying continually to make cost savings, often only small ones, from one time period to the next during the production stage of the product life cycle. *p. 170*

Key performance indicator (KPI) Financial and/or non-financial measure that reflects the critical success factors of a business. *p. 27*

Lead time The time lag between placing an order for goods or services and their delivery to the required location. *p. 460*

Learning curve The graph that represents the tendency for people to carry out tasks more quickly as they become more experienced in doing them. *p. 263*

Limiting factor Some aspect of the business (for example, lack of sales demand) that will prevent it achieving its objectives to the maximum extent. *p. 199*

Management accounting The measuring and reporting of accounting information for the managers of a business. *p. 16*

Management accounting information system The system used within a business to identify, record, analyse and report accounting information. *p. 23*

Management by exception A system of control, based on a comparison of planned and actual performance, that allows managers to focus on areas of poor performance rather than dealing with areas where performance is satisfactory. *p. 202*

Margin of safety The extent to which the planned level of output or sales lies above the break-even point. *p. 76*

Marginal analysis The activity of decision making through analysing variable costs and revenues, ignoring fixed cost. *p. 88*

Marginal cost The additional cost of producing one more unit. This is often the same as the variable cost *p. 88*

Marginal cost pricing Pricing output on the basis of its marginal cost, normally with a loading for profit. *p. 392*

Marginal costing *See* Variable costing. *p. 138*

Market price (as transfer price) Using a price set by the market outside the business as a suitable price for internal, inter-divisional transfers. *p. 431*

Master budget A summary of individual budgets, usually consisting of a budgeted income statement, a budgeted statement of financial position and, perhaps, a summarised cash budget. *p. 199*

Materiality The requirement that information should only be reported in the financial statements if it is significant and its omission could affect users' decisions. *p. 19*

Mission statement A concise declaration of the overriding purpose of the business. *p. 7*

Negotiated price (as transfer price) Transfer price that is derived as a result of negotiation between managers of the divisions concerned, possibly with the involvement of the business's central management as well. *p. 434*

Net present value (NPV) A method of investment appraisal based on the present value of all relevant cash flows associated with an investment. *p. 292*

Non-controllable cost A cost for which a specific manager is not held responsible. *p. 415*

Non-operating-profit variance Difference between budgeted and actual performance that does not lead directly to difference between budgeted and actual operating profit. *p. 257*

Objective probability Probability based on verifiable information, usually gathered from past experience. *p. 339*

Operating cash cycle (OCC) The period between the outlay of cash to buy supplies and the ultimate receipt of cash from the sale of goods. *p. 484*

Operating gearing The relationship between the total fixed and the total variable costs for some activity. Also known as operational gearing. *p. 79*

Opportunity cost The cost incurred when one course of action prevents an opportunity to derive some benefit from another course of action. *p. 42*

Outlay cost A cost that involves the spending of money or some other transfer of assets. *p. 43*

Outsourcing Subcontracting activities to (sourcing goods or services from) organisations outside of the business. *p. 93*

Overhead absorption (or recovery) rate The rate at which overheads are charged to cost units (jobs), usually in a job costing system. *p. 116*

Overheads *See* Indirect cost. *p. 111*

Past cost A cost that has been incurred in the past. *p. 43*

Payback period (PP) The time taken for the initial outlay for an investment to be repaid from its future net cash inflows. *p. 288*

Penetration pricing Setting prices at a level low enough to encourage wide market acceptance of a product or service. *p. 395*

Periodic budget A budget developed on a one-off basis to cover a particular planning period. *p. 198*

Position analysis A step in the strategic planning process in which the business assesses its present position in the light of the commercial and economic environment in which it operates. *p. 9*

Post-completion audit A review of the performance of an investment project to see whether actual performance matched planned performance and whether any lessons can be drawn from the way in which the investment was appraised and carried out. *p. 315*

Practical standard Standard that does not assume perfect operating conditions. Although demanding a high level of efficiency, account is taken of possible lost production time, defects and so on. Designed to be challenging yet achievable. *p. 262*

Price skimming Setting prices at a high level to make the maximum profit from the product or service before the price is lowered to attract the next strata of the market. *p. 396*

Process costing A technique for deriving the full cost per unit of output, where the units of output are exactly similar or it is reasonable to treat them as being so. *p. 108*

Product cost centre An area, object, person or activity for which cost is separately collected, in which cost units have cost added. *p. 126*

Profit centre Some area, object, person or activity for which its revenues and expenses are compared to derive a profit figure, for which the manager is held accountable. *p. 407*

Profit–volume (PV) chart A graphical representation of the contributions (revenue less variable cost) of some activity, at various levels, which enables the break-even point, and the profit at various activity levels, to be identified. *p. 81*

Quality cost The cost of establishing procedures which promote the quality of output, either by preventing quality problems in the first place or by dealing with them when they occur. *p. 182*

Relevance The ability of accounting information to influence decisions. Relevance is regarded as a key characteristic of useful accounting information. *p. 18*

Relevant cost A cost that is relevant to a particular decision. *p. 43*

Relevant range The range of output within which a particular business is expected to operate. *p. 83*

Residual income (RI) A divisional performance measure. The operating profit of a division, less an interest charge based on the business's investment in the division. *p. 421*

Responsibility accounting An arrangement where management is held accountable, usually through the budgetary control system, for its area of responsibility. *p. 408*

Responsibility centre Some aspect of a business for which a particular manager can be held accountable. *p. 407*

Return on capital employed (ROCE) A profitability ratio that expresses the operating profit (that is, profit before interest and taxation) for a period as a percentage of the long-term funds (equity and borrowings) invested in the business during the same period. *p. 285*

Return on investment (ROI) A divisional performance measure. The operating profit of a division expressed as a percentage of the business's investment in the division. *p. 417*

Risk The extent and likelihood that what is projected to occur will not actually occur. *p. 329*

Risk-adjusted discount rate A discount rate applied to investment projects that is increased (decreased) in the face of increased (decreased) risk. *p. 342*

Risk premium The additional return required from an investment, owing to a perceived level of risk; the greater the perceived risk, the larger the required risk premium. *p. 342*

Rolling budget *See* Continual budget. *p. 198*

Sales price variance The difference between the actual sales revenue figure for the period and the sales revenue figure as shown in the flexed budget. *p. 247*

Sales volume variance The difference between the operating profit as shown in the original budget, and the operating profit as shown in the flexed budget for the period. *p. 245*

Scenario analysis Creating a model of a business decision, usually on a computer spreadsheet, enabling the decision maker to look at the effect of different assumptions on the decision outcome, sometimes known as *scenario building*. *p. 334*

Semi-fixed (or semi-variable) cost A cost that has an element of both fixed and variable cost. *p. 68*

Sensitivity analysis An examination of the key variables affecting a decision (for example, an investment project), to see how changes in each input might influence the outcome. *p. 329*

Service cost centre Some area, object, person or activity for which cost is collected separately, in which cost units do not have cost added, because service cost centres only render services to product cost centres and to other service cost centres. *p. 126*

Standard quantities and costs Planned quantities and costs (or revenue) for individual units of input or output. Standards are the building blocks used to produce the budget. *p. 261*

Stepped fixed cost A fixed cost that does not remain fixed over all levels of output but which changes in steps as threshold levels of output are reached. *p. 67*

Strategic management The process of setting a course to achieve the business's objectives, taking account of the commercial and economic environment in which the business operates. *p. 6*

Strategic management accounting Providing management accounting information that will support the strategic plans and decisions made within a business. *p. 352*

Subjective probabilities Probabilities based on opinion rather than verifiable data. *p. 339*

Sunk cost A cost that has been incurred in the past; the same as a past cost. *p. 46*

Sunk cost fallacy The refusal to abandon an attachment to an irrecoverable investment. *p. 47*

SWOT analysis A framework in which many businesses set a position analysis. Here the business lists its strengths, weaknesses, opportunities and threats. *p. 9*

Target costing An approach to deriving product costs where the business starts with the planned selling price and from it deduces the target cost per unit that must be met to enable the business to meet its profit objectives. *p. 168*

Timeliness The quality that ensures that information is provided in time for users to make appropriate decisions. *p. 19*

Total cost The sum of variable and fixed costs. *p. 68*

Total direct labour variance The difference between the actual direct labour cost and the direct labour cost according to the flexed budget (budgeted direct labour hours for the actual output). *p. 249*

Total direct materials variance The difference between the actual direct materials cost and the direct materials cost according to the flexed budget. *p. 248*

Total life-cycle costing Reporting all of the costs that will be incurred during the entire life of a product or service. *p. 165*

Total quality management (TQM) A management philosophy that is concerned with providing products that meet or exceed customers' requirements all of the time. *p. 180*

Trade receivables to sales ratio Trade receivables outstanding at the end of the period divided by the sales revenue for the period. *p. 477*

Transfer pricing The activity of setting prices at which products or services will be transferred from one division to another division of the same business. *p. 426*

Understandability The requirement that accounting information should be understood by those for whom the information is primarily compiled. Lack of understandability will limit the usefulness of accounting information. *p. 19*

Value chain analysis Analysing each activity undertaken by a business to identify any that do not add value to the output of goods or services. *p. 174*

Value drivers Factors that create wealth, such as employee satisfaction, customer loyalty and the level of product innovation. *p. 364*

Variable cost A cost that varies according to the volume of activity. *p. 65*

Variable (or marginal) costing An approach to costing in which only those costs that vary with the level of output are included in the product cost. *p. 138*

Variance The financial effect, usually on the budgeted profit, of the particular factor under consideration being more or less than budgeted. *p. 245*

Verifiability The quality that provides assurance to users that information represents what it is supposed to represent and that this can be supported with evidence. *p. 19*

Vision statement A concise declaration of what the business seeks to achieve. *p. 8*

Work in progress Partially completed units of output. *p. 109*

Working capital Current assets less current liabilities. *p. 453*

XYZ inventories management A system of managing inventories that classifies inventories into three categories according to variability of customer demand. *p. 469*

Zero-base budgeting (ZBB) An approach to budgeting, based on the philosophy that all spending needs to be justified annually and that each budget should start as a clean sheet. *p. 210*

Appendix B

SOLUTIONS TO SELF-ASSESSMENT QUESTIONS

Chapter 2

2.1 JB Limited

(a)   £

Material M1

400 × 3 @ £5.50   6,600   The original cost is irrelevant since any
                                                                             inventories used will need to be replaced.

Material P2

400 × 2 @ £2.00   1,600   The best alternative use of this material is
(that is, £3.60 − £1.60)   as a substitute for P4 – an effective
                                                                             opportunity cost of £2.00/kg.

Part number 678

400 × 1 @ £50   20,000
Labour
Skilled 400 × 5 @ £12   24,000   The effective cost is £12/hour.
Semi-skilled 400 × 5 @ £10   20,000
Overheads   3,200   It is only the additional cost which is
                                                                             relevant; the method of apportioning total
                                                                             overheads is not relevant.

Total relevant cost   75,400
Potential revenue
400 @ £200   80,000

Clearly, on the basis of the information available it would be beneficial for the business to undertake the contract.

(b) There are many possible answers to this part of the question, including:

- If Material P2 had not already been held, it may be that it would not have been possible to buy it in and still leave the contract as a beneficial one. In this case, the business may be unhappy about accepting a price under the particular conditions that apply, which could not be accepted under other conditions.
- Will the replacement for the skilled worker be able to do the normal work of that person to the necessary standard?
- Is JB Limited confident that the additional semi-skilled employee can be made redundant at the end of this contract without cost to the business?

Chapter 3

3.1 Khan Ltd

(a) The break-even point, if only the Alpha service were rendered, would be:

$$\frac{\text{Fixed costs}}{\text{Sales revenue per unit} - \text{Variable cost per unit}} = \frac{£40,000}{£30 - £(15 + 6)} = 4,445 \text{ units (a year)}$$

(Strictly it is 4,444.44, but 4,445 is the smallest number of units of the service that must be rendered to avoid a loss.)

(b)

	Alpha	Beta	Gamma
Selling price (£/unit)	30	39	20
Variable materials (£/unit)	(15)	(18)	(10)
Variable production cost (£/unit)	(6)	(10)	(5)
Contribution (£/unit)	9	11	5
Staff time (hr/unit)	2	3	1
Contribution/staff hour	£4.50	£3.67	£5.00
Order of priority	2nd	3rd	1st

(c)

	Hours		Contribution
			£
Provide:			
5,000 Gamma using	5,000	generating (that is, 5,000 × £5 =)	25,000
2,500 Alpha using	5,000	generating (that is, 2,500 × £9 =)	22,500
	10,000		47,500
		Fixed cost	(40,000)
		Profit	7,500

This leaves a demand for 500 units of Alpha and 2,000 units of Beta unsatisfied.

Chapter 4

4.1 Hector and Co. Ltd

(a) Pricing on job-costing basis

			£
Materials:	Metal wire	1,000 × 2 × £2.20*	4,400
	Fabric	1,000 × 0.5 × £1.00*	500
Labour:	Skilled	1,000 × (10/60) × £12.00	2,000
	Unskilled	1,000 × (5/60) × £7.50	625
Indirect cost		1,000 × (15/60) × (50,000/12,500)	1,000
Total cost			8,525
Profit loading		12.5% thereof	1,066
Total tender price			9,591

* In the traditional approach to full costing, historic costs of materials tend to be used. It would not necessarily have been incorrect to have used the 'relevant' (opportunity) costs here.

(b) Minimum contract price (relevant cost basis)

			£
Materials:	Metal wire	1,000 × 2 × £2.50 (replacement cost)	5,000
	Fabric	1,000 × 0.5 × £0.40 (scrap value)	200
Labour:	Skilled	(there is no effective cost of skilled staff)	–
	Unskilled	1,000 × 5/60 × £7.50	625
Minimum tender price			5,825

The difference between the two prices is partly that the relevant costing approach looks to the future, partly that it considers opportunity costs, and partly that the job-costing basis total has a profit loading.

Chapter 5

5.1 Psilis Ltd

(a) Full cost (present basis)

	Basic £		Super £	
Direct labour (all £10/hour)	40.00	(4 hours)	60.00	(6 hours)
Direct material	15.00		20.00	
Overheads	18.20	(£4.55* × 4)	27.30	(£4.55* × 6)
	73.20		107.30	

* Total direct labour hours worked = (40,000 × 4) + (10,000 × 6) = 220,000 hours. Overhead recovery rate = £1,000,000/220,000 = £4.55 per direct labour hour.

Thus the selling prices are currently:

Basic: £73.20 + 25% = £91.50
Super: £107.30 + 25% = £134.13

(b) Full cost (activity cost basis)

Here, the cost of each cost-driving activity is apportioned between total production of the two products.

Activity	Cost £000	Basis of apportionment	Basic £000		Super £000	
Machine set-ups	280	Number of set-ups	56	(20/100)	224	(80/100)
Quality inspection	220	Number of inspections	55	(500/2,000)	165	(1,500/2,000)
Sales order processing	240	Number of orders processed	72	(1,500/5,000)	168	(3,500/5,000)
General production	260	Machine hours	182	(350/500)	78	(150/500)
Total	1,000		365		635	

The overheads per unit are:

Basic: $\dfrac{£365,000}{40,000} = £9.13$

Super: $\dfrac{£635,000}{10,000} = £63.50$

Thus, on an activity basis the full costs are as follows:

	Basic £		Super £	
Direct labour (all £10/hour)	40.00	(4 hours)	60.00	(6 hours)
Direct material	15.00		20.00	
Overheads	9.13		63.50	
Full cost	64.13		143.50	
Current selling price	91.50		134.13	

(c) It seems that the Supers are being sold for less than they cost to produce. If the price cannot be increased, there is a very strong case for abandoning this product. At the same time, the Basics are very profitable to the extent that it may be worth considering lowering the price to attract more sales revenue.

The fact that the overhead costs can be related to activities and, more specifically, to products does not mean that abandoning Super production would lead to immediate overhead cost savings. For example, it may not be possible or desirable to dismiss machine-setting staff overnight. It would certainly rarely be possible to release factory space occupied by machine setters and make immediate cost savings. Nevertheless, in the longer term it is possible to avoid these costs, and it may be sensible to do so.

(d) Useful measures may include:

- Percentage of sales revenue consumed in processing sales orders
- Average time taken to process each order received from wholesalers
- Average time taken to process each order received through mail order
- Average total cost of processing each order received from wholesalers
- Average total cost of processing each order received through mail order
- Average staff cost of processing each order received from wholesalers
- Average staff cost of processing each order received through mail order
- Average number of sales orders processed per staff member of sales processing department
- Number of processing errors per 100 sales orders received from wholesalers
- Number of processing errors per 100 sales orders received through mail order
- Percentage of sales orders requiring no human intervention to modify or fulfil
- Percentage of sales order enquiries resolved on first contact with staff member.

(e) Team members should ideally have the following skills:

- *Interpersonal skills*. This will include an ability to work as a member of a team and to deal effectively with negative attitudes displayed by employees towards the benchmarking exercise.
- *Communication skills*. This will include an ability to argue persuasively, to write reports fluently and to listen carefully to issues being raised by team members and others.
- *Relevant expertise*. Previous experience and training in benchmarking as well as in the sales order processing function would help to ensure the best results.
- *Commitment*. A keen interest in, and commitment to, the success of the exercise is needed, particularly when faced with difficult challenges.
- *Credibility*. Individuals who are held in high regard within the business are more likely to win approval for any changes proposed as a result of the exercise.
- *Project management skills*. An ability to set the agenda of work and to ensure that it is completed within the agreed timeframe is needed.

Although an individual team member may not possess all of the above attributes, the team as a whole should do so.

Chapter 6

6.1 Antonio Ltd

(a) (1) Raw materials inventories budget for the six months ending 31 December (physical quantities):

	July Units	Aug Units	Sept Units	Oct Units	Nov Units	Dec Units
Opening inventories (current month's production)	500	600	600	700	750	750
Purchases (balance figure)	600	600	700	750	750	750
	1,100	1,200	1,300	1,450	1,500	1,500
Issues to production (from question)	(500)	(600)	(600)	(700)	(750)	(750)
Closing inventories (next month's production)	600	600	700	750	750	750

Raw material inventories budget for the six months ending 31 December (in financial terms, that is, the physical quantities × £8):

	July £	Aug £	Sept £	Oct £	Nov £	Dec £
Opening inventories	4,000	4,800	4,800	5,600	6,000	6,000
Purchases	4,800	4,800	5,600	6,000	6,000	6,000
	8,800	9,600	10,400	11,600	12,000	12,000
Issues to production	(4,000)	(4,800)	(4,800)	(5,600)	(6,000)	(6,000)
Closing inventories	4,800	4,800	5,600	6,000	6,000	6,000

(2) Trade payables budget for the six months ending 31 December:

	July £	Aug £	Sept £	Oct £	Nov £	Dec £
Opening balance (current month's payment)	4,000	4,800	4,800	5,600	6,000	6,000
Purchases (from raw materials inventories budget)	4,800	4,800	5,600	6,000	6,000	6,000
	8,800	9,600	10,400	11,600	12,000	12,000
Payments	(4,000)	(4,800)	(4,800)	(5,600)	(6,000)	(6,000)
Closing balance (next month's payment)	4,800	4,800	5,600	6,000	6,000	6,000

(3) Cash budget for the six months ending 31 December:

	July £	Aug £	Sept £	Oct £	Nov £	Dec £
Inflows						
Trade receivables (40% of sales revenue of two months previous)	2,800	3,200	3,200	4,000	4,800	5,200
Cash sales revenue (60% of current month's sales revenue)	4,800	6,000	7,200	7,800	8,400	9,600
Total inflows	7,600	9,200	10,400	11,800	13,200	14,800
Outflows						
Payables (from payables budget)	(4,000)	(4,800)	(4,800)	(5,600)	(6,000)	(6,000)
Direct costs	(3,000)	(3,600)	(3,600)	(4,200)	(4,500)	(4,500)
Advertising	(1,000)	–	–	(1,500)	–	–
Overheads: 80%	(1,280)	(1,280)	(1,280)	(1,280)	(1,600)	(1,600)
20%	(280)	(320)	(320)	(320)	(320)	(400)
New plant	–	–	(2,200)	(2,200)	(2,200)	–
Total outflows	(9,560)	(10,000)	(12,200)	(15,100)	(14,620)	(12,500)
Net inflows/(outflows)	(1,960)	(800)	(1,800)	(3,300)	(1,420)	2,300
Balance c/f	5,540	4,740	2,940	(360)	(1,780)	520

The cash balances carried forward are deduced by subtracting the deficit (net outflows) for the month from (or adding the surplus for the month to) the previous month's balance.

Note how budgets are linked; in this case the inventories budget to the trade payables budget and the payables budget to the cash budget.

(b) The following are possible means of relieving the cash shortages revealed by the budget:

- Make a higher proportion of sales on a cash basis.
- Collect the money from credit customers more promptly, for example during the month following the sale.
- Hold lower inventories, both of raw materials and of finished goods.
- Increase the trade payables payment period.
- Delay the payments for advertising.
- Obtain more credit for the overhead costs; at present only 20 per cent are on credit.
- Delay the payments for the new plant.

A combination of two or more of these ways might be used.

Chapter 7

7.1 Toscanini Ltd

(a)

	Original	Flexed		Actual	
	Budget				
Output (units) (production and sales)	4,000	3,500		3,500	
	£	£		£	
Sales revenue	16,000	14,000		13,820	
Raw materials	(3,840)	(3,360)	(1,400 kg)	(3,420)	(1,425 kg)
Labour	(3,200)	(2,800)	(350 hr)	(2,690)	(345 hr)
Fixed overheads	(4,800)	(4,800)		(4,900)	
Operating profit	4,160	3,040		2,810	

	£	
Sales volume variance (4,160 − 3,040)	(1,120)	(A)
Sales price variance (14,000 − 13,820)	(180)	(A)
Materials price variance ((1,425 × 2.40) − 3,420)	0	
Materials usage variance (((3,500 × 0.4) − 1,425) × £2.40)	(60)	(A)
Labour rate variance ((345 × £8) − 2,690)	70	(F)
Labour efficiency variance (((3,500 × 0.10) − 345) × £8)	40	(F)
Fixed overhead spending variance (4,800 − 4,900)	(100)	(A)
Total net variances	(1,350)	(A)
Budgeted profit	4,160	
Less Total net variance	1,350	
Actual profit	2,810	

(b) Manager to be held accountable:

- Sales volume variance – sales manager
- Sales price variance – sales manager
- Materials usage variance – production manager
- Labour rate variance – human resources manager
- Labour efficiency variance – production manager
- Fixed overhead spending variance – various, depending on the nature of the overheads.

(c) Feasible explanations include the following:

- *Sales volume*. Ineffective marketing, though a drop in general demand for the product and unavailability of supply, could also be possibilities.
- *Sales price*. Ineffective marketing seems the only logical reason.
- *Materials usage*. Inefficient usage of material, perhaps because of poor performance by labour, or substandard materials.
- *Labour rate*. Less overtime worked or lower production bonuses paid as a result of lower volume of activity.

- *Labour efficiency*. More effective working.
- *Overheads*. Ineffective control of overheads.

(d) Clearly, not all of the sales volume variance can be attributed to poor marketing, given a 10 per cent reduction in demand.

It will probably be useful to distinguish between that part of the variance that arose from the shortfall in general demand (a planning variance) and a volume variance, which is more fairly attributable to the manager concerned. Thus accountability will be more fairly imposed.

	£
Planning variance (10% × 4,000) × £2.24*	896
'Revised' sales volume variance (4,000 − (10% × 4,000) − 3,500) × £2.24	224
Original sales volume variance	1,120

* £2.24 is the budgeted contribution per unit.

Chapter 8

8.1 Beacon Chemicals plc

(a) Relevant cash flows are as follows:

	Year 0 £ million	Year 1 £ million	Year 2 £ million	Year 3 £ million	Year 4 £ million	Year 5 £ million
Sales revenue		80	120	144	100	64
Loss of contribution		(15)	(15)	(15)	(15)	(15)
Variable cost		(40)	(50)	(48)	(30)	(32)
Fixed cost (Note 1)		(8)	(8)	(8)	(8)	(8)
Operating cash flows		17	47	73	47	9
Working capital	(30)					30
Capital cost	(100)					
Net relevant cash flows	(130)	17	47	73	47	39

Notes:

1 Only the elements of fixed cost that are incremental to the project (only existing because of the project) are relevant. Depreciation is irrelevant because it is not a cash flow.

2. The research and development cost is irrelevant since it has been spent irrespective of the decision on X14 production.

(b) The payback period is found as follows:

	Year 0 £ million	Year 1 £ million	Year 2 £ million	Year 3 £ million
Cumulative cash flows	(130)	(113)	(66)	7

The equipment will have repaid the initial investment by the end of the third year of operations. The payback period is, therefore, three years.

(c) The net present value is found as follows:

	Year 0 £ million	Year 1 £ million	Year 2 £ million	Year 3 £ million	Year 4 £ million	Year 5 £ million
Discount factor	1.00	0.926	0.857	0.794	0.735	0.681
Present value	(130.00)	15.74	40.28	57.96	34.55	26.56
Net present value	45.09	(That is, the sum of the present values for years 0 to 5.)				

(d) To have the effect of reducing the NPV to zero, the additional loss of contribution would have to be such that its present value would be £45.09 million. As the loss of contribution arises in each year (1 to 5), letting A = the additional loss of contribution:

$$45.09 = (A \times 0.926) + (A \times 0.857) + (A \times 0.794) + (A \times 0.735) + (A \times 0.681)$$
$$A = 45.09/3.993$$
$$A = £11.29 \text{ million}$$

This means that the loss of contribution would have to move from £15 million to £26.29 million – an increase of 75% – before a possible misestimation of this value would, taken alone, cause the project to be wealth destructive. In other words, the potential success of the project is not very sensitive to the estimate of the loss of contribution.

Chapter 9

9.1 Simtex Ltd

(a) Net operating cash flows each year will be:

	£000
Sales revenue (160 × £6)	960
Variable cost (160 × £4)	(640)
Relevant fixed costs	(170)
	150

The estimated net present value of the new product can then be calculated:

	£000
Annual cash flows (150 × 3.038*)	456
Residual value of equipment (100 × 0.636)	64
	520
Initial outlay	(480)
Net present value	40

* This is the sum of the discount factors over four years (that is 0.893 + 0.797 + 0.712 + 0.636 = 3.038). Where the cash flows are constant, it is a quicker procedure than working out the present value of cash flows for each year and then adding them together.

(b) (1) Assume the discount rate is 18%. The net present value of the project would be:

	£000
Annual cash flows (150 × 2.690*)	404
Residual value of equipment (100 × 0.516)	52
	456
Initial outlay	(480)
Net present value	(24)

* That is 0.847 + 0.718 + 0.609 + 0.516 = 2.690.

Thus an increase of 6%, from 12% to 18%, in the discount rate causes a fall from +40 to −24 in the net present value: a fall of 64, or 10.67 (that is, 64/6) for each 1% rise in the discount rate. So a zero net present value will occur with a discount rate approximately equal to 12 + (40/10.67) = 15.75%. (This is, of course, the internal rate of return.)

This higher discount rate represents an increase of about 31% on the existing cost of capital figure.

(2) The initial outlay on equipment is already expressed in present-value terms and so, to make the project no longer viable, the outlay will have to increase by an amount equal to the net present value of the project (that is, £40,000) – an increase of 8.3% on the stated initial outlay.

(3) The change necessary in the annual net cash flows to make the project no longer profitable can be calculated as follows:

Let Y = change in the annual operating cash flows. Then ($Y \times$ cumulative discount rates for a four-year period) − NPV = 0. This can be rearranged as:

$$Y \times \text{cumulative discount rates for a four-year period} = \text{NPV}$$
$$Y \times 3.038 = £40,000$$
$$Y = £40,000/3.038$$
$$= £13,167$$

In percentage terms, this is a decrease of 8.8% on the estimated cash flows.

(4) The change in the residual value required to make the new product no longer profitable can be calculated as follows:

Let V = change in the residual value. Then ($V \times$ discount factor at end of four years) − NPV of product = 0. This can be rearranged as:

$$V \times \text{discount factor at end of four years} = \text{NPV of product}$$
$$V \times 0.636 = £40,000$$
$$V = £40,000/0.636$$
$$= £62,893$$

This is a decrease of 62.9% in the residual value of the equipment.

(c) The net present value of the product is positive and so it will increase shareholder wealth. Thus, it should be produced. The sensitivity analysis suggests the initial outlay and the annual cash flows are the most sensitive variables for managers to consider.

Chapter 10

10.1 Peverell plc

(a) (1) NOPAT adjustment

	£m
Operating profit	38.0
EVA® adjustments (to be added back to profit)	
Marketing costs (4/5 × 40.0)	32.0
Excess allowance	8.0
	78.0
Tax (20%)	(15.6)
Adjusted NOPAT	62.4

(2) EVA® calculation

EVA® can be calculated as follows:

$$\text{EVA}^® = \text{NOPAT} − (\text{R} \times \text{C}) = £62.4m − (12\% \times £150m)$$
$$= £44.4m \text{ (to one decimal place)}$$

(b) Three major differences between the cost-plus approach and the target costing approach to pricing are as follows:

■ With the cost-plus approach, the price of a product is determined by its cost, whereas, with the target costing approach, it is the other way around.

■ With the cost-plus approach, cost efficiencies are normally achieved after the product is developed, whereas, with the target costing approach, cost efficiencies are built into the design process.

■ With the cost-plus approach, cost management is not driven by the demands of the market, whereas, with the target costing approach, cost management is market-driven.

(c) Three non-financial measures that could act as lead indicators concerning the internal business processes of a laptop manufacturer are

- number of new products brought to market;
- percentage of customers requiring after-sales service; and
- time taken to process new orders.

(d) It is difficult for these different approaches to coexist in a highly competitive economy. The pursuit of shareholder value may be necessary in order to attract funds and to ensure that managers retain their jobs. A stakeholder approach, which is committed to satisfying the needs of a broad group of constituents, can be difficult to sustain in such an environment.

It has been claimed that other stakeholders have been adversely affected by the pursuit of shareholder value. It has been suggested that the application of various techniques to improve shareholder value, such as hostile takeovers, cost cutting and large management incentive bonuses, have badly damaged the interests of certain stakeholders such as employees and local communities. However, a commitment to shareholder value must take account of the needs of other stakeholders if it is to deliver long-term benefits. Dissatisfaction among other stakeholders is likely to lead to loss of shareholder value.

(e) Businesses are often overcapitalised because insufficient attention is given to the capital investment that is required. Management incentive schemes that are geared towards generating a particular level of profits or achieving a particular market share without specifying the level of capital invested can help create such a problem. EVA® can help by highlighting the cost of capital, through the capital charge.

Chapter 11

11.1 Andromeda International plc

(a) Return on investment

	Jupiter	Mars
(1)	$(260/1,330) \times 100\% = 19.5\%$	$(50/1,380) \times 100\% = 3.6\%$
(2)	$(275/1,420^*) \times 100\% = 19.4\%$	$(80/1,680†) \times 100\% = 4.8\%$

* The profit will increase by £15,000 ((£250,000 × 0.30) − £60,000). Assets will increase by £90,000.
† Profit will increase by £30,000 (£90,000 − £60,000 depreciation). Assets will increase by £300,000.

(b) The investment opportunity for Jupiter division will result in an ROI of 16.7% (that is, 15/90) which is above the cost of capital for the business. As a result, central management is likely to view the opportunity favourably. However, the effect of taking the opportunity will be to lower the existing ROI of the division. This may mean that the divisional manager will be reluctant to take on the opportunity.

The investment opportunity for the Mars division provides an ROI of 10% (that is, 30/300), which is below the cost of capital of the business. As a result, central management would not wish for this opportunity to be taken up. However, the opportunity will increase the ROI of the Mars division overall and so the divisional manager may be keen to invest in the opportunity.

There may be reasons for investing in each opportunity which are not given in the question but which may be compelling. For example, it may be necessary to introduce the new product into the Jupiter division to try to ensure that the range of products offered to customers is complete. Failure to do so may result in a decline in overall sales. It may be that investment in the Mars division is important to ensure that productivity over the longer term does not slip behind that of its competitors.

(c) Ideally, ROI should be calculated using the current value of the assets employed. By so doing, we can see whether or not the returns are satisfactory as compared with the alternative use of those resources. Using cost (or cost less accumulated depreciation) as the basis for ROI will be measuring current performance against past outlays.

Gross book value (that is the amount before depreciation is charged) fails to take account of the age of the assets held. It may be that the assets are all near the end of their useful lives and are, therefore, highly depreciated. In such a case, the gross book value may produce a low ROI and may provide too high a 'hurdle' rate for new investment opportunities. Gross book value in such circumstances would also provide a poor approximation to the current value of the assets.

Using net book value (that is, the amount after depreciation has been charged) would overcome the problem mentioned above but, during a period of inflation, this measure may be significantly lower than the current value of the assets employed. In addition, there is the problem that ROI can improve over time simply because of the declining value of the assets employed. Divisional managers may be less willing to replace old assets where this will lead to a decline in ROI.

(d) The main objectives in setting transfer prices are to enable the performance of each division to be evaluated separately, to promote divisional autonomy and to encourage good decision making within each division, to the extent that they will pursue the best interests of the business as a whole, as a result of pursuing their own best interests.

In principle, the best transfer price is the opportunity cost. This is the price that the buying division (Jupiter) would have to pay the cheapest (for acceptable quality) outside supplier. For Mars (the selling division), it is the best alternative outside price for its output.

In this case, the best transfer price will depend on the particular circumstances of Mars. If it has spare capacity, its opportunity cost would be just the variable costs of the work that it will do for Jupiter. If it is operating at full capacity, the opportunity cost will be the price at which it sells its output to outsiders. This is because it will need to refuse to supply outsiders to enable it to free time for its work supplying the component to Jupiter. A problem is that this latter figure may be greater than the price that Jupiter is currently paying outside suppliers.

Chapter 12

12.1 Town Mills Ltd

(a) Operating cash cycle

	Days
Inventories holding period	
$192/652 \times 365$	107
Trade receivables settlement period	
$202 \times (105/110)/903 \times 365$ (Note 1)	78
	185
Trade payables settlement period	
$260 \times (105/110)/652 \times 365$ (Notes 1 and 2)	(139)
Operating cash cycle	46

Notes:
1. Since the closing level of trade receivables/payables was 10 per cent higher at the end of the year than at the start, the average balance would be 105/110 of the end of year balance.
2. Since inventories were the same at both ends of the year, purchases equal cost of sales.

Knowledge of the length of the operating cash cycle (OCC) helps the business to monitor it over time, perhaps relative to other businesses or some target. It is not possible to draw any helpful conclusion from looking at just one figure; there needs to be a basis of comparison.

A problem with using the 'bottom line' figure for the OCC is that values within it are not equivalent. In the case of Town Mills, one day's sales are worth £2,474, whereas one day's purchases or inventories holding are worth £1,786. So, while an extra day of trade receivables period coupled with an extra day of trade payables period would leave the OCC unchanged at 46 days, it would involve an additional £700 or so of investment in working capital.

(b) As mentioned in (a) above, knowledge of the number of days of the OCC tells us little without some basis of comparison.

The acid test (quick assets) ratio for this business is very low at 0.55:1 (trade receivables divided by trade payables plus overdraft). If the inventories were fairly fast-moving with a short trade receivables period, this might not be a worry but, as it stands, it is a concern.

The current ratio is close to 1:1 (current assets divided by current liabilities), which looks low, but it is not possible to say too much without a comparison with similar businesses or this business over time.

The level of the overdraft looks worrying. It represents almost 20% of the total financing of the business, according to statement of financial position values. The statement of financial position may well understate the value of equity, but it still seems that there is a lot of short-term finance that could be recalled instantly which, in practice, probably means within a couple of months. A term loan might be a better arrangement than an overdraft.

The level of trade payables also seems high, compared with trade receivables. This too could be a problem. It depends on the relative market positions of Town Mills and its suppliers.

Overall, the liquidity does not look strong and probably needs to be reviewed. It is not possible to be too dogmatic on this with very limited bases of comparison.

(c) The types of risk and cost that might be associated with high inventories levels of a whole-saler include:

- *Financing cost*. Inventories normally need to be financed. Usually the availability of free trade credit covers some of this. In Town Mills case, trade payables are greater than the value of inventories. The credit is linked to purchases rather than inventories levels so, if inventories levels were to be reduced, the level of payables need not.
- *Storage costs*. These are likely to be less where inventories are lower. The significance of these costs is likely to depend on the nature of the inventories. Those which are high-value and/or need special treatment are typically more expensive to store than other inventories.
- *Insurance cost*. This is likely to be subject to the same considerations as storage cost, of which it can be seen as being part.
- *Obsolescence cost*. The more inventories held, the greater the risk they will lose value either through physical deterioration or through obsolescence. A spare part for a machine no longer used may be in perfect condition and, in principle, usable, but if the machine is no longer being used, the spare part may be worthless.

Appendix C
SOLUTIONS TO REVIEW QUESTIONS

Chapter 1

1.1

Students	Whether to enrol on a course of study. This would probably involve an assessment of the university's ability to continue to operate and to fulfil students' needs.
Other universities and colleges	How best to compete against the university. This might involve using the university's performance in various aspects as a 'benchmark' when evaluating their own performance.
Employees	Whether to take up or to continue in employment with the university. Employees might assess this by considering the ability of the university to continue to provide employment and to reward employees adequately for their labour.
Government/funding authority	How efficient the university is in undertaking its various activities.
Local community representatives	Whether to allow/encourage the university to expand its activities. To assess this, the university's ability to continue to provide employment for the community, to use community resources and to help fund environmental improvements might be considered.
Suppliers	Whether to continue to supply the university at all; also whether to supply on credit. This would involve an assessment of the university's ability to pay for any goods and services supplied.
Lenders	Whether to lend money to the university and/or whether to require repayment of any existing loans. To assess this, the university's ability to meet its obligations to pay interest and to repay the principal would be considered.
Board of governors and other managers (faculty deans, and so on)	Whether the performance of the university requires improvement. Here, current performance would be compared with plans or some other 'benchmark' to decide whether action needs to be taken. Whether there should be a change in the university's future direction. In making such decisions, management will need to look at the university's ability to perform and at the opportunities available to it.

In principle, there is no difference between the ways in which the user groups concerned with a university and those concerned with a private sector business would use accounting information.

1.2 Most businesses are far too large and complex for managers to be able to see and assess everything that is going on in their own areas of responsibility merely by personal observation. Managers need information on all aspects within their control. Management accounting reports can provide them with this information, to a greater or lesser extent. These reports can be seen, therefore, as acting as the eyes and ears of the managers, providing insights not necessarily obvious without them.

1.3 The following accounting information relating to a new service might be useful to a manager:

- the cost of providing the service;
- the expected revenues from the service;
- the level of profit that will arise given different levels of demand for the service;
- the capital investment that is necessary to enable the business to provide the service; and
- a comparison of expected outcomes from the proposed service with other opportunities available and/or with similar services already provided.

1.4 There is no doubt that the onus is on accountants to make their reports as easy to understand as they can possibly be. A key aspect of accountants' work is communicating to non-accountants, and they should never overlook this. At the same time, accounting information cannot always be expressed in such a way that someone with absolutely no accounting knowledge can absorb it successfully. The onus is also therefore on managers to acquire a working knowledge of the basis on which accounting reports are prepared and what they mean.

Chapter 2

2.1 The three attributes are:
1 They must relate to the objective(s) that the decision is intended to work towards. In most businesses, this is taken to be wealth enhancement.
2 They must relate to the future. Past costs are irrelevant.
3 They must differ between the options under consideration. Where a cost will be the same irrespective of the outcome of the decision that is to be taken, it is irrelevant. It is only on the basis of things that differ from one outcome to another that decisions can be made.

2.2 A sunk cost is a past and, therefore, an irrelevant cost in the context of any decision about the future. Thus, for example, the cost of an item of inventories already bought is a sunk cost. It is irrelevant in any decision involving the use of the inventories, because this cost will be the same irrespective of the decision made.

An opportunity cost is the cost of being deprived of the next best option to the one under consideration. For example, where using an hour of a worker's time on Activity A deprives the business of the opportunity to use that time in a profitable Activity B, the benefit lost from Activity B is an opportunity cost of pursuing Activity A.

2.3 Cost may be defined as the amount of resources, usually measured in monetary terms, sacrificed to achieve a particular objective.

2.4 A committed cost is like a past cost in that an irrevocable decision has been made to incur the cost. This might be because the business has entered into a binding contract, for example to rent some accommodation for the next two years. Thus it is effectively a past cost even though the payment (for rent, in our example) has yet to be made. Since the business cannot avoid a committed cost, it cannot be a relevant cost.

Chapter 3

3.1 A fixed cost is one that is the same irrespective of the level of activity or output. Typical examples of costs that are fixed include rent of business accommodation, salaries of supervisory staff and insurance. A variable cost is one that varies with the level of activity or output. Examples include raw materials and power for machinery. It also includes labour where payment is made according to the level of output.

Note that it is in relation to the level of activity that costs are fixed. These costs are affected by inflation and the time period involved.

For a particular product or service, knowing which costs are fixed and which are variable helps managers to predict the total cost for a given level of activity. It also helps them to focus only on variable costs where a short-term decision does not alter the fixed costs.

3.2 The BEP is the break-even point, that is, the level of activity, measured either in units of output or in value of sales revenue, at which the sales revenue exactly covers all of the costs, both fixed and variable.

Break-even point is calculated as

Fixed costs/(sales revenue per unit − variable costs per unit)

which may alternatively be expressed as

Fixed costs/Contribution per unit

Thus break-even will occur when the contributions for the period are sufficient to cover the fixed costs for the period.

The break-even point can be used to compare with the planned level of activity. This can help in assessing the riskiness of the activity.

3.3 Operating gearing refers to the proportion of fixed cost in relation to the total cost of some activity. Where the fixed cost forms a relatively high proportion of the total cost (at the business's normal level of activity), we say that the activity has high operating gearing.

Typically, high operating gearing is present in environments where there is a relatively high level of mechanisation (that is, capital-intensive environments). These environments tend to have relatively high fixed costs, such as depreciation and maintenance, together with relatively low variable costs.

High operating gearing means that changes in the level of activity have an accentuated effect on operating profit. For example, a 20% decrease in output of a particular service will lead to a greater than 20% decrease in operating profit (assuming no cost or price changes).

3.4 In the face of a restricting scarce resource, profit will be maximised by using the scarce resource on output where the contribution per unit of the scarce resource is maximised.

This means that the contribution per unit of the scarce resource (for example, hour of scarce labour or unit of scarce raw material) for each competing product or service needs to be identified. It is then a question of allocating the scarce resource to the product or service that provides the highest contribution per unit of the particular scarce resource.

The logic of this approach is that the scarce resource is allocated to the activity that uses it most effectively, in terms of contribution and, therefore, profit.

Chapter 4

4.1 In process costing, the total production cost for a period is divided by the number of completed units of output for the period to deduce the full cost per unit. Where there is work in progress at the beginning and/or the end of the period, complications arise.

The problem is that some of the completed output incurred cost in the preceding period. Similarly, some of the cost incurred in the current period leads to completed production in the subsequent period. Account needs to be taken of these facts, if reliable full cost information is to be obtained.

Making the necessary adjustment involves calculating the equivalent units of production that the work in progress represents. This is the equivalent amount of completed units that could have been made given the effort and resources invested.

4.2 The only reason for distinguishing between direct and indirect costs is to help to deduce the full cost of a unit of output in a job-costing environment. In this environment, the products or services provided are quite distinct. Where all units of output are identical, or near identical, a process-costing approach will be taken. This means that an average cost can be applied to each identical unit. This avoids the need to separately identify direct and indirect costs.

Direct cost forms that part of the total cost of pursuing some activity that can be identified with, and measured in respect of, that particular activity. Examples of direct cost items in a typical job-costing environment include direct labour and direct materials. Indirect cost is the remainder of the cost of pursuing some activity.

4.3 The notion of direct and indirect cost is concerned only with the extent to which particular elements of cost can be identified with, and measured in respect of, a particular cost unit, usually a product or service. The distinction between the two costs is made exclusively for the purpose of calculating the full cost of some cost unit, where each cost unit produced is different. Thus, it is typically in the context of job costing, or some variant of it, that the distinction between direct and indirect cost is useful.

The notion of variable and fixed cost is concerned entirely with how costs behave in the face of changes in the volume of output. By distinguishing between fixed and variable cost, predictions can be made as to the total cost incurred at different levels of volume and/or the changes to total cost that occur if the volume of output is reduced or increased.

Thus the notions of direct and indirect cost, on the one hand, and of variable and fixed cost, on the other, are not related. In practice, some elements of direct cost are variable, while some are fixed. The same is true for indirect cost.

4.4 Full cost includes all of the cost of pursuing the cost objective, including a 'fair' share of the overheads. This means that, if the business were to sell its output at a price exactly equal to the full cost (manufacturing and non-manufacturing cost), the sales revenues for the period would exactly cover all of the cost. In other words, the business would break even.

Chapter 5

5.1 ABC is a means of dealing with charging overheads to units of output to derive full cost in a multi-product (job or batch costing) environment.

The traditional absorption costing approach tends to treat overheads as a common cost to be applied to jobs using the same formula, normally based on direct labour hours. ABC takes a much more enquiring approach to overheads. It follows the philosophy that overheads occur for a reason. They must be driven by activities. Assume, for example, a certain product takes up a disproportionately large part of supervisors' time. The traditional approach would simply accept that supervisory salaries are an overhead that needs to be apportioned along with other overheads. ABC, on the other hand, would charge an appropriate proportion of supervisors' salaries to the product that drives the cost.

5.2 One criticism is on the issue of the cost–benefit balance. It is claimed that the cost of analysing activities and identifying cost drivers exceeds the benefits from the improved quality of full cost information generated.

A further criticism is that where a business offers similar products or services, involving similar activities, the more accurate measurements provided by ABC will not provide very different outcomes to those provided under traditional absorption costing

It may also be difficult to identify certain overheads with particular activities. Failure to do so, however, can lead to arbitrary overhead cost allocations.

Finally, it is claimed that full cost information is of rather dubious value for decision making purposes, irrespective of how the full cost information is deduced. Full cost information is flawed by the fact that it is based on past costs and takes no account of opportunity cost.

5.3 The main categories of quality costs are:

- *Prevention costs.* These are involved with procedures to prevent products being produced that are not up to the required quality.
- *Appraisal costs.* These are concerned with monitoring raw materials, work in progress and finished products to ensure that they achieve the quality standards that have been set.
- *Internal failure costs.* These include the costs of rectifying substandard products before they reach the customer as well as the costs of scrap arising from quality failures.
- *External failure costs.* These include the costs of rectifying quality problems with products that have been passed to the customer.

By categorising costs in this way, we have an opportunity to manage them. For example, through investing in prevention costs, appraisal and failure costs may be reduced. This may lead to considerable cost savings.

5.4 The three phases of the product life cycle are:

- The *pre-production phase.* This is the period that precedes production of the product or service. During this phase, research and development – both of the product or service and of the market – is conducted. The necessary production facilities are also established.

- The *production phase* comes next, being the one in which the product is made and sold or the service is rendered to customers.
- The *post-production phase* comes last. During this phase, costs may be incurred to correct faults that arose with products or services sold (after-sales service).

Target costing can be applied at the pre-production phase. Careful planning at this phase of the product's life can prevent future manufacturing costs from becoming 'locked in'. Thus, having determined a target price for the product, costs may be managed through redesign and so on to ensure that the total costs incurred allow room for an acceptable profit to be made. Kaizen costing aims to reduce the manufacturing cost of a particular product to below that of the previous period. Hence it is employed at the production phase.

Chapter 6

6.1 A budget can be defined as a financial plan for a future period of time. Thus it sets out the intentions which management has for the period concerned. Achieving the budget plans should help to achieve the long-term plans of the business. Achievement of the long-term plans should mean that the business is successfully working towards its strategic objectives and mission.

A budget differs from a forecast in that a forecast is a statement of what is expected to happen without the intervention of management, perhaps because they cannot intervene (as with a weather forecast). A plan is an intention to achieve.

Normally management would take account of reliable forecasts when making its plans.

6.2 The five uses of budgets are as follows:
1 Budgets tend to promote forward thinking and the possible identification of short-term problems. Managers must plan and the budgeting process tends to force them to do so. In doing so, they are likely to encounter potential problems. If these can be identified early enough, solutions might be easily found.
2 Budgets can be used to help co-ordination between various sections of the business. It is important that the plans of one area of the business fit in with those of other areas; a lack of co-ordination could have disastrous consequences. Having formal statements of plans for each aspect of the business enables a check to be made that plans are complementary.
3 Budgets can motivate managers to better performance. It is believed that people are motivated by having a target to aim for. Provided that the inherent goals are achievable, budgets can provide an effective motivational device.
4 Budgets can provide a basis for a system of control. Having a plan against which actual performance can be measured provides a potentially useful tool of control.
5 Budgets can provide a system of authorisation. Many managers have 'spending' budgets such as research and development, staff training and so on. For these people, the size of their budget defines their authority to spend.

6.3 Control can be defined as 'compelling things to occur as planned'. This implies that control can only be achieved if a plan exists. Budgets are financial plans. This means that, if actual performance can be compared with the budget (plan) for each aspect of the business, divergences from plan can be spotted. Steps can then be taken to bring matters back under control where they are going out of control.

6.4 A budget committee is a group of senior staff that is responsible for the budget preparation process within an organisation. The existence of the committee places the budget responsibility clearly with an identifiable group of people. This group can focus on the tasks involved.

Chapter 7

7.1 Feedforward controls try to anticipate what is likely to happen in the future and then assist in making the actual outcome match the desired outcome. They contrast with feedback controls, which simply compare actual to planned outcomes after the event. Feedforward controls are therefore more proactive.

7.2 A variance is the effect on budgeted profit of the particular cost or revenue item being considered. It represents the difference between the budgeted profit and the actual profit assuming everything except the item under consideration had gone according to budget. From this it must be the case that:

Budgeted profit + favourable variances − unfavourable variances = actual profit

The purpose of analysing variances is to identify whether, and if so where, things are not going according to plan. If this can be done, it may be possible to find out the cause of things going out of control. If this can be discovered, it may then be possible to put things right for the future.

7.3 Where the budgeted and actual volumes of output do not coincide, it is impossible to make valid comparison of 'allowed' and actual costs and revenues. Flexing the original budget to reflect the actual output level enables a more informative comparison to be made.

Flexing certainly does not mean that output volume differences do not matter. Flexing highlights (as the difference between flexed and original budget profits) the effect on profit of output volume differences.

7.4 Deciding whether variances should be investigated involves the use of judgement. Often management will set a threshold of significance, for example 5 per cent of the budgeted figure for each variance relating to revenue or cost items. All variances above this threshold would then be investigated. Even where variances are below the threshold, any sign of a systemic variance, shown, for example, by an increasing cumulative total for the factor, should be investigated.

Knowledge of the cause of a particular variance may well put management in a position to take actions that will be beneficial to the business in the future. Investigating variances, however, is likely to be relatively expensive in staff time. A judgement needs to be made on whether the value or benefit of knowing the cause of the variance will be justified by the cost of this knowledge. As with most investigations of this type, it is difficult to judge the value of the knowledge until after the variance has been investigated.

Chapter 8

8.1 NPV is usually considered the best method of assessing investment opportunities because it takes account of

- *the timing of the cash flows.* By *discounting* the various cash flows associated with each project according to when it is expected to arise, it recognises the fact that cash flows do not all occur simultaneously. Associated with this is the fact that, by discounting, using the opportunity cost of finance (that is, the return that the next best alternative opportunity would generate), the net benefit after financing costs have been met is identified (as the NPV);
- *the whole of the relevant cash flows.* NPV includes all of the relevant cash flows irrespective of when they are expected to occur. It treats them differently according to their date of occurrence, but they are all taken account of in the NPV and they all have, or can have, an influence on the decision;
- *the objectives of the business.* NPV is the only method of appraisal where the output of the analysis has a direct bearing on the wealth of the owners of the business. (Positive NPVs enhance wealth; negative ones reduce it.) Since most private sector businesses seek to increase their owners' wealth, NPV clearly is the best approach to use.

NPV provides clear decision rules concerning acceptance/rejection of projects and the ranking of projects. It is fairly simple to use, particularly with the availability of modern computer software that takes away the need for routine calculations to be done manually.

8.2 The payback period method, in its original form, does not take account of the time value of money. However, it would be possible to modify the payback method to accommodate this requirement. Cash flows arising from a project could be discounted, using the cost of finance as the appropriate discount rate, in the same way as in the NPV and IRR methods. The discounted payback approach is used by some businesses (for example Kingfisher plc – see Real World 8.14, page 317) and represents an improvement on the original approach described in the chapter. However, it still retains the other flaws of the original payback approach that were discussed.

For example, it ignores relevant data after the payback period. Thus, even in its modified form, the PP method cannot be regarded as superior to NPV.

8.3 The IRR method does appear to be similar in popularity to the NPV method among practising managers. The main reason for this appears to be a preference for a percentage return ratio rather than an absolute figure as a means of expressing the outcome of a project. This preference for a ratio may reflect the fact that other financial goals of the business are often set in terms of ratios, for example return on capital employed.

8.4 Cash flows are preferred to profit flows because cash is the ultimate measure of economic wealth. Cash is used to acquire resources and for distribution to shareholders. When cash is invested in a project, an opportunity cost is incurred, as the cash cannot be used in other investment projects. Similarly, when positive cash flows are generated by the project, the cash can be used to reinvest in other projects.

Profit, on the other hand, is relevant to reporting the productive effort for a period. This measure of effort may have only a tenuous relationship to cash flows for a period. The conventions of accounting may lead to the recognition of gains and losses in one period and the relevant cash inflows and outflows occurring in another period.

Chapter 9

9.1 The two main limitations are:

- It assumes that only one of the variables will differ from its predicted value; in other words, sensitivity analysis is too static. In reality, the variables will probably all differ to some extent from the predicted values.
- It is difficult to interpret the results. This would be equally true even if the first limitation were overcome by using a scenario-building approach.

9.2 Approach (a) has the advantage that all possible outcomes, and their probability of occurrence, can be identified. This will give a feel for the distributions of possible outcomes, or it will allow the calculation of the standard deviation.

The number of possible outcomes could, in real life, be vast, which would make such an approach untenable.

Approach (b) is much more practical because it will be relatively easy to carry out the calculations. Since averages are used throughout, it is not possible to gain any feel, or deduce statistics, about the spread of possible outcomes and, therefore, of the risk involved.

9.3 Objective probabilities (OPs) are based on demonstrable facts, whereas subjective probabilities (SPs) are based on opinions. On the face of it, this might seem to imply that OPs are more reliable than SPs. This may not necessarily be true because:

- OPs are inevitably based on past experience and the past may not be a good guide to the future; and
- SPs, though based on opinions, can be based on the opinions of independent experts.

9.4 The word 'expected', in the context of expected values does not have the same meaning as in its normal use. This is because an expected value may not actually be capable of occurring because it is the weighted average of possible outcomes, rather than the single value that is most likely to occur.

Chapter 10

10.1 Possible reasons for A Ltd being preferred to B Ltd as a customer include:

- A Ltd may place fewer orders than B Ltd, so saving the business's order handling costs.
- A Ltd may have the service provided in larger quantities than B Ltd. This might lead to savings in travel costs or similar, if the service is provided on the customers' premises.
- A Ltd may require fewer visits by sales representatives than B Ltd.
- A Ltd may be a quicker payer than B Ltd, assuming that sales are on credit.

There may well be other reasons.

10.2 The four main areas in the balanced scorecard are:

1 *Finance.* In this area targets for measures such as return on capital employed will be stated.
2 *Customer.* The market/customers that the business will aim for is established, as will be targets for such things as measures of customer satisfaction and rate of growth in customer numbers.
3 *Internal business process.* Here the processes that are vital to the business will be established. This might include levels of innovation, types of operation and after-sales service.
4 *Learning and growth.* In this area, issues relating to growing the business and development of staff are identified and targets set.

10.3 Generally, a rise in the price of a commodity causes a fall in demand. A commodity is said to have elastic demand where it reacts strongly (stretches more) in the face of a particular price alteration. Elastic demand tends to be associated with commodities that are not essential, perhaps because there is a ready substitute.

It can be very helpful for those involved with pricing decisions to have some feel for the elasticity of demand of the commodity that will be the subject of a decision. The sensitivity of the demand to the decision is obviously much greater (and the pricing decision more crucial) with commodities whose demand is elastic than with commodities whose demand is inelastic.

10.4 A business will make the most profit from one of its products or services at the point where marginal sales revenue equals marginal cost of production or, in other words, the point where the increase in total sales revenue that will result from selling one more unit equals the increase in total costs that will result from selling the unit.

It is at this point that the cost curve and the revenue curve are furthest from one another and so profit is largest.

Chapter 11

11.1 Reporting non-financial measures may pose a number of problems. These include:

- resistance to the introduction of new measures (and, by implication, new ways of being assessed);
- scepticism of proposed measures (the latest 'flavour of the month');
- the cost of reporting new measures;
- data integrity (the lack of common measurement bases and objectivity associated with many non-financial measures); and
- the difficulty of measuring the benefits (for example, establishing the link between a particular non-financial measure and the achievement of business objectives).

11.2 Four possible measures may include:

- sales per employee;
- output per employee;
- total output during the period; and
- sales to assets employed.

Other measures may have been suggested which are equally valid.

11.3 Three non-financial measures might include:

- turnover of staff during the period;
- new clients obtained during the period; and
- level of client satisfaction during the period.

11.4 We saw in the chapter that negotiated prices can create problems for both the efficient use of resources and divisional autonomy. They can also tie up central management in arbitrational matters and deflect them from their more strategic role. This method is best used when there is an external market for the services or goods of both buying and selling divisions and when divisional managers are free to reject offers made by other divisions.

Market-based prices are, generally speaking, more appropriate as they reflect the opportunity cost of the services or goods. However, where the division is operating below capacity, a variable cost-based approach is more appropriate.

Chapter 12

12.1 Although the credit manager is responsible for ensuring that receivables pay on time, Tariq may be right in denying blame. Various factors could create the situation described and may be beyond the control of the credit manager. These include:

- a downturn in the economy leading to financial difficulties among credit customers;
- decisions by other managers within the business to liberalise credit policy in order to stimulate sales;
- an increase in competition among suppliers offering credit, which is being exploited by customers;
- disputes with customers over the quality of goods or services supplied; and
- problems in the delivery of goods leading to delays.

You may have thought of other factors.

12.2 The level of inventories held will be affected in the following ways.

(a) An increase in production bottlenecks is likely to result in an increase in raw materials and work in progress being processed within the plant. Therefore, inventories levels should rise.

(b) An increase in the cost of capital will make holding inventories more expensive. This may, in turn, lead to a decision to reduce inventories levels.

(c) The decision to reduce the range of products should result in a lower level of inventories being held. It would no longer be necessary to hold certain items in order to meet customer demand.

(d) Switching to a local supplier may reduce the lead time between ordering an item and receiving it. This should, in turn, reduce the need to carry such high levels of the particular item.

(e) A deterioration in the quality of bought-in items may result in holding higher levels of inventories to take account of possible defects. It may also lead to an increase in the inspection time for items received. This too could lead to a rise in inventories levels.

12.3 Inventories are held:

- to meet customer demand;
- to avoid the problems of running out of inventories; and
- to take advantage of profitable opportunities (for example, buying a product that is expected to rise steeply in price in the future).

The first reason may be described as transactionary, the second as precautionary and the third as speculative. They are, in essence, the same reasons why a business holds cash.

12.4 (a) The costs of holding too little cash are:

- failure to meet obligations when they fall due, which can damage the reputation of the business and may, in the extreme, lead to the business being wound up;
- having to borrow and thereby incur interest charges; and
- an inability to take advantage of profitable opportunities.

(b) The costs of holding too much cash are

- failure to use the funds available for more profitable purposes; and
- loss of value during a period of inflation.

Appendix D
SOLUTIONS TO SELECTED EXERCISES

Chapter 1

1.1 Strategic management involves five steps:

1. *Establish mission, vision and objectives.* The mission statement is usually a brief statement of the overriding purpose of the business. The vision statement sets out the aspirations of the business. The objectives are more specific than the mission and need to be consistent with the mission and vision. These objectives are often quantified.

2. *Undertake a position analysis.* Here the business is seeking to establish how it is placed relative to its environment (competitors, markets, technology, the economy, political climate and so on), given the business's mission and objectives. This is often approached within the framework of an analysis of the business's strengths, weaknesses, opportunities and threats (a SWOT analysis). Strengths and weaknesses are internal factors that are attributes of the business itself, whereas opportunities and threats are factors expected to be present in the environment in which the business operates. The SWOT framework is not the only approach to undertaking a position analysis, but it seems to be a very popular one.

3. *Identify and assess the strategic options.* This involves identifying possible courses of action that will enable the business to reach its objectives in the light of the position analysis undertaken in Step 2.

4. *Select strategic options and formulate plans.* Here the business will select what seems to be the best of the courses of action or strategies (identified in Step 3) and will formulate a plan to implement the strategies.

5. *Perform, review and control.* In this final step, the business pursues the plans derived in Step 4. It then exercises control by comparing actual performance against planned performance and taking corrective action where necessary.

1.2 SWOT analysis of Jones Dairy Ltd

Strengths

- A portfolio of identifiable customers who show some loyalty to the business.
- Good cash flow profile. Although credit will be given, a week is the normal credit period.
- An apparently sound distribution system.
- A monopoly of doorstep delivery in the area.
- Barriers to entry. There are probably relatively high entry costs to the market, which implies a 'critical mass' of volume is necessary.
- Good employees and ease of recruitment.
- Differentiated product; clearly different from what is supplied by the supermarket in that it is delivered to the door.
- Good customer relationship, since the decline in business is less than the national average.
- Good knowledge of the local market.
- Tendency for people to shop infrequently means that doorstep delivery may be the only practical means of having fresh milk.

Weaknesses

- Ageing managers.
- Success might be dependent on the present management team continuing.
- Narrow product range.

- High price necessary to generate acceptable level of profit.
- Available substitute – that is, non-delivered milk.
- Single supplier.

Opportunities

- Possibility of extending the product range to include other dairy and non-dairy products to existing customers.
- Possible geographical expansion to cover other local towns and villages.
- Possibly move to act as a wholesaler to local stores at differentiated prices. It is probable that the bottlers would supply Jones more cheaply than they would supply individual small stores.
- Using plant for some other purpose, such as leasing cold store facilities.

Threats

- Trend against doorstep delivery driven by price differential.
- Trend away from dairy products for health/cultural reasons.
- The probability that Jones is entirely dependent on the only local bottler. More geographically remote bottlers may not be prepared to supply at an acceptable price.
- Strength of supermarket buying, distribution and marketing power.

Chapter 2

2.1 Lombard Ltd

Relevant costs of undertaking the contract are:

	£
Equipment costs	200,000
Component X (20,000 × 4 × £5)	
Any of these components used will need to be replaced.	400,000
Component Y (20,000 × 3 × £8)	
All of the required units will come from inventories and this will be an effective cost of the net realisable value.	480,000
Additional costs (20,000 × £8)	160,000
	1,240,000
Revenue from the contract (20,000 x £80)	1,600,000

From a purely financial point of view, the project is acceptable. (Note that there is no relevant labour cost since the staff concerned will be paid irrespective of whether the contract is undertaken.)

2.2 The local authority

(a) Net benefit of accepting the touring company proposal:

	£
Net reduction in ticket revenues (see workings below)	(20,000)
Savings on: Costumes:	5,600
Scenery	3,300
Casual staff	3,520
Net deficit	(7,580)

Since there is a net deficit, on financial grounds, the touring company's proposal should be rejected.

Note that all of the following are irrelevant, because they will occur irrespective of the decision:

- non-performing staff salaries;
- artistes' salaries;
- heating and lighting;
- administration costs;
- refreshment revenues and costs; and
- programme advertising.

Workings

Normal ticket sales revenue:

	£
200 @ £24 =	4,800
500 @ £16 =	8,000
300 @ £12 =	3,600
	16,400

Ticket revenue at 50 per cent capacity for 20 performances:

$$(£16,400 \times 50\% \times 20) = £164,000$$

Touring company ticket sales:

Total revenue for each performance for a full house:

	£
200 @ £22 =	4,400
500 @ £14 =	7,000
300 @ £10 =	3,000
	14,400

		£
Ticket revenue	(£14,400 × 10 × 50%)	72,000
	(£14,400 × 15 × ⅔ × 50%)	72,000
		144,000
Net loss of revenue (£164,000 − £144,000)		£20,000

(b) Other possible factors to consider include:

- The reliability of the estimates, including the assumption that the level of occupancy will not alter programme and refreshment sales revenue.
- A desire to offer theatre-goers the opportunity to see another group of players.
- Dangers of loss of morale of staff not employed, or employed to do other than their usual work.

2.3 Andrews and Co. Ltd

Minimum contract price

			£
Materials	Steel core:	10,000 × £2.10	21,000
	Plastic:	10,000 × 0.10 × £0.10	100
Labour	Skilled:		–
	Unskilled:	10,000 × ⁵⁄₆₀ × £7.50	6,250
Minimum tender price			27,350

2.6 The local education authority

(a) One-off financial net benefits of closing:

	D only	A and B	A and C
Capacity reduction	800	700	800
	£m	£m	£m
Property developer (A)	–	14.0	14.0
Shopping complex (B)	–	8.0	–
Property developer (D)	9.0	–	–
Safety (C)	–	–	3.0
Adapt facilities	(1.8)	–	–
Total	7.2	22.0	17.0
Ranking based on total one-off benefits	3	1	2

(Note that all past costs of buying and improving the schools are irrelevant.)

Recurrent financial net benefits of closing:

	D only £m	A and B £m	A and C £m
Rent (C)	–	–	0.3
Administrators	0.2	0.4	0.4
Total	0.2	0.4	0.7
Ranking based on total of recurrent benefits	3	2	1

On the basis of the financial figures alone, closure of either A and B, or A and C, looks best. It is not possible to add the one-off and the recurring costs directly, but the large one-off cost saving associated with closing schools A and B makes this option look attractive. (In Chapter 8 we shall see that it is possible to add one-off and recurring costs in a way that should lead to sensible conclusions.)

(b) The costs of acquiring and improving the schools in the past are past costs and, therefore, irrelevant. The cost of employing the chief education officer is a future cost, but irrelevant because it is not dependent on future outcomes.

(c) There are many other factors, some of a non-quantifiable nature. These include:

- Accuracy of projections of capacity requirements.
- Locality of existing schools relative to where potential pupils live.
- Political acceptability of selling schools to property developers.
- Importance of purely financial issues in making the final decision.
- The quality of the replacement sporting facilities compared with those at school D.
- Political acceptability of staff redundancies.
- Possible savings/costs of employing fewer teachers, which might be relevant if economies of scale are available by having fewer schools.
- Staff morale.

2.7 Rob Otics Ltd

(a) The minimum price for the proposed contract would be:

	£
Materials	
Component X (2 × 8 × £180)	2,880
This inventories' item is in constant use by the business. This means that the 10 units held will ultimately need to be replaced, as well as a further 6 units needing to be purchased. All of these will need to be bought at the new price.	
Component Y	0
The history of the components held in inventories is irrelevant because it applies irrespective of the decision made on this contract. Since the alternative to using the units on this contract is to scrap them, the relevant cost is zero.	
Component Z [(75 + 32) × £20] − (75 × £25)	265
The relevant cost here is how much extra the business will pay the supplier as a result of undertaking the contract.	
Other miscellaneous items	250
Labour	
Assembly (25 + 24 + 23 + 22 + 21 + 20 + 19 + 18) × £48	8,256
The assembly labour cost is irrelevant because it will be incurred irrespective of which work the members of staff do. The relevant cost is based on the sales revenue per hour lost if the other orders are lost less the material cost per hour saved; that is £60 − £12 = £48.	
Inspection (8 × 6 × £12 × 150%)	864
Total	12,515

Thus the minimum price is £12,515.

(b) Other factors include:

- Competitive state of the market.
- The fact that the above figure is unique to the particular circumstances – for example, having Component Y available but having no use for it. Any subsequent order might have to take account of an outlay cost.
- Breaking even (that is, just covering the costs) on a contract will not fulfil the business's objective.
- Charging a low price may cause marketing problems. Other customers may resent the low price for this contract. Furthermore, the current enquirer may expect a similar price in future.

Chapter 3

3.1 Motormusic Ltd

(a) Break-even point = fixed costs/contribution per unit = (80,000 + 60,000)/[60 − (20 + 14 + 12 + 3)] = 12,727 radios.
These would have a sales value of £763,620 (that is, 12,727 × £60).

(b) The margin of safety is 7,273 radios (that is, 20,000 − 12,727). This margin would have a sales value of £436,380 (that is, 7,273 × £60).

3.3 Gandhi Ltd

(a) Given that the spare capacity could not be used by other services, the Standard service should continue to be offered. This is because it generates a positive contribution.

(b) The Standard service generates a contribution per unit of £15 (that is, £80 − £65), or £30 during the time it would take to produce one unit of the Nova service. The Nova service would generate a contribution of only £25 (that is, £75 − £50).
The Nova service should, therefore, not replace the Standard service.

(c) Under the original plans, the following contributions would be generated by the basic and standard services:

		£
Basic	11,000 × (£50 – £25)	275,000
Standard	6,000 × (£80 – £65)	90,000
		365,000

If the Basic took the Standard's place, 17,000 units (that is, 11,000 + 6,000) of them could be produced in total. To generate the same total contribution, each unit of the Standard service would need to generate £21.47 (that is, £365,000/17,000) of contribution. Given the basic's variable cost of £25, this would mean a selling price of £46.47 each (that is, £21.47 + £25.00).

3.6 Products A, B and C

(a) Total time required on cutting machines is:

$$(2,500 \times 1.0) + (3,400 \times 1.0) + (5,100 \times 0.5) = 8,450 \text{ hours}$$

Total time available on cutting machines is 5,000 hours. Therefore, this is a limiting factor.
Total time required on assembling machines is:

$$(2,500 \times 0.5) + (3,400 \times 1.0) + (5,100 \times 0.5) = 7,200 \text{ hours}$$

Total time available on assembling machines is 8,000 hours. Therefore, this is not a limiting factor.

	A (per unit)	B (per unit)	C (per unit)
	£	£	£
Selling price	25	30	18
Variable materials	(12)	(13)	(10)
Variable production costs	(7)	(4)	(3)
Contribution	6	13	5
Time on cutting machines	1.0 hour	1.0 hour	0.5 hour
Contribution per hour on cutting machines	£6	£13	£10
Order of priority	3rd	1st	2nd

Therefore, produce:

3,400 product B using	3,400 hours
3,200 product C using	1,600 hours
	5,000 hours

(b) Assuming there is no saving in variable production costs by subcontracting, it would be worth paying up to the contribution per unit (£5) for product C, which would therefore be £5 × (5,100 − 3,200) = £9,500 in total.

Similarly, it would be worth paying up to £6 per unit for product A – that is, £6 × 2,500 = £15,000 in total.

3.7 Darmor Ltd

(a) Contribution per hour of skilled labour of Product X is

$$\frac{£(30 - 6 - 2 - 12 - 3)}{(6/12)} = £14$$

To be indifferent between the products, given the scarcity of skilled labour, the contribution per skilled labour hour must be the same. Thus, for Product Y the selling price must be:

$$(£(14 \times (9/12)) + 9 + 4 + 25 + 7) = £55.50$$

(that is, the contribution plus the variable costs), and for Product Z the selling price must be:

$$(£(14 \times (3/12)) + 3 + 10 + 14 + 7) = £37.50$$

(b) The business could pay up to £26 an hour (£12 + £14) for additional hours of skilled labour. This is the potential contribution per hour, before taking into account the labour rate of £12 an hour.

3.8 Intermediate Products Ltd

(a)

	A	B	C	D
Total costs per unit (£)	(65)	(41)	(36)	(46)
Less Fixed cost (£)	20	8	8	12
Variable cost per unit (£)	(45)	(33)	(28)	(34)
Buying/selling price per unit (£)	70	45	40	55
Contribution per unit (£)	25	12	12	21
Hours on special machine	0.5	0.4	0.5	0.3
Contribution per hour (£)	50	30	24	70
Order of preference	2nd	3rd	4th	1st

Optimum use of hours on special machine

			Balance of hours
D	3,000 × 0.3 =	900	5,100 (that is, 6,000 − 900)
A	5,000 × 0.5 =	2,500	2,600 (that is, 5,100 − 2,500)
B	6,000 × 0.4 =	2,400	200 (that is, 2,600 − 2,400)
C	400 × 0.5 =	200	
		6,000	

Therefore, make all of the demand for Ds, As and Bs plus 400 (of 4,000) Cs.

(b) The contribution per hour from Cs is £24, which is the maximum amount per hour that it would be worth paying to rent the machine. This is for a maximum of 1,800 hours (that is, 3,600 × 0.5), which is the time necessary to make the remaining demand for Cs.

(c) Other possible actions to overcome the shortage of machine time include the following:

■ Alter the design of the products to avoid the use of the special machine.

■ Increase the selling price of the product so that demand will fall, making the available machine time sufficient and making production more profitable.

Chapter 4

4.1 Offending phrases and explanations

Offending phrase	*Explanation*
'Necessary to divide up the business into departments'	This can be done, but it will not always be of much benefit. Only in quite restricted circumstances will it give a significantly different job cost.
'Fixed costs (or overheads)'	This implies that fixed cost and overheads are the same thing. They are not really connected with one another. 'Fixed' is to do with how cost behaves as the level of output is raised or lowered; 'overheads' are to do with the extent to which cost can be directly measured in respect of a particular unit of output. Although it is true that many overheads are fixed, not all are. For example, power for machinery. All of the other references to fixed and variable costs are wrong. The person should have referred to indirect and direct costs.
'Usually this is done on the basis of area'	Where overheads are apportioned to departments, they will be apportioned on some logical basis. For certain elements of cost – for example, rent – the floor area may be the most logical. For others, such as machine maintenance cost, the floor area would be inappropriate.
'When the total fixed costs for each department have been identified, this will be divided by the number of hours that were worked'	Where overheads are dealt with on a departmental basis, they may be divided by the number of direct labour hours to deduce a recovery rate. However, this is only one basis of applying overheads to jobs. For example, machine hours or some other basis may be more appropriate to the particular circumstances involved.

4.4 Promptprint Ltd

(a) The plan (budget) may be summarised as:

	£	
Sales revenue	196,000	
Direct materials	(38,000)	
Direct labour	(32,000)	
Total indirect cost	(77,000)	(2,400 + 3,000 + 27,600 + 36,000 + 8,000)
Profit	49,000	

The job may be priced on the basis that both indirect cost and profit should be apportioned to it on the basis of direct labour cost, as follows:

	£	
Direct materials	4,000	
Direct labour	3,600	
Overheads	8,663	(£77,000 × 3,600/32,000)
Profit	5,513	(£49,000 × 3,600/32,000)
	21,776	

This answer assumes that variable overheads vary in proportion to direct labour cost.

Various other bases for charging overheads and profit loading the job could have been adopted. For example, materials cost could have been included (with direct labour) as the basis for profit loading, or even apportioning overheads.

(b) This part of the question is, in effect, asking for comments on the validity of 'full cost-plus' pricing. This approach can be useful as an indicator of the effective long-run cost of doing the job. On the other hand, it fails to take account of relevant opportunity cost as well as the state of the market and other external factors. For example, it ignores the price that a competitor printing business may quote.

Revised estimates of direct material cost for the job:

	£	
Paper grade 1	1,500	(£1,200 × 125%) (this item of inventories needs to be replaced)
Paper grade 2	0	(it has no opportunity cost value)
Card	510	(£640 − £130: using the card on another job would save £640, but cost £130 to achieve that saving)
Inks and so on	300	(this item of inventories needs to be replaced)
	2,310	

4.5 **(a)** Charging overheads to jobs on a departmental basis means that overheads are collected 'product' cost centre (department) by 'product' cost centre. This involves picking up the overheads that are specific to each department and adding to them a share of overheads that are general to the business as a whole. The overheads of 'service' cost centres must then be apportioned to the product cost centres. At this point, all of the overheads for the whole business are divided between the 'product' cost centres, such that the sum of the 'product' cost centre overheads equals those for the whole business.

Dealing with overheads departmentally may provide more accurate and useful information to decision makers. This is because different departments may have different overheads. Assigning overheads on a departmental basis takes this into account when calculating the cost of a job.

In theory, dealing with overheads on a departmental basis is more costly than on a business-wide basis. In practice, however, it may not make much difference to the cost of collecting the information. Businesses are usually divided into departments, and cost information is collected departmentally, as part of the normal routine.

(b) To make a difference to the job cost by dealing with overheads departmentally, rather than on a business-wide basis, the following *both* need to be the case:

- the overheads per unit of the basis of charging (for example direct labour hours) need to be different from one department to the next; and
- the proportion (but not the actual amounts) of total overheads charged to jobs must differ from one job to the next.

Assume that direct labour hours are used as the basis of charging overheads in all departments. Also assume that there are three departments, A, B and C.

There will be no difference to the overheads charged to a particular job if the rate of overheads per direct labour hour is the same for all departments. Obviously, if the charging rate is the same in all departments, that same rate must also apply to the business taken as a whole.

Also, even where overheads per direct labour hour differ significantly from one department to another – if all jobs spend, say, about 20 per cent of their time in Department A, 50 per cent in Department B and 30 per cent in Department C – it will not make any difference whether overheads are charged departmentally or overall.

These conclusions do not depend on the basis of charging overheads or even whether overheads are charged on the same basis in each department.

The points made above mean that, in practice, departmentalising overheads may not provide information that is significantly different from that when overheads are charged to jobs on a business-wide basis.

4.6 Products A, B and C

Allocation and apportionment of overheads to product cost centres:

	Basis of apportionment	Department				
		Cutting	Machining	Pressing	Engineering	Human resources
		£	£	£	£	£
Total		154,482	64,316	58,452	56,000	34,000
Human resources	Specified	18,700 (55%)	3,400 (10%)	6,800 (20%)	5,100 (15%)	(34,000)
		173,182	67,716	65,252	61,100	–
Engineering	Specified	12,220 (20%)	27,495 (45%)	21,385 (35%)	(61,100)	
		185,402	95,211	86,637	–	–

Note that the human resources services overheads were reapportioned to the other cost centres first. This is because human resources renders a service to the engineering services department, but does not receive a service from it.

Calculation of the overhead absorption (recovery) rates

In both the cutting and pressing departments, no machines seem to be used, and so a direct labour hour basis of overhead absorption seems reasonable.

In the machining department, machine hours are far in excess of labour hours and the overheads are probably machine-related. In this department, machine hours seem a fair basis for cost units to absorb overheads.

Total planned direct labour hours for the cutting department are thus:

		Hours
Product A	4,000 × (3 + 6)	36,000
Product B	3,000 × (5 + 1)	18,000
Product C	6,000 × (2 + 3)	30,000
		84,000

The overhead absorption rate for the cutting department is £185,402/84,000 = £2.21 per direct labour hour.

Total planned machine hours for the machining department are:

		Hours
Product A	4,000 × 2.0	8,000
Product B	3,000 × 1.5	4,500
Product C	6,000 × 2.5	15,000
		27,500

The overhead absorption rate for the machining department is £95,211/27,500 = £3.46 per machine hour.

Total planned direct labour hours for the pressing department are:

		Hours
Product A	4,000 × 2	8,000
Product B	3,000 × 3	9,000
Product C	6,000 × 4	24,000
		41,000

The overhead absorption rate for the cutting department = £86,637/41,000 = £2.11 per direct labour hour.

(a) Cost of one completed unit of product A:

		£
Direct materials		7.00
Direct labour		
Cutting department – skilled	(3 × £16)	48.00
– unskilled	(6 × £10)	60.00
Machining department	(0.5 × £12)	6.00
Pressing department	(2 × £12)	24.00
Overheads		
Cutting department	(9 × £2.21)	19.89
Machining department	(2 × £3.46)	6.92
Pressing department	(2 × £2.11)	4.22
		176.03

(b) Cost of one uncompleted unit of product B:

		£
Direct materials		4.00*
Direct labour		
Cutting department – skilled	(5 × £16)	80.00
– unskilled	(1 × £10)	10.00
Machining department	(0.25 × £12)	3.00
Overheads		
Cutting department	(6 × £2.21)	13.26
Machining department	(1.5 × £3.46)	5.19
		115.45

* This assumes that all of the materials are added in the cutting or machining departments.

4.8 Bookdon plc

(a) To answer this question, we need first to allocate and apportion the overheads to product cost centres, as follows:

Cost	Basis of apportionment	Total	Machine shop	Fitting section	Canteen	Machine maintenance section
		£	£	£	£	£
Allocated items:	Specific	90,380	27,660	19,470	16,600	26,650
Rent, rates, heat, light	Floor area	17,000	9,000	3,500	2,500	2,000
			(3,600/ 6,800)	(1,400/ 6,800)	(1,000/ 6,800)	(800/ 6,800)
Depreciation and insurance	Book value	25,000	12,500	6,250	2,500	3,750
			(150/300)	(75/300)	(30/300)	(45/300)
Canteen	Number of employees	–	10,800	8,400	(21,600)	2,400
			(18/36)	(14/36)		(4/36)
					–	34,800
Machine maintenance section	Specified %	–	24,360	10,440	–	(34,800)
			(70%)	(30%)		
		132,380	84,320	48,060	–	–

Note that the canteen overheads were reapportioned to the other cost centres first. This is because the canteen renders a service to the machine maintenance section but does not receive a service from it.

Calculation of the overhead absorption (recovery) rates can now proceed:

(1) Total budgeted machine hours are:

	Hours
Product X (4,200 × 6)	25,200
Product Y (6,900 × 3)	20,700
Product Z (1,700 × 4)	6,800
	52,700

Overhead absorption rate for the machine shop is

$$\frac{£84,320}{52,700} = £1.60/\text{machine hour}$$

(2) Total budgeted direct labour cost for the fitting section is:

	£
Product X (4,200 × £12)	50,400
Product Y (6,900 × £3)	20,700
Product Z (1,700 × £21)	35,700
	106,800

Overhead absorption rate for the fitting section is

$$\frac{£48,060}{£106,800} \times £100\% = 45\%$$

or £0.45 per £ of direct labour cost.

(b) The cost of one unit of product X is calculated as follows:

	£
Direct materials	11.00
Direct labour:	
Machine shop	6.00
Fitting section	12.00
Overheads:	
Machine shop (6 × £1.60)	9.60
Fitting section (£12 × 45%)	5.40
	44.00

Therefore, the cost of one unit of product X is £44.00.

Chapter 5

5.1 Comments

(a) It does not necessarily follow that, in order to improve the quality of output, total costs must increase. Quality costs may be divided into four categories: prevention, appraisal, internal failure and external failure. By investing resources into the prevention of faults and errors, through staff training, more advanced equipment and so forth, it may be possible to reduce costs relating to appraisal (such as inspection), internal failure (such as reworking products) and external failure (such as after-sales service). This means that the additional prevention costs incurred may be offset by the decrease in other quality-related costs.

(b) The TQM approach is concerned with improving quality, while kaizen costing is concerned with cost reduction; nevertheless, there are similarities in the approaches used. They include:

- a commitment to continuous improvement;
- recognition of the importance of continuous improvement in a competitive environment;
- the involvement of employees in the quest for improvements;
- detailed investigations of existing processes in order to identify areas for improvement; and
- the use of a range of possible methods to achieve the required improvements.

(c) Target costing is particularly useful for manufacturers producing goods with short life cycles. This is because cost savings are likely to be greatest where there is a need to make frequent updates to existing products and/or to develop a constant stream of new products.

It is less relevant for businesses where product development is not such a significant issue, which will include most service businesses. Nevertheless, opportunities to use this costing approach may still arise. An example was given in the chapter of a firm of management consultants bidding for a contract. Other service providers, such as IT specialists, auditors and lawyers, may find themselves in a similar position.

5.2 Target costing versus kaizen costing

The main similarities between the two methods are as follows:

- Both methods involve the setting of targets and the comparison of actual performance against target performance.
- Both methods are aimed at reducing costs of production.
- Both can be linked to the concept of total life-cycle costing.
- They were both developed by Japanese businesses in response to an increasingly competitive environment.
- They both employ cross-functional work teams as a means of identifying and reducing costs.
- Neither is a cost measurement method but rather each is a framework within which various cost reduction methods can be employed.

The main differences between the two methods are:

- Target costing is most suitable for the pre-production phase of a product's life whereas kaizen costing is most suitable for the production phase.
- Target costing normally has the potential for much greater cost savings than kaizen costing.
- Kaizen costing involves making many small changes whereas target costing may make significant changes.
- Kaizen costing is concerned with continuous improvement and so extends over a longer time period than target costing.
- Target costing is less relevant to manufacturers where product development is not a significant issue. Kaizen costing can be highly relevant to all manufacturers operating within a competitive environment.

5.3 Saxos plc The main problems that may be encountered include:

- Introducing benchmarking can be time-consuming and costly.
- Finding a suitable successful business against which to benchmark may be difficult.
- Even if a successful business can be found, it may be reluctant to engage in the exercise. This may be because it considers that it has little to gain, or fears the loss of confidential information.
- An inappropriate business may be used for benchmarking purposes, due to differences in process or culture.
- The benchmarks developed may be poorly defined leading to wasted effort.
- The benchmarks chosen may not capture the key aspects of operating efficiency.

5.4 Kaplan plc

(a) The business makes each model of suitcase in a batch. The direct materials and labour costs will be recorded in respect of each batch. To these costs will be added a share of the overheads of the business for the period in which production of the batch takes place. The basis of the batch absorbing overheads is a matter of managerial judgement. Direct labour hours spent working on the batch is a popular basis. This is not the 'correct' way, however. There is no single correct way. If the activity is capital-intensive, some machine hour basis of dealing with overheads might be more appropriate. Overheads might be collected, cost centre by cost centre (department by department), and charged to the batch as it passes through each product cost centre. Alternatively, all of the overheads for the entire production facility might be totalled and dealt with business-wide. It is only in restricted circumstances that overheads charged to batches will be significantly affected by a decision to deal with them by cost centres, rather than business-wide.

Once the 'full cost' (direct costs plus a share of indirect costs) has been calculated for the batch, the cost per suitcase can be established by dividing the batch cost by the number in the batch.

(b) The uses to which full cost information can be put have been identified as:

■ *For pricing purposes.* Sometimes, full costs are used as the basis of pricing. Here the full cost is deduced and a percentage is added on for profit. This is known as cost-plus pricing. A solicitor handling a case for a client usually provides an example of this.

  Most of the time, however, suppliers are not in a position to deduce prices on a cost-plus basis. Where there is a competitive market, a supplier will probably need to accept the price that the market offers – that is, most suppliers are 'price takers' not 'price makers'.

■ *For income-measurement purposes.* To provide a valid means of measuring a business's income, expenses must be matched in the same accounting period with the revenue that they generate. Where manufactured products are made, or partially made, in one period but sold in the next, or where a service is partially rendered in one accounting period but the revenue is generated in the next, the full cost (including an appropriate share of overheads) must be carried from one accounting period to the next. Unless we can identify the full cost of work done in one period, which then becomes the subject of a sale in the next, the profit figures for both periods are meaningless.

■ *For planning and control.* Often planned performance is set out in terms of full costs. If plans are used as the yardsticks by which actual performance is to be assessed, the information on actual performance should also be expressed in the same full cost terms.

■ *General decision making.* Knowing the full cost of the suitcases might be helpful in making a decision as to whether to continue to make all or some of the models. It can be argued, however, that identifying the relevant costs would provide a more helpful basis for the decision.

(c) Whereas the traditional approach to overheads is simply to accept that they exist and deal with them in a fairly arbitrary manner, ABC takes a much more enquiring approach. It recognises that overheads do not just 'occur', they are caused or 'driven' by 'activities'. It is then a question of discovering which activities are driving the costs and how much cost they are driving.

  For example, a significant part of the costs of making suitcases of different sizes might be resetting machinery to cope with a batch of a different size from its predecessor batch. Where a particular model is made in very small batches, because it has only a small market, ABC would advocate that this model is charged directly with its machine-setting costs. The traditional approach is to treat machine setting as a general overhead, which the individual suitcases (irrespective of the model) might bear equally. Thus, ABC should lead to more accurate product costing and to a more accurate assessment of profitability.

(d) An advantage of pursuing an ABC philosophy and identifying cost drivers is that, once the drivers have been identified, it may be possible to bring them under control. Managers are provided with a deeper insight to business operations and so can take whatever action is required.

5.7 Moleskin Ltd

(a) Price using absorption costing
Overhead absorption rate = total overheads/total direct labour hours = £280,000/4,000 = £70 per direct labour hour.

	JT101	GR27
	£	£
Direct materials	16.00	15.00
Direct labour	8.00	8.00
Overheads: ½ × £70	35.00	35.00
Total cost	59.00	58.00
Mark-up at 35%	20.65	20.30
Price per metre	79.65	78.30

(b) Price using activity-based costing

Cost driver rates:

Alpha Process	£96,000/480	£200 per hour
Omega Process	£44,800/1,280	£35 per hour
Set-ups	£42,900/260	£165 per set up
Handling	£45,600/380	£120 per movement
Other overheads	£50,700/4,000	£12.68 per direct labour hour

Prices for the two products:

		JT101 £		GR27 £
Direct materials		16.00		16.00
Direct labour		8.00		8.00
Alpha Process	(100 × £200)/1,000	20.00		–
Omega Process			(25 × £35)/50	17.50
Set-ups	£165/1,000	0.17	(2 × £165)/50	6.60
Ordering		–	(3 × £90)/50	5.40
Handling	£120/1,000	0.12	(5 × £120)/50	12.00
Other overheads	½ × £12.68	6.34	½ × £12.68	6.34
Total cost		50.63		71.84
35% mark-up		17.72		25.14
Price per metre		68.35		96.98

(c) Points for the management

- Under the traditional approach, the prices of the two products are quite similar because the direct costs are quite similar, which also leads to a similar allocation of overheads (because these are absorbed on the basis of direct labour hours).
- With ABC, the prices are quite different between the products. This is because the GR27s cause much more overhead cost than the JT101s and ABC reflects this fact.
- Management should reconsider its pricing policy. If the traditionally-based price is, in fact, the current selling price, the GR27s are earning only a small margin on the ABC cost.
- If the market will not bear a higher price for the GR27s, management may consider dropping them and concentrating its efforts on the JT101s. Projected market demand for the two products will obviously have a major bearing on the final decision.

(d) Practical problems of using ABC

- Identifying the cost driving activities and determining cost driver rates can be difficult and expensive. It is sometimes necessary to use arbitrary approaches to certain parts of the overheads, as with 'other overheads' in the Joists/Girders example above.
- The costs of introducing ABC may outweigh the benefits.
- Changing the culture necessary to introduce ABC may pose difficulties. There may be resistance to a new approach.
- On a positive note, ABC may have benefits beyond cost determination and pricing. Careful analysis of costs and what drives them can provide a basis for exercising better control over them.

Chapter 6

6.1 Prolog Ltd

(a) Cash budget for the six months to 30 June:

	Jan	Feb	Mar	Apr	May	June
	£000	£000	£000	£000	£000	£000
Receipts						
Credit sales revenue (Note 1)	<u>100</u>	<u>100</u>	<u>140</u>	<u>180</u>	<u>220</u>	<u>260</u>
Payments						
Trade payables (Note 2)	112	144	176	208	240	272
Operating expenses	4	6	8	10	10	10
Shelving	–	–	–	12	–	–
Taxation	<u>–</u>	<u>–</u>	<u>25</u>	<u>–</u>	<u>–</u>	<u>–</u>
	116	150	209	230	250	282
Cash flow	(16)	(50)	(69)	(50)	(30)	(22)
Opening balance	(68)	(84)	(134)	(203)	(253)	(283)
Closing balance	(84)	(134)	(203)	(253)	(283)	(305)

Notes:

1 Sales receipts will equal the month's sales revenue, but be received two months later. For example, the January sales revenue = £2,000 × (50 + 20) = £140,000, to be received in March.

2 Payments to suppliers will equal the next month's sales requirements, payable the next month. For example, January purchases = £1,600 × (50 + 40) = £144,000, payable in February.

(b) A banker may require various pieces of information before granting additional overdraft facilities. These may include:

- Security available for the loan.
- Details of past profit performance.
- Profit projections for the next 12 months.
- Cash projections beyond the next six months to help assess the prospects of repayment.
- Details of the assumptions underlying projected figures supplied.
- Details of the contractual commitment between Prolog Ltd and its supplier.
- Details of management expertise. Can they manage the expansion programme?
- Details of the new machine and its performance in relation to competing models.
- Details of funds available from owners to finance the expansion.

6.3 Nursing home

(a) The rates per patient for the variable overheads, on the basis of experience during months 1 to 6, are as follows:

Expense	Amount for 2,700 patients	Amount per patient
	£	£
Staffing	59,400	22
Power	27,000	10
Supplies	54,000	20
Other	<u>8,100</u>	<u>3</u>
	148,500	55

Since the expected level of activity for the full year is 6,000, the expected level of activity for the second six months is 3,300 (that is, 6,000 − 2,700).

Thus the budget for the second six months will be:

	£	
Variable element:		
Staffing	72,600	(3,300 × £22)
Power	33,000	(3,300 × £10)
Supplies	66,000	(3,300 × £20)
Other	9,900	(3,300 × £3)
	181,500	(3,300 × £55)
Fixed element:		
Supervision	60,000	6/12 of the annual figure
Depreciation/finance	93,600	ditto
Other	32,400	ditto
	186,000	(per patient = £56.36 (that is, £186,000/3,300))
Total (second six months)	367,500	(per patient = £111.36 (that is, £56.36 + £55.00))

(b) For the second six months, the actual activity was 3,800 patients. For a valid comparison with the actual outcome, the budget will need to be revised to reflect this activity.

	Actual costs	Budget (3,800 patients)	Difference
	£	£	£
Variable element	203,300	209,000 (3,800 × £55)	5,700 (saving)
Fixed element	190,000	186,000	4,000 (overspend)
Total	393,300	395,000	1,700 (saving)

(c) Relative to the budget, there was a saving of nearly 3 per cent on the variable element and an overspend of about 2 per cent on fixed costs. Without further information, it is impossible to deduce much more than this.

The differences between the budget and the actual may be caused by some assumptions made in framing the budget for 3,300 patients in the second part of the year. There may be some element of economies of scale in the variable costs; that is, the costs may not be strictly linear. If this were the case, basing a relatively large activity budget on the experience of a relatively small activity period would tend to overstate the large activity budget. The fixed-cost budget was deduced by dividing the budget for 12 months by two. In fact, there could be seasonal factors or inflationary pressures at work that might make such a crude division of the fixed cost element unfair.

6.4 Linpet Ltd

(a) Cash budgets are extremely useful for decision-making purposes. They allow managers to see the likely effect on the cash balance of the plans that they have set in place. Cash is an important asset and it is necessary to ensure that it is properly managed. Failure to do so can have disastrous consequences for the business. Where the cash budget indicates a surplus balance, managers must decide whether this balance should be reinvested in the business or distributed to the owners. Where the cash budget indicates a deficit balance, managers must decide how this deficit should be financed or how it might be avoided.

(b) Cash budget for the six months to 30 November:

	June £	July £	Aug £	Sept £	Oct £	Nov £
Receipts						
Cash sales revenue (Note 1)	4,000	5,500	7,000	8,500	11,000	11,000
Credit sales revenue (Note 2)	–	–	4,000	5,500	7,000	8,500
	4,000	5,500	11,000	14,000	18,000	19,500
Payments						
Purchases (Note 3)	–	29,000	9,250	11,500	13,750	17,500
Overheads	500	500	500	500	650	650
Wages	900	900	900	900	900	900
Commission (Note 4)	–	320	440	560	680	880
Equipment	10,000	–	–	–	–	7,000
Motor vehicle	6,000	–	–	–	–	–
Leasehold	40,000	–	–	–	–	–
	57,400	30,720	11,090	13,460	15,980	26,930
Cash flow	(53,400)	(25,220)	(90)	540	2,020	(7,430)
Opening balance	60,000	6,600	(18,620)	(18,710)	(18,170)	(16,150)
Closing balance	6,600	(18,620)	(18,710)	(18,170)	(16,150)	(23,580)

Notes:

1 50 per cent of the current month's sales revenue.
2 50 per cent of the sales revenue of the previous two months.
3 To have sufficient inventories to meet each month's sales will require purchases of 75 per cent of the month's sales inventories figures (25 per cent is profit). In addition, each month the business will buy £1,000 more inventories than it will sell. In June, the business will also buy its initial inventories of £22,000. This will be paid for in the following month. For example, June's purchases will be ((75% × £8,000) + £1,000 + £22,000) = £29,000, paid for in July.
4 This is 5 per cent of 80 per cent of the month's sales revenue, paid in the following month. For example, June's commission will be (5% × 80% × £8,000) = £320, payable in July.

6.5 Lewisham Ltd

(a) The finished goods inventories budget for the three months ending 30 September (in units of production) is:

	July '000 units	Aug '000 units	Sept '000 units
Opening inventories (Note 1)	40	48	40
Production (Note 2)	188	232	196
	228	280	236
Inventories sold (Note 3)	(180)	(240)	(200)
Closing inventories	48	40	36

(b) The raw materials inventories budget for the two months ending 31 August (in kg) is:

	July '000 kg	Aug '000 kg
Opening inventories (Note 1)	40	58
Purchases (Note 2)	112	107
	152	165
Production (Note 4)	(94)	(116)
Closing inventories	58	49

(c) The cash budget for the two months ending 30 September is:

	Aug £	Sept £
Inflows		
Receivables – current month (Note 5)	493,920	411,600
– preceding month (Note 6)	151,200	201,600
Total inflows	645,120	613,200
Outflows		
Payments to trade payables (Note 7)	168,000	160,500
Labour and overheads (Note 8)	185,600	156,800
Fixed overheads	22,000	22,000
Total outflows	375,600	339,300
Net inflows/(outflows)	269,520	273,900
Balance carried forward	289,520	563,420

Notes:

1 The opening balance is the same as the closing balance from the previous month.
2 This is a balancing figure.
3 This figure is given in the question.
4 This figure derives from the finished inventories budget (July, 188,000 × 0.5 = 94,000).
5 This is 98 per cent of 70 per cent of the current month's sales revenue.
6 This is 28 per cent of the previous month's sales revenue.
7 This figure derives from the raw materials inventories budget (July, 112,000 × £1.50 = £168,000).
8 This figure derives from the finished inventories budget (August, £232,000 × £0.80 = £185,600).

6.7 Newtake Records

(a) The cash budget for the period to 30 November is:

	June £000	July £000	Aug £000	Sept £000	Oct £000	Nov £000
Cash receipts						
Sales revenue (Note 1)	227	315	246	138	118	108
Cash payments						
Administration (Note 2)	(40)	(41)	(38)	(33)	(31)	(30)
Goods purchased	(135)	(180)	(142)	(94)	(75)	(66)
Repayments of borrowings	(5)	(5)	(5)	(5)	(5)	(5)
Selling expenses	(22)	(24)	(28)	(26)	(21)	(19)
Tax paid	–	–	(22)	–	–	–
Shop refurbishment	–	(14)	(18)	(6)	–	–
	(202)	(264)	(253)	(164)	(132)	(120)
Cash surplus (deficit)	25	51	(7)	(26)	(14)	(12)
Opening balance	(35)	(10)	41	34	8	(6)
Closing balance	(10)	41	34	8	(6)	(18)

Notes:

1 (50% of the current month's sales revenue) + (97% × 50% of that sales revenue). For example, the June cash receipts will be ((50% × £230,000) + (97% × 50% × £230,000)) = £226,550.
2 The administration expenses figure for the month *less* £15,000 for depreciation (a non-cash expense).

(b) The inventories budget for the six months to 30 November is:

	June £000	July £000	Aug £000	Sept £000	Oct £000	Nov £000
Opening balance	112	154	104	48	39	33
Inventories purchased	180	142	94	75	66	57
	292	296	198	123	105	90
Cost of inventories sold (60% of sales revenue)	(138)	(192)	(150)	(84)	(72)	(66)
Closing balance	154	104	48	39	33	24

(c) The budgeted income statement for the six months ending 30 November is:

	£000
Sales revenue	1,170
Cost of goods sold	(702)
Gross profit (40%)	468
Selling expenses	(136)
Admin expenses	(303)
Credit card charges	(18)
Interest charges	(6)
Profit for the period	5

(d) We are told that the business is required to eliminate the bank overdraft by the end of November. However, the cash budget shows that this will not be achieved. There is a decline in the overdraft of nearly 50 per cent over the period, but this is not enough and ways must be found to comply with the bank's requirements. It may be possible to delay the refurbishment programme that is included in the plans, or to obtain an injection of funds from the owners or other investors. It may also be possible to stimulate sales in some way. However, there has been a decline in the sales revenue since the end of July and the November sales revenue is approximately one-third of the July sales revenue. The reasons for this decline should be sought.

The inventories levels will fall below the preferred minimum level for each of the last three months. However, to rectify this situation it will be necessary to purchase more inventories which will, in turn, exacerbate the cash flow problems of the business.

The budgeted income statement reveals a very low net profit for the period. For every £1 of sales revenue, the business is only managing to generate 0.4p in profit. The business should look carefully at its pricing policies and its overhead expenses. The administration expenses, for example, absorb more than one-quarter of the total sales revenue. Any reduction in overhead expenses will have a beneficial effect on cash flows.

Chapter 7

7.1 True or false

(a) A favourable direct labour rate variance can only be caused by something that leads to the rate per hour paid being less than standard. Normally, this would not be linked to efficient working. Where, however, the standard envisaged some overtime working, at premium rates, the actual labour rate may be below standard if efficiency has removed the need for the overtime.

(b) The statement is true. The action will lead to an adverse sales price variance and may well lead to problems elsewhere, but the sales volume variance must be favourable.

(c) It is true that below-standard materials could lead to adverse materials usage variances because there may be more than a standard amount of scrap. This could also cause adverse labour efficiency variances because working on materials that would not form part of the output would waste labour time.

(d) Higher-than-budgeted sales revenue could well lead to an adverse labour rate variance because producing the additional work may require overtime working at premium rates.

(e) The statement is true. Nothing else could cause such a variance.

7.2 Overheard remarks

(a) Flexing the budget identifies what the profit would have been, had the only difference between the original budget and the actual figures been concerned with the difference in volume of output. Comparing the original budget profit figure with that in the flexed budget reveals the profit difference (variance) arising solely from the volume difference (sales volume variance). Thus, flexing the budget does not mean at all that volume differences do not matter. Flexing the budget is the means of discovering the effect on profit of the volume difference.

In one sense, all variances are 'water under the bridge', to the extent that the past cannot be undone, and so it is impossible to go back to the last control period and put in a better performance. Identifying variances can, however, be useful in identifying where things went wrong, which should enable management to take steps to ensure that the same things do *not* go wrong in the future.

(b) Variances will not tell you what went wrong. They should, however, be a great help in identifying the manager within whose sphere of responsibility things went wrong. That manager should know why it went wrong. In this sense, variances identify relevant questions, but not answers.

(c) Identifying the reason for variances may well cost money, usually in terms of staff time. It is a matter of judgement in any particular situation, of balancing the cost of investigation against the potential benefits. As is usual in such judgements, it is difficult, before undertaking the investigation, to know either the cost or the likely benefit.

In general, significant variances, particularly adverse ones, should be investigated. Persistent (over a period of months) smaller variances should also be investigated. It should not automatically be assumed that favourable variances can be ignored. They indicate that things are not going according to plan, possibly because the plans (budgets) are flawed.

(d) Research evidence does not show this. It seems to show that managers tend to be most motivated by having as a target the most difficult goals that they find acceptable.

(e) Budgets normally provide the basis of feedforward and feedback control. During a budget preparation period, potential problems (for example, an inventories shortage) might be revealed. Steps can then be taken to revise the plans in order to avoid the potential problem. This is an example of a feedforward control: potential problems are anticipated and eliminated before they can occur.

Budgetary control is a very good example of feedback control, where a signal that something is going wrong triggers steps to take corrective action for the future.

7.3 Pilot Ltd

(a)

	Budget			Actual	
	Original	Flexed			
Output (units) (production and sales)	5,000	5,400		5,400	
	£	£		£	
Sales revenue	25,000	27,000		26,460	
Raw materials	(7,500)	(8,100)	(2,700 kg)	(8,770)	(2,830 kg)
Labour	(6,250)	(6,750)	(675 hr)	(6,885)	(650 hr)
Fixed overheads	(6,000)	(6,000)		(6,350)	
Operating profit	5,250	6,150		4,455	

	£	
Sales volume variance (5,250 − 6,150)	900	(F)
Sales price variance (27,000 − 26,460)	(540)	(A)
Materials price variance (2,830 × 3) − 8,770	(280)	(A)
Materials usage variance ((5,400 × 0.5) − 2,830) × £3)	(390)	(A)
Labour rate variance ((650 × £10) − 6,885)	(385)	(A)
Labour efficiency variance ((5,400 × 7.5/60) − 650) × £10)	250	(F)
Fixed overhead spending variance (6,000 − 6,350)	(350)	(A)
Total net variances	(795)	(A)

	£
Budgeted profit	5,250
Less Total net variance	(795)
Actual profit	4,455

(b) Sales volume variance: sales manager; sales price variance: sales manager; materials price variance: buyer; materials usage variance: production manager; labour rate variance: human resources manager; labour efficiency variance: production manager; fixed overhead spending variance: various, depending on the nature of the overheads.

7.5 Bradley-Allen Ltd

(a)

	Budget			Actual	
	Original	Flexed			
Output (units) (production and sales)	800	950		950	
	£	£		£	
Sales revenue	64,000	76,000		73,000	
Raw materials – A	(12,000)	(14,250)	(285 kg)	(15,200)	(310 kg)
– B	(16,000)	(19,000)	(950 m)	(18,900)	(920 m)
Labour – skilled	(4,000)	(4,750)	(475 hr)	(4,628)	(445 hr)
– unskilled	(10,000)	(11,875)	(1,484 hr)	(11,275)	(1,375 hr)
Fixed overheads	(12,000)	(12,000)		(11,960)	
Operating profit	10,000	14,125		11,037	

Sales variances

Volume: $10,000 - 14,125 = £4,125$ (F)

Price: $76,000 - 73,000 = £3,000$ (A)

Direct materials A variances

Usage: $[(950 \times 0.3) - 310] \times £50 = £1,250$ (A)

Price: $(310 \times £50) - £15,200 = £300$ (F)

Direct materials B variances

Usage: $[(950 \times 1) - 920] \times £20 = £600$ (F)

Price: $(920 \times £20) - £18,900 = £500$ (A)

Skilled direct labour variances

Efficiency: $[(950 \times 0.5) - 445] \times £10 = £300$ (F)

Rate: $(445 \times £10) - £4,628 = £178$ (A)

Unskilled direct labour variances

Efficiency: $[(950 \times 1.5625) - 1,375] \times £8 = £875$ (F)

Rate: $(1,375 \times £8) - £11,275 = £275$ (A)

Fixed overhead variances

Spending: $(12,000 - 11,960) = £40$ (F)

Budgeted profit				£10,000
Sales:	Volume	4,125	(F)	
	Price	(3,000)	(A)	1,125
Direct material A:	Usage	(1,250)	(A)	
	Price	300	(F)	(950)
Direct material B:	Usage	600	(F)	
	Price	(500)	(A)	100
Skilled labour:	Efficiency	300	(F)	
	Rate	(178)	(A)	122
Unskilled labour:	Efficiency	875	(F)	
	Rate	(275)	(A)	600
Fixed overheads:	Expenditure			40
Actual profit				£11,037

(b) The statement in (a) is useful to management because it enables them to see where there have been failures to meet the original budget and to quantify the extent of such failures. This means that junior managers can be held accountable for the performance of their particular area of responsibility.

7.8 Varne Chemprocessors

(a) The standard usage rate of UK194 per litre of Varnelyne is 200/5,000 = 0.04. The standard price is £392/200 = £1.96 per litre of UK194.

Materials usage variance (UK194) is

$$((637,500 \times 0.04) - 28,100) \times £1.96 = £5,096 \text{ (A)}$$

Materials price variance is

$$(28,100 \times £1.96) - £51,704 = £3,372 \text{ (F)}$$

(b) The net variance on UK194 was, from the calculations in (a), £1,724 (A) (that is, £5,096 – £3,372). This seems to have led directly to savings elsewhere of £4,900, giving a net cost saving of over £3,000 for the month.

Unfortunately things may not be quite as simple as the numbers suggest. The non-standard mix to make the Varnelyne might lead to a substandard product, which could have very wide-ranging ramifications in terms of potential loss of market goodwill.

There is also the possibility that the material for which the UK194 was used as a substitute was already held in inventories. If this were the case, is there any danger that this material may deteriorate and, ultimately, prove to be unusable?

Other possible adverse outcomes of the non-standard mix could also arise.

The question is raised by the analysis in part (a) (and by the production manager's comment) of why the cost standard for UK194 had not been revised to take account of the lower price prevailing in the market.

(c) The variances, period by period and cumulatively, for each of the two materials are given as follows:

Period	UK500		UK800	
	Period	Cumulative	Period	Cumulative
	£	£	£	£
1	301 (F)	301 (F)	298 (F)	298 (F)
2	(251) (A)	50 (F)	203 (F)	501 (F)
3	102 (F)	152 (F)	(52) (A)	449 (F)
4	(202) (A)	(50) (A)	(98) (A)	351 (F)
5	153 (F)	103 (F)	(150) (A)	201 (F)
6	(103) (A)	zero	(201) (A)	zero

Without knowing the scale of these variances relative to the actual costs involved, it is not possible to be too dogmatic about how to interpret the above information.

UK500 appears to show a fairly random set of data, with the period variances fluctuating from positive to negative and giving a net variance of zero. This is what would be expected from a situation that is basically under control, but with small variances occurring.

UK800 also shows a zero cumulative figure over the six periods, *but* there seems to be a more systematic train of events, particularly the four consecutive adverse variances from period 3 onwards. This looks as if it may be out of control and worthy of investigation.

Chapter 8

8.1 Mylo Ltd

(a) The annual depreciation of the two projects is:

$$\text{Project 1: } \frac{(\pounds100,000 - \pounds7,000)}{3} = \pounds31,000$$

$$\text{Project 2: } \frac{(\pounds60,000 - \pounds6,000)}{3} = \pounds18,000$$

Project 1

(1) Net present value

	Year 0	Year 1	Year 2	Year 3
	£000	£000	£000	£000
Operating profit/(loss) before depreciation		60	30	33
Capital cost	(100)			
Residual value				7
Net cash flows	(100)	60	30	40
10% discount factor	1.000	0.909	0.826	0.751
Present value	(100.00)	54.54	24.78	30.04
Net present value	9.36			

(2) Internal rate of return

Clearly the IRR lies above 10%. Try 15%:

15% discount factor	1.000	0.870	0.756	0.658
Present value	(100.00)	52.20	22.68	26.32
Net present value	1.20			

Thus the IRR lies a little above 15%, perhaps around 16%.

(3) Payback period

To find the payback period, the cumulative cash flows are calculated:

Cumulative cash flows	(100)	(40)	(10)	30

Thus the payback will occur after three years if we assume year-end cash flows.

Project 2

(1) NPV

	Year 0	Year 1	Year 2	Year 3
	£000	£000	£000	£000
Operating profit/(loss) before depreciation		36	16	22
Capital cost	(60)			
Residual value				6
Net cash flows	(60)	36	16	28
10% discount factor	1.000	0.909	0.826	0.751
Present value	(60.00)	32.72	13.22	21.03
Net present value	6.97			

(2) IRR

Clearly the IRR lies above 10%. Try 15%:

15% discount factor	1.000	0.870	0.756	0.658
Present value	(60.00)	31.32	12.10	18.42
Net present value	1.84			

Thus the IRR lies a little above 15%, perhaps around 17%.

(3) Payback Period

The cumulative cash flows are:

Cumulative cash flows	(60)	(24)	(8)	20

Thus, the payback will occur after three years (assuming year-end cash flows).

(b) Assuming that Mylo Ltd is pursuing a wealth-enhancement objective, Project 1 is preferable since it has the higher net present value. The difference between the two net present values is not significant, however.

8.3 Newton Electronics Ltd

(a) Option 1

	Year 0 £m	Year 1 £m	Year 2 £m	Year 3 £m	Year 4 £m	Year 5 £m
Plant and equipment	(9.0)					1.0
Sales revenue		24.0	30.8	39.6	26.4	10.0
Variable cost		(11.2)	(19.6)	(25.2)	(16.8)	(7.0)
Fixed cost (excluding depreciation)		(0.8)	(0.8)	(0.8)	(0.8)	(0.8)
Working capital	(3.0)					3.0
Marketing cost		(2.0)	(2.0)	(2.0)	(2.0)	(2.0)
Lease	–	(0.1)	(0.1)	(0.1)	(0.1)	(0.1)
	(12.0)	9.9	8.3	11.5	6.7	4.1
Discount factor 10%	1.000	0.909	0.826	0.751	0.683	0.621
Present value	(12.0)	9.0	6.9	8.6	4.6	2.5
Net present value	19.6					

Option 2

	Year 0 £m	Year 1 £m	Year 2 £m	Year 3 £m	Year 4 £m	Year 5 £m
Royalties	–	4.4	7.7	9.9	6.6	2.8
Discount factor 10%	1.000	0.909	0.826	0.751	0.683	0.621
Present value	–	4.0	6.4	7.4	4.5	1.7
Net present value	24.0					

Option 3

	Year 0	Year 2
Instalments	12.0	12.0
Discount factor 10%	1.000	0.826
Present value	12.0	9.9
Net present value	21.9	

(b) Before making a final decision, the board should consider the following factors:

- The long-term competitiveness of the business may be affected by the sale of the patents.
- At present, the business is not involved in manufacturing and marketing products. Would a change in direction be desirable?
- The business will probably have to buy in the skills necessary to produce the product itself. This will involve costs, and problems may be encountered. Has this been taken into account?
- How accurate are the forecasts made and how valid are the assumptions on which they are based?

(c) Option 2 has the highest net present value and is therefore the most attractive to shareholders. However, the accuracy of the forecasts should be checked before a final decision is made.

8.4 Dirk plc

(a) (1) NPV

Net relevant cash flows are:

	Year 0 £m	Year £m	Year 2 £m	Year 3 £m	Year 4 £m
Sales revenue		9.0	9.6	7.2	3.0
Loss of contribution		(0.8)	(0.8)	(0.8)	
Variable cost		(1.0)	(1.2)	(1.2)	(0.7)
Fixed cost (Note 2)		(1.7)	(1.7)	(1.7)	(1.7)
Operating cash flows		5.5	5.9	3.5	0.6
Working capital	(1.8)				1.8
Capital cost (Note 3)	(10.5)	—	—	—	0.5
Net relevant cash flows	(12.3)	5.5	5.9	3.5	2.9

The NPV is:

	Year 0 £m	Year 1 £m	Year 2 £m	Year 3 £m	Year 4 £m
Net relevant cash flows	(12.3)	5.5	5.9	3.5	2.9
Discount rate (8%)	1.000	0.926	0.857	0.794	0.735
Present value	(12.3)	5.1	5.1	2.8	2.1
NPV	2.8				

NPV 2.8 (that is, the sum of the present values for years 0 to 4).

Notes:

1 The development cost of £0.4 million is irrelevant as it is a past cost.

2 Only that part of the fixed cost that arises as a direct result of the project is relevant. Depreciation is irrelevant as it is not a cash flow.

3 The residual value of the equipment is (£10.5m − (4 × £2.5m)) = £0.5m.

(2) IRR

To calculate the IRR, a higher discount figure (12%) will be applied.

	Year 0 £m	Year 1 £m	Year 2 £m	Year 3 £m	Year 4 £m
Net relevant cash flows	(12.3)	5.5	5.9	3.5	2.9
Discount rate (12%)	1.000	0.893	0.797	0.712	0.636
Present value	(12.3)	4.9	4.7	2.5	1.8
NPV	1.6				

Trial	Discount rate %	Net present value £000
1	8	2.8
2	12	1.6
Difference	4	1.2

For every 1 per cent change in the discount rate, the change in NPV will be:

$$1.2/4 = 0.3$$

The increase in the 12% discount rate necessary to achieve a zero NPV will be:

$$1.6/0.3 = 5.3\%$$

Thus the approximate IRR is:

$$(12.0 + 5.3) = 17.3\%$$

(b) The NPV of the project is positive and the IRR of the project exceeds the cost of capital. Acceptance of the project will therefore enhance shareholder wealth. The NPV, however, is not very high, and an analysis of the sensitivity of the key inputs to the decision may be useful to help assess the riskiness of the project.

8.7 Chesterfield Wanderers

(a) Player option

	Year 0 £000	Year 1 £000	Year 2 £000	Year 3 £000	Year 4 £000	Year 5 £000
Sale of player	2,200					1,000
Purchase of Bazza	(10,000)					
Sponsorship and so on		1,200	1,200	1,200	1,200	1,200
Gate receipts		2,500	1,300	1,300	1,300	1,300
Salaries paid		(800)	(800)	(800)	(800)	(1,200)
Salaries saved		400	400	400	400	600
	(7,800)	3,300	2,100	2,100	2,100	2,900
Discount factor 10%	1.000	0.909	0.826	0.751	0.683	0.621
Present values	(7,800)	3,000	1,735	1,577	1,434	1,801
Net present value	1,747					

Ground improvement option

	Year 1 £000	Year 2 £000	Year 3 £000	Year 4 £000	Year 5 £000
Ground improvements	(10,000)				
Increased gate receipts	(1,800)	4,400	4,400	4,400	4,400
	(11,800)	4,400	4,400	4,400	4,400
Discount factor 10%	0.909	0.826	0.751	0.683	0.621
Present values	(10,726)	3,634	3,304	3,005	2,732
Net present value	1,949				

(b) The ground improvement option provides the higher net present value and is therefore the preferable option, based on the objective of shareholder wealth enhancement.

(c) A professional football club may not wish to pursue an objective of shareholder wealth enhancement. It may prefer to invest in quality players in an attempt to enjoy future sporting success. If this is the case, the net present value approach will be less appropriate because the club is not pursuing a strict wealth-related objective.

8.8 Dallan plc

Differential cash flows of introducing the Dynamotor and abandoning the Powermite, compared to retaining the Powermite and not introducing the Dynamotor.

	20X0 £	20X1 £	20X2 £	20X3 £	20X4 £	20X5 £
Differential sales revenue		1,000,000	1,500,000	2,000,000	1,500,000	1,000,000
Variable costs		(400,000)	(600,000)	(800,000)	(600,000)	(400,000)
Fixed costs		(250,000)	(250,000)	(250,000)	(250,000)	(250,000)
Redundancy	(120,000)					
Plant	(1,200,000)					
	(1,320,000)	350,000	650,000	950,000	650,000	350,000
Discount factor	1.000	0.870	0.756	0.658	0.572	0.497
PV	(1,320,000)	304,500	491,400	625,100	371,800	173,950
NPV	646,750 (positive)					

The decision on the basis of NPV must be to abandon the Powermite and make the Dynamotor.

Chapter 9

9.1 Parklife Ltd A good answer would raise most of the following points and explain them:

Use of the payback period method of appraisal
- Claimed by some as a means of assessing the riskiness of a project.
- Dubious risk assessment method as it only considers the risk that the project will end prematurely; also projects with high early projected cash flows may in fact be just the ones that are most risky.

Use of basic sensitivity analysis
- Potentially very useful.
- Allows the decision maker to gain a clear impression of the crucial areas.
- Highlights areas of most doubt that could trigger closer observation of those areas.
- Difficult to interpret the results.
- Tends to be a rather static approach since only one factor assessed at a time.

Scenario building
- Similar to sensitivity analysis but looks at changes in input values to a number of factors.
- If the analysis can be set up on a spreadsheet very easy to use.
- Valuable insights can be gained.
- No rules on how to interpret the results.

Probabilities and expected values
- Probabilities can be ascribed to various possible actual values for the various inputs and an 'expected value' and standard deviation deduced.
- Difficult to ascribe probabilities.
- Dubious usefulness for a smaller business and a significantly sized project.

Use of risk adjusted discount rate
- Having assessed the riskiness of the inputs, say via scenario building, the discount rate can be loaded for the perceived level of riskiness.
- Attitudes to risk of the management/shareholders is a crucial issue here.

9.2 Easton Ltd

(a) *Differential cash flows of Machine A*

Year		2,000 demand £	3,000 demand £	5,000 demand £
0		(15,000)	(15,000)	(15,000)
1	(£4 – £1)/unit	6,000	9,000	15,000
2		6,000	9,000	15,000
3		6,000	9,000	15,000
	Discount factor	£	£	£
0	(1.000)	(15,000)	(15,000)	(15,000)
1	(0.943)	5,658	8,487	14,145
2	(0.890)	5,340	8,010	13,350
3	(0.840)	5,040	7,560	12,600
		1,038	9,057	25,095

Expected net present value = $(0.2 \times 1,038) + (0.6 \times 9,057) + (0.2 \times 25,095) = £10,661$.

Differential cash flows of Machine B

Year		2,000 demand £	3,000 demand £	5,000 demand £
0		(20,000)	(20,000)	(20,000)
1	(£4 − £0.5)/unit	7,000	10,500	17,500
2		7,000	10,500	17,500
3		7,000	10,500	17,500
	Discount factor	£	£	£
0	(1.000)	(20,000)	(20,000)	(20,000)
1	(0.943)	6,601	9,902	16,503
2	(0.890)	6,230	9,345	15,575
3	(0.840)	5,880	8,820	14,700
		(1,289)	8,067	26,778

Expected net present value = (0.2 × (−1,289)) + (0.6 × 8,067) + (0.2 × 26,778) = £9,938

A more direct route to expected net present values would be to take the 'expected' demand [(0.2 × 2,000) + (0.6 × 3,000) + (0.2 × 5,000) = 3,200] and then find the NPV assuming that level of demand for each year.

(b) If the business is selecting investment opportunities on the basis of expected NPV, it would buy Machine A. An added attraction of Machine A over Machine B is that, at all three levels of demand, there is a positive NPV. At the 2,000 demand level, Machine B gives a negative NPV.

9.3 Easton Ltd

(a) NPV

The expression for the NPV of this particular project may be put as follows:

$$NPV = D(S − V) \times 2.673 − I$$

where D is annual demand (in units), S is the selling price per unit, V is the variable cost per unit and I is the initial investment. 2.673 is the sum of years 1 2 and 3 discount factors at 6 per cent (see solution to Exercise 9.2 (above)).

$$NPV = [2,000(4 − 1) \times 2.673] − 15,000 = £1,038$$

Since the NPV is a significant positive figure the machine should be acquired.

(b) Sensitivity analysis

(1) *Annual demand*

This requires setting NPV at zero, putting in all inputs except annual demand, and solving for annual demand. That is:

$$[D(4 − 1) \times 2.673] − 15,000 = 0$$

$$D = \frac{15,000}{3 \times 2.673} = 1.871 \text{ units}$$

(2) *Selling price per unit*

$$2,000(S − 1) \times 2.673 = 15,000$$

$$S = \frac{15,000}{2,000 \times 2.673} + 1 = £3.806$$

(3) *Variable cost per unit*

$$2,000(4 - V) \times 2.673 = 15,000$$

$$V = \frac{-15,000}{2,000 \times 2.673} + 4 = \underline{£1.194}$$

(4) *Initial investment*

$$I = 2,000(4 - 1) \times 2.673 = £16,038$$

Table of sensitivities

Factor	Original estimate	Break-even point	Difference	Difference as % of original
D	2,000 units	1,871 units	129 units	6%
S	£4	£3.806	£0.194	5%
V	£1	£1.194	£0.194	19%
I	£15,000	£16,038	£1,038	7%

Note that it would also have been possible to derive the sensitivities of the cost of capital and the life of the project.

9.5 Kernow Cleaning Services Ltd

(a) The first step is to calculate the expected annual cash flows:

Year 1	£	Year 2	£
£80,000 × 0.3	24,000	£140,000 × 0.4	56,000
£160,000 × 0.5	80,000	£220,000 × 0.4	88,000
£200,000 × 0.2	40,000	£250,000 × 0.2	50,000
	144,000		194,000

Year 3		Year 4	
£140,000 × 0.4	56,000	£100,000 × 0.3	30,000
£200,000 × 0.3	60,000	£170,000 × 0.6	102,000
£230,000 × 0.3	69,000	£200,000 × 0.1	20,000
	185,000		152,000

The expected net present value (ENPV) can now be calculated as follows:

Period	Expected cash flow £	Discount rate 10%	Expected PV £
0	(540,000)	1.000	(540,000)
1	144,000	0.909	130,896
2	194,000	0.826	160,244
3	185,000	0.751	138,935
4	152,000	0.683	103,816
ENPV			(6,109)

(b) The *worst possible outcome* can be calculated by taking the lowest values of savings each year, as follows:

Period	Cash flow £	Discount rate 10%	PV £
0	(540,000)	1.000	(540,000)
1	80,000	0.909	72,720
2	140,000	0.826	115,640
3	140,000	0.751	105,140
4	100,000	0.683	68,300
NPV			(178,200)

The probability of occurrence can be obtained by multiplying together the probability of *each* of the worst outcomes above, that is 0.3 × 0.4 × 0.4 × 0.3 = 0.014.

Thus, the probability of occurrence is 1.4%, which is very low.

9.7 Hi Fido plc

Cash flows

	20X0 £000	20X1 £000	20X2 £000	20X3 £000
Plant	(1,000)			
Tracker revenue		2,160	2,208	1,104
Materials cost		(756)	(773)	(386)
Additional labour		(97)	(99)	(50)
Lost Repro contributions		(432)	(442)	(221)
Management	120	(48)	(48)	(188)
Working capital	(243)	(5)	124	124
	(1,123)	822	970	383
Discounted at 8%	(1,123)	761	831	304
Net Present Value	773 (positive)			

On the basis of this analysis, the project should go ahead.

Workings

Expected sales (units)

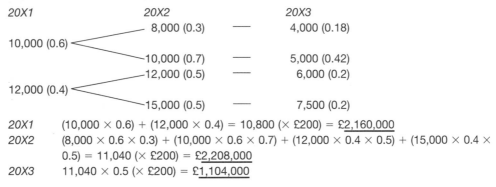

20X1	20X2	20X3
	8,000 (0.3) —	4,000 (0.18)
10,000 (0.6)		
	10,000 (0.7) —	5,000 (0.42)
	12,000 (0.5) —	6,000 (0.2)
12,000 (0.4)		
	15,000 (0.5) —	7,500 (0.2)

20X1   (10,000 × 0.6) + (12,000 × 0.4) = 10,800 (× £200) = £2,160,000

20X2   (8,000 × 0.6 × 0.3) + (10,000 × 0.6 × 0.7) + (12,000 × 0.4 × 0.5) + (15,000 × 0.4 × 0.5) = 11,040 (× £200) = £2,208,000

20X3   11,040 × 0.5 (× £200) = £1,104,000

Additional labour

Hours required per pair of Trackers = 3

Hours released per pair of Repros = 4

Additional hours required per pair of Trackers = 3 − (4/2) = 1, paid at £9

Effective loss of contribution per Repro sale

For each unit lost = £100 − 20 = £80

Working capital

	20X1 £000	20X2 £000	20X3 £000
Tracker sales revenues	2,160	2,208	1,104
Lost Repro revenue	(540)	(552)	(276)
Net increase in revenue	1,620	1,656	828
15% thereof	243	248	124

Chapter 10

10.2 Cost-plus pricing

Cost-plus pricing means that prices are based on calculations/assessments of how much it costs to produce the good or service, and include a margin for profit. 'Cost' in this context might mean relevant cost, variable cost, direct cost or full cost. Usually cost-plus prices are based on full costs. These full costs might be derived using a traditional or an ABC approach.

If a business charges the full cost of its output as a selling price, it will in theory break even. This is because the sales revenue will exactly cover all of the costs. Charging something above full cost will yield a profit. Thus, in theory, cost-plus pricing is logical.

If a cost-plus approach to pricing is to be taken, the issue that must be addressed is the level of profit required from each unit sold. This must logically be based on the total profit that is required for the period. Normally, businesses seek to enhance their wealth through trading. The extent to which they expect to do this is normally related to the amount of wealth that is invested to promote wealth enhancement. Businesses tend to seek to produce a particular percentage increase in wealth. In other words, they seek to generate a particular return on capital employed. It seems logical, therefore, that the profit loading on full cost should reflect the business's target profit and that the target should itself be based on a target return on capital employed.

An obvious problem with cost-plus pricing is that the market may not agree with the price. To put this another way, cost-plus pricing takes no account of the market demand function (the relationship between price and quantity demanded). A business may fairly deduce the full cost of some product and then add what might be regarded as a reasonable level of profit, only to find that a rival producer is offering a similar product for a much lower price, or that the market simply will not buy at the cost-plus price.

Most suppliers are not strong enough in the market to dictate pricing; most are 'price takers', not 'price makers'. They must accept the price offered by the market or they do not sell any of their wares. Cost-plus pricing may be appropriate for price makers, but it has less relevance for price takers.

The cost-plus price is not entirely useless to price takers, however. When contemplating entering a market, knowing the cost-plus price will tell the price taker whether it can profitably enter the market or not. As has been said above, the full cost can be seen as a long-run break-even selling price. If entering a market means that this break-even price, plus an acceptable profit, cannot be achieved, then the business should probably stay out. Having a breakdown of the full cost may put the business in a position to examine where it might be possible to cut costs in order to bring the full cost-plus profit to within a figure acceptable to the market.

Being a price maker does not always imply that the business dominates a particular market. Many small businesses are, to some extent, price makers. This tends to be where buyers find it difficult to make clear distinctions between the prices offered by various suppliers. An example of this might be a car repair. Though it may be possible to obtain a series of binding estimates for the work from various garages, most people would not normally do so. As a result, garages normally charge cost-plus prices for car repairs.

10.2 Woodner Ltd

A	B	C	D	E	F	G	H
Output units	Sales price per unit	Total sales revenue (A × B)	Marginal unit sales revenue	Total variable cost (A × £20)	Total cost (variable cost + £2,500)	Marginal cost per unit	Profit/ (loss)
£	£	£	£	£	£	£	£
0	0	0	0	0	2,500	–	(2,500)
10	95	950	95	200	2,700	20	(1,750)
20	90	1,800*	85†	400	2,900	20	(1,100)
30	85	2,550	75	600	3,100	20	(550)
40	80	3,200	65	800	3,300	20	(100)
50	75	3,750	55	1,000	3,500	20	250
60	70	4,200	45	1,200	3,700	20	500
70	65	4,550	35	1,400	3,900	20	650
80	60	4,800	25	1,600	4,100	20	700
90	55	4,950	15	1,800	4,300	20	650
100	50	5,000	5	2,000	4,500	20	500

* (20 × £90)
† ((1,800 − 950)/(20 − 10))

An output of 80 units each week will maximise profit at £700 a week. This is the nearest, given the nature of the input data, to the level of output where marginal cost per unit equals marginal revenue per unit. (For the mathematically minded, calculus could have been used to find the point at which slopes of the total sales revenue and total cost lines were equal.)

10.3 Sharma plc

Analysis of trading with Lopez Ltd during last year

		£
Gross sales revenue	(40,000 × £20)	800,000
Discount allowed	(£800,000 × 5%)	(40,000)
Manufacturing cost	(40,000 × £12)	(480,000)
Sales order handling	(22 × £75)	(1,650)
Delivery costs	(22 × 120 × £1.50)	(3,960)
Customer sales visits	(30 × £230)	(6,900)
Credit costs	((£800,000 − £40,000) × $\frac{1}{12}$ × 2%)	(2,533)
		(535,043)
Profit from the customer for the year		264,957

10.4 Virgo plc

There is no single correct answer to this problem. The suggestions set out below are based on experiences that some businesses have had in implementing a management bonus system based on EVA® performance.

In order to get the divisional managers to think and act like the owners of the business, it is recommended that bonuses based on divisional performance, as measured by EVA®, should form a significant part of their total rewards. Thus, around 50 per cent of the total rewards paid to managers could be related to the EVA® that has been generated for a period. (In the case of very senior managers it could be more, and for junior managers less.)

The target for managers to achieve could be a particular level of improvement in EVA® for their division over a year. A bonus rate can then be set for achievement of the target level of improvement. If this target level of improvement is achieved, 100 per cent of the bonus should be paid. If the target is not achieved, an agreed percentage (below 100 per cent) could be paid according to the amount of shortfall. If, on the other hand, the target is exceeded, an agreed percentage (with no upper limits) may be paid.

The timing of the payment of management bonuses is important. In the question, it was mentioned that Virgo plc wishes to encourage a longer-term view among its managers. One approach is to use a 'bonus bank' system whereby the bonus for a period is placed in a 'bank' and a certain proportion (usually one-third) can be drawn in the period in which it is earned. If the target for the following period is not met (presumably the case in Year 2 for Virgo), there can be a charge against the bonus bank so that the total amount available for withdrawal is reduced. This will ensure that the managers try to maintain improvements in EVA® consistently over the years.

In some cases, the amount of bonus is determined by three factors: the performance of the business as a whole (as measured by EVA®); the performance of the division (as measured by EVA®); and the performance of the particular manager (using agreed indicators of performance). The performance for the business as a whole is often given the most weighting, and individual performance the least weighting. Thus, 50 per cent of the bonus may be for corporate performance, 30 per cent for divisional performance and 20 per cent for individual performance.

10.6 Sillycon Ltd

(a) Overhead analysis

	Electronics £000	Testing £000	Service £000
Variable overheads	1,200	600	700
Apportionment of service dept (800:600)	400	300	(700)
	1,600	900	–
Direct labour hours ('000)	800	600	
Variable overheads per direct labour hour	£2.00	£1.50	
Fixed overheads	2,000	500	800
Apportionment of service dept (equally)	400	400	(800)
	2,400	900	–
Direct labour hours ('000)	800	600	
Fixed overheads per direct labour hour	£3.00	£1.50	

Product cost (per unit)

		£	
Direct materials		7.00	
Direct labour:	Electronics	40.00	(2 × £20.00)
	Testing	18.00	(1½ × £12.00)
Variable overheads:	Electronics	4.00	(2 × £2.00)
	Testing	2.25	(1½ × £1.50)
Total variable cost		71.25	(assuming direct labour to be variable)
Fixed overheads:	Electronics	6.00	(2 × £3.00)
	Testing	2.25	(1½ × £1.50)
Total 'full' cost		79.50	
Add Mark-up, say 30%		23.85	
		103.35	

On the basis of the above, the business could hope to compete in the market at a price that reflects normal pricing practice.

(b) At this price, and only taking account of incremental fixed overheads, the break-even point (BEP) would be given by:

$$BEP = \frac{\text{Fixed costs}}{\text{Contribution per unit}} = \frac{£150,0000^*}{£103.35 - £71.25} = 4,673 \text{ units}$$

*(£13,000 + £100,000 + £37,000) namely the costs specifically incurred.

As the potential market for the business is around 5,000 to 6,000 units a year, the new product looks viable.

Chapter 11

11.1 Divisionalised organisations

(a) A divisionalised organisation is one that divides itself into operating units in order to deliver its range of products or services. Divisionalisation is, in essence, an attempt to deal with the problems of size and complexity.

Autonomy of action relates to the amount of discretion the managers of divisions have been given by central management over the operations of the division. Two popular forms of autonomy are profit centres and investment centres. Though divisionalisation usually leads to decentralisation of decision making, this need not necessarily be the case.

(b) The benefits of allowing divisional managers autonomy include:
- better use of market information;
- increase in management motivation;
- providing opportunities for management development;
- making full use of specialist knowledge;
- giving central managers time to focus on strategic issues; and
- permitting a more rapid response to changes in market conditions.

(c) There are certain problems with this approach which include:
- goal conflict between divisions or between divisions and central management;
- risk avoidance on the part of divisional managers;
- the growth of management 'perks'; and
- increasing costs due to inability to benefit from economies of scale.

Transfers between divisions can create problems for a business. Managers of the selling division may wish to obtain a high price for the transfers in an attempt to achieve certain profit objectives. However, the managers of the purchasing division may wish to buy as cheaply as possible in order to achieve their own profit objectives. This can create conflict, and central managers may find that they are spending time arbitrating disputes. It may be necessary for central managers to impose a solution on the divisions where agreement cannot be reached which will, of course, undermine the divisions' autonomy.

11.2 Financial performance measures

(a) *Contribution* represents the difference between the total sales revenue of the division and the variable expenses incurred. This is a useful measure for understanding the relationship between costs, output and profit. However, it ignores any fixed expenses incurred and so not all aspects of operating performance are considered.

The *controllable profit* deducts all expenses (variable and fixed) within the control of the divisional manager when arriving at a measure of performance. Many view this as the best measure of performance for divisional managers as they will be in a position to determine the level of expenses incurred. However, in practice, it may be difficult to categorise expenses as being either controllable or non-controllable. This measure also ignores the investment made in assets. For example, a manager may decide to hold very high levels of inventories, which may be an inefficient use of resources.

Return on investment (ROI) is a widely used method of evaluating the profitability of divisions. The ratio is calculated in the following way:

$$\text{ROI} = \frac{\text{Division profit}}{\text{Divisional investment (assets employed)}} \times 100\%$$

The ratio is seen as capturing many of the dimensions of running a division.

When defining divisional profit for this ratio, the purpose for which the ratio is to be used must be considered. When evaluating the performance of a divisional manager, the controllable contribution is likely to be the most appropriate, whereas for evaluating the performance of a division, the divisional contribution is likely to be more appropriate. Different definitions can be employed for divisional investment. The net assets or total assets figure may be used. In addition, assets may be shown at original cost or some other basis such as current replacement cost.

(b) There are several non-financial measures available to evaluate a division's performance. Examples of these measures have been cited in the chapter. Further examples include:

- plant capacity utilised;
- percentage of rejects in production runs;
- ratio of customer visits to customer orders; and
- number of customers visited.

If a broad range of financial and non-financial measures covering different time horizons is used, there is a better chance that all of the major dimensions of management and divisional performance will be properly assessed. Focusing on a few short-term financial objectives incurs the danger that managers will strive to achieve these at the expense of the longer-term objectives. Clearly, ROI can be increased in the short term by cutting back on discretionary expenditure such as staff training and research and development and by not replacing heavily depreciated assets.

11.4 ABC Corporation

(a) (1) Residual income calculation – original plan:

	£000
Sales revenue	1,200
Variable costs	(800)
Contribution	400
Fixed costs	(250)
Divisional profit	150
Capital charge (£500,000 × 20%)	(100)
Residual income	50

(2) Residual income calculation – original plan and Option X:

	£000
Sales revenue ((100,000 × £12) + (20,000 × £11))	1,420
Variable costs (120,000 × £8)	(960)
Contribution	460
Fixed costs (250,000 + (80,000/4))	(270)
Divisional profit	190
Capital charge (£580,000 × 20%)	(116)
Residual income	74

(3) Residual income calculation – original plan and Option Y:

	£000
Sales revenue ((80,000 × £12) + (20,000 × £10))	1,160
Variable costs	(800)
Contribution	360
Fixed costs	(250)
Divisional profit	110
Capital charge (£500,000 × 20%)	(100)
Residual income	10

We can see that the highest residual income for Division A arises when only Option X is added to the original plan and that the lowest residual income arises when only Option Y is added to the original plan.

(b) Division A is unlikely to find the price reduction for Division B attractive. Division B, on the other hand, will benefit by £40,000 (20,000 × £2) from the price reduction. However, overall, the total profits of the business will be unaffected as the increase in Division B's profits will be cancelled out by the decrease in Division A's profit.

If an outside supplier is used, the profits of the business overall will fall by the amount of the lost contribution (20,000 × (£10 − £8) = £40,000).

Another option would be to allow the outsiders to supply Division B and to use the released production capacity to sell outside customers 20,000 units at £11 per unit. In this way, additional equipment costs would be avoided.

11.5 Telling Company

(a) (1) $\text{ROI} = \dfrac{\text{Divisional profit}}{\text{Divisional investment}} \times 100\%$

$= \dfrac{25,000}{150,000} \times 100\%$

$= 16.7\%$

(2)

	£
Divisional profit	25,000
Required return (20% × £150,000)	(30,000)
Residual income (loss)	(5,000)

(3) The results show that the ROI is less than the required return of 20 per cent and the residual income is negative. The results must therefore be considered unsatisfactory.

(b) **RI with the additional sales**

	£
Increase in sales revenue (£7.50 × 10,000)	75,000
Increase in variable costs (£6 × 10,000)	(60,000)
Increase in contribution	15,000
Increase in fixed costs	(5,000)
Increase in divisional profit	10,000
Increase in cost of capital (20% × £20,000)	(4,000)
Increase in RI	6,000

(c) (1) Though the divisional profits of Goodman and Sharp will each be affected by a change in the transfer price, the total profits of Telling Co. will be unaffected. The increase in profit occurring in one division will be cancelled out by the decrease in profit in the other division and so the overall effect will be nil.

(2) If the work goes outside, Goodman would lose £20,000 in contribution (that is, 10,000 × £2) and Sharp would gain £8,000 by the reduction in the buying-in price (that is, 10,000 × (£8 – £7.20)). The net effect on the business as a whole will therefore be a loss of £12,000 (that is, £20,000 – £8,000).

11.6 Glasnost plc

(a)

	West £000	East £000
Residual income:		
300 – (2,500 × 10%)	50	
100 – (500 × 10%)		50
Return on investment (ROI):		
Based on profit for the period		
(250/2,500) × 100%	10%	
(80/500) × 100%		16%
Based on divisional profit		
(300/2,500) × 100%	12%	
(100/500) × 100%		20%
Expenses to sales revenue ratio:		
Direct manufacturing	30%	53%
Indirect manufacturing	22%	12%
Selling and distribution	18%	10%
Central overhead	5%	5%

(b) The ROI ratios indicate that East is the better performing division. However, we are told in the question that East has older plant than West, which has recently modernised its production lines. This difference in the age of the plant is likely to mean that the ROI of East is higher due, at least in part, to the fact that the plant has been substantially written down. Some common base is required for comparison purposes (for example, unadjusted historical cost).

We are told that ROI is used as the basis for evaluating performance. We can see that, whichever measure of ROI is used, the two divisions meet the minimum returns required. If ROI is being used to assess managerial performance then the divisional profit rather than the profit for the period figure should be used in the calculation. This is because the profit for the period figure is calculated after non-controllable central overheads have been deducted.

The business should consider the use of RI as another measure of divisional performance. This measure reveals the same level of performance for the current year from each division.

The expenses to sales revenue ratios are revealing. West has a lower direct manufacturing cost to sales revenue ratio but a higher indirect manufacturing cost to sales revenue ratio than East. This is consistent with the introduction of modern labour-saving plant.

West has a higher selling expenses to sales revenue ratio than East. This is probably due to the fact that inter-business transfers are minimal whereas for East they represent 50 per cent of total sales revenue.

Chapter 12

12.2 Hercules Wholesalers Ltd

(a) The business is probably concerned about its liquidity position because:

- it has a substantial overdraft, which together with its non-current borrowings means that it has borrowed an amount roughly equal to its equity (according to statement of financial position values);
- it has increased its investment in inventories during the past year (as shown by the income statement); and
- the liquid current assets (that is current assets, excluding inventories) are only around 60 per cent of the maturing current liabilities.

(b) The operating cash cycle can be calculated as follows:

Number of days

Average inventories turnover period:

$$\frac{((\text{Opening inventories} + \text{Closing inventories})/2) \times 365}{\text{Cost of inventories}} = \frac{((125 + 143/2)) \times 365}{323} \qquad = 151$$

Add Average settlement period for receivables:

$$\frac{\text{Trade receivables} \times 365}{\text{Credit sales revenue}} = \frac{163}{452} \times 365 \qquad = \underline{132}$$

$$283$$

Less Average settlement period for payables:

$$\frac{\text{Trade payables} \times 365}{\text{Credit purchases}} = \frac{145}{341} \times 365 \qquad = \underline{155}$$

Operating cash cycle $\qquad \underline{128}$

(c) The business can reduce the operating cash cycle in a number of ways. The average inventories turnover period seems quite long. At present, average inventories held represent about five months' inventories usage. Reducing the level of inventories held can reduce this period. Similarly, the average settlement period for receivables seems long at more than four months' sales revenue. Imposing tighter credit control, offering discounts, charging interest on overdue accounts and so on may reduce this. However, any policy decisions concerning inventories and receivables must take account of current trading conditions.

Extending the period of credit taken to pay suppliers would also reduce the operating cash cycle. For reasons mentioned in the chapter, however, this option must be given careful consideration.

12.4 Plastics Manufacturers Ltd

Ratio analysis – Plastic Toys Ltd

	Year 1	Year 2	Year 3
ROCE	16.7%	16.9%	(26.1%)
Operating profit margin	12.5%	11.2%	(23.4%)
Current ratio	1.2	1.1	0.9
Acid test ratio	0.5	0.5	0.3
Inventories turnover period*	91 days	82 days	183 days
Average settlement period for trade receivables	64 days	60 days	91 days

* Using sales revenue figure rather than cost of sales, which is unavailable.

The above figures reveal that year 3 was a disaster for Plastic Toys Ltd (PT). Sales revenue and profitability fell dramatically. The fall in sales revenue does not seem, however, to have been anticipated as inventories levels rose dramatically. The fall in profitability and increase in inventories have created a strain on liquidity that should cause acute concern. The liquidity position is very bad and the business seems to be in a perilous state. Extreme caution must therefore be exercised in any dealings with the business.

Before considering the proposal to supply, Plastics Manufacturers Ltd (PM) should establish why Plastic Toys Ltd wishes to change its suppliers. In view of the problems that it faces, there may well be problems with current suppliers. If three months' credit were to be granted, PM will be committed to supplying 6,000 kilos before payment is due. At a marginal cost of £7 a kilo, this means an exposure of £42,000. The risks of non-payment seem to be very high unless there is information concerning PT that indicates that its fortunes will improve in the near future. If PM is determined to supply the goods to PT then some kind of security should be required in order to reduce the risk to PM.

12.6 Mayo Computers Ltd

New proposals from credit control department

	£000	£000
Current level of investment in receivables		
(£20m × (60/365))		3,288
Proposed level of investment in receivables		
((£20m × 60%) × (30/365))	(986)	
((£20m × 40%) × (50/365))	(1,096)	(2,082)
Reduction in level of investment		1,206

The reduction in overdraft interest as a result of the reduction in the level of investment will be £1,206,000 × 14% = £169,000.

	£000	£000
Cost of cash discounts offered (£20m × 60% × 2.5%)		300
Additional cost of credit administration		20
		320
Bad debt savings	(100)	
Interest charge savings (see above)	(169)	(269)
Net cost of policy each year		51

These calculations show that the business would incur additional annual cost if it implemented this proposal. It would therefore be cheaper to stay with the existing credit policy.

12.7 Boswell Enterprises Ltd

(a)

	Current policy		New policy	
	£000	£000	£000	£000
Trade receivables				
((£3m × 1/12 × 30%) + (£3m × 2/12 × 70%))		425.0		
((£3.15m × 1/12 × 60%) + (£3.15m × 2/12 × 40%))				367.5
Inventories				
((£3m − (£3m × 20%)) × 3/12)		600.0		
((£3.15m − (£3.15m × 20%)) × 3/12)				630.0
Cash (fixed)		140.0		140.0
		1,165.0		1,137.5
Trade payables				
((£3m − (£3m × 20%)) × 2/12)	(400.0)			
((£3.15m − (£3.15m × 20%)) × 2/12)			(420.0)	
Accrued variable expenses				
(£3m × 1/12 × 10%)	(25.0)			
(£3.15m × 1/12 × 10%)			(26.3)	
Accrued fixed expenses	(15.0)	(440.0)	(15.0)	(461.3)
Investment in working capital		725.0		676.2

(b) The expected profit for the year

	Current policy		New policy	
	£000	£000	£000	£000
Sales revenue		3,000.0		3,150.0
Cost of goods sold		(2,400.0)		(2,520.0)
Gross profit (20%)		600.0		630.0
Variable expenses (10%)	(300.0)		(315.0)	
Fixed expenses	(180.0)		(180.0)	
Discounts (£3.15m × 60% × 2.5%)	–	(480.0)	(47.3)	(542.3)
Profit for the year		120.0		87.7

(c) Under the proposed policy we can see that the investment in working capital will be slightly lower than under the current policy. However, profits will be substantially lower as a result of offering discounts. The increase in sales revenue resulting from the discounts will not be sufficient to offset the additional cost of making the discounts to customers. It seems that the business should, therefore, stick with its current policy.

12.8 Goliath plc

(a) (1) The existing operating cash cycle can be calculated as follows:

Number of days

$$\text{Inventories turnover period} = \frac{\text{Inventories at year end}}{\text{Cost of sales}} \times 365$$

$$= \frac{560}{1,440} \times 365 = \qquad 142$$

$$\text{Receivables settlement period} = \frac{\text{Receivables at year end}}{\text{Sales revenue}} \times 365$$

$$= \frac{565}{2,400} \times 365 = \qquad \underline{86}$$

$$228$$

$$\textit{Less} \text{ Payables settlement period} = \frac{\text{Payables at year end}}{\text{Purchases}} \times 365$$

$$= \frac{451}{1,450} \times 365 = \qquad \underline{(114)}$$

Operating cash cycle $\qquad \underline{114}$

The new operating cash cycle is:

Number of days

$$\text{Inventories turnover period} = \frac{(560 \times 1.15)}{(2{,}400 \times 1.10) \times 0.60^*} \times 365 \qquad 148$$

Receivables settlement period = 86 + 20   106
          254
Less Payables settlement period = 114 + 15   (129)
          125

	Number of days
New operating cash cycle	125
Existing operating cash cycle	(114)
Increase in operating cash cycle (days)	11

* Cost of sales is 60% of sales revenue (see the income statement).

(2)

	£000
Increase/(decrease) in inventories held ((560 × 1.15) − 560)	84.0
Increase/(decrease) in receivables (((2,400 × 1.1) × (106/365)) − 565)	201.7
	285.7
(Increase)/decrease in payables (1,668 × (129/365) − 451)	(138.5)
Increase/(decrease) in net investment	147.2

(3)

	£000	£000
Gross profit increase ((2,400 × 0.1) × 0.40)		96.0
Adjust for:		
Administration expenses increase (15%)	(45.0)	
Bad debts increase	(120.0)	
Interest (10%) on borrowing for increased net investment in working capital (147.2)	(14.7)	(179.7)
Increase (decrease) in profit before tax		(83.7)
Decrease in tax charge for the period (25% × 83.7)		20.9
Decrease in profit for the year		(62.8)

(b) There would be an increase in the operating cash cycle, which will have an adverse effect on liquidity. The existing trade payables and inventories turnover periods already seem quite high. Any increase in either of these must be justified. The planned increase in the trade payables period must also be justified since it may risk the loss of goodwill from suppliers. Although there is an expected increase in sales revenue of £240,000 from adopting the new policy, the profit for the year will decrease by £62,800. This represents a substantial decrease when compared with the previous year. (The increase in bad debts is a major reason why the profit for the period is adversely affected.) There is also a substantial increase in the net investment in inventories, trade receivables and trade payables, which seem high in relation to the expected increase in sales revenue. The new policy requires a significant increase in investment and is expected to generate lower profit than is currently being enjoyed. It should, therefore, be rejected.

Appendix E

PRESENT VALUE TABLE

Present value of £1, that is, $1/(1 + r)^n$
where r = discount rate
  n = number of periods until payment

					Discount rates (r)						
Periods (n)	1%	2%	3%	4%	5%	6%	7%	8%	9%	10%	
1	0.990	0.980	0.971	0.962	0.952	0.943	0.935	0.926	0.917	0.909	1
2	0.980	0.961	0.943	0.925	0.907	0.890	0.873	0.857	0.842	0.826	2
3	0.971	0.942	0.915	0.889	0.864	0.840	0.816	0.794	0.772	0.751	3
4	0.961	0.924	0.888	0.855	0.823	0.792	0.763	0.735	0.708	0.683	4
5	0.951	0.906	0.863	0.822	0.784	0.747	0.713	0.681	0.650	0.621	5
6	0.942	0.888	0.837	0.790	0.746	0.705	0.666	0.630	0.596	0.564	6
7	0.933	0.871	0.813	0.760	0.711	0.665	0.623	0.583	0.547	0.513	7
8	0.923	0.853	0.789	0.731	0.677	0.627	0.582	0.540	0.502	0.467	8
9	0.914	0.837	0.766	0.703	0.645	0.592	0.544	0.500	0.460	0.424	9
10	0.905	0.820	0.744	0.676	0.614	0.558	0.508	0.463	0.422	0.386	10
11	0.896	0.804	0.722	0.650	0.585	0.527	0.475	0.429	0.388	0.350	11
12	0.887	0.788	0.701	0.625	0.557	0.497	0.444	0.397	0.356	0.319	12
13	0.879	0.773	0.681	0.601	0.530	0.469	0.415	0.368	0.326	0.290	13
14	0.870	0.758	0.661	0.577	0.505	0.442	0.388	0.340	0.299	0.263	14
15	0.861	0.743	0.642	0.555	0.481	0.417	0.362	0.315	0.275	0.239	15

					Discount rates (r)						
Periods (n)	11%	12%	13%	14%	15%	16%	17%	18%	19%	20%	
1	0.901	0.893	0.885	0.877	0.870	0.862	0.855	0.847	0.840	0.833	1
2	0.812	0.797	0.783	0.769	0.756	0.743	0.731	0.718	0.706	0.694	2
3	0.731	0.712	0.693	0.675	0.658	0.641	0.624	0.609	0.593	0.579	3
4	0.659	0.636	0.613	0.592	0.572	0.552	0.534	0.516	0.499	0.482	4
5	0.593	0.567	0.543	0.519	0.497	0.476	0.456	0.437	0.419	0.402	5
6	0.535	0.507	0.480	0.456	0.432	0.410	0.390	0.370	0.352	0.335	6
7	0.482	0.452	0.425	0.400	0.376	0.354	0.333	0.314	0.296	0.279	7
8	0.434	0.404	0.376	0.351	0.327	0.305	0.285	0.266	0.249	0.233	8
9	0.391	0.361	0.333	0.308	0.284	0.263	0.243	0.225	0.209	0.194	9
10	0.352	0.322	0.295	0.270	0.247	0.227	0.208	0.191	0.176	0.162	10
11	0.317	0.287	0.261	0.237	0.215	0.195	0.178	0.162	0.148	0.135	11
12	0.286	0.257	0.231	0.208	0.187	0.168	0.152	0.137	0.124	0.112	12
13	0.258	0.229	0.204	0.182	0.163	0.145	0.130	0.116	0.104	0.093	13
14	0.232	0.205	0.181	0.160	0.141	0.125	0.111	0.099	0.088	0.078	14
15	0.209	0.183	0.160	0.140	0.123	0.108	0.095	0.084	0.074	0.065	15

Periods (n)	Discount rates (r)										
	21%	22%	23%	24%	25%	26%	27%	28%	29%	30%	
1	0.826	0.820	0.813	0.806	0.800	0.794	0.787	0.781	0.775	0.769	1
2	0.683	0.672	0.661	0.650	0.640	0.630	0.620	0.610	0.601	0.592	2
3	0.564	0.551	0.537	0.524	0.512	0.500	0.488	0.477	0.466	0.455	3
4	0.467	0.451	0.437	0.423	0.410	0.397	0.384	0.373	0.361	0.350	4
5	0.386	0.370	0.355	0.341	0.328	0.315	0.303	0.291	0.280	0.269	5
6	0.319	0.303	0.289	0.275	0.262	0.250	0.238	0.277	0.217	0.207	6
7	0.263	0.249	0.235	0.222	0.210	0.198	0.188	0.178	0.168	0.159	7
8	0.218	0.204	0.191	0.179	0.168	0.157	0.148	0.139	0.130	0.123	8
9	0.180	0.167	0.155	0.144	0.134	0.125	0.116	0.108	0.101	0.094	9
10	0.149	0.137	0.126	0.116	0.107	0.099	0.092	0.085	0.078	0.073	10
11	0.123	0.112	0.103	0.094	0.086	0.079	0.072	0.066	0.061	0.056	11
12	0.102	0.092	0.083	0.076	0.069	0.062	0.057	0.052	0.047	0.043	12
13	0.084	0.075	0.068	0.061	0.055	0.050	0.045	0.040	0.037	0.033	13
14	0.069	0.062	0.055	0.049	0.044	0.039	0.035	0.032	0.028	0.025	14
15	0.057	0.051	0.045	0.040	0.035	0.031	0.028	0.025	0.022	0.020	15

INDEX

Note: page references in **bold** refer to terms defined in the Glossary